Women's Ordination

Sources for Additional Research

For further information on the religious groups covered in this publication, consult J. Gordon Melton's *Encyclopedia of American Religions*, which contains information on approximately 1,600 churches, sects, cults, temples, societies, missions, and other North American religious organizations.

For additional information on the beliefs held by the religious groups covered in this publication consult the *Encyclopedia of American Religions: Religious Creeds*, a companion volume to the *Encyclopedia of American Religions*, which provides the creeds, confessions, statements of faith, and articles of religion of the groups covered.

To locate organizations concerned with the topics covered in this publication, consult the following terms in the Name and Keyword Index to Gale's *Encyclopedia of Associations*:

- Ministers
- Ministry
- Ordination
- Religion
- Women
- Women's

ISSN 1043-9609

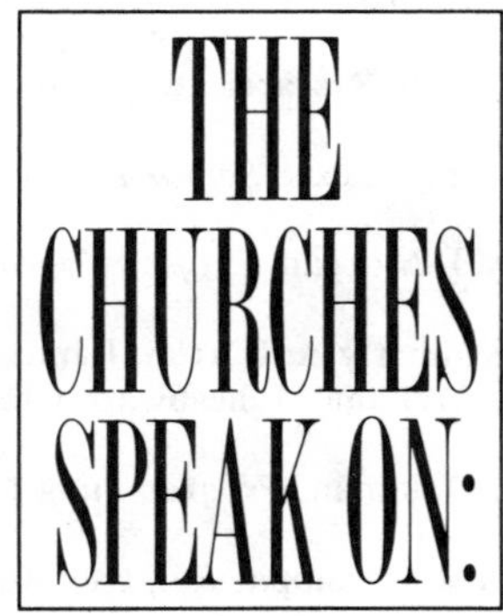

Women's Ordination

Official Statements from Religious Bodies and Ecumenical Organizations

J. Gordon Melton

Gary L. Ward, Contributing Editor

• DETROIT • NEW YORK • LONDON

J. Gordon Melton

Gary L. Ward, *Contributing Editor*

Gale Research Inc. Staff

Amy Lucas, *Senior Editor*

Bradley J. Morgan, *Project Coordinator*

Aided by: Peg Bessette, Kimberly A. Burton, Pamela Dundas, Terri Kessler, Ruth E. Littman, Archana Maheshwari, Christine Tomassini

Donald G. Dillaman, *Programming Consultant*

Victoria B. Cariappa, *Research Manager*
Jack Radike, *Research Supervisor*
Lisa Lantz, *Editorial Associate*

Mary Beth Trimper, *Production Manager*
Marilyn Jackman, *External Production Associate*
Mary Winterhalter, *External Production Assistant*

Arthur Chartow, *Art Director*
C. J. Jonik, *Keyliner*

Laura Bryant, *Production Supervisor*
Louise Gagné, *Internal Production Associate*
Yolanda Y. Latham, *Internal Production Assistant*

The paper used in this publication meets the minimum requirements of American National Standard for Information Sciences—Permanence Paper for Printed Library Materials, ANSI Z39.48-1984. ™

835 Penobscot Bldg.
Detroit, MI 48226-4094

ISBN 0-8103-7647-4
ISSN 1043-9609

Printed in the United States of America

Published simultaneously in the United Kingdom
by Gale Research International Limited
(An affiliated company of Gale Research Inc.)

Contents

Statements

Roman Catholic Church

Statements in this section are arranged chronologically by issuing date.

Protestant and Eastern Orthodox Churches

This section is arranged alphabetically by individual church, religious body, or ecumenical organization; the statements issued by each organization are presented chronologically within that organization.

Jewish Groups

This section is arranged alphabetically by individual religious organization; the statements issued by each organization are arranged chronologically within that organization.

Other Religious Bodies

Statements in this section are arranged chronologically by issuing date.

Preface

The Churches Speak is a quarterly series of monographs which systematically brings together the major official pronouncements of North American religious bodies and ecumenical organizations on the issues dominating today's headlines. Each monograph is devoted to a single topic and provides an overview of the topic itself, its historical background, and the full range of opinions found in the individual church statements. The statements themselves provide a unique and conveniently arranged survey of opinion on important contemporary issues, cutting across theological and denominational boundaries to influence the climate of social and political thought in our culture.

The formal statements issued by churches and other religious bodies are intended primarily to inform and guide their members, adherents, and supporters on the issue in question. These statements often attain additional importance, however, since they also exert influence on the actions of the religious agencies, clergy, and church administrators who initiate, direct, and regulate organizational programs. Church statements are also indirectly aimed at nonchurch members in an attempt to alter public policy, mobilize public opinion, or advocate changes in legislation. And they can also become the focal point of intense controversy, functioning as the bulwark against which many people direct their dissent on a given issue. This controversy can become magnified within the issuing organization itself when a significant minority of its members dissent from the positions taken by its hierarchies, judicatories, and boards of social concerns.

Focus is on Contemporary Topics From Major Religious Bodies

Each issue of *The Churches Speak* focuses on a single topic or a few closely related topics chosen for their high current public interest. Topics covered represent a wide range of vital social and political issues, such as AIDS, abortion, racism, the Middle East, euthanasia, capital punishment, and the ordination of women. Statements of major North American churches and religious organizations are included for each topic, providing comprehensive representation of the full range of opinions held on each topic.

The documents included in *The Churches Speak* were obtained through a mailing to all of the religious bodies in North America with more than 100,000 members. On any given issue, additional churches and religious organizations (including some outside of North America), and even some secular organizations known to have a special interest in the topic under consideration, were also solicited for their statements. Other statements have been identified in the files of the Institute for the Study of American Religion in Santa Barbara, California.

While most large churches and religious bodies make formal statements on important issues, it should be noted that many of the more than 1,500 denominations and religious organizations located in North America will not formulate any official statement or speak out on such issues. A number of religious bodies, including some of the largest denominations, do not make such statements as a matter of principle. Rather, they choose to leave actions and beliefs concerning social issues strictly up to individual effort and opinion.

Authentic Texts Used for All Statements

The statements presented in this series are in their authentic form, although obvious typographical errors have been corrected. The original wording, grammar, and punctuation of each statement remains intact. No attempt has been made to introduce foreign material or explanatory notes into the body of the statement's text.

Arrangement and Content

Each issue of *The Churches Speak* begins with an introductory essay which provides an overview of the topic itself and traces its recent historical manifestations. This essay also summarizes, compares, and contrasts the opinions found in the individual statements, allowing the user to place each one in the appropriate context. Each essay concludes with bibliographic citations to sources for further reading on the topic.

The statements presented in each monograph are arranged into four main sections based on broad religious families or traditions: The Roman Catholic Church (which represents the single largest religious body in the United States); Protestant and Eastern Orthodox Churches; Jewish Groups; and Other Religious Bodies.

Within the Roman Catholic Church section, statements are arranged chronologically by issuing date. The remaining sections are subarranged alphabetically by individual churches, religious bodies, or ecumenical organizations; the statements issued by each organization are presented chronologically within that organization.

Each of the four religious family sections is preceded by a note which provides background information on the family and analysis of its perspective on the issue in question. Individual statements contain the following elements:

Issuing organization. The name of the religious body or ecumenical organization issuing the statement.

Statement name. The actual or formal title of the statement. When no formal title is given, a descriptive title has been assigned.

Text of statement. The text of the statement is presented in its original form.

Notes. These appear in italic type following the text of each statement. When applicable, these remarks provide background information on the issuing organization's membership size and geographic distribution, and details about the circumstances under which the statement was made—including when it was passed, why it was passed, and whether or not it is binding on church members.

Index to Organizations, Statements, and Subjects Provided

To facilitate access to the material presented, each issue of *The Churches Speak* contains an Index to Organizations, Statements, and Subjects included in that issue. The index lists, in a single alphabetical sequence, the full titles of all the statements, the names of all religious bodies and ecumenical organizations mentioned in the statements' texts and notes, specifically named individuals, and specific subjects covered within the statements. Statement titles and organization names are also listed by important keywords that appear in their titles/names. Citations in the index refer to page numbers; page numbers rendered in boldface after an organization name indicate the location of that organization's statement(s) within the main text.

Sources of Additional Information

Additional information on many of the religious bodies covered in *The Churches Speak* can be found in the *Encyclopedia of American Religions.* The *Encyclopedia* provides details on approximately 1600 religious and spiritual groups in the United States and Canada, and is divided into two parts. The first part contains an essay covering the development of American religion, an essay providing a historical survey of religion in Canada, and historical essays grouped by general religious family. The second part contains directory sections listing individual churches and groups constituting the religious families discussed in the historical essays.

A companion volume, the *Encyclopedia of American Religions: Religious Creeds,* provides a comprehensive compilation of 464 religious creeds, confessions, statements of faith, summaries of belief, and articles of religion currently acknowledged by many of the churches or religious groups described in the *Encyclopedia of American Religions.* It also includes extensive notes on the history and textual variations of creeds, reflecting changing social, political, and doctrinal climates throughout the centuries. The material is arranged by major religious families, following, with minor variations, the approach used in the *Encyclopedia.*

Institute for the Study of American Religion

The Institute for the Study of American Religion was founded in 1969 for the purpose of researching and disseminating information about the numerous religious groups in the United States. More recently, the Institute's scope has been expanded to include religious groups in Canada, making it the only research facility of its kind to cover so broad a range of activity. After being located for many years in Evanston, Illinois, the Institute moved to Santa Barbara, California, in 1985. At that time, its collection of more than 25,000 books and its extensive files covering individual religious groups were donated to the Special Collections department of the library of the University of California—Santa Barbara. *The Churches Speak* has been compiled in part from the Institute's collection.

Suggestions Are Welcome

Users with particular questions about a religious group, suggested topics for coverage in or changes to *The Churches Speak,* or other information are invited to write to the Institute in care of its Director:

Dr. J. Gordon Melton
Institute for the Study of American Religion
Box 90709
Santa Barbara, CA 93190-0709

Introductory Essay:

A Survey of the Women's Ordination Issue by Gary L. Ward

In 1986 there were an estimated 20,730 female clergy in the United States, an increase of almost 100 percent just since 1977, and amounting to 7.9 percent of the total clergy in those denominations that ordain women. During that same time, the number of women enrolled in ordination programs in seminaries increased 110 percent. Prior to 1950 the ordination of women was mostly the province of a relatively small number of groups in the Pentecostal and Holiness families. However, a 1986 survey of 221 religious groups in the United States showed that 84 did ordain women, 82 did not, there was uncertainty about 49, and six had no clergy.[1] The direction, speed, and magnitude of these changes show no sign of reduction or alteration as we move into the 1990s, and there is every indication that more and more denominations will open their holy orders to women. This generation is witnessing shifts which, both literally and figuratively, are changing the face of religion.

Where do these changes come from? Is the ordination of women really a new thing? What are the different arguments that are used, pro and con? How have the religious groups been affected by this controversy? These are a few of the many questions that arise when the topic is women's ordination. A sociological assessment of why some groups ordain women when they do depends on the fact that religious groups relate on many levels with the surrounding culture. As the general environment shifts in its relation to women, it would be surprising not to see some corresponding shifts within religious groups. We thus see a number of churches granting ordination to women in the late 1800s, corresponding to the beginning of suffrage and temperance organizations and the increased role of women as settlers of the West. Another set of churches ordained women in the decade before and the decade after the passage of women's suffrage in 1920. Another set of churches ordained women in the 1950s, following the new roles women played in World War II. A larger set began ordaining women in the 1970s and 1980s, in the wake of the modern women's liberation movement, which may be said to have begun in 1963 with the publication of Betty Friedan's *The Feminine Mystique*. The issue of ordaining women presented the same tensions within the churches that the new roles for women presented outside the churches.

Some Early Historical Landmarks

Even in pre-Civil War years, women preachers were not unknown. The Quakers especially had a long tradition of women preachers, though the Quakers have no ordained clergy. Maria Cook (1779-1835) became a well known preacher for Universalism in the Pennsylvania and New York area. In 1848, Elizabeth Cady Stanton, Lucretia Mott, and others met in a Wesleyan Methodist church in Seneca Falls, New York. They drafted a statement called "Declaration of Sentiments," marking the organizational beginning of the women's rights movement in America. Three years later, in 1851, Lydia Sexton became the first female licensed preacher (a step below ordination) in the Church of the United Brethren in Christ. In 1853,

Antoinette Brown became the first American woman fully ordained to Christian ministry, at the Congregational Church of South Butler, New York. This action was without the full authority of the Congregational General Conference, which protested the action. Nevertheless, the United Church of Christ (successor body of the Congregational Church) today asserts its claim as the first denomination in North America to have an ordained woman minister.

The first woman ordained with the full authority and blessing of her denomination was Olympia Brown, a Universalist who was ordained by the St. Lawrence Association of Universalists in 1863. That year, she also became the first female graduate of Canton Theological School at St. Lawrence University. Prior to that point, it had been said at St. Lawrence "first, that women could not preach; second, that they would not preach; third, that if they did nobody would listen to them; and fourth, that, however much people might like to hear them, they never could be pastors of societies." Five years after Brown's graduation, it was noted that, "women preach, the people hear them gladly, and they are pastors of societies."[2] In 1869, Margaret Newton Van Cott became the first female licensed preacher in the Methodist Episcopal Church (in that same year, the two major women's suffrage associations began). In 1871 the Unitarians ordained their first female minister, Celia Burleigh, in Brooklyn, Connecticut. Other denominations authorizing the ordination of women in the 1800s include Advent Christian Church (1860), American Baptist Churches in the U.S.A., (ca.1893), Christian Church (Disciples of Christ) (1888), Christian Congregation (1887), Church of God (Anderson, Indiana) (1880), International Council of Community Churches (nineteenth century), Salvation Army (1880), Seventh Day Baptist General Conference (1885), and Wesleyan Church (nineteenth century).

In 1889, Emma Curtis Hopkins, who had previously founded the Independent Christian Science Theological Seminary in Chicago, Illinois, saw her first group of students graduate. Assuming the office of bishop, Hopkins ordained 22 of her students, which effectively launched what is today known as the New Thought. Several years later, Melinda Cramer (one of Hopkins students), began to ordain both men and women in the Divine Science movement, and Charles and Myrtle Fillmore began to ordain ministers with the Unity School of Christianity. Today, women make up a majority of the ordained ministry in the New Thought metaphysical churches, and the Unity movement, under the leadership of president Connie Fillmore, appears to be the largest religious group in America led by a female.

In the second and third decades of the twentieth century, surrounding the achievement of women's suffrage in 1920, a number of other denominations began ordaining women. These included the Apostolic Overcoming Holy Church of God (1916), Assemblies of God (1914), Church of the Nazarene (1908), Free Methodist Church (1911), General Conference Mennonite Church (1911), General Association of General Baptists (ca. 1925), and International Church of the Foursquare Gospel (1927).[3] What is evident about these early ordinations is that most of the denominations belong to the Pentecostal or Holiness families. This implies that in addition to social/cultural factors, there are theological/structural factors involved in the decision to ordain women.

The Holiness and Pentecostal families emphasize direct contact of the individual with God, or the indwelling Holy Spirit. The emphasis is not on the church as God's channel of salvation, but rather on salvation through personal communion with the Holy Spirit. This is the position of the "left wing" of the Reformation, eschewing organization constraints to allow God's voice to speak freely, wherever and however it will. Some groups, like the Quakers (or Friends), eliminated the role of clergy altogether. Because these families of churches understood the Spirit to operate very personally and often outside human-made structures, there was little theological warrant to prevent women from preaching. Thus, the majority of early female preachers or evangelists were not part of what today would be considered "liberal" churches like the Universalist or Unitarian churches. Rather, they were from otherwise very strict, often "hellfire" style churches. Even today, according to a report by Constant H. Jacquet, Jr., of the National Council of Churches, the denomination with the largest number of female clergy is the Assemblies of God (over 3,700), followed by the Salvation Army (over 3,200). It has also been reported, however, that among the historically black denominations, the African Methodist Episcopal Church estimated that of its 19,000 ministers, one-third are women.[4] That would give it the largest number of female clergy.

After the passage of the 19th Amendment gave women the right to vote in 1920, the fortunes of female ministers fell considerably. As an example, in 1920 there were 88 Universalist and 42 Unitarian women in the ministry, but by 1930, with the coming of the Depression, there were very few who could find jobs anywhere. Even after the Depression ended, the situation persisted for those two denominations and a number of others, and did not change until the 1960s.[5] Between 1927 and 1956 only two new denominations, Church of God General Conference (Oregon, Illinois) in 1940 and the Fundamental Methodist Church in 1950 began ordaining women. It has often been noted that for the secular women's movement, the period of 1920 to 1960 marked the time of withdrawal and inactivity between the early women's movement and the modern women's movement, thus paralleling the decline in women's ordination in the churches.

Recent Milestones

In the 1950s and early 1960s, in the wake of World War II, many changes were in the air. The first meeting of the World Council of Churches in Amsterdam in 1948 provided the forum for an international discussion of the "Life and Work of Women in the Church." In preparation for that meeting, Inez Cavert of the Federal Council of Churches (predecessor of the National Council of Churches) prepared the study "Women in American Church Life." After the meeting, Kathleen Bliss interpreted the national reports of the conference in a landmark work, *The Service and Status of Women in the Churches* that was published in 1952. Also in 1952, *Christian Century* magazine, commenting on Bliss's work, initiated a series of articles on women in the church and called for women's ordination. At the same time the United Church Women of the National Council of Churches called for continued study of the role of women in the churches.[6] Not long after this activity began, a number of churches began ordaining women, including the precursors of the United Methodist Church and the Presbyterian Church (U.S.A.) in 1956, the Church of the Brethren (1958), Latvian Evangelical Lutheran Church in America (1960), Apostolic Faith Mission Church of God (1963), and Bible Church of Christ (1964).[7] This number grew rapidly throughout the 1970s and 1980s, largely as a result of the contemporary women's movement. Churches ordaining during this period included the Schwenkfelder Church in America (1969), American Lutheran Church (1970), Lutheran Church in America (1970), Moravian Church in America (Northern Province) (1970), Moravian Church in America (Southern Province) (1970), Mennonite Church (1973), Association of Evangelical Lutheran Churches (1976), Episcopal Church (1976), Reformed Church in America (1981), and Reorganized Church of Jesus Christ of Latter Day Saints (1984). In 1990 the Christian Reformed Church made a preliminary vote to allow the ordination of women, but will not finalize it until 1992. Also during this time, Reform Judaism ordained its first female rabbi (1972), as did Reconstructionist Judaism (1974) and Conservative Judaism (1985).

The trend has been the same on the international scene. The Lutheran Church of Denmark has ordained women since 1948. In 1958, the Church of Sweden (Lutheran) voted to ordain women, as did the Lutheran Church in Czechoslovakia. In 1961, the first woman was ordained in the Lutheran Church of Norway. In 1962, the Church of France voted to ordain women. In 1970, approximately one-third of the member bodies of the World Council of Churches ordained women, and that percentage has continued to increase. Worldwide, the churches of Western Europe and North America have shown the greatest inclination to ordain women. Cultural attitudes toward women, especially in Asia and Latin America, have inhibited the number of groups ordaining women in other regions. In 1990, for example, the 55th World conference of the Seventh-day Adventist Church rejected a proposal to open ordination to women, despite strong support for women's ordination in the North American segment of the church. In many of the other 190 countries represented at the conference, however, there was no such support for ordination. In Africa, traditional culture has often given women leadership roles in religion, which leads many to ascribe the low rank of women in the Christian churches there to imported Western notions about the role of women.[8]

Since the 1950s, the main characterization of the ordination movement has been the fact that many of the larger, more mainstream churches have begun ordaining women. These churches, like the Lutherans and Methodists, have a different ecclesiastical structure than many of the churches which earlier had ordained women. They are less oriented to the experiences of individuals or to the autonomy of congregations and more oriented to a theology of the whole church as the "body of Christ" and the channel of salvation. These mainstream churches tend to strike a balance between the two emphases, sometimes described as "low church" and "high church," or sometimes as ministry of the Word vs. sacramental theology. Moving more in the direction of high church is the Episcopal/Anglican Church, with the Roman Catholic Church at the far end of that spectrum. It is more difficult for those who follow the high church ideal to ordain women because there is a far greater emphasis on the importance of church tradition. Because most of Christian history shows no priestly roles given to women, the sheer weight of tradition among the high church groups lobbies against their ordination. High church groups also attach more symbolism and theological importance to the offices of the church, including the priesthood. If the priesthood is opened to women, this involves rethinking certain theological and ecclesiastical assumptions which are less an issue for low church groups.

For this reason, it was considered of particular importance when the Anglican Church of Canada (in 1975) and the Episcopal Church in America (in 1976) voted to ordain women. This put pressure on other members of the worldwide Anglican Communion (especially the Church of England), and also on the Roman Catholic Church, which has maintained its position against the ordination of women. In 1978, the decennial Lambeth Conference (which brings together the bishops of the worldwide Anglican Communion) accepted women's ordination in principle. The 1988 Lambeth Conference was divided on the issue of female bishops and stated that provinces may appoint a female bishop, but no province is obliged to and all are asked to respect each other's viewpoint. On September 24, 1988, the Reverend Barbara C. Harris was elected Suffragan (assisting) Bishop of Massachusetts, becoming the first female bishop of the Episcopal Church. In 1989 the Reverend Penelope Ann Bansall Jamieson was elected bishop to head the Diocese of Dunedin for the Anglican Church of New Zealand, becoming the first woman to head a diocese anywhere in the worldwide Anglican Communion.

In 1975, the Church of England voted affirmatively that "there are no fundamental objections to ordination of women to the priesthood," though it voted against removing barriers to such ordination. In 1987, the church ordained its first female deacons, and in 1988 voted approval of legislation which could ultimately enable the ordination of women priests. Because of various legislative hurdles that must yet be cleared, 1993 would be the earliest possible time for the actual ordination of a female priest in the Church of England.[9] Out of 27 Anglican Provinces, five already ordain female priests: Hong Kong, New Zealand, Canada, United States, and Brazil. Some Ugandan and Kenyan bishops have ordained women, but this is not yet the general policy of their provinces. In 1988, the Church in Australia decided against ordaining women as priests.

Arguments Against Ordination

The specific arguments that have been used against the ordination of women have varied greatly but can be broadly grouped under four categories:

1. Social/Sexual Arguments

A 1985 survey of member churches of the World Alliance of Reformed Churches noted that those churches that did not ordain women did not typically base their opposition on theological/biblical arguments, but rather on arguments based more on perceived sexual differences or on social conditions (e.g., "up to now we have always found sufficient men"). On occasion, Reformed churches have been reluctant to ordain women if their church was only a tiny minority within an almost exclusively Roman Catholic society, or if some other strong ethos against female clergy existed.[10] Social/sexual arguments tend to be cast as practical concerns: "One hears that women's voices cannot be heard, or that women ought not to be out alone at night or in all kinds of weather...[or] that a woman will use her pulpit to attract men erotically and this will break up families."[11]

When the United Church of Canada began ordaining women in 1936, it ordained only single women. When it agreed to ordain married women 20 years later, there was considerable new debate. The major argument on this point was that the demands of the ministry and the peculiar demands of motherhood were mutually incompatible. There was also the sense that the status of marriage highlighted the woman's sexual and reproductive activity. It signified that she was having sexual relations, and her position as a sexual being and perhaps temptress was already an issue for many. Further, since biblical times there have been beliefs about the uncleanness of women during menstruation and after childbirth. Thus, many have argued that it was "inappropriate for a menstruating, married, or pregnant woman to preside at the eucharist or lead in worship."[12] In 1962 the United Church of Canada debated whether female candidates for ordination should be required to have a physician's medical certificate to indicate their emotional stability. Many considered that women, by and large, did not have the emotional stability to do proper ministry. Another social/sexual argument states that, by letting women into leadership positions, the church would lose its masculine edge and become soft, unable to function as adequately in a tough world. "The ordination of women would feminize our Church, and this process has already gone far enough," stated one theologian.[13]

2. Theological/Biblical Arguments

At some point in the religious dialogue about the ordination of women, there is an inevitable turn to the Bible. One passage that is often used in arguments against ordaining women is the second creation story of Genesis 2:18–23. Here Eve is described as being created second, after the male, and her role is to be Adam's "helper." Adam's primacy of place is reinforced by the story of the "fall" in Genesis 3:1–6, where Eve is interpreted as the weaker partner and temptress. Her punishment is to include bearing children in pain and being ruled over by her husband. This ordering of male/female relationships is held by opponents of women's ordination to be plainly visible throughout the Bible and is subscribed to by most church fathers. The anthropological model portrayed in Genesis is most notably cited by St. Paul in I Corinthians 11:3–15:

> Christ is the head of every man, and the husband is the head of his wife...a man ought not to have his head veiled, since he is the image and reflection of God, but woman is the reflection of man. Indeed, man was not made from woman, but woman from man. Neither was man created for the sake of woman, but woman for the sake of man.

The two other passages most often quoted are I Corinthians 14:34–35:

> Women should be silent in the churches. For they are not permitted to speak, but should be subordinate, as the law also says. If there is anything they desire to know, let them ask their husbands at home. For it is shameful for a woman to speak in church.

and I Timothy 2:11–15:

> Let a woman learn in silence with full submission. I permit no woman to teach or to have authority over a man; she is to keep silent. For Adam was formed first, then Eve; and Adam was not deceived, but the woman was deceived and became a transgressor. Yet she will be saved through childbearing, provided they continue in faith and love and holiness, with modesty.

Those arguing against the ordination of women suggest that these passages should be the guideline for the role of women in the churches. In 1832, the General Assembly of the Presbyterian Church in the U.S.A. sent a pastoral letter to its member churches, which included this statement:

> Meetings of pious women by themselves for conversation and prayer, whenever they can be conveniently held, we entirely approve. But let not the inspired prohibition of the great apostle to the gentiles, as found in his Epistles to the Corinthians and to Timothy, be violated. To teach and exhort or to lead in prayer, in public and promiscuous assemblies, is clearly forbidden in the Holy Oracles.[14]

Those opposed to the ordination of women will vary in their interpretation of these Scriptures. For example, some will emphasize the matter of wifely submission and secondary status. Others say that it is not that women are inferior or unequal, but rather simply have different roles to play. The fact that a man cannot give birth and a woman cannot be a priest are not value judgments, but merely the way creation has been ordered. Adam was created before Eve in a headship structure that is not affected by the fall or redemption.

A difficult area has been exactly what tasks women may or may not perform. Most churches have women who teach Sunday school classes, or who occasionally lead a group in prayer. Are these roles permitted? May a woman ask a question at a Bible class? May women vote on church issues? These questions were directly confronted in a paper issued by the Lutheran Church-Missouri Synod (see index). It concluded that what must be reserved for the male pastor are: 1) preaching in the services of the congregation; 2) leading formal public services of worship; 3) the public administration of the sacraments; and 4) the public administration of the office of the keys. Women may vote, since it is the whole assembly that thus exercises authority and not the individual woman. Women may read the Scriptures in worship, teach classes, and do other things, provided there is no confusion over their appropriate roles. The pastor, for instance, always has the authority of overseeing the teaching of classes, but may delegate the actual teaching responsibilities to others, including women.

Whatever the varieties of particular application of these passages, opponents of women's ordination, especially among the fundamentalist churches, would likely agree with this statement from a Missouri Synod pastor:

> Granted, the apostle Paul may not be popular with many people today. But the fact remains that he was a hand-picked apostle of Jesus Christ. What he wrote was not personal opinion (unless identified as such). Knowingly or not, people who object to Scripture object not only to the views of the human writer —Paul, for example —but also to Christ Jesus.[15]

The Bible is also used to provide precedent with regard to the roles of women in the early Christian church. Acts 21:9 and I Corinthians 11:5 clearly show women functioning as prophets at that time. Based upon the list in Ephesians 4:11, this may be interpreted by opponents of women's ordination as different from regular preaching or serving as pastor. Rather, it can be understood as occasional inspiration from the Holy Spirit, which may come to anyone. The New Testament also clearly shows women serving as deacon (or deaconess), as in Romans 16:1–2. The Greek word for deacon translates approximately as "servant," and although Paul used this word to describe his own work, opponents of women's ordination say that this does not mean that women deacons were on a par with bishops or elders. It is true, opponents will say, that some extra-biblical writings, such as the Acts of Paul, indicate that women were often known for their missionary teaching and preaching. An early church father, John Chrysostom, however, explained that the early church did not apply I Timothy 2:12 to the mission field: "But, when the man is not a believer and the plaything of error, Paul does not exclude a woman's superiority, even when it involves teaching."[16]

Finally, in terms of biblical precedents, is the ministry of Jesus himself. Opponents of women's ordination will point out that Jesus was a man, and picked only men as disciples. It is true that women were among Jesus' close companions and supporters, and that Jesus treated women in a manner surprisingly progressive for that time. However, this makes the argument all the stronger that Jesus could have broken with custom even further and named a woman as one of the 12, but he did not.

Theologically, the Roman Catholic Church in particular argues that the image of spousal love is crucial for understanding God's love and the role of the church. For the prophet Isaiah, the woman-bride is Israel, God's Chosen People, whom God loves, even when Israel is not faithful. This symbolism explains God's Covenant with Israel. In the New Testament, Christ is to be understood as the bridegroom (e.g., John 3:27–29 and Mark 2:19–20), and the church is the bride. This symbolism explains God's new Covenant. Jesus was known as the "son of man," and was also a real, flesh and blood male. Thus the symbolism of the Christ and the bridegroom must be masculine. In the words of Pope John Paul II:

> Since Christ, in instituting the Eucharist, linked it in such an explicit way to the priestly service of the Apostles, it is legitimate to conclude that he

> thereby wished to express the relationship between man and woman, between what is "feminine" and what is "masculine." It is a relationship willed by God both in the mystery of creation and in the mystery of Redemption. It is the Eucharist above all that expresses the redemptive act of Christ the Bridegroom towards the Church the Bride. This is clear and unambiguous when the sacramental ministry of the Eucharist, in which the priest acts "in persona Christi," is performed by a man.[17]

In this argument, the priest functions as the representation of Christ, as the new Adam, to overcome the work and world of the old Adam. The male sex of the priest is therefore very important, and admitting women to that position would seriously undermine the whole structure. A related perspective, but with a different emphasis, is expressed by a representative of the Old Catholic churches:

> There is one view of sacramental ministry which I think precludes women from being ordained. I have never heard it adequately countered by those in favour of women's ordination. It is that if God is Creator and Redeemer, then the sign of sexual difference, so obvious and essential in the Creation, must also be evident again in the eucharist which is the symbol of the Redemption. We have a sign of the importance of sexual differences in the celebration of the eucharist if we assume that those receiving communion are regarded as God's Church, the bride, and therefore as female. It then follows that the ministering priest who represents Christ, the bridegroom, must be male. How can we express a sign of the importance of this sexual difference in God the Redeemer if women are ordained in an equal manner as men?[18]

Another style of theological argument is to suggest that the church is letting the secular world set its agenda in terms of including women in arenas previously closed to them. Referring to the ordination of women, a Reformed minister said in 1921, "If we heed the politicians and the world, we are following the wrong leader."[19]

3. Unity/Ecumenical Arguments

Examples of objections to women's ordination on the basis of church unity may be found in the Reformed Church in America's struggle with the issue. In 1918 the General Synod said, "The submission of the proposed amendment to the Classes will work injury through friction and division out of all proportion to any possible good that might accrue to any portion of our church." A similar response was given in 1932. The ecumenical argument is concerned with how having female clergy will affect relations with other churches, and is often used as an objection to female clergy. When the World Council of Churches confronts the ordination question, unity is a primary issue. In 1958, when the Church of Sweden (Lutheran) decided to ordain women, a major concern was how it would affect relations with the Church of England. The Lutheran Council in the U.S.A. has also raised this issue (see index).

4. Tradition/Other Arguments

Perhaps the strongest tradition-oriented position against the ordination of women is taken by the Orthodox Church. In the words of Nicolae Chitescu, "In the Orthodox Church the opinions of theologians do not count. The only thing that matters is the traditional regulations established by the Church as a whole in its canons and in its practice."[20] In a search of that canonical tradition, the Rev. Archimandrite Georges Khodre of the Diocese of Tripoli of the Patriarchate of Antioch found that it "excludes women from the ministry. The sole ministry which they exercised as deaconesses was that of charity, and some other minor liturgical tasks."[21] To these men, two thousand years worth of tradition should not be thrown over lightly.

"Other" arguments against ordaining women are varied in scope. various. In 1951, the General Synod of the Reformed Church in America noted that "opening the offices of elder and deacon to women might tend to diminish men's sense of responsibility in the life and work of the Church." In 1921, it was predicted by a prominent church leader that the ordination of women "would import heresy, fanaticism, distortion, and perversion into church doctrine."

Arguments In Support of Ordination

To contradict the arguments that the ministry of women would lead to perversions or a decline in quality, proponents point to the long and illustrious history of women in the mission field. Churches have unanimously hailed the achievements of women missionaries in spreading the gospel around the world, and yet many of those same churches have balked at having women in the same roles closer to home. Experience has shown women to be capable leaders, not just in ministry, but in all kinds of professions previously unavailable to them.

Biblically, proponents argue that one can adduce as many Scriptures to support the ordination of women as oppose it. There is no need to use the second creation story in Genesis as the model for male-female relations when the first creation story (Genesis 1:1–2:4) offers a better alternative. In this story there is no subordination of the woman to the man; both were made at the same time, in God's image. Even in the second creation story (Genesis 2:5–25), it may simply be cultural prejudice that we see in it the subordination of women. The woman is created to be Adam's "helper," a term which in English implies a subordinate. The Hebrew word, however, never refers to a subordinate, and often refers to a superior form of help, including God (e.g., Psalm 46:1).

Jesus, proponents note, gave women an uncommon degree of regard and responsibility, including them among his band of followers (e.g., Luke 8:2–3). As the first witnesses to the Resurrection, the women were advised to "Go and tell" (Matthew 28:7). Proponents suggest that just because Jesus did not include a woman among the 12 disciples is no warrant to exclude women from the ordained ministry. After all, Jesus did not include a gentile among the disciples either. The story of Mary and Martha in Luke 10:38–42 indicates that women should participate in spiritual matters rather than just with household concerns.

Proponents of women's ordination deal in various ways with the problematic Pauline injunctions. There is wide agreement among scholars that Paul did not write I Timothy, and some have implied that the passage therefore has somewhat less authority. Commentators have also noted the apparent contradiction between the many passages which describe the warm support Paul shows for women who were deacons, prophets, and other active leaders in the early church (e.g., Acts 18:18–26, I Corinthians 11:5, Philippians 4:3, Romans 16:1–16), and the passages in which Paul apparently prefers women to be silent and submissive. A common assessment of those in favor of women's ordination is that Paul was inconsistent and did not always live up to his highest beliefs and capacities. In some cases he allowed himself to be captured by the limited cultural prejudices of the time, and in other cases his Christian convictions allowed him to attain a more beatific vision. It is said that in Galatians 3:28 he reached such a vision: "There is no longer Jew or Greek, there is no longer slave or free, there is no longer male and female; for all of you are one in Christ Jesus." Proponents have offered other examples of Paul falling short of his full Christian potential, such as Titus 2:9–10, where he tells slaves to "be submissive to their masters." They note that few today will quote Paul as approving the system of slavery because it is commonly understood to be a more culture-bound, less worthy passage than that of Galatians.

Among the "mainstream" Protestant churches, a change in view towards the ordination of women often corresponds with a change in view towards the Scriptures in general. In 1954, Floyd Filson, New Testament professor at McCormick Theological Seminary, said that the decision about the ordination of women depends upon whether or not one views the Bible literally. "The New Testament does not lay down binding and permanent laws about church officers. Those who hold literalistic views, and claim that we are permanently bound by the literal statements of the New Testament, can never consistently accept the idea of ordaining women to the ministry."[23] This means that to a large extent, proponents of the ordination of women accept a more liberal view of Scripture. One does not just ask what the Bible says, but asks what the historical context of the passage was, and how it is to be understood in the light of other passages in the Bible. If relation to a particular historical context is important, this means that not all parts of the Bible are considered to be equally binding or equally applicable in all other times and places, as with the Titus passage on slavery, and as with passages on women being silent or wearing veils.

Theologically, those in favor of women's ordination also recognize the Reformation notion of the "priesthood of all believers." Although this was Martin Luther's dictum, he believed that women still should not be priests in order to preserve order and decency, and because of women's "inferior aptitudes."[24] Proponents suggest that perhaps now we should see the priesthood of all believers as a vision we can more nearly approximate today, not unlike including blacks and women in the meaning of the words of the United States Constitution, "all men are created equal," even though the framers of that Constitution did not necessarily have that in mind. It thus becomes, for those in this camp, a matter of ethics, of justice, that women be allowed ordination.

As for the position that the priest must be a male to represent Jesus and the new Adam, a question for proponents is whether maleness is really the essential thing to represent. If only males can be ordained because Jesus was a male, maybe only Jews should be ordained because Jesus was a Jew. Should we not rather emphasize the divine incarnate in the human? The image of spousal love is but one among many that can be used to express the divine-human relationship. Even if we do focus on this image, must the Christ-figure always be male? Jesus as a human was male, but is Christ as part of the Trinity to be thought of as male? Few theologians would accept that, maintaining that the Trinity is supra-sexual. Even beyond this consideration, proponents suggest, the eucharist need not necessarily be considered as an exchange with the church as the bride, but as a reconciliation with all persons. One who has argued against the Roman Catholic position is the distinguished Roman Catholic theologian Hans Kung, a church insider, who has stated of women in the priesthood that "there are no dogmatic or biblical reasons against it."[25]

Proponents of women's ordination also point out that in some ways, arguments based on ecumenical concerns are less relevant now than they may have been at one time, since chances are about equal that a proposed merger or intercommunion would be as hampered by lack of women's ordination as enhanced. Many feel that the fear of disunity within a church has negligible power as an argument against women's ordination, since the same argument was used in churches to maintain promotion or acceptance of slavery. For a tradition to be alive, they say, it must be flexible and open to new currents. Since we know women had significant leadership roles in the early church, why, proponents ask, should there be such a sense of discontinuity? The order of deaconess was present in the Orthodox Church until the twelfth century.[26] The importance of tradition did not seem to apply to women when that order disappeared.

Charges of Sexism

Beyond arguments for the ordination of women that point to different Bible passages or to women's leadership abilities, there is the argument which charges that the underlying reason for the lack of women clergy is not Scriptural injunctions per se, nor theology, nor tradition, nor anything else but simply patriarchy and sexism. As one woman put it,

> Anthropologists and psychologists suggest that patriarchy is rooted in misogyny—a hatred of women. This hatred is based on fear: fear of women's creative power; fear, retained from infancy, of the omnipotence of the mother; fear of being found lacking as a man, whether in the husband or son relation; and fear of women's ability to form a society exclusive of men. Patriarchy is reflected in Old Testament references to the God of Abraham, Isaac, Jacob, and is reinforced by the interpretation which holds Eve responsible for the "fall." It is also demonstrated in such New Testament passages as I Timothy 2:9–15, I Corinthians 11:4–12.[27]

It is not difficult, proponents say, to find quotes from the early church fathers and theologians to support the position that women have not been respected as full human beings within the Christian tradition. Tertullian, a third century theologian, said of women,

> You are the devil's gateway: you are the unsealer of that tree: you are the first deserter of the divine law: you are she who persuaded him whom the devil was not valiant enough to attack: you destroyed so easily God's image, man. On account of your desert—that is, death, even the Son of God had to die.[28]

From this point of view, women would seem to be responsible for sin, death, and Christ's crucifixion. St. Augustine equated irrationality with sin and rationality with the divine, and argued that since women made men irrational, they were the embodiment and perpetrators of sin.[29] St. John of Damascus (ca. 675–749), a Doctor of the Church, said, "Woman is a sick she-ass...a hideous tapeworm...the advance post of hell."[30] St. Thomas Aquinas referred to women as "misbegotten males," subscribing to the theory that at conception all fetuses are naturally male and only become female through accident or injury in development. Aquinas also said, "Woman is secondary both in purpose (sex) and in material (body)...This has a negative effect on her moral discernment."[31] Martin Luther, architect of the Reformation, defined marriage as the "plaster God had made for the sore of incontinency," and defined women as "Priests of the Evil One." He also said, "If a woman dies in childbirth, it matters not, because it was for this that she was created by God."[32]

The examples could continue, but the point for some proponents of women's ordination is that the pervasive sexism that these quotes reveal cannot be separated from the theologies that these religious leaders shaped. The problem is not simply misinterpretation of certain biblical passages or choosing a certain theological emphasis. Rather, the problem is understanding and dealing with a long-standing, religiously supported view of women that most of contemporary society now finds unhealthy. Women who have stayed within the church often maintain that it is only as women are ordained and accepted as theologians in greater and greater numbers that sexism in the church will be diminished.

Arguments Within Judaism

Arguments in Judaism for and against female rabbis cover some of the same ground as discussed above, but also some different areas. Those who oppose female rabbis can point to the fact that the Levitic priesthood was restricted to Aaron and his male descendants (Exodus 27:21; Leviticus 16:32), and that women occupied an inferior status among the people of Israel (Deuteronomy 29:10–11). Women, of course, were excluded from circumcision, considered to be the key symbol of inclusion in the Covenant. Those supporting female rabbis point out the role played by Deborah, who led Israel as both a prophet and a judge (Judges 4–5). Genesis 1:26 is often cited as the basis for the principle of equality. Genesis 3:16 ("and he shall rule over you") is taken in that context to mean that male dominance is the result of sin. The ideal state is thus understood to be equality, and Jews are to move toward that until it is fully realized in the messianic age.[33]

Beyond individual texts, however, what is important in Judaism is how the tradition of Jewish law has dealt with the issue. For example, Deuteronomy 6:4–5 gives an important summary of the faith known as the *Shema*. Tradition exempted women from all positive time-bound commandments such as the duty of reciting the *Shema* and putting on *tefillin* (phylacteries), and Deuteronomy 6:7, "Recite them to your children," was interpreted to mean "to your sons and not to your daughters" (*Kiddushin* 29b). The main reasoning for this was that in her duties as wife and mother the woman would often be prevented from performing many of the religious duties imposed upon the men. Since she was exempt from these duties, she naturally could not act as religious leader or representative of the congregation. In the *Midrash* (Num. R. X, 5), it is quoted as a well known and established principle that women may not have the authority to render decisions in religious or ritual matters. To ordain women as rabbis, opponents say, would thus be too radical a break with tradition, and could splinter Judaism. Those opposed to women as rabbis add that a female rabbi who was married could not also properly attend to family duties.[34]

In Reform Judaism, proponents of female rabbis note that there have been many previous breaks with tradition, meaning that the ordination of women would not be a unique event in Reform history. For Reform (and in part for Reconstructionist) Judaism, the tradition is a source of guidance and not governance. Therefore, the decision to ordain women was more of a practical matter, one that involved relating the faith to contemporary understandings and overcoming prejudices against women in new spheres of activity. Orthodox Judaism maintains that *Halakhah* (the body of Jewish law) is an unchanging presentation of God's will. Thus, since there have not been female rabbis in the past, there should not be female rabbis in the future.

The problem of whether or not to ordain women rabbis has been most acute in Conservative Judaism, which has tied itself most strongly to the *Halakhah* as revelatory, yet which also understands the tradition to be dynamic. "The traditional *Halakhah* of the past clearly assigns [women] a position of inferiority in law and status," yet that same *Halakhah* reveals a trend toward the equality of both sexes.[35] The 1979 decision of the Commission for the Study of the Ordination of Women as Rabbis to allow women as rabbis indicated an awareness that the contemporary role of the rabbi is very different from anything discussed in the classical Jewish texts, and that there is no specific *halakhic* category relating to the rabbinate. Instead, *halakhic* problems are connected with ancillary functions that the rabbi might perform, such as serving as a witness in judicial proceedings. Of these problems, the tradition that women could not be appointed to any office of communal responsibility was considered to have been superseded by the practice of including women in high-level positions, an example of which would be Golda Meir. In response to other objections, the Conservative Movement had already made some changes toward the inclusion of women. In the early 1900s, *Bat Mitzvah* was introduced, and women were urged to study the Torah on a basis equal to men. In 1955, women were allowed to read the

Torah at services; in 1973, women were permitted to be counted as part of the *minyan* (quorum) for public worship; and in 1974, a minority of the Law Committee voted to allow women to serve as witnesses in legal proceedings. According to the rules of the committee, a minority of more than two (in this case there were six) allows that vote the status of a legitimate option. The ultimate decision, therefore, was to allow women as rabbis in Conservative Judaism.

Reform Judaism: A Detailed Review

While the above paragraphs provide insight into how the issue of women's ordination has been handled by Jewish groups, a more detailed study of how Reform Judaism has addressed the issue provides additional historical context. In 1875, Rabbi Isaac Mayer Wise established the Hebrew Union College in Cincinnati as a Reform theological seminary and was among the first Jews in America to champion the cause of women's rights. In 1846, he admitted women into the synagogue choir, and in 1851, he integrated the pews. Women attended Hebrew Union College nearly from its beginning, but not with an eye toward ordination. In the 1890s, a woman named Ray Frank developed a reputation as a preacher, lecturer, and journalist along the Pacific Coast. Her name first gained prominence in 1890 when her Day of Atonement sermon to a group of Jews in Spokane Falls, Washington, inspired them to build a house of worship. In 1893, she went to study at Hebrew Union College. She was only there for one semester to study ethics and philosophy, but some newspapers erroneously reported that she had been ordained as the first female rabbi.[36]

The subject of women's ordination was not broached at Hebrew Union College until 1921, when Martha Neumark petitioned the faculty to be assigned to lead High Holy Day services in the fall. The faculty vote was a tie, and the president of the college, Kaufman Kohler, broke the tie with an affirmative vote, provided the congregation approved. He also formed a joint committee of faculty and the Board of Governors to study the larger issue of women's ordination. The majority of the committee decided that, while no specific reason existed to prevent women from being rabbis, it did not want to encourage women in that goal. The Board of Governors felt unable to make a final ruling, and asked for a faculty opinion. The faculty as a whole then voted unanimously to approve a resolution stating: "In view of the fact that Reform Judaism has in many other instances departed from traditional practice, it cannot logically and consistently refuse the ordination of women."[37] The Board of Governors then referred the matter to the Central Conference of American Rabbis, which voted 56–11 to ordain women. Nevertheless, in February 1923, the Board of Governors decided "that no change should be made in the present practice of limiting to males the right to matriculate for the purpose of entering the rabbinate."[38]

From 1928 until her death in 1963, Lily Montague was the chair and spiritual leader of the London West Central Liberal Jewish Congregation and the first Jewish woman to gain formal recognition as a "lay minister." At the 1928 World Union for Progressive Judaism Conference, she preached at the Reform Synagogue in Berlin, becoming the first Jewish woman to occupy a pulpit in Germany. At one point she wrote, "German women must come down from the galleries and take part literally and in a real sense in the construction of and struggle for a living religion for the entire community."[39]

In 1939, Helen Hadassah Levinthal completed the entire rabbinical course at the Jewish Institute of Religion (which merged with Hebrew Union College around 1950). The faculty considered ordaining her, and the great historian of the *Halakhah,* Chaim Tchernowitz (known as Rav Za'ir), favored such a move.[40] The final decision was that the time was not yet right. As a compromise, she was given a Master of Hebrew Literature degree and a certificate stating that she had completed the curriculum. Also in the late 1930s, Regina Jones completed rabbinical studies at the *Hochschule fur die Wissenschaft des Judentums* (Berlin Academy for the Science of Judaism). The faculty refused to ordain her, and she then secured private ordination from Rabbi Max Dienemann of Offenbach, thereby becoming the first female rabbi in history. She served as a rabbi in several social service agencies until 1940, when she was taken by the Nazis and sent to the concentration camp in Theresienstadt, where she later died.

In November 1950, Rabbi William Ackerman, leader of the Beth Israel Reform congregation in Meridian, Mississippi, died, and his wife, Paula Ackerman, stepped in to lead the congregation until a replacement could be found. That replacement was not found until 1954. Even without ordination, she thus became the first woman to serve as spiritual leader of a Jewish congregation in the United States.

The issue of women's ordination was raised again in 1956. A committee of the Central Conference of American Rabbis affirmed the 1922 support of women as rabbis. Nelson Glueck, then president of Hebrew Union College, maintained that the school was ready to ordain any woman who passed the required courses. In the 1960s some women actually entered the rabbinical program, and on June 3, 1972, Sally J. Priesand was ordained as the first female rabbi in the United States.

How Specific Denominations Have Handled the Ordination Question

It should be made clear that the vote of a denomination at some point for or against women's ordination is generally only the tip of the iceberg in relation to the full ordination story. The Church of Sweden, for example, made the basic decision to ordain women in 1958 but then faced numerous obstacles to accomplishing that, since bishops who were opposed to female clergy could block such actions in their dioceses. It wasn't until 1988 that the church's annual assembly eliminated the last possible way to exclude women from the ministry. Bishop Bertil Gaertner of Goeteborg was the only remaining bishop who refused to ordain women, and the assembly voted to allow other bishops to perform ordinations in the Goeteborg Cathedral.[41] A look at how other denominations have handled the ordination problem provides a glimpse at the often dramatic stories surrounding the controversial topic.

Episcopal Church

The Episcopal Church has experienced a great deal of drama as a result of the struggle for women's ordination. In 1964, the General Convention changed the canons to read that deaconesses are "ordered" rather than "appointed," just as male deacons. In 1965, Bishop James Pike, on the basis of the previous year's legislation, formally recognized Phyllis Edwards as a deacon because of her ordination as a deaconess. As a result of the controversy of this action, the House of Bishops opened a new study on ordination of women, which then requested further word from the next Lambeth Conference. The 1968 Lambeth Conference decided to return to its original 1920 decision to regard deaconesses as part of the diaconate and therefore within Holy Orders. In 1971, Suzanne Hiatt became the first woman in the United States to be ordained to the diaconate under the new canon. It has been noted that "it was largely under her leadership that an identifiable movement for ordination actually emerged."[42]

After the General Convention of 1973 rejected the ordination of women to the priesthood, a number of members planned ordinations anyway, in protest. On July 29, 1974, at Philadelphia's Church of the Advocate, two retired and one resigned bishop ordained 11 female deacons to the priesthood. A diocesan bishop was also present, but did not participate in the ordination. Some of the women afterward voluntarily agreed to abstain from priestly functions, and others were prevented from serving as priests by the bishops of their respective dioceses. In August, the bishops of the Episcopal Church issued a statement declaring that the action of the ordaining bishops was a "violation of collegiality" and that the ordinations were not valid. The 11 women stated that they could not accept that conclusion. Dr. Charles Willie resigned from the House of Deputies in protest. In October, three of the women celebrated an Episcopal eucharist in New York's Riverside Church. Since this was not an Episcopal Church, no further action could be taken by church authorities. However, in November the Rev. William Wendt invited one of the women, the Rev. Alison Cheek, to celebrate the eucharist at St. Stephen's and the Incarnation in Washington, D.C., and Wendt was subsequently charged and tried for violations of the canons. The Rev. Peter Beebe in Oberlin, Ohio, was later similarly charged for inviting two of the women to preside at services.

In July 1975, the General Synod of the Church of England passed a motion stating that "there are no fundamental objections to ordination of women to the priesthood," though it declined to actually remove the barriers to women as priests. This basic philosophic support for female priests was, however, extremely important to the Episcopal Church in America as it moved toward its 1976 Convention and another decision about the ordination of women. Another very important influence came in September 1976, when the Anglican Church of Canada agreed to ordain women as priests (actually ordaining its first woman in November 1976). These factors were crucial in the decision of the Episcopal Church in September 1976 to ordain women to the priesthood and to the episcopate.

One year later, the St. Louis Conference of the Fellowship of Concerned Churchmen was held. It was attended by some 1,700 Episcopalians who were frustrated by the decision to ordain women, by the new Episcopal Prayer Book, and by a number of other things, including secular humanism and the activities of the National and World Councils of Churches. The conference concluded with the "Affirmation of St. Louis," a declaration of the intention to leave the Episcopal Church and form the Anglican Catholic Church.

In the October 1977 meeting of the Episcopal Bishops, Presiding Bishop Rt. Rev. John Maury Allin made a statement that shocked the assembly:

> ...I have prayed to be open to any new understanding of either priesthood or human sexuality which may be given to me. Thus far my understanding of Christian priesthood, of the inter-relatedness of the Christian ministry, of New Testament imagery and symbolism, of the roles and interrelations of human sexuality prevent my believing that women can be priests any more than they can become fathers or husbands...I remain unconvinced that women can be priests.[43]

Allin went on to say that he would not let his ideas interfere with the performance of his office, but he would neither ordain a woman himself nor participate in the consecration of a female bishop. He noted that he was attempting to head off a schism of conservatives by making public his personal feelings, which were in sympathy with them. He said he was willing to resign his office if the other bishops felt he was no longer able to lead the church. The House of Bishops then drafted a "conscience clause" as a message of inclusion for both Allin and potential schismatics that they need not leave the church: "...no bishop, priest, deacon or lay person should be coerced or penalized in any manner, nor suffer any canonical disabilities as a result of his or her conscientious objection" to the church's decision to ordain women.[44]

The actual impact on the church of the ordination of women has been less drastic than some of the more negative predictions. The wholesale loss of membership has not occurred, although about five percent of the membership did leave to join traditionalist denominations such as the Anglican Catholic Church.[45] For these persons, the ordination of women was but one of several reasons for departure. The church has continued a general membership decline that began in the 1960s, long before it ordained women; the decline has also affected many other major Protestant churches. The national office of Women in Mission and Ministry points out that actual worship attendance has increased about 25 percent since the ordination of women.[46]

There are still a dozen or so of the 99 domestic dioceses in the church that do not accept female priests. In 1988, the same year that the church elected its first female bishop, one of those dioceses, Quincy in southern Illinois, chose a new bishop whose job description required the candidate to be opposed to women in the priesthood. Proponents of female priests believed such a requirement to be canonically illegal and protested strongly, though the election was upheld. For most of the church, however, the ordination of women as priests is no longer much of an issue. Recent surveys have shown that the majority of both male and female members of the Episcopal Church would (or do) accept a female priest in their diocese. As of 1988 the Episcopal Church had 1,752 ordained women out of a total of 15,000 clergy.

Southern Baptist Convention

That the Southern Baptists have any female clergy at all often comes as a surprise to outsiders, yet the church has had quite a number of female leaders. In the 1700s, the Separate Baptists (the Southern Baptist Convention was not organized until 1845) recognized both deaconesses and eldresses who were set apart in a manner similar to their male counterparts. Some, like Martha Stearns Marshall, became quite well known for their preaching and praying styles. Many Southern Baptist churches continued to have deaconesses well into the twentieth century, but reactions against the suffragette movement and the rise of the modern church committee caused that office to disappear almost entirely.[47]

On August 9, 1964, Addie Davis was ordained at the Watts Street Baptist Church in Durham, North Carolina, the first woman formally ordained to ministry in a Southern Baptist church, although she was not able to find a church to pastor. No woman was ordained between 1964 and 1972.[48] In that year, Druecillar Fordham became the Southern Baptist Convention's second ordained woman, its first female pastor, and also its first black ordained female pastor.[49] It has been estimated that about 450 women have since been ordained in Southern Baptist churches.[50] The vast majority of these women have been unable to pastor churches, and have instead taken positions as counselors, directors of missions, and in other places beyond the local church. More and more women are finding at least small churches to pastor—the largest church with a woman as senior pastor is the Prescott Memorial Baptist Church in Memphis, Tennessee, with about 235 members. There are even perhaps a dozen clergy couples in Southern Baptist Convention churches. One woman among those couples, Anne Rosser of Richmond, Virginia, baptized three converts in 1980, the first ordained female minister known to have baptized in a Southern Baptist church.[51] Female deacons (no longer deaconesses) have seen a resurgence, and are far more numerous than are female clergy.

Reactions to these female clergy have, of course, been varied. A 1977 survey found that about 17 percent of Southern Baptists favored female pastors, 24 percent favored ordination for women as chaplains, and over 75 percent favored ordination for women in the fields of religious education, youth ministries, or social work. About two-thirds believed that Southern Baptist attitudes toward women in ministry would change in favor of acceptance in the next 25 years.[52] In 1974 the Washington, D.C., association of Southern Baptist churches actually encouraged the ordination of women, but most associations and state conventions have remained silent on the issue. Some have excluded from fellowship churches that have supported women's ordination. In 1984, the Southern Baptist Convention adopted a resolution opposing women's ordination (see index), a resolution which provoked a negative reaction from many. Even many of those opposed to women's ordination believed that the resolution was an un-Baptist violation of local church autonomy. Meanwhile, some infrastructures have been developing for female clergy. *Folio*, a newsletter for Southern Baptist women in ministry, was begun in 1983, and in 1987, the newly organized Southern Baptist Alliance pledged financial support to ordained female pastors who had lost such support from the Home Mission Board.

Lutheran Church-Missouri Synod

The Lutheran Church-Missouri Synod (LCMS), which has continued to affirm its position against the ordination of women, nevertheless has a number of internal pressures working in the other direction. The most public tension surrounds the proposed heresy trial of Daniel Bruch, a teacher of sociology at the synod's Concordia College in St. Paul, Minnesota. In May 1988, when Bruch was still a campus minister for the LCMS at the University of Wisconsin, he published an article in *Inter-Connections*, a journal of the synod's campus ministry division. As per standard practice, the article was first approved by the synod's commission on doctrinal review. The article did not directly discuss women's ordination, but suggested that the church ought to follow society's lead in allowing women to perform tasks traditionally not open to them. After publication of the article, critics charged that the article was contrary to LCMS doctrine on the role of women in the church, and particularly understood it to be a challenge to the current stand on the ordination of women. After the criticism surfaced, the committee on doctrinal review took a second look at the article and withdrew its certification. In 1989, three LCMS pastors formally charged Bruch with heresy and sought a trial to expel him. The issue is still unresolved.

A similar situation exists with Dr. Alvin J. Schmidt. Formerly a professor at the LCMS seminary, Concordia, in Fort Wayne, Indiana, he was fired after arguing that there were no valid theological or biblical grounds for excluding women from the ministry. In 1989, the American Association of University Professors formally charged the seminary with violations of academic freedom in relation to the firing of Schmidt. Incidents such as these are not likely to disappear and will be difficult for the LCMS.

What The Future Will Bring

For those religious groups already ordaining women, the future will likely bring a continued increase in the percentage of female clergy and in the percentage of women in positions of denominational power, such as senior clergy of large churches and as bishops or other high administrative positions. The advancement of women into these ranks is considered an indication of acceptance, and remains a significant barrier. In the United Church of Christ, for example, out of 1,460 female clergy in 1986, only 277 (19 percent) were heads of a pastoral staff. This is the case despite the fact that the United Church of Christ (then the Congregational Church) was the first Protestant church to ordain a woman (1853).[53]

Also slated for continued increase is the sheer number of female clergy. In 1987 there were 6,108 women enrolled in ordination programs in seminaries (an increase of 110 percent since 1976), accounting for approximately 25 percent of the total seminary enrollment.[54] In some denominations, women account for more than 50 percent of seminary students. A number of commentators have suggested that the ministry will become more like other social service professions, such as nursing, which have been relegated to women; as the social prestige of the ministry declines, men will look elsewhere for career opportunities.

For those groups that do not ordain women, the trend suggests that more and more of them will. It is likely that sometime in the 1990s (1993 at the earliest), the Church of England will agree to ordain women as priests. This will be highly influential for those Anglican bodies worldwide that do not yet ordain women as priests, and will probably lead them to follow suit. In Orthodox Judaism there are a few people who are already voicing support for female rabbis. Change will not be fast, but may take place in gradual steps over the next few generations. One supporter is Blu Greenberg, who wrote in 1984 that even in Orthodoxy, "young girls study Talmudic texts in a way that was not done even a bare decade ago."[55]

Within the Roman Catholic Church, support (at least within the United States) is growing rapidly for female priests. A 1979 Gallup Poll showed that 40 percent of the membership agree with the ordination of women, an increase from 36 percent in 1977 and from 29 percent in 1974.[56] Since that time the percentage in support has become a majority. In 1975, in Detroit, the First Roman Catholic Women's Ordination Conference was held, a landmark event. In 1978, in Baltimore, an even larger Second Roman Catholic Women's Ordination Conference was held, with 2,000 participants attending. The U.S. Catholic bishops are aware of the struggle on women's issues, and this has both stimulated activity and blocked concrete steps. As of late 1990, the Pastoral Letter from the U.S. bishops on women, which has been in process for nine years, has still not been completed and released. A draft of April 3, 1990, titled "One in Christ Jesus: A Pastoral Response to the Concerns of Women for Church and Society," retreated from the more liberal tone and content of an initial draft released in 1988. It has been difficult for the bishops to satisfy the many audiences which will respond to their Pastoral Letter.

An additional element in the Roman Catholic conflict is the fact that every year there are fewer active diocesan priests, while the church as a whole is growing. There are now over 1,000 parishes without a priest, run instead by "pastoral administrators" or nuns filling that role. Practical necessity has led to innovations in the functions of ministry. Lay ministers now can administer communion, whereas in the past that was strictly the province of the priest. Some have suggested that the lack of male priests alone will put tremendous pressure on the church to make changes in the concept of ministry, which might include the admission of women.

Overall, this generation is witnessing a significant crossroads in the mission and ministry of religious groups worldwide, as new arenas are opened up to women. These changes will not just be visible ones, like seeing a different face behind the pulpit, but will also be conceptual ones. The struggle over female clergy has already related significantly with changes in how people interpret the Bible and tradition, and the increasing presence of women will undoubtedly lead to further alterations in how the churches think of themselves and how they act in the world. Only time will reveal the complete dimensions of these transformations.

Endnotes

1 Jacquet, 3–8.

2 Hitchings, 4. The two quotes that Hitchings uses are from an article in the Universalist newspaper *Star in the West* from February 8, 1868.

3 I am indebted to Constant Jacquet's paper for many of these dates.

4 Ari L. Goldman, "Black Women's Bumpy Path to Church Leadership," *New York Times*, Metropolitan section, Sunday, 29 July 1990, p.1.

5 Hitchings, 6.

6 Brereton and Klein in Reuther and McLaughlin, 319.

7 The Southern Baptist Convention ordained its first woman in 1964, but this was the decision of a local congregation only, not of the convention as a whole.

8 Bam, 3–4.

9 John Barton, "Fact Sheet on the Ordination of Women," Church of England Broadcasting Department, 1989.

10 Dirks-Blatt, 440–441.

11 Harkness, 217–218.

12 Parvey, 34.

13 Dirks-Blatt, 436–437.

14 Carson and Price, 245.

15 Dirk van der Linde, "Why Can't Women Be Pastors?" *Lutheran Witness* (April 1990): 5.

16 In the paper "Women in the Church: Scriptural Principles and Ecclesial Practice" from the Lutheran Church-Missouri Synod (see index), see the section titled "Excursus on the Service of Women in the Early Church."

17 Pope John Paul II, *On the Dignity and Vocation of Women (1989):* 98.

18 As quoted in Parvey, 8.

19 Dirks-Blatt, 436–437.

20 Nicolas Chitescu, "The Ordination of Women," in *Concerning the Ordination of Women* (Geneva: World Council of Churches, 1964), 57.

21 Georges Khodre, "The Ordination of Women," in *Concerning the Ordination of Women* (Geneva: World Council of Churches, 1964), 63.

22 Quoted in Dirks-Blatt, 436–437.

23 Carson and Price, 250.

24 Harkness, 208.

25 As quoted in Harkness 208.,

26 Chitescu, P. 57,

27 Parsons in Davy, 173–174.

28 Quoted in Boldrey, 40.

29 Parsons in Davy, 174.

30 Quoted in Chittester, 7.

31 Quoted in Chittester, 2.

32 Reuther, 71, and McGrath, 94.

33 Blu Greenberg, "Will There Be Orthodox Women Rabbis?" *Judaism* 33:1 (Winter 1984): 26–27.

34 See the argument presented by Joseph K. Lauterbach, in the 1922 statement from the Central Conference of American Rabbis (see index).

35 Robert Gordis, "The Ordination of Women—A History of the Question." *Judaism* 33:1 (Winter 1984): 6–7.

36 Umansky in Reuther and McLaughlin, 343.

37 Ibid., 340.

38 Ibid.

39 Quoted in Umansky, 344.

40 Gordis, 8.

41 *The Lutheran* (December 14, 1988): 30.

42 Carter in Reuther and McLaughlin, 359.

43 Hyer, 281.

44 Ibid., 282.

45 This membership loss in the Episcopal Church is apparently the smallest loss associated with the influx of women clergy among the denominations which have made that change. In all cases, predictions of large-scale defections have proven groundless. In addition, ecumenical relations have also by and large survived among churches where women have entered the clergy. There were fears that the 1958 decision of the Church of Sweden (Lutheran) to ordain women would jeopardize relations with the Church of England. Despite some tension, however, the relationship remained intact.

46 From "Women Priests and the Episcopal Church in the USA" (see index).

47 H. Leon McBeth, *The Baptist Heritage* (Nashville: Broadman Press, 1987), 690–691.

48 H. Leon McBeth, "The Ordination of Women." *Review and Expositor* 78 (1981): 516.

49 Blevins, 45.

50 *Christianity Today* (October 16, 1987): 40.

51 McBeth, *The Baptist Heritage*, 691.

52 Ibid., 692.

53 Jacquet, 7. See also "Women Clergy Still Experiencing Discrimination, UCC Survey Finds," Office of Communication, United Church of Christ, December 18, 1986.

54 Jacquet, 8.

55 Greenberg, 30.

56 Pomerleau et al., 299.

57 George W. Cornell, "Analyst Finds Church Responsibilities Are Shifting." *Home News* (September 1, 1990): B-4.

Selected Sources

Bam, Brigalia, ed. *What Is Ordination Coming To?* Geneva: World Council of Churches, 1970.

Blevins, Carolyn DeArmond, "Patterns of Ministry Among Southern Baptist Women," *Baptist History and Heritage* XXII:3 (July, 1987): 41–49.

Bliss, Kathleen. *The Service and Status of Women in the Churches.* London: SCM Press, 1952.

Boldrey, Richard, and Joyce Boldrey. *Chauvinist or Feminist?: Paul's View of Women.* Grand Rapids, Michigan: Baker Book House, 1976.

Bozarth-Campbell, Alla. *Womanpriest: A Personal Odyssey.* New York: Paulist Press, 1978.

Brunner, Peter. *The Ministry and the Ministry of Women.* St. Louis: Concordia Publishing House, 1971.

Calkins, Gladys Gilkey. *Follow Those Women.* New York: National Council of Churches, 1961.

Carson, Mary Faith, and James J. H. Price, "The Ordination of Women and the Function of the Bible," *Journal of Presbyterian History* 59,2 (Summer 1981): 245–265.

Chittester, Joan. *Women, Ministry and the Church.* New York: Paulist Press, 1983.

Concerning the Ordination of Women. Geneva: World Council of Churches, 1964.

Davy, Shirley, ed. *Women Work and Worship in the United Church of Canada.* United Church of Canada, 1983.

Demarest, Victoria Booth. *Sex and Spirit: God, Women, and Ministry.* St. Petersburg, Florida: Valkyrie Press, 1977.

Dirks-Blatt, Henny G., "The Ordination of Women to the Ministry in the Member Churches of the World Alliance of Reformed Churches," *Reformed World* 38,8 (1985): 434–489.

Ermarth, Margaret Sittler. *Adam's Fractured Rib.* Philadelphia: Fortress Press, 1970.

Hageman, Alice L. *Sexist Religion and Women in the Church: No More Silence!* New York: Association Press, 1974.

Hamilton, Michael P., and Nancy S. Montgomery, eds. *The Ordination of Women: Pro and Con.* New York: Morehouse-Barlow Co., 1975.

Harkness, Georgia. *Women in Church and Society: A Historical and Theological Inquiry.* Nashville: Abingdon Press, 1972.

Hewitt, Emily C. and Suzanne R. Hiatt. *Women Priests: Yes or No.* New York: The Seabury Press, 1973.

Hitchings, Catherine F. *Universalist and Unitarian Women Ministers.* 2nd ed. Unitarian Universalist Historical Society, 1985.

Hyer, Marjorie, "Bloodletting, Episcopal Style: How Not to Heal Wounds," *Christianity and Crisis* 37 (November 28, 1977): 281–3.

Jacquet, Constant H., Jr. *Women Ministers in 1986 and 1977: A Ten Year Review.* New York: National Council of Churches, 1988.

Jewett, Paul King. *The Ordination of Women: An Essay on the Office of Christian Ministry.* Grand Rapids, Michigan: Wm. B. Eerdmans Publishing Co., 1980.

Judaism. 33,1 (Winter 1984): 6–90

Keller, Rosemary, Louise Queen, and Hilah Thomas, eds. *Women in New Worlds*. Vol. 2. Nashville: Abingdon Press, 1982.

Lotz, David W., ed. *Altered Landscapes*. Grand Rapids, Michigan: Wm. B. Eerdmans Publishing Co., 1989.

Lynch, John E., "The Ordination of Women: Protestant Experience in Ecumenical Perspective," *Journal of Ecumenical Studies* 12 (Spring 1975), 173–97.

Maitland, Sara. *A Map of the New Country: Women and Christianity*. London: Routledge and Kegan Paul Ltd., 1983.

McBeth, H. Leon. *The Baptist Heritage*. Nashville, Tennessee: Broadman Press, 1987.

________. "The Ordination of Women," *Review and Expositor* 78 (1981): 515–530.

McGrath, Sister Albertus Magnus. *Women and the Church*. Garden City, New York: Image Books, 1976.

Parvey, Constance F., ed. *Ordination of Women in Ecumenical Perspective*. Geneva: World Council of Churches, 1980.

Pomerleau, Dolly, Maureen Fiedler, and William R. Callahan, "Women Priests: A Research Report," *America* (November 17, 1979): 299–300.

Priesand, Sally. *Judaism and the New Woman*. New York: Behrman House, 1975.

Ruether, Rosemary R. *Women-Church: Theology and Practice of Feminist Liturgical Communities*. San Francisco: Harper and Row, 1985.

Ruether, Rosemary R. and Eleanor McLaughlin, eds. *Women of Spirit: Female Leadership in the Jewish and Christian Traditions*. New York: Simon and Schuster, 1979.

Swidler, Leonard and Arlene Swidler. *Women Priests: A Catholic Commentary on the Vatican Declaration*. New York: Paulist Press, 1977.

Tiemeyer, Raymond, ed. *The Ordination of Women*. Augsburg Publishing House, 1970.

Wakelin, Rosemary. *Call Accepted: Reflections on Women's Ordination in the Free Churches*. London: The Movement for Ordination of Women, 1988.

Zerbst, Fritz. *The Office of Woman in the Church: A Study in Practical Theology*. St. Louis: Concordia Publishing House, 1955.

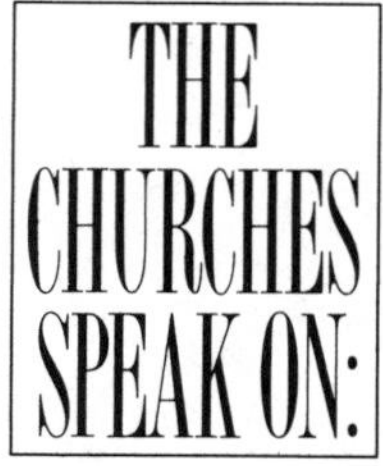

Women's Ordination

Roman Catholic Church

The Roman Catholic Church, which is the largest Christian church in the world, is headquartered in Vatican City. With more than 50,000,000 members in the United States and an additional 10,000,000 in Canada, it is also the largest religious body in North America. Its tremendous size, influence, and resources have both required and enabled it to make statements on the pressing issues of the world, including women's ordination.

The first major statement of the Roman Catholic Church on the issue of the ordination of women was in 1976. It was the first time in history that the issue had become important enough to warrant clear explanation and justification from the church's highest authorities. Since that time, pressure from the world ecclesiastical community to ordain women has grown, with approximately half of the member bodies of the World Council of Churches now ordaining women. The church also faces increasing internal pressure from portions of its membership as well as a consistent shortage of persons (i.e., males) entering the priesthood. Due to these factors, the Catholic church will bear watching in the future to see how its opinion on this issue develops.

ROMAN CATHOLIC CHURCH—SACRED CONGREGATION FOR THE DOCTRINE OF THE FAITH

DECLARATION ON THE QUESTION OF THE ADMISSION OF WOMEN TO THE MINISTERIAL PRIESTHOOD (1976)

Introduction

The Role of Women in Modern Society and the Church

Among the characteristics that mark our present age, Pope John XXIII indicated, in his Encyclical *Pacem in Terris* of April 11, 1963, "the part that women are now taking in public life. . . . This is a development that is perhaps of swifter growth among Christian nations, but it is also happening extensively, if more slowly, among nations that are heirs to different traditions and imbued with a different culture".[1] Along the same lines, the Second Vatican Council, enumerating in its Pastoral Constitution *Gaudium et Spes* the forms of discrimination touching upon the basic rights of the person which must be overcome and eliminated as being contrary to God's plan, gives first place to discrimination based upon sex.[2] The resulting equality will secure the building up of a world that is not levelled out and uniform but harmonious and unified, if men and women contribute to it their own resources and dynamism, as Pope Paul VI recently stated.[3]

In the life of the Church herself, as history shows us, women have played a decisive role and accomplished tasks of outstanding value. One has only to think of the foundresses of the great religious families, such as Saint Clare and Saint Teresa of Avila. The latter, moreover, and Saint Catherine of Siena, have left writings so rich in spiritual doctrine that Pope Paul VI has included them among the Doctors of the Church. Nor could one forget the great number of women who have consecrated themselves to the Lord for the exercise of charity or for the missions, and the Christian wives who have had a profound influence on their families, particularly for the passing on of the faith to their children.

But our age gives rise to increased demands. "Since in our time women have an ever more active share in the whole life of society, it is very important that they participate more widely also in the various sectors of the Church's apostolate".[4] This charge of the Second Vatican Council has already set in motion the whole process of change now taking place: these various experiences of course need to come to maturity. But as Pope Paul VI also remarked,[5] a very large number of Christian communities are already benefitting from the apostolic commitment of women. Some of these women are called to take part in councils set up for pastoral reflection, at the diocesan or parish level; and the Apostolic See has brought women into some of its working bodies.

For some years now various Christian communities stemming from the sixteenth-century Reformation or of later origin have been admitting women to the pastoral office on a par with men. This initiative has led to petitions and writings by members of these communities and similar groups, directed towards making this admission a general thing; it has also led to contrary reactions. This therefore constitutes an ecumenical problem, and the Catholic Church must make her thinking known on it, all the more because in various sectors of opinion the question has been asked whether she too could not modify her discipline and admit women to priestly ordination. A number of Catholic theologians have even posed this question publicly, evoking studies not only in the sphere of exegesis, patrology and Church history but also in the field of the history of institutions and customs, of sociology and of psychology. The various arguments capable of clarifying this important problem have been submitted to a critical examination. As we are dealing with a debate which classical theology scarcely touched upon, the current argumentation runs the risk of neglecting essential elements.

For these reasons, in execution of a mandate received from the Holy Father and echoing the declaration which he himself made in his letter of November 30, 1976,[6] the Sacred Congregation for the Doctrine of the Faith judges it necessary to recall that the Church, in fidelity to the example of the Lord, does not consider herself authorized to admit women to priestly ordination. The Sacred Congregation deems it opportune at the present juncture to explain this position of the Church. It is a position which will perhaps cause pain but whose positive value will become apparent in the long run, since it can be of help in deepening understanding of the respective roles of men and of women.

1. The Church's Constant Tradition

The Catholic Church has never felt that priestly or episcopal ordination can be validly conferred on women. A few heretical sects in the first centuries, especially Gnostic ones, entrusted the exercise of the priestly ministry to women: this innovation was immediately noted and condemned by the Fathers, who considered it as unacceptable in the Church.[7] It is true that in the writings of the Fathers one will find the undeniable influence of prejudices unfavorable to women, but nevertheless, it should be noted that these prejudices had hardly any influence on their pastoral activity, and still less on their spiritual direction. But over and above considerations inspired by the spirit of the times, one finds expressed—especially in the canonical documents of the Antiochian and Egyptian traditions—this essential reason, namely, that by calling only men to the priestly Order and ministry in its true sense, the Church intends to remain faithful to the type of ordained ministry willed by the Lord Jesus Christ and carefully maintained by the Apostles.[8]

The same conviction animates medieval theology,[9] even if the Scholastic doctors, in their desire to clarify by reason the data of faith, often present arguments on this point that modern thought would have difficulty in admitting or would even rightly reject. Since that period and up to our own time, it can be said that the question has not been raised again, for the practice has enjoyed peaceful and universal acceptance.

The Church's tradition in the matter has thus been so firm in the course of the centuries that the Magisterium has not felt the need to intervene in order to formulate a principle which was not attacked, or to defend a law which was not challenged. But each time that this tradition had the occasion to manifest itself, it witnessed to the Church's desire to conform to the model left to her by the Lord.

The same tradition has been faithfully safeguarded by the Churches of the East. Their unanimity on this point is all the more remarkable since in many other questions their discipline admits of a great diversity. At the present time these same Churches refuse to associate themselves with requests directed towards securing the accession of women to priestly ordination.

2. The Attitude of Christ

Jesus Christ did not call any woman to become part of the Twelve. If he acted in this way, it was not in order to conform to the customs of his time, for his attitude towards women was quite different from that of his milieu, and he deliberately and courageously broke with it.

For example, to the great astonishment of his own disciples Jesus converses publicly with the Samaritan woman (cf. Jn 4:27); he takes no notice of the state of legal impurity of the woman who had suffered from haemorrhages (cf. Mt 9:20-22), he allows a sinful woman to approach him in the house of Simon the Pharisee (cf. Lk 7:37 ff.); and by pardoning the woman taken in adultery, he means to show that one must not be more severe towards the fault of a woman than towards that of a man (cf. Jn 8:11). He does not hesitate to depart from the Mosaic Law in order to affirm the equality of the rights and duties of men and women with regard to the marriage bond (cf. Mk 10:2-11; Mt. 19:3-9).

In his itinerant ministry Jesus was accompanied not only by the Twelve but also by a group of women: "Mary, surnamed the Magdalene, from whom seven demons had gone out, Joanna the wife of Herod's steward Chuza, Susanna, and several others who provided for them out of their own resources" (Lk 8:2-3). Contrary to the Jewish mentality, which did not accord great value to the testimony of women, as Jewish law attests, it was nevertheless women who were the first to have the privilege of seeing the risen Lord, and it was they who were charged by Jesus to take the first paschal message to the Apostles themselves (cf. Mt 28:7-10; Lk 24:9-10; Jn 20:11-18), in order to prepare the latter to become the official witnesses to the Resurrection.

It is true that these facts do not make the matter immediately obvious. This is no surprise, for the questions that the Word of God brings before us go beyond the obvious. In order to reach the ultimate meaning of the mission of Jesus and the ultimate meaning of Scripture, a purely historical exegisis of the texts cannot suffice. But it must be recognized that we have here a number of convergent indications that make all the more remarkable the fact that Jesus did not entrust the apostolic charge[10] to women. Even his Mother, who was so closely associated with the mystery of her Son, and whose incomparable role is emphasized by the Gospels of Luke and John, was not invested with the apostolic ministry. This fact was to lead the Fathers to present her as the example of Christ's will in this domain; as Pope Innocent III repeated later, at the beginning of the thirteenth century, "Although the Blessed Virgin Mary surpassed in dignity and in excellence all the Apostles, nevertheless it was not to her but to them that the Lord entrusted the keys of the Kingdom of Heaven".[11]

3. The Practice of The Apostles

The apostolic community remained faithful to the attitude of Jesus towards women.

Although Mary occupied a privileged place in the little circle of those gathered in the Upper Room after the Lord's Ascension (cf. Acts 1:14), it was not she who was called to enter the College of the Twelve at the time of the election that resulted in the choice of Matthias: those who were put forward were two disciples whom the Gospels do not even mention.

On the day of Pentecost, the Holy Spirit filled them all, men and women (cf. Acts 2:1; 1-14), yet the proclamation of the fulfillment of the prophecies in Jesus was made only by "Peter and the Eleven" (Acts 2:14).

When they and Paul went beyond the confines of the Jewish world, the preaching of the Gospel and the Christian life in the Greco-Roman civilization impelled them to break with Mosaic practices, sometimes regretfully. They could therefore have envisaged conferring ordination on women, if they had not been convinced of their duty of fidelity to the Lord on this point. In the Hellenistic world, the cult of a number of pagan divinities was entrusted to priestesses. In fact the Greeks did not share the ideas of the Jews: although their philosophers taught the inferiority of women, historians nevertheless emphasize the existence of a certain movement for the advancement of women during the Imperial period. In fact we know from the book of the Acts and from the Letters of Saint Paul that certain women worked with the Apostle for the Gospel (cf. Rom 16:3-12; Phil 4:3). Saint Paul lists their names with gratitude in the final salutations of the Letters. Some of them often exercised an important influence on conversions: Priscilla, Lydia and others; especially Priscilla, who took it on herself to complete the instruction of Apollos (cf. Acts 18:26); Phoebe, in the service of the Church of Cenchreae (cf. Rom 16:1). All these facts manifest within the Apostolic Church a considerable evolution vis-a-vis the customs of Judaism. Nevertheless at no time was there a question of conferring ordination on these women.

In the Pauline Letters, exegetes of authority have noted a difference between two formulas used by the Apostle: he writes indiscriminately "my fellow workers" (Rom 16:3; Phil 4:2-3) when referring to men and women helping him in his apostolate in one way or another; but he reserves the title "God's fellow workers" (1 Cor 3:9; cf. 1 Thess 3:1) to Apollos, Timothy and himself, thus designated because they are directly set apart for the apostolic ministry and the preaching of the Word of God. In spite of the so important role played by women on the day of the Resurrection, their collaboration was not extended by Saint Paul to the official and public proclamation of the message, since this proclamation belongs exclusively to the apostolic mission.

4. Permanent Value of the Attitude of Jesus and the Apostles

Could the Church today depart from this attitude of Jesus and the Apostles, which has been considered as normative by the whole of tradition up to our own day? Various arguments have been put forward in favor of a positive reply to this question, and these must now be examined.

It has been claimed in particular that the attitude of Jesus and the Apostles is explained by the influence of their milieu and their times. It is said that, if Jesus did not entrust to women and not even to his Mother a ministry assimilating them to the Twelve, this was because historical circumstances did not permit him to do so. No one however has ever proved—and it is clearly impossible to prove—that this attitude is inspired only by social and cultural reasons. As we have seen, an examination of the Gospels shows on the contrary that Jesus broke with the prejudices of his time, by widely contravening the discriminations practiced with regard to women. One therefore cannot maintain that, by not calling women to enter the group of the Apostles, Jesus was simply letting himself be guided by reasons of expediency. For all the more reason, social and cultural conditioning did not hold back the Apostles working in the Greek milieu, where the same forms of discrimination did not exist.

Another objection is based upon the transitory character that one claims to see today in some of the prescriptions of Saint Paul concerning women, and upon the difficulties that some aspects of his teaching raise in this regard. But it must be noted that these ordinances, probably inspired by the customs of the period, concern scarcely more than disciplinary practices of minor importance, such as the obligation imposed upon women to wear a veil on the head (1 Cor 11:2-16); such requirements no longer have a normative value. However, the Apostle's forbidding of women "to speak" in the assemblies (cf. 1 Cor 14:34-35; 1 Tim 2:12) is of a different nature, and exegetes define its meaning in this way: Paul in no way opposes the right, which he elsewhere recognizes as possessed by women, to prophesy in the assembly (cf. 1 Cor 11:5); the prohibition solely concerns the official function of teaching in the Christian assembly. For Saint Paul this prescription is bound up with the divine plan of creation (cf. 1 Cor 11:7; Gen 2:18-24): it would be difficult to see in it the expression of a cultural fact. Nor should it be forgotten that we owe to Saint Paul one of the most vigorous texts in the New Testament on the fundamental equality of men and women, as children of God in Christ (cf. Gal 3:28). Therefore there is no reason for accusing him of prejudices against women, when we note the trust that he shows towards them and the collaboration that he asks of them in his apostolate.

But over and above these objections taken from the history of apostolic times, those who support the legitimacy of change in the matter turn to the Church's practice in her sacramental discipline. It has been noted, in our day especially, to what extent the Church is conscious of possessing a certain power over the sacraments, even though they were instituted by Christ. She has used this power down the centuries in order to determine their signs and the conditions of their administration: recent decisions of Popes Pius XII and Paul VI are proof of this.[12] However, it must be emphasized that this power, which is a real one, has definite limits. As Pope Pius XII recalled: "The Church has no power over the substance of the sacraments, that is to say, over what Christ the Lord, as the sources of Revelation bear witness, determined should be maintained in the sacramental sign".[13] This was already the teaching of the Council of Trent, which declared: "In the Church there has always existed this power, that in the administration of the sacraments, provided that their substance remains unaltered, she can lay down or modify what she considers more fitting either for the benefit of those who receive them or for respect towards those same sacraments, according to varying circumstances, times or places".[14]

Moreover, it must not be forgotten that the sacramental signs are not conventional ones. Not only is it true that, in many respects, they are natural signs because they respond to the deep symbolism of actions and things, but they are more than this: they are principally meant to link the person of every period to the supreme Event of the history of salvation, in order to enable that person to understand, through all the Bible's wealth of pedagogy and symbolism, what grace they signify and produce. For example, the sacrament of the Eucharist is not only a fraternal meal, but at the same time the memorial which makes present and actual Christ's sacrifice and his offering by the Church. Again, the priestly ministry is not just a pastoral service; it ensures the continuity of the functions entrusted by Christ to the Apostles and the continuity of the powers related to those functions. Adaptation to civilizations and times therefore cannot abolish, on essential points, the sacramental reference to constitutive events of Christianity and to Christ himself.

In the final analysis it is the Church, through the voice of her Magisterium, that, in these various domains, decides what can change and what must remain immutable. When she judges that she cannot accept certain changes, it is because she knows that she is bound by Christ's manner of acting. Her attitude, despite appearances, is therefore not one of archaism but of fidelity: it can be truly understood only in this light. The Church makes pronouncements in virtue of the Lord's promise and the presence of the Holy Spirit, in order to proclaim better the mystery of Christ and to safeguard and manifest the whole of its rich content.

This practice of the Church therefore has a normative character: in the fact of conferring priestly ordination only on men, it is a question of an unbroken tradition throughout the history of the Church, universal in the East and in the West, and alert to repress abuses immediately. This norm, based on Christ's example, has been and is still observed because it is considered to conform to God's plan for his Church.

5. The Ministerial Priesthood in the Light of the Mystery of Christ

Having recalled the Church's norm and the basis thereof, it seems useful and opportune to illustrate this norm by showing the profound fittingness that theological reflection discovers between the proper nature of the sacrament of Order, with its specific reference to the mystery of Christ, and the fact that only men have been called to receive priestly ordination. It is not a question here of bringing forward a demonstrative argument, but of clarifying this teaching by the analogy of faith.

The Church's constant teaching, repeated and clarified by the Second Vatican Council and again recalled by the 1971 Synod of Bishops and by the Sacred Congregation of the Doctrine of the Faith in its Declaration of June 24, 1973, declares that the bishop or the priest, in the exercise of his ministry, does not act in his own name, *in persona propria:* he represents Christ, who acts through him: "the priest truly acts in the place of Christ", as Saint Cyprian already wrote in the third century.[15] It is this ability to represent Christ that Saint Paul considered as characteristic of his apostolic function (cf. 2 Cor 5:20; Gal 4:14). The supreme expression of this representation is found in the altogether special form it assumes in the celebration of the Eucharist, which is the source and center of the Church's unity, the sacrificial meal in which the People of God are associated in the sacrifice of Christ: the priest, who alone has the power to perform it, then acts not only through the effective power conferred on him by Christ, but *in persona Christi,*[16] taking the role of Christ, to the point of being his very image, when he pronounces the words of consecration.[17]

The Christian priesthood is therefore of a sacramental nature: the priest is a sign, the supernatural effectiveness of which comes from the ordination received, but a sign that must be perceptible[18] and which the faithful must be able to recognize with ease. The whole sacramental economy is in fact based upon natural signs, on symbols imprinted upon the human psychology: "Sacramental signs," says Saint Thomas, "represent what they signify by natural resemblance."[19] The same natural resemblance is required for persons as for things: when Christ's role in the Eucharist is to be expressed sacramentally, there would not be this "natural resemblance" which must exist between Christ and his minister if the role of Christ were not taken by a man: in such a case it would be difficult to see in the minister the image of Christ. For Christ himself was and remains a man.

Christ is of course the firstborn of all humanity, of women as well as men: the unity which he re-established after sins is such that there are no more distinctions between Jew and Greek, slave and free, male and female, but all are one in Christ Jesus (cf. Gal 3:28). Nevertheless, the Incarnation of the Word took place according to the male sex: this is indeed a question of fact, and this fact, while not implying an alleged natural superiority of man over woman, cannot be disassociated from the economy of salvation: it is, indeed, in harmony with the entirety of God's plan as God himself has revealed it, and of which the mystery of the Convenant is the nucleus.

For the salvation offered by God to men and women, the union with him to which they are called—in short, the Covenant—took on, from the Old Testament Prophets onwards, the privileged form of a nuptial mystery: for God the Chosen People is seen as his ardently loved spouse. Both Jewish and Christian tradition has discovered the depth of this intimacy of love by reading and rereading the Song of Songs; the divine Bridegroom will remain faithful even when the Bride betrays his love, when Israel is unfaithful to God (cf. Hos 1-3; Jer 2). When the "fullness of time" (Gal 4:4) comes, the Word, the Son of God, takes on flesh in order to establish and seal the new and eternal Covenant in his blood, which will be shed for many so that sins may be forgiven. His death will gather together again the scattered children of God; from his pierced side will be born the Church, as Eve was born from Adam's side. At that time there is fully and eternally accomplished the nuptial mystery proclaimed and hymned in the Old Testament: Christ is the Bridegroom; the Church is his Bride, whom he loves because he has gained her by his blood and made her glorious, holy and without blemish, and henceforth he is inseparable from her. This nuptial theme, which is developed from the Letters of Saint Paul onwards (cf. 2 Cor 11:2; Eph 5:22-23) to the writings of Saint John (cf. especially Jn 3:29; Rev 19:7,9), is present also in the Synoptic Gospels: the Bridegroom's friends must not fast as long as he is with them (cf. Mk 2:19); the Kingdom of Heaven is like a king who gave a feast for his son's wedding (cf. Mt 22:1-14). It is through this Scriptural language, all interwoven with symbols, and which expresses and affects man and woman in their profound identity, that there is revealed to us the mystery of God and Christ, a mystery which of itself is unfathomable.

That is why we can never ignore the fact that Christ is a man. And therefore, unless one is to disregard the importance of this symbolism for the economy of Revelation, it must be admitted that, in actions which demand the character of ordination and in which Christ himself, the author of the Covenant, the Bridegroom and Head of the Church, is represented, exercising his ministry of salvation—which is in the highest degree the case of the Eucharist—his role (this is the original sense of the word *persona*) must be taken by a man. This does not stem from any personal superiority of the latter in the order of values, but only from a difference of fact on the level of functions and service.

Could one say that, since Christ is now in the heavenly condition, from now on it is a matter of indifference whether he be represented by a man or by a woman, since "at the resurrection men and women do not marry" (Mt 22:30)? But this text does not mean that the distinction between man and woman, insofar as it determines the identity proper to the person, is suppressed in the glorified state; what holds for us holds also for Christ. It is indeed evident that in human beings the difference of sex exercises an important influence, much deeper than, for example, ethnic differences: the latter do not affect the human person as intimately as the difference of sex, which is directly ordained both for the communion of persons and for the generation of human beings. In Biblical Revelation this difference is the effect of God's will from the beginning: "male and female he created them" (Gen 1:27).

However, it will perhaps be further objected that the priest, especially when he presides at the liturgical and sacramental functions, equally represents the Church: he acts in her name with "the intention of doing what she does." In this sense the theologians of the Middle Ages said that the minister also acts *in persona Ecclesiae,* that is to say, in the name of the whole Church and in order to represent her. And in fact, leaving aside the question of the participation of the faithful in a liturgical action, it is indeed in the name of the whole Church that the action is celebrated by the priest: he prays in the name of all, and in the Mass he offers the sacrifice of the whole Church. In the new Passover, the Church, under visible signs, immolates Christ through the ministry of the priest.[20] And so, it is asserted, since the priest also represents the Church, would it not be possible to think that this representation could be carried out by a woman, according to the symbolism already explained? It is true that the priest represents the Church, which is the Body of Christ. But if he does so, it is precisely because he first represents Christ himself, who is the Head and Shepherd of the Church. The Second Vatican Council[21] used this phrase to make more precise and to complete the expression *in persona Christi*. It is in this quality that the priest presides over the Christian assembly and celebrates the Eucharistic sacrifice "in which the whole Church offers and is herself wholly offered."[22]

If one does justice to these reflections, one will better understand how well-founded is the basis of the Church's practice; and one will conclude that the controversies raised in our days over the ordination of women are for all Christians a pressing invitation to meditate on the mystery of the Church, to study in greater detail the meaning of the episcopate and the priesthood, and to rediscover the real and pre-eminent place of the priest in the community of the baptized, of which he indeed forms part but from which he is distinguished because, in the actions that call for the character of ordination, for the community he is—with all the effectiveness proper to the sacraments—the image and symbol of Christ himself who calls, forgives, and accomplishes the sacrifice of the Covenant.

6. The Ministerial Priesthood Illustrated by the Mystery of the Church

It is opportune to recall that problems of sacramental theology, especially when they concern the ministerial priesthood, as is the case here, cannot be solved except in the light of Revelation. The human sciences, however valuable their contribution in their own domain, cannot suffice here, for they cannot grasp the realities of faith: the properly supernatural content of these realities is beyond their competence.

Thus one must note the extent to which the Church is a society different from other societies, original in her nature and in her structures. The pastoral charge in the Church is normally linked to the sacrament of Order: it is not a simple government, comparable to the modes of authority found in States. It is not granted by people's spontaneous choice: even when it involves designation through election, it is the laying on of hands and the prayer of the successors of the Apostles which guarantee God's choice; and it is the Holy Spirit, given by ordination, who grants participation in the ruling power of the Supreme Pastor, Christ (cf. Acts 20:28). It is a charge of service and love: "If you love me, feed my sheep" (cf. Jn 21:15-17).

For this reason one cannot see how it is possible to propose the admission of women to the priesthood in virtue of the equality of rights of the human person, an equality which holds good also for Christians. To this end use is sometimes made of the text quoted above, from the Letter to the Galatians (3:28), which says that in Christ there is no longer any distinction between men and women. But this passage does not concern ministries: it only affirms the universal calling to divine filiation, which is the same for all. Moreover, and above all, to consider the ministerial priesthood as a human right would be to misjudge its nature completely: baptism does not confer any personal title to public ministry in the Church. The priesthood is not conferred for the honor or advantage of the recipient, but for the service of God and the Church; it is the object of a specific and totally gratuitous vocation: "You did not choose me, no, I chose you; and I commissioned you . . ." (Jn 15:16; cf. Heb 5:4).

It is sometimes said and written in books and periodicals that some women feel that they have a vocation to the priesthood. Such an attraction, however noble and understandable, still does not suffice for a genuine vocation. In fact a vocation cannot be reduced to a mere personal attraction, which can remain purely subjective. Since the priesthood is a particular ministry of which the Church has received the charge and the control, authentication by the Church is indispensable here and is a constitutive part of the vocation: Christ chose "those he wanted" (Mk 3:13). On the other hand, there is a universal vocation of all the baptized to the exercise of the royal priesthood by offering their lives to God and by giving witness for his praise.

Women who express a desire for the ministerial priesthood are doubtless motivated by the desire to serve Christ and the Church. And it is not surprising that, at a time when they are becoming more aware of the discriminations to which they have been subject, they should desire the ministerial priesthood itself. But it must not be forgotten that the priesthood does not form part of the rights of the individual, but stems from the economy of the mystery of Christ and the Church. The priestly office cannot become the goal of social advancement; no merely human progress of society or of the individual can of itself give access to it: it is of another order.

It therefore remains for us to meditate more deeply on the nature of the real equality of the baptized which is one of the great affirmations of Christianity: equality is in no way identity, for the Church is a differentiated body, in which each individual has his or her role. The roles are distinct, and must not be confused; they do not favor the superiority of some vis-á-vis the others, nor do they provide an excuse for jealousy; the only better gift, which can and must be desired, is love (cf. 1 Cor 12:13). The greatest in the Kingdom of Heaven are not the ministers but the saints.

The Church desires that Christian women should become fully aware of the greatness of their mission: today their role is of capital importance, both for the renewal and humanization of society and for the rediscovery by believers of the true face of the Church.

His Holiness Pope Paul VI, during the audience granted to the undersigned Prefect of the Sacred Congregation on October 15, 1976 approved this Declaration, confirmed it and ordered its publication.

Given in Rome, at the Sacred Congregation for the Doctrine of the Faith, on October 15, 1976, the feast of Saint Teresa of Avila.

FRANJO CARDINAL SEPĚR
Prefect

F. Jerome Hamer, O.P.
Titular Archbishop of Lorium
Secretary

Notes

1 *Acta Apostolicae Sedis* 55 (1963), pp. 267-268.

2 Cf. Second Vatican Council, Pastoral Constitution *Gaudium et Spes,* 29 (December 7, 1965): AAS 58 (1966), pp. 1048-1049.

3 Cf. Pope Paul VI, Address to the members of the Study Commission on the Role of Women in Society and in the Church and to the members of the Committee for International Women's Year, April 18, 1975: AAS 67 (1975), p. 265.

4 Second Vatican Council, Decree *Apostolicam Actuositatem,* 9 (November 18, 1965): AAS 58 (1966), p. 846.

5 Cf. Pope Paul VI, Address to the members of the Study Commission on the Role of Women in Society and in the Church and to the members of the Committee for International Women's Year, April 18, 1975: AAS 67 (1975), p. 266.

6 Cf. AAS 68 (1976), pp. 599-600; cf. *ibid.,* pp. 600-601.

7 Saint Irenaeus, *Adversus Haereses,* I, 13, 2: PG 7, 580-581; ed. Harvey, I, 114-122; Tertullian, *De Praescrip. Haeretic.* 41, 5: CCL 1, p. 221; Firmilian of Caesarea, in Saint Cyprian, *Epist.,* 75: CSEL 3, pp. 817-818; Origen, *Fragmentum in 1 Cor.* 74, in *Journal of Theological Studies* 10 (1909), pp. 41-42; Saint Epiphanius, *Panarion* 49, 2-3; 78, 23; 79, 2-4: vol. 2, GCS 31, pp. 243-244; vol. 3, GCS 37, pp. 473, 477-479.

8 *Didascalia Apostolorum,* ch. 15, ed. R. H. Connolly, pp. 133 and 142; *Constitutiones Apostolicae,* bk. 3, ch. 6, nos. 1-2; ch. 9, nos. 3-4: ed F. H. Funk, pp. 191, 201; Saint John Chrysostom, *De Sacerdotio* 2, 2: PG 48, 633.

9 Saint Bonaventure, *In IV Sent.,* Dist. 25, art, 2, q1, ed. Quaracchi, vol. 4, p. 649; Richard of Middleton, *In IV Sent.,* Dist. 25, art. 4, n.1, ed. Venice, 1499, f° 177^{r}; John Duns Scotus, *In IV Sent.,* Dist. 25: *Opus Oxoniense,* ed. Vives, vol. 19, p. 140; *Reportata Parisiensia,* vol. 24, pp. 369-371; Durandus of Saint-Pourcain, *In IV Sent.,* Dist. 25, q.2, ed. Venice, 1571, f° 364^{v}.

10 Some have also wished to explain this fact by a symbolic intention of Jesus: the Twelve were to represent the ancestors of the twelve tribes of Israel (cf. *Mt* 19-28; *Lk* 22:30). But in these texts it is only a question of their participation in the eschatological judgment. The essential meaning of the choice of the Twelve should rather be sought in the totality

of their mission (cf. *Mk* 3:14): they are to represent Jesus to the people and carry on his work.

[11] Pope Innocent III, *Epist.* (December 11, 1210) to the Bishops of Palencia and Burgos, included in *Corpus Iuris, Decret. Lib.* 5, tit. 38, *De Paenit,* ch. 10 *Nova:* ed. A. Friedberg, vol. 2, col. 886-887; cf. *Glossa in Decretal. Lib. 1,* tit. 33, ch. 12 *Dilecta, v° Iurisdictioni.* Cf. Saint Thomas, *Summa Theologiae, III,* q.27, a.5 ad 3; Pseudo-Albert the Great, *Mariale,* quaest. 42, ed. Borgnet 37, 81.

[12] Pope Pius XII, Apostolic Constitution *Sacramentum Ordinis,* November 30, 1947: AAS 40 (1948), pp. 5-7; Pope Paul VI, Apostolic Constitution *Divinae Consortium Naturae,* August 15, 1971; AAS 63 (1971), pp. 657-664; Apostolic Constitution *Sacram Unctionem,* November 30, 1972: AAS 65 (1973), pp. 5-9.

[13] Pope Pius XII, Apostolic Constitution *Sacramentum Ordinis: loc. cit.,* p. 5.

[14] Session 21, chap. 2: Denzinger-Schonmetzer, *Enchiridion Symbolorum* 1728.

[15] Saint Cyprian, *Epist,* 63, 14: PL 4, 397 B; ed. Hartel, vol. 3, p. 713.

[16] Second Vatican Council, Constitution *Sacrosanctum Concilium,* 33 (December 4, 1963): ". . . by the priest who presides over the assembly in the person of Christ . . ."; Dogmatic Constitution *Lumen Gentium,* 10 (November 21, 1964): "The ministerial priest, by the sacred power he enjoys, molds and rules the priestly people. Acting in the person of Christ, he brings about the Eucharistic Sacrifice, and offers it to God in the name of all the people . . ."; 28. "By the powers of the sacrament of Order, and in the image of Christ the eternal High Priest . . . they exercise this sacred function of Christ above all in the Eucharistic liturgy of synaxis. There, acting in the person of Christ . . ."; Decree *Presbyterorum Ordinis,* 2 (December 7, 1965): ". . . priests, by the anointing of the Holy Spirit, are marked with a special character and are so configured to Christ the Priest that they can act in the person of Christ the Head"; 13: "As ministers of sacred realities, especially in the Sacrifice of the Mass, priests represent the person of Christ in a special way"; cf. 1971 Synod of Bishops, *De Sacerdotio Ministeriali I,* 4; Sacred Congregation for the Doctrine of the Faith, *Declaratio circa catholicam doctrinam de Ecclesia,* 6 (June 24, 1973).

[17] Saint Thomas, *Summa Theologiae,* III, q.83, art. 1, ad 3: "It is to be said that [just as the celebration of this sacrament is the representative image of Christ's Cross: *ibid.* ad 2], for the same reason the priest also enacts the image of Christ, in whose person and by whose power he pronounces the words of consecration".

[18] "For since a sacrament is a sign, there is required in the things that are done in the sacraments not only the 'res' but the signification of the 'res'", recalls Saint Thomas, precisely in order to reject the ordination of women: *In IV Sent.,* dist. 25, q.2, art. 1, quaestiuncula 1ª corp.

[19] Saint Thomas, *In IV Sent.,* dist. 25, q.2, quaestiuncula 1ª ad 4um.

[20] Cf. Council of Trent, Session 22, chap. 1: *DS* 1741.

[21] Second Vatican Council, Dogmatic Constitution *Lumen Gentium,* 28: "Exercising within the limits of their authority the function of Christ as Shepherd and Head"; Decree *Presbyterorum Ordinis,* 2; "that they can act in the person of Christ the Head"; 6: "the office of Christ the Head and the Shepherd". Cf. Pope Pius XII, Encyclical Letter *Mediator Dei:* "the minister of the altar represents the person of Christ as the Head, offering in the name of all his members": AAS 39 (1947), p. 556; 1971 Synod of Bishops, *De Sacerdotio Ministeriali,* I, 4; "[The priestly ministry] . . . makes Christ, the Head of the Community, present . . .".

[22] Pope Paul VI, Encyclical Letter *Mysterium Fidei,* September 3, 1965: AAS 57 (1965), p. 761.

Commentary on the Declaration of the Sacred Congregation for the Doctrine of the Faith on the Question of the Admission of Women to the Ministerial Priesthood

Circumstances and Origin of the Declaration

The question of the admission of women to the ministerial priesthood seems to have arisen in a general way about 1958, after the decision by the Swedish Lutheran Church in September of that year to admit women to the pastoral office. This caused a sensation and occasioned numerous commentaries[1]. Even for the communities stemming from the sixteenth-century Reformation it was an innovation: one may recall, for example, how strongly the *Confessio Fidei Scotiae* of 1560 accused the Roman Church of making improper concessions to women in the field of ministry[2]. But the Swedish initiative gradually gained ground among the Reformed Churches, particularly in France, where various National Synods adopted similar decisions.

In reality, the admission of women to the pastoral office seemed to raise no strictly theological problem, in that these communities had rejected the sacrament of Order at the time of their separation from the Roman Church. But a new and much more serious situation was created when ordinations of women were carried out within communities that considered that they preserved the apostolic succession of Order[3]; in 1971 and 1973 the Anglican Bishop of Hong Kong ordained three women with the agreement of his Synod[4]; in July 1974 at Philadelphia there was the ordination in the Episcopal Church of eleven women—an ordination afterwards declared invalid by the House of Bishops. Later on, in June 1975, the General Synod of the Anglican Church in Canada, meeting in Quebec, approved the principle of the accession of women to the priesthood; and this was followed in July by the General Synod of the Church of England: Dr. Coggan, Archbishop of Canterbury, frankly informed Pope Paul VI "of the slow but steady growth of a consensus of opinion within the Anglican Communion that there are no fundamental objections in principle to the ordination of women to the priesthood"[5]. These are only general principles, but they might quickly be followed by practice, and this would bring a new and serious element into the dialogue with the Roman Catholic Church on the nature of the ministry.[6] It has provoked a warning, first by the Archbishop for the Orthodox in Great Britain, Athenagoras of Thyateira[7], and then, more recently, by Pope Paul VI himself in two letters to the Archbishop of Canterbury[8]. Furthermore, the ecumenical sectors brought the question to the notice of all the Christian denominations, forcing them to examine their positions of principle, especially on the occasion of the Assembly of the World Council of Churches at Nairobi in December 1975[9].

A completely different event has made the question even more topical: this was the organization under United Nations' auspices of International Women's Year in 1975. The Holy See took part in it with a Committee for International Women's Year, which included some members of the Commission for the Study of the Role of Women in Society and the Church, which had already been set up in 1973. Ensuring respect for and fostering the respective rights and duties of men and women leads to reflection on participation by women in the life of society on the one hand, and in the life and mission of the Church on the other. Now, the Second Vatican Council had already set forth the task: "Since in our times women have an ever more active share in the whole life of society, it is very important that they participate more widely also in the various fields of the Church's apostolate"[10]. How far can this participation go?

It is understandable that these questions have aroused even in Catholic quarters intense studies, indeed passionate ones: doctoral theses, articles in reviews, even pamphlets, propounding or refuting in turn the biblical, historical and canonical data and appealing to the human sciences of sociology[11], psychology and the history of institutions and customs. Certain famous people have not hesitated to take sides boldly, judging that there was "no basic theological objection to the possibility of women priests"[12]. A number of groups have been formed with a view to upholding this claim, and they have sometimes done this with insistence, as did the conference held in Detroit (U.S.A.) in November 1975 under the title "Women in Future: Priesthood Now, a Call for Action".

The Magisterium has thus been obliged to intervene in a question being posed in so lively a fashion within the Catholic Church and having important implications from the ecumenical point of view. Archbishop Bernardin of Cincinnati, President of the United States National Conference of Catholic Bishops, declared on October 7, 1975 that he found himself "obliged to restate the Church's teaching that women are not to be ordained to the priesthood"; Church leaders, he said, should "not seem to encourage unreasonable hopes and expectations, even by their silence"[13]. Pope Paul VI himself had already recalled the same teaching. He did so at first in parenthetical fashion, especially in his address on April 18, 1975 to the members of the Study Commission on the Role of Women in Society and in the Church and the Committee for the Celebration of International Women's Year: "Although women do not receive the call to the apostolate of the Twelve and therefore to the ordained ministries, they are nonetheless invited to follow Christ as disciples and co-workers. . . . We cannot change what our Lord did, nor his call to women"[14]. Later he had to make an express pronouncement in his exchange of letters with Dr. Coggan, Archbishop of Canterbury: "Your Grace is of course well aware of the Catholic Church's position on this question. She holds that it is not admissible to ordain women to the priesthood, for very fundamental reasons"[15]. It is at his order that the Sacred Congregation for the Doctrine of the Faith has examined the question in its entirety. The question has been complicated by the fact that on the one hand arguments adduced in the past in favor of the traditional teaching are scarcely defensible today, and on the other hand the reasons given by those who demand the ordination of women must be evaluated.

To avoid the rather negative character that must mark the conclusions of such a study, one could have thought of inserting it into a more general presentation of the question of the advancement of women. But the time is not ripe for such a comprehensive exposition, because of the research and work in progress on all sides. It was difficult to leave unanswered any longer a precise question that is being posed nearly everywhere and which is polarizing attention to the detriment of more urgent endeavors that should be fostered. In fact, apart from its non-acceptance of the ordination of women, the document points to positive matters: a deeper understanding of the Church's teaching and of the ministerial priesthood, a call to spiritual progress, an invitation to take on the urgent apostolic tasks of today. The bishops, to whom the document is primarily addressed, have the mission of explaining it to their people with the pastoral feeling that is theirs and with the knowledge they have of the milieu in which they exercise their ministry.

The Declaration begins by presenting the Church's teaching on the question. This in fact has to be the point of departure. We shall see later how necessary it is to follow faithfully the method of using *loci theologici.*

Tradition

It is an undeniable fact, as the Declaration notes, that the constant tradition of the Catholic Church has excluded women from the episcopate and the priesthood. So constant has it been that there has been no need for an intervention by a solemn decision of the Magisterium.

"The same tradition", the document stresses, "has been faithfully safeguarded by the Churches of the East. Their unanimity on this point is all the more remarkable since in many other questions their discipline admits of a great diversity. At the present time these same Churches refuse to associate themselves with requests directed towards securing the accession of women to priestly ordination"[16].

Only within some heretical sects of the early centuries, principally Gnostic ones, do we find attempts to have the priestly ministry exercised by women. It must be further noted that these are very sporadic occurrences and are moreover associated with rather questionable practices. We know of them only through the severe disapproval with which they are noted by Saint Irenaeus in his *Adversus Haereses*[17], Tertullian in *De Praescriptione Haereticorum*[18], Firmilian of Caesarea in a letter to Saint Cyprian[19], Origen in a commentary on the First Letter to the Corinthians[20], and especially by Saint Ephiphanius in his *Panarion*[21].

How are we to interpret the constant and universal practice of the Church? A theologian is certain that what the Church does she can in fact do, since she has the assistance of the Holy Spirit. This is a classical argument found again and again in Saint Thomas with regard to the sacraments[22]. But what the Church has never done—is this any proof that she cannot do it in the future? Does the negative fact thus noted indicate a norm, or is it to be explained by historical and by social and cultural circumstances? In the present case, is an explanation to be found in the position of women in ancient and mediaeval society and in a certain idea of male superiority stemming from that society's culture?

It is because of this transitory cultural element that some arguments adduced on this subject in the past are scarcely defensible today. The most famous is the one summarized by Saint Thomas Aquinas: *quia mulier est in status subiectionis*[23]. In Saint Thomas' thought, however, this assertion is not merely the expression of a philosophical concept, since he interprets it in the light of the accounts in the first chapters of Genesis and the teaching of the First Letter to Timothy (2:12-14). A similar formula is found earlier in the *Decretum of Gratian*[24], but Gratian, who was quoting the Carolingian Capitularies and the false Decretals, was trying rather to justify with Old Testament prescriptions the prohibition—already formulated by the ancient Church[25]—of women from entering the sanctuary and serving at the altar.

The polemical arguments of recent years have often recalled and commented on the texts that develop these arguments. They have also used them to accuse the Fathers of the Church of misogyny. It is true that we find in the Fathers' writings the undeniable influence of prejudices against women. But it must be carefully noted that these passages had very little influence on their pastoral activity, still less on their spiritual direction, as we can see by glancing through their correspondence that has come down to us. Above all it would be a serious mistake to think that such considerations provide the only or the most decisive reasons against the ordination of women in the thought of the Fathers, of the mediaeval writers and of the theologians of the classical period. In the midst of and going beyond speculation, more and more clear expression was being given to the Church's awareness that in reserving priestly ordination and ministry to men she was obeying a tradition received from Christ and the Apostles and by which she felt herself bound.

This is what had been expressed in the form of an apocryphal literature by the ancient documents of Church discipline from Syria, such as the *Didascalia Apostolorum* (middle of the third century)[26] and the Apostolic Constitutions (end of the fourth or beginning of the fifth century)[27], and by the Egyptian collection of twenty pseudo-apostolic canons that was included in the compilation of the Alexandrian *Synodus* and translated into many languages[28]. Saint John Chrysostom, for his part, when commenting on chapter twenty-one of John, understood well that women's exclusion from the pastoral office entrusted to Peter was not based on any natural incapacity, since as he remarks, "even the majority of men have been excluded by Jesus from this immense task."[29]

From the moment that the teaching on the sacraments is systematically presented in the schools of theology and canon law, writers begin to deal *ex professo* with the nature and value of the tradition that reserved ordination to men. The canonists base their case on the principle formulated by Pope Innocent III in a letter of December 11, 1210 to the Bishops of Palencia and Burgos, a letter that was included in the collection of Decretals: "Although the Blessed Virgin Mary was of higher dignity and excellence than all the Apostles, it was to them, not her, that the Lord entrusted the keys of the Kingdom of Heaven"[30]. This text became a *locus communis* for the *glossatores*[31].

As for the theologians, the following are some significant texts: Saint Bonaventure: "Our position is this: it is due not so much to a decision by the Church as to the fact that the sacrament of Order is not for them. In this sacrament the person ordained is a sign of Christ the Mediator''[32]. Richard of Middleton, a Franciscan of the second half of the thirteenth century: ''The reason is that the power of the sacraments comes from their institution. But Christ instituted this sacrament for conferral on men only, not women''[33]. John Duns Scotus: ''It must not be considered to have been determined by the Church. It comes from Christ. The Church would not have presumed to deprive the female sex, for no fault of its own, of an act that might licitly have pertained to it''[34]. Durandus of Saint-Pourcain: ''. . . the male sex is of necessity for the sacrament. The principal cause of this is Christ's institution . . . Christ ordained only men . . . not even his Mother. . . . It must therefore be held that women cannot be ordained, because of Christ's institution''[35].

So it is no surprise that until the modern period the theologians and canonists who dealt with the question have been almost unanimous in considering this exclusion as absolute and having a divine origin. The theological notes they apply to the affirmation vary from ''theologically certain'' (*theologice certa*) to, at times, ''proximate to faith'' (*fidei proxima*) or even ''doctrine of the faith'' (*doctrina fidei*)[36]. Apparently, then, until recent decades no theologian or canonist considered that it was a matter of a simple law of the Church.

In some writers of the Middle Ages however there was a certain hesitancy, reported by Saint Bonaventure without adopting it himself[37] and noted also by Joannes Teutonicus in his gloss on *Caus. 27*, q. 1, c. 23[38]. This hesitancy stemmed from the knowledge that in the past there had been deaconesses: had they received true sacramental ordination? This problem has been brought up again very recently. It was by no means unknown to the seventeenth- and eighteenth-century theologians, who had an excellent knowledge of the history of literature. In any case, it is a question that must be taken up fully by direct study of the texts, without preconceived ideas; hence the Sacred Congregation for the Doctrine of the Faith has judged that it should be kept for the future and not touched upon in the present document.

The Attitude of Christ

In the light of tradition, then, it seems that the essential reason moving the Church to call only men to the sacrament of Order and to the strictly priestly ministry is her intention to remain faithful to the type of ordained ministry willed by the Lord Jesus Christ and carefully maintained by the Apostles. It is therefore no surprise that in the controversy there has been a careful examination of the facts and texts of the New Testament, in which tradition has seen an example establishing a norm. This brings us to a fundamental observation: we must not expect the New Testament *on its own* to resolve in a clear fashion the question of the possibility of women acceding to the priesthood, in the same way that it does not on its own enable us to give an account of certain sacraments, and especially of the structure of the sacrament of Order. Keeping to the sacred text alone and to the points of the history of Christian origins that can be obtained by analyzing that text by itself would be to go back four centuries and find oneself once more amid the controversies of the Reformation. We cannot omit the study of tradition: it is the Church that scrutinizes the Lord's thought by reading Scripture, and it is the Church that gives witness to the correctness of its interpretation.

It is tradition that has unceasingly set forth as an expression of Christ's will the fact that he chose only men to form the group of Twelve. There is no disputing this fact, but can it be proved with absolute certainty that it was a question of a deliberate decision by Christ? It is understandable that the partisans of a change in discipline bring all their efforts to bear against the significance of this fact. In particular, they object that, if Christ did not bring women into the group of the Twelve, it was because the prejudices of his time did not allow him to: it would have been an imprudence that would have compromised his work irreparably. However, it has to be recognized that Jesus did not shrink from other ''imprudences'', which did in fact stir up the hostility of his fellow citizens against him, especially his freedom with regard to the rabbinical interpretations of the Sabbath. With regard to women his attitude was a complete innovation: all the commentators recognize that he went against many prejudices, and the facts that are noted add up to an impressive total.

For this reason greater stress is laid today on another objection: if Jesus chose only men to form the group of the Twelve, it was because he intended them to be a symbol representing the ancestors of the twelve tribes of Israel (''You who have followed me will also sit on twelve thrones and judge the twelve tribes of Israel'': Mt 19:28; cf. Lk 22:30); and this special motive, it is added, obviously referred only to the Twelve and would be no proof that the apostolic ministry should thereafter always be reserved to men. It is not a convincing argument. We may note in the first place how little importance was given to this symbolism: Mark and John do not mention it. And in Matthew and Luke this phrase of Jesus about the twelve tribes of Israel is not put in the context of the call of the Twelve (Mt 10:1-4) but at a relatively late stage of Jesus' public life, when the Apostles have long since been given their ''constitution''; they have been called by Jesus, have worked with him and been sent on missions. Furthermore, the symbolism of Mt 19:28 and Lk 22:30 is not as certain as is claimed: the number twelve could designate simply the whole of Israel. Finally, these two texts deal only with a particular aspect of the mission of the Twelve: Jesus is promising them that they will take part in the eschatological judgment[39]. Therefore the essential meaning of their being chosen is not to be sought in this symbolism but in the totality of the mission given them by Jesus: ''he appointed twelve; they were to be his companions and to be sent out to preach'' (Mk 3:14). As Jesus before them, the Twelve were above all to preach the Good News (Mk 3:14; 6:12). Their mission in Galilee (Mk 6:7-13) was to become the model of the universal mission (Mk 12:10; cf. Mt. 28:16-20). Within the messianic people the Twelve represent Jesus. That is the real reason why it is fitting that the Apostles should be men: they act in the name of Christ and must continue his work.

It has been described above how Pope Innocent III saw a witness to Christ's intentions in the fact that Christ did not communicate to his Mother, in spite of her eminent dignity, the powers which he gave to the Apostles. This is one of the arguments most frequently repeated by tradition: from as early as the third century the Fathers present Mary as the example of the will of Jesus in this matter[40]. It is an argument still particularly dear to Eastern Christians today. Nevertheless it is vigorously rejected by all those who plead in favor of the ordination of women. Mary's divine motherhood, the manner in which she was associated with the redeeming work of her Son, they say, put her in an altogether exceptional and unique position; and it would not even be fair to her to compare her with the Apostles and to argue from the fact that she was not ranked among them. In point of fact these assertions do have the advantage of making us understand that there are different functions within the Church: the equality of Christians is in harmony with the complementary nature of their tasks, and the sacramental ministry is not the only rank of greatness, nor is it necessarily the highest: it is a form of service of the Kingdom. The Virgin Mary does not need the increase in ''dignity'' that was once attributed to her by the authors of those speculations on the priesthood of Mary that formed a deviant tendency which was soon discredited.

The Practice of the Apostles

The text of the Declaration stresses the fact that, in spite of the privileged place Mary had in the Upper Room after the Ascension, she was not designated for entry into the College of the Twelve at the time of the election of Matthias. The same holds for Mary Magdalen and the other women who nevertheless had been the first to bring news of the Resurrection. It is true that the Jewish mentality did not accord great value to the witness of women, as is shown by Jewish law. But one must also note that the Acts of the Apostles and the Letters of Saint Paul stress the role of women in evangelization and in instructing individual converts. The Apostles were led to take a revolutionary decision when they had to go beyond the circle of a Jewish community and undertake the evangelization of the Gentiles. The break with Mosaic observances was not made without discord. Paul had no scruples about choosing one of his collaborators, Titus, from among the Gentile converts (Gal 2:3). The most spectacular expression of the change which the Good News made on the mentality of the first Christians is to be found precisely in the Letter to the Galatians: "For as many of you as were baptized into Christ have put on Christ. There is neither Jew nor Greek, there is neither slave nor free, there is neither male nor female; for you are all one in Christ Jesus" (Gal 3:27-28). In spite of this, the Apostles did not entrust to women the strictly apostolic ministry, although Hellenistic civilization did not have the same prejudices against them as did Judaism. It is rather a ministry which is of another order, as may perhaps also be gathered from Paul's vocabulary, in which a difference seems to be implied between "my fellow workers" *(synergoi mou)* and "God's fellow workers" *(Theou synergoi)*[41].

It must be repeated that the texts of the New Testament, even on such important points as the sacraments, do not always give all the light that one would wish to find in them. Unless the value of unwritten traditions is admitted, it is sometimes difficult to discover in Scripture entirely explicit indications of Christ's will. But in view of the attitude of Jesus and the practice of the Apostles as seen in the Gospels, the Acts and the Letters, the Church has not held that she is authorized to admit women to priestly ordination.

Permanent Value of this Practice

It is the permanency of this negative decision that is objected to by those who would have the legitimacy of ordaining women admitted. These objections employ arguments of great variety.

The most classic ones seek a basis in historical circumstances. We have already seen what is to be thought of the view that Jesus' attitude was inspired solely by prudence, because he did not want to risk compromising his work by going against social prejudices. It is claimed that the same prudence was forced upon the Apostles. On this point too it is clear from the history of the apostolic period that there is no foundation for this explanation. However, in the case of the Apostles, should one not take into account the way in which they themselves shared these prejudices? Thus Saint Paul has been accused of misogyny and in his Letters are found texts on the inferiority of women that are the subject of controversy among exegetes and theologians today.

It can be questioned whether two of Paul's most famous texts on women are authentic or should rather be seen as interpolations, perhaps even relatively late ones. The first is 1 Cor 14:34-35: "The women should keep silence in the churches. For they are not permitted to speak, but should be subordinate as even the Law says". These two verses, apart from being missing in some important manuscripts and not being found quoted before the end of the second century, present stylistic peculiarities foreign to Paul. The other text is 1 Tim 2:11-14: "I do not allow a woman to teach or to exercise authority over men." The Pauline authenticity of this text is often questioned, although the arguments are weaker.

However, it is of little importance whether these texts are authentic or not: theologians have made abundant use of them to explain that women cannot receive either the power of magisterium or that of jurisdiction. It was especially the text of 1 Timothy that provided Saint Thomas with the proof that woman is in a state of submission or service, since (as the text explains) woman was created after man and was the person first responsible for original sin. But there are other Pauline texts of unquestioned authenticity that affirm that "the head of the woman is the man" (1 Cor 11:3; cf. 8-12; Eph 5:22, 24). It may be asked whether this view of man, which is in line with that of the books of the Old Testament, is not at the basis of Paul's conviction and the Church's tradition that women cannot receive the ministry. Now this is a view that modern society rejects absolutely, and many present-day theologians would shrink from adopting it without qualifying it. We may note however that Paul does not take his stand on a philosophical level but on that of biblical history: when he describes, in relation to marriage, the symbolism of love, he does not see man's superiority as domination but as a gift demanding sacrifice, in the image of Christ.

On the other hand there are prescriptions in Paul's writings which are unanimously admitted to have been transitory, such as the obligation he imposed on women to wear a veil (1 Cor 11:2-16). It is true that these are obviously disciplinary practices of minor importance, perhaps inspired by the customs of the time. But then there arises the more basic question: since the Church has later been able to abandon prescriptions contained in the New Testament, why should it not be the same with the exclusion of women from ordination? Here we meet once again the essential principle that it is the Church herself that, in the different sectors of her life, ensures discernment between what can change and what must remain immutable. As the Declaration specifies, "When she judges that she cannot accept certain changes, it is because she knows that she is bound by Christ's manner of acting. Her attitude, despite appearances, is therefore not one of archaism but of fidelity: it can be truly understood only in this light. The Church makes pronouncements in virtue of the Lord's promise and the presence of the Holy Spirit, in order to proclaim better the mystery of Christ and to safeguard and manifest the whole of its rich content."

Many of the questions confronting the Church as a result of the numerous arguments put forward in favor of the ordination of women must be considered in the light of this principle. An example is the following question dealt with by the Declaration: why will the Church not change her discipline, since she is aware of having a certain power over the sacraments, even though they were instituted by Christ, in order to determine the sign or to fix the conditions for their administration? This faculty remains limited, as was recalled by Pius XII, echoing the Council of Trent: the Church has no power over the substance of the sacraments.[42] It is the Church herself that must distinguish what forms part of the "substance of the sacraments" and what she can determine or modify if circumstances should so suggest.

On this point, furthermore, we must remember, as the Declaration reminds us, that the sacraments and the Church herself are closely tied to history, since Christianity is the result of an event: the coming of the Son of God into time and to a country, and his death on the Cross under Pontius Pilate outside the walls of Jerusalem. The sacraments are a memorial of saving events. For this reason their signs are linked to those very events. They are relative to one civilization, one culture, although destined to be reproduced everywhere until the end of time. Hence historical choices have taken place by which the Church is bound, even if speaking absolutely and on a speculative level other choices could be imagined. This, for instance, is the case with bread and wine as matter for the Eucharist, for the Mass is not just a fraternal meal but the renewal of the Lord's Supper and the memorial of his Passion and thus linked with something done in history.[43]

It has likewise been remarked that in the course of time the Church has agreed to confer on women certain ministerial functions that antiquity refused to give them in the very name of the example and will of Christ. The functions spoken of are above all the administration of baptism, teaching and certain forms of ecclesiastical jurisdiction.

As regards baptism, however, not even deaconesses in the Syriac-speaking East were permitted to administer it, and its solemn administration is still a hierarchical act reserved to bishop, priest and, in accessory fashion, deacon. When urgently required, baptism can be conferred not only by Christians but even by unbaptized people whether men or women. Its validity therefore does not require the baptismal character, still less that of ordination. This point is affirmed by practice and by theologians. It is an example of this necessary discernment in the Church's teaching and practice, a discernment whose only guarantee is the Church herself.

As regards teaching, a classical distinction has to be made, from Paul's Letters onwards. There are forms of teaching or edification that lay people can carry out and in this case Saint Paul expressly mentions women. These forms include the charisms of "prophecy" (1 Cor 11:15). In this sense there was no obstacle to giving the title of Doctor to Teresa of Avila and Catherine of Siena, as it was given to illustrious teachers such as Albert the Great or Saint Laurence of Brindisi. Quite a different matter is the official and hierarchical function of teaching the revealed message, a function that presupposes the mission received from Christ by the Apostles and transmitted by them to their successors.

Examples of participation by women in ecclesiastical jurisdiction are found in the Middle Ages: some abbesses (not abbesses in general, as is sometimes said in popularizing articles) performed acts normally reserved to bishops, such as the nomination of parish priests or confessors. These customs have been more or less reproved by the Holy See at different periods: the letter of Pope Innocent III quoted earlier was intended as a reprimand to the Abbess of Las Huelgas. But we must not forget that feudal lords arrogated to themselves similar rights. Canonists also admitted the possibility of separating jurisdiction from Order. The Second Vatican Council has tried to determine better the relationship between the two; the Council's doctrinal vision will doubtless have effects on discipline.

In a more general way, attempts are being made, especially in Anglican circles, to broaden the debate in the following way: is the Church perhaps bound to Scripture and tradition as an absolute, when the Church is a people making its pilgrim way and should listen to what the Spirit is saying? Or else a distinction is made between essential points on which unanimity is needed and questions of discipline admitting of diversity: and if the conclusion reached is that the ordination of women belongs to these secondary matters, it would not harm progress towards the union of the Churches. Here again it is the Church that decides by her practice and Magisterium what requires unanimity, and distinguishes it from acceptable or desirable pluralism. The question of the ordination of women impinges too directly on the nature of the ministerial priesthood for one to agree that it should be resolved within the framework of legitimate pluralism between Churches. That is the whole meaning of the letter of Pope Paul VI to the Archbishop of Canterbury.

The Ministerial Priesthood in the Light of the Mystery of Christ

In the Declaration a very clear distinction will be seen between the document's affirmation of the datum (the teaching it proposes with authority in the preceding paragraphs) and the theological reflection that then follows. By this reflection the Sacred Congregation for the Doctrine of the Faith endeavors "to illustrate this norm by showing the profound fittingness" to be found "between the proper nature of the sacrament of Order, with its specific reference to the mystery of Christ, and the fact that only men have been called to receive priestly ordination". In itself such a quest is not without risk. However, it does not involve the Magisterium. It is well known that in solemn teaching infallibility affects the doctrinal affirmation, not the arguments intended to explain it. Thus the doctrinal chapters of the Council of Trent contain certain processes of reasoning that today no longer seem to hold. But this risk has never stopped the Magisterium from endeavoring at all times to clarify doctrine by analogies of faith. Today especially, and more than ever, it is impossible to be content with making statements, with appealing to the intellectual docility of Christians: faith seeks understanding, and tries to distinguish the grounds for and the coherence of what it is taught.

We have already discarded a fair number of explanations given by mediaeval theologians. The defect common to these explanations is that they claimed to find their basis in an inferiority of women vis-á-vis men; they deduced from the teaching of Scripture that woman was "in a state of submission", of subjection, and was incapable of exercising functions of government.

It is very enlightening to note that the communities springing from the Reformation which have had no difficulty in giving women access to the pastoral office are first and foremost those that have rejected the Catholic doctrine on the sacrament of Order and profess that the pastor is only one baptized person among others, even if the charge given has been the object of a consecration. The Declaration therefore suggests that it is by analyzing the nature of Order and its character that we will find the explanation of the exclusive call of men to the priesthood and episcopate. This analysis can be outlined in three propositions: 1) in administering the sacraments that demand the character or ordination the priest does not act in his own name *(in persona propria)*, but in the person of Christ *(in persona Christi)*; 2) this formula, as understood by tradition, implies that the priest is a sign in the sense in which this term is understood in sacramental theology; 3) it is precisely because the priest is a sign of Christ the Savior that he must be a man and not a woman.

That the priest performs the Eucharist and reconciles sinners in the name and place of Christ is affirmed repeatedly by the Magisterium and constantly taught by Fathers and theologians. It would not appear to serve any useful purpose to give a multitude of quotations to show this. It is the totality of the priestly ministry that Saint Paul says is exercised in the place of Christ: ''We are acting as ambassadors on behalf of Christ, God, as it were, appealing through us''—in fact this text from 2 Corinthians has in mind the ministry of reconciliation (5:18-20)—''you have received me as an angel of God, even as Christ Jesus'' (Gal 4:14). Similarly Saint Cyprian echoes Saint Paul: ''The priest truly acts in the place of Christ''.[44] But theological reflection and the Church's life have been led to distinguish the more or less close links between the various acts in the exercise of the ministry and the character of ordination and to specify which require this character for validity.

Saying ''in the name and place of Christ'' is not however enough to express completely the nature of the bond between the minister and Christ as understood by tradition. The formula *in persona Christi* in fact suggests a meaning that brings it close to the Greek expression *mimêma Christou*.[45] The word *persona* means a part played in the ancient theatre, a part identified by a particular mask. The priest takes the part of Christ, lending him his voice and gestures. Saint Thomas expresses this concept exactly: ''The priest enacts the image of Christ, in whose person and by whose power he pronounces the words of consecration''.[46] The priest is thus truly a *sign* in the sacramental sense of the word. It would be a very elementary view of the sacraments if the notion of sign were kept only for material elements. Each sacrament fulfills the notion in a different way. The text of Saint Bonaventure already mentioned affirms this very clearly: ''the person ordained is a sign of Christ the mediator''.[47] Although Saint Thomas gave as the reason for excluding women the much discussed one of the state of subjection *(status subjectionis)*, he nevertheless took as his starting point the principle that ''sacramental signs represent what they signify by a natural resemblance'',[48] in other words the need for that ''natural resemblance'' between Christ and the person who is his sign. And, still on the same point, Saint Thomas recalls: ''Since a sacrament is a sign, what is done in the sacrament requires not only the reality but also a sign of the reality''.[49]

It would not accord with ''natural resemblance'', with that obvious ''meaningfulness'', if the memorial of the Supper were to be carried out by a woman; for it is not just the recitation involving the gestures and words of Christ, but an action, and the sign is efficacious because Christ is present in the minister who consecrates the Eucharist, as is taught by the Second Vatican Council, following the Encyclical *Mediator Dei*.[50]

It is understandable that those favoring the ordination of women have made various attempts to deny the value of this reasoning. It has obviously been impossible and even unnecessary for the Declaration to consider in detail all the difficulties that could be raised in this regard. Some of them however are of interest in that they occasion a deeper theological understanding of traditional principles. Let us look at the objection sometimes raised that it is ordination—the character—not maleness, that makes the priest Christ's representative. Obviously it is the character, received by ordination, that enables the priest to consecrate the Eucharist and reconcile penitents. But the character is spiritual and invisible *(res et sacramentum)*. On the level of the sign *(sacramentum tantum)* the priest must both have received the laying on of hands and take the part of Christ. It is here that Saint Thomas and Saint Bonaventure require that the sign should have natural meaningfulness.

In various fairly recent publications attempts have been made to reduce the importance of the formula *in persona Christi* by insisting rather on the formula *in persona Ecclesiae*. For it is another great principle of the theology of the sacraments and liturgy that the priest presides over the liturgy in the name of the Church, and must have the intention of ''doing what the Church does''. Could one say that the priest does not represent Christ, because he first represents the Church by the fact of his ordination? The Declaration's reply to this objection is that, quite on the contrary, the priest represents the Church precisely because he first represents Christ himself, who is the Head and Shepherd of the Church. It indicates several texts of the Second Vatican Council that clearly express this teaching. Here there may well be in fact one of the crucial points of the question, one of the important aspects of the theology of the Church and the priesthood underlying the debate on the ordination of women. When the priest precides over the assembly, it is not the assembly that has chosen or designated him for this role. The Church is not a spontaneous gathering. As its name of *ecclesia* indicates, it is an assembly that is convoked. It is Christ who calls it together. He is the head of the Church, and the priest presides ''in the person of Christ the Head'' *(in persona Christi capitis)*. That is why the Declaration rightly concludes ''that the controversies raised in our days over the ordination of women are for all Christians a pressing invitation to meditate on the mystery of the Church, to study in greater detail the meaning of the episcopate and the priesthood, and to rediscover the real and pre-eminent place of the priest in the community of the baptized, of which he indeed forms part but from which he is distinguished because, in the actions that call for the character of ordination, for the community he is—with all the effectiveness proper to the sacraments—the image and symbol of Christ himself who calls, forgives, and accomplishes the sacrifice of the Covenant.''

However, the objectors continue: it would indeed be important that Christ should be represented by a man if the maleness of Christ played an essential part in the economy of salvation. But, they say, one cannot accord gender a special place in the hypostatic union: what is essential is the human nature—no more—assumed by the Word, not the incidental characteristics such as the sex or even the race which he assumed. If the Church admits that men of all races can validly represent Christ, why should she deny women this ability to represent him? We must first of all reply, in the words of the Declaration, that ethnic differences ''do not affect the human person as intimately as the difference of sex''. On this point biblical teaching agrees with modern psychology. The difference between the sexes however, is something willed by God from the beginning, according to the account in Genesis (which is also quoted in the Gospel), and is directed both to communion between persons and to the begetting of human beings. And it must be affirmed first and foremost that the fact that Christ is a man and not a woman is neither incidental nor unimportant in relation to the economy of salvation. In what sense? Not of course in the material sense, as has sometimes been suggested in polemics in order to discredit it, but because the whole economy of salvation has been revealed to us through essential symbols from which it cannot be separated, and without which we would be unable to understand God's design. Christ is the new Adam. God's covenant with men is presented in the Old Testament as a nuptial mystery, the definitive reality of which is Christ's sacrifice on the Cross. The Declaration briefly presents the stages marking the progressive development of this biblical theme, the subject of many exegetical and theological studies. Christ is the Bridegroom of the Church, whom he won for himself with his blood, and the salvation brought by him is the New Covenant: by using this language, Revelation shows why the Incarnation took place according to the male gender, and makes it impossible to ignore this historical reality. For this reason, only a man can take the part of Christ, be a sign of his presence, in a word ''represent'' him (that is, be an effective sign of his presence) in the essential acts of the Covenant.

Could one do without this biblical symbolism when transmitting the message, in contemplating the mystery and in liturgical life? To ask this, as has been done in certain recent studies, is to call into question the whole structure of Revelation and to reject the value of Scripture. It will be said, for example, that ''in every period the ecclesial community appeals to the authority it has received from its founder in order to choose the images enabling it to receive God's revelation.'' This is perhaps to fail even more profoundly to appreciate the human value of the nuptial theme in the revelation of God's love.

The Ministerial Priesthood in the Mystery of the Church

It is also striking to note the extent to which the questions raised in the controversy over the ordination of women are bound up with a certain theology of the Church. We do not of course mean to dwell on the excessive formulas which nonetheless sometimes find a place in theological reviews. An example is the supposition that the primitive Church was based on the charisms possessed by both women and men.[51] Another is the claim that "the Gospels also present women as ministers of unction".[52] On the other hand, we have already come across the question of the pluralism that can be admitted in unity and seen what its limits are.

The proposal that women should be admitted to the priesthood because they have gained leadership in many fields of modern life today seems to ignore the fact that the Church is not a society like the rest. In the Church, authority or power is of a very different nature, linked as it normally is with the sacrament, as is underlined in the Declaration. Disregard of this fact is indeed a temptation that has threatened ecclesiological research at all periods: every time that an attempt is made to solve the Church's problems by comparison with those of States, or to define the Church's structure by political categories, the inevitable result is an impasse.

The Declaration also points out the defect in the argument that seeks to base the demand that the priesthood be conferred on women on the text Galations 3:28, which states that in Christ there is no longer any distinction between man and woman. For Saint Paul this is the effect of baptism. The baptismal catechesis of the Fathers often stressed it. But absolute equality in baptismal life is quite a different thing from the structure of the ordained ministry. This latter is the object of a vocation within the Church, not a right inherent in the person.

A vocation within the Church does not consist solely or primarily in the fact that one manifests the desire for a mission or feels attracted by an inner compulsion. Even if this spontaneous step is made and even if one believes one has heard as it were a call in the depths of one's soul, the vocation is authentic only from the moment that it is authenticated by the external call of the Church. The Holy Office recalled this truth in its 1912 letter to the Bishop of Aire to put an end to the Lahitton controversy.[53] Christ chose "those he wanted" (Mk 3:13).

Since the ministerial priesthood is something to which the Lord calls expressly and gratuitously, it cannot be claimed as a right, any more by men than by women. Archbishop Bernardin's declaration of October 1975 contained the sound judgment: "It would be a mistake . . . to reduce the question of the ordination of women to one of injustice, as is done at times. It would be correct to do this only if ordination were a God-given right of every individual; only if somehow one's human potential could not be fulfilled without it. In fact, however, no one, male or female, can claim a 'right' to ordination. And, since the episcopal and priestly office is basically a ministry of service, ordination in no way 'completes' one's humanity".[54]

The Declaration of the Sacred Congregation for the Doctrine of the Faith ends by suggesting that efforts in two directions should be fostered, efforts from which the pastors and faithful of the Church would perhaps be distracted if this controversy over women's ordination were prolonged. One direction is in the doctrinal and spiritual order: awareness of the diversity of roles in the Church, in which equality is not identity, should lead us—as Saint Paul exhorts us—to strive after the one gift that can and should be striven after, namely love (1 Cor 12-13). "The greatest in the Kingdom of Heaven are not the ministers but the saints", says the Declaration. This expression deserves to be taken as a motto.

The other direction for our efforts is in the apostolic and social order. We have a long way to go before people become fully aware of the greatness of women's mission in the Church and society, "both for the renewal and humanization of society and for the rediscovery by believers of the true countenance of the Church". Unfortunately we also still have a long way to go before all the inequalities of which women are still the victims are eliminated, not only in the field of public, professional and intellectual life, but even within the family.

NOTES

1 Note especially: J.E. HAVEL, *La question du pastorat féminin en Suède,* in *Archives de sociologie des religions,* 4, 1959, pp. 207-249; F. R. REFOULE, *Le problème des femmes-prêtrés en Suède,* in *Lumière et Vie,* 43, 1959, pp. 65-99.

2 No. 22 (W. NISEL, *Bekenntnisschriften und Kirchenordnungen . . .* , Munchen, 1939, p. 111): "quod . . . foeminis, quae Spiritus sanctus ne docere quidem in Ecclesia patitur, illi [papistae] permittunt ut etiam Baptismum administrarent".

3 The position of the Catholic Church on this point was made clear by Leo XIII in the Letter *Apostolicae Curae* of September 13, 1896 (Leonis XIII Acta, 16, 1897, pp. 258-275).

4 Earlier, in 1944, his predecessor Bishop Hall called a woman to the priesthood, but she had to refrain from exercising the ministry because of the energetic intervention of the Archbishops of York and Canterbury, who for ecumenical motives repudiated the action of the Bishop of Hong Kong.

5 Letter of July 9, 1975 to the Pope, in *L'Osservatore Romano* (English edition), September 2, 1976.

6 Cardinal Wilebrands stated this to some United States Episcopal Bishops in September 1974, according to the account published in *Origins—NC Documentary Service,* October 9, 1975.

7 Italian translation published in *L'Osservatore Romano,* June 16-17, 1975.

8 Letters of Paul VI to Dr. Coggan, November 30, 1975 and February 10, 1976: cf. AAS 68(1976), pp. 599-601.

9 At the WCC's Assembly in New Delhi in 1961, the Department on Faith and Order was asked to prepare, in collaboration with the Department on Cooperation of Men and Women in Church, Family and Society, a study on the theological questions raised by the problem of women's ordination (cf. Nouvelle Delhi 1961, Neuchâtel, 1962, pp. 166, 169). On the discussion of the problem at the Nairobi Assembly, see E. LANNE, *Points chauds de la Ve Assemblée mondial du Conseil oecuménique des Eglises a Nairobi . . .* , in *Revue théologique de Louvain,* 7, 1976, pp. 197-199: *Les Femmes dans l'Eglise.*

10 Second Vatican Council, Decree *Apostolicam Actuositatem,* 9.

11 This intrusion of sociology into hermeneutics and theology is perhaps one of the most important elements in the controversy. This has been rightly stressed by B. LAMBERT, *L'Eglise catholique peut-elle admettre des femmes à l'ordination sacerdotale,* in *Documentation Catholique* 73, 1976, p. 774: "en corrigeant dans l'interprétation de la Tradition et de l'Ecriture ce qui était lié à des formes socio-culturelles, historiquement nécessaires et conditionnées, mais aujourd'hui dépassées, à la lumière de l'évolution de la société et de L'Eglise".

12 The very phrase (reported in *Le Monde* of September 19-20, 1965) used by J. DANIELOU during the Council at a meeting of the Alliance Internationale Jeanne d'Arc. He returned to the subject, introducing perhaps more shades of meaning, in the interview he gave at the time of his promotion to Cardinal, *L'Express,* 936, 16-22 June 1969, pp. 122, 124: "Il faudrait examiner oú sont les vraies raisons qui font que l'Eglise n'a jamais envisagé le sacerdoce des femmes."

13 *Origins—NC Documentary Service,* October 16, 1975: "Honesty and concern for the Catholic community . . . require that Church leaders not seem to encourage unreasonable hopes and expectations, even by their silence. Therefore I am obliged to restate the Church's teaching that women are not to be ordained to the priesthood."

[14] *AAS* 67 (1975), p. 265.

[15] Letter of November 30, 1975: AAS 63(1976), p. 599.

[16] Cf., for example, the theological conversations between Catholics and Russian Orthodox at Trent, June 23-28, 1975: *L'Osservator Romano,* July 7-8, 1975; *Documentation Catholique,* 71, 1975, p. 707.

[17] 1, 13, 2: PG 7, col 580-581; Harvey edition 1, 114-122.

[18] 41, 5: CCL 1, p. 221.

[19] In the Letters of Saint Cyprian, 75: CSEL 3, pp. 817-818.

[20] Fragments published in *Journal of Theological Studies,* 10 (1909), pp. 41-42 (No. 74).

[21] *Panarion,* 49, 2-3: GCS 31, pp. 243-244;—78, 23 and 79, 2-4; GCS 37, pp. 473, 477-479.

[22] St. Thomas, *Summa Theol.,* 2^{a} 2^{ae}, p.10, a.12; 3^{a} pars, q.66, a.10; q.72, a.4 and a.12; q.73, a.4; q.78, a.3 and a.6; q.80, a.12; q.82, a.2; q.83, a.3 and a.5;—cf. *In IV Sent.* Dist. 20, q.1, a.4, q.^{a} 1 ff; *Dist.* 23, q.1, a.4, q.^{a} 1, etc.

[23] St. Thomas, *In IV Sent.* Dist. 19, q.1, a 1 q^{a} 3 ad 4um; Dist. 25, q.2, a.1, q^{a} 1; cf. q.2, a.2, q^{a} 1, ad 4: *Summa Theol.,* 2^{a} 2^{ae}, q. 177, a.2.

[24] *Dictum Gratiani in Caus.* 34, q.5, c.11, ed. FRIEDBERG, t. 1, col. 1254; cf. R. METZ, *La femme en droit canonique médiéval,* in *Recueil de la société Jean Bodin,* 12, 1962, pp. 59-113.

[25] Canon 44 of the collection called after the Council of Laodicea; H. T. BRUNS, *Canones Apostolorum et Conciliorum* . . . t. 1, Bertolini 1839, p. 78; St. Gelasius, *Epist.* 14, *ad universos episcopos per Lucaniam, Brutios et Siciliam constitutos,* March 11, 494, no. 26: A. THIEL, Epistolae *Romanorum pontificum* . . . , t. 1, Brunsbergae, 1868, p. 376.

[26] Chap. 15: ed. R. H. Connolly, pp. 133 and 142.

[27] Lib. 3, c.6 nn.1-2; c.9, 3-4; ed. F. X. Funk, pp. 191, 201.

[28] Can. 24-28;—Greek text in F. X. Funk, *Doctrina Duodecim Apostolorum,* Tubingen, 1887, p. 71; T. SCHERMANN, *Die allgemeine Kirchenordnung* . . . , t. 1, Paderborn, 1914, pp. 31-33;—Syriac text in *Octateuque de Clément,* Lib. 3, c. 19-20; Latin text in the Verona ms., Bibl. capit. LV, ed. E. TIDNER, *Didascaliae Apostolorum, Canonum Ecclesiasticorum, Traditionis Apostolicae Versiones Latinae,* Berlin, 1965 (TU 75), pp. 111-113. The Coptic, Ethiopian and Arabic versions of the *Synodos* have been translated and published chiefly by G. HORNER, *The Statutes of the Apostles or Canones Ecclesiastici,* Oxford University Press, 1915 (=1904).

[29] *De Sacerdotio* 2, 2: PG 48, 633.

[30] *Decretal,* Lib. V. tit. 38, *De paenit.,* can. 10 Nova A. FRIEDBERG, t. 2, col. 886-887: *Quia licet beatissima Virgo Maria dignior et excellentior fuerit Apostolis universis, non tamen illi, sed istis Dominus claves regni caelorum commisit.*

[31] e.g., *Glossa in Decretal.* Lib. 1, tit. 33, c.12 *Dilecta,* V° *lurisdictioni.*

[32] *In IV Sent.,* Dist. 25, art. 2, q.1: ed. Quaracchi, t.4, p. 649: *Dicendum est quod hoc non venit tam ex institutione Ecclesiae, quam ex hoc quod eis competit Ordinis sacramentum. In hoc sacramento persona quae ordinatur significat Christum mediatorem.*

[33] *In IV Sent.* Dist. 25, a.4, n°1; ed. Bocatelli, Venice, 1499 [PELLECHET—POLAIN, 10132/9920], f° 177^{R}: *Ratio est quod sacramenta vim habent ex sua institutione: Christus autem hoc sacramentum instituit conferri masculis tantum, non mulieribus.*

[34] *In IV Sent., Dist. 25, Opus Oxoniense,* ed. Vivés, t. 19, p. 140; cf. *Reportata Parisiensia,* ed. Vives, t. 24, pp. 369-371. *Quod non est tenendum tamquam praecise per Ecclesiam determinatum, sed habetur a Christo: non enim Ecclesia praesumpsisset sexum muliebrem privasse sine culpa sua actu qui posset sibi licite competere.*

[35] *In IV Sent.,* Dist. 25, p. 2; ed. Venice, 1571, f° 364ᵛ: . . . *sexus virilis est de necessitate sacramenti, cuius causa principalis est institutio Christi . . . Christus non ordinavit nisi viros . . . nec matrem suam . . . Tenendum est igitur quod mulieres non possunt ordinari ex institutione Christi.*

[36] Details of these theological notes can be found in E. DORONZO, *Tractatus Dogmaticus de Ordine,* t.3, Milwaukee, Bruce, 1962, pp. 395-396; cf. also F. HALLER, *De Sacris Electionibus,* 1636, quoted in J. P. MIGNE, *Theologiae Cursus Completus,* t.24, col. 821-854; many present-day objections are surprisingly anticipated in this work, which goes so far as to qualify as *periculosa in fide* the opinion that would admit women's ordination in general, and as *haeretica* that which would admit them to the priesthood, col. 824; cf. also H. TOURNELY, *Praelectiones Theologicae de Sacramento Ordinis, Parisiis,* 1729, p. 185, notes as an error *contra fidem* this assertion with regard to episcopate, priesthood and diaconate. Among canonists: X. WERNZ, *Ius Decret.,* t.2, Romae, 1906, p. 124: *iure divino* (he quotes several writers); P. GASPARRI, *Tractatus Canonicus de Sacra Ordinatione,* t.1, *Parisiis,* 1893, p. 75; *Et quidem prohibentur sub poena nullitatis: ita enim traditio et communis doctorum catholicorum doctrina interpretata est legem Apostoli: ed ideo Patres inter haereses recensent doctrinam qua sacerdotalis dignitas et officium mulieribus tribitur.*

[37] St. BONAVENTURE, In IV Sent., Dist. 25, art. 2, q.1, ed. Quaracchi, t.4, p. 650: *Omnes consentiunt quod promoveri non debent, sed utrum possint, dubium est* (the doubt arises from the case of the deaconesses); he concludes: *secundum saniorem opinionem et prudentiorum doctorum non solum non debent vel non possunt de iure, verum etiam non possunt de facto.*

[38] This canon deals with deaconesses. At the word ordinari, Johannes Teutonicus states: *Respondeo quod mulieres non recipiunt characterem, impediente sexu et constitutione Ecclesiae: unde nec officium ordinum exercere possunt . . . nec ordinatur haec: sed fundebatur super eam forte aliqua benedictio, ex qua consequebatur aliquod officium speciale, forte legendi homilias vel evangelium ad matutinas quod non licebat alii. Alii dicunt quod si monialis ordinetur, bene recipit characterem quia ordinari facti est et post baptismum quilibet potest ordinare.*

[39] *Cf. J. DUPONT, Le Logion des douze trônes,* in *Biblica,* 45, 1964, pp. 355-392.

[40] The documents cited in notes 26-28 above. Note also the curious *Mariale,* falsely attributed to Albert the Great, quaest. 42, ed. Borgnet, t. 37. pp. 80-81.

[41] I. DE LA POTTERIE, *Titres missionnaires due chrétien dans le Nouveau Testament* (Rapports de la XXXIème semaine de Missiologie, Louvain, 1966), Paris, Desclée de Brouwer, 1966, p. 29-46, cf. pp. 44-45.

[42] Council of Trent, sess. 21, c.2 and Pius XII, Constitution *Sacramentum Ordinis,* November 30, 1947, quoted in the Declaration.

[43] Cf. Ph. DELHAYE, *Rétrospective et prospective des ministéres féminins dans l'Eglise,* in *Revue théologique de Louvain* 3, 1972, pp. 74-75.

[44] Epist. 63, 14: ed. Hartel, CSEL t.3, p. 713: *sacerdos vice Christi vere fungitur.*

[45] *St. Theodore the Studite, Adversus Iconomachos cap.* 4; PG 99, 593; *Epist. lib.* 1, 11: *PG* 99, 945.

[46] *Summa Theol.,* III, q.83, a.1 ad 3um.

[47] Above, note 32: *persona quae ordinatur significat Christum mediatorem.*

[48] *In IV Sent.*, Dist. 25, q.2, a.2, q[a] 1, ad 4[um]: *signa sacramentalia ex naturali similitudine repraesentent.*

[49] *Ibid. in corp. quaestiunculae: Quia cum sacramentum sit signum, in eis quae in sacramento aguntur requiritur non solum res, sed significatio rei.*

[50] II Vatican Council, Constitution *Sacrosanctum* on the Liturgy, no. 7; Pius XII, Encyclical *Mediator Dei,* November 20, 1947, AAS 39 (1947), p. 528.

[51] Cf. Concilium III, 1975, *La femme dans l'Eglise,* French edition, pp. 19, 20, especially 23: "Au temps de Paul, les fonctions de direction étaient réparties et reposaient sur l'autorité charismatique".

[52] *Theological Studies* 36, 1975, p. 667.

[53] *AAS* 4, 1912, p.485.

[54] In *Origins—NC Documentary Service,* October 16, 1975.

Notes: *This 1976 document was produced by the Sacred Congregation for the Doctrine of the Faith, the Vatican section charged with maintenance of proper doctrinal teaching for the Roman Catholic Church. The introduction notes that this statement on women in the priesthood has been made necessary by the increasing number of churches around the world that have begun ordaining women and by the increasing number of voices within the Roman Catholic Church calling for such action. This became even more acute in 1976 when the Episcopal Church in the United States, closer to the Roman Catholic Church than some of the other churches, also authorized admitting women to the priesthood. The Sacred Congregation emphasizes the Church's opposition to women priests, but its argument does not follow the same lines as does, for example, the Lutheran Church—Missouri Synod. Unlike the Missouri Synod, the Catholic argument does not focus exclusively on the Bible, and there is comparatively little stress placed on those passages which would suggest an order of creation in which women play a submissive role. Rather, the focus is on the sacramental nature of the priesthood, in which the priest represents, both metaphysically and physically, the figure of Jesus the Christ, a man.*

ROMAN CATHOLIC CHURCH—POPE JOHN PAUL II

ON THE DIGNITY AND VOCATION OF WOMEN (MULIERIS DIGNITATEM) (1988)

VII

The Church—The Bride of Christ

The "Great Mystery"

23. Of fundamental importance here are the words of the Letter to the Ephesians: "Husbands, love your wives, as Christ loved the Church and gave himself up for her, that he might sanctify her, having cleansed her by the washing of water with the word, that he might present the Church to himself in splendour, without spot or wrinkle or any such thing, that she might be holy and without blemish. Even so husbands should love their wives as their own bodies. He who loves his wife loves himself. For no man ever hates his own flesh, but nourishes and cherishes it, as Christ does the Church, because we are members of his body. 'For this reason a man shall leave his father and mother and be joined to his wife, and the two shall become one flesh'. *This mystery is a profound one,* and I am saying that *it refers to Christ and the Church*" (5:25-32).

In this Letter the author expresses the truth about the Church as the bride of Christ, and also indicates how this truth *is rooted in the biblical reality of the creation of the human being as male and female.* Created in the image and likeness of God as a "unity of the two'', both have been called to a spousal love. Following the description of creation in the Book of Genesis (2:18-25), one can also say that this fundamental call appears in the creation of woman, and is inscribed by the Creator in the institution of marriage, which, according to Genesis 2:24, has the character of a union of persons (*''communio personarum''*) from the very beginning. Although not directly, the very description of the ''beginning'' (cf. *Gen* 1:27; 2:24) shows that the whole ''ethos'' of mutual relations between men and women has to correspond to the personal truth of their being.

All this has already been considered. The Letter to the Ephesians once again confirms this truth, while at the same time comparing the spousal character of the love between man and woman to the mystery of Christ and of the Church. *Christ is the Bridegroom of the Church—the Church is the Bride of Christ.* This analogy is not without precedent; it transfers to the New Testament what was already contained *in the Old Testament,* especially in the prophets Hosea, Jeremiah, Ezekiel and Isaiah.[48] The respective passages deserve a separate analysis. Here we will cite only one text. This is how God speaks to his Chosen People through the Prophet: ''Fear not, for you will not be ashamed; be not confounded, for you will not be put to shame; for you will forget the same of your youth, and the reproach of your widowhood you will remember no more. *For your Maker is your husband,* the Lord of hosts is his name; and the Holy One of Israel is *your Redeemer,* the God of the whole earth he is called. For the Lord has called you like a wife forsaken and grieved in spirit, like a wife of youth when she is cast off, says your God. For a brief moment I forsook you, but with great compassion I will gather you. In overflowing wrath for a moment I hid my face from you, but with everlasting love I will have compassion on you, says the Lord, your Redeemer. . . . For the mountains may depart and the hills be removed, *but my steadfast love shall not depart from you,* and my covenant of peace shall not be removed, says the Lord, who has compassion on you'' (*Is* 54:4-8, 10).

Since the human being—man and woman—has been created in God's image and likeness, God can speak about himself through the lips of the Prophet using language which is essentially human. In the text of Isaiah quoted above, the expression of God's love is ''*human*'', but the *love* itself *is divine.* Since it is God's love, its spousal character is properly divine, even though it is expressed by the analogy of a man's love for a woman. The woman-bride is Israel, God's Chosen People, and this choice originates exclusively in God's gratuitous love. It is precisely this love which explains the Covenant, a Covenant often presented as a marriage covenant which God always renews with his Chosen People. On the part of God the Covenant is a lasting ''commitment''; he remains faithful to his spousal love even if the bride often shows herself to be unfaithful.

This *image of spousal love,* together with the figure of the divine Bridegroom—a very clear image in the texts of the Prophets—finds crowning confirmation in the Letter to the Ephesians (5:23-32). *Christ* is greeted as the bridegroom by John the Baptist (cf. *Jn* 3:27-29). Indeed Christ applies to himself this comparison drawn from the Prophets (cf. *Mk* 2:19-20). The Apostle Paul, who is a bearer of the Old Testament heritage, writes to the Corinthians: ''I feel a divine jealousy for you, for I betrothed you to Christ to present you as a pure bride to her one husband'' (2 *Cor* 11:2). But the fullest expression of the truth about Christ the Redeemer's Love, according to the analogy of spousal love in marriage, is found in the Letter to the Ephesians: ''*Christ loved the Church and gave himself up for her*'' (5:25), thereby fully confirming the fact that the Church is the bride of Christ: ''The Holy One of Israel is your Redeemer'' (*Is* 54:5). In Saint Paul's text the analogy of the spousal relationship moves simultaneously in two directions which make up the whole of the ''great mystery'' (*''sacramentum magnum''*). The covenant proper to spouses ''explains'' the spousal character of the union of Christ with the Church, and in its turn this union, as a ''great sacrament'', determines the sacramentality of marriage as a holy covenant between the two spouses, man and woman. Reading this rich and complex passage, which *taken as a whole is a great analogy,* we must *distinguish* that element which expresses the human reality of interpersonal relations from that which expresses in symbolic language the "great mystery" which is divine.

The Gospel "Innovation"

24. The text is addressed to the spouses as real women and men. It reminds them of the "ethos" of spousal love which goes back to the divine institution of marriage from the "beginning". Corresponding to the truth of this institution is the exhortation: "*Husbands, love your wives*", love them because of that special and unique bond whereby in marriage a man and a woman become "one flesh" (*Gen* 2:24; *Eph* 5:31). In this love there is a fundamental *affirmation of the woman* as a person. This affirmation makes it possible for the female personality to develop fully and be enriched. This is precisely the way Christ acts as the bridegroom of the Church; he desires that she be "in splendour, without spot or wrinkle" (*Eph* 5:27). One can say that this fully captures the whole "style" of Christ in dealing with women. Husbands should make their own the elements of this style in regard to their wives; analogously, all men should do the same in regard to women in every situation. In this way both men and women bring about "the sincere gift of self ".

The author of the Letter to the Ephesians sees no contradiction between an exhortation formulated in this way and the words: "Wives, be subject to your husbands, as to the Lord. For the husband is the head of the wife" (5:22-23). The author knows that this way of speaking, so profoundly rooted in the customs and religious tradition of the time, is to be understood and carried out in a new way: as a "*mutual subjection out of reverence for Christ*" (cf. *Eph* 5:21). This is especially true because the husband is called the "head" of the wife *as* Christ is the head of the Church; he is so in order to give "himself up for her" (*Eph* 5:25), and giving himself up for her means giving up even his own life. However, whereas in the relationship between Christ and the Church the subjection is only on the part of the Church, in the relationship between husband and wife the "subjection" is not one-sided but mutual.

In relation to the "old" this is evidently something "new": it is an innovation of the Gospel. We find various passages in which the apostolic writings express this innovation, even though they also communicate what is "old": what is rooted in the religious tradition of Israel, in its way of understanding and explaining the sacred texts, as for example the second chapter of the Book of Genesis.[49]

The apostolic letters are addressed to people living in an environment marked by that same traditional way of thinking and acting. The "innovation" of Christ is a fact: it constitutes the unambiguous content of the evangelical message and is the result of the Redemption. However, the awareness that in marriage there is mutual "subjection of the spouses out of reverence for Christ", and not just that of the wife to the husband, must gradually establish itself in hearts, consciences, behaviour and customs. This is a call which from that time onwards, does not cease to challenge succeeding generations; it is a call which people have to accept ever anew. Saint Paul not only wrote: "In Christ Jesus . . . there is no more man or woman", but also wrote: "There is no more slave or freeman". Yet how many generations were needed for such a principle to be realized in the history of humanity through the abolition of slavery! And what is one to say of the many forms of slavery to which individuals and peoples are subjected, which have not yet disappeared from history?

But *the challenge presented by the "ethos" of the Redemption* is clear and definitive. All the reasons in favour of the "subjection" of woman to man in marriage must be understood in the sense of a "mutual subjection" of both "out of reverence for

Christ''. The measure of true spousal love finds its deepest source in Christ, who is the Bridegroom of the Church, his Bride.

The Symbolic Dimension of the ''Great Mystery''

25. In the Letter to the Ephesians we encounter *a second dimension* of the analogy which, taken as a whole, serves to reveal the ''great mystery''. This is *a symbolic dimension.* If God's love for the human person, for the Chosen People of Israel, is presented by the Prophets as the love of the bridegroom for the bride, such an analogy expresses the ''spousal'' quality and the divine and non-human character of God's love: ''For your Maker is your husband . . . the God of the whole earth he is called'' (*Is* 54:5). The same can also be said of the spousal love of Christ the Redeemer: ''For God so loved the world that he gave his only Son'' (*Jn* 3:16). It is a matter, therefore, of God's love expressed by means of the Redemption accomplished by Christ. According to Saint Paul's Letter, this love is ''like'' the spousal love of human spouses, but naturally it is not ''the same''. For the analogy implies a likeness, while at the same time leaving ample room for non-likeness.

This is easily seen in regard to the person of the ''bride''. According to the Letter to the Ephesians, the bride *is the Church,* just as for the Prophets the bride was Israel. She is therefore *a collective subject* and not *an individual person.* This collective subject is the People of God, a community made up of many persons, both women and men. ''Christ has loved the Church'' precisely as a community, as the People of God. At the same time, in this Church, which in the same passage is also called his ''body'' (cf. *Eph* 5:23), he has loved every individual person. For Christ has redeemed all without exception, every man and woman. It is precisely this love of God which is expressed in the Redemption; the spousal character of this love reaches completion in the history of humanity and of the world.

Christ has entered this history and remains in it as the Bridegroom who ''has given himself''. ''To give'' means ''to become a sincere gift'' in the most complete and radical way: ''Greater love has no man than this'' (*Jn* 15:13). According to this conception, *all human beings—both women and men—are called* through the Church, *to be the ''Bride'' of Christ, the Redeemer of the world.* In this way ''being the bride'', and thus the ''feminine'' element, becomes a symbol of all that is ''human'', according to the words of Paul: ''There is neither male nor female; for you are all *one* in Christ Jesus'' (*Gal* 3:28).

From a linguistic viewpoint we can say that the analogy of spousal love found in the Letter to the Ephesians links what is ''masculine'' to what is ''feminine'', since, as members of the Church, men too are included in the concept of ''Bride''. This should not surprise us, for Saint Paul, in order to express his mission in Christ and in the Church, speaks of the ''little children with whom he is again in travail'' (cf. *Gal* 4:19). In the sphere of what is ''human''—of what is humanly personal—*''masculinity'' and ''femininity'' are distinct,* yet at the same time they *complete and explain each other.* This is also present in the great analogy of the ''Bride'' in the Letter to the Ephesians. In the Church every human being—male and female— is the ''Bride'', in that he or she accepts the gift of the love of Christ the Redeemer, and seeks to respond to it with the gift of his or her own person.

Christ is the Bridegroom. This expresses the truth about the love of God who ''first loved us'' (cf. 1 *Jn* 4:19) and who, with the gift generated by this spousal love for man, has exceeded all human expectations: ''He loved them to the end'' (*Jn* 13:1). The Bridegroom—the Son consubstantial with the Father as God—became the son of Mary; he became the ''son of man'', true man, a male. *The symbol of the Bridegroom is masculine.* This masculine symbol represents the human aspect of the divine love which God has for Israel, for the Church, and for all people. Meditating on what the Gospels say about Christ's attitude towards women, we can conclude that *as a man,* a son of Israel, he *revealed* the dignity of the "daughters of Abraham" (cf. *Lk* 13:16), *the dignity belonging to women* from the very "beginning" on an equal footing with men. At the same time Christ emphasized the originality which distinguishes women from men, all the richness lavished upon women in the mystery of creation. Christ's attitude towards women serves as a model of what the Letter to the Ephesians expresses with the concept of "bridegroom". Precisely because Christ's divine love is the love of a Bridegroom, it is the model and pattern of all human love, men's love in particular.

The Eucharist

26. Against the broad background of the "great mystery" expressed in the spousal relationship between Christ and the Church, it is possible to understand adequately the calling of the "Twelve". *In calling only men as his Apostles,* Christ acted *in a completely free and sovereign manner.* In doing so, he exercised the same freedom with which, in all his behaviour, he emphasized the dignity and the vocation of women, without conforming to the prevailing customs and to the traditions sanctioned by the legislation of the time. Consequently, the assumption that he called men to be apostles in order to conform with the widespread mentality of his times, does not at all correspond to Christ's way of acting. "Teacher, we know that you are true, and teach the way of God truthfully, and care for no man; for *you do not regard the position of men*" (*Mt* 22:16). These words fully characterize *Jesus of Nazareth's behaviour.* Here one also finds an explanation for the calling of the "Twelve". They are with Christ at the Last Supper. They alone receive the sacramental charge, "Do this in remembrance of me" (*Lk* 22:19; 1 *Cor* 11:24), which is joined to the institution of the Eucharist. On Easter Sunday night they receive the Holy Spirit for the forgiveness of sins: "Whose sins you forgive are forgiven them, and whose sins you retain are retained" (*Jn* 20:23).

We find ourselves at the very heart of the Paschal Mystery, which completely reveals the spousal love of God. Christ is the Bridegroom because "he has given himself": his body has been "given", his blood has been "poured out" (cf. *Lk* 22:19-20). In this way "he loved them to the end" (*Jn* 13:1). The "sincere gift" contained in the Sacrifice of the Cross gives definitive prominence to the spousal meaning of God's love. As the Redeemer of the world, Christ is the Bridegroom of the Church. *The Eucharist* is *the Sacrament of our Redemption.* It is *the Sacrament of the Bridegroom and of the Bride.* The Eucharist makes present and realizes anew in a sacramental manner the redemptive act of Christ, who "creates" the Church, his body. Christ is united with this "body" as the bridegroom with the bride. All this is contained in the Letter to the Ephesians. The perennial "unity of the two" that exists between man and woman from the very "beginning" is introduced into this "great mystery" of Christ and of the Church.

Since Christ, in instituting the Eucharist, linked it in such an explicit way to the priestly service of the Apostles, it is legitimate to conclude that he thereby wished to express the relationship between man and woman, between what is "feminine" and what is "masculine". It is a relationship willed by God both in the mystery of creation and in the mystery of Redemption. It is *the Eucharist* above all that expresses *the redemptive act of Christ the Bridegroom towards the Church the Bride.* This is clear and unambiguous when the sacramental ministry of the Eucharist, in which the priest acts *"in persona Christi"*, is performed by a man. This explanation confirms the teaching of the Declaration *Inter Insigniores,* published at the behest of Paul VI in response to the question concerning the admission of women to the ministerial priesthood.[50]

The Gift of the Bride

27. The Second Vatican Council renewed the Church's awareness of the universality of the priesthood. In the New Covenant there is only one sacrifice and only one priest: Christ. *All the baptized share in the one priesthood of Christ,* both men and women, inasmuch

as they must ''present their bodies as a living sacrifice, holy and acceptable to God (cf. *Rom* 12:1), give witness to Christ in every place, and give an explanation to anyone who asks the reason for the hope in eternal life that is in them (cf. *Pt* 3:15)''.[51] Universal participation in Christ's sacrifice, in which the Redeemer has offered to the Father the whole world and humanity in particular, brings it about that all in the Church are ''a kingdom of priests'' (*Rev* 5:10; cf. 1 *Pt* 2:9), who not only share in the priestly mission but also in the prophetic and kingly mission of Christ the Messiah. Furthermore, this participation determines the organic unity of the Church, the People of God, with Christ. It expresses at the same time the ''great mystery'' described in the Letter to the Ephesians; *the bride united to her Bridegroom;* united, because she lives his life; united, because she shares in his threefold mission (*tria munera Christi*); united *in such a manner as to respond* with a ''sincere gift'' of self *to the inexpressible gift of the love of the Bridegroom,* the Redeemer of the world. This concerns everyone in the Church, women as well as men. It obviously concerns those who share in the ''ministerial priesthood'',[52] which is characterized by service. In the context of the ''great mystery'' of Christ and of the Church, all are called to respond—as a bride—with the gift of their lives to the inexpressible gift of the love of Christ, who alone, as the Redeemer of the world, is the Church's Bridegroom. The ''royal priesthood'', which is universal, at the same time expresses the gift of the Bride.

This is of *fundamental importance for understanding the Church in her* own *essence,* so as to avoid applying to the Church—even in her dimension as an ''institution'' made up of human beings and forming part of history—criteria of understanding and judgment which do not pertain to her nature. Although the Church possesses a ''hierarchical'' structure,[53] nevertheless this structure is totally ordered to the holiness of Christ's members. And holiness is measured according to the ''great mystery'' in which the Bride responds with the gift of love to the gift of the Bridegroom. She does this ''in the Holy Spirit'', since ''God's love has been poured into our hearts through the Holy Spirit who has been given to us'' (*Rom* 5:5). The Second Vatican Council, confirming the teaching of the whole of tradition, recalled that in the hierarchy of holiness it is *precisely the ''woman'',* Mary of Nazareth, who is the ''figure'' of the Church. She ''precedes'' everyone on the path to holiness; in her person ''the Church has already reached that perfection whereby she exists without spot or wrinkle (cf. *Eph* 5:27)''.[54] In this sense, one can say that the Church is *both* ''Marian'' and ''Apostolic-Petrine''.[55]

In the history of the Church, even from earliest times, there were side-by-side with men *a number of women,* for whom the response of the Bride to the Bridegroom's redemptive love acquired full expressive force. First we see those women who had personally encountered Christ and followed him. After his departure, together with the Apostles, they ''devoted themselves to prayer'' in the Upper Room in Jerusalem until the day of Pentecost. On that day the Holy Spirit spoke through ''the sons and daughters'' of the People of God, thus fulfilling the words of the prophet Joel (cf. *Acts* 2:17). These women, and others afterwards, played *an active and important role in the life of the early Church,* in building up from its foundations the first Christian community—and subsequent communites—*through their own charisms and their varied service.* The apostolic writings note their names, such as Phoebe, ''a deaconess of the Church at Cenchreae'' (cf. *Rom* 16:1), Prisca with her husband Aquila (cf. 2 *Tim* 4:19), Euodia and Syntyche (cf. *Phil* 4:2), Mary, Tryphaena, Persis, and Tryphosa (cf. *Rom* 16:6, 12). Saint Paul speaks of their ''hard work'' for Christ, and this hard work indicates the various fields of the Church's apostolic service, beginning with the ''domestic Church''. For in the latter, ''sincere faith'' passes from the mother to her children and grandchildren, as was the case in the house of Timothy (cf. 2 *Tim* 1:5).

The same thing is repeated down the centuries, from one generation to the next, as *the history of the Church* demonstrates. By defending the dignity of women and their vocation, the Church has shown honour and gratitude for those women who—faithful to the Gospel—have shared in every age in the apostolic mission of the whole People of God. They are the holy martyrs, virgins, and mothers of families, who bravely bore witness to their faith and passed on the Church's faith and tradition by bringing up their children in the spirit of the Gospel.

In every age and in every country we find many "perfect" women (cf. *Prov.* 31:10) who, despite persecution, difficulties and discrimination, have shared in the Church's mission. It suffices to mention: Monica, the mother of Augustine, Macrina, Olga of Kiev, Matilda of Tuscany, Hedwig of Silesia, Jadwiga of Cracow, Elizabeth of Thuringia, Birgitta of Sweden, Joan of Arc, Rose of Lima, Elizabeth Ann Seton and Mary Ward.

The witness and the achievements of Christian women have had a significant impact on the life of the Church as well as of society. Even in the face of serious social discrimination, holy women have acted "freely", strengthened by their union with Christ. Such union and freedom rooted in God explain, for example, the great work of Saint Catherine of Siena in the life of the Church, and the work of Saint Teresa of Jesus in the monastic life.

In our own days too the Church is constantly enriched by the witness of the many women who fulfill their vocation to holiness. Holy women are an incarnation of the feminine ideal; they are also a model for all Christians, a model of the *"sequela Christi"*, an example of how the Bride must respond with love to the love of the Bridegroom.

VIII

"The Greatest of These is Love"

In the Face of Changes

28. "The Church believes that Christ, who died and was raised up for all, can through his Spirit offer man the light and the strength to respond to his supreme destiny".[56] We can apply these words of the Conciliar Constitution *Gaudium et Spes* to the present reflections. The particular reference to the dignity of women and their vocation, precisely in our time, can and must be received in the "light and power" which the Spirit grants to human beings, including the people of our own age, which is marked by so many different transformations. The Church "holds that in her Lord and Master can be found the key, the focal point, and the goal" of man and "of all human history", and she "maintains *that beneath all changes there are many realities which do not change and which have their ultimate foundation in Christ,* who is the same yesterday and today, yes and forever".[57]

These words of the Constitution on the Church in the Modern World show the path to be followed in undertaking the tasks connected with the dignity and vocation of women, against the background of the significant changes of our times. We can face these changes correctly and adequately only if *we go back* to the foundations which are to be found in Christ, to those *"immutable" truths and values* of which he himself remains the "faithful witness" (cf. *Rev.* 1:5) and Teacher. A different way of acting would lead to doubtful, if not actually erroneous and deceptive results.

The Dignity of Women and the Order of Love

29. The passage from the Letter to the Ephesians already quoted (5:21-33), in which the relationship between Christ and the Church is presented as the link between the Bridegroom and the Bride, also makes reference to the institution of marriage as recorded in the Book of Genesis (cf. 2:24). This passage connects the truth about marriage as a primordial sacrament with the creation of man and woman in the image and likeness of God (cf. *Gen* 1:27; 5:1). The significant comparison in the Letter to the

Ephesians gives perfect clarity to *what is decisive for the dignity of women both in the eyes of God*—the Creator and Redeemer—*and in the eyes of human beings*—men and women. In God's eternal plan, woman is the one in whom the order of love in the created world of persons takes first root. The order of love belongs to the intimate life of God himself, the life of the Trinity. In the intimate life of God, the Holy Spirit is the personal hypostasis of love. Through the Spirit, Uncreated Gift, love becomes a gift for created persons. *Love, which is of God, communicates itself to creatures:* "God's love has been poured into our hearts through the Holy Spirit who has been given to us" (*Rom* 5:5).

The calling of woman into existence at man's side as "a helper fit for him" (*Gen* 2:18) in the "unity of the two", provides the visible world of creatures with particular conditions so that "the love of God may be poured into the hearts" of the beings created in his image. When the author of the Letter to the Ephesians calls Christ "the Bridegroom" and the Church "the Bride", he indirectly confirms through this analogy *the truth about woman as bride*. The Bridegroom is the one who loves. The Bride is loved: *it is she who receives love, in order to love in return.*

Rereading Genesis in light of the spousal symbol in the Letter to the Ephesians enables us to grasp a truth which seems to determine in an essential manner the question of women's dignity, and, subsequently, also the question of their vocation: *the dignity of women is measured by the order of love,* which is essentially the order of justice and charity.[58]

Only a person can love and only a person can be loved. This statement is primarily ontological in nature, and it gives rise to an ethical affirmation. Love is an ontological and ethical requirement of the person. The person must be loved, since love alone corresponds to what the person is. This explains *the commandment of love,* known already in the Old Testament (cf. *Deut* 6:5; *Lev* 19:18) and placed by Christ at the very center of the Gospel *"ethos"* (cf. *Mt* 22:36-40; *Mk* 12:28-34). This also explains the *primacy of love* expressed by Saint Paul in the First Letter to the Corinthians: "the greatest of these is love" (cf. 13:13).

Unless we refer to this order and primacy we cannot give a complete and adequate answer to the question about women's dignity and vocation. When we say that the woman is the one who receives love in order to love in return, this refers not only or above all to the specific spousal relationship of marriage. It means something more universal, based on the very fact of her being a woman within all the interpersonal relationships which, in the most varied ways, shape society and structure the interaction between all persons—men and women. In this broad and diversified context, a *woman represents a particular value by the fact that she is a human person,* and, at the same time, this particular person, *by the fact of her femininity.* This concerns each and every woman, independently of the cultural context in which she lives, and independently of her spiritual, psychological and physical characteristics, as for example, age, education, health, work, and whether she is married or single.

The passage from the Letter to the Ephesians which we have been considering enables us to think of a special kind of "prophetism" that belongs to women in their femininity. The analogy of the Bridegroom and the Bride speaks of the love with which every human being—man and woman—is loved by God in Christ. But in the context of the biblical analogy and the text's interior logic, it is precisely the woman—the bride—who manifests this truth to everyone. This *"prophetic" character of women in their femininity* finds its highest expression in the Virgin Mother of God. She emphasizes, in the fullest and most direct way, the intimate linking of the order of love—which enters the world of human persons through a Woman—with the Holy Spirit. At the Annunciation Mary hears the words: "The Holy Spirit will come upon you" (*Lk* 1:35).

Awareness of a Mission

30. A woman's dignity is closely connected with the love which she receives by the very reason of her femininity; it is likewise connected *with the love which she gives in return.* The truth about the person and about love is thus confirmed. With regard to the truth about the person, we must turn again to the Second Vatican Council: "Man, who is the only creature on earth that God willed for its own sake, cannot fully find himself except through a sincere gift of self".[59] This applies to every human being, as a person created in God's image, whether man or woman. This ontological affirmation also indicates the ethical dimension of a person's vocation. *Woman can only find herself by giving love to others.*

From the "beginning", woman—like man—was created and "placed" by God in this order of love. The sin of the first parents did not destroy this order, nor irreversibly cancel it out. This is proved by the words of the Proto-evangelium (cf. *Gen* 3:15). Our reflections have focused on *the particular place occupied by the "woman"* in this key text of revelation. It is also to be noted how the same Woman, who attains the position of a biblical "exemplar", also appears within the eschatological perspective of the world and of humanity given in the Book of Revelation.[60] She is *"a woman clothed with the sun",* with the moon under her feet, and on her head a crown of stars (cf. *Rev* 12:1). One can say she is a Woman of cosmic scale, on a scale with the whole work of creation. At the same time she is "suffering the pangs and anguish of childbirth" (*Rev* 12:2) like Eve "the mother of all the living" (*Gen* 3:20). She also suffers because "before the woman who is about to give birth" (cf. *Rev* 12:4) there stands "the great dragon . . . that ancient serpent" (*Rev* 12:9), already known from the Proto-evangelium: the Evil One, the "father of lies" and of sin (cf. *Jn* 8:44). The "ancient serpent" wishes to devour "the child". While we see in this text an echo of the Infancy Narrative (cf. *Mt* 2:13, 16), we can also see that the struggle with evil and the Evil One marks the biblical exemplar of the "woman" from the beginning to the end of history. It is also *a struggle for man, for his true good, for his salvation.* Is not the Bible trying to tell us that it is precisely in the "woman"—Eve-Mary—that history witnesses a dramatic struggle for every human being, the struggle for his or her fundamental "yes" or "no" to God and God's eternal plan for humanity?

While the dignity of woman witnesses to the love which she receives in order to love in return, the biblical "exemplar" of the Woman also seems to reveal *the true order of love which constitutes woman's own vocation.* Vocation is meant here in its fundamental, and one may say universal significance, a significance which is then actualized and expressed in women's many different "vocations" in the Church and the world.

The moral and spiritual strength of a woman is joined to her awareness that *God entrusts the human being to her in a special way.* Of course, God entrusts every human being to each and every other human being. But this entrusting concerns women in a special way—precisely by reason of their femininity—and this in a particular way determines their vocation.

The moral force of women, which draws strength from this awareness and this entrusting, expresses itself in a great number of figures of the Old Testament, of the time of Christ, and of later ages right up to our own day.

A woman is strong because of her awareness of this entrusting, strong because of the fact that God "entrusts the human being to her", always and in every way, even in the situations of social discrimination in which she may find herself. This awareness and this fundamental vocation speak to women of the dignity which they receive from God himself, and this makes them "strong" and strengthens their vocation. Thus the "perfect woman" (cf. *Prov* 31:10) becomes an irreplaceable support and source of spiritual strength for other people, who perceive the great energies of her spirit. These "perfect women" are owed much by their families, and sometimes by whole nations.

In our own time, the successes of science and technology make it possible to attain material well-being to a degree hitherto unknown. While this favours some, it pushes others to the edges of society. In this way, unilateral progress can also lead to a gradual *loss of sensitivity for man, that is, for what is essentially human.* In this sense, our time in particular *awaits the manifestation* of that "genius" which belongs to women, and which can ensure sensitivity for human beings in every circumstance: because they are human!—and because "the greatest of these is love" (cf. 1 *Cor* 13:13).

Thus a careful reading of the biblical exemplar of the Woman—from the Book of Genesis to the Book of Revelation—confirms that which constitutes women's dignity and vocation, as well as that which is unchangeable and ever relevant in them, because it has its "ultimate foundation in Christ, who is the same yesterday and today, yes and forever".[61] If the human being is entrusted by God to women in a particular way, does not this mean that *Christ looks to them for the accomplishment of the "royal priesthood"* (1 *Pt* 2:9), which is the treasure he has given to every individual? Christ, as the supreme and only priest of the New and Eternal Covenant, and as the Bridegroom of the Church, does not cease to submit this same inheritance to the Father through the Spirit, so that God may be "everything to everyone" (1 *Cor* 15:28).[62]

Then the truth that "the greater of these is love" (cf. 1 *Cor* 13:13) will have its definitive fulfillment.

IX

Conclusion

"If You Knew the Gift of God"

31. "If you knew the gift of God" (*Jn* 4:10), Jesus says to the Samaritan woman during one of those remarkable conversations which show his great esteem for the dignity of women and for the vocation which enables them to share in his messianic mission.

The present reflections, now at an end, have sought to recognize, within the "gift of God", what he, as Creator and Redeemer, entrusts to women, to every woman. In the Spirit of Christ, in fact, women can discover the entire meaning of their femininity and thus be disposed to making a "sincere gift of self " to others, thereby finding themselves.

During the Marian Year *the Church desires to give thanks to the Most Holy Trinity* for the "mystery of woman" and for every woman—for that which constitutes the eternal measure of her feminine dignity, for the "great works of God", which throughout human history have been accomplished in and through her. After all, was it not in and through her that the greatest event in human history—the incarnation of God himself—was accomplished?

Therefore *the Church gives thanks for each and every woman:* for mothers, for sisters, for wives; for women consecrated to God in virginity; for women dedicated to the many human beings who await the gratuitous love of another person; for women who watch over the human persons in the family, which is the fundamental sign of the human community; for women who work professionally, and who at times are burdened by a great social responsibility; for *"perfect"* women and for "weak" women—for all women as they have come forth from the heart of God in all the beauty and richness of their femininity; as they have been embraced by his eternal love; as, together with men, they are pilgrims on this earth, which is the temporal "homeland" of all people and is transformed sometimes into a "valley of tears"; as they assume, together with men, *a common responsibility for the destiny of humanity* according to daily necessities and according to that definitive destiny which the human family has in God himself, in the bosom of the ineffable Trinity.

The Church gives thanks *for all the manifestations of the feminine "genius"* which have appeared in the course of history, in the midst of all peoples and nations; she gives thanks for all the charisms which the Holy Spirit distributes to women in the history of the People of God, for all the victories which she owes to their faith, hope and charity: she gives thanks for all *the fruits of feminine holiness.*

The Church asks at the same time that these invaluable "manifestations of the Spirit" (cf. 1 *Cor* 12:4ff.), which with great generosity are poured forth upon the "daughters" of the eternal Jerusalem, may be attentively recognized and appreciated so that they may return for the common good of the Church and of humanity, especially in our times. Meditating on the biblical mystery of the "woman", the Church prays that in this mystery all women may discover themselves and their "supreme vocation".

May *Mary,* who "is a model of the Church in the matter of faith, charity, and perfect union with Christ",[63] obtain for all of us *this same "grace",* in the Year which we have dedicated to her as we approach the third millennium from the coming of Christ.

With these sentiments, I impart the Apostolic Blessing to all the faithful, and in a special way to women, my sisters in Christ.

Given in Rome, at Saint Peter's, on 15 August, the Solemnity of the Assumption of the Blessed Virgin Mary, in the year 1988, the tenth of my Pontificate.

Endnotes

[48] Cf. for example, *Hos* 1:2; 2:16-18; *Jer* 2:2; *Exek* 16:8; *Is* 50:1;54: 5-8.

[49] Cf. *Col* 3:18; 1 *Pt* 3:1-6; *Tit* 2:4-5; *Eph* 5:22-24; 1 *Cor* 11:3-16; 14:33-35; 1 *Tim* 2:11-15.

[50] Cf. CONGREGATION FOR THE DOCTRINE OF THE FAITH, Declaration Concerning the Question of the Admission of Women to the Ministerial Priesthood *Inter Insigniores* (15 October 1976): *AAS* 69 (1977), 98-116.

[51] Cf. SECOND VATICAN ECUMENICAL COUNCIL, Dogmatic Constitution on the Church *Lumen Gentium,* 10.

[52] Cf. *ibid.,* 10.

[53] Cf. *ibid.,* 18-29.

[54] *Ibid.* 65; cf. also 63; cf. Encyclical Letter *Redemptoris Mater,* 2-6: *loc. cit.,* 362-367.

[55] "This *Marian* profile is also—even perhaps more so—fundamental and characteristic for the Church as is the *apostolic* and *Petrine* profile to which it is profoundly united. . . . The Marian dimension of the Church is antecedent to that of the Petrine, without being in any way divided from it or being less complementary. Mary Immaculate precedes all others, including obviously Peter himself and the Apostles. This is so, not only because Peter and the Apostles, being born of the human race under the burden of sin, form part of the Church which is 'holy from out of sinners', but also because their triple *function* has no other purpose except to form the Church in line with the ideal of sanctity already programmed and prefigured in Mary. A contemporary theologian has rightly stated that Mary is 'Queen of the Apostles without any pretensions to apostolic powers: she has other and greater powers' (H.U. VON BALTHASAR, *Neue Klarstellungen)*". *Address* to the Cardinals and Prelates of the Roman Curia (22 December 1987): *l'Osservatore Romano,* 23 December 1987.

[56] SECOND VATICAN ECUMENICAL COUNCIL, Pastoral Constitution on the Church in the Modern World *Gaudium et Spes,* 10.

[57] *Ibid.,* 10.

[58] Cf. SAINT AUGUSTINE, *De Trinitate,* L. VIII, VII, 10X, 14: *CCL* 50, 284-291.

[59] SECOND VATICAN ECUMENICAL COUNCIL, Pastoral Constitution on the Church in the Modern World *Gaudium et Spes*, 24.

[60] Cf. in the Appendix to the works of SAINT AMBROSE, *in Apoc.* IV, 3-4: *PL* 17, 876; SAINT AUGUSTINE, *De symb. ad catech. sermo* IV: *PL* 40, 661.

[61] SECOND VATICAN ECUMENICAL COUNCIL, Pastoral Constitution on the Church in the Modern World *Gaudium et Spes*, 10.

[62] Cf. SECOND VATICAN ECUMENICAL COUNCIL, Dogmatic Constitution on the Church *Lumen Gentium*, 36.

[63] Cf. *ibid.*, 63.

Notes: *These are the final three chapters of Pope John Paul II's 1988 apostolic letter, which has the authority of a church teaching but not the infallibility of a papal encyclical. In earlier chapters, Pope John Paul II takes pains to place women in a positive light by emphasizing that both man and woman share in the original sin, and that in the person of Mary, the mother of Jesus, woman "is to be found at the center of this salvific event." The role of women is shown to be uplifted by Jesus's activities and relationships with women; women, in fact, are the first witnesses of the Resurrection. In chapter six, motherhood and virginity are defined as the two major callings of women.*

The chapters printed here are perhaps the most germaine to the question of ordination. In chapter seven's section on the Eucharist, the Pope says that "in calling only men as his Apostles, Christ acted in a completely free and sovereign manner," and did not pick only men in conformity with current cultural customs. In the "spousal love of God," Christ is the bridegroom and the church is the bride. "It is the Eucharist above all that expresses the redemptive act of Christ the Bridegroom towards the Church the Bride." In choosing male Apostles and linking their work to the institution of the Eucharist, Christ "thereby wished to express the relationship between man and woman." This argument against women as priests is not one which would easily lend itself to a future policy change.

Protestant and Eastern Orthodox Churches

While the Roman Catholic Church is the single largest religious body in North America, the Protestant and Eastern Orthodox churches together number more than 800 distinct church bodies and contain more than half of the religiously affiliated individuals in North America. Statements in this section show some of the diversity one would expect of such a wide-ranging group. Statements on women's ordination tend to be longer and more complex than those on other issues. This is because women's ordination involves more than just taking a stand; it requires an evaluation of the core of one's religious identity. Thus this section includes fewer but longer statements than others in the series.

The issue of women's ordination is unique in that once a particular Protestant or Eastern Orthodox body approves of it, debate within that group usually ceases. Energy is then focused on the acceptance and placement of women clergy. Statements in this section focus on those groups for whom the ordination of women either is now or has recently been a "live" issue. Most of the groups still do not ordain women or have done so only since 1970. Two exceptions to this are the United Church of Canada, which approved ordination in 1935, and the Presbyterian Church (U.S.A.) (its predecessor, the Presbyterian Church in the USA, approved in 1956).

Where possible, a number of different statements from the same group are included in order to show how a group may adopt different approaches to the issue at different points in time. Multiple statements can also reveal the sometimes lengthy turmoil and internal struggle an issue can arouse. A case in point is the Reformed Church in America, which first dealt with women's ordination in 1918, but did not finally allow it until 1981.

EPISCOPAL CHURCH

PROGRESS REPORT TO THE HOUSE OF BISHOPS FROM THE COMMITTEE TO STUDY THE PROPER PLACE OF WOMEN IN THE MINISTRY OF THE CHURCH (1966)

The creation of the Committee to Study the Proper Place of Women in the Ministry of the Church was authorized by the House of Bishops in September, 1965, and its members were subsequently appointed by the Presiding Bishop. The Committee consists of

The Bishop of Rochester, *Chairman*
Mrs. Irvin Bussing of California, *Secretary*
The Bishop of New Hampshire
The Bishop of Oklahoma

Mrs. Charles M. Hawes III of the Virgin Islands
Rev. Dr. Alden D. Kelley of Bexley Hall
Mrs. Theodore O. Wedel of New York

Of the women serving on the Committee, one has been an executive in public relations and advertising, another has been engaged in professional Church work for many years, both in this Church and on an ecumenical level, and the third has recently received a Bachelor of Divinity degree.

The Committee presents this preliminary Report, indicating the direction of its thinking and making some initial recommendations to the House of Bishops.

Scope and Urgency

The Committee presents this preliminary Report, indicating the place of women in the Church's Ministry demands the facing of the question of whether or not women should be considered eligible for ordination to any and all Orders of that Ministry. No one would deny that women are part of the lay ministry of the Church, and the Committee does not think that another examination of the status of Deaconesses alone would do justice to the matter.

The Committee is convinced that a number of factors give the question a new urgency, require a fresh and unprejudiced look at the whole issue, and warn against uncritical acceptance of beliefs, attitudes, and assumptions that have been inherited from the past and strongly persist at the present time. Three such factors seem especially important:

a. *The growing place of women in professional, business, and public life,* in medicine, in teaching, in politics and government, in the Armed Forces, even in high executive positions within this Church.

b. *The development of new forms of ministry* that permit greater flexibility and call for many more specialized skills than is the case when the ministry is limited largely to one priest in charge of one parish, a generalist rather than a specialist. As one member of the Committee put it, "We need to stop talking or thinking of the ministry as though it were a single unitary vocation. Rather, we need to think of the many functions of ministry which are needed today—the sacramental ministry, preaching, theological and Biblical research, teaching, pastoral work and counseling, social service, etc. In an age of specialization and of a tremendous explosion of knowledge we must face the fact that no one person can possibly be adequate in all these areas. . . . We need to encourage specialization according to a person's gifts and interests and organize our corporate life to use specialists." This fact requires consideration of how women may be used in a changing and increasingly specialized ministry.

c. *The growing importance of the issue in ecumenical relationships.* The question is being discussed in many parts of the Anglican Communion. . . . The initiation of a study of the experiences of ordained women was urged by the World Conference on Church and Society, meeting at Geneva in the Summer of 1966. In this country, the Consultation on Church Union has reached the point of considering the drafting of a plan of union, involving this Church and a number of others that now admit women to the ordained ministry, and the question of the ordination of women in such a united Church obviously must be faced as the negotiations proceed.

Nor does it seem that the question of the ordination of women in the Orthodox and Roman Churches can be regarded as finally and forever decided in the negative, particularly in view of other changes that have occurred, especially in the Roman Church.

There is a sentence in one of the official documents of Vatican II that reads, "Since in our times women have an ever more active share in the whole life of society, it is very important that they participate more widely also in the various fields of the Church's apostolate." *The Documents of Vatican II,* Walter M. Abbott, S. J., General Editor. Guild Press, New York. 1966, page 500.) The Archbishop of Durban, South Africa, Dr. Dennis Hurley, recently predicted that "there are going to be some fantastic developments" in the role of women in the Church. (See *Christian Century,* September 15, 1966.) And in an interview with the Secretary of this Committee, given on October 11, 1966, the Rev. Dr. Hans Kung, Professor in the University of Tubingen (Germany) stated, "There are two factors to consider regarding the ordination of women to the Sacred Ministry of the Church. The first is that there are no dogmatic or biblical reasons against it. The second is that there are psychological and sociological factors to be considered. The solution to the problem depends on the sociological conditions of the time and place. It is entirely a matter of cultural circumstances."

Burden of Proof

The Committee has become increasingly convinced that the burden of proof is on the negative in this matter.

For, to oppose the ordination of women is either to hold that the 'whole trend of modern culture is wrong in its attitude toward the place of women in society, or to maintain that the unique character of the ordained ministry makes that ministry a special case and justifies the exclusion of women from it.

Reasons Given Against the Ordination of Women

Mental and Emotional

The alleged mental and emotional characteristics of women are said to make them unsuitable to serve as clergymen. Such arguments are never very clear, consistent, or precise. Sometimes, the weakness of women is stressed, despite the fact that women are healthier and live longer than men. Or, it is claimed that women think emotionally rather than rationally and that they over-personalize problems or decisions.

The same sort of arguments can be used to show that women are unfit for almost any business, professional, or public responsibility. They were used against the admission of women to higher education, to the practice of medicine and law, and against women suffrage. They are still being used against the admission of women to the House of Deputies of the General Convention.

None of these negative arguments has been borne out in any other walk of life. Women have proved to be capable, often brilliant, lawyers, statesmen, scientists, and teachers. They have enriched the practice of medicine, and politics have neither been redeemed nor debased by their participation.

As experience has demonstrated, only experience can show the extent to which women might fulfill a useful role in the ordained ministry, as well as ways in which their role might be different from the role of men. Here, as in other callings, women would need to be better than men in order to compete with them.

Emil Brunner states, "It is absolutely impossible to put down in black and white, as a universal rule, which spheres of activity 'belong' to women and which do not. This can only become clear through experience; and for this experience, first of all the field must be thrown open."

Because the field has not been thrown open, any judgement based on the Church's experience with professional women workers is limited and inadequate. With the highest respect for the contributions these women are now making, the Committee is convinced that an absolute bar at the level of ordination has a deterring effect upon the number of women of high quality who enter professional Church work or undertake theological study, and that this same bar places theologically trained women in a highly uncomfortable and anomalous position.

Marriage versus Ministry

There is alleged the impossibility or impracticality of combining the vocation of a clergyman with domestic responsibilities, with marriage, as well as the bearing and care of children. Would it be possible for a wife and mother of a family to bring to the priesthood the required degree of commitment, concentration, and availability?

First, it must be said that many women choose careers and never marry, others combine marriage and careers. The Church recognizes that the latter is an entirely legitimate vocation, both in the secular world and in the Church itself.

Secondly, the question of married women is partly answered by the fact that married men are permitted to serve as bishops, priests, and deacons in the Anglican Communion. Such permission implies an acknowledgment of the strong claims that the wife and family of a married clergyman rightfully have upon his time, his money, and the conduct of his vocation. All would grant that a clergyman has a duty, as well as a right, to take into account his wife's health, or his children's education, in considering a call, in negotiating about his salary, in determining his standard of living and the amount of money he will give away.

While other, and perhaps more serious, problems might exist for a woman who wished to combine ordination with marriage, the Commission is by no means convinced that such a combination would not prove practical in many instances. Even such demanding professions as teaching and medicine are finding ways of using skilled and trained married women with children, both on a part-time and a full-time basis. Many intelligent women find that they are better wives and mothers by combining an outside calling with the care of a family. Many also can look forward to years of full-time professional work after their children are grown.

The Commission would ask whether the leadership of the Church does not possess resourcefulness and imagination similar to that displayed by other institutions in using married women, if not often as ministers in charge of parishes, yet as assistants, or for the specialized types of ministry that are sure to develop much more rapidly in the future. It is thought unlikely that any great number of women would seek ordination, considering the very real difficulties involved. But difficulty is not impossibility, and at the least there need be no fear that women will "take over" the Church.

Theological Arguments

Then there are certain theological objections which seem to the Committee to present a strange mixture of tradition and superstition.

Biblical

Some of the objections rest on a rather literal approach to the Bible and fail to take into account the degree to which the Bible is conditioned by the circumstances of its time. It is not necessary to dwell upon the Creation Story, in which woman is created after man and taken from him, nor be influenced by the fact that women were excluded from the covenant-relation of God with Israel, any more than one would support polygamy or slavery because both have clear sanction in the Old Testament. Nor is one moved by the familiar argument that our Lord chose only men to be his apostles. Any sound doctrine of the Incarnation must take full account of the extent to which Jesus lived and thought within the circumstances and environment of his own time. To deny such facts is to deny the full humanity of Jesus and to subscribe to a grotesque Docetism. Our Lord did choose women as close associates, even if he did choose men as the transitional leaders of the new Israel. The Committee also believes that St. Paul, as well as the authors of *Ephesians* and the Pastoral Epistles, were sharing in the passing assumptions of their own time, as well as advising wise strategy for the First Century Church, in recommending that women keep silent at services, cover their heads, and be subordinate to their husbands; just as St. Paul thought it wise to send a run-away slave back to his master. Much more permanent and basic are St. Paul's words, "There is neither Jew nor Greek . . . slave nor free . . . male nor female; for you all are one in Christ Jesus."

Image of God

Then there is a cluster of theological objections based on the assumption that the female is a less true or complete image of God than the male; and that, therefore, woman is less capable, or is quite incapable, of representing God to man and man to God in the priesthood, and of receiving the indelible grace of Holy Orders.

This line of reasoning has a number of curious sources. In the Bible, God is thought and spoken of as "he", for the most part, as would be entirely natural in a culture first militant and warlike, always patriarchal, and with a developing monotheism. Even so, God can be compared with a mother who comforts her child.

Jesus Christ was born a man. Obviously, God's unique child would need to be born either a man or woman; and, again, in a patriarchal culture, only a man could fulfill the role of Messiah, Lord, or Son of God. When one calls God personal, one can mean no more than that human personality is the best clue we have to the nature of God. Perhaps male personality is a better clue than female personality in a masculine-dominated society, but who would presume to project such sexual differentiation upon the very nature of God? The first of the Anglican Articles of Religion states that God is "without body, parts, or passions". To call God "he", implies no more than to call the entire human race "man" or "mankind".

The view that the female is a less true or complete image of God than the male is sometimes still supported by a tradition coming from Aristotle and St. Thomas Aquinas, which holds that woman is an incomplete human being, "a defective and/or misbegotten male". This tradition was based upon the pre-scientific biology which held that woman was an entirely passive partner in reproduction. On this subject, the Rev. Dr. Leonard Hodgson has commented, "We should be unwise to base our theological conclusions on notions of a pre-scientific biology which has never heard of genes or chromosomes."

Emotional and Psychological Pressures

The Commission is also aware that all the intellectual arguments against the ordination of women are connected with and reflect strong emotional and psychological pressures. These pressures *may* point to profound truth about men and women and their relationship to each other. Or, they *may* reflect magical notions of priesthood and Sacraments that linger on in the most sophisticated minds. Or, they *may* reflect the fact that our deepest emotional experiences in the life of the Church, experiences often associated with the birth and baptism of children, maturity and Confirmation, worship and Sacraments, the pastoral ministry in times of crisis, joy and sorrow, are all closely associated with an episcopate and a priesthood that is exclusively male. Or, they *may* illustrate the sad fact that historical and psychological circumstances frequently make the Church the last refuge of the fearful and the timid in a changing world and that, the more rapidly the world changes, the stronger become the pressures to keep the Church safe and unchanged. Or, they *may* represent a threat to the present ordained ministers, to their wives, to lay men or lay women. The Commission is disturbed by the scorn, the indifference, the humorless levity, that is occasioned by the question of seating women in the House of Deputies, let alone their admission to ordination.

Finally, one cannot place much weight upon the common opinion that women themselves do not wish to be ordained. Who knows? Most women obviously do not, just as most men do not wish to become clergymen. But some women do. Kathleen Bliss has written, "This is not a woman's question, it is a Church question." The Church's answer must be determined, not primarily by what is good for women, but what is good for the Church.

Recommendations

Upon the basis, then, of its work up to now, the Commission makes the following proposals:

- That the Lambeth Conference of 1968 be asked to study the question of the ministry of women again in a fresh and thorough manner.

  The fact that Lambeth has dealt with the question before is hardly decisive. In 1920, the Lambeth Conference condemned contraception; in 1930, it gave it rather grudging approval; but, in 1958, it implied that family-planning was a marital decision.

- That this Committee be continued, or that a similar one be appointed by the Presiding Bishop, to carry forward the study of the proper place of women in the ministry of the Church, keeping abreast of new developments and the wealth of new material appearing on the subject, and reporting any significant trends to this House, to the Presiding Bishop, and, through him, to those responsible for preparing for the Lambeth Conference.
- That the Committee be asked to communicate with other groups in the Anglican Communion making similar studies.
- That the Joint Commission on Ecumenical Relations be asked to explore the implications of the issue in its negotiations and conversations with other Christian Churches, Protestant, Orthodox, and Roman, and that the studies of the Committee be made available to them for such purpose.
- That the Committee be asked to collaborate with the Division of Christian Ministries of the Executive Council, with the Committee now studying theological education under the chairmanship of the President of Harvard University, with the Joint Commission on Education for Holy Orders, and with the Joint Commission on Women Church Workers, and that this last Commission be commended and encouraged in its efforts to improve the training, canonical and professional status, and compensation of the lay women now engaged in professional Church work or who shall be so engaged in the future.

Notes: *This report made to the House of Bishops of the Episcopal Church (approximately 2,750,000 members) during a special meeting in 1966 just prior to the 1967 General Convention is the first major examination of the issue made by the church. Citing social and ecclesiastical changes taking place worldwide, the committee felt that the burden of argument lay on those opposed to the ordination of women, and that the usual arguments of that position could not bear that weight. The House of Bishops adopted the resolutions from the committee, which sought a continued discussion of the topic, especially at the 1968 Lambeth Conference, the once-a-decade gathering of the bishops of the world-wide Anglican Communion. The House of Bishops also rejected a resolution which would have eliminated women from ordination. At the 1967 General Convention, the House of Bishops voted to follow up the committee report by establishing a joint commission with the House of Deputies to study the issue further. The House of Deputies, however, which consists of both lay and clergy orders, did not agree to such a study.*

EPISCOPAL CHURCH

RESOLUTION ON LAMBETH CONFERENCE RECOMMENDATIONS (1969)

House of Bishops—Fifth Day

The Bishop Coadjutor of Massachusetts, for the Committee on Memorials and Petitions, reported affirmatively with regard to a Resolution submitted by the Executive Council's *ad hoc* Committee on the Laity, and moved the following Resolution:

> *Whereas,* The Lambeth Conference of 1968 asked the Churches of the Anglican Communion to respond to their Resolutions Numbers 32, 34, 35, and 38, concerning the Diaconate and the ordination of women to the Priesthood; therefore, be it

Resolved, the House of Deputies concurring, That this Special General Convention direct the appropriate Joint Committees and Joint Commissions of the General Convention to study, and make recommendations to a subsequent meeting of the General Convention for a response from this Church to the following Resolutions of the Lambeth Conference of 1968; to wit:

The Diaconate

32. The Conference recommends:

    a. That the diaconate, combining service of others with liturgical functions, be open to

        i. men remaining in secular occupations,

        ii. full-time church workers,

        iii. those selected for the priesthood

    b. That Ordinals should, where necessary, be revised

        i. to take account of the new role envisaged for the diaconate,

        ii. by the removal of reference to the diaconate as "an inferior office,"

        iii. by emphasis upon the continuing element of diakonia in the ministry of bishops and priests.

    c. That those made deaconesses by laying on of hands with appropriate prayers be declared to be within the diaconate. (For, 221. Against, 183.)

    d. That appropriate canonical legislation be enacted by provinces and regional Churches to provide for those already ordained deaconesses.

Ordination of Women to the Priesthood

34. The Conference affirms its opinion that the theological arguments as at present presented for and against the ordination of women to the priesthood are inconclusive.

35. The Conference requests every national and regional Church or province to give careful study to the questions of the ordination of women to the priesthood and to report its findings to the Anglican Consultative Council (or Lambeth Consultative Body) which will make them generally available to the Anglican Communion.

38. The Conference recommends that, in the meantime, national or regional Churches or provinces should be encouraged to make canonical provision, where this does not exist, for duly qualified women to share in the conduct of liturgical worship, to preach, to baptize, to read the epistle and gospel at the Holy Communion, and to help in the distribution of the elements.

Resolution adopted

[Communicated to the House of Deputies by Message No. 47.]

House of Deputies—Fifth Day

Message No. 47 was received from the House of Bishops at the close of session on this Day and referred to the Committee on Theological Education.

House of Deputies—Sixth Day

Because of the shortness of time, and the press of other business, the Report of the Committee on Theological Education in respect of House of Bishops Message No. 47 was not called for.

The legislation, therefore, was incomplete, for lack of action on the part of the House of Deputies.

Notes: *The House of Bishops voted to form joint committees with the House of Deputies in order to respond to the Lambeth Conference's recommendations on the diaconate and the ordination of women. In 1920, the Lambeth Conference had decided that deaconesses are in holy orders just as deacons are, though this decision was reversed in 1930. In 1968 it altered its position once again, asserting that deaconesses are indeed "within the diaconate," i.e. in ordained holy orders. The House of Deputies did not have time to respond to this motion, and thus the legislation remained incomplete.*

EPISCOPAL CHURCH

RESOLUTION ON WOMEN'S ORDINATION (1970)

Ordination of Women

The Rev. Mr. Long of Pennsylvania presented Report #2 of the Committee on Theological Education, as follows:

Your Committee on Theological Education, to which was referred HD 41, on the subject of *Ordination of Women,* reports as follows:

Your Committee is of the opinion that the following Resolution is appropriate to afford this House an opportunity to express its opinion on the subject matter of HD 41, and accordingly moves the adoption of the following Resolution:

Resolved, the House of Bishops concurring, That, subject to the resolution of any constitutional or canonical questions, the Sixty-third General Convention of the Church affirm that women are eligible to seek and accept ordering to the diaconate and to the priesthood and to be ordained and consecrated to the episcopate.

In the event of the adoption of this Resolution, your Committee will report further as to its implementation.

The matter was debated at great length.

The Rev. Mr. Gillett of New Hampshire moved a Substitute Resolution, as follows:

Resolved, the House of Bishops concurring, That the question of the eligibility of women to seek and accept ordination to the Diaconate, the Priesthood, and the Episcopate, be submitted to the widest Anglican and ecumenical discussion and debate during the next triennium, including the Anglican Consultative Body; and that this question be immediately referred to our Joint Commission on Ecumenical Relations, in order that the question may be discussed with those Christian bodies with whom we are engaged in dialogue, looking toward unity.

The Substitute was debated, and, in the course of the debate, the Rev. Mr. Stevens of Massachusetts, on behalf of the Clerical and Lay Deputations of that Diocese, demanded that the vote be taken by orders and Dioceses.

Before the scheduled conclusion of the debate, but when it appeared that both sides had adequately stated their arguments, and no more speakers were in line to be heard, Mr. Cheney of Mississippi moved that the Special Rules be amended, and that debate be terminated.

Motion carried

A vote by orders and Dioceses on the Gillett Substitute was announced.

The Clerical and Lay Deputations of Connecticut and the Clerical Deputation of Long Island asked to be polled, with the following results:

Connecticut—clerical
Read—Yes
Beecher—No
Van Winkle—No

Vote: NO

Connecticut—lay
Lamb—No
Bakewell—Yes
Hartt—No
Attwood—No

Vote: NO

Long Island—clerical
Lemoine—Yes
MacLean—No
Capon—No
Penny—No

Vote: NO

The results of the vote by orders and Dioceses on the Gillett Substitute were announced, as follows:

Clerical
Yes, 39; No, 35; Divided, 16

Lay
Yes, 33½; No, 46; Divided, 10

Substitute defeated

The Clerical Deputation of Los Angeles demanded a vote by orders and Dioceses on the Original Question, being Report #2 of the Committee on Theological Education.

Five Clerical Deputations asked to be polled, with the following results:

Harrisburg
Lloyd—Yes
Mintz—No
Weitzel—No
Trost—Yes

Vote: DIVIDED

Hawaii
Crane—Yes
Yoshida—No
Smith—No
Kennedy—Yes

Vote—DIVIDED

Long Island
Lemoine—No
MacLean—Yes
Capon—Yes
Penny—Yes

Vote: YES

Northern Michigan
Robertson—No
Wiedrich—Yes
Heimer—Yes
Gerdau—Yes

Vote: YES

Spokane
Mason—No
Fox—No
Fowler—Yes
Coombs—No

Vote—NO

The Results of the vote were announced, as follows:

Clerical
Yes, 49¼; No, 28¾; Divided, 21.

Lay
Yes, 49¼; No, 28¾; Divided, 13.

There being no concurrence of the orders, the Resolution was declared to have lost.

Notes: *This 1970 resolution from the House of Deputies declaring women to be eligible for the priesthood and other ordained offices caused significant debate. In the final vote, the laity passed the resolution, with more than 50% of its total number voting affirmatively. The clergy did not pass the resolution, however, and therefore it failed. That same year, though, the General Convention voted to ordain women to the diaconate.*

EPISCOPAL CHURCH

REPORT OF SPECIAL COMMITTEE OF THE HOUSE OF BISHOPS, ON THE ORDINATION OF WOMEN (1972)

At the 1971 meeting of the House of Bishops, a resolution was presented by the Committee on Ministry (Bishop of Newark), in substance asking the House to state that it was "the mind of the House that it endorses the principle of the Ordination of Women to the Priesthood and of the Ordination and Consecration of Women to the Episcopate", and further asking the Committee on Canons to prepare the amendments necessary to establish this principle at the 1973 General Convention. After discussion, on motion, the matter was referred to a Special Committee of the House. It is now the privilege of that Committee to report.

We were not asked to make a specific proposal or proposals to the House for action, and we do not do so. A committee of seven Bishops is a small fraction of the House; and any attempt on our part to count our own noses and possibly emerge with some such verdict as "2 Yes/2 No/2 Wait/1 Undecided" would have been stultifying and useless to the House as a guide for action.

In our two meetings and in the various circulated drafts, we uncovered a surprising degree of unanimity among ourselves as to the considerations which seem to us the fundamental ones on which, in our judgment, the Church's decisions should be based. The differences among us as to the specific issues were clear; but we were in substantial agreement as to the main biblical and theological evidence which must be considered in reaching any conclusion. We came to feel that our usefulness to the House might lie in a report which would sketch these fundamental considerations and thus perhaps provide a somewhat disciplined theater for debate and decision. In other words, what follows is mainly a discussion of the matters which all of us felt were the decisive elements in the debate. On these we were generally of one mind, even though we might differ quite sharply on what we should therefore do about the specific issues. The report is in four parts, dealing, respectively, with The Ministry; Scripture, Tradition and Images; Evangelism and Development; and A Penumbra of Practicalities.

I: The Ministry

A. *The Diaconate* is the one order of sacred ministers to which women are ordained, in our Church. That this is so no doubt reflects the fact that the diaconate, in the New Testament, seems clearly a ministry to which women were admitted (*cf.* Romans 16:1, Acts 9:36). By the time 1 Timothy (3:8-13) was written, the diaconate seems to be a recognized "holy order". St. Paul's use of the word *diakonos* for Phoebe may well not have echoed those more formalized overtones, but C. H. Dodd's comment is appropriate, that "we may fairly suppose that the order of deacons which emerges in the second century . . . had its origin in Paul's own time; and that it included women as well as men". (*The Epistle of Paul to the Romans,* p. 235).

The ministry of the deacon, as generally understood in the contemporary Church, is murky and confused. To some it is no more than a "one-armed priesthood"—a brief stepping-stone in a professional career. To others it seems almost indistinguishable from the ministry of a lay person, save for the privilege of reading the Gospel at public worship. Perhaps because of such confusion, the admission of women to this order has appeared to present few serious difficulties, particularly because the New Testament evidence supports it. The main exception to this is the resistance of some to the substitution of "deacon" for the traditional "deaconess". In our mind, the fact that women are accepted as deacons is true to the New Testament evidence, and may well lead to a long-needed, fresh statement of the work of the ordained deacon. We think, however, that it bears only indirectly, if at all, on the present issue.

If the ordained diaconate is not merely a vestigial historical fragment, or an apprenticeship, it seems clearly to be a ministry of service. It may be distinguished from the service to which all Christians are called simply by intensity and by the authority and accountability conveyed in ordination, of which perhaps the liturgical privilege of reading the Gospel is a token. In Christian history, administration and teaching have been two ministries frequently associated with the diaconate. Further, the diaconate has also been closely associated with the Bishop. The liturgical aspects of the diaconate—baptism, administration of the Holy Communion, unction, *et al*—now tend to be blurred by the increasing participation of un-ordained persons in those functions. Should the diaconate by seen as primarily a work of advocacy of the poor, the sick, the dispossessed? All this enters into the Church's need for a fresh statement. But it is clear that the diaconate is a ministry for both men and women, with firm scriptural authority, which needs and deserves to be seen in its own unique terms, however they may be phrased. Yet we have not come to the core of the matter until we look at priesthood and episcopacy.

B. *The Priesthood:* What we say here about priesthood is a brief statement of a contemporary understanding of ordained priesthood which we generally share. The mystery of the priesthood far outruns any attempt to "describe" it. The New Testament seems to know of only one Priest, the Lord, in Whom the ancient High Priesthood of Israel culminates and is once for all fulfilled (Hebrews 5). The "Royal Priesthood" of 1 St. Peter 2:9 is derivative from Christ's High Priesthood—it refers to the ministry of loving service which all Christians share because of their inclusion, through baptism, in His Priestly Body. The word "priest" as applied to individual ministers seems not to have found its way into the Church's vocabulary until the end of the second century. Any developed doctrine of ministerial priesthood is still slower to appear; indeed it may be said that the Church, in our time, is still unfolding the truths about the ministry of the ordained and the un-ordained, alike hidden in the mystery of priesthood.

Some things seem to have been securely learned. The ministry shared and exercised by those ordained as priests partakes in and expresses both the High Priesthood of Christ and also the Royal Priesthood into which Christians enter in baptism. Priesthood is also perceived in the way in which this reconciling act is mediated, generation after generation, in and through Christ's Body, the Church, and all its members share in that mediation. The ordained priest is deeply linked to both these perceptions. By ordination, certain members of the Body are called of God and authorized by the Body to speak and act for the High Priest toward the Church and the world. They also speak and act for the Church and the world in making offering for them, through the Son, to the Father. To say, as we do, that ordained priesthood is "representative" is to say that the priest is, in ways far beyond our understanding, acting for both the Lord and His Church. His priesthood is not derived from the Church nor has anyone a right to claim priesthood; the priest is called to receive a gift, in ordination, which comes from the Father. But his call and the gifts are alike recognized and ratified by the Church; he acts for them in receiving and exercising the gift. Thus the authority and accountability conveyed in ordination has a double reference. No man exercises priesthood in a vacuum.

The priest is not set "above" the *Laos,* or against it. He is rather within the *Laos* as a particular focus, or symbol, or effective means of Christ's action toward the Church and the world, and of the Church's thankful response, through Christ, to the Father. This duality in no way implies two separate authorities or credentials or accountabilities. There is only One Priest. In Fr. Hebert's words, "The whole meaning of priesthood and sacrifice in the Church is gathered up in the one Priesthood and Sacrifice of Christ. He is recorded to have committed to the leader of the apostles the keys of stewardship, and to have instituted a sacrificial and sacramental rite; but the Christian minister does not hold a separate and individual priesthood. . . . In whatever sense the Church and its ministers are priestly, Christ must remain the one Priest. . . . As He has once for all offered Himself up for us, so that same sacrificial oblation is continued in us . . ." (*The Apostolic Ministry,* p. 519).

In sum, we found ourselves often using the word "representative", in its two separate contexts, as expressive of part of the central mystery of priesthood. This duality of role, in quite different ways, seemed to several of us to pose the question whether representation implied or required male-ness as a necessary attribute. In Part II some further thoughts on this are recorded.

C. *The Episcopate,* again, and in still greater depth, seems to usmarked by the mystery of representation. All that has been said of priesthood applies to the Bishop, of course. What is added is his peculiar ministry of continuity, of unity, of wholeness, of oversight. This ministry, shared with the clergy and laity, and fully collegial, is an incarnation of Christ's actions and qualities. The Bishop represents the Lord to His Body and the world. That is to say, it is the eternity of the Son which is the continuity mediated through ordination; it is the complex unity of the person of Jesus Christ—a unity of disciplined, single-minded obedience to mission—which is the source of the unity of the Church; it is the health and wholeness of the Incarnate Lord which is given in the whole state of His Church; it is Christ's compassionate and vigilant care which is mediated in the ministry of the overseer and the pastor. And in all this, the Bishop represents the Church and the world before the Father, in and through the Son. He is the called, authorized, accountable personification of these gifts of God in Christ, and of the Church's stewardship of them. More than one of us felt deeply that the accountability of the Bishop is a primary factor in keeping him faithful in the midst of the perplexities and demands he faces.

In the case of episcopacy as in that of priesthood, the suggestion of a duality of representative roles raised in some of our minds the question as to the significance of male-ness as a necessary attribute or characteristic of the Bishop. Perhaps even more than the priest, the episcopal Father-in-God imagery is that of a male figure, and none of us doubts the extraordinary tensions and problems which would confront the Church were women to be chosen to be Bishops. But the question remains, in some of our minds, whether it can be said that female-ness is a diriment impediment to their consecration as Bishops. We have recited these statements about the Church's ordained ministry simply to set down a broad outline of the understandings we all felt we shared and within which we approached the question of the ordination of women. Now we turn to that question.

II: Scripture, Tradition and Images

(N.B. Rather than attempting to conflate two divergent drafts on this theme, they are both included as clear statements of thoughtful points of view. In both cases, the Committee felt the statements presented arguments and evidences which had to be considered and faced. The two writers remain in full communion.

The following material . . . presents the position of an opponent to the ordination of women.)

The New Testament takes it for granted that men will usually exercise the ministry of bishop-presbyter or deacon. Romans 16:1-2 is an exception, where Phoebe is spoken of as *diakonos* of the church in Cenchrea. In I Timothy 3:11, the writer may be speaking of female deacons, or of the deacons' wives. The use of *hosautos* ('even so') shows a close connection between the women and the deacons and suggests that a new class is being introduced, analogous to the preceding order of deacons. Another argument for this is that no special requirements have been mentioned for the wives of bishop-presbyters. Certainly, the solemnity of the requirement that these women shall be *pistas en pasi,* ('absolutely faithful', says Moffat) seems to point to the requirements of some office in the Church. Junia, apparently the wife of Andronicus (Romans 16:7), is like him 'eminent among the Apostles'. Dr. Dodd has pointed out that the word 'apostle' is not used in the New Testament to mean only one of the Twelve, but is applied to one 'properly commissioned by the church to preach the Gospel'. Another husband-wife team is that of Priscilla and Aquila. These women are teachers and evangelists, but there is no evidence that they were bishop-presbyters. Other women who are prominent in the formation of the early Church are Euodia and Syntyche (Philippians 4:2) who 'labored with me in the Gospel', and Dorcas (Acts 9:36).

Dorcas is a special case, for to her alone is the technical name *mathetria* given. The plain sense of the passage is that she had been a disciple of the Lord in the days of his flesh, and that 'disciple' must be given its official and technical meaning. There are other evidences of women's ministries: in Acts 21:9 the four daughters of Philip are 'Prophets', and women are said to pray and prophesy in the meetings of the church in Corinth (I Corinthians 11:5), though St. Paul wishes them to observe the conventions about head coverings as they do so. In Acts and the Pauline epistles there is ample evidence of the part that women played in the establishing of the Christian Church. Contrary to vulgar superstition, Paul welcomed his women colleagues, and praised them highly and judiciously.

In this he only follows the example of his Lord. It appears from the linguistic usage in Luke 17:27 and Mark 12:25 *(egamoun, egamizonto, gamousin, gamiskontai)* that there is no 'equality' between the sexes, in Jesus' teaching; but we never hear a derogatory word from Him concerning women. His parables often illustrate the anxieties and joys of women. He will observe the proprieties (Mark 5:40), but he will also break with Jewish customs and laws when it is necessary. He is surrounded by a band of women who travel with him (Luke 3:2) and help to support him. Women are near him in his suffering (Mark 15:40ff) and in his triumph (John 20). But he does not choose a woman to be one of the Twelve, nor (unless Dorcas is an exception, unnamed in the Gospels) to be one of the Seventy.

In the Apostolic Church there is no doubt about the full membership of women (Acts 1:14, 12:12); and as Christian men are called 'brothers', so the technical word for a woman Christian is 'sister', as in Romans 16, I Corinthians 9, and elsewhere. In the teaching of St. Paul, woman is equal to man in Baptism (Galatians 3:26ff), yet she is subordinate to man in leadership, and the full removal of sexual distinction must await the Coming Age (I Corinthians 7:29-31). Much perverse ingenuity has been expended in pitting Galatians against Corinthians, and we have had to endure the unedifying spectacle of Galatians 3:26*ff* being canonized by those who reject the traditional Catholic doctrine of the inspiration of the Holy Scriptures. Nevertheless, to belong to the cultic ministry is no part of the perfection of Christian membership in Christ. That the Church acted as if it were, and as if lay people were second-class Christians, is only too true. It is only too true that lay women have been excluded from the decision-making processes of the Church; this is one of the causes of their present anger and frustration. But we cannot right this wrong by committing another.

That the 'marriage-image' that Scripture uses to denote the relationship between God and his people must not be pressed too far in our thinking, is a common-place. Those who have anxieties about these images (more than forty references to bride-bridegroom in the Old Testament and New Testament) must ask themselves whether their concern is to understand them, or to explain them away.

Fr. John Heidt (Marquette University) has pointed out that the Christian priest, unlike the pagan priest, is a sacrament of the givenness of the Christian religion—of the initial creative and recreative act of God towards mankind. On the human level, this is symbolized in masculinity as biologically expressed in the male. A woman priest, therefore, must lack the full symbolic expression of the meaning of Christian priesthood, and to that extent must be defective. The difficulties that many people have with symbolic statement and practice are too evident. 'Masculine' is always interpreted as 'male', although, as C. S. Lewis has reminded us, maleness is only a part of masculinity, and the same is true of femaleness and femininity, while masculinity and femininity are part of the make-up of both men and women. In religion (and this is the usual language of Holy Scripture), mankind is feminine towards God, in that we receive and respond to Him. He is masculine towards us, in that He gives and creates.

All of this does not mean that men only give and never respond, or that women only respond and never give. All men and women do both. It is possible, where no real alternative exists, for a woman to perform a masculine role—or how would the children of widows grow into real adulthood? But a woman cannot symbolize a masculine role; she is not the visible sacrament of God's giving act towards mankind. On the other hand, if it were not for the gross devaluation of womanhood in our culture, would not a sensitive mind see in a woman the visible sacrament of the soul's openness and receptivity towards God?

In the Report of the Archbishops' Commission on Women and Holy Orders (CIO London, 1966), Canon Demant reminds us that in the non-theistic cults, religion centers in men's response to nature's fertility. In these cults, a female priesthood is common and appropriate. But the Christian cultic minister symbolizes the fact that the Church exists through the initiating act of God as transcending nature, and this symbolism is normally and adequately expressed in a male priesthood. I should add to this statement the thought that the ordained Christian priest must act officially in the person of Christ, and male-ness is therefore required for a priest to act in this way.

All of this has its background in the Old Testament. The cultic priesthood there belongs to males, by divine ordinance. One must not exaggerate the significance of this for women's participation. Women are not religious nonentities in the Old Testament. They have part in the national festivals (2 Samuel 6:19, Deuteronomy 12:12); they lead the cultic dances (Judges 21:12); they have a part in the sacrificial meals, and in the Passover. They too enter into Covenant with Yahweh in Deuteronomy 29:10ff. Some of them are God's prophets—Miriam, Huldah, and others—and some of them serve the Tent of Revelation in Exodus 38:8. Nevertheless, they are not chosen by God to serve the altar; that belongs in the Old Testament to males alone. The usual explanation given for all of this is that the Old Testament culture was a 'patriarchal' one, and that women were subordinated to men in that culture. The discovery that there are other cultures known to human history is not a new one, but the inferences being drawn from this discovery are new—the inference, for instance, that Scripture need not be right in saying that humanity comes in two kinds, masculine and feminine; that the woman is not inferior to the man (although not 'equal' to him, for his is the task of leadership). There are some matters that cannot be settled by comparative anthropology alone, just as there are matters in Scripture that demand the light of all the science at our command. The existence of two stories of creation cannot be said to invalidate the insights about man and woman that are found in chapter 2 of Genesis. The Genesis I story speaks in completely general terms; the second deals from a rather different standpoint with a single locality and a specific pair of individuals. The dramatic narrative in chapter 2 of Genesis is meant to exemplify the biblical idea of monogamic marriage. It should not be used to nullify the plain teaching of Scripture in other places, that man has a special responsibility of leadership in the man-woman unity.

Such is the background of Our Lord's ministry. To speculate that He would have done this or that if things had been all different is a sign of skepticism. What Jesus did is normative for His people. The Apostles had no doubt about that. They chose another man to replace Judas, although there were women present who fulfilled the other conditions that are mentioned in Acts 1:21 and 22. When they admitted first Samaritans, and then Gentiles, to the infant Church, they did so in response to a direct intervention by the Spirit of Jesus. On the basis of this experience, they formed their attitude towards circumcision. Those who represent such matters as mere happenstance offer us an amazingly a-pneumatic Church, and substitute ideologies for evidences.

But is there no place for development in doctrine and practice in the Church? If it is true (and the evidence is overwhelming) that there are no women presbyters in the early Church, may it not now be the time to admit women to the priesthood and episcopate? Questions of 'The Spirit of the Age' must be set aside, and will be by all candid persons. The existence of a demand for priesthood by some women is not *a priori* evidence of an unmistakable intervention by the Holy Spirit, such as we find in Acts. To the plea that some women now genuinely believe themselves called by God to priesthood, one must reply that it has always been the duty of the Church to tell a man whether or not he has a true vocation to priesthood, and the Church has this task today. If the Church says 'No' to these aspirants, it would seem proper to assume that their question had been answered by the guidance of the Holy Spirit.

That there have been developments in the life of the Church is undeniable. The canon of the Holy Scripture was a development. The Threefold Ministry was a development. The full Conciliar faith about the person of Christ was a development. They were developments of that which was implicitly present from the beginning. From the beginning of the Church, the cultic priesthood of the Church has been restricted to males, and no new light has broken forth from God's Holy Word on this matter. For the Scriptures are not just a troublesome ghost; they are the 'lively oracles of God', as the old Prayer Book said. Those who relativize certain passages that are troublesome to them, cannot stop there. Then they have put Scripture out of court as a guide. And the Church, all its life long, must stand under the judgment of Scripture. There is no other guide for her and for the Christian.

Some of the confusion in the Episcopal Church on this question stems from the fact that in 1970 the General Convention affirmed that it is the mind of our Church that deaconesses, so-called, are simply women deacons. Many (even professors of theology) have gone on to say 'then why can't women be admitted to full orders'? They betray the fallen state of our Church in saying so. The Diaconate is 'full' ordination. In the New Testament, it is the only Order exercised by a woman. (To speak of it simply as 'Order' in the New Testament is anachronistic to some extent, but the intention is clear.) Women had their place in the ministry of the early Church, and it was a prominent and honored place. They have an honored place today, and that place will be fully understood only when the Church reforms herself, and understands that the only authority of ministry is the authority of service. But diaconate is not presbyterate.

On the evidence, to admit women as Bishops and priests is to overturn the practice of the New Testament Church, and the Catholic Church ever since. (And it is not the mark of a reactionary to believe that the universal and unanimous testimony of the Catholic Church may be thought binding upon a man's conscience.) The evidence of the Bible may seem to some to be insufficient to declare women incapable of priesthood. It is strong enough to establish a very great improbability that women should be admitted to priesthood and episcopate. In the light of this, such a revolution of Christian practice cannot be undertaken by us. The abolition of clerical celibacy at the Reformation was not a parallel—like the restoration of the chalice to the laity, that was a taking back of something illegitimately denied. To marry is a natural right. There is no natural right to priesthood. This momentous step must not be taken by a small branch of a particular Catholic Church on its own initiative, without reference to the remainder of catholic Christendom, and I am sure, against the convictions and sentiments of a majority of its own members.''

(N.B. The following portion of Part II presents the position of an advocate of the ordination of women. It covers the same basic ground as does the preceding draft.)

There is no question that, in the New Testament, women are the exception and not the rule, in the ministry of the Church. It is only in the diaconate that the ministry of a woman can be established with assurance. The inclusion of Junia (and perhaps others) among 'The Apostles' has significance according to what meaning is attached to the word, but in any case it does not refer to Bishop or presbyter. To teach, to pray, to 'prophesy', to evangelize—again, these are not functions restricted to men, but neither are they limited to Bishops or presbyters. Nor is there any question as to the Old Testament evidence. Women exercised many ministries, but not that of priesthood.

But to argue that because women were not included in various forms of ministry—Aaronic priesthood, episcopate/presbyterate—they never should or can be, simply cannot be sustained. If the adoption of the Canon of Holy Scripture or the three-fold ministry or the conciliar faith can be defended as legitimate development of what was implicit in the revelation of God in Christ from the beginning, there is no reason why the ordination of women cannot similarly be defended.

Those who say that it cannot be defended guard their position by arguments from four quarters: The relation of man and woman in Creation; the analogy of Christian priesthood to the Aaronic priesthood or pagan priesthood; the argument, broadly put, that God is male toward humanity, and humanity female toward God; and the fact that the Church has overwhelmingly said that women may not—or even can not—be ordained. Comments on these four areas follow.

A. *The evidence of the two accounts of Creation:* It is claimed that the Bible sees God as establishing in the natural order a hierarchy in which man, for purposes of the government and preservation of the race, is set over woman. The root evidence for this view is the account of Creation and the Fall in Genesis 2:4b - 3:24. In this account the male was created first; the female was taken from him; the female yielded to the tempting serpent; the female led the male to join her in eating; the female was condemned by God to sorrow in childbirth and to domination by the male.

From this basic source flow most of the arguments for the male/female hierarchy. The other account of Creation (Genesis 1:1-2:4a) knows nothing of such a hierarchy. God creates male and female together, in His image; together they are to share God's blessing; together they are to subdue and rule the earth. If this account were all we had, the Biblical root of the common hierarchical understanding would have been decisively cut. But it is not the only account, and therefore the teaching in Genesis about hierarchy in Creation is not as unambiguously clear as is often claimed. Professor André Dumas (in an article included in the 1964 WCC report *Concerning the Ordination of Women)* has an important comment on this:

''Genesis de-sexualised God the Creator, by correcting the sacred myths and rites of the Middle East. On the other hand it strongly insisted on the importance of the sex-differentiation among mankind. It is the only differentiation between human beings which is described as inherent, preceding the fall; it is also the only differentiation which is directly related to the likeness of God (Gen. 1:26 and 27: ''So God created man in his own image. . .: male and female He created them'') and to God's purpose in the creation (the whole of Genesis, chapter 2, especially verse 18: "It is not good that the man should be alone; I will make him a helper fit for him"). The origins of these two accounts are very different: the sacerdotal source (which is quite recent) is a "genealogy of the heavens and of the earth" (Gen. 2:4a) formulated so that Israel should have a creed about the creation of the world, with which to confront the cosmogonies of the nations by which it was surrounded. The Jahvist source, which is older, is quite different. It is an aetiological description of what happens between man and woman in their intimate relationship, where man's sex-instinct attracts him to the woman and proves stronger than his patriarchal attachment to his parents (v.24). This relationship also includes shame, fear and enmity between the sexes (Gen. 3:7, 12, 16), and after this perversion it also includes the desire to propagate and have children (Gen. 3:20) until the possible day of deliverance, after the necessary time of fragility and protection. But although these two versions are so different, they both stress that originally there was a human couple. In this respect they complete one another. Genesis, chapter 1, describes God's creative act in entrusting dominion over the creation not to man in the singular, but in the plural. This plural is used already in verse 26b, even before the mention of "male and female" in verse 27. Note also that their common mission is primarily to rule (v.26b and 28b), while their fruitfulness (expressed in the same terms as the fruitfulness of the fish and the birds on the 5th day of creation, v.28a = v.22) is described as God's blessing upon them. But human fruitfulness is not a sign of the species, as animal fruitfulness is ("according to their kinds", v.21, 24, 25); it is placed under the sign of that joint authority which characterizes the mission of man and woman. Genesis, chapter 2, in a sense confirms in human terms the order of divine creation described by chapter 1. The male exercises his authority by giving names to all the living animals. But this leaves him with "no helper like himself" (2:20). God then created woman, and in her man discovered his feminine counterpart.

"If one stops at this stage in reading "the order of creation", one sees that it consists of a "joint authority" entrusted by God to man and woman over the whole creation (Gen. 1). This joint authority is ratified by the male, who felt very lonely in his domination until God created his counterpart (Gen. 2). In that case, the order of creation would be the joint exercise of authority, thus expressing the likeness of God." (*Ibid,* pp. 24-25)

Dumas goes on to point out that in the New Testament, notably in the Pauline Epistles, the emphasis is heavily on the second account (Genesis 2:4b-3:24). Indeed St. Paul seems never to have quoted Genesis 1. In approaching this, Dumas describes three main factors which operated (in the Old Testament world) to discourage the inclusion of women in the priesthood. One was the patriarchal regime of the nation, in which women were part of their husbands' households. The second was the often-mentioned fear of women leading people astray (as Potiphar's wife, for example) culminating in the exegesis of Ecclesiasticus 25:24: "It is through woman that sin began, and it is because of woman that we shall all die". This exegesis (as in 1 Timothy 2) played a powerful role in the beginning Church.

The third factor—Dumas says it is 'the only one which is really theological'—was that before the birth of Christ, woman was blessed as the mother of all living people. 'Her true and special priesthood was to bring into the world sons who would perpetuate the Chosen People until the coming of the Messiah. . . . By giving the people male children, women mediated the grace of God; whereas men mediated that grace through sacrifice and (in Judaism after the Exile) more and more through the Torah.'

What of those factors carried over to the New Testament? The patriarchal regime, much modified, certainly did. The fear of seduction into idolatry again carried over, as in I Corinthians 11:10 or Revelation 2:20, but against this must be balanced the Bride images and the many others which testify to the sanctifying grace of women. The third, the most significant factor, disappeared completely. "Since the birth of Christ maternity in itself is no longer a vocation which mediates grace."

Dumas summarizes thus: "Of the three reasons for excluding women from the priesthood in the Old Testament, the New Testament therefore regards the first two as conventions observed for reasons of prudence, and it fundamentally rejects the third as an anti-messianic regression. Therefore one can no longer say: The ministry is for men, and maternity is for women'. (*Ibid.*, p. 33)

To quote so extensively from Prof. Dumas is in no way to propose his answers as authoritative for us. It is, rather, to present important Biblical consideration as concisely as possible. To this member of the Committee, the conclusion reached by Dumas seems correct. To another it may not. In any case, the complex evidence must be dealt with reverently and carefully.

B. *The analogy of Christian priesthood with Aaronic or pagan priesthood:* The Christian priesthood is analogous to the Aaronic priesthood only for purposes of contrast—"Types and shadows have their ending . . ." In Christ's High Priestly offering and sacrifice, the old priesthood of Israel was completed, fulfilled, ended. Whatever priesthood is to develop in the Church will be in no way a continuation or revival of the old; it will be, in some way, an expression of the totally new ministry of the crucified and risen Lord. Therefore it would be misleading to draw on a supposed analogy, as if the Epistle to the Hebrews had never been written. The Royal Priesthood into which all the baptized enter is a far wider concept than the later doctrines about the ministry of ordained priests. But both priesthoods are rooted in a new fact, a new creation. As circumcision has given way to baptism, as a new Israel has taken the place of the old, as men and women alike have 'put on Christ' and 'put off the old nature', so has priesthood found a totally new meaning.

It must also be clear that Christian and pagan priesthoods are not analogous, unless one wishes to remain at the level of trivialities, such as the fact that both Christian and Shinto priests wear curious hats, both Christian and animist altars often have flowers on them, both Christian and voodoo celebrations involve considerable talk of death, etc. The basically sexual frame of reference of so much ancient (and contemporary) pagan worship has no counterpart in Christian understandings of priesthood. The control over deity characteristic of so much pagan worship has no counterpart in Christian faith. So one could continue; but the commanding fact remains, the fact of the new creature in Christ, which is not analogous to anything, for there has never been anything like it. To press for analogies is anthropological pettifoggery.

C. *God is male toward humanity; humanity is female toward God:* This includes the implication that therefore priesthood must be male toward the Church and female toward God. There are significant meanings to be discerned here, and also significant correctives. For example, the notion of creation or creativity has often been perceived in a basically masculine or male frame of reference, no doubt phallic at base. In earlier times, many of the great myths of creation were of this character. The gods were seen as super-men and women, of often stupendous erotic capability, who in their coupling create the heavens and the earth or whatever. No doubt this sexual reference was widespread because it reflected very deep human awarenesses.

The cardinal truth is that the religion of Yahweh came into existence in the midst of a galaxy of such myths, and from the very beginning rejected them. Yahweh was alone. To pluck phrases from Prof. Dumas again, "Yahweh is the Creator; but He is never the procreator, as Baal was, in the form of a bull (Exodus 32, I Kings 12:28-30). The Person of God is completely severed from the web of myths and rites which worshipped sexuality. God is unique, which means that He is not in the likeness of man, nor of woman, nor of them together." (*Ibid*, p. 22) As in the Priestly Creation story (Genesis 1) man and woman together are in the image of God; He holds both maleness and femaleness in Himself, yet He is not limited to them or by them.

This is corrective reflection, not an attempt to say that male or female imagery is automatically untrue in human experience. There is a giving-ness about God which we call love or revelation or providence, and it is the sense of the divine initiative in that which we, in our habitual cultural milieu, commonly associate with the responsible initiative of male figures—husband, father. Indeed we come honestly by both those images. There is, equally a notion of humanity's receiving God's gifts which, again quite understandably, we commonly associate with female figures—wife, daughter.

The point here is not to attempt to rule out the reality of such imagery, but, rather, to see it in both its power and its limitations. Its power is derived from deep springs in the human spirit and from important forces in our culture and history. Insofar as it reflects truths about masculinity and femininity, it can be a significant instrument in our grappling with reality. Its limitations lie, of course, in the fact that there is no analogy in Deity to such imagery, no way to identify in Deity the anguish and the beauty inescapably part of the man-woman differentiation in humanity.

The whole question of imagery is extraordinarily complex, not to say murky, and it would be folly to try to pretend to any of the easy approaches to it. Mere rationality—*i.e.*, the approach which simply denies the reality of the 'primordial mythologies in the unconscious background of the race'—is of no importance. Mere egalitarianism—*i.e.*, the approach which simply asserts the 'equality' of men and women—is of no assistance. Neither is it of value to write off the influence of cultural and historical forces in developing social attitudes and expectations. The attitudes of western men and women toward each other are the result of many forces which have played on us through our history, as well as of interior forces which in their turn have found certain outlets and acceptable forms of expression. It is not helpful to brush all this aside as irrelevant to the theological issue. Neither is it helpful to canonize particular understandings and attitudes as being *de fide*.

Are we then doomed to paralysis, not knowing what we wish we did about ourselves, fearful lest we cast ourselves and our companions in mistaken roles, anxious not to leave a known set of images to seek others? The answer cannot simply be that we will not change—we are changing, we are being changed by the immense cultural changes going on in our society, for good or ill. If we decide to keep our present arrangements, we shall be keeping them with men and women who are themselves profoundly changed. For a woman of today to choose to play the part her grandmother played in society would be an exercise in dramatic lunacy, and the same is true of a man. The problem for Christians is not how to get back to what was, but to bear their witness in the midst of what is; and even the choice to stay where we are, if we make it, will be a choice of a new position which has got to be made in the presence of real people, not ghostly memories.

To say this much is not to say that the only answer is to admit women to priest's and Bishop's orders, though many will wish to do so. It is rather to point out the very positive and indeed decisive character of whatever the Church decides; there is no safety in doing nothing.

D. *The fact that the Church has overwhelmingly denied women admission to priest's and Bishop's orders:* This is a fact, though currently "overwhelmingly" may be fairly said to be a rather strong modifier to use. More than 70 member Churches of the WCC now admit women to all orders or ministry as against 48 fifteen years ago. More than 85 women are now studying in our Episcopal seminaries alone, 62 of them candidates for the M.Div degree. This compares with 55 last year, 27 being M.Div. candidates.

What does this say to us? It certainly does not say that such statistics answer our question for us. No decision that this Church makes can be a right decision if it is in truth a surrender to a popularity contest or to the women's liberation movement. No doubt, if we do in the end decide to admit women to priesthood our action will be seen in those terms—there is no help for that. But it should not be a surrender, and it need not be. The question we are facing is not how to keep up with the pack or how to live in peace with crusading women. The question is, Is God now calling women to priesthood?

We add to these two statements this note: It should be recorded that several members of the Committee, while recognizing both the fact and the urgency of the male imagery of priesthood, wished also to note the fact and the cogency of female imagery. Mention was made of this in Part I, when we touched on the two directions of priesthood—toward the Church, toward God. Receiving, molding, delivering the Word of God, for example, is analogous to the role of the Blessed Virgin, but we do not therefore feel that it is wrong for men to preach, or particularly appropriate for women to do so. The shepherd is a male image, no doubt, but the passionate search of a woman for her lost money is not, even though it speaks as clearly as the shepherd does of the obligations of a pastor. The members who share this feeling about female imagery wonder whether it is not true that Christ's priesthood is too comprehensive to be contained by the symbolism of one sex, that in fact its variety and depth call for full sacramental feminine expression in order to represent a God who sustains both masculinity and femininity? If this is true, might we not be on the threshold of a new dimension and awareness of the unsearchable riches of Christ? Far from confusing sexual roles or affirming unisex values, might not the ordination of women assure the enrichment of our understanding of humanity in Christ by guaranteeing the presence of both its components visibly present in the offering of the Oblation which is Christ's and ours?

III: Evangelism and Development

One of the Church's greatest departures from tradition, in order and doctrine, occurred in the first century when the Council of Jerusalem (Acts 15) ruled that persons could become Christians without circumcision. The decision was buttressed by theology, scriptural references, and close reason. The dynamic for its consideration was inspired by visions and dreams, and the issue took on the coloration of a liberal-conservative polarization already present among the disciples. However, the root reason for the decision to eliminate circumcision as a requirement for admission to the Church was the overwhelming imperative of missionary strategy, before which even the Master's words, "I am not sent but unto the lost of the House of Israel", were overridden.

At that Council, the issue was clearly stated by Peter, and even more vividly illustrated by the leadership of Paul and Barnabas. Circumcision, that ancient and honorable symbol of man's covenant with God, must go. The rite of circumcision was freighted with sexual imagery, religious symbolism, and anthropological significance; but against the imperative of spreading the gospel it could not stand. Once the decision was made, the implications and consequences of it grew apparent, and the Church's life was deepened and strengthened in many ways. The parallel with our present situation is not exact. We are not first-century Christians, and there is no Peter or Paul or Barnabas to move us. Even more important, there is now no equivalent to the single household of "the apostles and elders" which met in Jerusalem. Some would reject the parallel out of hand and say that this is precisely the point—for our Church to go on its own, without waiting for the Roman Church and the Orthodox to act with us, is to violate the pattern of the Jerusalem Council.

We wonder whether the parallel can be that easily dismissed. All across the land, indeed across the world, the accepted patterns of sexual behavior and of the respective roles of men and women in society are explosively changing. As in the case of racism, the confrontation with the women's liberation movement has helped to open many eyes to the damage men and women do to each other, often without recognizing it, and our need to cleanse our hearts and our ways of the "sexist" stereotypes which hurt so many and make it so appallingly difficult for men and women to be with each other the partners in life and work which Genesis 1 portrays. This is to say that there can be a prophetic character about confrontation, in that it often opens our eyes to saving judgment. In the fifties and sixties, Christians were confronted by the civil rights movement and then the harsher movement toward ethnic self-determination, and the eyes of many were open to judgment for the sins of the often-unintended and un-examined racism implicit in attitudes and institutions pervading our national life and indeed the Church's life. Something like that is happening now, in the movement for women's liberation, again testing the Church's capacity to see itself, and hear itself, and open itself again to the cleansing judgment of God. And this open-ness is part of the secret of the Jerusalem Council.

In that instance, the judgment was perceived in terms of the missionary imperative. In the present instance, the judgment may be perceived broadly in terms of the promise of fuller life and more mature relationships, under God, between men and women—in terms of a liberation not to be measured only in equal pay, or equal opportunity in employment, or equal obedience to moral and ethical standards, but as a genuine freeing of men and women to be in each other's eyes more nearly what the Biblical revelation says we are made to be.

Whatever one thinks about the ordination issue, there are few who doubt that the Church and all its institutions and ways is being tested, weighed, by our society in respect of this issue as we are in respect of race. To the outsider, certainly, indeed to many who are inside the Church, our theological statements often seem to serve the interests of those who oppose change in the stereotypes men and women have about each other, who oppose the new freedom which is promised. Bishops may know that the imagery of Fatherhood and Sonship are analogical and not substantive, but the untutored do not know that. To them we are heard to say that God is male, and therefore the authority-figures of the Church are male, and therefore the woman in the Church is automatically a second-class citizen. It is no wonder that many men and women now reject an institution which seems to go on saying that, and thereby deny themselves access to the liberating gospel of God in Christ.

This Committee is not prepared to say that with one mind that we agree that the Church should open all its orders of ministry to women. What we are saying is that the issue of liberation must be seen and taken in utter seriousness and in very great depth, even as the men in Jerusalem took the issue of the Gentiles. The cause of the liberation of men and women, in the sense in which we see it and describe it, is not going to be served by token re-adjustment of quotas and the like. Nor will the Church and we who rejoice in the Church be cleansed by the confrontation if we do not deeply share its pain and its hope, and open every possible door to the full partnership of men and women in the Church's life. If the Church has, as the Committee unitedly believes, a peculiar mission to men and women caught in the perplexities of our society and struggling to learn how to become what they really are, the Church must seize every way it finds to re-establish lost credibility and to take the initiative and regain its capacity to serve its mission to contemporary humanity.

Once again we say that this demand on us does not solve the problem of the ordination of women to the priesthood and episcopate. If there is diriment impediment to that in anyone's mind, then of course he or she must vote against the proposal. But the debate must be open and clear; the issue must not be evaded by maneuver; and it must be plain for the world to see that we are in deadly earnest about the mission to which we are called. It is the mission that matters.

With respect to "development", most of the Committee—perhaps all—would probably agree that only that can be developed which is implicit in the original revelation. From the first draft in Part II it is clear that at least one of us does not believe that the opening of these orders to women would be faithful to this doctrine of implication, and from the second draft it is clear that not all accept this judgment. It is difficult for them to accept a judgment that inclusion within the Royal Priesthood, which plainly is open to men and women on identical terms, does not carry with it an equal right to share in the ordained priesthood which is its minister. It is difficult for them to see what St. Paul meant when he said that humanity was all one in Christ Jesus, neither Jew nor Greek, bond nor free, male nor female, if he was not saying that baptism into Christ has created a new life in which old limitations and distinctions may no longer rule. To those of us who share those views, the development of what is implicit in the two passages in question, among others, could certainly extend to the opening of every order of ministry to women as well as men. But we record this, remembering those who, in all honesty, cannot accept such ordination as implicit in the New Testament deposit and who do feel that it is explicitly ruled out by the fact that women were not chosen by Christ or the apostolic Church for certain ministries.

IV: Penumbra of Practicalities

What we identify in this part is a variety of problems, novelties, unknowns, which must be kept in mind in considering the main question. We group them under four heads. The first category are the more-or-less obvious questions of selection, training, deployment, and continuing education. What changes would be required in the selection and screening process, for example? Many Dioceses have already gone into this, in connection with women preparing for the diaconate, and no doubt the practical steps needed to adapt to the inclusion of women are not all that complicated. Experience also suggests that the inclusion of women in seminary education is not nearly as complicated as it was once thought to be. But there will undoubtedly be curricular changes and enlargements as experience teaches us. The problems of employment are more complicated. No matter how effective our deployment system becomes, the introduction of women priests into it will bring new pressures into play. Some congregations will not accept them; some of the clergy will find it impossible to work with women; some women will be so emotionally involved that systematic placement will be extraordinarily difficult. Should the Church choose to admit women to priesthood and episcopacy, there is bound to be a fairly-extended period of time while we come to terms with a highly charged situation and find out how to deal with it effectively. This process would undoubtedly be at its most severe in the case of episcopate, where the image of the Father in God has for so long characterized the chief pastor and minister of the Church. That comment would be notably true in the context of the following paragraph.

The second category is related to the last-mentioned—it is the group of problems the Church will face in establishing the place of women in the clergy generally. We imagine that these will be less vexing in a large, experienced congregation where a sizeable staff might allow the addition of a woman, particularly in some specialised area of ministry, with a minimum of tension. By contrast, the problem of establishing a satisfactory and accepted place for a few women in the ranks of the clergy of a Diocese could be painful indeed. Clearly the burden of this would fall on the ordained women, but we think of it not as a problem for the women to solve but for the Church to solve, and it will not be easy. As so often with non-parochial and non-stipendiary men, the inherited sense that the full-time parish ministry of men is the norm and standard will continue to get in the way of any rational, theologically informed understanding of the collegiality of the Church's ministry.

Thirdly, we have discussed the strains the ordination of women can lay on their families, if they are married, and on themselves, because of the unavoidable fact of novelty, of sexual rivalry, of the animosity which often would greet them, of the sense of crusade which would be bound to surround them, whether or not they shared it. There are probably relatively few—certainly of the male clergy over thirty—who would be free enough to be able to accept and work maturely and positively with women colleagues. This might be equally true of the freedom of some of the women. We say this not to blame the persons concerned, men or women, but rather to remind ourselves of the long inheritance both men and women have—particularly in the Church—of defensiveness and advantage. To learn new ways would be hard, and the process would be costly and abrasive, in many cases. This is not to argue one way or the other on the substantive issue, of course; it is only a cautionary reflection on the new care which must be provided to minister to those caught in such a situation.

Fourthly, the ecumenical issues implicit in the main question are of significance. Doubtless, in some instances, the argument that to ordain women would "imperil" our relationship with this or that community of Christians is self-serving and masks the real feeling behind it. Equally so is, sometimes, the argument that the ordination of women is inevitable and therefore right. It seems to us misleading to approach the question in a spirit of coming to terms with the women's liberation movement, or the *Zeitgeist*, or the counter-culture, or whatever. Whatever of greatness there has been in the history of the Church was given it by its willingness to follow a different drum than the world, at any given time. The "inevitability" of the ordination of women, in our liberated society, is a vain and idle argument. The question is whether God is now calling women to priesthood and episcopate. If He is, then the Church must respond in obedient faith. If He is not, then no popularity contest can ever make it right for the Church to ordain them.

We have already commented on the increasing number of Churches in which all ministerial orders are open to women. Yet those Churches together do not number nearly as many Christians as those in the Roman Catholic and Orthodox Churches; and it would be reckless to imagine any swift change in Roman Catholic discipline, and probably even more so with respect to Orthodoxy. The recent statement of the Pope on the subject of woman's place in the formal ministries of the Church is a chilling warning, at best, in this regard. Yet it remains true that there is an increasing restlessness on the subject in most responsible circles and it is not likely that a papal regulation *motu proprio* will put an end to it. The Roman Church, in these times, is very far from providing the monolithic, certain guidance one once could take for granted.

We agree that it would be idle to say that a decision to ordain women as priests or Bishops would make no difference in our ecumenical engagements. No doubt such a decision would, for good and ill. Very much would depend on the basis for our decision, and the clarity of our reasoning, and the soundness of the theology which informs our reasoning. But the question cannot be, What is best for our ecumenical relationships? It must be, Is God now calling women to ordination as priests and bishops?

Recommendation

1. We believe that the Resolution which has been referred to us should be debated by this House, at this meeting, looking forward to further debate and canonical action at Louisville.
2. We make no recommendation as a Committee, favorable or unfavorable.
3. We believe that the debate should cover at least the issues identified in this report.
4. We believe that the issue should be met head-on, not as something to be resolved by tinkering with the meaning of words, not as something to be resolved by unilateral action by individual Bishops or groups of Bishops.
5. We believe that justice must be seen to have been done by the manner and content of our debate.
6. We most deeply plead for a steady understanding of the gravity of the issue as it is perceived on both sides. This means to us that the members of this House must be the first to reach out with compassion and supportive love to those on both sides—those hurt by what seems to them a Church bent on keeping them as second-class members and those hurt by what seems to them a Church throwing away its credentials of catholicity for the sake of momentary popularity. It means to us that the members of the House must find every way to minister to those souls caught on both sides—priests and lay people whose life-long faith in their Church seems to be attacked; priests and lay people whose eager hope for a more just society seems to be denied. It means to us that, as in every great decision we ever face, we the members of this House are called to stand together on common ground, and know that we do so, and act accordingly in the patience and openness we show in our debate and in what issues from it.

Respectfully submitted,

Stanley H. Atkins
Stephen F. Bayne, Chairman

Robert F. Gibson, Jr.
John M. Krumm
Paul Moore, Jr.
C. Kilmer Myers
Samuel J. Wylie

Ordination of Women

The Bishop of Newark, Chairman of the Committee on Ministry, called on Bishop Bayne, Chairman of the Special Committee on Ordination of Women, who reported that a letter from Virginia Seminary had been referred to their Committee and that the information had been distributed to the House.

Bishop Bayne then moved that the Committee on Ordination of Women, having submitted its report and completed its work, be discharged.

Motion carried

The Presiding Bishop, on behalf of the House, expressed deep gratitude to the Committee for its work.

The Bishop of Newark, for the Committee on Ministry, thanked the Special Committee for help to his Committee. He thereupon moved Bishop Bayne's motion on the Ordination of Women.

Bishop Smith (P.A.) presented the findings of the group discussion on the Ordination of Women, as follows:

"The House of Bishops, on the issue of the Ordination of Women to the priesthood and to the episcopate, manifested in its small-group discussions a divided mind, just as did its Special Committee in its report on the subject to the House.

- By some it was stated there were no real Biblical or theological objections. By others it was stated that more Biblical exegesis was needed and also further theological input.
- Some have a feeling that we are committed to such ordination because of the diaconate's having already been opened to women. Others have a feeling that we do not have a clear definition either of diaconate or priesthood. Women feel called by God to priesthood, but the Church needs to call its ministers.
- Women have special gifts and qualities to bring to the priesthood, yet there are potential strains for women in the priesthood as in the family situation.
- There needs to be more grass-roots involvement and education first, but the Bishops must also exercise leadership on such issues.
- Whatever Bishops do must be done openly and with knowledge. Yet a secret ballot is desired on this issue.
- Unilateral action by this Church is not deemed good, yet such action might be helpful to other Churches.
- God calls in new ways, such as women to the priesthood, yet such a serious breach with tradition is ill-advised and present arguments are not sufficient to make the change.
- Cultural circumstances do matter in such issues, yet cultural pressures should not carry the day.
- The Church must face the issue without delay, yet it needs to do more study to prepare the Church for change.
- Such a move is viewed as good in terms of evangelism in some places, yet as unhelpful in others.

- There is a fear of schism if the change is approved, and a serious attrition of women in the Church if it is not.
- Some Roman Catholic authorities are quoted as saying it would be an obstacle to ecumenical relations, yet other Roman Catholic authorities are quoted as saying it would not be and might even provide good leadership to Rome.
- It is not good for the Bishops to decide on this issue ahead of the 1973 General Convention, yet the House of Bishops is looked to for leadership in the matter.
- Some Bishops will vote for it, in principle, yet will not be able to offer employment for women as priests in their Dioceses.
- Sexuality must be taken out of consideration in the matter of priesthood, yet the psycho-sexual aspects of the matter must be faced.
- Jesus Christ was a man, yet humanity, not maleness, is the crux of the matter.

"A further index of the divided mind of the House is reflected in the straw-votes of the ten discussion groups:

3 voted for such ordination

2 voted against it

1 recorded a split vote

2 took no vote at all

2 want no vote of the House at this time on the issue

"The Committee on Ministry at its meeting following the receiving of the small-group reports decided that the House needed further discussion of the whole matter, and voted to recommend favorable action on the Resolution moved by Bishop Bayne, as follows:

Whereas, The Special Meeting of the House of Bishops, on October 23, 1970, at Houston, referred for consideration by the House at this meeting the following statement: "It is the mind of this House that it endorses the principle of the Ordination of Women to the Priesthood and to the Ordination and Consecration of Women to the Episcopate"; therefore, be it

1. *Resolved, That this present House adopt this statement as the mind of the House; and be it further*
2. *Resolved, That the Committee on Canons be instructed to prepare the necessary canonical changes to put this Resolution into effect for presentation at the General Convention of 1973.*

The Bishop of West Texas asked that the Resolution be referred to the Committee on Constitution and the Committee on Canons.

So ordered

The Bishop of West Virginia moved that the question be divided.

Motion carried

The time previously set for the celebration of the Eucharist having arrived, the Presiding Bishop announced that further discussion would continue at 2:00 p.m.

The Bishop of Missouri moved that discussion not be interrupted, and that Holy Communion be postponed until 4:00 p.m.

Motion defeated

The Presiding Bishop called the House to order at 2:03 p.m.

The Bishop of Rhode Island, reporting for the Committee on the Dispatch of Business, moved the following Motion, setting procedures in the debate on the Ordination of Women:

Resolved, That speeches be limited to four minutes; that no member of the House speak twice on the subject until everyone has had a chance to speak; and that members in favor of, and opposed to, the Resolution speak in alternate order.

The Bishop of West Missouri moved to amend by increasing the time-limit on speeches from 4 to 5 minutes.

Amendment defeated
Motion carried

After eight Bishops (four on each side of the debate) had spoken, the Bishop of Lexington moved for re-consideration of the procedural Motion. A Motion for re-consideration required a two-thirds majority to prevail.

Motion defeated
(Yes, 66; No, 56)

Debate resumed, and an additional 21 Bishops spoke, making a total of 31 Bishops who spoke during the debate.

At the conclusion of the debate, there was a two-minute recess and the House reconvened at 4:02 p.m.

The Bishop of California then moved that the words, "and to the Ordination and Consecration of Women to the Episcopate", be stricken from the resolution.

Amendment failed

The Bishop of Northern California, the Bishop of Fond du Lac, and the Bishop of Lexington, joined in a request for a roll-call vote.

Motion carried

The Bishop of Western New York moved that the House be allowed to cast undecided or abstaining votes.

The Presiding Bishop ruled that a Bishop may say, "Present but not voting", which will be recorded, and that a majority would be considered as a majority of those actually voting.

The Presiding Bishop announced the results, as follows: Yes, 74; No, 61; Present but not Voting, 5.

Resolution adopted

The Bishop of Oregon moved the following implementation for the original Resolution:

Resolved, That the ordination of women to the Priesthood, or the ordination and consecration of women to the Episcopate, be implemented and authorized only after full consideration and approval by the next Lambeth Conference, and full discussion through our Joint Commission on Ecumenical Relations with the other Christian bodies, and reports of their action made to the Bishops of the House.

Motion defeated

The second Resolution was put.

Resolution adopted

The Resolutions on the Ordination of Women thus adopted by the House read as follows:

Whereas, The Special Meeting of the House of Bishops, on October 23, 1970, at Houston, referred for consideration by the House at this meeting the following statement: "It is the mind of this House that it endorses the principle of the Ordination of Women to the Priesthood and to the Ordination and Consecration of Women to the Episcopate"; therefore, be it

1. *Resolved. That this present House adopt this statement as the mind of the House; and be it further*

2. *Resolved, That the Committee on Constitution and the Committee on Canons be instructed to prepare the necessary constitutional and canonical changes to put this Resolution into effect for presentation at the General Convention of 1973.*

Notes: *The House of Bishops resolution in 1970 to support the ordination of women was brought up again in 1971 and referred to a special committee of the house. Printed here is the committee's 1972 report, along with the resulting discussion and final vote. The report is in four parts, the second of which includes statements both opposing and affirming women's ordination; the other parts (along with the conclusion) take a neutral position. The discussion mirrors the ambivalence of the committee, as it includes both the views of the Bible and the early church, as well as the weight merited by other factors. In the end, the vote to adopt the original resolution was passed 74 to 61, with five not voting.*

EPISCOPAL CHURCH

STATEMENT ON BEHALF OF THE ORDINATION OF WOMEN (1973)

The Bishop of Indianapolis, on a point of personal privilege, and speaking for 60 Bishops in favor of the ordination of women, asked that a statement be entered into record of this Meeting.

So ordered

A Statement of Conviction Concerning Ordination of Women

As has so frequently happened in the history of civilization, human societies have developed rules and traditions to enshrine the rights and responsibilities of a ruling or dominant segment of each age. In so doing, such rights have denied equal access to other segments of that time. Finally, and inevitably, the sense of justice prevails, and it becomes essential to see that all human rights are available to all human beings.

We, the undersigned members of the House of Bishops, have already expressed our position on the theological right and moral justice of opening ordination to the Priesthood and the Episcopate in the Episcopal Church to all adult human persons who have felt God's call to this vocation and have been examined by appropriate Church officials. We wish to underscore this conviction at this time, since we have not been allowed such expression, because of the inadequacy of our present procedures in our General Conventions, to repeat our voice of conscience on this subject.

We respect the rights of those who differ with us on this question to make their conviction known, but we ask, as leaders bearing responsibility in the Espicopal Church to have our view equally stated and respected. We have come to this position from many different routes, all of which have been stated at various times previously, and need no repetition here as possibly argumentative statements, but we do accept the responsibility to speak to our Church.

We should not be true to the guidance of the Holy Spirit through our own consciences if we did not now speak.

So we affix our names as evidence of this conviction in favor of the ordination of women, in profound trust in divine guidance, to let this Church know that this issue of moral justice and theological justification must not rest until all have known equal treatment in their search for vocation.

Bishop of Indianapolis
Bishop of Pennsylvania
Bishop of Newark
Bishop of Central New York

Suffragan Bishop of New York
Bishop Blanchard
Bishop of Alaska
Bishop of Nevada

Bishop of Rochester
Bishop of Wyoming
Bishop of Delaware
Bishop of Missouri
Bishop of Ohio
Bishop of Puerto Rico
Bishop of Costa Rica
Bishop Coadjutor of Virginia
Bishop of Massachusetts
Bishop Coadjutor of Pennsylvania
Bishop of Michigan
Bishop of Bethlehem
Bishop of Pittsburgh
Bishop of Washington
Bishop Coadjutor of Newark
Bishop of Western Kansas
Bishop of New York
Bishop of Erie
Bishop of Eastern Oregon
Bishop of Mexico
Suffragan Bishop of Connecticut
Bishop of Southwestern Virginia
Bishop Burrill
Bishop of Minnesota
Bishop Coadjutor of Erie
Bishop Mosley
Bishop of Northern Michigan
Suffragan Bishop of Massachusetts
Bishop Kellogg (Paul)
Suffragan Bishop of Washington
Bishop Mills
Bishop of Nebraska
Bishop of Atlanta
Suffragan Bishop of Oklahoma
Bishop of Utah
Bishop of Taiwan
Bishop of Vermont
Bishop of Southern Virginia
Bishop of Southern Ohio
Bishop of West Virginia
Bishop of Iowa
Bishop of Central Pennsylvania
Bishop of Northern Philippines
Bishop of New Hampshire
Bishop of Rhode Island
Suffragan Bishop of Texas
Bishop of the American Churches in Europe
Bishop of the Rio Grande
Bishop of Virginia
Bishop of Alabama
Bishop of North Dakota
Bishop Coadjutor of West Virginia

Notes: *In this statement, sixty bishops registered their belief that the ordination of women be allowed. At the same General Convention, a Resolution on Collegiality and Loyalty was passed (53 to 40) in the House of Bishops, stating that bishops would respect the process and none would try to ordain women before it was properly allowed.*

EPISCOPAL CHURCH

RESOLUTION ON THE PHILADELPHIA ACTIONS (1974)

The House of Bishops in no way seeks to minimize the genuine anguish that so many in the Church feel at the refusal to date of the Church to grant authority for women to be considered as candidates for ordination to the priesthood and episcopate. Each of us in his own way shares in that anguish. Neither do we question the sincerity of the motives of the four Bishops and eleven deacons who acted as they did in Philadelphia. Yet in God's work, ends and means must be consistent with one another. Furthermore, the wrong means to reach a desired end may expose the Church to serious consequences unforeseen and undesired by anyone.

> *Whereas,* Our Lord has called us to walk the way of the Cross through the questions and issues before us, resulting from the service in Philadelphia on July 29, 1974, and
>
> *Whereas,* The Gospel compels us to be as concerned with equality, freedom, justice, and reconciliation, and above all love, as with the order of our common life and the exercise of legitimate authority; therefore, be it
>
> *Resolved,* That the House of Bishops, having heard from Bishops Corrigan, DeWitt, Welles, and Ramos the reasons for their action, express our understanding of their feelings and concern, but express our disagreement with their decision and action.

> We believe they are wrong; we decry their acting in violation of the collegiality of the House of Bishops, as well as the legislative process of the whole Church.
>
> Further, we express our conviction that the necessary conditions for valid ordination to the priesthood in the Episcopal Church were not fulfilled on the occasion in question; since we are convinced that a Bishop's authority to ordain can be effectively exercised only in and for a community which has authorized him to act for them, and as a member of the episcopal college; and since there was a failure to act in fulfillment of constitutional and canonical requirements for ordination.

And be it further

Resolved, That we believe it is urgent that the General Convention reconsider at the Minneapolis meeting the question of the ordination of women to priesthood, and be it further

Resolved, That this House call upon all concerned to wait upon and abide by whatever action the General Convention decides upon in this regard.

Notes: *This resolution was passed by the House of Bishops at a special meeting in 1974. Much of the meeting was spent responding to actions which had taken place one month earlier, on July 29, 1974, at Philadelphia's Church of the Advocate. There, two retired and one resigned bishop ordained eleven women deacons to the priesthood. These unauthorized actions sent the Episcopal Church into an uproar. The House of Bishops declared that the women involved were still only deacons, and chastised the bishops involved for violations of both "collegiality" and "the legislative process of the whole Church."*

EPISCOPAL CHURCH

RESOLUTION ON WOMEN'S ORDINATION (1976)

Ordination of Women

The Bishop of Maine, Chairman of the Advisory Committee to the House of Bishops, called upon Bishop Richards to outline further procedure for group meetings to continue discussion on the Ordination of Women. The Bishop of Chicago, Chairman of the Committee on Ministry, distributed a proposed Resolution to initiate discussion. The House recessed at 11:27 a.m. for the Bishops to convene with their groups.

The Presiding Bishop convened the House of Bishops at 2:04 p.m.

The Chairman of the Committee for the Dispatch of Business proposed that the First Report of the Committee on Ministry concerning the Ordination of Women be open to a two-hour debate.

The Bishop of Chicago, Chairman of the Committee on Ministry, reported and moved for the adoption of the Resolution B-5.

Resolved, the House of Deputies concurring, that a new Section 1. of Title III., Canon 9, be adopted, with renumbering of the present Section 1. and following, the said Section 1. to read as follows:

> Section 1. The provisions of these Canons for the admission of Candidates, and for the Ordination to the three Orders: Bishops, Priests and Deacons shall be equally applicable to men and women.

Bishop Gordon seconded the motion.

The Bishop of Oregon presented the following Resolution (Substitute—Ordination of Women):

> *Whereas,* requirements for Ordination are governed by the Constitution of the Episcopal Church in the U.S.A., and the Ordinal of the Book of Common Prayer, therefore be it
>
> *Resolved,* that Article VIII. of said Constitution be amended pursuant to the process set forth in Article XI., by substituting the words "he or she" for the word "he" in lines two and seven of paragraph one of Article VIII., and in line three of the last paragraph thereof, and be it further
>
> *Resolved,* that the appropriate Committees be directed to bring all Canons relating to Ministry, and the Ordinal of this Church into compliance with this Article as amended.
>
> The Bishop of East Carolina seconded the motion.

After discussion of the original and substitute motions, the Presiding Bishop called for the beginning of the two-hour debate at 2:40 p.m.

After two hours of debate, the Bishop of Dallas moved that the debate cease. Seconded by Bishop Mosley.

Motion carried

The Bishop of Colorado moved that the Rules of the House be suspended in order that a motion could be entertained to require a two-thirds vote on the motion for substitution.

Seconded by the Bishop of Lexington.

Motion defeated

The vote of substitution was then taken, and the substitution was defeated by a vote of 59 for, and 96 against.

The vote on the original motion B-5 as presented by the Committee on Ministry was 95 for, 61 against and 2 abstained.

Vote on Women's Ordination

The Chair announced the results of the ballot on concurring with House of Bishops Message No. 56, Resolution B-5 on the Ordination of Women as follows:

Clerical	*Lay*
114 votes cast	113 votes cast
58 votes needed for affirmative action	57 votes needed for affirmative action
60 votes yes	64 votes yes
39 votes no	36 votes no
15 votes divided	13 votes divided

The resolution carried in both orders.

The House concurred

Notes: *This statement includes the historic vote in 1976 of the House of Bishops and the House of Deputies (both lay and clerical orders) affirming the ordination of women. It is interesting that the House of Bishops was proportionately far more in favor of the action than either order of the House of Deputies. In both Houses, a minority statement was made which objected to the legislation on the grounds that it was contrary to the opinions of the Roman Catholic, Old Catholic, and Orthodox churches. This General Convention also decided that the 1974 ordinations of 11 women in Philadelphia would be regularized, but not repeated, and that after regularization those 11 women would be recognized as full priests.*

EPISCOPAL CHURCH

WOMEN PRIESTS AND THE EPISCOPAL CHURCH IN THE USA (1985)

The purpose of a report on "Women Priests and the Episcopal Church in the U.S.A." is to document the facts of the impact of women's ordination on the membership of the Episcopal Church. Official statistics of the National Church are presented to dispell any myths that the ordination of women caused defection of members.

I highly commend the efforts of the Rev. Sandra Boyd, who has diligently kept the statistics on women's ordination for the Episcopal Church, and Dr. Susan M. Cole-King, who has compiled and written this report.

My prayers of gratitude go to all those individuals who have and who are supporting women's ordination throughout the Anglican Communion.

Sincerely,
Ann Smith, Coordinator
Women in Mission & Ministry

In debating the issue of women's ordination at the 1976 General Convention, some opponents of ordination predicted that the decision would cause a major defection from the Church. A look at the actual membership figures, as published yearly by diocese in the *Episcopal Church Annual* disproves this prediction. No evident defection took place as illustrated in the graph in Fig. 1. In fact, the data show that:

1. The Episcopal Church has been declining in membership since the peak years of the late sixties, as have other "mainline" Protestant churches in America.
2. The period of most rapid decline was early on, from 1969 to 1973. In the years since the 1976 Convention, the decline has slowed down noticeably.
3. Baptisms (and in most provinces, confirmations), after many years of decline, have begun to increase, mostly in the last five years.
4. Worship attendance has increased steadily since 1977 showing an overall increase in attendance between 1977 and 1983.

Far from being a divided and unhappy Church on the decline, the Episcopal Church shows signs of increasing vitality. Its upturn in membership over recent years is illustrated by the fact that 72 dioceses have opened up new churches, and over 200 new congregations have been formed in the past five years (see Fig. 2).

The pattern of change has differed significantly across the eight provinces of the Church in the U.S., reflecting social and economic changes and subsequent population shifts. For example:

—Province IV (the American South) has grown steadily during the past twenty years; its rate of growth is now greater than at any other time since the mid-sixties.

—Province VII (the Southwest) and Province VIII (the West) have halted their decline and show signs of growth.

—The provinces of the industrial Northeast (I, II, and III) and the Midwest (V) continue to decline reflecting economic recession and population movements. It is clear that the "sunbelt" is growing at the expense of the older urban industrial centers. A focus on only one of these geographical areas, therefore, can be misleading if the overall pattern is not clearly seen.

As illustrated in the graph in Fig. 1, the major fall in membership occurred between 1972 and 1974; i.e. before any women priests were ordained. In these early years of the decade, communicants declined by almost 2% on average, but since 1976 there were only two years when the decline in communicants reached as much as 1%. That the decline is clearly levelling off is apparent in the trend in baptized members.[1]

Even more marked has been the steady increase in worship attendance since 1977. Attendance of baptized membership increased from 37% to 41%, with a total increase in church attendance of an overall 8.6% between 1977 and 1983. These figures are compiled by the *"State of the Church Committee of the General Convention"*, and are based on attendance at 4 key services.[2] Since 1976, when women priests were officially sanctioned, the percentage of baptized members attending services has risen from 32% to 41% by 1983 (the last available annual data).

This Parochial report analysis also illustrates a slight overall national increase in Church membership as a percentage of the total population. This has gone up by an average of 0.1% per year since 1980 nationally, but this increase is over 2% per year in some dioceses, most of which have women priests. While this increase in Church membership is still relatively small, it would appear that the decline of the early 70's has been reversed. The upturn in membership has occurred as ordained women clergy are being increasingly employed in parishes around the country. This analysis also shows the trends in giving per household per week which has also increased by 10% per year since 1973. The ordination of women seems not to have affected this trend.

It is clear from the above statistics that women priests have not contributed to any significant loss in membership in the Episcopal Church, contrary to what has sometimes been claimed by opponents to women's ordination. In fact, the figures show quite the reverse.

The Schisms

Exaggerated figures are often quoted about the extent of the rupture which occurred over the issue of women priests. What was the extent of the damage? It is difficult to estimate how far women's ordination, per se, contributed to the formation of split off churches during the seventies, some of which had begun prior to 1976. Four issues contributed to the reaction of some clergy and laity at this time. These were:

1. The revision of the prayer book.
2. The reaction against "Liberalism".
3. The reaction to Black Power.
4. The ordination of women.

In 1977, 400 priests and 1600 lay persons met in St. Louis in reaction against the 1976 Convention. There followed several years of turmoil, but by the end of the decade the split off segment of the Episcopal Church consisted of no more than 10-15,000 members, less than 5% of total members, and nowhere near the "third" that has sometimes been claimed. At present, there are nine Church bodies separated from the Episcopal Church which have 23 bishops and 250 congregations. Most of the 400 priests who protested in 1977 remained within the Episcopal Church. A few disgruntled individuals went over to the Roman Catholic Church and, at present, there are five "personal parishes" made up of ex-Episcopalians within the Roman Catholic Church. However, no Episcopal parish "went over" to the Roman Church as a parish.[3]

Some Statistics on Women in the Episcopal Church

By October of 1985, there were 968 women in Holy Orders: 629 priests (65%) and 339 deacons (35%). These women constitute over 7% of ordained ministers in the Episcopal Church. In seminaries, on average, 35% of student enrollment are women, and some seminaries have as many as 50% women. At the current rate of growth, the number of women clergy is doubling every three years and it is expected that parity will be achieved by 1994. From the deployment figures, however, it is apparent that women are less likely to be employed as rectors of parishes: only 14% of ordained women were rectors or vicars at the end of 1985. By contrast, many churches are increasingly hiring women as assistants or curates. Forty-five percent of ordained women were functioning as assistants/associates at the end of 1985. Only 1% of women, however, were reported to be unemployed.[4]

These statistics on women's deployment reflect an increasing popularity of women in parishes, although their positions in senior posts are still relatively limited. However, the fact that it has been only eight years since women were officially admitted to Holy Orders could well account for this. After nearly 2000 years of tradition it is remarkable that such a major change can take place in such a short period of time, and it reflects the rapid acceptance of women as priests in the Episcopal Church.

Attitudes Toward Women Priests

At present, only 11 out of the 94 North American dioceses do not ordain women. This situation, however, is constantly changing as alterations in the Church's leadership occur and as women priests become more accepted. Also, it is apparent that many who were originally opposed to women's ordination are changing their views.

A notable example of such a change in views is that of the Bishop of Central Florida, Bishop Folwell, an opponent of women's ordination at the 1976 Convention. In his diocesan publication of October 1983, Bishop Folwell writes:

> It is as a consequence of study, prayer, listening and observing, that I am now committed to the decision our Church made at the General Convention.

He goes on to state his reasons, which are both theological and practical.

> For seven years we have belonged to a Church which has authorized the ordination of women to the priesthood. It has also seen over 300 women ordained. We cannot live as members of this Church as though it never happened.

Bishop Folwell clearly reflects the views of many who were originally opposed to the ordination of women, but who have come to see the Holy Spirit at work in this fundamental change.

People's actual experience of women as priests contrasts with their early negative reactions to the abstract idea. Many stories are told about this. For example, in a small booklet about women in the priesthood, published by the Board for Clergy Deployment in 1979, it is reported that when a woman stepped in to assist a parish when the priest was ill, the parishoners changed their opinions of women in the priesthood from negative to positive because of her presence. The acceptance of women priests seems to come from having encountered them and realizing that they fulfill a need which was previously unrecognized.

Finally, does the increasing number of church members in recent years bear any relationship to the increasing number of women priests in America? It is impossible to document this statistically, as comparisons between dioceses which ordain women and those which do not cannot be made because of so many other variables, and because women still constitute small numbers, even in dioceses where women have been ordained for several years past. There are only six dioceses where women represent more that 10% of canonically resident clergy, and some of these are in areas where economic recession is causing migration.

On the other hand, as can be seen from the map in Fig. 2, many of the dioceses where no new churches are opening are also those which do not ordain women. Five out of the 11 dioceses which do not ordain women have no new churches. Again, however, economic and social factors may be the more important determinants influencing the opening of new churches. One interesting case which can be cited is the diocese of Virginia, where there is a relatively large number of women priests (31 by the end of 1984), many of whom are deployed as assistants (curates) in parishes. Church membership was declining by 0.4% per year on average from 1972 to 1976, but since that time it has been growing by 0.8% per year, and since 1980 by as much as 1.46% per year.

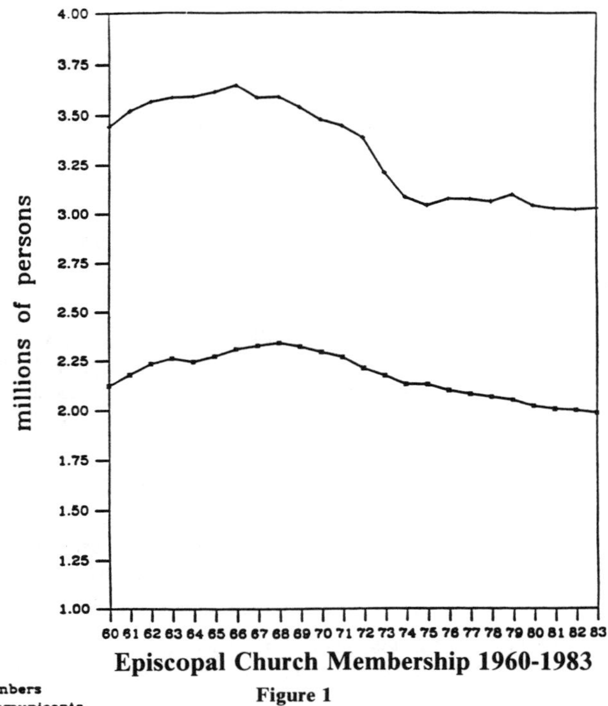

Episcopal Church Membership 1960-1983

— members
-•- communicants

Figure 1

In summary, far from being in a state of serious decline, the figures show that the Episcopal Church shows signs of increasing vitality and growth since the ordination of women became official policy. The statistics show more and more women being ordained and being employed in parishes and institutions around the country, reflecting the increasing acceptance of women in the Church, a change which has taken place in an amazingly short period of time.

The figures also show clearly that there has been a marked upturn in church attendance and membership in the years since women were ordained and began to be deployed in parishes.

Footnotes and Sources

1. This data has been prepared by Michael Sieman (currently a resident at General Theological Seminary), who is undertaking an analysis of the Episcopal Church Annual. Work in Progress, *Episcopal Church Membership: 1964-1983.*

2. *Committee on the State of the Church. Parochial Report Analysis.* Data obtained by Alison Warner from the Episcopal Women's Caucus.

3. These figures are from an editorial in *The Christian Challenge,* ''An Independent Episcopal Witness in the Anglican Tradition'', Vol. XXI, No. 11, Dec. 1982. This gives an historical account of the schisms in the Episcopal Church since the late sixties.

4. Data from the Rev. Sandra Boyd and the Rev. Susanne Hyatt of Episcopal Divinity School, Cambridge, Mass. Prepared for the Office of Women's Ministries at the Episcopal Church Center in New York City.

Other data and information cited is from the Office of Women's Ministries of the Episcopal Church Center, 815 Second Avenue, New York, NY 10017.

Acknowledgements
Mrs. Sharon Green, of General Theological Seminary, helped in preparing some of the tables and obtaining some of the information. I am also grateful for the considerable assistance and help given by the Office of Women's Ministries at the Episcopal Church Center, which supplied me with much of the data and information used in this paper.

Author

Dr. Susan M. Cole-King
General Theological Seminary
175 Ninth Avenue
New York, NY 10011

Notes: *What are the consequences of allowing women into the priesthood? This report, distributed by the Women in Mission and Ministry office at the Episcopal national headquarters, examined that question 10 years after the first Episcopal women priests were ordained. It found that the predictions of large-scale defections did not prove accurate, with only about a 5% loss in membership actually occurring. For those who did leave, the ordination of women was only one reason among many for dissatisfaction. Overall, the loss in membership which began in the 1960s slowed noticeably after 1976, and worship attendance has increased since then.*

EVANGELICAL LUTHERAN CHURCH IN AMERICA

REPORT OF THE COMMISSION ON THE COMPREHENSIVE STUDY OF THE DOCTRINE OF THE MINISTRY (1970)

The 1966 convention of the church adopted the following recommendations:

> "That the Comprehensive Study of the Doctrine of the Ministry, report thereon having been made to the 1966 convention of the Lutheran Church in America, be continued." (Minutes, p. 627)
>
> "That the president appoint a commission of not more than 15 persons for this purpose to report to the 1968 convention of the church." (Minutes, p. 627)
>
> "That the action of the convention directing the president to appoint a committee to study the role of women in the ministry (See p. 579) be rescinded, and that the studies called for in that action be assigned to the commission to continue the comprehensive study of the doctrine of the ministry." (Minutes, p. 743)

Pursuant to these actions, the president appointed the following persons to membership on the commission and designated the Rev. Edgar S. Brown, Jr., Th.D., as staff assistant.

Rev. Edmund A. Steimle, D.D., chrm., New York, N.Y.
Prof. Sidney E. Ahlstrom, Ph.D., New Haven, Conn.
Rev. H. George Anderson, Ph.D., Columbia, S.C.
Rev. Arnold E. Carlson, Th.D., Columbia, S.C.
Prof. Margaret S. Ermarth, Springfield, Ohio
Prof. Marianka Fousek, Th.D., River Forest, Ill.
Rev. Victor R. Gold, Ph.D., Berkeley, Calif.
Rev. Jacob W. Heikkinen, Th.D., Gettysburg, Pa.
Rev. Martin J. Heinecken, Ph.D., Philadelphia, Pa.
Rev. Albert H. Keck Jr., D.D., Hickory, N.C.
Rev. Richard W. Lundin, Wyomissing, Pa.

Prof. Floyd Martinson, Ph.D., St. Peter, Minn.
Sister Anna Melville, Gladwyne, Pa.
Rev. Ralph E. Peterson, New York, N.Y.
Rev. Alfred H. Stone, D.D., Seattle, Wash.

Meetings of the commission were held on the following dates: Jan. 23-24, 1967; April 3-4, 1967; May 25-26, 1967; Oct. 9-10, 1967; Jan. 11-12, 1968; May 16-17, 1968; Oct. 15-16, 1968; Jan. 7-8, 1969; Mar. 10-11, 1969; May 20-21, 1969; Oct. 20-21, 1969; Dec. 2-3, 1969; Jan. 13-14, 1970.

Preface

Who is a minister? What is the church? Once upon a time it may have been easy to answer these questions. Today, in a time of dramatic social change, the search for human community and the quest for authority challenge earlier definitions. Can ministry to a congregation be considered normative in these days of specialized chaplaincies and experimental missions? Must ministry be full-time, or are "tent-making" ministries possible? Should women be ordained?

Questions like these led the Lutheran Church in America to establish a Commission on the Comprehensive Study of the Doctrine of the Ministry in 1964. The original commission reported to the 1966 convention of the LCA, and then the present commission was appointed. This commission made a progress report to the 1968 convention and now presents its findings and recommendations.

One biblical affirmation has governed our thinking: all Christians are ministers. Therefore the word "ministry" cannot be reserved for the work of ordained clergy. Ministry is the task of the whole people of God*(Matthew 5:13-16, Romans 12:1-8, 1 Peter 1:9-10, 2 Corinthians 5:18-21). Every Christian is called to minister to his neighbor in the world, and this calling to ministry is performed through the Christian's life and work. It stems from the freedom given to all of us in baptism. In this sense the "Doctrine of the Ministry" applies to all Christians.

This renewed appreciation of lay ministry, however, has only intensified the need to re-examine the role of the ordained minister. Among all the tasks he performs, which tasks are uniquely his? Does he have any functions that differ from those of other baptized Christians? How essential is he in a society where others can communicate more effectively, counsel more expertly, and raise money more efficiently? Who needs him and for what? In short, what is his "identity"?

Traditionally Lutherans have answered these questions by referring to the "ministry of Word and Sacraments." Our commission too has used that concept as the basis for its work. But from the beginning we were conscious of two factors that have complicated current usage of "ministry of Word and Sacraments." First, we wanted to avoid the tendency to interpret "Word and Sacraments" solely in terms of what happens within a congregation. We were vividly aware of the many kinds of ministry to the world which clergymen perform on behalf of the church. Secondly, the congregation knows that in our kind of society the pastor spends a limited amount of his time in the activities usually associated with "Word and Sacraments." What about all the other things he does? Should he forget about them and concentrate on "what he was ordained to do"? With these questions in mind, the commission tried to analyze the meaning of "ministry of Word and Sacraments" as it appears in the Confessions (Augsburg Confession, V & VII) and as it is supplemented there by other definitions of clergymen's functions, such as "leaders of the community of God" (Formula of Concord: Solid Declaration, X, 10).

In such an analysis of "ministry of Word and Sacraments" two dimensions must be maintained. First, the Church is constituted by the "external Word" (Augsburg Confession V). That means that certain things must happen within the Church in order that it may exercise its ministry in the world. Its members live from a power beyond themselves. They receive before they can give; they are loved before they can love; they are forgiven before they forgive; they hear before they speak. Therefore, there must be persons among the people of God who are fluent enough in the language of Zion to translate its salt and savor into contemporary idioms; persons able to grasp the depth of God's love profoundly enough to hear the true thoughts of men's hearts and still declare, "Your sins are forgiven"; persons skilled enough in discerning the true mission of the Church to call each congregation of believers away from the hypnotic vortex of self-serving to the real work of discipleship.

The commission has chosen to call this first dimension of the ministry of Word and Sacraments a *representative* ministry. Other terms for this dimension, such as "basic," "fundamental," or "constitutive," might have been used, since they express the priority of this ministry in relation to all the other ministries of the Church. The term "representative" was chosen because it guards against the false notion that it is the clergy who constitute the Church. It stresses the fact that both ministry and Church are called into being by the Word. In this sense the ordained minister represents the Word; he does not create it by his mere presence.

Of course, the word "representative" is itself open to misinterpretation. On the one hand, it could be taken to mean that the ordained minister is merely the representative of other Christians, and that he is supposed to do their praying, serving and speaking for them. On the other hand, "representative" has been used to mean that the minister "re-presents" Christ in the Church. Neither of these interpretations reflects the intention of the commission. In actuality the representative dimension of the ministry of Word and Sacraments means that such a ministry . . . represents by life, word and activity God's act of reconciliation in Christ, his bringing a community into being and his utilization of persons in creating and maintaining this community." (World Council of Churches paper, "The Meaning of Ordination," Sec. I. D.) The ordained minister is the pastor of his people; as their shepherd he gives his life to and identifies his whole being with the reconciling work of God in Christ among them. Yet he is not a slave of his flock but a free man in Christ. By "rightly handling the word of truth," he leads others to the same freedom.

A second dimension of the ministry of Word and Sacraments relates to order. Luther and the Confessions speak of the "public" character of the ministry. This does not simply mean that a ministry is carried on "in the world" but that it is related to a specific "office." Since the Church has been given the ministry of Word and Sacraments, the Church must order the exercise of that ministry. Persons must be designated as qualified to testify to the Gospel as the church receives it and understands it, and in that sense their ministry is "official." Within a congregation the ordained minister exercises an official ministry because he has been designated and authorized by the Church. Furthermore, there are places in society where the church should be present, but where traditional structures are not available. To wait for congregations to develop would be folly; to ignore the need would be tragic. In such pioneering, experimental ministries, the ordained minister can act for the Church until such time as a community of faith may take root. Thus there is an "official" dimension to the ministry of Word and Sacraments in both congregation and world.

The ordained ministry is therefore created by the intersection of the "official" and "representative" dimensions of the ministry of Word and Sacraments. The "official" dimension calls attention to the *ordering* of this ministry, and the "representative" dimension reflects its *function*. Both dimensions are necessary to distinguish the ordained ministry from other ministries performed by individual Christians. For example, a synod may designate a layman to serve as treasurer, and in that sense he would have an "official" position. However, he would not be ordained for this office because his function would not be "representative" of the Gospel. On the other hand, any Christian fulfills the "representative" function on those occasions when he witnesses in life, word and activity to God's work of reconciliation. That would not mean, however, that he was exercising an "official" ministry of the Church.

Who is qualified to serve in this.official, representative capacity? Historically, the decision about qualifications for ordained ministers has rested with the church. Even denominations with highly individualistic traditions have vested the authority to call ministers in the congregation. In the Lutheran tradition, the rite by which persons have been so designated is ordination. To decide who should be ordained, therefore, is to decide who qualifies for the official, representative ministry. As the steward of the Gospel, the church must make this decision. The church, however, must realize that its decisions are fallible and not always identical with the will of God.[1]

The bases for deciding whether a person is to be ordained are both personal and professional. In addition to vocational commitment candidates should have personal endowments which qualify them to act responsibly. The church, however, must decide whether or not a person's motivations and endowments are capable of fruitful use. Secondly, candidates should possess sufficient professional education to equip them for exacting tasks of leadership in a complex society. Normally a degree from a seminary recognized and approved by the church would fulfill this requirement. Again, however, the mere possession of a degree does not guarantee that a candidate is able to assume an official ministry.

Service in the ordained ministry is always dependent on a call. ''Call'' and ''calling'' have not been identical in Lutheran usage. ''Calling'' has referred to the work of the Holy Spirit in summoning persons into the Christian life. In this sense every Christian has a calling. A ''call,'' on the other hand, is an official act of the church by which a specific assignment is given to a specific person whom the church believes God has called to ministry. Of course, not all specific tasks require an ordained clergyman. Calls, therefore, should be issued only for ministries which fulfill both of the following criteria: the ministry shall be related to the structure of the church and it shall be created by the interaction of the Gospel and the world. These criteria are simply another way of saying that the ordained ministry is both official and representative.

Once ordained, the clergyman needs effective support to help him face the immense demands of his ministry. This ministry requires the constant expenditure of personal resources in dealing with human need and conflict. The clergyman is sometimes called to work in lonely tasks without the support of an organized congregation. The church, therefore, must provide adequate means for him to renew his resources and to maintain a vision of his task within the total ministry of the people of God.

Several possibilities are available. Ordination itself provides the basis for such support. In ordination, prayer and the laying on of hands combine to assure the ordinand of God's own aid in his ministry. The ordained minister should also be provided with opportunities for continuing professional education to help him develop skills commensurate with his tasks. Finally, the church needs to demonstrate its concern for the individual clergyman through pastoral oversight exercised by appropriate officials. At present this responsibility is vested in the president of synod. He is to ''counsel with the ministers as their pastor.'' This function of the synodical president is so important that steps should be taken to prevent strictly administrative functions from eclipsing it.

The commission looks with favor on changing the title of ''synod president'' to ''bishop.'' The latter title has been used both in our Lutheran heritage and by other Christian bodies throughout the world to designate that official who serves as pastor to pastors. The title also has the advantage of biblical usage. Although a change in name would not guarantee that pastoral oversight would be exercised more conscientiously, the title ''bishop'' does not imply the preoccupation with administration that ''president'' conveys.

In all our deliberations the commission never seriously doubted the importance and viability of the parish ministry. We are cheerful about its future. We recognize the unique opportunity it gives for a steady ministry to persons through their whole life cycle. If our position statements and recommendations concentrate on other aspects of the ordained ministry, it is only because our assigned task demanded it.

In the following position statements the commission has tried to summarize the key points on which it reached consensus. We believe that these propositions speak to the crucial issues which must be resolved in order to formulate policies relating to the ordained ministry. In this sense we have not tried to produce a ''timeless'' document. Although our study of the doctrine of the ministry has been comprehensive, we have concentrated on those questions which are important for establishing guidelines here and now. A truly comprehensive study of the doctrine of the ministry must be an on-going study, since the shape of that ministry is hammered out in contact with the concrete demands of constant changes in the human community and environment.

Position Statements

1. The Church exists to bring the grace of God in Jesus Christ to bear upon the whole of life. It is uniquely responsible for the redemptive relationship of faith to which all of its other concerns are subordinate, and it takes its place with other humanitarian servants to ameliorate the human situation.
2. Ministry is entrusted to the whole people of God, not only to the ordained ministers. In the Christian tradition baptism serves as the individual's ''calling'' to the task of ministry. (See #4.) This calling is realized in his occupation as well as in all other areas of his life. The Christian's distinctive style of life is the individual expression of the ministry of God's people in the world.
3. For the sake of order and for regularizing and providing leadership, the church seeks out and ordains certain individuals to its official, representative ministry.
4. The ''call'' is a summons to exercise this official, representative ministry in a specific situation upon the initiative and at the discretion of the church. ''Call'' is distinct from ''calling'' for which every Christian is responsible. (See #2.)
5. Ordination, therefore, designates a member of the church as qualified by professional education and personal endowments to serve in the official, representative ministry. It presupposes a call. (See #4.) Both men and women are eligible for call and ordination.
6. In addition to personal endowments, the major qualification of the ordained ministry is professional education. Therefore, all ordained ministers serving in the official, representative ministry of the church are expected to engage in continuing professional education.
7. A person so called and ordained continues in the official, representative ministry of the church so long as he wishes, unless for valid reasons his services in this role are no longer desired by the church. Provisions for retirement allow for exception to this principle.
8. A person may voluntarily resign from the ordained ministry without prejudice. He may again be called to this ministry without prejudice.
9. Entrance upon or continuance in the ordained ministry shall not depend upon the source of income. Subject to the decision of the church an ordained minister may be employed outside the church if either through or alongside such an occupation he exercises an official, representative ministry.
10. The church must recognize the weight of its responsibility for its ordained and non-ordained leaders by the ordered and personalized nurture of their gifts and the effective deployment of their services. On their part, these leaders should exercise initiative in taking advantage of available resources to strengthen their ministries.
11. For the pastoral care and oversight of the congregations and other communities of faith and for their pastors and other ordained ministers in a specific jurisdiction, it is

necessary that a member of the ordained ministry order, guide and encourage the church's mission. The title "bishop" is appropriate for this office and need not imply tenure. Administrative responsibilities that interfere with the pastoral nature of the office should be assigned to assistants.

12. Flexibility and imagination are needed to move toward patterns of partnership that relate ministers and congregations to each other in new and diverse ways.
13. The changing needs of society require creativity and diversification in the ministry of the church. Accordingly, the mood and methods of experimentation will characterize the ministry of lay persons as well as of the ordained ministry.
14. Experimentation may result in ordered and recognized offices of ministry carried out by qualified laymen on either a full or part-time basis. These offices are not intended to supplant or imitate the pastoral office but to facilitate new patterns of ministry.
15. Laymen should be encouraged in every parish to participate in the leadership of public worship. Normally they may perform those liturgical acts not generally reserved to the clergy. Emergencies and other contingencies may require exceptions to the this norm.
16. Although baptism serves as the individual's calling to the task of ministry, a commissioning service for specific functions or offices as envisioned above may be appropriate.
17. It is urgent that new and diversified modes and patterns of theological education be developed for the preparation and training of leaders who will both serve the Lutheran church and also share in the mission of the whole Church to the world.

Recommendations

(Note: Words to be deleted are in *italics;* words to be added are in **bold-face** type.)

The commission respectfully recommends:

A. Concerning LCA Bylaws

1. That Section II, Item 1 of the LCA Bylaws be amended by striking the word "man" and inserting the word "person":

   > Item 1. A minister of this church shall be a *man* **person** whose soundness in the faith, aptness to teach, and educational qualifications have been examined and approved in the manner prescribed in the constitution, and who has been properly ordained; who accepts and adheres to the Confession of Faith of this church; who is diligent and faithful in the exercise of his ministry; and whose life and conduct are above reproach. He shall comply with the constitution, bylaws and enactments of this church and of the synod of which he is a member, and shall participate actively in their undertakings for Christ's Kingdom.

   Adopted. . . .

2. That Section II, Item 5 of the LCA Bylaws be amended by adding a third and a fourth sentence to the paragraph:

   > Item 5. No candidate for ordination or ministerial applicant for reception into this church who has failed to be approved by one synod or its examining committee may apply to another synod. Re-application, if any, shall be to the same synod to which the original application was made: **Exception to this ruling may be secured by requesting the president of the synod to confer with the president of another synod to which the candidate or applicant wishes to apply and with a third person acceptable to both presidents. The decision of the three shall be final.**

   Amended and Adopted. . . .

3. That Section II, Item 10 of the LCA Bylaws be amended by striking the present paragraph which reads:

> Item 10. *A minister may demit the ministry voluntarily by giving written notice of that fact to the president of the synod. The president, after consultation with the examining committee, may subsequently certify him as eligible to receive a call and upon his receipt and acceptance of such call, restore him to the ministerial roll.*

and substituting therefor the following:

> Item 10. **A minister may voluntarily resign from the ministry by giving written notice to the president of the synod. Request for reinstatement shall be submitted to the examining committee. Upon favorable action by the examining committee the president of the synod shall declare the person eligible for a call. Upon receipt of acceptance of a call the president of the synod shall reinstate the person on the ministerial roll and report to the next convention of the synod any such action of removal or restoration.**

Adopted. . . .

4. That Section II, Item 11 of the LCA Bylaws be amended by striking the present paragraph which reads:

> Item 11. *A minister who leaves the work of the ministry and engages in secular pursuits except as provided for in Item 12 of this section, or who enters such pursuits without the consent of the president of the synod while serving under a call, shall cease to be a minister of this church during the period of such business or employment. His name shall be removed from the ministerial roll by the president of the synod until such time as he resumes full-time work in the ministry with the consent of the president of the synod who shall then restore him to said roll, reporting to the next convention of the synod any such action of removal or restoration.*

and substituting therefor the following:

> Item 11. **A minister, serving under a call, who either leaves the work of the ministry or engages in another occupation without the consent of the president of the synod shall cease to be a minister of this church. His name shall be removed from the ministerial roll by the president of the synod. Request for reinstatement shall be submitted to the examining committee. Upon favorable action by the examining committee the president of the synod shall declare the person eligible for a call. Upon receipt of acceptance of a call the president of the synod shall reinstate the person on the ministerial roll. He shall report to the next convention of the synod any such action of removal or restoration.**

Adopted. . . .

5. That Section II, Item 14 of the LCA Bylaws be amended by adding a second and a third sentence to the paragraph:

> Item 14. A minister under discipline by a synod or otherwise removed by it from the ministerial roll must be restored by that synod to good standing before becoming eligible to acceptance by another synod. **Exception to this ruling may be secured by requesting the president of the synod to confer with the president of another synod to which the minister wishes to apply for reinstatement and with a third person acceptable to both presidents. The decision of the three shall be final.**

Amended and Adopted. . . .

B. Concerning the Approved Constitution for Synods

1. That Article Eleven, Section I, Item 2 of the Approved Constitution for Synods be amended by striking the words "young men" and inserting the word "persons":

> Item 2. Every pastor shall preach the Word, administer the Sacraments, and conduct public worship in consistency with the faith and practices of the Lutheran Church in America. He shall care for his people individually and as a congregation, give catechetical instruction, confirm, marry in accordance with the teaching of the church and with the laws of the state, visit the sick and distressed, and bury the dead. He shall inculcate piety in individual and family life and supervise all schools and auxiliary organizations of the congregation. He shall install regularly elected members of the church council, and, with the council, administer discipline. He shall seek out and encourage qualified *young men* **persons** to prepare for the ministry of the Gospel and strive to extend the Kingdom of God in the community, in the homeland and abroad. He shall impart knowledge of the church and its wider ministry through distribution of its periodicals and other publications and shall endeavor to increase the liberality of his congregation in support of the work of the Lutheran Church in America and of this synod.

Referred to the Executive Council for revision in view of the adoption of Recommendation A. 1. above. . . .

2. That Article Eleven, Section I, Item 5 of the Approved Constitution for Synods be amended by striking the present paragraph which reads:

> Item 5. *Each pastor shall submit a pastoral report to the president of the synod at least ninety days before each regular convention of the synod.*

and substituting therefor the following:

> Item 5. **Each minister on the roll of a synod shall submit a report of his ministry to the president of the synod at least ninety days before each regular convention of the synod.**

Executive Council requested to amend the Approved Constitution for Synods as indicated in the above recommendation. . . .

C. Concerning the Approved Constitution for Congregations

1. That Article V, Section 1 of the Approved Constitution for Congregations be amended by striking the word "man" and inserting the word "person":

> Section 1. A pastor of this congregation shall be a *man* **person** whose soundness in the faith, aptness to teach, and educational qualifications have been examined and approved by the church, and who has been properly ordained; who accepts and adheres to the Confession of Faith of the Lutheran Church in America and of this congregation (Article II); and whose life and conduct are above reproach.

Referred to the Executive Council for revision in view of the adoption of Recommendation A.1. above. . . .

2. That Article V, Section 5 of the Approved Constitution for Congregations be amended by striking the words "young men" and inserting the word "persons":

> Section 5. A pastor shall preach the Word, administer the Sacraments and conduct public worship in consistency with the faith and practices of the Lutheran Church in America. He shall care for his people individually and as a congregation, give catechetical instruction, confirm, marry in accordance with the teaching of the church and with the laws of the state, visit the sick and distressed, and bury the dead. He shall inculcate piety in individual and family life and supervise all schools and auxiliary organizations of the congregation. He shall install regularly elected members of the church council, and, with the council,

administer discipline. He shall seek out and encourage qualified *young men* **persons** to prepare for the ministry of the Gospel and strive to extend the Kingdom of God in the community, in the homeland and abroad. He shall impart knowledge of the church and its wider ministry through distribution of its periodicals and other publications and shall endeavor to increase the liberality of this congregation in support of the work of the Lutheran Church in America and of the synod.

Referred to the Executive Council for revision in view of the adoption of Recommendation A.1. above. . . .

D. Concerning the Standards of Acceptance Into and Continuance in the Ministry of the Lutheran Church in America*

1. That paragraph "a" of the "standards" be amended by striking the present paragraph which reads:

a. *A candidate for the ministry of the Lutheran Church in America, with the exceptions indicated in paragraph "d," shall be a graduate of an accredited college or university and of an approved theological seminary. He shall normally secure the full theological education required for ordination in a seminary of this church. In every case, except as hereinafter provided, he shall have been a student in residence at an LCA seminary for at least one academic year. A graduate of a non-LCA Lutheran theological seminary in North America may be exempted from the one-year residence requirement by the examining committee. A candidate for the ministry who is a graduate either of a theological faculty or seminary outside North America or of a non-Lutheran seminary in North America may alternatively be required by the examining committee to serve a year's internship in a parish approved by the Board of Theological Education or may be excused from both requirements by a panel consisting of the president of the church or his appointee, the president of the synod concerned, and the executive secretary of the Board of Theological Education.*

and substituting therefor the following:

a. A candidate for ordination, with the exception indicated in "d," shall be a graduate of an accredited college or university, and normally of a theological seminary of this church. If he has pursued his theological education elsewhere he shall:

1. give evidence that this has been done in an accredited theological school;

2. have fulfilled a year's internship, or its equivalent, acceptable to the appropriate synodical authorities and in a situation approved by the Board of Theological Education;

3. present satisfactory reports of regular and frequent contact with the synodical church vocations committee;

4. be subject to the same examining procedures administered to the graduates of the seminaries of this church.

Any variance from the above procedure shall require the approval of a panel consisting of the president of the church or his appointee, the president of the synod concerned, and the executive secretary of the Board of Theological Education.

Amended and Adopted. . . .

2. That paragraph "e" of the "standards" be deleted:

e. *A seminary graduate who has been called by the Board of World Missions shall be ordained when he is ready to depart for his field of service.*

Amended and Adopted. . . .

3. That paragraph "h" of the "standards" be amended by striking the number "3" in the parenthetical reference:

> h. A synod may, upon receipt of a recommendation from the Board of Theological Education, extend a call to special service to a minister of this church who is to engage in graduate study, each such call to be for a period of one year, and may upon like recommendation renew such call provided he remains actively engaged in such study. The rules regarding prior parish experience (as set forth in paragraph j. *3* below) shall apply to ministers desiring calls to special service in this category.

Amended and Adopted. . . .

4. That paragraph "i" of the "standards" be amended by striking the present paragraph which reads:

> i. *It shall be the duty of the synodical examining committee:*
>
> *1. to determine that each applicant for admission into the ministry of the Lutheran Church in America accepts and adheres to the confession of faith of this church prior to such admission;*
>
> *2. to ascertain, or authorize the president of the synod to ascertain, that each applicant for ordination to the LCA has completed the academic requirements prior to ordination;*
>
> *3. to verify that each applicant for admission into the ministry of the Lutheran Church in America is in possession of a proper call as specified in Article VII, Section 5 of the constitution of this church, and*
>
> *4. to ascertain that, if called to serve a congregation, he will carry out fully the functions of the pastoral office as defined in Article Eleven, Section 1, Item 2 of the Approved Constitution for Synods.*

and substituting therefor the following:

> i. **A candidate may be recommended for ordination or reception when the examining committee has met with him personally and has ascertained 1) his acceptance of and adherence to the confession of faith of this church; 2) his fulfillment of the academic requirements; 3) his possession of a proper call specified in Article VII, Section 5 of the constitution of this church; and 4) his personal qualifications for carrying out the functions of the ministry to which he has been called.**

Adopted. . . .

5. That paragraph "j" of the "standards" be amended by striking the present paragraph which reads:

> *j. The following rules shall obtain in regard to the parish experience required of a minister or candidate for ordination before he is permitted to enter into a specialized ministry and in that capacity be on the roll of a synod:*
>
> *1. prior parish experience shall not be required of a person called;*
>
> *a. by the Board of American Missions to be a mission developer;*
>
> *b. by the Board of World Missions to be a missionary;*
>
> *2. three years of parish experience or, alternatively, two years of such experience plus an academic year of approved internship in a congregation of the LCA, shall be required of men entering the military or federal civilian chaplaincy, except as this requirement may be waived by the president of the*

church for a man of unusually high academic standing and demonstrated ability and maturity;

3. *subject to exceptions that may be granted by a panel consisting of the president of the church or his appointee, the president of the synod concerned, and the executive secretary of the Board of Theological Education, three years of parish experience shall be required of a minister before he enters into:*

   a. *general work, such as service on the staff of this church (including its boards, commissions, and auxiliaries) or on the staff of a synod (including its educational and eleemosynary institutions and agencies); or*

   b. *service in the administration or on the teaching staff of theological seminaries or on the staff of such organizations as state and local councils of churches or inter-Lutheran agencies, the Lutheran Council in U.S.A., the Lutheran Council in Canada, National Lutheran Campus Ministry, Lutheran Student Foundations, the Lutheran World Federation, the National Council of the Churches of Christ in the U.S.A., or the World Council of Churches.*

and substituting therefor the following:

j. The practical experience which may be required prior to accepting a call to a specialized ministry (chaplaincy, general work of the church, teaching in a college or theological seminary, etc.) shall normally be gained through a parish ministry. The calling agency, however, shall determine the type and extent of the practical experience most appropriate for that ministry.

Amended and adopted. . . .

6. That a new paragraph be added to the "standards" and placed between paragraph "j" and "k" (see recommendation 11):

   11. **A minister may be engaged in another occupation provided he has the approval of the president of the synod and has a proper call. In the exercise of his ministry he shall continue to be responsible to the president of the synod. It is expected that the occupation of the minister will have a functional relationship to the purpose of the ordained ministry, either providing a secure basis for support or enabling him to enter strategic areas of life normally remote from a traditional parish ministry.**

Amended and adopted. . . .

7. That paragraph "k" of the "standards" be amended by striking the present paragraph which reads:

   k. *A minister who is an administrator or on the teaching staff of a theological seminary, college or university of this church, or who is in the full-time service of a church-owned or church-recognized eleemosynary institution or agency of this church shall be included on the ministerial roll of the church so long as he has a proper call.*

and substituting therefor the following:

k. **Persons in the following categories shall be admitted to the ministerial roll of this church and continue there so long as they possess a proper call:**

1. **Ministers who are on the administrative or teaching staffs of accredited theological seminaries;**
2. **Teachers of religion in accredited schools, colleges, or universities;**
3. **Chaplains and pastoral counselors serving, e.g., academic, military, healing, correctional, or eleemosynary institutions.**

Referred to Executive Council for consideration and action. . . .

8. That paragraph "l" of the "standards" be amended by striking the present paragraph which reads:

    l. *A minister who is an administrator or on the teaching staff of a non-LCA theological seminary, or who is a chaplain or teacher of religion in a non-LCA college or university or Bible School or who is a chaplain giving full-time service to a non-church (LCA)-owned or non-church (LCA)-recognized eleemosynary institution or agency shall be continued on the ministerial roll of the church so long as he has a proper call.*

    and substituting therefor the following:

    l. **Ministers occupying positions prior to July 1, 1970 that do not ordinarily require theological education or ordination—e.g., teachers in other college disciplines, institutional administrators, community development directors—shall be continued on the ministerial roll so long as they possess a proper call and remain in their present position.**

Referred to Executive Council for consideration and action. . . .

9. That paragraph "m" of the "standards" be amended by striking the present paragraph which reads:

    m. *Other ministers on the ministerial roll of the LCA on July 1, 1966 who are administrators or otherwise on the teaching staffs of non-LCA colleges or universities or who are in full-time service of non-church (LCA)-owned or non-church (LCA)-recognized eleemosynary institutions or agencies shall be continued on the roll so long as they have proper calls. Further additions to the roll in this category*

    1. *affecting men in such positions within the United States or Canada may be made by synods which will issue proper calls after securing the concurrence of the officers of this church, or*
    2. *affecting men in such positions elsewhere, by the Executive Council, if in the judgment of the synod concerned or of the Executive Council respectively such persons will fulfill by their vocation the purposes of the ordained ministry.*

    and substituting therefor the following:

    m. **Applicants for admission to or continuance on the ministerial roll after July 1, 1970 who wish to exercise a ministry through or alongside of another occupation not ordinarily requiring theological education or ordination shall be subject to the following procedures:**

    1. **Each application shall be decided on an individual basis by the appropriate synod or the Executive Council.**
    2. **The synod or Executive Council shall establish whatever controls may be necessary to insure that the occupation of the minister shall have a functional relationship to the purpose of the official, representative ministry, either providing a secure basis for support or enabling him to enter strategic areas of life normally remote from a traditional parish ministry.**
    3. **The call to or authorization for all such ministries shall be for a term of no more than four years. Renewal of this call or authorization shall require approval by the synod or Executive Council, after proper investigation, that the position continues to be essential for the official, representative ministry of the church.**
    4. **Persons serving in such positions will be responsible to the president of the synod as well as to the calling agency.**

5. **An applicant whose petition that a certain position qualify him for ministerial status has been denied may appeal to the President of the church whose decision shall be final.**
6. **The ordained ministry of the Lutheran Church in America is an official, representative ministry. It is "official" because it is performed under the official call; it is "representative" because its functions represent the gospel by word and activity.**

Amended and Adopted. . . .

10. That paragraph "p" of the "standards" be deleted:

> p. *All applications for restoration to the ministerial roll of the Lutheran Church in America shall be addressed to the synod in which the minister last held membership. The president of the synod shall consult with the examining committee before declaring a former minister of this church who has demitted the ministry voluntarily (LCA Bylaws, Section II, Item 10) or who is no longer continued on the ministerial role in the category of "awaiting a call" (LCA Constitution, Article VII, Section 5; LCA Bylaws, Section II, Item 12) to be eligible to receive and accept a call and subsequently restoring him to that roll.*

Referred to Executive Council for consideration and action. . . .

E. Additional Recommendations

1. That the Executive Council be instructed to arrange for the publication of a professional handbook on the ordained ministry that will incorporate, among other items, all pertinent materials in the official documents of the church (including the standards), the Preface and Position Statements of this commission's report, and related personnel and pension statements; and, to arrange for distribution to those holding offices of ministry and to those in training for such offices.

Referred to Executive Council for consideration and action. . . .

2. That, for provision to be made for a permanent on-going study of ministry of men and women in the church, the development of new forms of that ministry, and the integration of all functions of the church having to do with ministry,

a. the Executive Council be requested to study the present board and commission structure of the church in the interest of a possible realignment of these structures to provide a central agency whose responsibility it shall be to engage in a permanent, on-going study of ministry, the direction of enlistment, professional training, deployment, and the development of new forms of ministry appropriate to our world;

b. pending the outcome of such a proposed study, the Executive Council be instructed to commit to the Board of Theological Education the task of an on-going comprehensive study of the nature of ministry and that the board be instructed to report its findings to each future convention of the church.

Referred to Executive Council for consideration and action. . . .

3. That in view of the close relationship of programs which select, guide, and examine men and women for church occupations which serve all phases of the Church's mission, both national as well as world, and the growing recognition of functional tensions which might arise among synodical committees when there is an unclear delineation of responsibility, the Board of College Education and Church Vocations, the Board of Theological Education, the Board of World Missions, and the Board of Parish Education integrate as much as possible their present programs for the recruitment, guidance, and examination of candidates for professional leadership in the Lutheran Church in America.

Referred to Executive Council for consideration and action. . . .

4. *That the Board of American Missions, the Board of Theological Education, and the Board of College Education and Church Vocations, devise and execute vigorous strategies for the enlistment of members of minority groups for the ordained ministry as well as for other positions of leadership, and for methods of training appropriate to their ministries.*

Referred to Executive Council for consideration and action. . . .

5. *a. That the church endorse the principle of continuing education embodied in the PACE (Pastor's Aid for Continuing Education) program of the Board of Theological Education as an initial step toward a program of continuing education that will be mandatory for persons who wish to remain on the ministerial roll, provision for which shall be included on the face of the Call.*

   b. That the Board of Theological Education be requested to study the possibility of providing a plan for periodic career evaluation and guidance for those on the ministerial roll of the church.

Referred to Executive Council for consideration and action. . . .

6. *That the church look with favor on changing the title of Synod President to Bishop, and that the Executive Council be instructed to take the necessary steps toward the adoption of the title and to define the duties of the office resulting from that change.*

Referred to Executive Council for consideration and action. . . .

7. *That, whereas worship is properly the action of all the members of the community and therefore is most fitly expressed when leadership is shared by qualified persons, whether clergy or lay, the LCA*

   a. *encourage every congregation to train lay leaders who shall assist in the leadership of public worship guided by patterns provided in "Lay Assistants at Divine Services" (Commission on Worship, LCA, 1967);*

   b. *approve the following procedure whereby in an emergency or for a specified short term of no longer than six months and in a specified congregation including one other than his own, a lay person may perform functions normally reserved to the ordained ministry such as preaching and administration of the sacraments, subject to (1) authorization by the congregation with the approval of the president of the synod involved, and (2) the possession of appropriate training, skill and competence. If, in unusual circumstances, the lay person's services are required for more than six months, renewed authorization and approval may be given at the end of each six month period;*

   c. *discontinue the practice of setting men apart for the office known in the past variously as lay preacher or lay reader and, instead, encourage synods to use qualified lay assistants from the congregation or from neighboring congregations, where such services may be required following the procedures indicated in 7, b above.*

Amended and Adopted. . . .

8. *That the Executive Council be requested to provide for a study of the form and function of the ministry of deacons, and that it encourage experiments leading to a diaconate, male as well as female, that will effectively share in the ministry of the church.*

Referred to Executive Council for consideration and action. . . .

9. *That to achieve a consistent interpretation of the official, representative ministry throughout the church, synodical officials and all calling agencies shall be guided by the Preface and Position Statements embodied in this report and that the Conference of Synodical Presidents annually provide in its agenda a forum that will clarify what types of ministry each synod is sanctioning.*

Referred to Executive Council for consideration and action. . . .

Edmund A. Steimle, *Chairman*

Edgar S. Brown Jr., *Recorder*

The following position paper "The Role of Women in the Life of the Church" based on the findings of a subcommittee of the Commission on the Comprehensive Study of the Doctrine of the Ministry of the Lutheran Church in America is appended as information.

The Role of Women in the Life of the Church

In order to place its report to the commission in proper perspective, the subcommittee on the Role of Women in the Life of the Church found it imperative to make three basic statements.

One, the evidence is overwhelming that the effects and the implications for women of the world-wide revolution in the economic, political, and social structures of secular society are profound, pervasive, and immediate, and that they are filled with grave problems and enormous opportunities for the church.

Two, it is already too late for the church to exercise its genius for the role of pioneer, but not too late for the church to provide creative responses to a volatile situation it inadvertently helped to create, does not fully comprehend, and is now rather frantically trying to investigate. It is also displaying considerable reluctance in implementing the insights it already possesses. In other words, the church in its thinking and its action has up to this point lagged seriously behind secular society in trying to cope with a revolution in human affairs. The point has now been reached where a responsible church has no choice but to participate in the movement toward a greater freedom of thought and action for women.

Three, that insofar as this liberation movement pertains directly to the life of the church it must be considered in close conjunction with the church's teaching on creation, redemption, baptism, rite as over against sacrament, the concept of vocation, the freedom of the Christian, sacredness of individuality, ecumenism, and a new and dynamic concept of the ministries of the church.

Our reading of the evidences of the movement within the church indicates that it is most dramatically manifested among our Roman Catholic brethren. Among Protestant churches it seems more like a groundswell, a kind of unselfconscious assertion of a fact of life; it is, to change the figure of speech, washing rather quietly over the church and threatening to go far, far beyond it. Powerfully responsive to other related movements toward a greater freedom in every area of life (the civil rights revolution, the emphasis on individual fulfillment in a mass society, one-worldism, etc.), the gifted, religiously devoted woman, and especially the professionally trained woman has recognized that her abilities are most fruitfully used in secular society, and that they have been on the whole ignored, stereotyped, or downgraded by the church. Her response has been pragmatic, reflecting relatively little resentment or bitterness.

The problem of women and the church is a very old one; what is new is the element of urgency and the obvious fact that the consequences of non-response will most certainly be felt in all areas of the church's life. It also seems obvious that the Holy Spirit is attempting to tell us something.

I. Biblical and Theological Considerations

Early in its work the Commission on the Ministry came to the conclusion that there were no hard and fast biblical or theological reasons for denying ordination to women, and this conclusion was duly reported to the LCA Convention in Atlanta in June 1968. The conclusion was based upon the formulation of certain theological criteria to be used in interpreting the ministry of women in the church that would not be juridic or legalistic, but that would open the way to explore the vocation of women as servants of Christ in terms of the New Testament and in view of the actualities of the contemporary world. Theological study and biblical sources would indicate that there is a single ministry of the church dedicated to fulfilling God's purpose for his creation. There is oneness in service. In this service the sexes complement one another. Divisiveness and subordination within this service have risen out of cultural and social circumstances. Paul's pastoral judgments on the women's place should be understood in light of the social religious realities of the Hellenistic world. His abiding teaching is caught up in his continuous reiteration of the wholeness of the body of Christ, and expressed in succinct and classic form in the Galatian epistle: "For as many of you as were baptized into Christ have put on Christ. There is neither Jew nor Greek, there is neither slave nor free, there is neither male nor female; for you are all one in Christ Jesus." Under this interpretation there need be no special pleading for women in the name of equality and justice.

The missionary character of the church determines what spheres of labor it enters upon and who can do specific tasks most effectively. Preaching, teaching, administering of the sacraments may be done by every Christian. The major question is "By what authority?", since there must be order in the church.

The theologians, therefore, concluded that their study would justify a statement on the role of women in the church that would express:

1. An allegiance to the "faith once for all delivered to the saints," and not bound to times or conditions reflected in the New Testament, but to the life of faith and missionary responsibility to which the whole of the New Testament witnesses.
2. The wholeness of the community of faith, who "though many, are one body, and individually members one of another" (Romans 12:5).
3. The structure of authority in the household of God, with proper regard for the roles of leadership and the variety of functions.
4. Full recognition of the ministry of women in the "building up of the community of Christ" based upon the following considerations:
   a. Recognition of the fact that, according to God's on-going creative structuring of the world, there is no egality (sameness) of human beings, although there is *equality* of all God's children. Human life, therefore, is always a life of individuals-in-community.
   b. The sex differentiation also makes its constructive contribution to the life of individuals-in-community. This is so within marriage, in coitus and in the begetting, bearing and rearing of children. It is so also in whatever role a person may play in life which will be affected by that person's sexuality.
   c. Gifts, talents, abilities (such as intelligence, creative imagination, stamina, sense of humor, etc., etc.) are not differentiated according to sex. The differences are between individuals and not the sexes. Therefore, full equality must be extended to members of both sexes for the full development and exercise of whatever capacities they may possess. Then whatever talents are developed will reflect the person's sexuality and so make a constructive contribution to the life-in-community. This is the basis for full equality of women in our society (politically, economically, socially) without negating the fact that they are women. This applies then equally to the life and work of the church.
5. Since, within the community of the church, there is a variety of functions fitness for the exercise of that function will be determined by the possession and nurture of the necessary gifts.
6. There is nothing in the exercise of the "ordained ministry" as a functional office (the "office of Word and Sacrements," i.e., the official representative ministry—see the "Preface" to the Report of the Commission) which would exclude a woman because of her sex. The decisive thing is the possession of the necessary gifts and education and the "call" from the church. As women enrich the other ministries of the church they will also enrich its "ordained ministry."

II. The Historical Development of Women's Role in the Life of the Church

In the early church there was a great variety of ministries, and women had a part in carrying out several of them. In the New Testament times women served in the functions of "prophets," "widows," or "deacons." However, the rise of heretical movements, adjustment of the church to the social pattern of the late Roman society, and, finally, the deep inroads of asceticism into the church led to severe restrictions on the activities and functions performed by lay people and by women in and for the church. However, women continued to function as official "widows" or "deaconesses" in the life of the ancient parish. The fact that the whole city constituted a single "parish," with a team ministry, made for diversity and flexibility in the church's ministry, and provided a place for a variety of official ministries on the part of men as well as of women. Yet the monastic movement, which arose in the 4th century as a reaction against the secularization and popularization of the church at the time, served to remove women both from the public life and from their accustomed services in the congregations. Women, however, received positions of significant leadership in the monastic communities.

When the barbarian invasions broke up the urban-centered Roman society, the city-wide parish and with it the team-ministry gradually disappeared. In the Western world the Church's official ministry became in effect restricted to the rural priest resident in the small local community and to the more distant bishop with his cathedral staff, which consisted of priests and apprentices to the priesthood. A place was no longer provided for other public ministries, and the ecclesiastical services of women became confined to the cloister.

It is remarkable that the Reformation on the whole did not provide substitutes for the services which had been previously provided by nuns, prioresses and abbesses, or of the ancient deaconess, or "widow." Only within some of the radical sects did women receive ecclesial functions again.

From the 17th century on, Roman Catholic orders as well as lay groups and certain elements within the Protestant pietist movement again began to use women in the public life, in works of charity. In the 19th century the order of deaconesses was created and women became active as missionaries and Sunday School teachers. Among the laity in general, many organizations for women evolved to sustain the services of the church, but aside from the missionary and educational work, they were peripheral, derivative, and largely parochial in character. The activists in women's work were drawn off from "church work" into important secular philanthropic work and into the anti-slavery and feminist movements.

Secular society, and especially the Industrial Revolution, gradually emancipated women, but the church has dragged far behind. It may be that the ascendency of the primarily small local church is chiefly to blame, and that the greater variety of ministries demanded of the church in our day by a predominantly city culture will once more move the church to call upon the gifts that women can exercise in its ministry.

III. The Revolution in the Role of Women in Secular Society

The dramatic changes taking place in the role of women in secular life have produced a situation that is profoundly paradoxical: women have been drawn more and more into work outside the home, to the point where they constitute about one-third the labor force of the country. But this emancipation has tended to lock them into subordinate strata of the society where they have not only been deprived of advancement but have received lower wages, fewer fringe benefits, and much less security than their male counterparts.

Another paradox is that when both parents have jobs outside the home the consequences for the family are not always bad: often a kind of partnership develops between the parents centering upon the care of home and children and stimulating activities in which the whole family participates.[1] Especially during the last ten years sociologists, psychologists, economists, and politicians have attempted to analyze the interplay of factors involved in this new situation in a massive array of studies.

Two assumptions long held by secular and religious thinkers have now been largely discredited: that the emancipation of women would let loose on male-dominated institutions a flood of women who would compete for men's jobs on a static labor market; that there are psychological, emotional, and physical conditions that mark so elemental a difference between men and women that many tasks (ministries?) are almost automatically ruled out for one or the other sex. Instead, what has happened is that the technological and scientific revolution has combined with a larger and more diversified labor force to produce new types of jobs. Tasks which a few years ago had to be done by men are now open to both sexes, not only because of refined muscle-saving machinery, but also because of the newly developed capabilities of women. What the secular community has recognized, and what most of the religious community, including the women in it, has been blind to, is the fact that in very large measure the stereotyped notions about the basic attributes of man and woman no longer hold. Whereas contemporary secular society is adjusting to or even exploiting the concept of the team, i.e., the possibilities of male-female partnership in work, the church lags behind in many practical and obvious ways.[2]

It seems obvious that, should the creative concept of partnership be allowed to evolve to its full potential (and this does not necessarily include a strict and legal egalitarianism), the true emancipation of individuals in society—both secular and religious—will come nearer to realization. The way in which ordination is defined will both affect and be affected by this working concept. In short, both men and women have latent and untried potentialities that develop under new conditions and are challenged by newly defined tasks; and new tasks are *shaped* in order to make creative use of these potentialities. The idea that static confrontations between men and women are inevitable is yielding; but both men and women contribute to it, and it is to be found in every segment of secular and religious communities.[3]

In conclusion, an analysis of the census reports tell us that the picture of the employment of women, even of professionally trained women, in secular society is still not very bright, but that it is getting brighter. In contrast, and with no census reports available, with few researchers interested and few writers attracted to a patently unspectacular subject, it has been difficult to draw up a reliable account of the role women are now playing in the life of the church.

IV. Professional Women in the Work of the Church

To draw an accurate picture of the role of women in general in the work of the churches today has been termed difficult; reliable information about professional women who work for the church is simply not available. For example, the thorough and dependable *Monthly Labor Review* of the Department of Labor, surveyed for a period of the entire year of 1968, contained not one statistic or category to include women who were church workers or even parochial school teachers! Our commission attempted through a questionnaire to get some information from LCA synodical offices about attitudes toward women involved in professional work in the church, the numbers so employed, the experiences of these women in their work, etc. The results are important and interesting, but the objective data, the hard facts, do not surface. One thing, however, is clear: the *concern* about women in the contemporary church is very lively and is growing rapidly.[4] This concern is erupting into studies and rumors of studies being conducted by most of the major denominations. Those that have been made available reveal anxieties about the complexities of the problem, uncertainty as to the implications of their findings for the traditional work and structures of the church, and all of them complain about the necessity for making decisions under the pressure of the events within and outside the church.

The next message that comes through is that the need of the churches for intelligent and well-trained manpower is growing by leaps and bounds, regardless of how its ministries are defined, just at the same time many of its most able women are being absorbed into secular positions. The church positions simply do not attract women. However favorably they may be disposed, most professionally educated women don't even think of the church. Non-church publications for instance, designed to inform women college graduates on job opportunities, do not even mention occupations in church-related work.

The relative barrenness of women's work in the secular life—marked by monotony, apathy, and frustration even with a greater variety of opportunities available to them—is tragically pervasive in the church. In an incisive and shocking article in *Renewal* magazine, Peggy May, formerly a social welfare consultant to the Chicago City Missionary Society and presently on the faculty of the Divinity School of the University of Chicago, describes trenchantly the stereotypes of women's church groups we all know too well. She calls them the bane of the minister, an impediment to bona fide church renewal, a breeding ground for self-satisfaction and contentment with the status quo, and an offense especially to active and intelligent young women of the church who are ". . . accustomed to the give and take of conversation in a bisexual environment . . . [and] less apt to seek out the sexually 'proper' place for women which the church provides."[5] A further quote:

> "Yet even those who believe in such stereotypes must be helped to recognize them as only partial truths which mask other realities and potentialities. For example, it is often forgotten that most women in the Church are not only sincerely motivated, but are doing precisely that which Church leadership over the past fifty years has encouraged and provided opportunities for them to do.
>
> "It is a fact that formal Church leadership (need we state that it is predominantly male?) has counted on the women to raise money in whatever ways they could; to do 'good works' for the entire Church; and to keep themselves occupied in their own organizations and out of the sessions, vestries, church councils, presbyteries, etc.—where the real decisions concerning the Church are made.
>
> "If women have honestly sought to do just this, then the words of the elderly woman who told me: 'I don't understand—I've given my life to the circles, and now the new pastor tells us that they are all wrong'—are indeed plaintive.
>
> "Traditional women's groups are often branded as irrelevant, irreverent and banal. But they are no more so than the rest of the Church, and the truth is that the struggles for renewal now going on within them bespeak of the latent health of the entire Body of Christ.
>
> ***"Directions for Renewal***
>
> "Several years ago, a woman philosopher writing in the *Journal of Religion* suggested that theology tends to reflect masculine rather than feminine experience. And why not? Theologians are overwhelmingly men!
>
> "She also suggested that major theological emphasis upon pride as the condition for human sin reflects the traditional nature of male existence as embodying aggressiveness and power. False pride and temptation to misuse power thus create the masculine condition for sinfulness, and the theological plea is for greater humility and less confidence in one's own resources.
>
> "The situation is different for women. The nature of feminine existence has traditionally been more passive and self-denying. Yet the theological plea has emphasized even greater humility and self-abnegation. Few—if any—have recognized that too little pride, rather than too much pride, may be the condition of feminine sinfulness.
>
> "It is not a far step to suggest that the banality of much women's work in the Church is related to such a dynamic. In their false pride, men tend to protect women from the 'real world,' and in women's lack of pride, they tend to accept this and retreat into 'safe' roles. But if women do this, they must then accept the stereotyping, condescending and sentimental view of their work held by many churchmen. And

they are totally unprepared when a younger generation of Church leaders begins to look to them for programs of significance.

> "This dynamic affects all women in the Church. It is time to say openly that the Church treats its own professionally trained women, its Christian educators and pastors, as second-class citizens. If this is so, it is no wonder that women's groups have followed the directions they have taken. The recently passed legislation assuring 'equal pay for equal work' for women will be embarrassing to no organization more than the Church. But this is merely symbolic of the real gaps that exist between men and women Christians, whether in the various traditional ministries, or within the more recently emphasized ministry of the laity."

There are some bright spots in the picture: more women are being elected to local church councils and task forces, and to national church bodies in all denominations (except, so far as we know, the Lutheran Church—Missouri Synod).[6] There is a new willingness to use enlightened literature and other materials for women's study groups and for devotional purposes. The impact of such improvements is difficult to measure except in one way: the young are obviously keeping their distance; the old stereotype of empty irrelevance, sentimental charity, and extreme conservatism still holds for them.

Outside the U.S.A., the tradition of a non-functioning laity still largely obtains. A broad-gauged stewardship program begun in Germany after World War II got off to a brave beginning, but it, too, presently suffers from the stubbornness of the "cake of custom." Interestingly enough, European women in considerable numbers break this cake of custom not as lay persons working within a congregation but as professional persons—as theologians, who occasionally aspire to ordination, and as teachers, deaconesses, nurses, etc.

The research undertaken or sponsored by the subcommittee on the subject of the professional woman in the work of the church has been limited in scope for a number of reasons, particularly the pressure of time and the paucity of data in important areas. These factors govern the shape of the summary account included in the study booklet *Adam's Fractured Rib* (Philadelphia: Fortress Press, 1970). The account is neither definitive nor inclusive. The findings, however, do indicate trends rather clearly. In addition to the relevant printed materials and unpublished monographs listed in its bibliography, the subcommittee drew upon nine basic papers written at its behest by professional women who are now working within the church or who have worked in the church in the past, upon reports of interviews with girls who are being educated for work in the church, and upon answers to the questionnaires sent out to all presidents of synods, referred to elsewhere in this report.

As has been already pointed out, the barrenness and irrelevance of traditional forms of service for lay women in the local parishes have driven many able young women into the community to serve society on a voluntary basis. Their professionally trained sisters and other full-time women workers also find greater fulfillment in secular positions than in working for the church, even though in secular positions many of them enjoy less protection in their jobs than a Negro man. The women seem to be reacting to the same set of circumstances that influence a startling number of seminarians to reject or not to seek out positions within the parish ministry. Prominent among these circumstances are certain traditional and conservative attitudes within the church which seem to inhibit or blunt the new thrust of the church to involve itself in the great upheavals of our time.

V. Special Problems Attending the Emancipation of Women into Fuller Service Within the Church

Ten years ago, a Lutheran theologian could write as follows:

> "There exists, indeed, unanimity of opinion that the subordination which is required of the woman must find such a concrete expression in the life of the church as corresponds to the social and religious situation. In the Lutheran churches there is

> general agreement on the necessity to distinguish between that which transpires in the secular realm and that which transpires in the spiritual realm. An argument which believes it can derive a case for the ordination of women from the changed position of the woman in modern society has no validity in the church; it cannot be advanced as proof that the ordination of the woman to the pastoral office is in harmony with the subordination required of her.''[7]

Whether or not, in 1969, reactions of the clergy and the laity to the assumptions and arguments laid forth by Peter Brunner in the article quoted from above would be different from those in 1959 is an unanswerable question. No one need argue that the church must act in agreement with the secular world, but to respond to the need of that world is part of the mission of the church, and it is the duty and privilege of her people to assist her in meeting that need. Women will respond to a call from the church with the same basic gifts and potential they are offering in increasing numbers to challenges in the secular society. At this writing it would seem that on the whole women are simply not used to looking to the church for jobs that match their abilities and training, particularly at the professional level. And there is some justification for the opinion of many women that they can indeed render a fuller service to society outside the church, even though the secular society also has its ''orders of subordination'' for women.

The problems inherent in attempting to change the status of women in church work do not seem to be those familiar to the past. Male prejudice per se is no longer identified as such very often in the literature of the contemporary discussions. The basic concern is apt to be the future of the man-woman relationship, and there seems to be an increasing willingness to recognize that women as well as men can respond creatively and with new insight and powers to new situations that develop in society and in the church, and that even the traditional and ''natural'' roles they have played in that society can bring their own kinds of renewal to a church in a state of crisis. Dynamic interaction can operate; the powers of a woman can be *shaped* to a task; new and valuable tasks can be designed to make most fruitful use of her gifts and training.

More and more throughout society the lines of a good discrimination are drawn not on the lines of sex but on the lines of the person. There is, in short, less and less disposition to look upon women workers as intruding upon and competing for ''men's positions.'' Concomitantly, there is little disposition to eradicate as far as possible the differences between man and woman; rather, there is considerable evidence that our society is about ready to take advantage of the insights we have gained from the psychologists and sociologists to celebrate the differences and make them holy and wholly creative.

The concept of partnership, analyzed so brilliantly by Elisabeth Hahn in her book by that name, is gradually taking hold.[8] It was refreshing to read recently that the Episcopal women of a mid-western state moved to dissolve their ''circles'' in order to join with other lay organizations of the church in supporting a multi-faceted program that would call upon all the resources of the laity, both men and women. The blessings and strains of our technological society have brought an identity crisis upon *both* male and female. How they establish their identity and prepare to work and live fully in this society is apt to be less sex-linked than ever before. The church which has so often upheld the sanctity of the individual (his and her *personhood*), seems disposed now toward taking further steps to validate the principle within its own ranks.

In the little pamphlet, *A Study of the Man-Woman Relationship*, published in 1952 for the Commission on the Life and Work of Women of the Church of the World Council of Churches, there is a profound and provocative treatment of the idea that ''. . . there is a tension between an order of creation 'male and female made He them' and an order of redemption 'in Christ there is neither male nor female.''' Was Christ ''. . . the archetype of a fully united humanity and not of masculine humanity alone''? Are we at a point in human development where the church can speak more precisely of redemption *within* the society? ''Many Christians feel that the churches have no sense of the urgency of showing how our present-day situation in man-woman relationships can be redeemed. Meanwhile in secular society various groups are trying to work out a pattern of redemption in woman-man relationships, looking both to science and to their own partial understanding of the gospel for help.'' But now, seventeen tumultuous years later, the atmosphere is far more receptive to elevated, sober and productive debate on the subject of man-woman relationships within the church.

Diakonia

As we move into the eighth decade of this century, it is obvious that the rediscovery of the New Testament concept of *Diakonia,* which led to the creation of varying kinds of orders for deacons and deaconesses in the 19th century, and the much more drastic 20th century emphasis upon the service of the church to society will converge to effect drastic changes in the diaconate. The problem is already upon all the churches, and the signs of change already abundantly clear. They are to be seen in the turmoil within the Catholic clergy and especially, of course, the laity. The Anglican and the Presbyterian churches are seeking to bring the laity and the clergy closer together by a new definition of the authority, the duties, and the status of the deacon. Those churches which have long since settled upon a vocabulary that designates ''deacon'' as male and the ''diaconate'' as female—especially the Lutheran churches—are under pressure to clarify their understanding of the *Diakonia* as they have institutionalized it.

Strong indications of the direction in which the winds of change are blowing are to be seen in a series of ecumenical consultations, special projects, and subsequent studies in recent years.[9] The World Council of Churches has published three important studies: *The Role of The Diakonia of the Church in Contemporary Society* (1966); *The Ministry of Deacons* (1965); and *The Deaconess* (1966). Two years ago, in 1967, an Ecumenical Secretariat for the Diaconal Ministry of the Church was established in Geneva as a three-year experiment sponsored by the World Federation of Deaconess Associations and the Federation for Inner and Christian Social Work, in cooperation with the World Council of Churches. In the fall of 1968, a consultation between the Ecumenical Secretariat for the Diaconal Ministry of the Church and the Roman Catholic Information Center's special body for diaconate affairs was held in Switzerland. A summary of the discussions by Dr. Lukas Vischer and other reports from different churches points out that the traditional structure of the church has not given adequate expression to its diaconal responsibility. The Rev. Thure-Bengt Molander, presently executive secretary of the Ecumenical Secretariat mentioned above, made the following succinct statement in reporting on the consultation:

> ''At a time in history when the world is in deep crisis and in a process of renewal, the old structures of the churches themselves questioned and often felt quite obsolete, no fruitful research as to the specificity and function of the Ministry of Deacons can be pursued in isolation. It must be part of the great reappraisal and research for renewal which the churches themselves and the ministry in general must undergo. The Church must become a diaconal Church in the deepest and most forward-looking sense, or it will not be the Church. It is therefore important, in this diaconal perspective, that our Churches meet and challenge one another theologically, in a true ecumenical spirit. It is also important that the new needs of our times should challenge our churches, their theology and ministry. Only as these two currents influence one another can we be led to see what structures and ministries the churches really need. . . . Meanwhile in this process of renewal, the deacon and the deaconess by their presence, by the questions they pose to the Church, are reminders of the full diaconal dimension of the Churches' Ministry and should be incitements and not impediments to renewal.''

Three organizations of deaconesses are currently debating the issues involved in the new shape of a diaconate, including the implications for them as women. The *World Federation Of Deaconess Associations,* organized in 1947 in Copenhagen, now includes deaconess organizations from 21 countries and represents about 35,000 deaconesses. The tenth meeting of this ecumenical organization took place in July 1969, in Tampere, Finland, with about 500 delegates and visitors present. [At this writing, the results are not yet available.] The *North American Deaconesses Organization* held its first conference in Racine, Wisconsin, in August 1968, and drew about 100 delegates from nine denominational churches into a discussion of the role of the diaconate in a radically changing society. The *Lutheran Deaconess Conference,* representing all Lutheran churches in North America, has been meeting every two years since 1896, and is the oldest inter-Lutheran organization of America. The deaconesses of the Missouri Synod joined the Conference in 1968.

The women of the churches of all denominations have, consciously or unconsciously, voted their reactions to the problems relating to the diaconate and their confidence in its future for them by refusing to be recruited.

In the opinion of Sister Anna Ebert, Coordinator of the Brooklyn Project for the LCA Deaconess Community, the following questions require consideration:

1. If the Church is primarily to be understood as the people of God and the ministry is there solely for the strengthening of the people of God, how should the diaconal ministry be related to the priestly or pastoral ministry? Can it be a ministry among equal ministries and understood as each carrying out specific functions?
2. Just as there appear to be no scriptural or theological reasons for limiting the ordained ministry to men, is there any reason for continuing to limit the diaconate to women in the LCA? With the diaconate open to men and women, then its assignments can be more meaningful as "diaconal stimulators or enablers" in the church to enable God's people to fulfill their diaconal tasks.
3. Is there any merit in considering the diaconate as the office embracing the present diversity of professional church workers, e.g. directors of Christian education, social workers, teachers, with the present LCA Deaconess Community as one of its forms?
4. Since worship is the source from which diakonia arises and diakonia without worship is empty, what can be done to strengthen their relationship in a more effective manner to dramatize the responsibility of God's people to be a Church-for-others? Is the honest recognition of a diaconate part of the answer?

The Problem of Ordination

Ordination remains the most controversial and the most threatening of all problems. No matter at what point the discussion of the woman question begins, sooner or later the subject of ordination arises. (Semantically, it is a disaster that the word "subordination," and the conditions and feelings it invokes, follows so closely on the heels of "ordination.") Although the pressures for the ordination of women have been fairly strong among many Protestant groups in Europe and even among Catholic women's groups in Europe and America, no such organized efforts have been made by Protestant women in the United States. Here and there a lone woman appears ready to make a test case after she graduates from a theological seminary. Most of the evidence, however, seems to lead to the conclusion that women who wish to work for the church do not make a great point of insisting upon ordination. The crux of the matter is justice, and the major complaint is that traditionally the church has gone along with society in treating women as inferior human beings and stunting their ability to exploit their gifts to the fullest. To be barred from ordination perpetuates this tradition, and supports it on theological grounds that are at least questionable. Their position is roughly analogous to that of the Negro in the open-housing issue: "We don't necessarily *want* to live among the whites. We know the problems. But we should be free to choose." The few professionally trained women who are firmly pressing for this right feel, however, very strongly about it, primarily as a cause that must be fought for. It is anticipated that about a half-dozen test cases will, within a year or so, be presented to the Lutheran churches in the U.S.A. alone.

There is no question that the woman problem poses a threat to ecumenical fellowship between the Protestants and the Roman and Orthodox churches, and between other Protestant churches and the Anglican Communion. Fellowship between the more liberal Lutherans and the Lutheran Church—Missouri Synod is threatened as well. Two factors are powerfully at work, however, in this situation: the grassroots revolt that is an actuality in the Roman Church, and a very real possibility in the Missouri Synod. Secondly, the contemporary crisis in the church in all its branches may quite simply force a bona fide and practical cooperation among the churches to the point where the particular threat of women usurping functions traditionally assigned to males will seem irrelevant. Stranger developments than these are likely to occur within the foreseeable future.

The hope is bright that a redefinition of the ministry or ministries of the church in our time will bring with it the wisdom to identify the rites by which the church recognizes her ministers in such a way that the "most delicate matter" of women and ordination may well be subsumed under matters that are much more pressing for the whole community of God's people.

Professor Margaret S. Ermarth, the Rev. Albert H. Keck, Jr., Dr. Anderson, and the Rev. Alfred H. Stone presented the five proposed amendments to Section II of the by-laws, . . . properly signed by at least five delegates.

These proposed amendments were referred to the Executive Council for consideration and report. The Rev. Martin J. Heinecken drew attention to the items under "D. Concerning the Standards of Acceptance into and Continuance in the Ministry of the Lutheran Church in America". . . .

Edward W. Lautenschlager moved to strike "this has been done in" and insert "he is a graduate of" in a. 1). This change was made by common consent.

The chair ruled that the word "he" refers to a person regardless of sex.

The Rev. Clemens Zeidler moved to insert the word "normally" between "shall" and "be" in paragraph a.

The motion to insert was adopted (Yes—301, No—239).

The previous question was ordered and the vote taken on the proposed amendment to "a." of the Standards as amended.

The proposed amendment was adopted. . . .

End Notes

Preface

* A word of explanation is offered about terms used in the Preface and the following Position Statements. The terms "whole people of God" and "the Church" are the equivalent of the "One, Holy, Catholic and Apostolic Church." The word "church" without the capital letter refers to the Lutheran Church in America. "Congregation" means a corporate entity, as the term is used in other documents of the LCA. A local body of believers such as a seminary community, a group of people worshiping together but not necessarily organized as a congregation, or a gathered company working at a specific task has been called a "community of faith." "Pastor" refers to the pastor of a congregation and "ordained minister" to any member of the clergy whether or not he is serving as pastor of a congregation.

[1] All statements that refer to the church deciding who is qualified for ordination, officially designating persons for the representative ministry, and issuing calls should be understood to presuppose and acknowledge God's prior and basic choice of these persons. The call is from God, through the church. The church's action means that it acknowledges and accepts God's purpose in such choices.

Recommendations

* See *"Standards of Acceptance into and Continuance in the Ministry of the Lutheran Church in America" (pp. 781-783) as amended at this convention and, as authorized by this convention, at the October 1970 meeting of the Executive Council.*

The Role of Women in the Life of the Church

[1] The recreation and do-it-yourself industries have cashed in heavily on this significant development in "family togetherness."

[2] See especially Elisabeth Hahn's *Partnership,* the World Council of Churches *Revolution and Renewal,* the Archbishop of Canterbury and York's Commission report on *Women and Holy Orders,* Krister Stendahl's little book, *The Bible and the Role of Women,* and Ernst Kasemann's *Essays on New Testament Themes,* Chapter III.

[3] It may come as a surprise even to careful observers of the contemporary scene that the "woman problem" has split the ranks of the New Left and other radical groupings. For instance, Stokley Carmichael summed up SNCC's attitude crudely but succinctly thus: "The only position for women in SNCC is prone." Many women who have worked for SDS long and hard have been so insulted and injured by being ignored by policy-making units while they answered telephones, printed, folded, and stamped, that they have left the movement. They asserted, logically enough, that if there was not freedom for women in a movement dedicated to freeing minority groups there could be no freedom eventually for anyone. In bizarre and striking fashion a group of Antioch students supported the new liberation movement for women by appearing nude before a visiting parcel of men from *Playboy* magazine, thus demonstrating their rejection of the *Playboy* attitude toward women and sex.

[4] A simple measure is provided by the fact that three-fourths of the items in our large bibliography of books, brochures, and articles on the subject have become available since 1965. Objective data such as employment statistics, however, are elusive. The first survey on this subject was authorized by the Federal Council of Churches in 1921; but as late as 1969 it is still not possible for a dogged researcher to come up with a reliable estimate of the number of even the professionally educated women who are engaged in the work of the church.

[5] This article was reprinted and distributed in a sample copy of *Renewal* magazine. No date was given.

[6] The LCA will have two women representatives at the 1970 LWF Assembly in Brazil.

[7] Peter Brunner, "The Ministry and the Ministry of Women," *Lutheran World,* December, 1959, p. 270.

[8] Elisabeth Hahn, *Partnership* (1954). Written for the Commission on the Life and Work of Women in the Church, World Council of Churches.

[9] This treatment of the diaconate was provided by Sister Anna Ebert at the request of the Commission.

Notes: *This 1970 report of the Commission on the Comprehensive Study of the Doctrine of the Ministry is from the Lutheran Church in America, which in 1988 merged with the American Lutheran Church to form the Evangelical Lutheran Church in America (approximately 5,300,000 members. The study combines an effort to clearly define "ministry" with an examination of women's role in ministry. Many of the changes suggested in the first part of the document reflect ideas expressed in the second part of the document, which explores the role of women in the life of the church. In the second part, St. Paul's admonitions against some of the public activities of women are judged to be not applicable to today's social and cultural realities; emphasis should instead be placed upon the more abiding teaching that in Christ "there is neither male nor female." Other often-cited arguments* *against women's ordination are also refuted, and the church is urged to assume a more modern view of women. The entire report was adopted, and women clergy were allowed in the Lutheran Church in America. The first woman ordained was Elizabeth A. Platz, assistant chaplain at the University of Maryland, on November 22, 1970.*

EVANGELICAL LUTHERAN CHURCH IN AMERICA

REPORT ON ORDINATION OF WOMEN (1970)

At its meeting in March 1967 the Board of Theological Education took action to transmit to the Church Council the information that women who were then matriculated at one of the seminaries might request ordination. At its meeting in June 1967 the Church Council requested the Lutheran Council in the U.S.A., Division of Theological Studies, to study the question of the ordination of women. This information was reported to the 1968 General Convention by the Church Council (*1968 Reports and Actions,* p. 156).

1. Statement by Faculty of Luther Seminary

In October 1968 the faculty of Luther Theological Seminary adopted and submitted to the Church Council the following statement regarding the question of the ordination of women:

> Four sets of objections are urged against the ordination of women to the ministry: biblical, theological, practical, and ecumenical.
>
> 1. The New testament does not confront the question of ordination of women and therefore does not speak directly to it. On the other hand, nothing in the New Testament speaks decisively against it.
> 2. Although the ordination of women raises new and difficult questions, there is no decisive theological argument against the ordination of women.
> 3. The practical objections, however serious, do not by themselves settle the question for Lutherans. As long as no decisive biblical or theological objections are raised, the ordination of women remains a possibility.
> 4. The most serious objection is the ecumenical, that Lutherans ought not unilaterally in the present divided state of Christendom make decisions which affect all Christian churches. But inasmuch as other churches already have ordained women to the ministry, and some churches not presently ordaining women are open to discussion of its possibility, the exact weight of this objection is difficult to assess.
>
> In view of the considerations above, we can see no valid reason why women candidates for ordination who meet the standard normally required for admission to the ministry should not be recommended for ordination.

2. Report of Study by Lutheran Council

The report of the study of the ordination of women by the Division of Theological Studies of the Lutheran Council was made to the annual meeting of the Lutheran Council in February 1970. The presidents of the four member churches had a redaction of the theological papers prepared and a copy was mailed to each pastor of the member churches in May 1970.

3. Recommendations of Study Committee

The executive committee of the Church Council appointed the following committee to study the recommendations of the report submitted to the Lutheran Council and make recommendations to the June 1970 meeting of the Church Council. The committee consisted of Dr. Bruno Schlachtenhaufen, chairman, Dr. E. Clifford Nelson, Mrs. Adolph

Streng, Rev. Johan Thorson, Mrs. Erling Wold. This committee submitted the following resolutions:

Whereas, A Statement of Findings Relating to the Requested Study on the Subject of the Ordination of Women* has been adopted and made available by the Standing Committee of the Division of Theological Studies, Lutheran Council U.S.A.; and

Whereas, The *ad hoc* Committee on the Ordination of Women concurs in the Statement of Findings; and

Whereas, The American Lutheran Church accepted the following statement in 1964 with reference to ministry:

> "Since the ministerial office is not precisely defined in the New Testament, and since the duties of early officers were varied and interchangeable, and since the needs of the church down through the centuries are subject to variation, we are led to Luther's conclusion, namely, that God has left the details of the ministerial office to the discretion of the church, to be developed according to its needs and according to the leading of the Holy Spirit." (*1964 Reports and Actions,* p. 140);

and

Whereas, Men and women are both resources for ministry in the church and each other in the pastoral role; and

Whereas, Women are prepared to serve and have been certified for call and ordination; therefore be it

Resolved, That the Church Council be requested to recommend to the General Convention which will meet in San Antonio in October of 1970, that women be eligible for call and ordination in The American Lutheran Church.

4. District Memorials

a. Southwestern Minnesota District Memorial—Eligibility for Ordination, Women

The Southwestern Minnesota District submitted the following memorial:

Resolved, That this district approve in principle the ordination of women.

b. Eastern North Dakota District Memorial—Eligibility for Ordination, Women

The Eastern North Dakota District submitted the following memorial:

Whereas, There are women in The ALC who have been certified for call and ordination by a theological faculty of The ALC; and

Whereas, These women are open to call and desire ordination in The ALC; and

Whereas, LC/USA has, through the Division of Theological Studies, found through study that there is no basic reason why women should not be ordained; therefore be it

Resolved, That the Eastern North Dakota District of The American Lutheran Church assembled in convention memorialize The American Lutheran Church to consider and approve the ordination of women at the 1970 Convention of The American Lutheran Church.

5. Recommendations of the Church Council

- ACTION BY THE CHURCH COUNCIL:

C70.6.96 To recommend that women be eligible for call and ordination in The American Lutheran Church.

- ACTION BY THE CONVENTION:

GC70.24.77 To adopt.

(YES—560; NO—414; Abstention—1)

The Church Council recognized that, especially during the transitional period that would follow, should the General Convention approve the ordination of women, there would be many practical issues to be faced by women who will serve as parish pastors.

- ACTION BY THE CHURCH COUNCIL:

C70.6.99 To recommend that the seminaries give special counseling to women who may seek to matriculate at the seminaries.

- ACTION BY THE CONVENTION:

GC70.24.78 NOT to approve.

Endnote

* *The Ordination of Women,* condensed by Raymond Tiemeyer, Appendix, pp. 51-53.

Notes: *This 1970 statement is from the American Lutheran Church, which in 1988 merged with the Lutheran Church in America to form the Evangelical Lutheran Church in America (approximately 5,300,000 members). The church was influenced by the Luther Seminary faculty's support of women's ordination and by the Lutheran Council's opinion that women's ordination was an issue that could be either supported or denounced. The 1970 church convention approved the ordination of women 560 to 414.*

EVANGELICAL LUTHERAN CHURCH IN AMERICA

REPORTS FROM THE COMMITTEE ON INTER-CHURCH RELATIONS (1972)

Exhibit B

What Do The Scriptures Say About The Ministry Of Women In The Church?

Ministry is servanthood. What this means is spelled out in those famous gospel passages calling for men to humble themselves, not to be served but to serve, and acted out in the washing of Peter's feet (i.e., *diakonia.* Matt. 23:8-11; Mark 10:42-45; Luke 22:24-27; John 13:1-11 [cf. 1 Peter 5:3.] The Old Testament Greek term for the priestly office, *leiturgia,* is found, with two exceptions [Rom. 15:16; Phil. 2:17], only in connection with Christ.) And as we carry out this role of being a slave, we have no other authority, no other appeal, but that of the gospel.

Within the church various people carry out various ministries, but they are all carrying out the one ministry of the gospel. In the New Testament the lists describing such ministries differ and are incomplete (Rom. 12:6-8; 1 Cor. 12:28-31; Eph. 4:11-12). The church has felt free to drop certain of these ministries, expand and add others, and no ministry corresponding precisely to contemporary Lutheran concepts of "the ministry of the Word and sacraments" appears. Nor is ordination in our sense of the term to be found fully in the Scriptures, although the prototype of our "laying on of hands" is there. When we go to the Bible for guidance on the ministry of women in the church, we have these important guidelines to help us begin.

In practice, women in the New Testament carried out some very important roles. Women were the first to be told of our Lord's resurrection; they were the first to be commanded to tell others of our Lord's resurrection; and a woman was the first to see our resurrected Lord (Mark 16:7; Matt. 28:7; Luke 24:22-23; John 20:16). In this way they fulfilled a decisive function at the beginning of the history of salvation. They proclaimed the gospel as prophetesses (Luke 2:38; Acts 2:17; 21:9; 1 Cor. 11:5; cf. Rev. 2:20), they served as deaconesses (Rom. 16:1; 1 Tim. 3:11), they taught—a man (Acts 18:26). Moreover, women in the early church baptized.

[Perhaps in Pliny, *Epist.* 96,8 (according to W. Nauck, *Die Tradition und der Charakter des ersten Johannesbriefes,* Tübingen, 1957, p. 164). Thekla baptized (Act. Paul 3,40.), it is presupposed in SyrDidasc 15-16 that women at an earlier time baptized just as deaconesses were assisting in Baptism when SyrDidasc was written, and women among the heretics baptized according to Tertullian, *de praescr.* 41 and Epiphanius *haer.* 42.3.4, 49.2.1. In Irenaeus, *adv. haer* I, 13.2, women among the heretics are described as consecrating the elements at the Lord's Supper.] This should not surprise us because in the changed situation of the Reformation, Luther still would permit women to preach or even administer the sacraments in cases of necessity.

(WA 8, 424-425, 489, 497-498; 10, III, 171; 12, 180-181; 30, III, 524; 50, 633) We also permit women to baptize in cases of necessity, and we permit this not only because the Word and sacraments are effective without regard to the state of grace of the one who acts (the Donatist problem), but also because we know that a woman's female nature is no impediment to the Word and sacraments.

It would therefore appear that in the New Testament, distinctions in ministry were not made on the basis of sex, but rather of need, ability, and social custom. In contrast to Jewish practice, women entered the church by the same rite as men. As a matter of fact, specific statements in the New Testament indicate that in the Lord the distinction between male and female no longer determines one's place as it did in the world at that time.

"There is neither Jew nor Greek, there is neither slave nor free, there is neither male nor female; for you are all one in Christ Jesus" (Gal. 3:28).

"Nevertheless, in the Lord woman is not independent of man nor man of woman; for as woman was made from man, so man is now born of woman. And all things are from God" (1 Cor. 11:11-12).

We cannot dismiss such passages as applying only to the religious sphere and not to the sphere of everyday life or as dealing with an eschatological vision. To be sure, in the early church many refused to take the phrase, "neither Jew nor Greek," seriously; several decades passed before those supporting the exclusivity of the Jew were convinced. In fact, only the fall of Jerusalem in A.D. 70 resolved the Jewish question for the church. But finally this neither purely "religious" nor purely "social" but also physical distinction (circumcision/uncircumcision) was realized to be of no importance.

The second pair of opposites, "neither slave nor free," took centuries for the church to put across. We may excuse her, for there are New Testament passages which seem to support remaining "as you are" (1 Cor. 7:17-24; Philemon 16); yet would any one of us today dare to use the New Testament to prove that merely the "spiritual" distinction between slave and free had been abolished? The third pair of opposites, "neither male nor female," (recalling Gen. 1:27) although it has been used to make religious and social as well as physical distinctions, has also been abolished in the Christian community ("in Christ"). The differences, even physical differences such as circumcision, or sexuality, may be there, but they are no longer of any importance (cf. Eph. 2:15; 3:6).

But what of other passages, which some have understood to prove women should have a restricted ministry or none at all? Most would turn first to 1 Cor. 11:3-16:

3 But I want you to understand that the head of every man is Christ, the head of a woman is her husband, and the head of Christ is God.

4 Any man who prays or prophesies with his head covered dishonors his head,

5 but any woman who prays or prophesies with her head unveiled dishonors her head—it is the same as if her head were shaven.

6 For if a woman will not veil herself, then she should cut off her hair; but if it is disgraceful for a woman to be shorn or shaven, let her wear a veil.

7 For a man ought not to cover his head, since he is the image and glory of God; but woman is the glory of man.

8 (For man was not made from woman, but woman from man.

9 Neither was man created for woman, but woman for man.)

10 That is why a woman ought to have a veil on her head, because of the angels.

11 (Nevertheless, in the Lord woman is not independent of man nor man of woman;

12 for as woman was made from man, so man is now born of woman. And all things are from God.)

13 Judge for yourselves; is it proper for a woman to pray to God with her head uncovered?

14 Does not nature itself teach you that for a man to wear long hair is degrading to him,

15 but if a woman has long hair, it is her pride? For her hair is given to her for a covering.

16 If any one is disposed to be contentious, we recognize no other practice, nor do the churches of God.

Whatever else is said, it must be stressed that women are ''prophesying'' in public—the question is simply whether they cover their heads—and that men and women are defined as being interdependent (vv. 11-12). Great care must be taken with other parts of this section, so that we do not fall into error. We surely do not want to impose a heretical Christology on Paul, and therefore in verse 3 he cannot mean that Christ is ontologically subordinate to the Father, just as he does not mean that woman is subordinate to man in her nature. Paul is defending the decorum of his time and, in this kind of occasional writing, must not be pressed as if every verse had the same weight. Our final exegetical judgments about Paul's teaching must be made on the basis of the fundamental and total teaching of Scripture, on the very basis of the gospel itself. In the same fashion, in verse 7 Paul can hardly mean that woman was not made or is no longer made in the image of God, for this would conflict with Gen. 1:27. Again we can see that Paul, in his concern for the practice of his time, is not trying, in one verse, to spell out the whole of Christian anthropology or Christology. Finally, one very concrete question of interpretation is raised by our modern situation: when the gospel reaches a distant land where the men wear their hair long, is it necessary for them, for the sake of the gospel, to cut their hair (vv. 7, 14)?

More absolute, in the eyes of some, is the admonition in 1 Cor. 14:33b-36:

33b As in all the churches of the saints,

34 the women should keep silence in the churches. For they are not permitted to speak, but should be subordinate, as even the law says.

35 If there is anything they desire to know, let them ask their husbands at home. For it is shameful for a woman to speak in church.

36 What! Did the word of God originate with you, or are you the only ones it has reached?

However, if taken at face value, Paul would seem to be contradicting himself, for in 1 Cor. 11:5 his objection is not to women speaking, but to women speaking with their heads uncovered. The context would indicate that Paul is facing excesses in church practice and is trying to find a way to control them. In any case, what is the extent of this ''silence''? Are they allowed to sing and speak the liturgical responses? Are they allowed to speak their minds through a vote?

With these questions we have already begun to consider the issues in 1 Tim. 2:8-15:

8 I desire then that in every place the men should pray, lifting holy hands without anger or quarreling;

9 also that women should adorn themselves modestly and sensibly in seemly apparel, not with braided hair or gold or pearls or costly attire

10 but by good deeds, as befits women who profess religion.

11 Let a woman learn in silence with all submissiveness.

12 I permit no woman to teach or to have authority over men; she is to keep silent

13 For Adam was formed first, then Eve;

14 and Adam was not deceived, but the woman was deceived and became a transgressor.

15 Yet woman will be saved through bearing children, if she continues in faith and love and holiness, with modesty.

Women are to be sensible, silent, and submissive. The problem is: as we Christians take this passage strictly in all of its parts, do we therefore have to hold the line against braided hair, pearls, and gold ornaments? As soon as there are males over 20 years of age in a class in church, may no woman teach, not even indirectly through questions? How can we reconcile v. 14, that woman is to be subordinate because Adam was not deceived but the woman was, with Rom. 5:12-14, which speaks of sin beginning with Adam? By what method and with what authority can we use only part of this text or try to distill a central truth from the whole? Since we do not want to follow the traditional practice of the Jewish synagogue reflected here, we interpret, and we can only do justice in our interpretation when we use the gospel as our norm.

In several other places in the New Testament, reference is made to women being subordinate, and the important factor to consider is the context. In 1 Peter 3:1 wives are told to be submissive to their husbands, in order that they may be won not by a spoken but a visible word (cf. 1 Cor. 7:14); on the other hand, in 1 Peter 3:7 women, though the weaker sex, are called "joint heirs" of grace with their husbands (cf. Eph. 3:6). But of course we are reading here of marriage, not the ministry, as is also the case in Col. 3:18 and Eph. 5:21-33; as a consequence, these passages do not apply to our question. And yet in Eph. 5:21-33:

21 Be subject to one another out of reverence for Christ.

22 Wives, be subject to your husbands, as to the Lord.

23 For the husband is the head of the wife as Christ is the head of the church, his body, and is himself its Savior.

24 As the church is subject to Christ, so let wives also be subject in everything to their husbands.

25 Husbands, love your wives, as Christ loved the church and gave himself up for her,

26 that he might sanctify her, having cleansed her by the washing of water with the word,

27 that he might present the church to himself in splendor, without spot or wrinkle or any such thing, that she might be holy and without blemish.

28 Even so husbands should love their wives as their own bodies. He who loves his wife loves himself.

29 For no man ever hates his own flesh, but nourishes and cherishes it, as Christ does the church,

30 because we are members of his body.

31 "For this reason a man shall leave his father and mother and be joined to his wife, and the two shall become one."

32 This is a great mystery, and I take it to mean Christ and the church;

33 however, let each one of you love his wife as himself, and let the wife see that she respects her husband.

as in 1 Peter 3:7, the reciprocal and interdependent nature of the relationship between man and woman in Christ is brought out; in verse 21 it commands: "Be subject *to one another*" for Christ's sake, and in verse 25 husbands are to love their wives as Christ loved the church, giving himself up for her. The wife, on her part, does not have her being from her husband, nor does she have her significance from her husband, but she too is to follow Christ's example (vv. 22-24, 33); Christ is the true head (Col. 1:18) just as he is the true image God imparted in Baptism (Rom. 8:29; Col. 3:10), true man and not simply true male.

From the New Testament therefore we conclude that women, too, exercised the priesthood of all believers, and thus they, too, were involved in the whole gospel ministry. This is demonstrated by the fact that in the complex society of New Testament times, women carried out ministerial functions far in advance of their day; today when the limitations of that society are no longer with us, we should make use of the freedom and responsibility which we are given in the gospel.

Joseph A. Burgess

Regent, North Dakota

Exhibit C

Some Observations on the Orders of Creation and the Office of Ministry

1. The concept *kephale* is not applied to the apostolic ministry, or to any offices within the early Christian community, within the New Testament. Therefore, any application of this concept to apostolic ministry is an inference which does not have direct warrant in the text itself.

2. I must confess to being somewhat ill at ease with an absolute use of the orders of creation/fall. There is an order of creation which the Bible insists on all the way through. In Gen. 1:29f. plants rather than animals are given for food. This is modified (now an order of the fall?) in Gen. 9:2-4 to permit man to eat animal flesh, but not the blood of animals. In Acts 15:20; 21:25 this prohibition of eating blood is said to continue to be valid for Gentiles. Neither The Lutheran Church-Missouri Synod nor The American Lutheran Church has deemed it necessary to apply this, even though it is a general principle rooted in the order of creation which the New Testament continues to apply to all men. With what justification? Or is it purely arbitrary which of the "orders of creation/fall" continue to be applied strictly without it being regarded as a violation of Scripture?

3. I am not much more comfortable with an absolute application of the relation of man and woman as an order of creation—more properly in Genesis an order of the Fall (Gen. 3:16; 2:24 almost seem to imply a matriarchal society)—in terms of its concrete application. Generally it applies to the subordination of the wife to the husband in the family (Gen. 3:16; 1 Cor. 11:2-16; Eph. 5:21-33; Col. 3:18f.), although it seems to be extended more generally in 1 Cor. 14:33b-36 and 1 Tim. 2:8-15. In the Old Testament it does not seem to hinder God from making the prophetess Deborah judge over Israel or the Israelites from submitting to her rule. What does this mean practically for Israelis or Indians? Should they refuse to submit to their government because they are ruled by women which is a violation of God's will? If, as seems probable, the U.S. should elect a woman president in the not too distant future, will it be The LCMS's position that their people should refuse to submit to the government, since it would mean being ruled over by a woman in obvious violation of the will of God and the order of creation? Or does this order of creation/fall apply only within the redeemed community? When we encounter matriarchal societies in the mission fields, must they change their social structure in order to be Christian? It is far from clear to me how a rigid, absolutized use of the idea of orders of creation is to be applied concretely to life in the world in which we live. Not even God seems to have applied it strictly.

4. None of the passages which speak about women's role in the church speak about the apostolic ministry as such. It does seem clear that if these passages were applied in their literal sense, they would exclude women from functioning in the office of ministry, since they prohibit women from speaking in church and from teaching men, as well as prohibiting them from braiding their hair, wearing jewelry, and praying or prophesying without veiling their heads because of the angels (1 Cor. 11:2-16; 14:33b-36; 1 Tim. 2:8-15; 1 Peter 3:1-6). But it is clear that The LCMS does not regard it as necessary to apply these passages literally in their own practice, i.e., not applying them literally does not violate their commitment to and obedience to the will of God as revealed in Scripture. With what justification?

5. These passages make no distinction between general principles applicable at all times and the concrete applications they make. Any such distinction is imported into the text by the interpreter rather than being derived from the text itself. To make recognition of such a distinction normative is to abandon the Scripture principle and to make the interpreter lord over Scripture, not obedient to it. Indeed, the interpretation of LCMS that women praying or prophesying with their heads veiled only represents a custom that is therefore not binding (1 Cor. 11:16) in distinction from general principles, is completely contrary to what Paul himself says in the text. Paul says that he recognizes no other practice, nor do the churches of God (RSV).

6. One cannot accuse others of a lack of commitment to Scripture and its authority for failing to apply literally passages one does not himself apply literally.

Neither of our churches has deemed it necessary to apply the passages about women in the church in their direct, literal sense, and these passages do not speak directly about the office of apostolic ministry. If the objection is rooted in the orders of creation so that women are not to have authority over men, but are to be subordinate, the question takes the form: does the office of apostolic ministry involve authority over others?

1. In the gospels Jesus consistently rejects the idea that the apostles are called to positions of authority over others: "And Jesus called them to him and said to them, 'You know that those who are supposed to rule over the Gentiles lord it over them, and their great men exercise authority over them. But it shall not be so among you; but whoever would be great among you must be your servant, and whoever would be first among you must be slave of all.'" (Mark 10:42-44. See also Matt. 20:25-27 and Luke 22:24-27.) This is then grounded in Jesus having come not to be served but to serve. "But you are not to be called rabbi, for you have one teacher, and you are all brethren. And call no man your father on earth, for you have one Father, who is in heaven. Neither be called masters, for you have one master, the Christ. He who is greatest among you shall be your servant; whoever exalts himself will be humbled, and whoever humbles himself will be exalted" (Matt. 23:8-12). Thus, our Lord Jesus Christ does not grant authority over other people to the apostles, although he does give them authority over the unclean spirits (Mark 6:7).

2. To be sure, all authority in heaven and on earth belongs to Jesus. One may also speak of the authority of the gospel, or its power, which is associated with its relation to Jesus (he is the gospel), God, and the Holy Spirit. There is no clear evidence that those who are the ministers of that gospel are given authority over those to whom they proclaim it.

3. This same understanding of apostolic ministry in contrast to having authority over others characterizes Paul. In distinction from the Corinthians, who are rich and reign as kings, the apostles do not rule, but are weak, dishonored, suffering, cast off, etc. (1 Cor. 4:8-13; 3:21-23). Indeed, such weakness on the part of the apostle who proclaims the gospel is an essential part of his ministry and belongs to the character of the gospel (1 Cor. 1:17—2:5). Hence, although he is free from all men, he becomes a slave to all men for the sake of the gospel which he proclaims (1 Cor. 9:19-23). In the long discussion of the apostolic ministry in 2 Cor. 2:14—6:13 the same thing applies, so that Paul can say that they do not preach themselves, but Jesus Christ as Lord and themselves as the

Corinthians' servants (4:5). Hence the power of God and the life of Jesus is manifested in their weakness, in their always being given up to death for Jesus' sake (4:7-15). This same dialectic of their weakness as the vehicle for God's power is developed again (6:3-10). Hence Paul can insist again and again that they do not commend themselves and rejects those who pride themselves on a man's position and not on his heart (5:12). The same pattern is followed in Paul's defense of himself in 2 Corinthians 10-13, even though he can speak of his authority, which is for building them up and not destroying them (10:8; 13:10). But it is a strange kind of authority, which has the shape of weakness and suffering, which is the vehicle for God's power in them (13:3-4), so that Paul can be glad that he is weak and the Corinthians strong (13:9).

4. Hence, it appears in Jesus and in Paul that the concept of authority over others or the concept of *kephale* does not apply to the office of apostolic ministry, but is explicitly excluded. If this is so, no conclusions can be drawn from the order of creation which can be applied to the office of apostolic ministry, since the *kephale* structure does not seem to be valid for that function.

5. This is not different when it comes to the Office of the Keys, for, as Luther correctly emphasized ("Concerning the Ministry," *Luther's Works,* 40, pp. 25-28), the New Testament passages do not give this authority only to a particular class of Christians, but to all Christians. Indeed, the Office of the Keys is nothing other than the preaching of the gospel which, along with Baptism, is given to women as well as men (p. 25—in the section of the discussion of the administration of the Lord's Supper).

6. The two possible exceptions in the New Testament involve the use of the word *pro-histēmi* in 1 Thes. 5:12 and 1 Tim. 5:17, where the RSV translates it *rule*, or *be over*. First, as is well known, the relation of the office of the elder in the New Testament, which at times is simply a continuation of the office of the elders in the Jewish synagogue, to what we call the office of apostolic ministry is somewhat ambiguous. There is clearly a distinction between the office of elder and the office of an apostle. Second, while *pro-histēmi* may be translated "be at the head of, rule, direct" it can also have the meaning "be concerned about, care for, give aid," or even "engage in." Since it is a standard rule of interpretation that the ambiguous passage be interpreted in the light of the clear, the interpretation of this verb in these passages would have to focus on the second meaning, which also fits in the context. It is also of interest that Rom 16:2 uses a feminine nominal cognate of this verb of a deaconess Phoebe in her relation to Paul.

7. To be sure, one can speak of the authority of the apostolic ministry in a refracted sense, but not in the sense of having authority over others or ruling over others. It is a kind of authority that lies in weakness, in serving, in a lack of overt authority, that one cannot claim for one's own person or position. It is an authority or power that resides wholly in the gospel, i.e., in Christ or the Holy Spirit, which manifests itself as God's power precisely in our lack of power or authority. It is far from clear to me that for women to participate in this kind of ministry poses any kind of threat to the authority of husband over wife/men over women in the order of creation. If Luther can say (somewhat sarcastically in the context), "A woman can baptize and administer the Word of life, by which sin is taken away, eternal death abolished, the prince of the world cast out, heaven bestowed; in short by which the divine majesty pours itself forth through all the soul," what else is there that Scripture gives to the office of the apostolic ministry? (See *Luther's Works,* 40, p. 25.)

Duane A. Priebe
Wartburg Theological Seminary

Exhibit D

Statement by the Evangelical Lutheran Theological Seminary Faculty on the Ordination of Women

1. Purpose

President Knutson requested faculty responses to basic questions:

1. Do you find that the Scriptures forbid the ordination or service of women in the ministry of Word and sacrament?
2. Do you find in the Scriptures, orders of creation which enunciate a principle of women being subordinate to men which then pertains directly to the role women should serve in the ministry?

President Knutson included Luther Seminary's brief statement (Exhibit E) and Joseph A. Burgess' paper on the ministry of women in the church (Exhibit B). Our faculty voiced approval of both documents. However, we felt that we could best discharge our responsibility to the ALC committee meeting with Missouri if we would again review some of the basic passages and reconsider some of the interpretative principles involved. What follows is some of the information made available to the faculty to stimulate discussion.

2. Procedure

Exhibit A: New Testament

Brief Review of Situation—Ordination of Women

Primary Texts

Interpretative Difficulties

Major Hurdles

Exhibit B: Systematics

Exhibit C: Discussion

Note: Wherever possible, recent and available resources have been used and cited. Excellent discussions have appeared in print and therefore ought to be used.

3. Exhibit A—New Testament

a. A Brief Review of the Situation

A number of Lutheran churches ordained women before 1959, including Denmark, Norway, France, Holland, and Czechoslovakia. The Swedish debates of the late 1950s particularly brought the subject to the attention of many of the Lutheran laymen. The appearance of Krister Stendahl's study, *The Bible and the Role of Women* (Facet Series—Fortress) clarified many of the issues (the study appeared in Sweden in 1958 and was printed in English translation in 1966).

The debates and discussion in Sweden proved to Americans that the subject—ordination of women—was not a simple issue. Serious studies of various theologians confirmed this. Of those, two will be cited:

1. Peter Brunner—"The Ministry and the Ministry of Women" *Lutheran World,* December, 1959, Volume VI, no. 3, pp. 247-274. In this article he opposed the ordination of women. His arguments particularly centered around orders of creation and the Kephale structure.
2. Margaret Thrall—*Ordination of Women to the Priesthood* (1958) voices a strong approval of ordination. She rejected the use of criteria such as "the status of women in society generally" or emotionalism resulting from the very idea of women's

ordination. She based her argument particularly on the change in status for women which adheres in the "New Israel."

In addition to the publications of Brunner and Thrall, an ALC committee (1957) composed of Alfred Hoefner, Paul Leo, and Theodore Liefeld offered a fine analysis in their study entitled "The Status of Women in the Church." One conclusion of that report ought to be cited: "The question of ordination of women for the ministry presents special problems which exist to the same degree in other professions. Whether it would be wise to provide constitutionally for the ordination of women in the church is a question beyond our assignment or church-related competence to decide. But we do not find in 1 Corinthians 14 or 1 Timothy 2 a theological prohibition against such a procedure, because these passages cannot be applied as an ecclesiastical rule" (p. 7).

A review such as this provides a helpful introduction for our discussion. It shows also why the booklet entitled *The Ordination of Women* (condensed by Raymond Tiemeyer), published by LCUSA, was a necessary venture if there is to be clarity in discussions.

b. Primary Texts

Interpretations haven't always been the same, but the biblical texts have. Generally, three texts are cited as presenting the controversial crux of the problem: 1 Cor. 11:2-16; 14:33b-36; 1 Tim. 2:8-15. Before referring to the texts themselves, the fundamental insights suggested by Hoefner, Leo, and Liefeld can well be emphasized: (1) We can discover the heart of the message in these passages only in the broader context of Paul's teaching and that of the whole New Testament concerning men and women transformed by the experience of grace. (2) Any "issue" dealt with by Paul in the Corinthian church situation must be approached and seen in the light of a pervasive congregational problem—disorder. An evidently dominant concern in his mind, in view of developments there, is protection of the church against all sorts of disruptive, destructive, "non-edifying" influence. He feels the need for regulating the conduct of a church threatened by many irregularities.

In a delightful and positive (brief) article, "The Place of Woman: A Look at the Biblical Evidence" (*The Reformed Journal* [March 1972] pp. 7-12), Karen DeVos draws attention to another matter pertinent to our discussion. Concerning ordination she writes, "A church seeking God's guidance ought not to decide such questions simply on the basis of current social thought. Still, it should realize that trends in society can make it aware of prejudice in its interpretation of the biblical evidence" (p. 7).

1. 1 Corinthians 11:2-16

Context: This text is only a portion of the discussion regarding the Christian assembly. The next section, 11:17-34, focuses attention on the Lord's Supper. (Note: No attempt has been made to be exhaustive. Many details, significant and intriguing in themselves, are not pertinent to the discussion. For good discussion, see C.K. Barrett, *First Epistle to the Corinthians,* Harper, 1968).

Verse 2: Paul begins with a reference to the tradition which at this stage was handed on orally from evangelist and teacher to convert. From other descriptions we can assume that they were the central truths of the Christian's faith.

Verse 3: Here we encounter the *Kephale* structure. A chain of relationships is set up: God-Christ-Man-Woman. What kind of correspondence is intended? Note Burgess' statement: "We surely do not want to impose a heretical Christology on Paul, and therefore in verse 3 he cannot mean that Christ is ontologically subordinate to the Father, just as he does not mean that woman is subordinate to man in her nature." Obviously there are difficulties in interpreting this in a straight-forward fashion. The Burgess statement ought to lead us to be wary of overinterpretations. What does this mean?

Verses 4–5: In the verse itself, Paul writes about the *kephalen autou* and *kephalen autes* (or *heautes*). Does he in the first instance speak of the man's head or of Christ? In the second instance of the woman's head or of man? Interpretations vary—the main point is that what is appropriate for man is not necessarily appropriate for woman and vice versa. Throughout the chapter it seems that Paul is speaking to those in the married state. It seems correct also to assume that a woman can offer public prayer and utter prophecies. Paul, allowing for such matters, nevertheless is defending the decorum of his time.

Verse 6: Note that the character of the statement is rhetorical. Paul assumes that everyone will agree with it. This verse refers to a practice which is not very clear to us. The proper custom is that the woman is to be covered. The man disgraces his head by wearing a veil, the woman by not doing so.

Verse 7: Man is called an *Eikon* of God; what about the woman? Is she not an *Eikon?* Paul does not give specific answer to that question; but such a deduction hardly seems warranted (cf. Gen. 1:27f).

Verses 8-9: Paul now moves to Gen. 2:18-23. Barrett says (p. 253), "as Adam was brought forth directly from God and was made for his sole service, so the woman was brought forth from man, and was intended from the beginning to be his helper . . . this is her role in creation: it is not her role in Christ, in whom such distinctions are removed. . . ."

Verse 10: "That is why" (RSV) the previous statement is to clarify. But it really doesn't remove the difficulty of interpreting this verse. Difficulties: Why a reference to angels? Are the angels regarded as guardians of the divine order? The latter is a possible interpretation. Why a reference to exousia? Does the word simply refer to a veil-showing subjection? Is it a sign of her own (power) or dignity as a woman? These and other interpretations have been offered. Varied interpretations of verse 10 are possible, whichever one chooses. Paul's general point of view in the text seems to be supported (at least it is not contradicted).

Verses 11-12: This significant parenthesis interrupts the detailed argument concerning woman's subordinate position in creation and her relationship to her husband. Following these verses, Paul continues the argument about distinction.

Note the "in the head." Together, man and woman make a unity in which each is essential. *And all things are from God* (v. 12). Barrett says (p. 255), "Men and women alike owe their existence to God and depend on him."

Verses 13-15: Paul returns to the subject of dress in worship. He appeals to these Christians to reach a common sense decision. Note: *Prepon estin*—"it is fitting, proper, right."

Verse 16: It is difficult to conclude whether the statement stresses Paul's authority or conciliatory spirit. At any rate, here is a reference to a general Christian practice.

2. 1 Corinthians 14:33-36

   Context: In preceding sections, Paul speaks about all prophesying—one by one—of course, in the freedom of the Spirit.

   Verse 33: God is a God of peace.

   Verse 34: In our passage, we have to do with "silence in the church" *as the law says*. We are not told which law Paul has in mind. Possibly, he is referring to Gen. 3:16. Words—*ou gar epitrepetai autus lalein* (RSV) "For they are not permitted to speak"—women should keep silence (RSV):

   Verse 35: This verse shows us that there isn't to be a lack of interest. The verse evidently contemplates married women primarily; they are to ask husbands when they arrive home.

Verse 36: The Corinthians will be well advised to keep an eye to general practice. They do not have a monopoly on the gospel or on its interpretation (see Barrett, p. 333).

3. Comparison

   A great problem seems to arise when we compare the "injunction to silence" (1 Corinthians 14) with 1 Corinthians 11. The first impression seems to be that they are contradictory. But are the differences so basic? In 1 Cor. 11:5, the women can pray and prophesy in the presence of others. In 1 Cor. 14:34, the woman is not permitted to speak. Some interpreters conclude that the silence here stands in contrast to asking questions, not to preaching, teaching, or prophesying. There is, then, no real tension between this passage and the reference in Chapter 11 to the fact that women may prophesy. (One interpreter stressing the preceding is Krister Stendahl, *The Bible and the Role of Women,* p. 30.) Others obviously differ.

4. 1 Timothy 2:8-15

   Context: Chapter 2—prayer and worship. Basically, the author here offers a repeat of Pauline injunction of 1 Corinthians 14. 1 Tim. 2:11: Silence—the reason for subordination (2:11 ff)—is grounded in Gen. 2:18f and Gen. 3:16f. It again seems to stand in tension with that stated in 1 Cor. 11:4. The passage does not introduce any new major difficulties.

c. *Interpretative Difficulties and Problems*

(Tiemeyer, *The Ordination of Women,* p. 25ff)

1. Scripture is the norm, but the norm isn't always found by simple literal reading. For ordination, there is no simple problem as we know. The Bible does not use the word at all.
2. How does one tell which scriptural instructions were to apply to the time in which they were written and which to all times? The early church lived in complex surroundings. We must distinguish between timely and timeless instructions. Here it seems that the Missouri Synod (Exhibit B—Resolution 2.04) doesn't really come to grips with the question. (See second paragraph.) If they had, it seems that they would have carried through the instructions rigorously. Note Stendahl, *The Bible and the Role of Women,* p. 39, footnote 38.
3. Taking the Bible as a whole also enters in. We cannot always deal with Scripture in bits and pieces. The conflict of 1 Corinthians 11 and 14 has to be seen in a broad context, too. It has to be seen in the light of the major emphasis of the Old and New Age.
4. How does one allow for development which took place during the New Testament period and in subsequent centuries? Society's view of women has undergone change.

d. *Major Hurdles as Some Interpreters See Them*

In our discussions with Missouri, major hurdles have again been mentioned. As they see it, there are difficulties to ordination.

1. Commission on Theology and Church Relations—Missouri Synod. Woman's subordination to man is written into the very structure of the universe—"orders of creation" argument. (Tiemeyer, p. 10.)
2. Headship structures. Here the argument develops, in a sense, from the orders of creation. Subordination is considered because order is necessary in church and home (cf. 1 Tim. 3:1-5). But does the passage grow out of the orders of creation, or does it just come from the culture of the day? Is it rulership or leadership service that is being talked about?

Note Tiemeyer, page 16—"At the inter-Lutheran consultation in Dubuque, this difference was sharply marked. Those who said headship was basically a divinely-given, rulership power thought it would be violated if a woman were ordained. Those who said headship was basically leadership service *(diakonia)* thought a woman in the ranks would not destroy the order.

Note how Joseph Burgess begins his study.

4. Exhibit B—Systematics
Orders of Creation, Headship, and the Ordination of Women

The term *orders of creation (Schöpfungsordnungen)* originated in 19th century neo-Lutheranism and seems to have been coined by Adolf von Harless. Already Luther and Calvin advocated ideas similar to those contained in the term orders of creation, but they do not use the term. Neither does the New Testament use the term (RGG³). The idea of orders of creation has been under heavy attack, especially because of the unfortunate use of the term by some theologians who tried to give the ideology of a Germanic master race its metaphysical foundation. Thus the term has even been labeled heresy. Karl Barth, for instance, objected that we no longer live under the orders of creation, whether pertaining to the creation prior to or after the Fall, but that we live under the orders of Christ. This means we live in an eschatological and anticipatory context. Walter Künneth, on the other hand, objected that the term orders of creation neglects the preservational character of our existence and the reality of evil. Thus he suggested replacing the term orders of creation with the more realistic term *orders of preservation (Exhaltungsordnungen.* Cf. Künneth, *Politik zwischen Dämon und Gott).*

Werner Elert is the most influential Lutheran representative of the idea of orders of creation *(The Christian Ethos).* He attempts to show the dynamic structure of these orders by declaring that both mankind and nature have their being in specific is-contexts. While the is-context in nature can be gathered from the so-called laws of nature, the human is-context is presupposed in the biblical laws, such as the Ten Commandments. While laws of nature cannot be violated by nature or by mankind itself, the very fact that biblical laws are commanding laws shows that the human is-context is open to contradiction.

Orders in the human realm are orders of use or misuse and can pertain to us either as conditional or as unconditional orders. For instance, the good Samaritan found himself in the context of a conditional order to assist the one who had fallen among the robbers from the time he saw him until he was cared for. Then the condition of the order ceased. Unconditional orders, however, are not limited to a specific time span and depend either on our own decision or are given to us through birth. For instance, to enter a certain profession depends on our own decision and the agreement connected with it is binding for us once we make it. To be a citizen of a particular country or the son of certain parents, however, does not depend on our decision, because we are always born as citizens of a particular country as children of certain parents.

Yet these different levels of orders do not confer upon us a certain ethical quality, but denote the field of operation within which we live and for which we are responsible to God. Elert sees here an affinity to Luther's concept of *Stand,* a term which should not be confused with a certain social standing, but which signifies a certain area of responsibility. Elert mentions that it is one of the worst misunderstandings that could have happened to Luther to interpret his understanding of *Stände* as meaning different classes of people. And Elert finds it strange that this long refuted opinion still emerges every now and then (since the English translation is very free at this point) [*Christian Ethos,* 80 cf.] the German original: "Es ist, man muss schon sagen, obwohl auch heute wieder dieser alte Ladenhüter hervorgeholt wird, das schlimmste Missverständnis, das Luther an diesem Punkte widerfahren konnte" [*Das christlich Ethos,* 115].

Luther emphasizes that in whatever state *(Stand)* man is, he is responsible to God and the world according to the *ordo ecclesiasticus,* the *ordo occonomicus,* and the *ordo politicus*—ecclesiastical, economic, and political order (cf. Althaus, *Die Ethik Luthers,* 43). These orders are holy orders and instituted by God. We stand in these orders regardless of whether we are servants, widows, princes, or virgins. Thus the *ordo ecclesiasticus* is not reserved for the pastor and neither the *ordo politicus* for the prince. Though our social status is more anchored in one order than in the other, our belonging to all three is as necessary as the interdependent subdivisions of these three main orders, such as pastor, deacon, layman in the ecclesiastical order, or father, mother, child in the economic order. It is wrong to restrict anyone to one order or aspect of life. A child is not just a child and thus a member of the economic order, but also a layman and thus a member of the ecclesiastical order, and a subject or citizen in the political order. If we did not have responsibility in all three orders, Luther would hardly call the parents (not just the fathers!) "apostles, bishops, and pastors" of their children (Althaus, 100).

Of course, there are attempts made to read into the Bible an order principle by which certain people are restricted to certain classes. Francis Pieper, for instance, asserts that "there is no difference made between male and female in regard to participation in the gifts of Christ. . . . The woman shared with man also the dominion over the creatures." And yet he suggests that "Scripture teaches that woman in her relation to man occupied a position of subordination even before the Fall." Pieper therefore concludes that "woman is forbidden to exercise dominion over man" (*Dogmatics,* I, p. 524). His argument, however, gets completely out of hand when he assumes that this creational subordination excludes woman from attaining full participation in the ecclesiastical order. His quoting Paul as the authority for vetoing any public teaching of women in the church is not convincing either, even if Paul argues that according to the order of creation man was made first, then woman, and Adam was not deceived in the Fall but Eve. Pieper forgets that though on the level of the *ordo occonomicus* man certainly is the head of the family, both man and woman participate also in the other two *ordines.* It is primarily out of the social custom prevailing in Paul's time, namely of man being regarded superior to woman, that Paul in one instance forbids women to exalt themselves over men. But Paul does not argue his point by saying that women do not belong to the *ordo ecclesiasticus.*

Pieper himself borders on inconsistency when he attempts to use the order of creation scheme for prohibiting women from teaching publicly in church, saying: "It is universally acknowledged that woman is the most influential teacher of the human race. If women prove themselves good teachers in the home (Titus 2:3), they thereby wield a greater influence on the coming generation than the men, including the pastors and schoolteachers" (Pieper, p. 526). Teaching at home and teaching publicly in church is thus a formal (social) distinction which in no way affects the material content of what is being taught. This proves that a woman, having the position of a housewife or mother, is still not exempted from her responsibility in all three *ordines.*

As Paul did in his time, so we have to ask ourselves in our time how this responsibility can be brought to fruition in the best possible way. It might be good to remind ourselves of Paul Althaus, who, in the historic situation of emerging Nazi Germany, said in 1934: "Romantic conservativism of the 'good old law,' of the 'customs of our fathers' can be disobedience against the living will of the creator. To obey God also means: to take seriously the movements of history and the newness of each hour. Obeying God's order is not by necessity conservativism. God's order of property is not tied to the past human order of property, God's order of marriage is not the traditional bourgeoise marriage custom; God's law of inequality, dependencies, and relationships of command does not at all authorize us to cling to certain outmoded social orders as 'dependencies decreed by God'" (*Theologie der Ordnungen,* p. 13f.).

The term headship *(kephale)* is not so much a systematic as a biblical term. In gnostic terminology it indicates both the fundamental dominion of the *kephale* over the body and its union with the body. In the New Testament one of the most interesting and most controversial passages for the understanding of the *kephale* concept is 1 Cor. 11:2-16. In 1 Cor. 11:3, Paul presupposes a creational difference between man and woman which indicates that woman is ontologically dependent on man in a twofold sense (cf. Kittel, ThWB, III, p. 678): Woman is created from man and towards man (1 Cor. 11:8f.). Paul wants to emphasize in this passage the subordination of woman to man (cf. for the following Hans Conzelmann, *Der erste Brief an die Korinther,* pp. 216-225). Though in Christ the differences between man and woman no longer prevail (v. 4: men and women pray and prophesy in church services!), this does not remove the creational or natural differences between them. It becomes clear that Paul does not address himself in this passage to marriage problems but to the problems caused within the congregation by enthusiastic (gnostic) groups who want to tear down as no longer applicable all creational and natural differences between men and women. Though Paul urges the congregation to adhere to the traditional customs (v. 16), he attempts to back up his admonition with more than mere reference to what is customary in Christian congregations. He emphasizes that to cover her head is not just a custom for a woman, but it is an order of creation and therefore binding. Because of her natural weakness, the headcover symbolizes in a realistic way her protection against the cosmic powers (v. 10). Yet Paul does not go into details concerning an order of creation. In his conclusion (v. 16) he simply appeals to the Corinthians' sense of Christian unity and to the common customs. In other words, he rejects any enthusiastic egalitarianism that denies the eschatological "not yet" character of our Christian existence (see also 1 Corinthians 15). This means that there is no theological justification for obscuring the creational difference between man and woman, even if they function in the same way in the church. Concerning the ordination of women this would mean: Don't obscure the creational difference between men and women in attempting to make clergymen out of women, but let them preserve their female status, and let them be clergywomen with equal rights and functions.

Finally, a few remarks can be made concerning the ordination of women, which is neither implied in nor rejected by the idea of orders of creation or the concept of *kephale.* The Augsburg Confession Article VIII expressly mentions that Word and sacrament are efficacious even though they be administered by unworthy people. (Et sacramenta et verbum propter ordinationem et mandatum Christi sunt efficacia, etiamsi per malos exhibeantur). Thus to fulfill the conditions *in qua evangelium pure docetur et recte administrantur sacramenta* a superior (male) clergy is not constitutive. Further, the condition for publicly teaching in church or for administering the sacraments *(in ecclesia publice docere aut sacramenta administrare)* depends solely on being properly called *(vite vocatus).* It is left open in the Augsburg Confession, as well as in the New Testament passages which allude to or explicitly mention the priestly office, whether the one who is to be called should be male or female. In the Smalkald Articles (*Bekenntnisschriften,* p. 459) when Luther defines the church he does so by referring to the New Testament imagery of sheep and shepherd. Though the image of a shepherd might imply an authority figure, John 10 and other New Testament passages make it unmistakably clear that, notwithstanding the immense responsibility connected with the pastoral office, it involves by far more the role of a servant than that of dominion. This becomes even more obvious when Christ himself is referred to as the *kephale* of the church and the church, in turn, as his body (Eph. 1:22f.).

To sum it up: There is no sound theological reason that can be cited against ordination of women. One could only refer to tradition, saying: We have never done it, and we aren't about to change. Yet we can remember Luther's struggle with the problem of infant Baptism, where he rightly argued that one must have good reasons if one wants to change ancient customs. This would also apply to the custom of not ordaining women. Parenthetically we want to list two (good) reasons for ordaining women.

a. The position of the woman is no longer confined to homemaking and bearing and rearing children. Women make valuable contributions to all facets of life, and they could also make their contribution to the pastoral office of the church.

b. There are hardly any full-time avenues open for well educated and dedicated women who want to serve the church. In following the paths of Fliedner, Löhe, and other equal opportunity pioneers of the 19th century, it would be good for the church to accept and seek the full-time service of well educated and dedicated women even in its pastoral office.

5. Exhibit C—Discussion

In the discussion following the two presentations the following issues were raised:

a. Paul draws his analogy on the status of women from the Old Testament. But in the Old Testament, there is no single status of women set forth. Legislation reflects this, in that laws about women are adapted and updated, thus reflecting women's changing status.

b. In the New Testament, the "order of redemption" is primary and in many instances takes precedence over the orders of creation. The very nature of the gospel is that of redemptive freedom.

c. In Paul's interpretation of the Old Testament there are illustrative and homiletical allusions. These should not be taken as prescriptive statements.

d. All the New Testament passages studied refer to married women. Is there any significance here?

e. The passage in 1 Timothy 2 is a deliberate sacrificing of freedom in favor of order. Is this binding in every situation?

f. The question of ordination, either of men or women, is not discussed in the New Testament at all. The question of function is, and women are definitely included.

Following the discussion, a summary statement was drawn up by Dr. Liefeld:

a. It is quite evident that the apostle Paul reaffirms the orders of creation, as this system subordinates woman to man—not in personal *value* but in *status*. When he faces the question, "How can the status given to woman in creation find proper expression in her life and conduct?" his answer is in terms of the existing rules and customs of decency and feminine propriety, as standardized by conservative Jewish practice. The wearing of a veil or headdress was required for a Jewish woman. It was a matter of custom and decency that women did not speak in the synagogue. It may be seriously asked by what authority or reasoning the one directive becomes any less binding than the other in our day.

b. But there's a more important question. The case for perpetuating *either* of these directives in the present time is founded in a distinctly Old Testament orientation. What are the implications of a New Testament gospel orientation? What influence do the orders of creation have on the order of redemption (or perhaps better, vice versa)? Paul clearly declares the latter (gospel) in Gal. 3:28: "There is neither Jew nor Greek, there is neither slave nor free, there is neither male nor female; for you are all one in Christ Jesus." Christ calls men and women to be children of God. They participate in the same grace. This equality before the merciful God does not eliminate their differences, but it certainly influences and completely transforms their mutual relation, and it makes them true partners in their Christian life and true cooperators in the church with equal responsibilities.

c. It is amply evident that Jesus himself dealt with woman in a way widely different from the attitude reflected in the rabbinical Judaism of his day. It is also evident that Paul was wrestling with the problem of giving expression to this new attitude. The "growing edge" of his gospel insight manifests itself in the significant exceptions to the prevailing rule—the women who in some sense were coworkers with him in the propagation of the gospel

d. Priscilla (first named) and Acquila were "expounders" *(exethento)* to Apollos of the way of God (Acts 18:26), and both were his "coworkers" *(synergoi)* in Christ Jesus (Rom. 16:3). Phoebe, in the same passage, is identified not only as a "deaconess" *(diakonos),* but as one "set over others" (*prostatis*—supervisor, presider). Euodia and Synteche in Philippi were "competers together with Paul" *(synethlesan)* in the gospel (Phil. 4:3). And of course 1 Cor. 11:5 recognizes the "prophesying" *(propheteuo)* of women in the church (without some sort of audience the word would be meaningless). One thing at least seems evident: there were such instances of women functioning "in the gospel," and under Paul's recognition and apostolic authority.

Exhibit E

Statement by Luther Theological Seminary Faculty on the Ordination of Women

In relation to the first question, "Do you find that the Scriptures forbid the ordination or service of women in the ministry of Word and sacrament?" we reaffirm our statement of October 1968 to the Church Council and do not consider it necessary to formulate another.

In response to the second question, "Do you find in the Scriptures, orders of creation which enunciate a principle of women being subordinate to men which then pertains directly to the role women should serve in the ministry?" we submit the following:

1. We regard the entire Bible as the Word of God to be taken seriously as authority in all matters of faith and life. Yet there is no sentence or section which can be properly understood apart from its setting in a particular historical context. On the other hand, there is no sentence or section which can be ignored or disregarded as being no longer relevant. The task of biblical interpretation is to ask of the entire Scripture the question of contemporary meaning in the light of historical meaning.

2. The phrase "orders of creation" is not found explicitly in the Bible or in the Lutheran Confessions, but has been formulated theologically to assert the biblical and confessional confidence that God continues to work in and with his creation and that his desire is for cosmos (order) and not chaos. It is clear in the Bible itself that this ordering of the creation, in particular of society, utilizes different structures at different times and places. We are thus bound, for instance, to take seriously and regard as Word of God New Testament words about slaves being obedient to masters. But we are also bound to seek out ways to understand how the living God of the Bible is carrying out his work of ordering his creation in our time and place, particularly in relation to appropriate social and ecclesiastical institutions. Or, we receive the words "Be fruitful and multiply" as Word of God. But we believe that obedience to this command may require acknowledging changes that have taken place since the words were first given.

3. The churches in New Testament times worked in a culture which accepted as normal the subordination (and probably inferiority) of women to men as it did of slaves to masters. The remarkable thing is not that one finds expressions of this view in the New Testament, but rather that the way in which these relationships are treated in the New Testament has been instrumental, in cultures touched by the gospel, in the abandonment of the institution of slavery and the elevation of the status of women.

4. Ministry, with or without the definite article, is described in a number of ways in the New Testament. We consider the theme of "servanthood" to be more central and helpful than that of "authority," both in understanding (the) ministry in New Testament times and in carrying out (the) ministry in our present situation.

5. We do not, therefore, "find in the Scripture, orders of creation which enunciate a principle of women being subordinate to men which then pertains directly to the role women should serve in the ministry."

Exhibit F

Statement by Wartburg Theological Seminary Faculty on the Ordination of Women

The faculty of Wartburg Theological Seminary hereby submits its respectful and prayerful reply to your letter of March 24, 1972, which posed two questions about the ordination of women:

1. Do you find that the Scriptures forbid the ordination or service of women in the ministry of Word and sacrament?
2. Do you find in the Scriptures, orders of creation which enunciate a principle of women being subordinate to men which then pertains directly to the role women should serve in the ministry?

We have given serious thought and discussion to these questions, but especially to the biblical hermeneutics involved. Our answer to both questions is a unanimous "No!"

As concerned teachers in various departments of theology, our individual argumentations would differ in adducing and weighing exegetical, systematic, historical, practical, and sociological points and evidences. But in essence, we would cover and include such statements as the following:

The Ordination of Women

1. We hold that there exists no specific or direct reference to this question in the Scriptures. We agree with the opinion of the study sponsored by LCUSA, that such ordination is neither inculcated nor forbidden. Our general position must therefore be based on other, broader scriptural considerations.
2. Even *ordination* as used in the church is not discussed or prescribed in the Scriptures, though there is mention of the laying on of hands. The Scriptures do not delineate in a formal manner the practice of ordination as an exclusive rite, nor establish the divinely intended existence of an ordained clergy separated from other believers as a definitive order of Christian ministry.
3. Even less is there any indication in the Scriptures that ordination is subsumed under, or integrally related to, some order of creation, whatever that might be taken to be.
4. "Authority" to minister in the church is therefore, simply, to be empowered to serve, to proclaim the gospel, to edify the church of Christ. According to the Scriptures it is not a legal authority, a formal right, least of all a power to rule over others (medieval misuse of the "power of the keys"). Christ calls all believers to love, to serve, and to witness.
5. We therefore prefer to seek another approach than selecting single verses in Paul's contemporary epistles to his congregations, or linking these with supposed orders of creation set in Genesis and connected with past cultures of mankind.
6. For us the Lord of the church is Jesus Christ *(solus Christus),* and he represents the centrality of the Scriptures. In his name alone there is redemption and eternal life. The joyous privilege of the church is to teach, proclaim, and celebrate this gospel. The knowledge and possession of, and witness to, this good news is the happiness and the impulse of every believer.
7. Since the gospel must rule the whole life of the Christian, and is the final authority for the church in every matter of faith and life, it is also determinative for a proper understanding of the position of women in church and society.

8. The gospel emancipates. It sets free from former things, from the old life, from the curse and bondage of the Law, and brings us into the glorious liberty promised to the children of God. This emancipating power of the gospel has been clearly manifest in human history in the gradual elimination of serfdom, slavery, oppressive autocracy, and the denial of suffrage to women. It removes the fence between Jew and Gentile, between slave and master, It casts down color barriers and racisms of all kinds.

9. In Jesus Christ both men and women are rendered free and equal (Gal. 3:28). The gospel plays no favorites. It does not make men wholly free but women only partly free.

10. Guided by the Holy Spirit, living "in Christ," all—men and women—are to use those gifts with which God endows each person. These include intelligence, scriptural understanding, eloquence, empathy, as well as sex and temperament. Not to use these gifts, even as a body might refuse to use one of its members, can only mean the ultimate impoverishment both of the individual and of the group.

11. What the New Testament sets forth (and what *ordination* would refer to) is the "office" (Augsburg Confession, Article V) which the Holy Spirit governs, the duty and function and blessing of public proclamation. This office belongs to the church and to the individual congregation. They are, in our Lutheran understanding of the freedom of the New Testament, permitted and empowered to call, or employ, under proper regulations, qualified and fit persons to serve in proclamation, teaching, the diaconate, etc.

12. Ministry is a call to servanthood and not a special dignity of persons (*ordo* in the sense of the Roman Catholic priesthood and hierarchy). The Scriptures make us all kings and priests unto God (1 Peter 2:9-10; Rev. 1:6). We hold firmly to the priesthood of all believers. This universal priesthood advanced by Luther in 1520 is today accepted also in Roman Catholic theology.

13. In view of all the above, the question whether the church or some part of it may call and ordain—or call but not ordain—women is a matter of the church's freedom in exercising her function of sharing the gospel and administering the sacraments. No hermeneutical principles preloading the view we might take of the Scriptures, the confessions, of "orders" as theological constructs, or of the fitness or unfitness of change in human history over the centuries, should be allowed to obscure or curtain the freedom the church has, in Christ, to exercise its function of witness and proclamation.

14. We cannot for a moment concede an exegetical handling of Gal. 3:28 which interprets and translates this crucial verse as indeed expressing liberation, the elimination of bars or special preference, equality in Christ—for Jews and Greeks, for the slave and the free—but then goes on to assert another "ideal relationship" between man and woman which reestablishes a SUBordination, a submissive inferiority of woman under man before and in Christ. We believe one must take this passage, Gal. 3:28, as a cardinal statement in the Scriptures precisely FOR the emancipation of all men and of all women, in Christ, from the disabilities of past time, ancient pagan cultures, and the consequences of sin and the Fall—after which Christ has made us a new creation.

15. We therefore hold hermeneutically that Paul had to interpret the gospel in the context of the traditions, settings, and customs of his day. In the face of the obvious disorder in the new Corinthian congregation (quarreling parties, incest, lawsuits, disgraceful communion feasts), he had to insist on some basic regularities. He naturally adhered to the custom of the Jewish synagogues he knew, where women did keep silence and often sat behind a lattice or on a balcony reached by a separate entrance. But such directives of Paul, even regarding persons not known to us today, ought not be

interpreted as binding upon people with other cultural patterns or social relationships, providing these are not contrary to the gospel of Jesus Christ.

16. The Scriptures also testify in a number of passages that God made use of women as leaders, teachers, and prophetesses (Deborah in Judges 5; Huldah the prophetess in 2 Kings 22:14ff.; Priscilla in Acts 18:26, who taught Apollos more perfect knowledge). At Corinth it seems women did prophesy or speak the Lord's word (1 Cor. 11:5 where Paul seems to fault their behavior on another point, an uncovered head; see 11:3-4). On the other hand it appears that women also voluntarily kept silent in that modesty which Paul commends.

17. When we turn to the suggestion of orders of creation (or fallen creation) supposed to be established by God for mankind and in the church, we must again assert that the Scriptures do not know the term. Luther speaks of "stations and vocations" (Paul Althaus, *The Ethics of M. Luther,* pp. 36-42), in which God uses persons to serve him and their fellowman. Luther urged everyone to carry out such vocations in full loyalty and devotion to God.

18. But we note that *orders* in this sense came into theology in rather recent history as abstract concepts, devised by theologians who thought they would be helpful in speaking of human life and social structures. Yet we find much that has been said about orders is vague, abstract, incautious, and sweeping, without precise definition as to contents. Such concepts often obscure actual historical facts or block a true understanding of life.

19. We are willing to suffer the term if it is to mean "areas, fields, or arenas of human life in which the will of a loving God may be at work—ruling, guiding, advancing—redeeming, transforming, sanctifying—his own." In other words, if one will take them as *dynamic* concepts, subject to change under God.

20. We are very dubious about orders of creation (or fallen man) if they are to be understood in Christian theology and human life as *absolutes,* beyond alteration or correction. Such a view petrifies the status quo of the past millennia of mankind in its agonies and struggles and freezes humanity within a moralistic or legalistic straitjacket. This occurs frequently when the orders are said to be from God, but their form and content is not clearly and perceptively described, when they are even generalized.

21. Thus government (Greek *exousia,* Rom. 13:1) is said to be from God. But there is no definition of what sort of human government, and obviously these have varied enormously and are subject to periodic change. States have ranged from anarchy, cruel tyrannies, oligarchies, the divine right of absolute kings, and glorious and inglorious revolutions, to many types of democracies, to ochlocracy, or the dictatorships of communism. How much of this would we want to underwrite as divine? Lutheran fondness for *Romans* 13 (about an empire that disappeared a thousand years before Luther) has led to some doubtful past history in church-and-throne relations in German territorial states, especially when princes of poor spirituality and low morals were called *summi episcopi.* Law comes from God and so does justice—but legal systems vary in many lands, the legal codices are constantly modified by legislators, and precedents set in fallible, sometimes corrupt courts. The medieval church spoke about a "just price," without understanding much economics, and Luther denounced "usury," but modern civilization is build not without some reason on capital and interest.

22. Over against the loose employment of orders of creation when speaking of, or in direct support of, the state, the throne, the magistrate, the economic system we have, the legalized establishment (e.g., quandry of churchmen and officers vs. Hitler to whom they had taken a personal oath), there stands the curious attempt to establish some

concrete positiveness regarding the order of marriage, which is to affect, if not culminate in, the spiritual dependency of woman on male proclamation in the church of Christ.

23. We believe one is on sounder and more responsible ground hermeneutically when one puts aside the term *orders,* and reads Paul's specific comments on the behavior of women in the first century within the context of the culture, the social and religious mores, of that time, beginning with the Jewish synagogues and the somewhat harsh Jewish attitude toward women. We hold to the emancipating power of the gospel in all situations, including the relationship between the sexes.

24. Biblical hermeneutics must not merely weigh most carefully what the Scriptures say, as a whole and in individual parts, but also be alert to the opportunities in the constantly changing world to which the Word of God must apply. It is our historical judgment that we are living in a happier age of sensitivity to human rights, of changing social attitudes and institutional policies. Flexibility rather than firm rigidity is indicated for the church. Clinical studies and the various social sciences may help us to understand that opportunities for Christian nurture and service could be optimized, and the viability of the church enhanced, by the admission of qualified women to ordination and to service in the Word and sacraments. We may safely leave the future to the Holy Spirit.

Endnote

(*Note:* It has been objected that Paul shifts his Greek construction after the first two opposed pairs (Jew/Greek, slave/free), and then employs *kai* to link male and female in some different relation. Against this, we profess to see in Paul's slight shift of phrasing merely a faithful mental echo of the Septuagint's phrase for Gen. 1:27: ''male and female (*arsen kai thylu*) created he them.'' In Genesis 1 and 2, before the Fall, there is no hint of any *sub*-ordination of woman. She is also made in the fullness of the divine image, a fit counterpart, helpmate and partner to man. Note that Paul in Rom. 10:12, where he again juxtaposes Jew and Greek, uses the connectives *te kai* without any idea of above or below one another.)

(Editor's note: Portions of the preceding statement originally appeared in Greek; these phrases were transliterated to English to aid the reader.)

Notes: *After the American Lutheran Church began ordaining women, its relationship with the Lutheran Church—Missouri Synod became strained. The 1971 Conference of the Missouri Synod narrowly rejected a proposal to eliminate fellowship ties with the ALC, but it did pass legislation which halted further ecumenical programs. When the Missouri Synod asked the ALC to reconsider its position, ALC President Kent S. Knutson again polled seminaries and leading thinkers, and printed the results as part of the 1972 Convention Report of the Committee on Inter-Church Relations. Included here are papers by the Wartburg Theological Seminary, Luther Theological Seminary, the Evangelical Lutheran Theological Seminary, Joseph Burgess, and Duane A. Priebe. The statement of the Evangelical Lutheran Theological Seminary in particular addresses the primary points of conflict with the Missouri Synod—the orders of creation and headship.*

EVANGELICAL LUTHERAN CHURCH IN AMERICA

CAN WOMEN SERVE IN THE ORDAINED MINISTRY? (1973)

Introduction

The Church Council of The American Lutheran Church at its meeting on June 6, 1972, requested the general president, Dr. Kent S. Knutson, to arrange for the preparation of a paper on the ordination of women to be available for study groups in congregations. The council was concerned that congregation members have opportunity to examine and discuss the basis on which The American Lutheran Church authorized the ordination of women at its 1970 General Convention

The president asked a member of the Commission on Fellowship with the Lutheran Church—Missouri Synod, Dr. Joseph Burgess of Regent, North Dakota, to prepare a manuscript to fulfill the request of The Church Council. Dr. Burgess had presented a paper on this subject for that commission, which was included as an exhibit to the Report of the Inter-church Relations Committee to the 1972 General Convention of The American Lutheran Church (reference pages 465 to 469, *1972 Reports and Actions*). It was one of five exhibits related to the issue of the ordination of women that had been developed in response to the action of the Lutheran Church—Missouri Synod at their 1971 Convention. Dr. Knutson reviewed the manuscript prepared by Dr. Burgess prior to his illness following the 1972 General Convention.

Reports regarding the Lutheran Council study to which Dr. Burgess refers and studies within The American Lutheran Church were published in the *1968 Reports and Actions,* p. 156; the *1970 Reports and Actions,* pp. 141, 326-328; and *1972 Reports and Actions,* pp. 459-461, 463-468.

On behalf of the Church Council, I express appreciation to Pastor Joseph Burgess for his efforts in developing this booklet.

Arnold R. Mickelson

General Secretary,

The American Lutheran Church

Can Women Serve in the Ordained Ministry?

Does a woman have any business in the pulpit? Lutherans have long assumed that pastors should be male. To many, female pastors have seemed awkward, annoying, and absurd. Suddenly, it seems, women are preaching sermons, and one is even listed on the ALC clergy roster.

Why should these developments come as a surprise? Just as women today have taken their place in all other professions, they have also studied theology and requested ordination. Within the Lutheran family, Norway led the way. Since 1938 the government has had the right to appoint women pastors if they were not rejected by the congregation. However, the first woman was ordained in 1961. Denmark permitted the ordination of women in 1947, Czechoslovakia in 1953, Sweden in 1959, France prior to 1962, and most of Germany by 1968. Well over half of the Lutherans in the world belong to churches which now have women on their clergy rolls. Outside of the Lutheran family, the major churches permitting ordination include the Reformed churches of Switzerland, Germany, and the United States, the Methodists, the United Church of Christ, the Baptists, the Disciples of Christ, and the Pentecostals. The major exceptions are the Orthodox, the Roman Catholics, and the Anglicans.

In the United States all three major Lutheran bodies became involved in a study of this question within the Division of Theological Studies of the Lutheran Council in the USA. In 1970, at the invitation of the ALC, the presidents of these three bodies distributed a summary of this study to all of their pastors. On March 7-8, 1969, the Division of Theological Studies concluded: "In examining the biblical material and theological arguments we find the case both against and for the ordination of women inconclusive." Therefore "a variety of practices at any given time remains possible amid common confession." For this reason, the study pointed out, it would be unrealistic to expect individual Lutheran bodies to conform with all other Lutherans, "but it is hoped that any single church would seek to act only after consultation with fellow Lutherans and with sensitivity to the entire ecumenical spectrum."

After this consultation within the Lutheran Council, the Lutheran Church-Missouri Synod continued to oppose the ordination of women, but in 1970 both The American Lutheran Church and the Lutheran Church in America decided to ordain women.

How can Lutheran Churches which teach that Scripture is the Word of God disagree on the ordination of women?

Article 7 of the Augsburg Confession states: "For the true unity of the church it is enough to agree concerning the teaching of the Gospel and the administration of the sacraments." What is decisive is the Gospel. In Scripture we read the Gospel, God's Word to us, that Jesus Christ is Lord, that he died for our sins and was raised that we might have life.

Unfortunately some are not satisfied that the Gospel is enough. They insist that we must hold to "the Gospel and. . . ." Of course, we Lutherans have always been concerned with many points in theology, and we have even been preoccupied with the glories of theology. But when all is said and done, as Lutherans we confess that it is enough to agree on the Gospel and the administration of the sacraments. Nothing else is central; everything else is secondary. The ordination of women is at least several steps removed from the center. How can the question of whether or not women are to be ordained either add to or subtract from the Gospel? The Gospel is not affected by this or like matters on which Lutherans of even the same synodical body often differ. Therefore we may in good conscience agree to disagree on such matters.

But why have we not ordained women before?

Change is disturbing, but it may be necessary. The biblical writers presupposed a three-storey universe, but now we think of the universe as heavenly bodies which travel in orbits around each other. One of the weaknesses of Western civilization was its acceptance of slavery; Patrick Henry could declaim, "Give me liberty or give me death!", but he would have been surprised if at that point his slaves had asked him for their freedom. The church has always been very much a part of its time. When Western civilization in the eighteenth century began to change its attitude toward slavery, the church also began to change, and today we consider slavery unjust. Some Lutherans in America used to consider fire and life insurance unchristian; at present very few would agree. At one time there were serious tensions between German and Scandinavian Lutherans in the United States, but in recent times these tensions have disappeared. It was not too long ago that most Lutherans in North America used theological arguments to oppose birth control.

Our forefathers in America held that women's suffrage in church matters is unbiblical, yet around the turn of the century, as the movement for women's suffrage in public life grew, some Lutheran churches gave women the right to vote. After the United States Constitution was amended in 1919 to permit women to vote, the rest of American Lutheranism gradually followed suit, until finally in 1969 the Lutheran Church—Missouri Synod also allowed congregations to grant women voting rights.

And why ordain women now? The times have changed. Women have taken their places with men in our society. They are in all occupations except those requiring great physical strength. We have learned to consider women and men equal in the body of Christ. Dare we then make absolute the attitudes toward women that were held in biblical times? Shall we quote Scripture to insist that women be veiled in church, that they be separated in balconies during worship services, that they be forbidden to cut their hair?

Does the ordination of women change the effectiveness of the Word and sacraments?

The Word and sacraments are effective without regard to the state of grace of the one who acts (this question was settled in the early church), but also without regard to the sex of the minister. The Lord's Supper is not effective because Christ is male or because the celebrant happens to be male. We allow women to baptize in emergency situations. The Lutheran confessions declare:

> Besides, the ministry of the New Testament is not bound to places and persons, as the Levitical priesthood is, but is spread abroad through the whole world and exists wherever God gives his gifts, apostles, prophets, pastors, teachers. Nor is this ministry valid because of any individual's authority but because of the Word given by Christ.

The German version continues:

> The person adds nothing to this Word and office commanded by Christ. No matter who it is who preaches and teaches the Word, if there are hearts that hear and adhere to it, something will happen to them according as they hear and believe . . . ("Treatise on the Power and Primacy of the Pope," Section 26)

Luther would permit women to preach and even to administer the sacraments in cases of necessity. (We find such references in Luther's works, *Weimar Edition,* 8, 424-425, 489, 497-498; 10, 111, 171; 12, 180-181; 30, 111, 524; 50, 633).

What is ministry?

Ministry is servanthood. What this means is spelled out in those famous Gospel passages calling for men to humble themselves, not to be served but to serve, and acted out in the washing of Peter's feet.

> But you are not to be called rabbi, for you have one teacher, and you are all brethren. And call no man your father on earth, for you have one Father, who is in heaven. Neither be called masters, for you have one master, the Christ. He who is greatest among you shall be your servant; whoever exalts himself will be humbled, and whoever humbles himself will be exalted (Matt. 23:8-12).

We find similar references in Mark 10:42-45; Luke 22:24-27; John 13:1-11. Christ emptied himself, taking the form of a slave (Phil. 2:7). We are to be like him, pouring ourselves out for others, like a slave having no rights, never lording it over others (1 Peter 5:3). As slaves we have no other authority, no other appeal, than that of the Gospel.

Does the ministry of the ordained differ from the ministry of all other Christians?

The ministry rings a different bell in our ears. The Lord has given particular gifts to particular people for the sake of his church. These particular people are within the church, but at the same time they have a responsible relationship to the other members of the church. Their function is to study and know the Word of God (though this does not exempt the other members from being well-grounded in the Word). Ordained pastors use the Word of God to equip and inspire the pilgrim people on their march. Ordained clergy do not exercise power over the church in the way authorities do in political life, for they have no other authority, no other claim, than that of the Gospel. Like Christ, who never did his own will, but was obedient even to death on the cross, they are servants, emptying themselves for others. Persons in the ordained ministry are servants of the Word, and their power is only that of pointing to and exemplifying the Word.

In the New Testament the lists describing these particular ministries differ and are incomplete (Rom. 12:6-8; 1 Cor. 12:28-31; Eph. 4:11-12). No ministry corresponding precisely to contemporary Lutheran concepts of "the ministry of the Word and sacraments" appears. The church has felt free to drop certain of these ministries, and to expand and add others. All of this indicates that the church is free to use diverse models of the ministry as times change. Whenever a particular need is met by particular people pointing to and exemplifying the Word, their function is an authentic model of the ministry.

What then is ordination?

Ordination is not defined in Scripture. The Conféssions once call ordination a sacrament, but this is immediately limited to the Lutheran understanding of the ministry of the Word ("Apology of the Augsburg Confession," 13, 10-12). The New Testament does speak of "the laying on of hands," but Lutherans have not been divided over methods, rites, or ceremonies of ordination.

The power of the keys, the phrase used for the authority to declare forgiveness of sins, does not belong "to the person of one particular individual, but to the whole church . . . for the same reason the church especially possesses the right of vocation" ("Treatise on the Power and Primacy of the Pope," Sections 24-26). Therefore the basic issue with ordination is: has this person been "regularly called" by the church? ("Augsburg Confession," 14) To be "regularly called" means that the church is led by the Holy Spirit to recognize that God has equipped certain people to apply his Word to particular needs. Nothing in the church's power of the keys prevents a woman from being "regularly called."

But the New Testament says: "Women should keep silence in the churches."

The opponents of women's ordination stress three passages, which were all written by the Apostle Paul:

> [3]But I want you to understand that the head of every man is Christ, the head of a woman is her husband, and the head of Christ is God. [4]Any man who prays or prophesies with his head covered dishonors his head,[5]but any woman who prays or prophesies with her head unveiled dishonors her head—it is the same as if her head were shaven.[6]For if a woman will not veil herself, then she should cut off her hair; but if it is disgraceful for a woman to be shorn or shaven, let her wear a veil.[7]For a man ought not to cover his head, since he is the image and glory of God; but woman is the glory of man.[8](For man was not made from woman, but woman from man.[9]Neither was man created for woman, but woman for man.)[10]That is why a woman ought to have a veil on her head, because of the angels.[11](Nevertheless, in the Lord woman is not independent of man, nor man of woman;[12]for as woman was made from man, so man is now born of woman. And all things are from God.)[13]Judge for yourselves; is it proper for a woman to pray to God with her head uncovered?[14]Does not nature itself teach you that for a man to wear long hair is degrading to him,[15]but if a woman has long hair, it is her pride? For her hair is given to her for a covering.[16]If any one is disposed to be contentious, we recognize no other practice, nor do the churches of God. (1 Corinthians 11:3-16)

Whatever final conclusion is drawn as to the meaning of this passage, it is clear that women are prophesying and praying in public, and that men and women are defined as being interdependent (vv. 11-12). (The question is simply whether women cover their heads.) The context shows that Paul is defending the decorum of his time. Women are to be veiled in public. His arguments to support this can hardly be considered more timeless than the veiling itself, which today we think was only part of that time.

First: (v. 3) in one sense God is the head of Christ, for Christ was obedient to his Father, but in a very profound sense Christ is God himself, the creator of heaven and earth (Col 1:16). Just as Paul's statement here about Christ can only be used with great care, so his declaration that "the head of a woman is her husband" must be carefully restricted to only the marriage relationship, which in Ephesians 5:21 is described in very modern terms: "Be subject to one another" (See also Col. 3:18-19; 1 Pet. 3:1-7).

Second: (v. 7) Paul can hardly mean that woman was not made or is no longer in the image of God, for this would conflict with Genesis 1:26-27, which asserts that both men and women are made in the image of God.

Third: (v. 10) this verse is much discussed. Perhaps the angels are guardians of the created order, perhaps the woman should be veiled so that men are not distracted by her hair and

God alone is glorified during worship, and perhaps the veil, which also represents the covering of man's glory before God, is called "authority" because it symbolizes woman's new authority to pray and prophesy. What is certain is that Paul is arguing for veiling; the rest is uncertain.

Fourth: (vv. 7, 14) when the Gospel reaches a distant land where the men wear long hair, is it necessary for them, for the sake of the Gospel, to cut their hair? Is short hair a timeless decree from God?

> [33b]As in all the churches of the saints,[34]the women should keep silence in the churches. For they are not permitted to speak, but should be subordinate, as even the law says.[35]If there is anything they desire to know, let them ask their husbands at home. For it is shameful for a woman to speak in church.[36]What! Did the word of God originate with you, or are you the only ones it has reached? (1 Cor. 14:33b-36)

In 1 Cor. 11:5 Paul does not object to women speaking in public, but only to women speaking with their heads uncovered. However, as the context in 1 Cor. 14 shows, he confronts disorder in Corinth; for the sake of order in Corinth only two or three prophets are to speak (v. 29), one male prophet is to be silent when another begins (v. 30), and the women should be silent. But what is the extent of their "silence"? Are they allowed to sing and speak the liturgical responses? Are they allowed to pray? Are they allowed to speak their minds through a vote? Is this a law for all places and times?

> [8]I desire then that in every place the men should pray, lifting holy hands without anger or quarreling;[9]also that women should adorn themselves modestly and sensibly in seemly apparel, not with braided hair or gold or pearls or costly attire[10]but by good deeds, as befits women who profess religion.[11]Let a woman learn in silence with all submissiveness.[12]I permit no woman to teach or to have authority over men; she is to keep silent.[13]For Adam was formed first, then Eve; and Adam was not deceived, but the woman was deceived and became a transgressor.[15]Yet woman will be saved through bearing children, if she continues in faith and love and holiness, with modesty. (1 Tim. 2:8-15)

Women are to be sensible, silent, and submissive! Are we to hold the line against braided hair, pearls, and gold ornaments? As soon as there are males over twenty years of age in a class in church, may no woman teach—not even indirectly through questions? How are we to reconcile v. 14, that woman is to be subordinate because Adam was not deceived but Eve was, with Romans 5:12-14, which speaks of sin beginning with Adam? And does Paul really mean in v. 15. that only mothers will be saved?

Did the coming of Christ change the relationship between man and woman?

Although we continue to struggle with the old age, in Christ's new age all relationships are being transformed.

> There is neither Jew nor Greek, there is neither slave nor free, there is neither male nor female; for you are all one in Christ Jesus. (Gal. 3:28. See also 1 Cor. 11:10-11 above.)

In context this radical passage refers to baptism, but to be baptized into Christ means that both the religious and the social spheres are changed. All of life is changed. Nor does this passage refer exclusively to a glorious future to come. The resurrected Christ is effectively working now through Word and sacraments to transform life; in Christ we "have put on the new nature, which is being renewed in knowledge after the image of its creator." (Cor. 3:9-11. See also 2 Cor. 4:8-11, 5:17.)

To be sure, in the early Church many refused to take the phrase "neither Jew nor Greek" seriously. The early church debated the question as to whether the church should be more "Jewish" than "Greek" (Acts 15). The terrible tragedy of the fall of Jerusalem in 70 A.D. removed Jewish contact with the church to such a degree that the question no longer was a critical one. Finally this meant that not only "religious" but also "social" and "physical" distinctions (circumcision/uncircumcision) were considered unimportant. It took centuries for the church to assimilate the second pair of opposites, "neither slave nor free." We may excuse her, for there are New Testament passages which seem to support remaining "as you are" (1 Cor. 7:17-24; Philemon 16). Yet would any one of us today dare to use the New Testament to prove that merely the "spiritual" distinction between slave and free has been abolished? The third pair of opposites, "neither male nor female," is also no longer decisive "in Christ." Biological differences like circumcision and sex continue within the Christian community as a matter of course (for example, Paul's discussion of marriage in 1 Corinthians 7), but uncircumcision is transformed (Ephesians 2:15; 3:6) and the original equality of woman with man is restored (in Greek Paul shifts away from the exact parallelism of the other two pairs of opposites so that for the third he can quote from the Greek version of Gen. 1:27).

Women in the Old Testament were not considered members of Israel, but their status was continually changing as the laws were revised and improved. A few were even prophetesses (Exod. 15:20, see also Micah 6:4; Judges 4:4; 2 Kings 22:14; Neh. 6:14), and Deborah was a judge as well.

In contrast to all of this, women in the New Testament enter the church by the same rite as men. A woman was the first to see our resurrected Lord, women were the first to be told of our Lord's resurrection, and they were the first to be commanded to tell others of our Lord's resurrection (John 20:16; Mk. 16:7; Matt. 28:7; Luke 24:22-23). In this way they fulfilled a major function in the history of salvation. They proclaimed the Gospel as prophetesses (Luke 2:38; Acts 2:17, 21:9; 1 Cor. 11:5. See also Rev. 2:20), they served as deaconesses (Rom. 16:1; 1 Tim. 3:11), and Priscilla and Aquila, Paul's "fellow workers in Christ Jesus" (Rom. 16:3), "expounded the way of God more accurately" to Apollos (Acts 18:26).

To be sure, Jesus and the twelve apostles were male. But this was to be expected in the social context of the first century. Today we understand that Jesus Christ is the true image of God (Rom. 8:29; Col. 3:10), and also true man (completely human) and not simply true male.

Does the Bible describe a divine order of creation in which women are subject to men?

The term "orders of creation" means that God the Creator continues to uphold his creation (for example, nature, justice, marriage, and the state). Unfortunately the case made for orders of creation is often unclear and extreme. "Orders" are understood in a static sense, as if for all time God had determined a set pattern. Yet even the static approach to "orders" is not consistent, for those holding it do not require us to obey the natural order given in Genesis 1:29-30 to eat plants instead of animals, which then in Genesis 9:2-4 is amended to permit meat but not the blood, and in Acts 15:20, 21:25 is specifically applied to the Gentiles. And is the command to "be fruitful and multiply" in Genesis 1:28 to be carried out in an absolute sense?

God's ordering activity is dynamic. He is not a Creator who made a clock-like universe, wound it up, and then left it. Just as in his saving work God is conditional, judging if men disobey, restoring if men repent, so God continues to create. He continues to order his world in changed situations. When man fell, God allowed meat but restricted the blood. Man and woman were created free and equal within a harmonious world (Gen. 1:27-31), but after the fall man was subject to struggling with nature, and woman to childbirth and man's rule. (Gen. 3:16-19.) In spite of this, Deborah (Judges 4:4) ruled—and even as a married woman!

In the New Covenant the original cosmos is not only restored but also transformed by being in Christ. Women are no longer subordinate to men, but men and women are "subject to one another" in Christ (Eph. 5:21), interdependent in Christ (1 Cor. 11:11-12), joint heirs in

Christ (1 Pet. 3:7), and equal in Christ (Gal. 3:28). In Romans 16:2 the deaconess Phoebe is described as "a helper of many and of myself"; the word "helper" in this verse is the noun form of the verb translated "be over, rule" in 1 Thess. 5:12 and 1 Tim. 5:17. In the New Covenant neither a female church leader, nor a woman president of the United States, nor a matriarchal society is considered to be against God's will.

Does the ordination of women make any practical difference?

Yes and no. It is difficult to be so certain. Already women are ministering in ways that cover almost every function of the ordained ministry. They teach, lead in worship, counsel, organize and administer, baptize (every Christian nurse has done this), evangelize, study the Bible and lead in its study, write books of devotion and theology, encourage all in the faith, criticize and admonish, and serve with kindness and humility. And they preach—regularly on the mission fields, in Sunday school worship services, in hospitals, in classrooms, in meetings in their homes. Yet they do not preach in our pulpits! They head, sometimes, the whole religious education effort in a congregation or school. They assist in Holy Communion. Women are involved in every major decision made in a congregation. They are an inspiration of every stewardship program, the vanguard of every evangelism effort, the real workers in projects in the community, certainly the major work force in education.

Surely to add preacher from the pulpit and celebrant at the Lord's Supper to women's list of service opportunities is significant, but does it require of women any different talent or power or right that they do not already perform in the name of the Gospel?

I suspect that women will continue to choose marriage as their chief vocation, and as in the case of professions of law and medicine a relatively small percentage will prepare for the ordained ministry.

But practical differences? A few perhaps. A young woman who desires to be a pastor must consider seriously the effect of marriage on that vocation. Her duties to her husband and family would make her ministry a bit different from that of a man. She will remain a woman—and this may limit her effectiveness in some areas (whom she can effectively counsel) and increase it in others (as in her relations to women and in counseling areas that are difficult for a male pastor to handle). Just as a man may not be completely effective, because he is a man, so a woman may be limited by her womanhood.

In short, there are practical difficulties in the ordination of a man as well as in the ordination of a woman. These must be taken into account, but they are inconsequential when compared with the basic question, "Will ordaining women distort or lessen the Gospel?"

The answer is "no." Then what does hinder us?

Women *can* serve in the ordained ministry.

Notes: *This 1973 paper by Joseph Burgess was commissioned by the American Lutheran Church (which in 1988 merged with the Lutheran Church in America to form the Evangelical Lutheran Church in America) as a study guide to help the church membership understand why the 1970 decision to ordain women was made. Burgess reiterates that "a relatively small percentage [of women] will prepare for the ordained ministry," a belief expressed in many of the statements in this book. In many of the churches that first decided to ordain women, only a handful of women actually applied. Unforseen, however, was the drastic increase in the number of female ministers during the late 1970s and 1980s. Today, in fact, men and women students are about equal in number in many seminaries.*

LUTHERAN CHURCH-MISSOURI SYNOD

WOMEN IN THE CHURCH: SCRIPTURAL PRINCIPLES AND ECCLESIAL PRACTICE (1985)

Abbreviations

AC—Augsburg Confession

FC—Formula of Concord

Ep—Epitome of the Formula of Concord

SD—Solid Declaration of the Formula of Concord

Introduction

The twentieth century has witnessed a veritable revolution in the roles of women and men. To some degree this revolution is attributable to rapid societal and cultural change. For example, the continued process of urbanization has shifted the population from the farms with their relatively clear and traditional roles for women and men, into the increasingly bureaucratized cities, where traditional identities have become blurred. This transition and its concomitant upheavals have had some positive results. More opportunities are becoming available to women now than ever before. Their unique contributions to society are increasingly recognized. At the same time, dramatic changes in male-female roles have also produced confusion and uncertainty.

Perhaps this confusion and uncertainty has affected the church as much as any other institution. In the wake of the feminist movement, the campaign for the Equal Rights Amendment, and related sociological and political developments, various Christian denominations have become involved in discussions of the role of women in the life of the church. Should churches ordain women into the pastoral office? Should church polity be rewritten so that women may serve as elders or deacons? Is there any ecclesiastical position from which women should be excluded in principle? These and other similar questions have been prominent on the theological agenda of numerous church bodies.

The Lutheran Church—Missouri Synod has not been immune from these developments. Overtures to past conventions of the Synod, inquiries received by the Commission on Theology and Church Relations, and discussions in various forums reveal the need for careful study of this matter. In response to a specific request from the Synod that it study "the role of women in the church," the CTCR has therefore prepared this document in the hope that it will assist members of the Synod in their consideration of this important topic.[1]

As it prepared this study, the Commission was acutely aware of the difficulties attending an examination of this subject in a report of limited scope. A vast body of literature on the many aspects of women's involvement in the mission of the church exists, which continues to expand in the light of contemporary discussion. Moreover, fundamental issues relating to principles of Biblical interpretation are involved in the study of this question. The extent to which the Bible reflects the culture and customs of its own time and the relationship between Scriptural principles and their contemporary application are important examples of issues about which there is disagreement. Thus, the Commission acknowledges at the outset that not all issues ultimately pertaining to this subject can be addressed.

This study is comprised of three basic parts: first, a survey of the Biblical witness to the involvement of women in Israelite culture and worship, in the ministry of Jesus, and in the life of the apostolic church; second, a distillation of the primary principles which the Scriptures present concerning women in the church; and third, a discussion of the application of these principles in concrete matters of practice today. This report is not designed to be exclusively a study of the question of ordaining women to the pastoral office. While much of the content will impinge on that issue and while such a specific study may be desirable at some point in the future, the issue of women's ordination is not the focal question here. Similarly, the Commission does not intend this document to be a reworking of its 1968 report on "Woman Suffrage in the Church." Nor is the present document a study of male-female relationships in general societal or marital contexts, however important these may be.[2] Rather, the Commission seeks in this report to outline and integrate two themes clearly present in the Word of God: 1) the positive and glad affirmation of woman as a person completely equal to man in the enjoyment of God's unmerited grace in Jesus Christ and as a member of His Body, the church; and 2) the inclusion of woman (as well as man) in a divinely mandated order which is to be reflected in the work and worship life of the church. The proper correlation of these two Biblical teachings is crucial if the church's thinking on this topic is to be determined by Holy Scripture and not by the dictates of cultural demands. (John 8:31)

I. Women in the Scriptures: An Overview

The formulation and interpretation of principles regarding women in the church today must be carried out against the backdrop of the picture of women presented in the Scriptures. In both the Old and the New Testaments women are spoken of with deep respect for their personhood and for their vital work in the Kingdom of God. The commonplace contention that the Bible demeans women simply cannot be sustained if one takes seriously the Scriptures' recurrent affirmations of the service of women, who stand before God side by side with men as recipients of His gifts of grace.

A. The Old Testament

While Israelite culture was patriarchal in its structuring of family and clan, the Old Testament gives a prominent place to the character, leadership, and service of many women (indeed, two of its books—Ruth and Esther—are named for women). This truth is especially evident in the giving of the titles "prophetess" and "judge" to women and in the participation of women in individual and family worship of God.

1. The Old Testament prophet possesses a number of unique characteristics, but technically a prophet is one through whom God speaks. The Hebrew word for prophet is *nabi,* and its feminine form is *nebiak.* This term is used to refer to three specific women.[3]

   a. Miriam, the sister of Moses, was called a woman prophet when she sang a victory praise of God at the time of the Israelites' escape from Pharoah's army (Ex. 15:20-21). That she was one through whom God spoke is also clearly implied in Num. 12:1-2. Although there is little indication of her work beyond these passages, she is referred to as a leader on a par with Moses and Aaron in Mic. 6:3-4.

   b. Deborah, in Judges 4:4, is called a prophetess and also a judge in Israel. In the latter role Deborah exercised decisive leadership. When Israel was severely oppressed she called forth the will in the men of Israel to fight for freedom. The Israelite general said he would fight only if she led the way. Deborah gave the command to attack, and victory was secured (Judges 5). However unusual it may or may not have been for women to serve in major civil roles, the example of Deborah shows a woman raised up by God to govern and to deliver His people.

   c. The third woman given the title of prophetess was Huldah (2 Kings 22:14). When the high priest at the Jerusalem temple told Josiah he had discovered the book of the law of the Lord, the king sent his emissaries to find out what further message God had for him. They sought out Huldah who was well-known for her commitment to God and for her ability to speak for God. She told Josiah very clearly and specifically God's message.

2. In private and public worship in the Old Testament the participation of women went beyond the hearing and obeying of the law. They were free to approach God in prayer just as the men (Hannah, 1 Sam. 1:10; Rebekah, Gen. 25:22; Rachel, Gen. 30:6, 22).

God responded to their prayers (Gen. 25:23; 30:6, 22) and appeared to them (Gen. 16:7-14; Judges 13:3). They were also expected to take an independent part in bringing sacrifices and gifts before God. (Lev. 12:6; 15:29)

Women appear to have had certain circumscribed roles in the public worship, too. For instance, Hannah approached the sanctuary (1 Samuel 1). Women ministered at the door to the tent of meeting (Ex. 38:8), and while it is not clear what form this service took, it did play some part in the worship.[4] Women also participated in the great choirs and processionals of the temple (Ps. 68:25; 1 Chron. 25:5-7; Neh. 7:67). Although they were not permitted to serve as priests, this is never interpreted to mean that they were less than full members of the worshipping community.

In sum, although the Old Testament reflects the patriarchal nature of the society in which it was written and with which it is concerned, the relationship of women to their fathers and husbands did not stand in the way of their joyful participation in the worship life of God's people. In the words of Biblical scholar Mary J. Evans, "They had a significant role to play . . . not only in their role as mothers and in the home, but also as individuals, and they were not barred from leadership when the circumstances required it."[5]

B. The Ministry of Jesus

The New Testament manifests the same genuine appreciation and respect for women. Jesus' ready acceptance and inclusion of women in His life and work stands in sharp contrast to the disdainful and condescending attitudes toward women of so many of His contemporaries. He saw them as persons to whom and for whom He had come into the world. This can be seen in the interactions of the Lord with individual women, in the prominence of women in His parables, and in the actual participation of women in His ministry.

1. The encounters of Jesus with women illustrate both His willingness to associate with them and also His respect for their intelligence and faith. His conversation with the Samaritan woman (John 4:7-30) shows His willingness to dismiss conventions of men which stand in opposition to His purposes. Normally a Jew would not address a Samaritan and normally a man would not speak to a woman in public. However, the Lord's conversation with this woman shows how He disregards these conventions of society in order to communicate about Himself and the Kingdom. The Samaritan woman emerges in this conversation as a perceptive and articulate individual, fully capable of engaging in theologically profound discourse. Certainly, if Jesus had considered this woman to be an inferior being and unable to speak of spiritual matters, He would not have spoken to her in concepts presupposing prior knowledge (e.g., the concept of "living water," John 4:10). Nor would He have responded to her question about the place of worship (4:21). Her sex did not affect the manner of His approach to her. It is instructive to note that this woman is the first individual to whom Jesus, in the Johannine account, clearly reveals that He is the Messiah. She is also the first messenger of that revelation outside the circle of disciples (v. 29). The witness role of the Samaritan woman is emphasized by John. He says that the villagers "believed . . . because of the woman's word." (John 4:39)

   The conversation between Jesus and the Canaanite woman provides another example of the Lord's respect for women (Matt. 15:21-28). In this exchange it was the woman's faith in Him as the Messiah that Jesus perceived and that moved Him. She therefore receives a place in sacred history as the first Gentile convert.

   Many other encounters of Jesus with women demonstrate His striking concern for their faith and His brotherly love for them. Women were seldom pictured in Rabbinic literature as exemplifying trust in God or as possessing theological acumen. But Jesus sees women as exercising such virtues (the encounter with the repentant woman at the home of Simon, Luke 7:36-50; the woman who suffered with an issue of blood, Mark

5:25-34). Further, although the title "son of Abraham" was a standard phrase used throughout Hebrew and Jewish literature to refer to a member (male) of the chosen people, Jesus calls the woman he heals on the Sabbath "daughter of Abraham" (Luke 13:10-17). For Jesus, women were to be valued highly; He was interested in them as persons and received them as full-fledged participants in the blessings of the people and covenant of God. Their sex was an integral part but not the totality of their personhood.

2. The parables which Jesus tells presuppose, and thereby reveal, His acceptance of women as treasured members of the human family. They present women in ordinary activities which dramatically illustrate various points which Jesus wished to make. A woman mixing leaven in flour provides insights into the nature of God's Kingdom (Matt. 13:33). A woman looking for a lost coin illustrates the concern of God for lost sinners (Luke 15:8-10). The wise and foolish bridesmaids are examples of the need for everyone to be prepared for the unexpected moment of Christ's return (Matt. 25:1-13). A woman appears in a parable of Jesus to illustrate an aspect of the Kingdom of God such as perseverance in prayer (Luke 18:1-8). Thus, in dramatic contrast to His contemporaries, who frequently avoided mentioning women at all, Jesus often refers to women in His parables and sayings, always in a positive way.

3. Women were not only recipients of the Lord's ministry. St. Luke reveals that Jesus on numerous occasions gladly received the help and ministry of women (Luke 8:1-3). St. Mark attests that some women followed Jesus and ministered to Him when He was preaching in Galilee (Mark 15:40-41). Women were a part of His close circle of friends and companions. The verb *diakoneo* (to minister or serve), from which the English word "deacon" is derived, is used to describe what these women did in addition to "following" Jesus.[6]

   The inclusion of women among His close companions in a significant way witnesses to Jesus' positive attitude toward them. While it was not out of the ordinary for rabbis, for example, to receive support from women of means, it was most unusual that their followers should include women. But Jesus' attitude towards women encouraged them to take the extraordinary step of following Him, a striking breach of the custom of the day.

   When all the disciples except one had abandoned Jesus, women accompanied Him to the place of His crucifixion. They were present at His burial. These same women found the empty tomb, met the resurrected Christ and angels, and reported the news of His resurrection to His unbelieving disciples (Matt. 28:1-10; Mark 16:1-11; Luke 24:1-11; John 20:1-2, 11-18). None of them, however, is included among the number of the apostles; they were parallel to the disciples as traveling companions, but they were not included among the twelve.[7]

   Significantly, Jesus does not say anything about women having a specific role in life. He issues no commands that apply to women only. Rather, the value Jesus gives to women is displayed in His relationship with them. In these relationships He affirms their personhood and manifests a noticeable concern that they hear His message and understand it. He relates to them with love and respect. He speaks to them, teaches them, heals them. He never speaks of them in a contemptuous way and never treats them as if they were unimportant. Jesus never gives the impression that only men were "full Israelites." He regards women as One whose message and concern is for the whole people of Israel. Women stand alongside men as recipients of the universal invitation to the Kingdom through Christ. (Matt. 12:50)[8]

C. The Apostolic Church

Women were present in the upper room praying prior to Pentecost, when the Holy Spirit came upon the disciples (Acts 1:14; cf. 2:17-18). From that moment they, like men, were added to the Christian community, endured persecution and suffering, brought others to faith in Christ, and were involved in the building up of the body of Christians. The activities in which women participated varied, but they included prophesying, performing charitable services, and serving as missionary workers.[9]

1. Acts 21:9 and 1 Cor. 11:5 specifically indicate that women functioned as prophets in the early church. Commentators differ on exactly what kind of prophesying was done by women in the apostolic church—some take the association of prayer and prophecy as a description of officiating at public worship; others equate prophecy with preaching. While not much is said about the type of prophecy given, these interpretations are deficient. Prophesying is distinguished from preaching in Eph. 4:11. Preaching is a form of teaching, but the distinctive characteristic of prophecy is that it results from God having put His very words into the mouth of the one speaking (2 Pet. 1:21-22). In other words, the prophet depends on special inspiration to speak a message which is more than a product of human thought. While a prophetic inspiration could form the basis for an exhortation, prophecy was a message delivered as words from the Lord. It is evident that there were women in the apostolic church who were moved by the Spirit to prophesy. Certain women exercised a particular verbal gift.[10]

2. Charitable service—caring for the needy, the sick, the visitors—was a major activity among the early Christians, and the New Testament pictures women serving faithfully and actively in this way. Tabitha is described as being full of good works and charity (Acts 9:36). Widows, recognized as a group in the church (1 Tim. 5:3-16), dedicated themselves to prayer and intercession.

   This service role of women in the church is highlighted particularly by Paul's reference to Phoebe as a *diakonos* (Rom. 16:1-2). Many scholars connect this text with sources from the third century in which the office of deaconess appears clearly defined for the first time.[11] However, in the vast majority of its occurrences in the New Testament, the term *diakonos* means simply "servant" or "one who ministers" to another.[12] The apostle introduces himself, together with his co-workers, as a *diakonos* (servant, minister) of Christ, of the gospel, of the new covenant (1 Cor. 3:5; 2 Cor. 3:6; Eph. 3:7; 1 Thess. 3:2), and speaks of his apostolic work as a *diakonia* (Rom. 11:13). He also writes of Stephanas and his household who "have devoted themselves to the service of the saints". (1 Cor. 16:15)

   What Paul means, therefore, is that Phoebe, a representative of the Cenchreaean church, had been a helper of many, even of himself. The term "helper" *(prostatis)* most probably refers to a patron who by virtue of greater wealth is able to provide one with material assistance or moral support.[13] Phoebe's service is the basis for Paul's request to the Romans that they "take care of her in whatever manner she may have need of you" (v.2). They want to do for Phoebe what she has done for the apostle and others—assist them in their material requirements. Phoebe's ministry, then, like that of Stephanas and his household, was to assist the saints. This servanthood function was assumed by many men and women in the apostolic church.

3. The early church was very active in missionary endeavors. Christian communities sent many missionary workers from their home communities to plant new ones where there was no Christian church. While much of this missionary activity is mentioned, the New Testament focuses on St. Paul and his co-workers, many of whom were women.

   In Romans 16 the apostle greets some of these women by name and acknowledges their important contributions to the life and growth of the church. Priscilla is a woman who receives particular mention. She is greeted not only in Rom 16:3, but allusions to her also appear in Acts 18, 1 Cor. 16-19, and 2 Tim. 4:19. In Acts she is engaged with her husband, Aquila, in teaching the great orator Apollos. Priscilla must have been, therefore, well-educated in the teachings of the Christian faith and a most capable instructor.[14] Paul's reference to the couple as "fellow-workers" is to be noted. The term was used by the apostle for a number of persons who worked with him. (Rom. 16:9, 21; 1 Cor. 3:9; 2 Cor. 1:24; 8:23; Phil. 2:25; 4:3; Col. 4:11; 1 Thess. 3:2; Philemon 1, 24)

After Priscilla and Aquila, Paul greets still other women: Mary, Tryphaena, Tryphosa, and Persis, all of whom "worked hard" in the Lord (v. 12). Here Paul uses a term that commonly refers to the toil of proclaiming the Gospel (cf. 1 Cor. 4:12; 15:10; Gal. 4:11; Phil. 2:16; Col. 1:29; 1 Tim. 4:10). In Rom 16:13, 15 he greets the mother of Rufus and the sister of Nereus. In Phil. 4:2-3 he mentions two other women—Euodia and Syntyche—who have labored beside him in the gospel. Although it is impossible to determine from Paul's words what specific missionary tasks these women assumed, there is no doubt but that he often benefited from the cooperation of women in his apostolic labors and that women were no less fervent than men in spreading the gospel message.[15]

The early Christian churches followed the pattern established by Jesus of including women as integral members. They attended worship, participated vocally, were instructed, learned of the faith, and shared it with others. They also played a significant role in the life of the community, teaching men and women and caring for those in need.

Excursus on the Service of Women in the Early Church[16]

*Within the "official" ordering of the early church's life there were two primary orders of women: widows and deaconesses. From the beginning widows were recipients of the church's charity in return for which they were "appointed for prayer" (*Apostolic Tradition *11; cf. 1 Tim. 5:3ff.). According to Tertullian (c. 160-220 A.D.), the widows were an* ordo *(*Ad uxorem *1.7.4) and were assigned a place of honor within the assembled congregation parallel to that of the presbyters. In the third century, however, the widows received additional responsibilities. They exercised charity, especially to women, and they taught. Their teaching seems to have been restricted to inquiring unbelievers, for while widows could speak concerning idols and the unity of God, they could not speak about Christ and His work. Lest the pagans mock, inquirers about such matters were sent to the elders for instruction (for the widow, see* Didaskalia, Apostolic Constitutions*). In the* Testament of Our Lord Jesus Christ *(c. 450) widows were a part of clerical orders and had a broad range of responsibilities, primarily to women: teaching women catechumens, rebuking those who strayed, visiting the sick, anointing women being baptized and veiling them so that their nudity would not show, seeing to it that women attended church and that they did not dress in a provocative way. Obviously, many of the duties of the widows were dictated by concerns of modesty and social acceptance.*

The female diaconate was a very significant feature of the church within Greek and Syriac Christianity. The West did not have deaconesses until around the fifth century and then only reluctantly. From numerous sources (especially Didaskalia, Apostolic Constitutions*) an outline of the activities of the deaconess can be discerned. They*

1. *assisted the bishop in the baptism of women, especially in the anointing of the body. Here concern for modesty was uppermost.*
2. *assisted women who were in need or who were ill.*
3. *served as an intermediary between women and the male clergy.*
4. *guarded the door by which women entered and left the assembly and ensured that the younger women gave way to older women in the place reserved for them.*
5. *verified the corporal integrity of the virgins.*
6. *bore messages and traveled about on congregational business.*

7. *gave private instructions to catechumens when necessary.*
8. *within Syrian Christianity gave the Eucharist to women who were ill, to nuns, to young children and to their sisters (apparently other deaconesses), when a priest was not available.*

Indicative of the high status of deaconesses in the East was the fact that they were ordained as clergy. The Apostolic Constitutions *make this especially clear (8, 19, 20), but it is also confirmed by the wording of Canon 15 of the Council of Chalcedon (451 A.D.). On the other hand, Western, Latin sources are punctuated by prohibitions against the ordination of the deaconess.*

Yet, ordination did not give one access to all the functions of clergy. Ordination placed one into a specific ordo *with its own prescribed functions. Hence, a bishop could ordain, but a presbyter could not; a presbyter could baptize, but a deacon could not. Concerning the role of women, there is a general exclusion of them from priestly duties and from the public teaching. The patristic argument against women performing sacerdotal functions, while making use of Biblical passages such as Gen. 3:16; 1 Cor. 11:3ff; 1 Tim 2:12, 14, is often based on Scriptural history and Jesus' own ministry. Against the Collyridians, Epiphanius writes: "Never from the beginning of the world has a woman served God as priest" (*Panarion *79). He, then in litany fashion, reviews all those in the Old and New Testaments who served as priests. "But never," Epiphanius again concludes, "did a woman serve as priest." Similarly, the practice of Jesus is determinative: although Mary and other women were present with Jesus, he chose to be baptized by John and he sent the twelve apostles for preaching. Such an appeal to Biblical history and the practice of Jesus was not just an appeal to tradition. It was predicated upon the belief that Jesus was the incarnated Word of God by whom all things were made and through whom all things were redeemed. The* Apostolic Constitutions *make the point: Jesus did what He did, and He has delivered to His church no indication of women priests because He "knows the order of creation." What He did, being the Creator of nature, He did in agreement with the creative action. Similarly, since Jesus is the incarnate Word in whom the creation is being made new, He, as Head of the church, the new people of God, typified in His ministry the new life of the church not only in its "spiritual" but also in its fleshly contours.*

Corresponding to Priscilla, who taught Apollos, early Christian tradition was not devoid of women known for their missionary teaching and preaching. The Acts of Paul *(c. 170) tells of Thecla, who was commissioned by Paul to "go and teach" and who is depicted as teaching both men and women. The* Acts of Peter *mentions Candida, who instructed her husband in the faith. The* Acts of Philip *reports that Jesus sent out Mariamne with Philip and Bartholomew. One tradition makes Mary and Martha, together with Lazarus, missionaries to the Province (southeastern France). St. Nina is honored as the missionary who converted Georgia. The early church, therefore, did not apply the prohibition of 1 Tim. 2:12 to the mission context. John Chrysostom expressed the consensus: "But, when the man is not a believer and the plaything of error, Paul does not exclude a woman's superiority, even when it involves teaching."*

Nascent Christianity was located within a religious environment in which female deities and significant female religious leadership were not uncommon. The polytheism of Greece and Rome had both male and female deities (e.g., Juno, Minerva, Diana), and the mystery religions, oriented toward the natural cycle of birth-death-rebirth, not infrequently had primary female deities (e.g., Isis, Cybele). Not surprisingly, therefore, early Christian groups which evidenced syncretism often had women in prominent positions and assigned to them real theological significance.

In gnostic Christianity women frequently were regarded as the bearers of secret tradition and divine revelation. Sometimes they were conceived of as the very expression of divine thought (in direct analogy to the view of Jesus as "Word of God"). Simon Magus had a *female companion, Helen, whom he declared to be the "first thought of his mind." The gnostic Apelles was accompanied by Philoumene, a prophetess whose revelations he wrote down and who performed miracles and illusions. Elsewhere, Mary Magdalene was regarded as the bearer of secret knowledge (*Pistis Sophia, Gospel of Mary*), as was also Salome (*Egyptian Gospel*).*

*Irenaeus (c. 180) tells of a certain Marcus whose religious rites included the consecration of cups of wine by women (*Adversus omnes Haereses *1.134f). It is clear that "Marcosian gnosticism" was highly attractive to women of higher social rank. In addition, Marcosian tendencies were very resilient in Gaul (France), for at the beginning of the sixth century there were priests in Brittany who were assisted at the Eucharist by women.*

*Epiphanius of Salamis (c. 380) reports on two groups in which women were preeminent and possessed priestly status. The "Quintillians" honored Eve as the prototype of their female clergy, for she first ate of the tree of knowledge. They had women bishops and women presbyters, arguing that "in Christ there is neither male nor female" (*Pan. *49). (Interestingly, the "Quintillians" used Gal. 3:28 in the same way that contemporary "feminists" treat that passage.) The second group, the Collyridians, apparently consisted predominantly of women who venerated the Virgin Mary as a goddess and once a year on a special day offered up to her a loaf of bread from which all members partook (*Pan. *79). Firmilian of Caesarea (c. 260) tells of a prophetess in Cappadocia who celebrated the Eucharist and who baptized many.*

*Yet, within the church's own communal life the general prohibition of Tertullian seems to have been commonplace: "It is not permitted to a woman to speak in Church. Neither may she teach, baptize, offer, nor claim for herself any function proper to a man, least of all the sacerdotal office" (*De virg. vel. *9.1). This did not mean, however, that women were simply quiescent. They were not. Especially in the areas of Christian piety and spirituality women often exercised leadership and authority. Much of the early impetus toward monasticism was supplied by women of wealth and social rank such as Melania and Paula, whose monastic foundations were every bit the equal of parallel male foundations. The Eastern tradition knows of "spiritual mothers" as well as "spiritual fathers," and the sayings of three of them even occur in the "Sayings of the Desert Fathers." In contexts of martyrdom women by precept and example exercised real religious leadership (e.g., Blandina, Perpetua). Within Celtic Christianity dual monasteries of both monks and nuns not infrequently were governed by abbesses (e.g., Hilda of Whitby, who even participated in the "Council" of Whitby). But women were not permitted to hold the sacerdotal office in the early Christian church.*

II. Scriptural Principles

The foregoing overview of women in the Bible has shown that the New Testament is replete with affirmations of the personhood of women and of their valuable contributions to the work of the church. Women and men are equally members of the priesthood of all believers by faith in Jesus Christ. They are both called to "declare the wonderful deeds of Him who called you out of darkness into His marvelous light." (1 Peter 2:9)

Mindful of these positive declarations, we must now take into account specific directives in the Scriptures concerning the status of women in the church, as well as their theological foundation. That theological foundation—which dare not be distorted or ignored in attitude or action—is that both men and women have been created in the image of God (Genesis 1-2). The specific Scriptural directives regarding the service of women issue from the three texts most prominent in the contemporary discussions of women in the church: 1 Cor. 11:2-16, which speaks of the covering of the head; 1 Cor. 14:34-35, where silence on the part of women in the church is enjoined; and 1 Tim. 2:8-15, which restricts teaching and the exercise of authority by women in the church. These passages, in turn, entail four broader principles fundamental for providing counsel regarding what women may and may not do in the church today: 1) the proper appreciation of humankind as male and female equally created in the image of God; 2) the proper relationship between man and woman which God established at creation and how that relationship is to be specifically maintained in the church; 3) the proper understanding of ''headship'' and ''submitting oneself'' for defining male-female relationships in the church; and 4) the proper relationship between the distinctive functions of the pastoral office and the exercise of authority in the church.

A. Male and Female

The book of Genesis teaches that woman is a special creation of God (Gen. 1:26-27; 2:18-24). Like Adam, so Eve, ''the mother of all living'' (Gen. 3:20), was created in the image and likeness of the Creator. Although in Genesis 1 and 2 there are two accounts of the creation of humankind, they both express this truth.

1. *Genesis 1.* The emphasis of Genesis 1 is somewhat different from that of Genesis 2. A chronological schema is utilized to report the creative events which occur (day one, day two, etc.). Mankind is first mentioned in the account of the sixth day: ''So God created man (*Adam*) in his own image, in the image of God he created him; male and female he created them'' (Gen. 1:27). This passage refers to man in the generic sense, in two sexes. *Adam* is here used corporately and generically of the human pair or species.

   According to the Genesis 1 account of creation, male and female were both made in the image and likeness of God. That is, mankind's unique status among all other creatures derives from the relationship to the Creator. Mankind is not a physical replica of God nor an emanation of God; the image has to do with spiritual qualities—features that correspond and relate to the Creator. The Lutheran theological tradition has identified the *imago Dei* in the narrow sense with the original righteousness that mankind—male and female—enjoyed.[17] Luther writes, ''. . . the image of God is this: that Adam had it in his being and that he not only knew God and believed that He was good, but that he also lived in a life that was wholly godly; that is, he was without the fear of death or of any other danger, and was content with God's favor.''[18]

   Gen. 1:26-27 clearly shows that the woman, like the man, has been created in the image of God. Some scholars have argued that man was created in God's image and woman in man's image so that the image of God in woman is a reflected image. Others have suggested that since God reveals Himself as male (the Father and the Son), woman must be excluded from participation in the image. However, Genesis makes no such distinctions. There is no basis here for suggesting a superiority-inferiority relationship.[19] The New Testament continues to uphold this teaching of the equality of the image of God in both sexes (1 Cor. 11:7; Gal. 3:28; Col 3:10; Eph. 4:24). This equality is a spiritual equality of man and woman before God (*coram Deo*). The apostle Peter indicates that a woman must be granted honor as a fellow-heir of the grace of life. (1 Peter 3:7)[20]

   It is also clear from Genesis 1 that male and female are *equally* distinct from all other creatures made by God. God gave to both the command to ''be fruitful and multiply, and fill the earth and subdue it; and have dominion'' over the earth (Gen. 1:28). Male and female are given the same dominion. Both the blessing and commission of verse 28 assume that the man and the woman are equal before God in their relationships to the rest of creation.

2. *Genesis 2.* While Genesis 1 speaks in summary fashion of the creation of male and female, Genesis 2 gives a more detailed description of the creation of humankind. Gen. 2:7 describes the creation of a man as male. God created him from the dust and breathed into him the breath of life. He is commanded not to eat of the tree of the knowledge of good and evil. Then God says that it is not good for man (male) to be alone and that a

fitting helper (*ezer kenegdo*) must be found for him. The "helper" is the woman God creates. She is suitable for him as a "helper." She is not under his domination, but she stands alongside him in exercising that dominion which God has given to both. She is in every way his equal before the Creator.

When Adam saw the woman, he immediately recognized her oneness with himself. "This at last is bone of my bone and flesh of my flesh" (Gen. 2:23). As a creature of God, she is good. For man to seek some advantage over the woman would be defiance of the Creator whose very image she bears. Rather, man is to live under the Word of God which describes as good his relationship to the woman, his equal before the Creator.

To be sure, this spiritual equality does not preclude a distinction in identities between man and woman. Genesis 2 takes up also this matter, and its teaching is discussed later in this report under the concept of "order of creation." However, any such differentiation does not impair the validity of the clear principle laid down in the inspired record of creation: *Man and woman are equal in having the same relationship to God and to nature.*

B. Creation and Redemption

The concept of creation—God's work and will as revealed in the creation of humankind—is critical for dealing Scripturally with the issue of male-female identities. Also of great importance is the concept of "new" creation—God's work and will as revealed in redemption. Two more formal terms have come into general theological usage to indicate these realities:

1. *The Order of Creation.* This refers to the particular position which, by the will of God, any created object occupies in relation to others. God has given to that which has been created a certain definite order which, because it has been created by Him, is the expression of His immutable will. These relationships belong to the very structure of created existence.

2. *The Order of Redemption.* This refers to the relationship of the redeemed to God and to each other in the new creation established by Him in Jesus Christ (Gal. 6:15; 2 Cor. 5:17). This new creation constitutes participation in a new existence, in the new world that has come in Christ. It is a relationship determined by grace.

   These two terms, "Order of Creation" and "Order of Redemption," were popularized by Emil Brunner in his work *The Divine Imperative.*[21] However, the concepts which these terms denote are of long-standing importance in the Lutheran theological tradition. Luther, for example, spoke of the social relationships (such as marriage and family, people, state, and economy) in which everyone finds himself, including the Christian, and in which he is subject to the commandments which God gave as Creator to all people. Husband and wife, parents and children have their own respective positions in relation to each other. The obligatory character of these orders of things derives from the Creator Himself. Luther employed such terms as *Stand* ("station") and *Beruf* ("calling") to refer to the relationships in the order of creation.[22] Francis Pieper employs the term *Schoepferordnung* ("order of creation") in his *Christian Dogmatics.*[23] The modern theologian Werner Elert uses this same term, together with the expression *Seins-Gefuege* ("structure of being").[24]

How do these two orders relate to each other when applied to male-female identities? According to the order of creation, God has assigned individual identities to each sex. He "from the beginning made them male and female" (Matt. 19:4). The identities and functions of each are not interchangeable; they must remain distinct. This is the burden of the Pauline use of the opening chapters of Genesis in those passages concerned with women in the church.

1. 1 Corinthians 11:7-9. The apostle argues for male "headship" on the basis of Gen. 2:18-25, which teaches that the man did not come from the woman but the woman from the man and that the woman was created for the sake of the man.

2. 1 Corinthians 14:34. Paul cites the Law (very likely Genesis 2 in this particular context) as the basis for the subordination of woman.

3. 1 Timothy 2:13-14. Paul appeals to the temporal priority of Adam's creation ("Adam was formed first"; cf. Gen. 2:20-22), as well as to Eve's having been deceived in the fall (Gen. 3:6), to show that women should not teach or exercise authority over men in the church.[25]

Excursus On Genesis 2-3

The basis for the instructions set forth here by the apostle Paul is the relationship between man and woman presented in Genesis 2 and 3. Genesis 2, like Genesis 1, teaches that the woman is in every way equal, before God, to the man.[26] *But these passages also reveal an order in their relationship to one another: Equality before God—spiritual equality—does not mean sameness. The word which Paul uses to describe this order—subordination—(The Greek word for subordination is* hypotage, *which is formed from the word* tasso*—to appoint, to order, to arrange, and* hypo*—under.*[27]*)—does not carry with it any notion of inferior value or oppression. This term is used by Paul simply to refer to order in the relationship of man and woman to one another. St. Paul teaches in 1 Cor. 11:7-9, "For a man ought not to cover his head, since he is the image and glory of God; but woman is the glory of man. (For man was not made from woman, but woman from man. Neither was man created for woman, but woman for man.)"*

There are several factors in the creation account in Genesis 2 which provide for the basis for Paul's teaching about the relationship of man and woman.[28] *First, verse 7 stipulates that man was created first, before woman. He is the "first-born" and hence would have a natural precedence by birth. The creation of man as the first in sequence is integral to the narrative structure of Genesis 2. Second, the man is designated as* Adam *(v. 20), which is also the term used to describe the race. That the man is given this name suggests that he occupies the position as head of the relationship. Third, Adam immediately begins to exercise his authority by naming the animals (v. 10). He also names his wife "woman" (v. 23). Fourth, woman is created to be a helper for man. She is created from him and brought to him.*[29] *While the word "subordination" is not actually used in Genesis 2, this account of the creation presents the foundation for 1 Corinthians 11. Clark summarizes its thrust well:*

> *. . . it is a very specific kind of subordination—the kind that makes one person (sic) out of two. According to Genesis 2, woman was created to be a help to man, not to be a servant or a slave. She was created to be a complement to him, making a household and children possible. He in turn protected her, provided for her, and considered her part of himself, a partner in life. He was the head of the relationship, head of a relationship that was "one flesh."*[30]

When the New Testament talks about the origin *of the subordination of woman to man, it does so on the basis of Genesis 2 and not on the basis of Genesis 3. The foundation for this teaching is not the "curse" of the fall but the original purpose of God in creation.*[31]

Genesis 3 describes the disruption and distortion of the order of creation brought about by the fall into sin. The "curse" pronounced in Gen. 3:16 does not institute subordination as such, but it does make this relationship irksome for both parties. Man was woman's head from the first moment of her creation, but after the fall the will to self-assertion distorts this relationship into domination and/or independence.[32] *The disruption caused by sin is remedied by Christ's redemption, of course (Rom. 5:12-21; 2 Cor. 5:17; Col 3:10), and men and women who are in Christ should perform their respective functions without either oppression or defiance (Eph. 5:21-23). But their redemption is not yet fully manifest in them in this life. (Eph. 4:22-24; Rom 8:18-25)*

But what are the implications of the order of redemption for the relationship of male and female? Does not this new order which has come in Christ abrogate the old? Does not Paul say in Gal. 3:28 that in Christ there is "neither male nor female"? Much of the modern debate on the issue of women in the church revolves around just these questions, questions which stem in large measure from a confusion of the order of creation and the order of redemption.

1. Various interpretations are proposed by contemporary theologians for resolving an alleged contradiction between the Galatians passage and Paul's other references to the order of creation. One view candidly acknowledges that Paul directly bases his admonitions in 1 Corinthians and 1 Timothy on the order of creation, but he sees in the Galatians passage a "breakthrough" which transcends this understanding. This interpretation is set forth by Krister Stendahl in his study on *The Bible and the Role of Women*. He writes:

   > It is not difficult for us to recognize that we are not yet in the kingdom. But we need badly the reminder of that which is new. We are not in danger of overstating that. We need help to see the forces toward renewal and re-creation. A mere repetition of Paul's reminder of the order of creation is not our most crying need. When Paul fought those who defended the old—as in Galatia—his bold vision of the new expressed itself most strongly, as in Galatians 3:28.[33]

   Stendahl's point is that in Christ the dichotomy of male and female is overcome. He does not allow for the "hiddenness" of the present eschatological age in which Christians live.

   Even more radical is the position of Roman Catholic theologian David Tracy. He sees the issue of the relationship between male and female in terms of social equality. Since, according to his view, Christianity must always be on the side of radical egalitarianism, he cannot allow the order of creation to determine the believer's view of the role of women in the church. He argues for a "Christian transvaluation of all values." According to his analysis, the Christian belief that God is love means first to "negate," and that is what the Christian faith does even in terms of male-female relationships. The new creation completely abolishes the old.[34]

2. The Biblical view affirms that the New Testament discussion of male-female relationships is rooted in a divinely instituted order and that this order is not overthrown by the new creation. To be sure, the new creation begins to transform that which is sinful, but since the eschatological transformation in the resurrection from the dead has not yet taken place, the relationships between man and woman must bear the elements of the structure given in creation (Rom. 8:18-25; 1 Cor. 7:17-31). This interpretation is carefully articulated by Lutheran theologian Peter Brunner in his treatment of *The Ministry and the Ministry of Women*.[35]

   Gal. 3:28 in particular speaks about the new life in Christ. When the apostle says in 3:27 that those who have been baptized into Christ have put on Christ, he uses the verb *enduomai*—to clothe oneself in. The baptized individual has become completely united with Christ and one with Him. But in this act those who have been baptized also become united with one another. In baptism there can be no question about the differences which are important in the present age such as between Jew and Greek, slave and free. Neither is there in baptism any distinction between man and woman. The division into male and female established in the order of creation is not relevant in reference to baptism into Christ.[36] No one is baptized to be either man or woman. Rather, baptism is a baptism into Christ. The objective is union with Him which can be experienced in this life through faith, as Luther stressed, but which in its finality belongs to the age to come.

Through faith both men and women become children of God. Thereby a unity is created between Jew and Gentile, slave and free, man and woman.[37]

In this passage, then, one sees the vision of that one body into which Christians have been incorporated as living members together with all baptized believers—that Body of Christ in which He is the head and where racial, social, and sexual distinctions have no validity. All share in the blessings of Christ's redemption. As Luther observed, "But we are all priests before God if we are Christians. . . . For priests, the baptized, and Christians are all one and the same."[38]

However, the oneness of male and female in Christ does not obviate the distinction given in creation. Gal. 3:28 does not mean that the identity of man or woman can be exchanged any more than that Greeks can become Jews or *vice versa*. The individual characteristics of believers are not abolished by the order of redemption.[39] The things ordained by God in His creation and the divisions in *this* world which reflect in some measure the creation of God are not annulled. This text reveals how believers appear before God, but it does not speak to issues pertaining to order in the church or the specific functions of women in the congregation. To be sure, all the redeemed are equal before our gracious God, but equality does not suggest the interchangeability of male and female identities.

This analysis of the orders of creation and redemption leads to the formulation of a second principle, derived from the Holy Scriptures, for clarifying the function of women in the church today: *Distinctive identities for man and woman in their relation to each other were assigned by God at creation. These identities are not nullified by Christ's redemption, and they should be reflected in the church.*

C. Headship and Subordination

The idea that God desires man to be the head of woman and woman to be subordinate to man is rooted deeply in the Old and New Testaments. While this Biblical truth may offend the sensibilities of some because it is so easily subject to misunderstanding and abuse (even within the church itself), it is the Creator's intention that we gratefully recognize and receive the ordered relationship of headship/subordination as an arrangement whereby the welfare of others may be served.[40] We have not properly understood the interrelated concepts of headship (1 Cor: 11:3) and subordination (1 Cor. 14:34) if we take them to be equivalent to superiority or domination.[41]

1. *Headship.* In Eph. 5:23 St. Paul writes, "For the husband is the head of the wife. . . ." Having first enjoined mutual submission of husband and wife to one another (5:21), the apostle then speaks of the submission of the wife to her husband and of the church to Christ as a consequence of headship. However, headship does not imply superiority. The man is not the "head" of the woman because he is intrinsically better in any respect than the woman. This is made clear in 1 Cor. 11:3, where the apostle asserts that "the head of Christ is God." Indeed, the Scripture makes it abundantly clear that the second person of the Holy Trinity is co-equal with the Father in such attributes as majesty, deity, omnipresence, and omniscience.

   The Scriptural concept of subordination, rather than implying a superiority/inferiority structure, presents this headship structure as an "ordering into." Peter Brunner states it well:

   > The man is the head of the woman; Christ is the head of the man; God is the head of Christ. The "head" is that which is prior, that which determines, that which leads. The head is the power that begins, it is *principium, arche*.[42]

   Similarly, Zerbst notes that Paul believed "that for man, woman, and Christ there is something which has been ordinated over them; something which either has been established in creation or which has its foundation in the work of redemption, but which in either case expresses the will of God."[43] Every individual has his/her "head";

everyone has the obligation of rendering obedience in that position to which God has assigned him/her.

The headship of Ephesians 5 stands also as the backdrop for 1 Corinthians 11. Paul states that the appointive headship of the man applies in worship as well as in the home. The problem in Corinth was that women there had stepped out of the relationship assigned to them by the Creator. They were asserting their "freedom" by praying and prophesying with uncovered heads like the men (11:4). But, says Paul, the "newness of the kingdom" does not do away with the creational pattern. There is an order of headship which endures.

Excursus on Headcovering: Principle and Custom

Paul's discussion of headship in 1 Corinthians 11 focuses on the issue of headcovering. In worship services men should leave their heads uncovered, the apostle says, while women should wear something which covers their heads. The question is sometimes posed as to why Christians who today accept the Biblical principle of headship in 1 Corinthians 11 do not also insist on the practice of headcoverings for women in contemporary worship settings.

This issue is clarified by noting the distinction between a principle and its application in custom and practice. Although it is not possible to determine precisely which customs Paul had in mind (most probably Jewish customs of covering and veiling at worship is the source, though there seems to have been much variation in the synagogue practices of Paul's day), it is clear that the use of headcoverings in worship was a cultural expression which had particular meaning within the original context.

1 Corinthians 11 addresses a situation where women had disregarded their subordinate position by praying and prophesying with uncovered head like the men. Paul opposes this behavior by declaring that a man who prays and prophesies having his head covered dishonors his head and that a woman who prays and prophesies with uncovered head dishonors her head. In other words, the laying aside of the headcovering is regarded by the apostle as a repudiation of the relationship between man and woman established in creation. The ultimate significance of the headcovering consisted in its potential for expressing a particular differentiation between men and women. Paul's concern therefore is not simply with the maintenance of outward conduct. For order and unity in the family there must be leadership, and the primary responsibility for such leadership is that of the husband and father. The headcovering was a custom *(v. 15) subservient to a principle ("the head of the woman is the man," v. 3). The custom of headcovering functioned as woman's acknowledgment of the principle of headship.*

Even in earliest times this practice was not universally followed by Christian congregations, and in modern Western society headcovering or veiling is generally devoid of the significance attached to it in Paul's time.[44] *In fact, it has commonly been understood from the very beginning that these passages of Scripture which pertain to custom are not binding and that the principle involved can be manifested in various ways. We have the affirmation, for example, of the Savior that we should wash one another's feet (John 13:14), a practice highly significant in its original setting. But Christians have not generally regarded this exhortation as instituting a perpetual ordinance. The Christian principles signified by it—humility and love for others—can and should be manifested by other practices. The* principle *of humble love remains, but the* custom *has passed away. Leon Morris comments:*

> *The application of this principle (Paul's words on headship) to the situation at Corinth yields the direction that women must have their heads covered when they worship. The principle is of permanent validity, but we may well feel that the application of it to the contemporary scene need not yield the same result. In other*

> *words, in the light of totally different social customs, we may well hold that the fullest acceptance of the principle underlying this chapter does not require that in Western lands in the twentieth century women must always wear hats when they pray.*[45]

The concept of headship is not only misunderstood, but it is also frequently abused. It is a mistake, for example, to identify the Biblical model of headship with a chain of command. The Scriptures teach that headship exists for the sake of serving others, of building up others. Christ taught that His followers are to be servants. Self-willed assertion over another for one's own personal advantage violates and perverts the headship principle of which the apostle speaks.

2. *Subordination.* The same present-day connotations of superiority and oppression that attach to the Biblical concept of headship also adhere to the concept of subordination. It is true that the Scriptures use the word for subordination *(hypotasso)* in a dominative sense in some contexts (e.g., 1 Cor. 15:27, ''For God has put all things in subjection under his feet''; 1 Peter 3:22, ''angels, authorities, and powers in submission to him''). There is, in point of fact, a type of coercive subordination which results from force or domination. A slave or a prisoner experiences subordination in this sense.

   But there is a subordination which is freely recognized and accepted by the subordinate. The New Testament refers to this type of subordination whenever it speaks of the woman in home and church contexts. It is an attitude of looking to another, of putting first the desires of another, of seeking another's benefit. This is not a subordination imposed by the man on the woman from a position of superior authority or power. Rather, it is rooted in the order *(taxis)* instituted by God to which *both* are subject.

   There are also differences in the way subordination and governance are conducted. Governance in a subordinate relationship can be oppressive—a relationship that works for the benefit of the ruler and to the detriment of the subordinate. This relationship is characterized by obedience to command, a ''lording-it-over-the-other'' attitude. But a person can be subordinate without ever having to obey a command. Nowhere in Scripture is it ever said that power or authority *(exousia)* or rule *(arche)* is given to the man over the woman. All of the passages which speak of the subordination of the woman to the man, or of wives to their husbands, are addressed to the woman. The verbs enjoining subordination in these texts are in the middle voice in the Greek (reflexive). The woman is reminded, always in the context of an appeal to the grace of God revealed in Jesus Christ, that she has been subordinated to man by the Creator and that it is for this reason that she should willingly accept this divine arrangement. The Scriptures never tell the man that he is to ''keep his wife in subjection'' (unlike the exhortation concerning children in 1 Tim. 3:4) by the issuance of commands. People can be subordinate by serving others, by cooperating with another's purposes, or by following another's teaching. The more love and commitment to the interest of others (Phil 2:4) are present in the relationship of the man to the woman, the more this subordinate relationship conforms to the Scriptural ideal.[46]

   Significantly, subordination is not applied by the apostolic writers to secular society. In this sphere—in the absence of Scriptural guidance—one must resist attempts to identify certain stances as the Christian or Biblical ones. The fact that a woman may be ''over'' a man (such as a woman foreman on a construction crew or a woman judge in a legal proceeding) is not to be construed as a violation of the Scriptural concept of subordination.

   The Biblical material focuses on the areas of marriage and the church. However, whenever the subordination of women to men in marriage and in the church becomes a matter of domination and whenever anyone, man or woman, behaves in an autocratic, domineering way, such conduct stems not from the creation but from the fall. Men honor the rule of God by submitting themselves to His will concerning their attitude and conduct toward women. Attitudes and actions which suggest that women are insignificant or inferior, or that they have no valid existence apart from men, originate in the fall.

Moreover, such a posture toward women is inconsistent with the example of Jesus' governance of those who live in a subordinate relationship to Him (Eph. 5:25). At the same time, the fact that Scripture speaks of woman being subordinate to man does not rob women of their purpose in life or make them only appendages of men. Both male and female are members of the Body of Christ. They both share in ruling God's creation and in the proclamation of the gospel. A third principle emerges, then, to guide us in determining the service of women in the church today: *Subordination, when applied to the relationship of women and men in the church, expresses a divinely established relationship in which one looks to the other, but not in a domineering sense. Subordination is for the sake of orderliness and unity.*

D. The Exercise of Authority

The three previous Scriptural principles concerning women in the church converge in St. Paul's specific directives regarding their speaking and teaching in the congregation at worship. (1 Cor. 14:33b-35; 1 Tim. 2:11-15)

1. *Silence.* At first glance the apostle's presumption that women will pray and prophesy (1 Cor. 11:5) appears to be in contradiction to his command for silence in 1 Corinthians 14. Commentators have offered a variety of solutions to the difficulties which arise when 1 Corinthians 11 is compared with 1 Corinthians 14. One solution proposed is that a distinction should be made between two kinds of church meetings in these chapters, the one a family, nonplenary meeting (chapter 11), the other an assembly of the entire congregation (chapter 14). Another solution emphasizes a distinction between two kinds of speaking. According to this proposal "to speak" in chapter 14 means "to ask questions," while chapter 11 refers to ecstatic speech. Full clarity perhaps is not possible. However, the following conclusions seem warranted.

   First, that Paul is not commanding *absolute,*[47] unqualified silence is evident from the fact that he permits praying and prophesying in 1 Corinthians 11. The silence mandated for women in 1 Corinthians 14 does not preclude their praying and prophesying.[48] Accordingly, the apostle is not intimating that women may not participate in the public singing of the congregation or in the spoken prayers. It should be noted in this connection that Paul uses the Greek word *laleo* for "speak" in 1 Cor. 14:34, which frequently means to "preach" in the New Testament (See Mark 2:2; Luke 9:11; Acts 4:1; 8:25; 1 Cor. 2:7; 2 Cor 12:19; Phil. 1:4; et al.), and not *lego,* which is the more general term. (The claim that Paul has a different meaning in mind and that he uses it here to prohibit disturbing chatter is extremely improbable.) When *laleo* has a meaning other than religious speech and preaching in the New Testament, this is usually made clear by an object or an adverb (e.g., to speak like a child, 1 Cor. 13:11; to speak like a fool, 2 Cor. 11:23). Secondly, it must be underscored that Paul's prohibition that women remain silent and not speak is uttered with reference to the worship service of the congregation (1 Cor. 14:26-33). Any other interpretation is artificial and improbable. Thus, Paul is not here demanding that women should be silent at all times or that they cannot express their sentiments and opinions at church assemblies. The command that women keep silent is a command that they not take charge of the public worship service, specifically the teaching-learning aspects of the service.

2. *Teaching and Authority.* While the thrust of Paul's comments in 1 Tim. 2:11-15 is similar to that in 1 Corinthians 14, he makes a more explicit point in this passage. A woman is not to teach or to have authority over man.

   Here, too, the limits of what is forbidden to women by the apostle have been widely disputed. Some have understood Paul here to be excluding women from all forms of teaching and exercising authority, including teaching in a public school or serving in a vocation in which a woman has men under her direct supervision. This constitutes a serious misreading of Paul's words. His instructions are directed to the worship/church setting. No doubt the public prayer which is regulated in verse 8 would occur during a liturgical service. The expression "likewise" in verse 9 indicates that the women's activity occurs in the same domain. In 1 Tim. 3:14-15 the apostle explains the purpose of his letter to Timothy: "I am writing these instructions to you so that, if I am delayed, you may know how one ought to behave in the household of God. . . ." The context of this passage is that of worship/church.

Still, two alternatives remain: 1) women are absolutely prohibited from *every* form of teaching or public address; or 2) women are prohibited from *certain types* of teaching or public address, especially from that exercised by the "teaching office," that is, the pastoral office.

The teaching that Paul forbids women to perform is the latter, namely, that of the formal, public proclamation of the Christian faith. The word for teach *(didaskein)* is used uniformly in this way throughout 1 Timothy. This term is used in this epistle to refer to "false teachers" (1:3, 7); "overseers" (i.e., pastors) who are "able to teach" (3:2); the pastor Timothy, who is to "teach" (4:11), to "attend to the public reading of Scripture, to exhortation, to teaching" (4:13), to "take heed . . . to your teaching" (4:16), and to "teach and exhort these things" (6:2); the "elders . . . who labor in preaching and teaching" (5:17); and especially the apostle Paul himself, who is a "teacher of the Gentiles." (2:7)

Therefore, Paul is not contending that Christian women are to avoid teaching under any circumstances. Elsewhere the New Testament indicates that women did teach in a context other than the community worship service (e.g., Priscilla, Acts 18:26). The apostolic restriction in 1 Timothy 2 pertains to that teaching of God's Word which involves an essential function of the pastoral office. The word *didaskein* is inappropriately applied to the Sunday school teacher, the Christian day school teacher, the home Bible study teacher. As Bishop Bo Giertz of Sweden suggests, "When in 1 Tim. 2:12 the word *didaskein* is used, it is a rather pregnant expression (the word means: to be a teacher in the church and to be charged by God with the proclamation of His Word)." Teaching which does not "coincide with that commission to which the New Testament refers when using the words *didaskalos* or *didaskein*" is not in view here.[49]

3. *Authority*. The question now arises, what is the relationship between teaching, learning, and exercising "authority over man"? The verb Paul employs in 1 Tim. 2:12 *(authentein)* occurs only here in the New Testament and is never used in the Septuagint. Thus, there is no explicit Scriptural background for interpreting its meaning. Consequently, it is open to varying definitions, some of them quite incongruent with Paul's actual concern.

One writer has observed that some interpreters separate the components of Paul's instructions in these verses, making them independent of one another: that women a) learn in silence; b) be in all submission; c) not teach; and d) not exercise authority over men.[50] However, when the apostle's phrases are separated in this way and used to formulate a code of rules concerning the role of women, both the text and women are abused. The damage is compounded if they are severed from the context. The result of this way of proceeding is that this passage is taken to mean that women should never, under any circumstances, teach in the church and that they must always, in every circumstance, submit to men by never making any decisions which may impact on them.

In point of fact, however, a careful review of this passage indicates that the terms "teach" and "exercise authority" parallel each other. They are intentionally linked. The kind of teaching referred to in the passage is tied to exercising authority. The authority forbidden to women here is that of the pastoral office, that is, one "who labors in preaching and teaching." (1 Tim. 5:17; cf. 1 Thess. 5:12)

A proper understanding of Paul here is of enormous significance for the discussion of the service of women in the church. One cannot divorce the phrase "nor have authority over man" from the pastoral office and then apply it in rather arbitrary ways. For example, if we are to be faithful to the apostle's instructions in this passage, we cannot simply take the dictionary meaning of "authority" as "the power to act or make decisions" and then proceed, solely on that basis, to eliminate women from all congregational meetings or committees which have the power to act or make decisions.

The theological matrix for the apostle's inspired teaching on the silence of women in the church and the exercise of authority is, again, the order of creation. In 1 Tim. 2:13 Paul points to the order of creation as the basis for the instructions given in verses 11 and 12. God made Adam before Eve; that is, He created man and woman in a definite order. Turning from the creation to the fall, Paul adds that Adam was not deceived but that the woman was deceived and became a transgressor.[51] The conclusion drawn is that the leadership of the official, public teaching office belongs to men. Assumption of that office by a woman is out of place because it is a woman who assumes it, not because women do it in the wrong way or have inferior gifts and abilities.

Of course, the church in all ages stands under the mandate of Christ to preach the gospel to all peoples. This commission is addressed to each member of the Body of Christ. All men and women in the church have a share in the proclamation of the Word and the administration of the sacraments. However, God has decreed that the church carry out this mandate not only in the context of private, individual actions but by formally selecting individual members for the office of the public ministry. The nomenclature used in the New Testament to refer to this office varies ("bishops," 1 Tim. 3:1; "elder," 1 Tim. 5:17; "leaders," Heb. 13:17), but that the holders of this office are to be engaged specifically in preaching and teaching is consistently enunciated. The oversight and supervision exercised in the office of the public ministry is that of teaching the Word and administering the sacraments.[52] Paul's directives relating to women in the church in 1 Corinthians 14 and 1 Timothy 2 provide instructions concerning this position of leadership.[53]

A fourth principle of benefit in providing guidance for the service of woman in the church today can be formulated as follows: *The creational pattern of male headship requires that women not hold the formal position of the authoritative public teaching office in the church, that is, in the office of pastor.*

E. Summary

Although only four major principles regarding women in the church have been discussed above, it may be helpful to summarize more extensively several key points made in this treatment of the pertinent Biblical texts.

1. In sharp contrast to the deprecation and suppression of women in ancient cultures, and especially in Rabbinic Judaism, the Gospel record affirms their value and dignity. Jesus clearly shows His regard for women, created equally with men in the image and likeness of God.
2. In the order of creation, God has placed woman in a position subordinate to man. This relationship of subordination, however, is radically different from "secular" interpretations of it. The Scriptural concept of subordination is a matter of function between two persons of equal worth and not a matter of inferiority/superiority. The subordination of woman to man is not a dominative subordination. The subordination of wife to husband is analogous to the relationship which exists between Christ and the church.
3. The relationship between man and woman can also be defined as a headship structure of God-Christ-man-woman, each member of the order superordinated to the succeeding member. This is a theological and not merely a sociological relationship.
4. The order of redemption, while affirming that men and women are one in Christ and joint heirs of the grace of life, does not abolish the order established at the time of creation. The distortion of the order of creation brought about by the fall has been remedied by Christ's redemption, but it has not yet become fully manifest in the

redeemed. This will happen only in heaven. Therefore, far from annulling the order of creation, the order of redemption sanctifies it. The two orders are held together coordinately within God's purposes. The Lordship of Christ spans both creation and redemption.

5. 1 Cor. 14:33b-35 and 1 Tim. 2:11-15 speak of women's roles in the public worship service. The main application of these passages in the contemporary church is that women are not to exercise those functions in the local congregation which would involve them in the exercise of authority inherent in the authoritative public teaching office (i.e., the office of pastor).

6. Men who find themselves in positions of leadership and authority must assume the attitude which Jesus Himself required: ". . . rather let the greatest among you become as the youngest, and the leader as the one who serves" (Luke 22:26). Christian leadership and service must model Him.

7. Women have all of the God-given rights, privileges, and responsibilities of the priesthood of all believers that men do. God's people are called priests not to confer status but to commission all of them to declare His deeds of salvation. All Christians have been given the responsibility to live their Christian faith in their several callings, including the responsibility to profess and share the Christian faith and to judge all doctrine.

8. The inspired writers of Scripture do not discuss the implications of the order of creation for life in the civil estate. In Lutheran theology there is general agreement on the necessity of distinguishing carefully between that which happens in the civil sphere and that which takes place in the spiritual sphere.

III. Guidelines for Practice

How does one address the wide range of practical questions that arise in dealing with the topic of women in the church today? Lutherans recognize that the "prophetic and apostolic writings of the Old and New Testaments are the only rule and norm according to which all doctrines and teachers alike must be appraised and judged" (FC Ep Rule and Norm 1). This article of faith remains true also with respect to the relationship between man and woman. God has revealed His will regarding such a relationship in His Word. To be sure, the political and social milieu of a culture influences the church and always will. Nevertheless, a specific sociological "mindset" must never be allowed to be decisive for expressing theological judgments.

At the same time, principles alone do not describe reality. Each situation combines many details in a unique way. Faithful, consistent application of Biblical principles requires that each distinctive situation be carefully assessed. We must be sure that we truly understand both the situation or problem with which we are dealing and the full range of Scriptural principles which should be brought to bear on it. This is especially true of the question of the service of women in the church.

While it is impossible to deal with all the practical questions which arise in individual congregations, there are a number of inquiries which the Commission has received or which have been introduced in other contexts that can be addressed briefly in a study of this kind. The purpose of this section of the report is to suggest one approach for using the principles and theses enunciated in Part II and to illustrate that approach through succinct responses to the questions of 1) women's ordination to the pastoral office; 2) woman suffrage; and 3) additional practical applications for situations which emerge from the contemporary life of the church.

A. Applying Scriptural Principles: An Approach

James Hurley has proposed three preliminary guidelines for addressing specific questions related to women in the church.[54] These suggested guidelines are by no means exhaustive, but they do provide a helpful frame of reference for approaching the pertinent issues.

1. In response to questions regarding the service of women in the church, we must first ask whether God's Word expressly permits it or whether it expressly prohibits the activity. In the foregoing study of the Pauline passages it is clear that some activities are permitted while others carry restrictions.
2. We must also ask whether an activity is consonant with the purpose of Scripture but prevented by a technicality of human definition. To what extent have cultural definitions—of "authority" or "subjection," for instance—influenced our understanding of the Biblical passages? Or conversely, does an activity which is permitted on the basis of a technicality of definition effectively undermine, nevertheless, a Biblical norm?
3. The third guideline has to do with perceptions and the taking of offense (cf. 1 Corinthians 8; Romans 14; FC SD X). Is an action likely to be misunderstood or perceived in a way that it becomes a stumbling block for others? And, a perennial question in Lutheran theology at least, is this a situation in which an indifferent matter ceases to be a matter of indifference?

Some practical questions about the service of women in the church may be resolved on the basis of a clear mandate of Scripture. Other questions cannot be given a specific answer but will need to be considered according to individual circumstances from the perspective of definitions and/or perceptions. Frequently, all three guidelines will be employed in seeking to determine which ecclesiastical functions are appropriate for women to perform.

B. Women and the Pastoral Office

The ordination of women to the divinely instituted ministry of Word and sacraments is a question that can be addressed on the basis of the first guideline alone. For centuries Christendom has consistently opposed the practice as contrary to the express teachings of Scripture.

There are a number of issues which impinge on the question of women and the pastoral office which remain beyond the scope of the present report (e.g., the meaning of ordination itself[55]). However, the fundamental Scriptural principles (and corresponding theses) examined in this study demonstrate not only that the service of women in the pastoral office lacks Biblical foundation but, in point of fact, is expressly prohibited by the Scriptures.

First, the occupation of the pastoral office by women violates the headship structure rooted in God's order of creation. Peter Brunner writes:

> . . . the combination of pastoral office and being woman objectively and fundamentally destroys the *kephale*-structure of the relationship between man and woman and therefore also rejects the "ordering into" and "subordination to" *(hypotage)* which is demanded by God's will. That which contradicts the spiritual and creaturely order with which God has invested being cannot be the good that God wills! God does not contradict Himself in creation and redemption. The apostolic command to silence, as we find it in 1 Corinthians 14 and 1 Timothy 2, cannot be explained away as the result of the peculiar theological speculation of its author, who was bound by the cultural history and special circumstances of his day. These instructions are based much more on certain hidden, but yet extraordinarily incisive, fundamental laws and commands that God Himself established . . . .[56]

Second, women are not to be pastors nor perform the essential and unique functions of the pastoral office, since the pastoral office has oversight from God over the congregation, "the household of God" (1 Tim. 3:15). Properly speaking, of course, the only authority or power in the church is the Word of Christ, who is Head over all things (Eph. 1:22). However, as noted previously, there are those within the church who are entrusted with the office of the public ministry and are representatives of the Head of the church.

In its 1981 report on "The Ministry" the Commission acknowledges that no specific "checklist" of functions of the office of the public ministry is provided in the Scriptures.[57] At the same time, it was pointed out that the functions of the pastoral office involve public supervision of the flock. The pastor exercises this supervision through the public proclamation of the Word and the administration of the sacraments.[58] This, in turn, suggests that there are certain specific functions which should not be carried out by the laity (who may hold auxiliary offices) but which are to be exercised by the pastor.[59] Among them are the following:

1. preaching in the services of the congregation
2. leading the formal public services of worship
3. the public administration of the sacraments
4. the public administration of the office of the keys

Since the "headship" over the congregation is exercised through these functions unique to the office of the public ministry, the functioning of women in this specific office is precluded. Just as the woman should not be the "head" of the house, so a woman should not be the "head" over the "household of God" (cf., 1 Tim. 5:17; 1 Thess. 5:12; 1 Tim. 3:12). Article XIV of the Augsburg Confessions states: "It is taught among us that nobody should publicly teach or preach or administer the sacraments in the church without a regular call" *(nisi rite vocatus)*. Such a call is denied to women by a "command of the Lord."

Although the Scriptures teach that women may not hold the pastoral office or perform its distinctive functions, the service of women to the Lord and His church in various other offices established to facilitate the proclamation of the Word has been longstanding in the history especially of The Lutheran Church—Missouri Synod. The self-denying service, gladly given by the many faithful women who have served over the years in such offices as deaconess, Christian day school teacher, and parish worker, has been of immeasurable importance. Of these coworkers, too, it must be said that they "can never be sufficiently thanked and repaid."[60]

C. Woman Suffrage

Woman suffrage is an issue that must be decided largely on the basis of the second of the three guidelines noted above. One reason for this is that the matter of franchise is not discussed in the Scripture. A word which can be translated as "voting" (*cheirotoneo*—raising the hand) occurs in Acts 14:23 and 2 Cor. 8:19. However, when in the Corinthian passage the churches are described as choosing a representative to accompany Paul to Jerusalem, nothing is said about the method actually employed. In the Acts verse, the word appears to mean "appoint." No kind of franchise seems to be involved.[61]

In summary, the Scriptural passages employed for guidance on this question have been those verse of 1 Corinthians 11, 1 Corinthians 14, and 1 Timothy 2 which deal with woman's subordination, woman's silence in the church, and woman's exercise of authority. As has been noted, Paul is not addressing himself here to anything like a contemporary "voters' assembly." He is giving instructions to Christians regarding the arrangement of and order in public worship.[62]

Further, it has been shown that the prohibition in 1 Tim. 2:11-12 of woman's exercising authority is not a concept independent of "to teach." According to this text, the woman is prohibited from the teaching in the public worship assembly. To define "authority" simply as the power to make decisions is alien to the exegesis of the passage. There is no express Biblical ground for denying women the vote on issues which facilitate the work of the priesthood of all believers in the congregation.

The definition of "suffrage" is also significant. A "democratic" society of men and women is ruled by a majority vote. However, it is not an exercise of the authority prohibited to women in the Scriptures. In fact, according to this understanding of the matter, it is actually the assembly that exercises authority as a result of suffrage, not the individual voter. Furthermore, in the church, which is ruled by love, the casting of a ballot should also have the added dimension of being an act of service.

The Commission presented a study to the Denver Convention (1969) of The Lutheran Church—Missouri Synod on the issue of woman suffrage. It states by way of conclusion: "We find nothing in Scripture which prohibits women from exercising the franchise in voters' assemblies. Those statements which direct women to keep silent in the church, and which prohibit them to teach and to exercise authority over men, we understand to mean that women ought not to hold the pastoral office."[63] Subsequent study of the matter has provided no basis for altering these conclusions. The Commission reaffirms them.[64]

D. Additional Practical Applications

In applying the principles delineated above to concrete situations one must bear in mind that the New Testament presents no ceremonial law regulating the details of public worship. Also, in applying these principles, it is necessary to distinguish the one divinely instituted office of the public ministry of the Word and sacraments from all other offices which the church establishes in Christian freedom in response to various needs (Acts 6). Holy Scripture clearly excludes women from the office of the public ministry of Word and sacraments. For other offices we have no express "thus saith the Lord," and everything depends on the functions assigned to these offices. Differences in judgement can be expected here in decisions regarding the specific application of general principles. What follows, therefore, is to be understood not as "canon law" but as pastoral and collegial advice to be judged by the church in terms of its faithfulness to such clear Scripture as is relevant.

1. Should a woman participate in public worship in the capacity of reading the Scriptures for the day or in assisting with the formal liturgical service?

All Christians have access to the Scriptures. They do not require the church as an institution or another person to read and interpret them on their behalf. The reading of the Scriptures belongs to the priesthood of all believers, men and women.

Moreover, there is no ceremonial law in the New Testament regarding the reading of Scripture in the context of public worship. Nor is there explicit apostolic prohibition of such reading by women. Nevertheless, it is the opinion of the CTCR that the reading of the Scriptures is most properly the function of the pastoral office and should therefore not ordinarily be delegated to a lay person, woman or man. Pastors and congregations should therefore exercise great care in making decisions permitting the lay reading of the Scriptures or any other activity in the formal liturgical services which might be perceived as an assumption of the pastoral role or a disregard for the Scriptural principles concerning the service of women in the church (e.g., 1 Cor. 11:3-16; 14:33b-35). The third guideline listed above concerning the perceptions which certain actions may convey is also relevant and should be taken into account in answering this question.

2. May a woman address a congregation on a particular subject in which she possesses an expertise (lectures or presentations on social and ethical issues, etc.) and therefore "teach" in the church?

The answer to this question depends, in the first place, on the interpretation of Paul's statement in 1 Tim. 2:12 that woman may not teach. The passage does not expressly prohibit the instance envisioned in the above question. The sharing and teaching this question entails does not place the woman in the office of the pastor. She is not seeking to enforce her teaching with discipline and is not usurping the authority of any man. Paul did not forbid *all* teaching by women. In terms of perceptions or the giving of offense, such a presentation by a guest speaker on any topic should be arranged in such a way that the impression is not given that it replaces the sermon. There are women in the church who, through their education and experience, have much to contribute on a wide range of significant concerns. They should be encouraged to serve in such capacities as gifts of God to His church.

3. Does the above response also apply to the regular adult Bible class of a congregation which includes men?

Certainly there is a legitimate distinction between a special presentation to the congregation and the continued instruction offered by the adult Bible class instructor. However, there is also a distinction between "overseeing" the instruction carried on in an adult Bible class and the actual physical teaching of the class (just as there is a more general distinction between "office" and "function"). It is the responsibility of the called pastor to "oversee" the adult Bible class (as well as all of the formal educational programs of the congregation). He may, from time to time, have members of the church teach the class and such teachers could indeed be women with the gifts for such a service. Their participation would be within the bounds of the priesthood of all believers. At the same time, teaching an adult class may involve possible, but very real, confusion regarding the office of pastor for some in a congregation. No doubt the pastor would seek to allay any such misunderstanding by appropriate preparation of the class for the service of laypeople in this capacity.

4. May women hold office in a congregation, serve on committees of the congregation, chair committees of the congregation?

Women may hold any office and serve on any committee of the congregation which enhances the work of the priesthood of all believers. Women also have the privilege to chair congregational committees, since a "chair" does not "have authority over men" any more than the committee *per se* would have such authority in the New Testament sense. The only stricture would have to do with anyone whose official functions would involve public accountability for the function of the pastoral office (e.g., elders, and possibly the chairman of the congregation). The tasks of the elders in a congregation are often directly associated with the pastoral office and the public administration of the office of the keys. As stated in the introductory paragraph to this section, everything depends on the nature of functions assigned to various offices established by the church.

The same general position outlined above applies to various district or synodical committees and commissions. Affairs of the church have never been assigned only to those holding the office of the public ministry. Women offer valuable contributions to the work of such committees, boards, and commissions.

5. What about the service of women in other worship contexts such as devotions conducted in the chapels of synodical colleges and other institutions?

Here, especially in the tradition of The Lutheran Church—Missouri Synod, much has to do with definition and perception. While it is clear from the Scriptures that women should not preach or lead the formal public worship services of the church, many of the church's educational institutions conduct what has been referred to as extended "family devotions" and have asked women to serve in worship leadership capacities. These "devotions" should be differentiated from the formal (and to a great extent, public) worship services. Institutions that hold public worship services under the responsibility of one who is called to be chaplain, campus pastor, dean of the chapel, etc., would seem to be out of the realm of "family devotions" in any acceptable meaning of the phrase. In such contexts, women should not preach or lead the services of worship. In those other worship opportunities which may be appropriately understood as "devotions," the chaplain or other "spiritual head" of the community should make responsible decisions regarding the service of women, keeping in mind all of the guidelines presented in this report. It is impossible to anticipate all of the exigencies of such situations in a general study such as that offered in this document.

6. May women serve as assistants in the distribution of the Lord's Supper?

While some might argue that assisting the presiding minister in the distribution of the elements is not necessarily a distinctive function of the pastoral office, the commission strongly recommends that, to avoid confusion regarding the office of the public ministry and to avoid giving offense to the church, such assistance be limited to men.[65]

7. May young women serve in such capacities as acolytes or ushers in public worship services?

Since such service does not involve the exercise of distinctive functions of the pastoral office, there should be no objection to young women serving in such capacities. Pastoral wisdom requires that those who make decisions in this area be sensitive to such considerations as the effects of change in congregational worship practices, the need for appropriate instruction regarding the principles of Christian worship, and the importance of respectful and modest behavior and attire for those young men and women who perform such acts of service.

Conclusion

In its 1977 report the synodical Task Force on Women alerted the membership of the church to the continuing need for utilizing the gifts of women in the service of the Christian community. This report stated:

> It is the responsibility of the individual men and women to work together as equal, redeemed Christians, putting the welfare of the Kingdom ahead of prejudices, customs, or mind-sets. Women and men must realize that each Christian has a calling and a ministry and that the service of each individual is important and valuable to the life of the church.[66]

The present study has reviewed basic Biblical principles and directives which speak of women in the church today with this responsibility and concern in mind.

The nature of the topic itself has drawn attention to questions of headship and subordination in the man/woman relationship as pertinent to the church's life as a worshipping and serving community. To consider these themes in this report is appropriate. Christian men and women will want to know what God's word teaches and humbly submit to His authority in such matters. However, they will be just as willing to receive the apostle's inspired teaching that "the body is a unit, though it is made up of many parts; and though all its parts are many, they form one body" (1 Cor. 12:12 NIV). Every Christian individual possesses gifts which contribute to the function of the body, and they ought to be joyfully and thankfully received. Thus, the Christian community will affirm the unique and differing gifts of women, seeking ways to enlist them more fully in the church's life and work. But God did not call His church into being and give gifts to His people so that they would be concerned about how they might become the greatest in the Kingdom. Since the life of every Christian is to be characterized by obedience and submission on some level, any demand for "rights" and "power" is inappropriate. The Commission believes that a more precise understanding of the Biblical teaching about the service of women in the church will move further reflection on the topic to its appropriate level—how all members of the church can serve our Lord and one another within the order He has established. On this level there is no thought of inferiority or superiority, of rule and domination, but only of our Savior's words: "Truly, truly, I say to you, a servant is not greater than his master; nor is he who is sent greater than he who sent him. If you know these things, blessed are you if you do them." (John 13;16-17)

Endnotes

1 A call for increased participation of women in the corporate life of the church led to the appointment in 1973 of the Task Force on Women (1973 Res. 2-49 and 4-47). This Task

Force continued its work through 1977 and submitted to the Synod detailed reports on ways in which women may more fully participate in the life of the church. The 1977 convention adopted three recommendations of the Task Force. One of the recommendations was that the responsibility for studying the issues relating to women in the church be assigned to the CTCR (Res. 3-06). In 1981 and again in 1983 the Synod asked the CTCR to give priority to this study. In 1984 the President of the Synod appointed the Commission on Women and asked it to devote itself to six tasks: 1) review material prepared by the previous task force and evaluate the extent to which the recommendations have been implemented in the Synod; 2) gather additional data on the current involvement of women in various aspects of synodical and congregational life; 3) review current emphases and dimensions of the women's movement in society as these affect the church; 4) consult with the CTCR and advise it as it prepares a theological study on the service of women in the church; 5) recommend appropriate service and ministry opportunities for women at all levels of church life; and 6) explore the possibility of creating a network of forums on women's activity in the church through the districts of the Synod. Although work of the Commission on Women, including a Synodwide survey of the service of women, has not yet been completed, the CTCR has benefited from several consultations with the members of the Commission on Women. In the interest of sensitizing itself to the concerns of women in the Synod, the CTCR has also shared preliminary drafts of this report with other groups and individuals of the Synod (Council of Presidents, seminary faculties, college presidents, the CTCR's Social Concerns Committee, and staff at the International Center).

2 The Commission included a discussion of male-female relationships within the context of marriage as a major part of its 1981 study on "Human Sexuality: A Theological Perspective." Material from that study especially pertinent to the present report includes "The Relational Purpose of Marriage" (pp. 13-17) and "Headship Within Marriage" (pp. 29-32).

3 The term for "prophetess" is used for the false prophetess Noadiah in Neh. 6:14, and for Isaiah's wife in Isaiah 8:3. In the case of Isaiah's wife, the word likely means "the wife of a prophet." *Interpreter's Dictionary of the Bible,* 1962 ed., s.v. "Prophetess." Cf. George Buchanan Gray, *A Critical and Exegetical Commentary of the Book of Isaiah,* 3d ed. (Edinburgh: T&T. Clark, 1949), p. 144.

4 Clarence Vos, *Woman in Old Testament Worship* (Delft: Judels and Brinkman, 1968). pp. 164-67.

5 Mary J. Evans, *Woman in the Bible* (Downers Grove: Inter-Varsity Press, 1983), p. 32.

6 See discussion [elsewhere in this report].

7 This is clear not only from the negative fact that no call or commission is reported to have been given them, but from the sentence structure itself of Luke 8:1-3. Three groups are distinguished, "Jesus," "the twelve with him," and "some women." These women do not relate to Jesus and to His ministry in exactly the same way as do the Twelve. The women "served" them from "their own resources." The service of the women is explicitly that of material support. Also the plural "them" indicates that the Twelve were, with Jesus, recipients of the women's administrations. This, too, shows that they stood as a distinct group, apart from the Twelve, and not in possession of the selfsame service.

8 Jesus' practice and teaching regarding women certainly differs from Rabbinic Judaism. He was not of the opinion that "there is no wisdom in women except with the distaff" (*The Talmud,* London: Soncino Press, 1938, Vol 11, p. 311) or that a man should praise God "who hast not made me a heathen . . . a woman . . . a brutish man" *Ibid.*, Vol. 2, p. 264). However, the tendency in contemporary feminist literature to see Jesus' dealings with women as completely revolutionary is overdrawn. He went beyond the norms of Pharisaic or scribal interpretation of God's teaching that were wrong. His revolution had

to do with the nature of true righteousness and of the spiritual relationship of men and women alike before God, not with the obliteration of the differentiation between man and woman.

[9] Our discussion follows Stephen Clark, *Man and Woman in Christ* (Servant Books: Ann Arbor, 1980), pp. 103-23; James Hurley, *Man and Woman in Biblical Perspective* (Grand Rapids: Zondervan Publishing House, 1981), pp. 115-24; and Roger Gryson, *The Ministry of Women in the Early Church* (Collegeville: Liturgical Press, 1976), pp. 3-5.

[10] John refers to a woman of the church at Thyatira, Jezebel, as a prophetess (Rev. 2:20-24). Although he warns against her teachings, he does not say that a woman could not prophesy.

[11] The *Didascalia Apostolorum,* written in the first half of the third century, is the earliest full source for the role of deaconess. Deaconesses performed a great variety of services in the care of women, including burial and baptism of the women, the catechizing of women, and the caring for sick women at home. However, like the deacons, they were not heads of the community but served in a role auxiliary to that of the bishop and elders.

[12] The term *diakonos* can be used to refer to both men and women. The Greek definite article that occurs with the word determines the gender.

[13] F.F. Bruce, *The Pauline Circle* (Flemington Markets, New South Wales, Australia: The Paternoster Press, 1985), p. 88.

[14] It is noteworthy that in Acts and Romans Priscilla is mentioned before her husband, a possible indication that she was more prominent than her husband in the missionary work. F.F. Bruce, however, notes: "But in the secular society of the time, when one finds a wife being named before her husband, the reason usually is that her social status was higher than his" (p. 45).

[15] The characterization of St. Paul as an enemy of women is an unfounded prejudice. Actually, there is more evidence for his friendships with women than for Jesus'. The basis for the view that Paul was "anti-feminist" is the fact that most of the Scriptural passages which speak of a differentiation between men and women are in the Pauline epistles. However, Paul's love and admiration for women is not less than that of Jesus. See Clark's discussion of the New Testament approach to women in his *Man and Woman in Christ,* pp. 235-54.

[16] The most pertinent passages of the New Testament concerning the positive roles women could and did perform in the primitive church have been summarized in the previous discussion. The purpose of this brief excursus is to present representative evidence that reflects early Christian and patristic attitudes towards the participation of women in the church's worship and life, and to do this within the context of developments in heterodox and heretical Christian groups.

[17] Mankind is also spoken of as created in the image of God in the broad sense; that is, man and woman reflect from God a variety of attributes such as self-consciousness, the capacity for self-transcendence, and rationality.

[18] Martin Luther, *Luther's Works,* American Edition 1 (St. Louis: Concordia Publishing House, 1958), pp. 62-63.

[19] See Susan T. Foh, *Woman and the Word of God* (Grand Rapids: Baker Book House, 1980), pp. 51-52.

[20] 1 Peter 3:7 speaks of the woman as "the weaker sex" (vessel). It is perhaps best to understand this primarily in the sense of physical weakness (cf. E.G. Selwyn, *The First Epistle of St. Peter* [London: Macmilland Co. LTD, 1964], p. 187), though Martin Franzmann's caution is appropriate: "In common parlance this phrase has come to have a derogatory sense. But it is human male pride that made it depreciatory, not Peter. He uses

it to commend woman to man's love and care . . ." *Concordia Self-Study Commentary* (St. Louis: Concordia Publishing House, 1970), p. 262.

[21] Emil Brunner, *The Divine Imperative*, trans. Olive Wyan (Philadelphia: Westminster Press, 1947), pp. 208-33.

[22] See, for example, *Luther's Works*, American Edition, vol 13, p. 358, and vol. 41, p. 177.

[23] Franz Pieper, *Christliche Dogmatik*, 3 vols. (St. Louis: Concordia Publishing House, 1924), 1:629. See English edition, *Christian Dogmatics*, 4 vols. (St. Louis: Concordia Publishing House, 1950), 1:526.

[24] Werner Elert. *Morphologie des Luthertums*, 2 vols. (Munich: C.H. Beck Publishing Co., 1953), 2:37-49. See Elert's *Das Christliche Ethos* (Hamburg: Furche-Verlag, 1961), p. 37.

[25] The peculiarly Pauline meaning of "teaching" and "exercising authority" is treated in later sections of this document. See pp. 34-37.

[26] The creation of woman from man's "rib" indicates the sameness of nature between man and woman. Karl Barth writes in his *Church Dogmatics* (Edinburgh: T. and T. Clark, 1985), vol. 3, 1, p. 296: "She is not himself but something of and from himself. He is related to her as to another part or member of his own body. . . . With her special existence she fulfills something which he himself ought to fulfill in this special part or member but cannot, so that it awaits fulfillment in her existence. So close is she to him." In a 1525 sermon on marriage Luther spoke of what this would mean for the faithful husband: "He should not consider her a rag on which to wipe his feet; and, indeed, she was not created from a foot but from a rib in the center of man's body, so that the man is to regard her not otherwise than his own body and flesh . . . you should . . . not love *her* as much as you love your own body. Nay, nay, *your* wife you should love as your own body. . . ." Quoted in Ewald M. Plass, *This Is Luther* (St. Louis: Concordia Publishing House, 1948), p. 257.

[27] Fritz Zerbst offers the following definition in *The Office of Women in the Church* (St. Louis: Concordia Publishing House, 1955), p. 69: "*Hypotage* means subjection, *hypotassein:* to put in subjection, and *hypotassesthai:* to subject oneself, or, in the passive, to be subjected, to be under obedience. For the idealistic culture of personality this group of words connotes that which is limiting or restricting, even degrading and humiliating. In its original sense, however, 'to be in subjection' means to 'be placed in an order,' to be under definite *tagmata* (arrangement of things in order, as in ranks, rows, or classes). This original sense it is which evidently and chiefly underlies the New Testament use of the term *hypotage*." The implications of this definition are explored on pages 30-32 of this report.

[28] Michael F. Stitzinger, "Genesis 1-3 and the Male/Female Role Relationship," *Grace Theological Journal* (Spring, 1981), pp. 30-33.

[29] It has been argued that the word *ezer* does not necessarily imply subordination in any way. Sixteen of the twenty-one uses of the word in the Old Testament refer to God as a superior helper to human beings. The remaining three refer to men helping other men. But *ezer* must be seen in context. The phrase says that God created woman to be a help for man; that is to say, the purpose of her creation was to be a help to the man. There is apparently some kind of subordination indicated by the phrase. See Stitzinger, p. 31.

[30] Clark, p. 28.

[31] David P. Kuske, "The Order of Creation," *Wisconsin Lutheran Quarterly* (Winter, 1985), p. 31.

[32] Stitzinger, p. 38. See also Susan T. Foh, "What Is the Woman's Desire?" *Westminster Theological Journal* 37-38 (Fall 1974/Spring 1976), pp. 376-83.

[33] Krister Stendalh, *The Bible and the Role of Women* (Philadelphia: Fortress Press, 1966), p. 37.

[34] David Tracy, "Christian Faith and Radical Equality," *Theology Today* (January 1978), pp. 370-77.

[35] Peter Brunner, *The Ministry and the Ministry of Women* (St. Louis: Concordia Publishing House, 1971). Similar to Brunner's position is that of George M. Knight in *The New Testament Teaching on the Role Relationship of Male and Female* (Grand Rapids: Baker Book House, 1977).

[36] C.S. Lewis makes a similar point in his essay on "Priestesses in the Church?" when he writes, "The point is that unless 'equal' means 'interchangeable,' equality means nothing for the priesthood of women" (that is, for women in the pastoral office). *God in the Dock,* ed. Walter Hooper (Grand Rapids: William B. Eerdmans Publishing Company, 1970), p. 238.

[37] Although it would be anachronistic to read present day striving for equality into the words of Paul, it is obvious that a message such as his does remove the stigmata of the differences between Jew and Greek, slave and free, man and woman. As long as the gospel is a living power, differences in this world cannot become the basis for arrogance and oppression.

[38] Martin Luther, *Luther's Works,* American Edition 30 (St. Louis: Concordia Publishing House, 1967), p. 63.

[39] The Formula of Concord, Article II, notes that the relationship between male and female was created before the Fall. Sins associated with this relationship need to be redeemed, but the relationship itself, since it is created by God, does not stand in need of redemption.

[40] See the 1981 report of the CTCR on "Human Sexuality: A Theological Perspective," p. 256.

[41] The Commission recognizes that much could be said about how the headship/subordination relationship works itself out in marriage. However, it here limits its discussion of this concept to the service of women in the church.

[42] Brunner, p. 25.

[43] Zerbst, p. 32.

[44] Zerbst surmises that "the people of Paul's day felt much more keenly than do people of our day that the outward demeanor of a person is an expression of his inner life, specifically, of his religious convictions and moral attitude" (p. 40).

[45] Leon Morris, *The First Epistle of Paul to the Corinthians* (Grand Rapids: William B. Eerdmans Publishing Company, 1958), p. 156. See AC XXVIII, 53-56.

[46] Clark makes a discerning distinction between oppressive-subordination, care-subordination, and unity-subordination. The latter, summarized here, is described as "a relationship that is carried on for the sake of unity or a higher cause." *Man and Woman in Christ,* pp. 39-45.

[47] The term which Paul uses for "silence" in 1 Tim. 2:2, 11-12 also occurs in Acts 11:18, 21:14, and 22:24, where total silence is not implied.

[48] Cf. George Stoeckhardt's discussion (originally published in 1897) in "Von dem Beruf der Lehrerinnen an christlichen Gemeindeschulen," *Concordia Theological Monthly 5* (October 1934), pp. 764-73. Stoeckhardt writes, "No, the apostle's words will hardly allow another interpretation than that he finds nothing objectionable in the public praying and prophesying in itself, if only it occurs with a covered head. But thereby he has not in the least limited or weakened what he writes in 1 Cor. 14 regarding the silence of women. Neither the praying nor the prophesying belongs to that speaking which he forbids for

women directly in 1 Cor. 14:33-36. The women are not to teach in the assembly of the congregation. They are not to appear as teaching women, nor to instruct the men, nor to dispute publicly before and with men. This is, as we have recognized, the understanding of St. Paul in the latter passage quoted. Neither the praying nor the prophesying belongs in this category. Obviously the praying is not teaching or disputing'' (p. 769).

[49] Bo Giertz, ''Twenty-Three Theses on The Holy Scriptures, The Woman, and the Office of the Ministry,'' *The Springfielder* (March 1970), p. 14. Priscilla, together with Aquila, took Apollos in and expounded *(exethento)* the way of God more accurately. Neither *didaskein* nor any other closely related word is used (Acts 18:26).

[50] Hurley, pp. 200-201.

[51] The role of the deception of the woman in the teaching of Paul is viewed by many as an effort to exculpate Adam from guilt and picture women as naturally more subject to deception or prone to temptation than man. Such conclusions are unwarranted. They attempt to explain on the basis of the sexes what can be explained only on the basis of the order of creation which God established. There is no intimation that woman bears the primary responsibility for the fall. The point is simply that the woman was deceived. Being deceived was her role in the fall. See Zerbst, pp. 54-56.

[52] AC V and XIV speak of the ''ministry of teaching the Gospel and administering the sacraments'' on behalf of the church. This office is distinguished from auxiliary offices, which have been created by the church to carry out certain functions of the divinely mandated office of the public ministry. See the CTCR's 1981 report on ''The Ministry: Offices, Procedures, and Nomenclature,'' pp. 16-19.

[53] An expanded discussion of the functions of the office of the public ministry follows. . . .

[54] Hurley, p. 246.

[55] ''The Ministry,'' pp. 22-23.

[56] Brunner, p. 35. Also, Zerbst, p. 121: ''Whereas rule over the congregation is exercised through the proclamation of the Word and the administration of the Sacraments, the ordination of woman into this office is a practical invalidation of the proclamation governing woman's subordination. The demands that the office be opened completely to woman must be resisted, because they are essentially an attack upon the order of creation, which must be preserved.''

[57] ''The Ministry,'' p. 15.

[58] Ibid., pp. 13-14. As the Commission has stated in its document on ''The Ministry,'' the office of the *public* ministry and its functions are called ''public'' ''not because the functions are always discharged in public, but because they are performed on behalf of the church'' (p. 13).

[59] In an emergency situation a congregation may request a lay leader to perform some functions of the office of the public ministry. The fact that in unusual circumstances one performs such functions does not mean that one holds the office. Luther's celebrated comment that if ''no one were present . . . then a woman must step up and preach to the others, otherwise not,'' is not a basis for saying that a woman may occupy the office of the public ministry.

[60] Martin Luther, *Large Catechism,* 1, 130.

[61] Whether congregations establish and maintain a constitutionally organized voters' assembly is neither commanded nor forbidden by Scripture. For those congregations with a voting assembly, the words of Francis Pieper are pertinent: ''. . . the voting or balloting in the meetings of orthodox congregations has a different significance when it concerns Christian doctrine than when it concerns indifferent matters. The only purpose of voting in matters of doctrine is to see whether all now understand the teaching of the

divine Word and agree to it. . . . In *adiaphora* a vote is taken to ascertain what the majority regards as the best. The natural order is that in *adiaphora* the minority yields to the majority and acquiesces, not because the majority has the right to rule, but for love's sake.'' Pieper, *Christian Dogmatics,* 3:430. Such votes have no ultimate authority.

[62] See discussion on pp. 32, 33.

[63] ''Woman Suffrage in the Church,'' A Report of the CTCR, 1968, p. 3.

[64] The historical fact that in the past the Synod restricted woman suffrage does not mean that the 1969 report or the present one rests on a changed understanding of Scriptural authority or the principle of the subordination of women in the church. To a great extent what is reflected is a changed understanding of the nature and function of the franchise as practiced in the contemporary congregation. See 1972 opinion of the CTCR on ''Woman Suffrage,'' 1973 *Convention Workbook,* pp. 37-38.

[65] Quoted from the CTCR's 1983 report on ''Theology and Practice of the Lord's Supper,'' p. 30.

[66] Report of Task Force on Women, 1977 *Convention Workbook,* p. 54.

Notes: *This 1985 report of the Commission on Theology and Church Relations reinforces the tradition of the Lutheran Church-Missouri Synod (approximately 2,660,000 members) of denying ordained status to women. In 1969, the church gave women the right to vote within ecclesiastical structures based on the position that it is ''the assembly that exercises authority as a result of suffrage, not the individual voter.'' Otherwise, Scripture is understood as prohibiting women from teaching and exercising authority over men. This principle was not accepted by the Lutheran Council papers of 1970, resulting in a conflict with Missouri Synod beliefs. Nevertheless, throughout the 1970s the church conducted studies in an effort to increase the participation of women in the life of the church, short of ordination. The Missouri Synod believes that woman's subordination to man is built into the order of Creation, and is not part of a fallen relationship that needs to be redeemed. The church emphasizes that headship and subordination are not to be equated with superiority or domination. Woman is not less valuable; she is simply one part of a universal hierarchical structure which serves to order creation.*

LUTHERAN COUNCIL IN THE U.S.A.

THE ORDINATION OF WOMEN (1970)

Introduction

Whole Books Now?

For many centuries no one talked about ordaining women. No one even thought about it. Gradually, though, whispers were heard—all arguing against, of course. Then voices became quite audible, as when Thomas Acquinas said women are not up to ''that eminence of degree that is signified by priesthood.'' Others agreed, being sure that self-assertive women had ''been the occasion of much evil in the church.''

Eventually, a few began to favor public status for women. So more voices were heard—still almost all against. Bishop Martensen of Denmark speaking in 1892, for example, thought the movement to take women out of the home was the result of a perverted mania for free love.

Today whole books are being written on the subject, not all against, nor all for.

Why a booklet like this anyway? These chapters are a digest of research done through the Division of Theological Studies of the Lutheran Council in the U.S.A. A study had been requested by The American Lutheran Church which, along with the Lutheran Church in America, had been pressed by the question of ordaining women. The Division of Theological Studies was a natural choice for processing the study because it provides a forum for the ALC, the LCA, the Lutheran Church—Missouri Synod and the Synod of Evangelical Lutheran Churches to examine jointly questions of mutual concern.

A committee of four was assigned to the task. It carried out the research, sought counsel, and wrote its findings. The findings were adopted by the Division and reviewed by a consultation in Dubuque, Iowa, in September, 1969. The participants in that consultation were appointed by the respective church body presidents.

The research papers, the findings, and the report of the Dubuque consultation were presented to the annual meeting of the Lutheran Council in February, 1970. The Council gave a full evening's discussion to the material as it transmitted it without recommendation to the church presidents. In the spirit of that discussion, the presidents are having the main points of the documents distributed to the congregations in this abridged and popularized form.

The exact findings are reprinted in full in the appendix. In brief they said:

> Although the Gospel does not change, conditions do. New situations, differing customs, continued research, the on-going work of God, and the promptings of the Spirit demand constant reconsideration of previous assumptions. The Church must periodically ask whether its practices give the fullest expression of the will of the Lord.
>
> In the past the Church has hesitated to ordain women because scripture seemed to forbid it. Yet strict and literal enforcement of passages such as 1 Corinthians 11:2-16 and 14:33-36 has never been applied. In practice churches have given several kinds of leadership functions to women. Hence, and in the light of further examination of the biblical material, the case both against and for ordination is found to be inconclusive. Among the Lutheran church bodies, therefore, a variety of practices on this question ought not disrupt church fellowship.

Great credit must be given to those who did the research for the study. Unfortunately, the discipline of their scholarship will not be fully evident here. A digest would not be a digest if it retained the extensive footnotes, quotations, and citation of the original work.

Chapter 1: Is Scripture Against?

Woman was made only as an afterthought, and secondhand at that. She didn't even rate fresh dust—just a rib. Any man can spare a rib.

Though woman was made second, she was deceived first. Too gullible. She could never be trusted, especially to teach in church.

This, of course, is a glib treatment of Genesis 2 and 3. It is used here to show how serious arguments against the ordination of women do *not* begin. They come from a much deeper level of scripture interpretation, deep enough in fact to write off more shallow points of debate such as the first three to be given here.

Incapability

The Weaker Sex

Many have believed that woman is the weaker sex. In fact, they would say she is downright inferior. She is to be ruled by man because she is not capable of managing herself. "It is not the nature of the office of the ministry that excludes women, it is the nature of woman." Ordination would never "take."

Those in the Lutheran church who are against the ordination of women generally have not used this argument. When the representatives from the churches met in Dubuque to compare views on the question, some were strongly opposed to ordination, but no one argued that woman was by nature incapable of receiving God's charismatic gifts.

Neither did the representatives accept the God-is-male argument against female clergy.

God is Male

Incarnation is Male

God is Father and Jesus Christ is Son—the incarnation is male. The Bible has no time for goddesses. Jahweh has no consort. The male figure is a principle in understanding God. The Christ was not male just to be socially acceptable.

This is faulty logic, anyone could charge. It makes too much of an analogy. If carried to its conclusion, women would be excluded even from membership in Christ's body, the Church. But, to the contrary, Christ came as the new man showing the new humanity of men and women in Christ. As a matter of fact, God's love can be described like "a mother's for her child" (Deuteronomy 32:11; Isaiah 46:3, 51:1; Psalm 131:2).

The "God-is-male" contention was not only judged weak, it was rejected by all Lutherans who took part in the Council's study.

The Apostles were Male

The Twelve

Jesus chose only males for his twelve. He must have intended the ministry to be all male, for surely he knew what he was doing.

But can anyone be sure Jesus deliberately kept women out, or that he intended this selection to be a model for all time? If he did, no Gentile should be a minister, for Jesus chose only Jews. The requirement for being an apostle was to be a "witness to his resurrection" (Acts 1:22). Women were witnesses to his resurrection.

The apostles-were-male argument was also rejected by the study participants, because it is not a part of serious biblical theology.

Orders of Creation

Changeless or Changing

Genesis 2 and 3 is where the "orders of creation" argument usually begins. It says that woman's subordination to man is written into the very structure of the universe. The consultation had an intense discussion about this. Repeatedly, they asked whether God had ordained an eternal, unchanging subordination of woman to man, or whether, instead, he is actually changing the orders of creation by his constant action in history.

It is easy to see how, until recent years, man believed that the natural order always stayed the same. An oak was always just like an oak, and a woman was always just like a woman. The Bible seems to assume this permanence. Under such a view, even when God acted in history as in Christ, he was only trying to restore the original perfection.

But it is now evident that the static view is not so certain. Mutations can be observed. New strains can be developed. Barbarians can become civilized. Slave peoples can manage their freedom. Patriarchal and matriarchal societies can become democratic. A Priscilla can teach a man like Apollos "more accurately" (Acts 18:26), with the help of an Aquila, of course.

Then too, on closer look, maybe the subordination of woman wasn't an order of creation after all, but an order of judgment! It is only after the fall that God says to Eve, "your husband . . . shall rule over you" (Geneis 3:16). And maybe the orders of creation are all upstaged by the order of redemption.

The New Testament

Actually, though, the New Testament does little to erase the subordination argument. In fact, it substantiates it, telling women repeatedly to be silent and submissive. Yet, all the while it gives them a radical new freedom and recounts how they taught and prophesied in the early church.

Certain passages have been cited so convincingly through the years for the subordination of women and against their ordination that they must be examined in detail. Anyone who wants to be prepared for serious discussion on the subject should commit three of the citations to memory, 1 Corinthians 11 and 14 and 1 Timothy 2.

> 1 Corinthians 11:2-16: 2 I commend you because you remember me in everything
> and maintain the traditions even as I have delivered them to you. 3 But I want you to
> understand that the head of every man is Christ, the head of a woman is her husband,
> and the head of Christ is God. 4 Any man who prays or prophesies with his head
> covered dishonors his head. 5 But any woman who prays or prophesies with her head
> unveiled dishonors her head—it is the same as if her head were shaven. 6 For if a
> woman will not veil herself, then she should cut off her hair; but if it is disgraceful for
> a woman to be shorn or shaven, let her wear a veil. 7 For a man ought not to cover his
> head, since he is the image and glory of God; but woman is the glory of man. 8 (For
> man was not made from woman, but woman from man. 9 Neither was man created
> for woman, but woman for man.) 10 That is why a woman ought to have a veil on her
> head, because of the angels. 11 (Nevertheless, in the Lord woman is not independent
> of man nor man of woman; 12 for as woman was made from man, so man is now born
> of woman. And all things are from God.) 13 Judge for yourselves; is it proper for a
> woman to pray to God with her head uncovered? 14 Does not nature itself teach you
> that for a man to wear long hair is degrading to him, 15 but if a woman has long hair,
> it is her pride? For her hair is given to her for a covering. 16 If any one is disposed to
> be contentious, we recognize no other practice, nor do the churches of God.

Woman were prophesying and praying in the church assemblies at Corinth! That is made clear in verse 5. And Paul does not stop them. He only stresses that they should wear headgear. Several reasons come to his mind:

- Proper subordination of wives to husbands, verse 3.
- Woman was made for man, verse 8.
- Social custom (shorn hair is a disgrace), verse 5.
- Nature wants the woman's head covered as indicated by the long hair it gives her, verse 15.
- Because of the angels, verse 10, whatever that means. The sense is obscure.
- The practice in other churches, verse 16. This is the ecumenical argument.

But Paul also opens the door here a bit. Men should now recognize that they depend on women, just as women depend on men. Woman is not always second—man must be born from woman (verse 12). Man and woman are interdependent in the Lord (verse 11). So women may continue to prophesy.

Freedoms Need Limits

But Paul takes pains to keep the new freedom from going too far. Traditions should not be broken needlessly. That would cause unnecessary offense.

> 1 Corinthians 14:33b-36: As in all the churches of the saints, 34 the women should
> keep silence in the churches. For they are not permitted to speak, but should be
> subordinate, as even the law says. 35 If there is anything they desire to know, let
> them ask their husbands at home. For it is shameful for a woman to speak in church.

> 36 What! Did the word of God originate with you, or are you the only ones it has reached?

Should this instruction be brushed aside as no more binding than Paul's tastes in clothes and hairstyles? If it is taken seriously, a contradiction must be resolved. How can it be that Paul allowed the Corinthian women both to pray and prophesy in the previous passage, while in this one he forbids them to speak in church?

- It could be that these verse were added later. Some manuscripts have verses 34 and 35 following 40; the verses do seem out of context as they are here; and it is odd to hear Paul saying, "as even the law says."
- Maybe these are from two different letters, Paul having changed his mind in between.
- Maybe he was thinking of public worship here, and of house meetings in Chapter 11.
- He might have been giving permission to prophesy in Chapter 11, but stating his own preference against it here in 14.
- His term for women in this text (verse 34) likely means "wives" rather than "all women."
- He might just have been irked with wives who had interrupted.

Whatever the explanation, the puzzle makes this passage questionable grounds for prohibiting ordination.

The "ecumenical argument" does come through strongly though (verse 33b—unless 33b goes with 33a as in NEB note). The Corinthians had reveled in gifts of the spirit, especially prophecies. Too much to suit Paul. "Are you the only people God's word reached?" No, there are other congregations. Try to do as they do, not just as you think.

> 1 Timothy 2:11-14: Let a woman learn in silence with all submissiveness. 12 I permit no woman to teach or to have authority over men; she is to keep silent. 13 For Adam was formed first, then Eve; 14 and Adam was not deceived, but the woman was deceived and became a transgressor. 15 Yet woman will be saved through bearing children, if she continues in faith and love and holiness, with modesty.

Some think that a wave of emancipation was spreading through the young churches. These verses try to hold the line. Women were to remove the ornaments, replace the jewels with good deeds (verses 9-10), stop teaching and holding authority over men. Reason? Order of creation; order of judgment.

Women could take satisfaction in a few things though. They could bear children and be saved if they continued in the virtues of faith, love, holiness, and modesty.

The Timothy passage is "handled" in various ways:

- By pointing out that if it is taken literally, women may not teach in church school or parochial school, direct choirs, or even pray or sing aloud.
- By saying that this refers to the place of women in nature and society, not in the "order of salvation."
- By reasoning that this should be read "evangelically," not "legally," especially in view of the fact that women did teach in the early church.
- By re-emphasizing that this refers to the relation of wife to husband, not all women to men.

Ephesians 5:22: Wives, be subject to your husbands as to the Lord (cf. 1 Peter 3:1. Likewise you wives, be submissive to your husbands. . .)

Some think that Ephesians was not written by Paul, but that is beside the point. The passage is typical of a code morality which shows up in several New Testament references. It is a catechetical form perhaps taken over from the culture of the day.

The greatest objection to the use of these verses as arguments is that they concern only the married woman, not all women.

Headship Structures

Warning! Watch for shifts along the way here. The theme is subordination as an order of creation. That has not changed. It has been clearly set forth in passage after passage. But the discussion is looking at a variety of reasons for it. First it was because man was made ahead of woman and head over her. Then it was because the freedoms which were sweeping the Church had to have some traditional limits. Now, subordination is being considered because order is necessary in church and home. This latter is more precisely called "headship structures."

> 1 Timothy 3:1-5: 1 The saying is sure: If any one aspires to the office of bishop, he desires a noble task. 2 Now a bishop must be above reproach, the husband of one wife, temperate, sensible, dignified, hospitable, an apt teacher, 3 no drunkard, not violent, but gentle, not quarrelsome, and no lover of money. 4 He must manage his own household well, keeping his children submissive and respectful in every way; 5 for if a man does not know how to manage his own household, how can he care for God's church?

This famous passage is especially crucial to the discussion because it definitely connects the ruling of a family to the ruling of a church. All passages cited earlier were somewhat dismissed on the grounds that they referred only to husbands and wives, not to men and women in general, nor to ministers and laymen. This text, however, brings the argument of subordination back into full bloom.

But does this passage grow out of the orders of creation, or does it just come from the culture of the day? The Stoics liked to place family, city-state, and world in parallel. Paul may be reflecting their thought here. If so, can such orders be taken as eternal truth? Should they be the deciding factor for the Church's ministry? In a once-over-lightly reading the passage poses no problem, but read in detail it does: Must bishops (pastors) be married? Must they be fathers?. . .of submissive children? If these verses are saying that, the very design of nature demands that man be head, and the church must crusade for the subordination of women in all areas of society. But what then, about verses 8 and 11? Verse 8 says, "Deacons likewise must be serious." No problem. However, verse 11 says, "The women likewise must be serious, no slanderers, but temperate, faithful in all things." This seems directed at a class of women deacons who have some sort of ministry parallel to the deacons and bishops unless the women here were the wives of deacons.

No, the chapter as a whole cannot be taken to require absolute subordination of women. Its style is too casual to be church by-laws. It can be paralleled in Hellenistic lists of qualifications for military generals.

All of this aside, the passage is speaking about the bishop's responsibility to be a leader who serves so faithfully he inspires respect and obedience. It is not talking of the responsibility of subordinates to be duly subordinate, but of leaders to be good leaders.

Rulership or Leadership Service?

This calls for another shift of attention. Headship was first being seen as the need for order. Now consider it as the need to make someone responsible for good pastoral care. Contrast the two. Is power conferred from above? A divine right? Or is it granted by those who are served? The consent of the governed? Is "authority" the right of the office, or is it earned only in the service the office performs?

At the inter-Lutheran consultation in Dubuque, this difference was sharply marked. Those who said headship was basically a divinely-given, rulership power thought it would be violated if a woman was ordained. Those who said headship was basically leadership service *(diakonia),* thought a woman in the ranks would not destroy the order. This is a very important difference.

The Confessions

The Lutheran view of the ministry steers a tricky course between rulership and service. It does not make the pastor a special, sacred class of citizen; yet it calls for sufficient respect to make the office effective. The pastor stands with the people under God, yet also under God against the people as the voice of God's word.

The Reformers insisted that the office of the ministry be filled only by persons who are "rightly called" and ordained. The confessions even speak once of ordination as a sacrament.[1] But this ministry is servant to the Word. "The ministry of the New Testament is not bound to places and persons, as the Levitical priesthood is, but is spread abroad through the whole world and exists wherever God gives his gifts, apostles, prophets, pastors, teachers. Nor is this ministry valid because of any individual's authority but because of the Word given by Christ." The German goes on to say, "The person adds nothing to this Word and office commanded by Christ. No matter who it is who preaches and teaches the Word, if there are hearts that hear and adhere to it, something will happen to them according as they hear and believe because Christ commanded such preaching."[2] Such a ministry involves both the authority of the Word and the service to those addressed.

The current upheavals in society have much to do with the contrast between rulership as authority and as service. Young people hate "columns on courthouses." They want the institutions to earn respect solely on the basis of their record, not to induce it by awe-inspiring symbols. Institutions are not to hide unimpressive service behind impressive fronts. Responsible service needs no front. It can inspire respect on its own.

But can it? Does good service in and of itself inspire the respect it must have to function, or must it be supported by some pomp and circumstance, or some response conditioning, or some authority "from above"?

The freedoms which are sweeping society today are perhaps forcing authorities to serve with more sensitivity, but those gains might be lost if due respect for the authority does not then follow:

Which Way?

Should freedom and reform be further inflamed, or should such movements now be squelched? At this stage, would the effectiveness of the clergy be hurt more if the awe of their office were further diminished or if the new demands for credibility were eased off?

For some, the ordination of women would probably reduce the image of authority the office has enjoyed. But if authority is judged by duly dedicated service, then the admission of women might add to the respect. Luther held that women were more fervent in faith than men.

There are two more passages which illustrate the headship discussion:

> Hebrews 13:7, 17,: Remember your leaders, those who spoke to you the word of God; consider the outcome of their life, and. . . .17 Obey your leaders and submit to them; for they are keeping watch over your souls, as men will have to give account . . . (cf. verse 24, Greet all your leaders.)

The theme in Hebrews is the pilgrimage of the people of God. There is no stress on hierarchy in it (Christ is the high priest). The leaders mentioned in this text are to be respected because they speak God's word and faithfully care for souls. The word for leaders in this use is vague, coming from the Greek political world. The term for "submit" is also not the same as the one used previously in Ephesians 5. Respect is due "the ministry," but the authority seems to come from example.

A few scholars think that a woman, Priscilla, helped write the epistle!

> 1 Peter 5:1, 5: 1 I exhort the elders among you, as a fellow elder. . . . 2 tend the flock of God. . . . 5 Likewise you that are younger, be subject to the elders. Clothe yourselves, all of you, with humility toward one another. . . .

Many scholars see in verse 1 a technical use of the term "elders" *(presbyteroi)* as a "college of presbyters." In verse 5, however, the term *(hypotagete presbyterois)* seems to mean "elders" in the sense of older people in contrast to the younger (Beck translates, "You young people, be subject to those who are older.").

Like Hebrews, 1 Peter has a "people of God" theme. Distinctions between clergy and laity are not stressed. It seems to be urging due submission to pastoral leaders, again, for the care they give.

Reverse Thrust

Orders of creation, subordination, headship structures—several pages have been spent discussing this many-sided argument. The space is justified, though, because it was generally these principles which in the past caused the Church to decide against the ordination of women. And now these are the very points which are blunted by the arguments for ordination. In fact they are used as part of the basis to make the case in favor. Two examples have already been seen—that God's work continues in creation, and that headship is that service which is worthy of respect. The search for guidance now goes to other scripture concepts which might favor the ordination of women—image of God, new age, all-members-are-ministers, and women-ministered.

Chapter 2: Is Scripture For?

The Image of God

The Old Testament Image

The "image of God" argument goes back to Genesis also, but not to Genesis 2 where the orders of creation discussion began—rather to Genesis 1. It goes to the so-called first creation story with its seven days, instead of to the second with its dust and rib.

"God created man in his own image, in the image of God he created him; male and female he created them" (Genesis 1:27).

These words seem to make woman worth as much as man.

What is more, the image was not lost in the Genesis 3 fall. Adam still had it at the age of 130 when he was passing it on to Seth in Genesis 5:1 and 3, and it was still the basis for prohibiting murder in the Noah episode, 9:6.

The New Testament Image

The New Testament says it differently, or understands the "image" in a different way. There Jesus Christ alone is the image of God, and others attain it only by entering his body through baptism—a new creation! (1 Corinthians 15:49; 2 Corinthians 4:4; Romans 8:29; Colossians 1:15; 3:9 f.; Ephesians 4:24.)

Whether the image of God was kept after the fall, or whether baptism restores it as it had been before the fall, women seem to acquire equal status before God by partaking in it. The orders of creation argument against ordination of women is therefore weakened.

The catch though, is that the principles in the first creation story cannot be detached that easily from those in the second. At least that is what the counter argument might say. Woman may have the image in Genesis 1, but Genesis 2 could imply that it is merely derived from man. Thus woman could be said to be even spiritually below man. But if not spiritually subordinate, having the image still doesn't preclude orderly channels of authority. Just because the image of God grants certain spiritual qualifications doesn't mean equality of functions in the church's ministry. Thus, the image of God argument can be vulnerable too.

The New Age

The New Order

The "new age" is but a slight shift from the image of God argument. It focuses on the new order that has come in Christ. "Therefore, if anyone is in Christ he is a new creation, the old has passed away, behold, the new has come" (2 Corinthians 5:17).

> Galatians 3:27-28: For as many of you as were baptized into Christ have put on Christ. There is neither Jew nor Greek, there is neither slave nor free, there is neither male nor female; for you are all one in Christ Jesus.

Galatians has been dubbed "The Epistle of Freedom." In it, Paul stresses the entirely new status of all who are in Christ—women included. People had been giving thanks, as prayers put it, that they were not women, barbarians, unbelievers, or slaves. Their religion told them that the grace of God had saved them from being born a girl. But Paul is telling them here that women and slaves are not second-class citizens in Christ. Many believe that the Galatians text is the breakthrough which makes the ordination of women possible. In Christ "all barriers are down."

But look around you, anyone with reservations could say. See, the new age has not come, not even in the Body of Christ, the Church. See it as it is. The "Epistle of Freedom" is referring to future salvation, not to current social life.

Eschatology

This brings up the whole question of eschatology, that is, how everything comes out in the end. Has the new age already come, or is it yet to come? Or both? "Both/and" seems to be Paul's way of looking at it. Already, but not yet. Freedom has come, and with it the privilege to live to the full. But reality is still here, limiting what can be done. As in Paul's day, so with the church today. Christians live with a tension in deciding on matters like the ordination of women. Should the situation be seen in the terms of the new and of the fulfilled, or in terms of the old and creation? Has the new day dawned? Has it come partially, as in Paul's day, requiring some limitations?

Some suggest that women might be ordained now, but that the new limit be drawn at the eucharist. Ordination, perhaps; celebration, no. But comments at the Dubuque consultation expressly opposed preventing ordained women from giving communion. Here, in the sacrament, where the Church enjoys the new age most fully, there should be neither slave nor free, male nor female; all are one in Christ. In fact, this Galatians 3 text is understood by some to mean equality in the eucharist—exactly there, if not anywhere else.

Breakthrough to a new age, or restoration of the original image of God—both arguments have much substance, but still nothing conclusive.

All Members Are Ministers

Males only, and just those without blemishes at that, were admitted to the Old Testament's priesthood and temple offices. Nor were women allowed to be rabbis in Judaism. In a way, Israel's faith itself was reserved for men. Entry was by circumcision. There was no initiation rite for women. They were not regarded as worthy to study the Law. Women were even, some suspected, the source of idolatry. Neighboring cults had priestesses, and their gods had goddesses. Israel was different.

Baptism as Ordination

But by and large, there is agreement that the ministry of the Church of Jesus Christ is not particularly a continuation of the Old Testament priesthood. The New Testament deliberately changes it. There is a "royal priesthood" of all baptized believers (1 Peter 2:9). Christian baptism ordains all believers. Women, then, are "priests" by baptism.

But, a reply could say, there is a special, ordained ministry to be distinguished from the general ministry; and, for reasons already well noted, women have thus far been excluded from it.

Women Ministered in Israel and the Early Church

The Picture from History

Although care was taken to keep women out of the priesthood, they did get judgeships (Deborah). And they became prophetesses (Miriam, Hulda, Anna). Women were "ministering at the tent of meeting" (1 Samuel 2:22). Some, however, think this verse is a jibe at the laxity which was going on under the sons of Eli.

In the New Testament several references are made to the service of women:

- They minister to Jesus during his lifetime and at his death (Luke 8:3, Mark 15:41).
- They serve as prophetesses (1 Corinthians 11; Acts 21:9), perhaps "ordained" at Corinth, certainly speaking in the Lord's name under the Spirit.
- They are deaconesses, the sort of ministry Phoebe held (Romans 16:1), consequently recognized as an office (1 Timothy 3:8ff., 3:11). Later references suggest women serving as elders or bishops, but the terms involved could mean the wife of an elder or bishop.
- They are consecrated widows (1 Timothy 5:3ff.), possibly an order in the church.
- They have leadership roles—Lydia, Priscilla, Thecla.

The acid test, arguments could say, is whether women actually ministered in the New Testament. They did. But the evidence is thin. Need every woman who served in the Bible be considered a pastor? And why are there so few?

"Image of God," "new age," "all-members-are-ministers," "women-ministered." The scriptural concepts which seem to favor ordination are not conclusive either.

Chapter 3: What Does Scripture Say?—Hermeneutics

Maybe readers are saying, "Hold it!" because they have not agreed with the way scripture is being used here. A few may think the exegesis in this summary is too breezy, that it is not seriously searching the text for direction. Some may say that the exegesis is too forced. That it has been trying to make the scriptures answer questions they had never been asked. The answers may be new to still others. This brings the study tight up against the problem of hermeneutics. How should scripture be interpreted and applied?

Hermeneutical Problems

Seriously, Not Literally?

Scripture is to be considered normative and taken seriously, but it need not always be taken literally. That seems to be the practice of the church anyway. To take these passages literally would mean purging a lot of Bible classes, that is, dismissing women teachers and never letting women students publicly question a statement made by a man. In fact, just have women keep silent altogether. Let them be seen, not heard—and their faces shouldn't be seen at that. A veil please. No. In practice at least, the agreement is: scripture is the norm, but the norm is not always found by a simple literal reading.

In fact, finding the norm is often difficult. For ordination, there is a problem right off. The Bible does not use the word "ordination" as it is known today. A "laying on of hands" was practiced in Judaism as far back as Joshua, but it was used only for certain high offices and scholarship. The early Christians used it to bestow the Spirit, or to heal, which is something else again. Acts has some people being "sent forth" (13:1ff.), but that was more like the rite used for commissioning today. The Pastoral Epistles, Acts, and probably Matthew, suggest types of ordination, but no uniform practice can be detected, let alone a full-blown "theology of ordination." The Bible doesn't carry the whole mind of the Church because so many practices had to be worked out over the years.

Time Conditioning

The guidance sought is on ordination, and the scripture doesn't mention ordination. That is the first problem.

Second problem: how to tell which scriptural instructions were to apply to the time in which they were written, and which to all times?

The early church lived in complex surroundings. It was influenced by:

- The Old Testament
- First-Century Judaism
- Greek culture
- Roman culture
- The philosophies of the day
- The religions of the day

Some customs it accepted, some it rejected. Paul could use various Stoic sayings and ideas, while decrying pagan practices. In the same way, Christians adopted some of the current attitudes toward women while denouncing others.

For the most part, the surrounding cultures regarded women as subjects. The early Church was often as far ahead of its time in this respect as it could go. It gave women a radical new freedom. It allowed them the same rite of entry as man—baptism. It believed they could be saved just like men. It let them prophesy in some places.

In other ways, though, it set limits on this freedom. It acted out of the feelings for order that prevailed around it. Those feelings were often taught in the Church as a part of the basic Christian catechism. As was mentioned, some of the codes seem to have been transferred intact to the passages just studied.

Now, which practices are the everlasting will of the Lord and which are just time-conditioned?

If subordination was kept in some forms by the early church merely to avoid needless offense to the community, then maybe ordination should be the norm today—to avoid offense in a society which is beginning to resent male domination. If subordination is an order of creation for all times, however, then the norm is obvious.

And then, too, Paul and the early Christians may have been unable to distinguish clearly between what the Gospels implied and what the culture taught. That is, the influence of the culture may have caused Paul to assume that subordination was an order for all time. That would not settle the norm either.

Conflicts in Scripture?

Third problem: taking the Bible as a whole, not just in bits and pieces or proof texts. If a church tries to construct a norm for ordination from the overall view of scriptures, then it must deal with possible conflicts. One passage taken by itself says one thing, while another taken by itself says something else. Remember trying to resolve 1 Corinthians 11 and 14 where the differences occur within three chapters of each other. Remember the broader conflict between the old age and the new. Unfortunately, building a theology of ordination from the Bible as a whole isn't easy either.

Historical Evaluation

Fourth problem: to what extent should historical criticism be applied in the search for norms? How rigorously? Can some passages be marked as earlier and others as later and less central?

Development

Fifth problem: how to allow for the development which took place during the New Testament period and in subsequent centuries. The Church's view of ordination and society's view of woman's place have undergone much change. How is development weighted?

A Canon Within the Canon?

This brings up still a sixth problem: degrees of emphases. If the interpreter accepts the possibility that through the years development has taken place, passages reinterpreted, ideas added, emphasis changed, then the value of some texts is bound to be affected. Should some texts be weighted more heavily than others? Is there a "canon within the canon"? What is central in the Bible? Do some texts matter more than others? Does "the gospel" take precedence over any single verse?

This is hardly the place to try to wrestle to the floor the massive hermeneutical issues of our day. Enough to say that for every interpretation some objection can be raised and to every argument some weakness found.

But the problem remains unsolved. Is there any principle to guide in norm-finding?

A Case Study in Norm-Finding

An idea can be gained of the criteria which a church uses by observing it in the actual process of norm-finding. An example occurred in the recent decision of the Lutheran Church—Missouri Synod to allow congregations to let women vote. The Commission on Theology and Church Relations finished a study on woman's suffrage in 1969.

In its final report the CTCR refers, in passing, to ordination. It understands the scriptural injunctions to mean that women should not hold the pastoral office. This reference may have been in the report to separate the onus of ordaining women from the question of granting suffrage to them. The commission concluded against ordaining women, but for suffrage. The latter was voted at the 1969 Denver convention. The former certainly would not have been.

The norm-finding work of the commission was done very seriously and gives direction for the process. The master argument of the CTCR statement is subordination as an order of creation. The study believed voting would not be insubordination, but holding any office in the church which involves authority over men would. The fact that this subordination theme was chosen by the CTCR from the biblical complex offers a clue to a norm-finding principle which might be isolated.

In arguing its case, the CTCR did not explicitly use the statements (1) that a woman ought to wear a veil "because of the angels," (2) that man was not made for woman, but woman for man, (3) that Adam was made first or (4) that Eve was the first to be deceived. It did identify the passages which contain them, but it generalized from them; it did not apply them specifically.

The Selection Process

That is, from all those reasons which are given by biblical writers for subordination of women, the CTCR document did some selecting. The question is: why was the rule about veils bypassed and the rule about subordination applied? By what "higher criteria" are some of the Bible's specifics ignored and other principles retained? Is it that the general principles are to be taken seriously, but not detailed specifics? That is to be doubted. Is it really because there is no case today just like that of Paul's day in which wives publicly question their husband's revelations? What about the typical Bible class in which the leader, like the pastor himself, invites questions and sincerely wants the class, including his wife, to discuss what he says? Why isn't that forbidden? Not because the two situations are too specific to be connected. There must be another reason.

Could it be that times have changed, that some practices of Bible times are no longer binding because times are different; that the situation today is quite different from that of the New Testament? To many folks, the answer is "yes." This means that, to them, historical change is an important factor in finding the Bible's meaning for each new age.

History, the Guide

Like most American Lutherans at one time or another, the early Missouri Synod fathers had assumed, without expecting to be challenged, that the Bible made woman's suffrage invalid. However, the CTCR notes, woman's suffrage had not yet been established then in the American way of life. The question has taken on new significance for the church since women have had equal vote in society.

It may seem that the norms of scripture should direct the history of the Church and world. The fact is, though, history gives new understandings which permit reconsideration of earlier interpretations.

The CTCR study has made allowances for time-conditioning in norm-finding. That principle helps a great deal toward hermeneutical problem solving.

Humanization of History

Going even further: God's act in Christ might be "humanizing" history, making the status of women more humane. If that is true, then the action reported in scripture is shaping the history of the world. History is a reflection of the action in scripture!

There is nothing conclusive about all of this, of course, but it makes things previously thought to be conclusive less so. It suggests, again, that the orders of creation might not be static if God is at work in them. The orders might have a history and may be understood best in the light of the changes they have undergone.

Such a conclusion still need not imply ordination of women. It could be pointing, instead, to whole new forms of ministry and whole new meanings of ordination.

The work of the Church has branched out into a wide variety of new opportunities. There are ministries of music, ministries of mercy, educational ministries, streets ministries, and dozens more. Laymen work full time in social institutions, on parish staffs, in community services. The dividing line between the work of laymen and pastors is becoming more and more unclear. History has brought the opportunity for new definitions. Those who participated in the Council's ordination of women research strongly urged the churches to undertake a joint study of this broader question, the meaning of ordination itself. History has brought the need.

What does the Bible say? For all the hermeneutical problems, hopefully this discussion has made some progress. First the problems themselves were isolated to show that a conclusive case could not be made easily for or against a practice such as the ordination of women. Second came the realization that history does have a bearing on biblical understandings and that history brings new situations which require the reconsideration of previous assumptions. Third, history was seen as the possible arena for God's humanizing work, bringing new opportunities and the necessity for new definitions.

Is there a hint in all this that the Bible should be dropped altogether, with history becoming the norm? If there is, this study disclaims it. The fact that the major portion of the booklet is given to the search for scriptural norms is a witness to the place scripture holds.

If there be any hint, let it suggest that the histories of the church bodies involved in this study do differ slightly. Think how the histories of the various Lutheran churches throughout the world vary. Which is to say a practice which might be in the strongest interest of the Gospel for one, might not be for another. The representatives participating in the study found themselves again and again in agreement on the point that differing decisions on the ordination of women should not cause division in Lutheran fellowship.

Chapter 4: What Have Lutherans Said?—History

Lutheran History in Europe

Luther and the Confessions

Luther can be quoted on both sides. Sometimes he repeated the traditional views. Sometimes he was radically different. He based some of his reasoning on abilities, which he thought women generally lacked, but did not completely lack. If no men were able, he said, let women preach and administer the sacraments. Let the circumstances decide. But then, he added, the Spirit will surely see to it that capable men are not lacking.

The Lutheran confessions say nothing about the ordination of women. They do have points to make on the ministry, some of which have already been mentioned.

Lutheran Orthodoxy

In Europe, Lutherans, after the Reformation, generally decided the question by continuing past practice, not as the result of debate about doctrine. Until this century they gave little attention to the possibility of ordination. They were generally opposed when they did, and most assumed that biblical doctrine forbade it, but not all. A few early voices thought the matter was less than dogma, but they were ignored by most eighteenth and nineteenth century Europeans.

Matthias Flacius (1520-1575) thought that men rather than women should preach and minister, but considered this a human arrangement rather than divine command. He thought that order was at least partly to be based on the attitude of the whole community so long as there was fear of God in what was done.

Johann Gerhard (1621-1668) saw 1 Corinthians 14:34 and 1 Timothy 2:11, 12 as a rejection of the matriarchal ways of some sects, rather than as an absolute rule. He distinguished between church privileges in general and teaching in particular, public-church and private-home teaching, and routine rules and special cases. He believed women had all sorts of weaknesses of character and intellect, making them less fit.

Pietism

The Pietists broke down some of the separation between clergy and laity by insisting on a more active laity. They did not stir up sentiment for ordaining women though. *Phillip Jakob Spener* (1635-1705) found no scripture against having women teach, but wanted to control the extent to which the practice was permitted.

Johann Albrecht Bengel (1687-1752) admitted that there could be logical exceptions to the rule against ordination. The fact is, though, exceptional cases have been exceptionally few. Bengel emphasized that women are to have no authority over men.

19th Century

Little was said about ordination of women in the nineteenth century and little change took place in attitude toward it. The common feelings were against; one voice, for example, quite adamantly saying that women are "too easily excited." Bishop Martensen (1808-1884) of Denmark thought women had no real creative talents. F.H.R. Frank (1827-1894) wanted to let the inner brotherly love of the congregation decide the question.

Europe Today

By 1968 the ordination of women was permitted in the Lutheran churches in the following countries:

> *Norway.* Since 1938 the government has had the right to appoint women pastors, provided they were not rejected by the congregation. A 1956 law removed this veto power. The first woman was ordained in 1961.
>
> *Denmark.* A law permitting ordination has been in effect since 1947. Ordination has been practiced since 1948.
>
> *Czechoslovakia.* Women were pastors in Czechoslovakia as early as 1953, but they were not allowed to become chief pastors of parishes until 1959.
>
> *Sweden.* The law permitting ordination has been in effect since 1959, the practice since 1960.
>
> *France.* Reports available at the time of this research indicate that the Lutheran church of France already had several women pastors prior to 1962.
>
> *Germany.* As of February, 1968, of the twenty-seven member churches of the Evangelical Church in Germany (EKID), twenty permitted the ordination of women. Of the thirteen territorial churches in the United Evangelical Lutheran Church in Germany, seven admit women to the ministry. All of the territorial Lutheran churches in the German Democratic Republic permit ordination of women.

Women are not ordained in Finland yet. Nothing in its Public Worship Act prevents ordination, but a 1958 and 1962 refusal of the church to remove all legal doubts has prevented any exercise of the possibility. Since 1965, a type of parish service office has been open to male and female theological graduates.

When the shift came, it came fast. Over half of the Lutherans in the world are in churches which now have women on their clergy rolls. But none of these is in North America.

Lutheran History in America

American Lutherans, until recently, were unanimously opposed. Hardly anyone thought that the question was solely a matter of practice, neither enjoined nor forbidden by God in scripture. They presumably saw it settled by the Bible.

A sampling of American views ranging over the century:

> *Samuel S. Schmucker* (General Synod). Women shouldn't even lead in prayer.
>
> *Edmund Jacob Wolf* (General Synod). Subordination was not only established in creation, but made sure by history.
>
> *Henry Eyster Jacobs* (General Council). In 1897 said women may speak sometimes in public, but in 1899 he reverted to the rule that they must be silent "except there be no man."
>
> *C.F.W. Walther* (Missouri). Scripture excludes women from voting, teaching in public assemblies and having authority over men but does not forbid their teaching privately and in parish schools.
>
> *Franz Pieper* (Missouri). Was alarmed by woman suffrage. "Woman ought not be dragged from her place of honor into public life." Women were not even to ask questions publicly.

The break in ranks in America came on the question of vote and voice for women in congregational meetings. At the turn of the century, the General Synod's model congregational constitution gave the women vote but not office. In 1907, Augustana gave women vote and in 1930 allowed them to be delegates. In 1934, the United Lutheran Church decided that women could be delegates, church councilmen, and board and commission members. (The majority report said, though, that it would have agreed with the opposition's minority report had the question been ordination.) In 1969, the Missouri Synod allowed congregations to grant women voting rights.

Krister Stendahl believes the matter of vote and voice is the basic question anyway.

Lutherans in North America do not now ordain, but the ALC, LCA, and LC—MS are all at some stage of study on the matter.

The ALC's Board of Theological Education reported in 1966 that it permits enrollment of women in its theological seminaries to receive the B.D. degree, and allows adjustment of the curriculum with respect to the women students. It adopted this rule, however, fully understanding that the church's prevailing practice did not ordain women.

In 1967 the ALC's Church Council asked the board to have the question of women's ordination studied. The faculty of Luther Seminary reviewed four objections to ordination—biblical, theological, practical, and ecumenical. It found that there was nothing decisive in the first three and that the fourth, while serious, was difficult to assess because some churches are already ordaining and some that aren't are open to discussion of the possibility. In view of this, they saw no reasons why ordination shouldn't be permissible.

The LCA heard an interim report in 1968 by a Commission on the Comprehensive Study of the Doctrine of the Ministry which said the commission could see no biblical or theological reasons for denying women ordination.

The LC—MS's 1969 convention adopted a guide which referred to the scripture directing women to keep silent in the church and prohibiting them from teaching and exercising authority over men. The resolution said, "We understand [this] to mean that women ought not to hold the pastoral office or serve in any other capacity involving the distinctive functions of this office." The resolution stated the belief that the passages did not preclude women from service on boards, commissions, and committees and in congregational or synodical assemblies, so long as the order of creation was not violated. Congregations and the synod were thus at liberty to alter their polities accordingly but were urged to act cautiously and deliberately in the spirit of Christian love.

In January, 1970, the Synod's Commission on Theology and Church Relations assigned to its committee on theology a study on the ordination of women.

In Europe the shortage of pastors following World War II opened the way to the ordination of women. America did not experience that emergency. Challenges to the traditional view came only with a change in the position of woman in society and a development of principles of biblical interpretation which could permit basic reconsiderations.

Chapter 5: Is it Workable?—Pragmatics

Practicalities

This is the post-pill era. Practically speaking, women are already free. Ordination will hardly change that one way or the other. But what effects would ordination have? How would it work? How much resistance would be encountered? How would the churches be changed as a result? What rules of selection should be set? What would other churches think?

Even if scripture had a verse which said, "Women should be ordained in the American Lutheran churches beginning in 1970," practical preparations would be necessary.

If on the other hand scripture really neither forbids nor enjoins ordination, then the whole question might be a matter of practice altogether, something to be decided by the churches in the light of their God-given responsibilities and effectiveness. Practice instead of dogma.

Either way, this chapter tries to isolate some of the practical aspects by looking at sociological, psychological, and ecumenical factors.

How Has Woman's Status Changed?

- the right to vote, 1919
- decline in the double standard
- entrance into occupations
- more freedom from the home because of labor-saving devices and smaller families
- laws against discrimination

In 1840, only seven occupations were open to women in the United States: teaching, needlework, keeping boarders, working in cotton factories, typesetting, book binding, and housekeeping. Then came vast changes in technology, massive war efforts, and an exploding economy. Not enough men were available to fill all the jobs. The social system tremored a bit and admitted women.

History changed not only attitudes but methods of Bible interpretation as well. Herbert Alleman's *New Testament Commentary*, 1936, was probably the first American Lutheran commentary to say that the references in Corinthians and Timothy were "part of the intellectual-philosophical milieu of the writers."

History

Changes in society brought up the question of woman's status in the Church, and the new awarenesses in hermeneutics opened the way to reconsideration of practice. The practical developments of history had been the key.

What Will the People Think?

But what will people think if women are ordained? Facts are available to help answer that question. A study was made by Lawrence Kersten in the Detroit metropolitan area.[1] Several hundred Lutherans were surveyed. Response of Lutherans to the question: "Do you think women should have as equal a voice in the church decisions as men?" (Proportion answering "yes.")

TABLE I

	Laymen	Clergy
LCA	91%	98%
ALC	86%	98%
LC—MS	71%	40%
Wisconsin	49%	0%

Response of Lutherans to the question: "Should women be allowed to become ordained ministers?" (Proportion answering "yes.")

TABLE II

	Laymen	Clergy
LCA	73%	62%
ALC	68%	30%
LC—MS	47%	8%
Wisconsin	39%	0%

Laymen Least Opposed

The results of the study indicate several probabilities:

1. Laymen will be more receptive to the idea than clergymen.
2. Quite a bit of resistance can be expected from the clergy.
3. There is much difference depending upon church body. A proposal to ordain women:
   - would probably meet approval without many problems in the LCA
   - could possibly be approved with concerted effort in the ALC
   - would most likely be defeated the first two or three tries in the LC—MS
   - might as well be forgotten for a generation or two in the Wisconsin Synod

Although there is much opposition in the ALC and Missouri, the seeds of change are there, as shown by the feelings on equal voice for women. The gap between the Wisconsin clergy and laity also forbodes change.

There are also statistics showing the differences of opinion between men and women:

TABLE III

	Lay Men	Lay Women
Favoring equal voice	79%	71%
Favoring ordination of women	65%	51%

Men are less opposed than women!

So what will people think? There is no doubt that some will be repelled by the idea of a woman pastor. This will probably be based more on inner feelings than on scripture. From a psychological point of view, such feelings can change. Because some do not want change is no reason for the church's deciding against it though. Yet, the church must be concerned about feelings and must handle them with love and care. Attitudes are best changed by experience, and a few decades with women in some pulpits will probably quiet all fears.

What Will Others Think?

What will other churches think? Here are brief statements of their present and possible future practices with regard to ordination of women.

The Orthodox Church

The Orthodox Church ordains no women and has no interest in doing so. A few questions about the possibility are being raised as a result of contacts in the World Council of Churches; but unbroken tradition, Canon Law, and strict interpretation of 1 Corinthians and 1 Timothy discourage all discussion.

The Roman Catholic Church

The Roman Catholic Church? Certainly no ordination yet but it could come. Canon Law says that only men may be ordained but allows a woman's advance to the lower orders. Discussion, however, is lively and growing. Several prominent theologians propose ordination, including Rahner, Küng, Tavard and Haering. Küng says, for example, that ordination is entirely a matter of cultural circumstances; there are no biblical or dogmatic reasons against it.

The momentum of the discussion cannot be gauged easily. In the light of Vatican II, the consequences may be revolutionary.

The Anglican Communion

The Anglicans? Maybe. Woman's suffrage was the larger question among Anglicans until recently, but that right has advanced quickly.

The 1968 Lambeth conference decided that:

- arguments both for and against ordination are inconclusive. (This was in rejection of a report which said there were no conclusive reasons for withholding the clergy office from women.)
- the churches should study the question.
- the churches should allow women to lead worship, preach, baptize, read scripture, distribute sacramental elements, and enter the diaconate, though they would not thereby automatically become eligible for the priesthood.

The Reformed Family

Churches of the Reformed family have taken different positions. Those in Switzerland, Germany, and the United States do ordain. In 1956, the Presbyterian Church, U.S.A., said "Equality is proper both in terms of creation and redemption."

Other Churches

Other major bodies permitting ordination include Methodist, United Church of Christ, United Church of Canada, Baptist, Disciples of Christ, and Pentecostal.

Observations

Some observations can be made which might help in getting ready for a decision:

1. Lutherans should benefit from the study of a question such as this one to be aware of any effect an action by a church to ordain would have on inter-church relations.
2. The ecumenical factor should not be given undue weight, though, in the decision. When Swedish Lutherans decided to go ahead with the ordination of women, there were fears it would hurt their relations with the Church of England, but it hasn't.
3. "Ordination" and "ministry" carry different freight in different churches.
4. The ordination of women is far from the most critical problem in inter-church conversations.
5. The greater ecumenical problem for Lutherans in this regard may be intra-Lutheran rather than inter-denominational.
6. Over one-half of all Lutherans belong to churches which have women on their clergy roll.
7. Since arguments neither for nor against ordination are conclusive, a variety of practices is permissible within a common confession. This certainly was the case with regard to the question of women voting in the church. Neither would a compromise of the gospel be involved with the ordination of women. A decision by one church to ordain them, while another chooses not to do so, should not endanger their fraternal relationships. That was the finding emphasized by the inter-Lutheran consultation at Dubuque.

What Might Happen?

Perhaps the question should be re-worded. What are the most drastic changes that might come? There is little data which can be obtained from the experience of the other large churches which have begun ordaining. This study can only pose some possibilities:

1. The church might become more feminine. Already there is a trend to leave religion to the women. And women are generally more active members than men. This has not been so true among Lutherans, males having kept the leadership. Even in the Lutheran church, though, men and boys wonder whether religion is masculine enough for them. That gap would probably widen, mainly on the lower economic levels. Men would be reluctant to

go to a woman for counselling. Boys who already live in female-dominated homes and schools would have even less opportunity to identify with strong male figures.

2. The Church might get fewer men to go into the ministry. Public opinion ordinarily classifies pastors as somewhat effeminate. The ordination of women might reinforce this image. An argument can be made that the Church would even contribute to sex-role blur. On the other hand, ordination of women could have the opposite effect. If both the male and female elements were distinctively evident in the image of the ministry, the more masculine male might identify with it more easily than is now the case.

3. The Church might become more supportive. Men try to get a job done. Women try to see that people are happy while doing the job. Studies show that women in professional roles tend to program emotionally supportive, healing ministries, whereas men try for task fulfillment. This means:

   a. The Church might become more concerned about well-being and less about right-knowing. Doctrinal distinctions and scriptural constructs might receive less attention.

   b. The Church might do less evangelizing. The idea of saving people for the Church Triumphant might have less interest as healing and supportive ministries increase.

These hypotheses might be overdrawn, but they try to bring out the most drastic possibilites in order to deal with them clearly. Getting unduly upset might be unnecessary, though, because statistics indicate that few women would actually be ordained.

Few Would Apply

Eighty of 262 denominations in the United States ordain women. In the 1960 census, only 2.3 percent of all clergymen were women—4,727. That is a decline from 4.1 percent in 1950! Of 4,258 students in Lutheran seminaries in January, 1969, 109 were women. Only 17 were in B.D. programs—none in Missouri seminaries, 7 in ALC, 10 in LCA. (To look at the matter pragmatically, the issue of the ordination of women may actually have been decided when seminaries began admitting women to B.D. programs and some of the female students found internships.)

Only a small number of women who do enter the ministry serve the parish. In 1951, only fifty percent were in the parish ministry, including those in assistantships. The majority of those serving as pastors are in the Pentecostal and Holiness groups.

TABLE IV
DATA FROM OTHER PROFESSIONS

	1950	1960
Lawyers and Judges	3.5%	3.7%
Physicians, Surgeons	6.1%	7.0%
Social Workers	69.2%	57.4%
Teachers (elementary and secondary)	74.6%	72.6%

The length of the training period for a profession seemed to reduce the percentage of women directly.

The proportion of women in most of the professions has not been increasing. For women professors and administrators in colleges and universities, it was greater in 1930 than it is today. The proportion of women physicians and surgeons was greater in 1910!

Summing it up, the number of women in pastorates would probably be such a small proportion, for the predictable future at least, as to minimize the effects.

Vocational Factors

In this day of concept explosions, the definition of ordination itself has spread out into a wide range of understandings. The most pragmatic view would say that it is no more than a licensing process which qualifies certain individuals for certain specialized functions, just as a pharmacist must be registered and an accountant certified. This takes any supernatural and theological flavor out of the rite though and could be charged with being an understatement of the "holy office" of the ministry.

At the other extreme may be a highly sacramental definition which says ordination brings a change to the essential nature of the ordained. This could be charged with being an overstatement because it makes the change something "indelible," a principle rejected by Lutherans. This discussion doesn't wish to prejudice any study which might be undertaken by the Council on this broader question of ordination. The range is mentioned here though to point up the importance of entrance standards. Whether the need is for exceptional professional skills as illustrated in the certification extreme or for unique spiritual qualities as indicated by the sacramental view, standards are necessary.

Entrance Standards

But setting entrance standards is nervous business. The Church has not come far in making qualifications measurable. It has been bold only on two counts, poor grades and evident immorality. It probably should screen more finely against persons who exploit or who are so guilt loaded that their talk of the gospel comes through as law.

Maybe it is just as well though that the rules are not so specific. If they were, a particular type would be favored and the candidates would turn out looking like so many sausage links, all alike. How could a Luther or a Saint Francis get in then?

Exclusion of a Whole Sex?

Even if the standards were to require candidates to possess certain traits, women would not thereby be ruled out. Women are not completely devoid of any one particular quality found in men. They may not be as forceful as men, for example, but on the other hand they might be more humane. As a group they may have more of one quality while men have more of another. There is much overlap. A woman having the most of a quality not typical of her sex will have more of it than the man who has the least, and vice versa. The standards would have to exclude females explicitly if they intended to admit males only, which brings up the possibility that the female exclusion clause of some present standards is even illegal.

If women were admitted, would the standards which apply to them have to be tighter than those which apply to men? No, with one exception. When persons of one sex first enter a role which has previously been reserved to the other, a larger portion of them may tend to be deviant in some way. This deviation could either be in a good or bad direction. While this is still not cause for excluding women as a group, it would mean careful screening until the role is well established.

Motives

A vocation is chosen in many unconscious ways. Recent research has shown that no one makes choices in simple, straightforward, perfectly-reasoned ways. Behavior is too complex for that. Some women candidates might have unconscious motives such as feelings of protest against male domination. Some might be seeking a sort of holiness in the ministry because of a heavy guilt. Some might wish they were men. These motives would need some attention in the selection process, but they would not necessarily make vocational hopes invalid. Men have a mixture of motives too.

Happiness and Satisfaction

Can a woman be happy and satisfied as a pastor? The answer depends on her personal ability to cope with some inevitable problems. Anyone who assumes an unusual role will be criticized and discriminated against. Could she accept this? Could she function at ease with her colleagues when most are male? Is she ready to choose between profession and family rearing? Of course she could take leave from the ministry for a time, but she might find the dislocation difficult. This also raises a selection question: would the willingness to forego a family be desirable or undesirable? Some suggest that only married women should be ordained; others, only single women.

Credibility

Many say the Church is in a credibility crisis. How would the ordination of women affect this? If the Church gives the impression that its past rules on women were wrong and even unscriptural, it will add to a growing list of such admissions. The repercussions of these changes are just beginning. The confidence of the people in what the Church says is eroding. Support and commitment will decline. A shattering of many personal faith systems may result, and the entire Lutheran social system could be shaken—some could say.

This does not mean the Church should conceal anything it suspects to be truth. Part of the credibility crisis has already been caused by delayed admissions. Honest change here might actually have a positive effect. By facing reality, preparations could be made to minimize the bad consequences and strengthen the good. A pragmatic study cannot be conclusive for or against ordination, either. Its service is to tell what practical effects should be considered and what consequences might be expected.

Conclusion—Reconsider the Evidence

''Not fully persuasive''—that is the basic conclusion of this study. All major arguments *against* ordination of women are found to be less than decisive. The same is true of the arguments *for* ordination.

''Ordain Her, Ordain Her Not,'' was the title of a recent article.[1] The reader of the reciprocating arguments in this book probably feels that that is the way it has gone. The last petal was never plucked. The last word has yet to be said. And the churches themselves must say it, the decision must be theirs.

What is the last word? It is that what used to be the last word is not necessarily to be the last any longer. Enough new possibilities have arisen in the understanding of scripture to make reconsideration of previous conclusions permissible. The arguments are sufficiently inconclusive now that the churches may adopt differing practices in this regard without violating the gospel.

So,''variety.'' That is another important word. A variety of practices is permissible on this matter within a common confession without endangering fellowship.

The exact wording of the ''Statement of Findings Relating to the Requested Study on the Subject of the Ordination of Women'' is printed in full in the appendix immediately following. It is the official summary of the 123-page study committee report which formed the basis for this booklet and which was transmitted by the Lutheran Council to the presidents of its member churches.

Appendix

A Statement of Findings Relating to the Requested Study on the Subject of the Ordination of Women

A. 1. Until recent times it has been the case in Lutheran churches, as in Christendom generally, that the ordained ministry be limited to men because of long-standing and inherited custom, sociological and psychological factors, and, more specifically, biblical references, notably at I Corinthians 11:2-16 and 14:33-36, which preclude women teaching or speaking in church.

2. In actual practice, however, strict and literal enforcement of what these passages say has probably nowhere fully existed, and women in different Lutheran churches have thus increasingly been permitted to go without veils; take part in public worship, join in liturgy and hymns; lead worship in choirs; speak and teach in church schools, on Sundays and weekdays, asking questions of teachers and instructing males as well as females; vote and hold positions of leadership in the church; and in some cases be ordained to a ministry which is partial or total.

3. Today, in a time of widespread change, women are achieving new dignity, rights, and responsibilities in all areas of life in the world, so that one can properly speak of a "revolution" in the status of women.

4. While the Gospel is determinative for the church's ministry, not contemporary developments, and that Gospel does not change from age to age, nonetheless it is necessary to ask from time to time whether areas of the church's life such as practices regarding the ordained ministry do properly reflect that Gospel and the will of the church's Lord in the world amid the new situations. We must ask whether what we have been accustomed to continues warranted in the face of what we are actually doing in some instances and amid what is happening in God's world, and is the fullest expression currently possible of faith and of the Spirit's activity. Lest we miss the ongoing work of God and promptings of his Spirit, we are called to consider anew what we have readily assumed.

B. 1. In examining the biblical material and theological arguments we find the case both against and for the ordination of women inconclusive.

a. "Ordination" in our sense of the term is not a topic addressed in the New Testament—there has been a long history of development—and the ordination of women was not a question discussed in the Lutheran confessions.

b. The biblical passages and theological arguments invoked against the ordination of women are not fully persuasive because, e.g., of exegetical obscurities (are "women generally" or only "wives" referred to in them?), possible internal contradictions (does I Corinthians 14 give the same answer as I Corinthians 11?), and the impossibility (and undesirability) of consistent literal application (veils; total silence of women in church?). In short, for every interpretation some objection can be raised, and to every argument some objection found.

On the other hand, passages and arguments employed to urge ordination of women are likewise not fully decisive either, and here, too, objections and exceptions occur.

Some of the arguments offered on both sides are inconsistent or rest on unbiblical, unevangelical assumptions.

2. There are also, besides these arguments, sociological and psychological considerations, pro and con. We are convinced that such factors are significant and that assessing such non-biblical factors is indeed "biblical." But neither the objections to the ordination of women, serious as they are, nor the positive potentials which some see, settle the issue.

3. The "ecumenical argument" concerning the relation of the decision by one church to what other Lutherans and other Christians do on this question deserves serious weighing, but does not decide the issue either; if some groups appear irrevocably set against the ordination of women, others, it is to be noted, have already begun the practice, and some churches assumed to be most opposed to the practice are or seem to be open to discussion of it.

C. 1. Thus no one argument or set of arguments settles the matter clearly one way or another at this point for us.

2. It would not be realistic to insist that individual Lutheran bodies should tailor their decisions or delay them indefinitely so as to conform with all other Lutherans, let alone the whole ecumenical world (the fact is that varying degrees of difference of practice already exist), but it is hoped that any single church would seek to act only after consultation with fellow Lutherans and with sensitivity to the entire ecumenical spectrum.
3. If there are no conclusive grounds for forbidding the ordination of women and no definitive ones for demanding it, it follows that a variety of practices at any given time remains possible amid common confession; indeed, question can be raised to what extent doctrinal matters in the strict sense are here involved (theological aspects, yes, but whether "in the doctrine of the Gospel" is another matter).
4. We have been forced to observe again and again in our study that the ordination of women is part of larger questions: (a) the ordained ministry; (b) the work of the laity in ministry of the whole people of God today; (c) the church. Also involved is a hermeneutical question which lies not fully resolved among Lutherans on how one interprets and applies scripture.
5. We urge, therefore, that appropriate commissions of the participating churches share in further joint study of broader topics of the "ministry," "laity," and "church" as a context in which such specific questions must be addressed, and invite representatives of the churches to join with us in exploring fully these areas.

(Adopted by the Standing Committee of the Division of Theological Studies, March 7-8, 1969)

Members of the Subcommittee on the Study on the Ordination of Women by the Lutheran Council in the U.S.A.:

Dr. John Reumann, Chairman
Dr. Robert W. Bertram
The Rev. Stephen G. Mazak
Dr. Fred W. Meuser
Dr. Paul D. Opsahl (Staff)

Study Papers reviewed in this book were by the above persons and:

Dr. Harold I. Haas
Dr. Ronald L. Johnstone

Participants in the Inter-Lutheran Consultation on the Ordination of Women, Dubuque, Iowa, September 20-22, 1969:

The subcommittee and staff named above

American Lutheran Church
Dr. Roy A. Harrisville
Dr. William Larsen
Dr. Stanley D. Schneider

Lutheran Church in America
Mrs. Margaret Ermath
Dr. Martin J. Heinecken
Rev. Ralph E. Peterson

Lutheran Church—Missouri Synod
Dr. Fred Kramer
Dr. Martin H. Scharlemann
Dr. Edward H. Schroeder

Synod of Evangelical Lutheran Churches
Professor Kenneth Ballas

Endnotes

Chapter 1

[1] *Apology XIII.10: cf. 12, Tappert ed., 212.*

[2] *Treatise on the Power and Primacy of the Pope, 26; Tappert ed., p. 324.*

Chapter 5

[1] *Cf. Kersten's forthcoming book, The Lutheran Ethic, Detroit: Wayne State University Press, 1970.*

Conclusion

[1] *Constance Parvey, Dialog, Summer, 1969.*

Notes: *This 1970 document is a digest of papers written for the Lutheran Council in the U.S.A., an ecumenical body consisting of representatives from the American Lutheran Church, the Lutheran Church in America, the Lutheran Church-Missouri Synod, and the Synod of Evangelical Lutheran Churches. (In 1988, the Lutheran Church in America and the American Lutheran Church merged to form the Evangelical Lutheran Church in America.) The study found that the issue of women's ordination is biblically ambiguous, and therefore a variety of church practices ought not to disrupt ecumenical fellowship.*

The surveys done to determine reaction to women's ordination within the various Lutheran churches were especially valuable. Overall, men were somewhat more favorable towards ordination than women, and the laity significantly more favorable than clergy. The predictions about how ordination would be received in each denomination have so far proven accurate. The American Lutheran Church approved women's ordination at the same time as the Lutheran Church in America, but its members were more resistant. The Lutheran Church-Missouri Synod has thus far disallowed women ministers, but some signs of change are apparent.

The Council study, though couched in mostly neutral terms, did suggest that churches ought to be able to make their own decisions regarding this issue. Though this finding was not binding on the member churches, it did influence the American Lutheran Church in particular to approve the ordination of women. The Missouri Synod church was displeased with the study and in 1971 reaffirmed its position against the ordination of women.

PRESBYTERIAN CHURCH (U.S.A.)

REPORT ON THE OFFICIAL RELATION OF WOMEN IN THE CHURCH (1920)

The Special Committee on the Official Relation of Women in the Church presented its report, through its Chairman, Rev. S. Hall Young, D.D. The report was adopted and is as follows:

The constitution of your Committee was on this wise:

The General Assembly of 1919 received three overtures. The Presbytery of Columbia River asked that Women be made eligible to ordination both as ministers and ruling elders; the Presbytery of Saginaw overtured that they be ordained as ruling elders; and the Presbytery of Dallas asked that a committee be appointed to investigate the whole question of enlarged opportunities for women in the Church.

These overtures were referred to the Assembly's Committee on Polity. A majority of the Committee recommended that the Assembly take no action; a minority report asked that a committee be appointed to take under consideration the whole matter of enlarging opportunities for women in the Church, and to report to the next Assembly. The minority report was adopted and the Committee appointed by the Moderator. In composing the Committee the Moderator selected one each from those voting for the majority and the minority reports of the Committee on Polity.

At the first meeting of the Committee held September 23, 1919, the following sub-committees were appointed: Dr. Young, to obtain and tabulate the consensus of opinion of prominent men and women in the Church on this subject; Dr. Work, to examine the teachings of Scripture on the question; Dr. Barrett, to ascertain the deliverances and practice of other ecclesiastical bodies; Mr. Manson, to review the case of Mrs. Chapman which was before the last Assembly, and other similar cases; and Mr. Taggart, to report on the law and equity of the question.

It was decided that as far as possible public discussion of the question should be avoided until after the report of the Committee should be rendered; and that Presbyteries and Synods and their officers should not be consulted officially until the Assembly should decide whether or not it would send an overture or overtures on this subject to the Presbyteries.

On December 30, 1919, a meeting of the Committee was held at which all the members were present, with the exception of Dr. Work who was ill. However, he presented his report.

The facts and conclusions arrived at by your Committee at this meeting and from subsequent investigation and correspondence are as follows:

Personal letters were sent to over a hundred ministers and elders and to forty women asking their opinion on these three questions: (1) Should women be admitted to ordination as ruling elders? (2) Should they be received into the ministry? (3) Should they be made eligible to sit in the courts and councils of the Church on an equality with men?

The names of the men to whom this letter was sent were selected from those prominent in the Presbyterian Church and representing the different synods and the various theological seminaries. The women addressed were generally officers in missionary organizations, or of wide reputation in other lines of Christian work.

In addition requests for letters on the subject were inserted in various church papers; and the sub-committees corresponded concerning their special subjects.

Many letters have been received in reply, evincing a general, intelligent and growing interest in this question. These were distributed among the sub-committees, tabulated and discussed in Committee. After laying aside those letters which were indefinite or expressed no decided convictions, a hundred letters have been examined and compared, with these results:

I. From a Scriptural standpoint, the question was discussed keenly, pro and con, by professors in our theological seminaries and others, strong on the Old and New Testaments. After examining these arguments and after independent investigation your Committee is of the opinion that the Scriptures do not forbid either women elders or women preachers.

II. The sub-committee appointed to investigate the usages of other ecclesiastical bodies corresponded with the leading representatives of seven Protestant denominations, receiving courteous and informing replies in every case. In brief, this is the sum of these replies:

   1. Three of these denominations, namely the Methodist Protestant, the Christian, and the Congregational, ordain women to the ministry. However but few women have availed themselves of the privilege.

   2. The other four denominations interrogated, viz. the Lutheran, Baptist, Episcopal and Methodist Episcopal do not have women preachers, nor does there seem to be any particular inclination in these Churches to accord them this office.

3. Where women preach their labors are generally limited to small fields.
4. In practically all of these seven churches women are admitted to every other official position in the Church except the ministry. They serve on official boards, are trustees, deaconesses, etc., and there is a growing tendency to admit them to official equality with men in the matter of counsel and oversight in the government and service of the Church.
5. If the experience of other denominations is to be considered in helping us to reach a decision, the evidence is favorable to women in the office of the eldership, but is, on the whole, unfavorable to women in the ministry.

III. The case of the appeal of Rev. Robert C. Hallock, D.D., against the Presbytery of Chemung for licensing Mrs. Wm. A. Chapman to preach. The Assembly sent the case back to the Synod of New York and it came before the Judicial Commission at the fall meeting of the Synod.

The appellant had three counts in his plea: first, that the licensing of a woman to preach was irregular; second, that it was unconstitutional; third, that it was unscriptural.

The Judicial Commission refused to pronounce upon any of these counts but the first, that the licensing was irregular. It found against the Presbytery and directed that the license of Mrs. Chapman be rescinded, reminding the Presbytery that the proper way to reach such a license would be by overture to the Assembly. The papers in the case were handed to this Committee by the Chairman and Clerk of the Synod's Judicial Commission.

The fact that the Presbytery's attorney moved that the Synod overture the General Assembly that women be granted the right of licensure and ordination; and that the motion was voted down, was taken by some of our Presbyterian papers to mean that the Synod of New York had gone on record as opposed to giving women the right to preach. The officers of the Synod's Commission made it plain that this was not the case. The Synod did not act upon the merits of the question, but only upon the irregularity of such licensure under the present order of things, and the impropriety of the Synod's sending up such an overture.

IV. As to the propriety and equity of ordaining women as ruling elders and ministers, the hundred letters which were carefully examined and tabulated by your Committee and considered as fairly representing sentiment in our Church, were most interesting and illuminating. Seventy of these were from ministers and elders of the Church, sixty-three ministers and seven elders, all men of weight and influence in the Church; thirty were from women of like prominence.

Of these seventy men, forty-two, or sixty per cent. favored the ordination of women to the eldership; thirty-four, or forty-eight and one-half per cent. advocated their right of ordination to both ministry and eldership; six thought they ought to have the right to a seat in the courts and councils of the Church, but without ordination; while but twenty-two, or thirty-one and one-half per cent. opposed any change in the present usage of the Church.

Of the thirty women whose letters were listed, eighteen favored granting women the right of ordination to both ministry and eldership, two advocated admission as commissioners to presbytery and assembly without ordination, while but seven opposed their advancement in any respect or degree in the Church.

One very significant item must be recorded here. Seven of these ladies who wrote to your Committee took the question to the missionary and other organizations of which they were officers, and a vote of sentiment was taken. In each case the majority was in favor of the ordination of women.

Among the arguments advanced by those opposed to any change in the present usage of the Church, in addition to the Scriptural, are these: That woman's sphere is the home. That her family duties would interfere with her functions as minister and elder. That her ordination would result in lowering the dignity of the office. That it would afford an excuse for men to shirk *their* duties. That it would retard, and perhaps defeat the hoped for union of the Presbyterian Church in the U.S.A. with other Presbyterian bodies; that it would keep men away from the Church; that it would lend countenance to and accelerate a dangerous feministic movement.

Some of the arguments urged by those who advocate the ordination of women to one or both these church offices, in addition to the argument from Scripture, are these: The ordination of women belongs to the spirit of the age, her civil equality is assured in our own and other nations—who deny her ecclesiastical equality? A considerable majority of the membership of the Presbyterian Church is composed of women and girls, and they do more missionary and other church work than the other sex; hence they are entitled to the honors as well as the labors of the Church. In many cases, especially on the frontiers, the organization of new churches is hindered and sometimes made impossible because of the lack of suitable material for elders among the men of the community, whereas there is abundance of good "elder-timber" among the Christian women. Women elders and ministers would in thousands of cases be able to do useful and necessary work for the children and the poor which is impossible for male officers. The call to minister in holy things is of God and is not limited to one sex; when this call is heard by a woman it is not seemly in man to say her nay.

Other arguments on both sides were advanced. It is proper to report that the ladies advocating the ordination of women to the ministry or eldership in each case disclaimed any wish to occupy the office themselves but claimed the right for their sisters.

Your Committee declines to express an opinion upon the merits of this important question. It is divided in sentiment, a majority having expressed themselves as conservative. But it is united in the opinion that the question is of sufficient moment and has excited such widespread interest as to demand discussion and settlement by the Church at large.

As the question of admitting women to the office of ruling elder has commanded the support of the larger number, and seems most urgently to call for the decision of the Church upon it, your Committee has decided to present only the one subject to the Assembly. The admission of women to presbytery, synod and Assembly without ordination would involve radical changes in our Constitution, while this right naturally follows ordination. Your Committee respectfully presents the following resolution and urges its adoption:

Resolved, That the Stated Clerk be directed to prepare and send to the Presbyteries for their action the following Overture:

"Shall the Constitution of the Presbyterian Church in the U.S.A. be so amended as to admit properly qualified and elected women to ordination as Ruling Elders, with all the rights and duties pertaining to this office."

Respectfully submitted,

S. Hall Young, *Chairman*.

Notes: *This 1920 report of the Committee on the Official Relation of Women in the Church is, like the rest of the statements in this section, from the Presbyterian Church in the U.S.A., which in 1958 merged with the United Presbyterian Church in North America to form the United Presbyterian Church in the U.S.A. The United Presbyterian Church in the U.S.A. later merged with the Presbyterian Church in the United States in 1983 to form the Presbyterian Church (U.S.A.), which has approximately 3,000,000 members. As the report says, the issue of women's ordination was first broached in 1919 by three separate overtures, and in response a committee was selected to study the topic. The committee found sufficient support to seek a general vote on women being ordained as elders, but not as* *ministers. The vote was 139 for and 125 against, with 37 presbyteries not voting. Passage required a majority of all existing presbyteries, however, so the measure failed by 12 votes.*

PRESBYTERIAN CHURCH (U.S.A.)

OVERTURE ON WOMEN DEACONS (1921)

Overture 1425. The Presbytery of Transylvania requests an overture sent down to the Presbyteries on "Women Deacons." The majority of the Committee on Polity recommend that the Assembly send down to the Presbyteries the following *Overture*—"Shall the Form of Government, Chapter 13, section 2, be amended by adding—'With the exception that deacons may be either male or female.' "

Notes: *The proposal to include women as deacons was approved 210 to 52 in a church-wide vote and was thus adopted.*

PRESBYTERIAN CHURCH (U.S.A.)

PETITION TO REMOVE BARRIERS TO WOMEN (1924)

Petition 1. Asking the General Assembly to remove from Presbyterian rules and regulations the restrictions in connection with the participation of women in the affairs of the Church: and to authorize the organization of a Woman's Missionary Society of the Presbyterian Church in the U.S.A.

From various individuals and Women's Missionary Societies.

Notes: *This petition stems largely from the initiative of Louise Blinn, an advocate of sexual equality and president of the Women's Missionary Society of Cincinnati, Ohio. In 1923, the Women's Boards of Home and Foreign Missions were absorbed into the male structures. Because only men could serve as commissioners to the General Assembly and its committees, the women had no say in these actions; many felt betrayed. The purpose of this petition was not only to provide women with access to all official positions, including ordained, but to also recreate a Women's Missionary Society. Response to this petition was postponed until 1925, when it was finally rejected. Reasons for the rejection were sent in a personal letter from Clarence Macartney, chair of the General Council, to Louise Blinn. A similar petition in 1926 to remove barriers to the participation of women at all levels was also rejected. That same year, the report of a special committee to investigate "causes of unrest" in the church showed, among other things, that some church members "regarded as unjust the lack of representation of women in the church."*

PRESBYTERIAN CHURCH (U.S.A.)

REPORT OF THE SPECIAL COMMITTEE ON THE STATUS OF WOMEN IN THE CHURCH (1929)

A. Special Committee on Status of Women in the Church

At the meeting of the Council in Chicago in November, 1928, Mrs. Bennett and Miss Hodge, vice presidents of the Boards of National and Foreign Missions, and corresponding members of the Council, presented a paper entitled, "Causes of Unrest Among the Women of the Presbyterian Church in the United States of America." This was a very thoughtful and disturbing paper and the Council gave it careful consideration. Instead of, at that time, taking any action or even giving general distribution to the paper the Council deemed it wise to call a Conference with fifteen representative women of the Church to study with them the whole question of the relation of women to the life and work of the Church together with the problems which at this time confront the women's organizations in the Church. A whole day was devoted to this conference in Chicago in November, 1928, and at its meeting in Philadelphia in March, 1929, the Council received a full report of this Conference and considered the recommendations of the committee of the Council which had arranged for the conference and had been charged with the duty of recommending to the Council any actions which it might be deemed wise to present to the Assembly.

This committee, which consisted of two members of the Council, and Mrs. Bennett and Miss Hodge, brought before the Council two important recommendations. The first recommendation had to do with a request from the women's committees of the boards of Missions of the Church that the General Council should call a conference of the following three groups:

1. The women members of all the Boards.
2. An equal number of women who were associated with the present forms of church service, such as the Missionary Society, Women's Association or Federation, the Ladies' Aid Society.
3. Some women who, while church women, are quite outside of the organized service of the women of the Church.

This Conference would make a survey of the whole field of women's service to the Church and of the types of women's organizations in the Church best suited to present conditions. The Council voted to approve such a Conference to be held in St. Paul in May in connection with the biennial meetings of the women's societies; the Conference to be limited to approximately one hundred women, one half consisting of women members of the boards of the Church, the other half representing, as far as possible, all sections and types of women in the membership of the Church. The expenses of the women from the Mission Boards to be met by the Boards, and the expenses of the women from the Church at large to be met out of the funds of the General Assembly.

In accordance with the request of the women's committees this Conference is to report to the General Council and the General Council agreed to defer any action with regard to women's organizations in the Church until it had received the report of this Conference. A committee consisting of Miss Hodge, Mrs. Bennett, Mrs. Coy, Mrs. Waid and Mrs. Flemming was appointed to make arrangements for the Conference.

The other important recommendation of the Committee dealt with the official relations of women to the ecclesiastical organization of the Church. This matter had been carefully considered by the General Assemblies of 1919 and 1920 and a special committee was appointed by the General Assembly of 1919 which made a full report to the Assembly in 1920. This Committee reported:

''From a Scriptural standpoint the question was discussed keenly pro and con by professors in our theological seminaries and others strong on the Old and New Testaments. After examining these arguments and after independent investigation, your committee is of the opinion that the Scriptures do not forbid either women elders or women preachers.''

The Committee recommended, however, that it was desirable at that time to submit only a proposal in favor of the admission of women to the eldership. The report of the Committee in full was adopted by the General Assembly and the following overture was ordered sent down to the Presbyteries:

''Shall the Constitution of the Presbyterian Church in the United States of America be so amended as to admit properly qualified and elected women to ordination as ruling elders, with all the rights and duties pertaining to this office?''

This overture was voted upon by the Presbyteries and it was reported to the General Assembly of 1920 that 139 Presbyteries had voted for its adoption and 125 against it and that 37 Presbyteries had not voted. Of the Presbyteries which voted accordingly the majority favored the overture. However, as a majority vote of all existing Presbyteries (at that time 301) is required in favor of a given overture if the Form of Government is to be amended in accordance with its provision this overture failed of adoption but only by twelve votes.

The Committee of the Council laid before the Council the following three alternative proposals:

1. The re-submission to the Presbyteries of the substance of the overture which was approved by the majority of the Presbyteries which voted in 1920-21.
2. A re-submission of this matter with an additional proposition providing for the licensure of women as evangelists wherever Presbyteries believe that it is desirable.
3. The removal from the Form of Government of any form of speech which is inconsistent with the recognition of the complete equality of men and women in the life and work of the Church. This could be effected very simply by amending the Form of Government.

   a. making Chapter III, Section II, to read

      "The ordinary and perpetual officers in the Church, *who may be of either sex*, are Bishops or Pastors; the representatives of the people, usually styled Ruling Elders; and Deacons." Or in similar language.

   b. making Chapter XIII, Section II, read

      "Every congregation shall elect persons to the office of ruling elder, and to the office of deacon, or either of them, in the mode most approved and in use in that congregation. In all cases the persons elected must be members in full communion in the church in which they are to exercise their office."

   c. and by making a few (minor) verbal changes elsewhere, as for example in Chapter XII, Section VII," and in Constitutional Rule No. 1.

The Committee unanimously recommended to the Council the approval of the third of these alternatives. After long discussion the General Council, by a vote of 13 to 6, adopted this recommendation of the Committee, and herewith recommends to the General Assembly that the Stated Clerk be instructed to send to the Presbyteries for their action the following overtures:

A. On the Election and Ordination of Women as Bishops or Pastors, and as Ruling Elders.

To the Presbyteries of the Presbyterian Church, U.S.A.:

The General Assembly of the Presbyterian Church in the U.S.A., meeting in St. Paul, Minnesota, May 23-29, 1929, adopted the following:

"Resolved, That the Stated Clerk be directed to prepare and send to the Presbyteries for their action the following Overture:

a. "Shall the Form of Government, Chapter III, Section II, be amended by the addition of the following words: 'These officers may be either men or women, and wherever this provision is applicable, directly or impliedly, there the terms employed are to be interpreted in harmony therewith', so that the Form of Government, Chapter III, Section II, shall read as follows:

   "II. The ordinary and perpetual officers in the Church are Bishops or Pastors; the representatives of the people, usually styled Ruling Elders; and Deacons. These officers may be either men or women, and wherever this provision is applicable, directly or impliedly, there the terms employed are to be interpreted in harmony therewith."

b. "Shall the Form of Government, Chapter XIII, Section II, be amended by the omission of the following words: 'provided, that men shall be eligible to election to the office of ruling elder, and that men and women shall be eligible to election to the office of deacon', so that it shall read as follows:

"II. Every congregation shall elect persons to the office of ruling elder, and to the office of deacon, or either of them, in the mode most approved and in use in that congregation. In all cases the persons elected must be members in full communion in the church in which they are to exercise their office."

c. "Shall the personal pronouns, "he", "his", "him", be followed by the personal pronouns, ("she"), ("her"), ("her"), respectively, in the sections of the Form of Government where forms of record or of personal address, or of commission, are prescribed, namely, The Form of Government, Chapter XIV, Section VIII; Chapter XV, Section XIII; Chapter XXII, Section II."

Pursuant to this action by the General Assembly, the Presbyteries of the Presbyterian Church, U.S.A., are asked to express their approval or disapproval of this Overture as a whole including (a) (b) and (c) by giving a single direct affirmative or negative answer thereto.

B. On the Election and Ordination of Women as Ruling Elders.

To the Presbyteries of the Presbyterian Church, U.S.A.:

The General Assembly of the Presbyterian Church in the U.S.A., meeting in St Paul, Minnesota, May 23-29, 1929, adopted the following:

"Resolved, That the Stated Clerk be directed to prepare and send to the Presbyteries for their action the following Overture:

"Shall the Form of Government, Chapter XIII, Section II, be amended by the omission of the following words: 'provided, that men shall be eligible to election to the office of ruling elder, and that men and women shall be eligible to election to the office of deacon', so that it shall read as follows:

"II. Every congregation shall elect persons to the office of ruling elder, and to the office of deacon, or either of them, in the mode most approved and in use in that congregation. In all cases the persons elected must be members in full communion in the church in which they are to exercise their office."

Pursuant to this action by the General Assembly, the Presbyteries of the Presbyterian Church U.S.A. are asked to express their approval or disapproval of this Overture, by giving a direct affirmative or negative answer thereto.

C. On the Licensure of Local Evangelists.

To the Presbyteries of the Presbyterian Church, U.S.A.:

The General Assembly of the Presbyterian Church in the U.S.A., meeting in St. Paul, Minnesota, May 23-29, 1929, adopted the following:

"Resolved, That the Stated Clerk be directed to prepare and send to the Presbyteries for their action the following Overture:

Shall Constitutional Rule No. 1 adopted in 1893 and entitled "Local Evangelists" be amended to read as follows:

It shall be lawful for presbytery, after proper examination as to piety, knowledge of the scriptures, and ability to teach, to license, as a local evangelist, any communicant member of the church, who, in the judgment of presbytery is qualified to teach the gospel publicly, and who is willing to engage in such service under the direction of presbytery. Such license shall be valid for but one year unless renewed, and such licensed local evangelist shall report to the presbytery at least once each year, and any license may be withdrawn at any time at the pleasure of the presbytery. Communicant members securing such licenses may be ordained to the gospel ministry, should they be eligible and desire to enter it, only when they shall have served at least four years as local evangelists, and shall have pursued and been examined upon what would be equivalent to a three years' course of study in theology, homiletics, Church history, Church polity, and the English Bible, under the direction of presbytery."

Pursuant to this action by the General Assembly, the Presbyteries of the Presbyterian Church, U.S.A., are asked to express their approval or disapproval of this Overture, by giving a direct affirmative or negative answer thereto.

The Secretary of the General Council was requested to add at this point in the report of the General Council to the General Assembly a note stating that certain members of the General Council voted in the negative *upon the question of transmitting to the Presbyteries* the overtures herewith submitted relating to the status of women in our Church, believing it to be for the best interests of the Church that the submission of this matter to the Presbyteries for their votes should be *postponed for a one year period*. The members of the General Council who desired to have their names associated with this note were Dr. Mark A. Matthews, Dr. John Timothy Stone, Dr. Henry C. Swearingen, Mr. Fred B. Shipp and Mr. S. Frank Shattuck.

Later, at the meeting of the General Council held at St. Paul, on May 22, 1929,

On motion of Dr. Stone, seconded by Dr. Thompson, the action of the Council at the March meeting recommending that the next General Assembly send down to the Presbyteries for their votes the overtures relating to the Status of Women in the Church, was reconsidered. The motion to postpone the sending down of the overtures relating to women for one year, namely, until the 1930 General Assembly, was lost by a vote of 19 to 2, the Chairman, Dr. Hugh K. Walker, being ineligible to vote and Dr. Swearingen being absent.

The Council then ordered that the Chairman in conference with the Stated Clerk, Dr. Speer and Dr. Matthews, arrange for a mutually agreeable time for the presentation to the General Assembly of the question of the submission to the Presbyteries of the Overtures on the Status of Women in the Church.

Notes: *In 1927, Katherine Bennett and Margaret Hodge were asked by the General Council to study the specific causes of unrest among Presbyterian women and report back the following year. They did, and the Council heard a "very thoughtful and disturbing paper." The result was another special committee which presented this report in 1929. The presbyteries then voted on three proposals—one to allow women as pastors, one as elders, and one as local evangelists—and approved two of them. As a result, starting in 1930 women could become elders or local evangelists. Approval of women as elders or local evangelists came in 1930. The issue then focused on the third area, women's ordination as pastor or minister.*

PRESBYTERIAN CHURCH (U.S.A.)

REPORT OF THE SPECIAL COMMITTEE ON THE ORDINATION OF WOMEN (1955)

Ordination of Women

The Special Committee on the Ordination of Women presented its Report through its Chairman, the Rev. C. Vin White. The order of the day having arrived, the time was extended ten minutes. The Report was received and approved, and its recommendation adopted, as follows:

In response to *Overture 3*, 1953, from the Presbytery of Rochester, the 165th General Assembly adopted the resolution that "no action" be taken "by this General Assembly, but that the Moderator of the General Assembly appoint a representative committee of seven persons, consisting of three ministers, and four ruling elders, two of whom shall be women."

The Overture is as follows:

Overture 3—On the Ordination of Women to the Gospel Ministry—from the Presbytery of Rochester.

The Christian faith has been history's most potent force in elevating the position of women in our civilization and in using their special gifts. God has called a number of women to the Gospel Ministry and has set his seal to their ordination by other denominations with the fruit of salvation of souls and the prosperity of churches. Because of her home responsibilities, it is not often possible for a woman to accept the stringent demands of the parish ministry. Yet when a woman is led of God so to dedicate her life, it would be difficult to discover truly Christian grounds to deny her request for ordination.

The Church has never interpreted Paul's teaching as prohibiting women from serving the church as teachers of the Bible, as missionaries or as leaders in the promotion of missionary work.

Inasmuch as the Presbyterian Church has already approved the ordination of women as ruling elders, it has accepted as of permanent validity the teaching of Paul that, "There can be neither Jew nor Greek, there can be neither bond nor free, there can be no male or female, for ye are all one in Christ Jesus." (Gal. 3:27) It has thus decided that Paul's various strictures on the place of women in the Church were addressed to a contemporary situation.

Our age sees many other evidences of the leadership of women. A woman can be a teacher, a lawyer, a business executive, a diplomat, a doctor; yet in our Church she cannot be ordained to preach the Gospel! The whole emphasis of organized Christianity has been the extension rather than the limitation of the number of those called into the service of Christ. Let us follow the spirit of our Master and no longer discriminate against any person because of sex.

The Presbytery of Rochester, meeting in Calvary Presbyterian Church, Rochester, on February 17, 1953, therefore, respectfully overtures the General Assembly of the Presbyterian Church in the United States of America, meeting in Minneapolis, Minnesota, May 28, 1953, to initiate such actions as may be necessary to permit the ordination of women to the Ministry of Jesus Christ.

The General Assembly instructed the Committee "to consider the whole subject and report to the 166th General Assembly."

The Committee was constituted of the following:

Mr. D. Luther Evans, Columbus, Ohio
Mr. Edward B. Hodge, Bryn Mawr, Pennsylvania
Rev. Hugh T. Kerr, Jr., Princeton, N.J.
Rev. Frank L. McCormick, Fort Morgan, Colorado
Mrs. Frank A. Remde, Pasadena, California
Mrs. L. Irving Woolson, Birmingham, Michigan, Secretary
Rev. C. Vin White, Lincoln, Nebraska, Chairman
Rev. Eugene Carson Blake, Philadelphia, Penna., Advisor

After an initial all-day meeting at which time it was decided to study in detail the Biblical, theological and sociological issues of this subject, the Committee reported to the 166th General Assembly meeting in Detroit, Michigan, May, 1954, that: "Because of the time required to complete these studies now in progress, and because the Committee's report should be substantiated by such findings, the Committee, therefore, respectfully requests

General Assembly to continue the Committee for another year, thus permitting it to make its report to the 167th General Assembly meeting in 1955.'' The request was granted.

The committee now feels that it has completed its study of these issues and it herewith submits the following report and recommendation:

Whereas, the previous actions of General Assembly since 1832, regarding the ordination of women to the Gospel ministry in the Presbyterian Church in the United States of America have been reviewed;

Whereas, the ''Statement Regarding the Position of Women in the Presbyterian Church in the United States of America,'' prepared for the General Department of the United Church Women of the National Council of the Churches of Christ, (October 1953) reveals that women in the Presbyterian Church in the United States of America:

1. Are now ordained as deacons and ruling elders;
2. May be commissioned by a Presbytery as church workers and lay preachers;
3. Constitute one-third of the membership of the program boards, and also are included on the General Council and the Board of Pensions;
4. May be elected or appointed to any administrative or policy making bodies;
5. As ruling elders, may be elected to the Moderatorship of Presbytery, Synod and General Assembly;

Whereas, material from the Commission on the Life and Work of Women in the Church, of the World Council of Churches, indicates clearly that the ordination of women is a live issue before many Churches throughout the world;

Whereas, there is an increasing cooperation between men and women in business, industry, government, professional life and the Church, whereby each makes room for the other to develop his or her special potentialities, and each recognizes the other as a partner on equal footing;

Whereas, the general trend throughout the world is toward increasing the opportunities for women to take leadership along with men;

Whereas, special studies have been prepared by and for the Committee regarding:

1. The Biblical view of women in society and the Church;
2. The doctrinal implications of the Reformed Faith as they pertain to the place of women in the Church and the ministry;

Whereas, the Bible teaches:

That ''in Christ Jesus there is neither male nor female'';

That neither sex is inferior to the other in access to God's grace and gifts;

That women did serve as deaconesses and did hold other positions in the Apostolic Church;

Whereas, the Bible does not prescribe a permanent and specific social structure for the Church or society; and

Whereas, the Bible neither provides specific direction for nor prohibits the ordination of women to the Gospel ministry;

Whereas, the Reformed doctrinal view, as it pertains to the place of women in the Church, as well as the Reformed view of the ministry, set forth:

That it is proper to speak of equality of status for men and women both in terms of their creation and their redemption;

That it is proper to speak of equality of status for men and women in the Church and its ministry;

That there is no theological ground for denying ordination to women simply because they are women;

That structure in the Christian Church, is essentially functional in character;

That officers of the Church and the form of its organization were designed by Jesus Christ to serve the best interests of the Church, to fulfill His purpose for the Church;

That there is no theological barrier against the ordination of women if ordination would contribute to the edification and nurturing of the Church in its witness to the Lord of the Church;

Whereas, in the Presbyterian form of government, ordination to the ministry is the only way for a full-time church worker to participate fully and responsibly in Presbytery and in the other courts of the Church;

Whereas, the ministry of our Church is becoming more and more diversified, with increasing opportunities not only for pastors and preachers, but for teachers, missionaries, directors of religious education, chaplains, social workers, and other church vocations;

Whereas, the ordination of women would enable the Church to give status to women now serving the Church and would also encourage others to undertake the work of the ministry;

Therefore, the Committee recommends that the 167th General Assembly approve the following Overture and propose it to the Presbyteries for action:

Overture B, 1955

Shall the Form of Government, Chapter IV, Section 1, ''Of Bishops or Pastors, and Associate Pastors,'' be amended by the addition of the following sentence, which would become the last sentence of the Section:

''Both men and women may be called to this office.''

Notes: *In 1953, 24 years after women were first ordained as elders, the Presbytery of Rochester petitioned the General Assembly to allow women to be ordained as ministers. The assembly took no action, but instead appointed a committee to investigate the issue and report back the following year. The committee was still working on the report in 1954, so it was not issued until 1955. The report, printed here, found no theological barrier to the ordination of women, and suggested that such action would in fact contribute to the growth of the church. In 1956 the assembly approved the report by a vote of 205 to 35, thus allowing the ordination of women.*

REFORMED CHURCH IN AMERICA

REPORT OF THE COMMITTEE ON THE ORDINATION OF WOMEN (1957)

Fathers and Brethren:

Your committee hereby makes its second report and presents for your consideration a number of studies bearing upon the question whether women should be eligible to the offices recognized in our Constitution. You will notice that we have studied Scripture with respect to woman's place in the life of the New Covenant both in the Old and New Testaments. That, we believe, is basic. Your committee, however, was of the opinion that other studies should be made regarding the question. Accordingly, you will find an essay regarding previous deliberations of your body, one regarding the practice of women officers in other denominations, one regarding the nature and function of the office, and one regarding practices in the early and post-apostolic church.

There is a further question on which your committee is making a study. We recognize that practical considerations as well as sociological differences within the R.C.A. must be honestly faced and given full weight in arriving at a decision regarding changes in our Constitution as to who should and who should not be eligible to office. This study we may have to publish and distribute separately. Time failed us in doing it in time for inclusion in the "Reports for General Synod."

There is another matter to which we call your attention. All the studies are signed by individual members of the committee. This means that the original work of each study was done by the person who signed it. Every study, however, has had the scrutiny, criticism, and evaluation of the committee as a whole. The members of the committee are agreed in viewpoint and occupy the same position regarding the question of women's ordination. It may appear, however, that here and there the vocabulary differs from essay to essay. We regret that laboring under the pressures of time, we could not do otherwise than accept the vocabulary of each writer, even though it may mean an added difficulty in reading.

Your committee is not ready to bring a recommendation to this session of General Synod. It is our hope that you will adopt our recommendation that these studies be separately published and distributed to the several consistories for study. Out of such a study the committee hopes that it will glean new evidence that should be taken into consideration before a recommendation can or should be made.

It is not needless to ask that the consistories and the church be admonished to take the study of the question seriously. The right answer to the question the Holy Spirit can not indicate to a church that refuses to listen what the "Spirit saith to the churches." This study and any reflections should be made and sent to the committee prior to the spring meeting of classes, otherwise there will not be time for the committee to digest the material sent to it. We hope that the Stated Clerk, in sending the committee's work to the consistories for study and comment, will be asked to stress the importance of prompt action.

In order that the church may give serious thought to the question regarding opening the offices to women, which is discussed in the six studies here presented, and in order that the decision of the Reformed Church in America may be based not on emotion but on knowledge, we make the following recommendations:

1. that the studies here presented regarding the question of women's ordination be separately published in sufficient quantity for every member of all the consistories for study, criticism, and evaluation.

2. that the remaining sum of the money allocated to the committee for this year be used to publish these studies supplemented by money from the General Synod budget.

3. that the Stated Clerk be instructed to mail copies to every member of each consistory with a letter urging prompt action and replies to the chairman of the committee before February 1st, 1958.

4. that the committee be continued for another year, and that the Board of Direction be directed to include $750.00 in its budget for the work of the committee.

Respectfully submitted,

Vernon Kooy
A. W. Meyer
Richard Oudersluys
Lambert J. Ponstein
G. T. Vander Lugt,
Chairman

I

Ordination of Women in the Reformed Church

By GERRIT T. VANDER LUGT

The General Synod of 1955 appointed a committee to study the question of whether in the Reformed Church in America women should be ordained as deacons, elders and ministers. Dr. Daniel Y. Brink, at that time president of the General Synod, appointed the following committee, Dr. G. T. Vander Lugt, chairman, the Rev. Lambert Ponstein, Dr. Vernon Kooy, Dr. Richard Oudersluys, Elder Andrew Meyer.

During the year 1955-56, the committee met to consider the question and a progress report was given to the General Synod of 1956 as follows:

> Your committee is making a progress report. We have worked under handicap of Synod not providing an appropriation for the work of the committee. We were, however, able to meet as a committee to survey the question and to plan for its study, with a view to making a full and detailed report later. Your committee feels that Synod should be prepared with an adequate document indicating a full study of the historical and Biblical problems involved. Accordingly, the subject under study has been divided and aspects of the problem have been assigned to individual members of the committee.
>
> Your committee is prepared to proceed and ask Synod to continue the committee, and to allow an appropriation of $1,000 to carry on the study which will be used in part for travel and in part for bibliography.
>
> Your committee, however, asks that Synod seriously face what is involved should these two requests be granted. We are not unmindful that the question of the ordination of women was proposed very hastily at the conclusion of last year's meeting of the General Synod. Your committee is not certain that this question is one that the General Synod is convinced needs serious consideration. We, as a committee, are ready to devote time and energy to the problem to the end that the membership of the Reformed Church in America might be enlightened and take action accordingly, if it is assured by General Synod that the committee is authorized to proceed in faith that its study of the question needs to be done for the best interests of the Reformed Church in America and for the cause of Christ.

Dr. G. T. Vander Lugt is the president of Central College in Pella, Iowa.

Apparently, the General Synod of 1956 desired that the question of the ordination of women be considered seriously and, accordingly, voted the allowance and continued the committee.

As the report to the General Synod indicates, the question of the ordination of women has several aspects, and one each was assigned to the individual members of the committee. The first aspect that needs study is the historical, to see what light is thrown on the problem by past deliberations of the General Synod. The study of this aspect was assigned to the chairman of the committee.

Accordingly, the deliberations and actions of the General Synod were studied to see what former Synods, reflecting the mind of the Reformed Church in America, had said about the ordination of women. Of course, in reviewing the past, we should remember that previous deliberations and decisions do not necessarily answer the question. The past is an invaluable but not infallible teacher. The Word of God comes to every generation, and every generation must interpret and respond. In doing so, however, it is always well to listen to what those who have preceded us have said.

When we turn to the sources, we find, as is to be expected, that prior to the close of the first World War, the question simply was not raised. Since then, several overtures have appeared before the General Synod, the first one in 1918 from the Particular Synod of Albany and the Classis of Montgomery, asking that the constitution be amended by omitting the word "male" from Article IV, Section 42, of the constitution. Similar overtures have appeared from the Classis of Philadelphia, the Particular Synod of New Brunswick, and the Particular Synod of Albany. Philadelphia repeated its request in 1922. In 1932, the Classis of Westchester made an overture; in 1936, the Classis of Bergen; in 1941, the Classis of Long Island; in 1945, the Classis of Newark; and in 1951, once again, the Classis of Westchester—all asking that something be done regarding the ordination of women as elders and deacons. It was not, however, until 1952 that several voices at once began to assert themselves both for and against the question of ordination. There were in that year 13 overtures, seven of which opposed any change in the constitution, and six once again asking for a deletion of the word "male" from Article IV, Section 42.

The reason or reasons, if any, that have been given for ordination of women can easily be summarized as follows:

1. "To grant women the same rights and privileges as are now enjoyed by male members."
2. "In recognition of the full share of the work of our Reformed Church in America which has been done by women, and in accord with the action of our country in civil matters, and with the teachings of democracy, justice and equal opportunity by our Lord when on earth."
3. "The retention of this wording (that of the constitution as it is at present, that 'elders and deacons shall be chosen from the male members of the church. . . .') was an anachronism which discriminates against the most interested and helpful members of our churches and is outmoded in an age when women are accorded equal rights and privileges by the civil law of the land."

Further, the several Synods have given the following reasons for not giving the classes an opportunity to vote on the proposed amendment. The dates and pages given after each reason refer to the minutes of the General Synod of the Reformed Church in America. (I am deferring consideration for the present of the action of the 1952 Synod.)

1. "The submission of the proposed amendment to the Classes will work injury through friction and division out of all proportion to any possible good that might accrue to any portion of our church." (1918, p. 479 ff.)
2. "The time for such changes as these overtures call for has not yet come, and therefore recommends no action in the matter." (1921, p. 500).
3. "The time does not seem ripe for the action suggested." (1922, p. 833).
4. "Your committee finds no indications of a general desire at the present time for such a change in the Constitution and is informed that strong objections to such a change may arise in certain quarters. It recommends, therefore, that the request be not granted." (1932, p. 121)
5. "Where God created male and female, each have their distinctive functions. They are our equals—what is more, our superiors—in many of their qualifications, not to mention consecration. We, however feel that should they be given the office of Elders and Deacons in our churches, such would rather hinder than progress the work of the kingdom. The men would become content to let the women assume responsibilities which properly are theirs." (1936, p. 393)
6. "Your committee desires to pay its most sincere tribute to the invaluable services rendered by the noblest women of our Church, in very many departments of our work, yet sees no immediate advantage in any particular study of the matter." (1941, p. 147).
7. "The necessity for this provision is not generally apparent in the Reformed Church in America. Also, opening the offices of elder and deacon to women might tend to diminish men's sense of responsibility in the life and work of the Church. Moreover, it is the opinion of the committee that the Church is not ready for this change." (1951, p. 124).

The most serious thought was given to the matter at the 1952 meeting of the General Synod. At that time, I repeat, there were thirteen overtures, some for and some against the ordination of women. In its deliberations, Synod's committee could not come to a unanimous recommendation, and so, there was a majority report from twelve members and a minority report from four. The minority report recommended that no action be taken for the following reasons:

1. "As to principle, the weight of Biblical evidence is against the practice of women serving as elders and deacons in the church.

   a. Jesus appointed men only to be His disciples, even though capable and devoted women were available.

   b. When the place of Judas among the Twelve was to be filled, the approximately 120 disciples selected men and not women as candidates for the office (Acts 1:15-26). Women were free to pray with the disciples (Acts 1:14) but they were not chosen to office.

   c. When deacons were chosen in Acts 6, even though the occasion for the office involved women, only men were chosen.

   d. I Cor. 11:1-12 teaches that in the ordinances of Creation, God gave man a position superior to that of women, not that he is superior to women intellectually or spiritually, but that God has nonetheless given man a preferential status. The tenor of Scripture supports the contention that one way in which this leadership ought to be manifested and employed is in spiritual office in the Church.

   e. 'In Christ there is neither male nor female.' (Gal. 3:28) This is the only alleged Scriptural ground presented by the Westchester Classis and it is wholly irrelevant. Paul refers to the equal and full participation of male and female in the Covenant of Grace and salvation in Christ. This has no bearing on the question of women serving as elders and deacons. The custom of women holding office was not practiced in the apostolic Church.

2. "As to expediency:

   a. We reaffirm the position adopted by General Synod, 1951, that 'opening the offices of elder and deacon to women might tend to diminish men's sense of responsibility in the life and work of the church.'

   b. It is most unlikely that the change proposed by the Westchester Classis would receive the approval of 2/3 of the classes required by the Constitution, RCA (Sec. 181) and the discussion and dissension on the subject would inevitably place a strain upon the peace of our Reformed Church." (1952, p. 110 ff.)

The majority report recommended that General Synod give the classes opportunity to vote on the proposed amendment to the constitution of the Reformed Church in America which would delete the word "male" from Article IV, Section 42. This majority report was adopted, and the classes were given an opportunity to vote.

At the 1953 meeting of the General Synod, its Stated Clerk reported that the motion to delete the word "male" from Article IV, Section 42, had been lost.

There the matter rested until the appointment of the present committee at the 1954 Synod.

II.

The Practice of other Churches in the Ordination of Women

By ANDREW W. MEYER AND LAMBERT J. PONSTEIN

Now that we as a church are studying the Scriptural basis for the ordination of women, we are interested in what other churches have done. Are we studying a question with which many of the churches are concerned? Is this of interest to churches beyond our own borders?

Have other Reformed Churches asked this same question? In this paper we want to make a survey of what others have done or are doing. We shall deal first with those which are in the Reformed tradition, and then with those churches outside that group.

First we go to the Netherlands Reformed Church (De Hervormde Kerk). This church had appointed a study committee to ascertain whether or not there was a Scriptural basis for the ordination of women. The committee suggested several different ways in which women could be given a greater degree of responsibility in the church. All of these were considered by the committee to have a Scriptural warrant. The Synod, after a thorough discussion of the problem, decided to admit women to all offices of the church. Throughout the discussion, which was thorough, there was an insistence that the Bible should be the basis on which the decision should be made.

In the Gereformeerde Kerken of the Netherlands, the question of women's place in the church has not gone beyond a study of her right to vote at congregational meetings. This was granted. However, this discussion has prompted Dr. N. J. Hommes, a minister in that denomination, to make a thorough study of the place of women in the church. In this study he comes very close to the position taken by the Netherlands Reformed Church.

In the British churches we find various solutions to the problem. The Church of Scotland, in both 1934 and 1946, voted overwhelmingly against admission of women to the eldership. In 1947 the General Assembly voted against granting women an official standing in the Councils of the Church. The Presbyterian Church of Wales allows women to hold the office of elder, and has a number of women in this office at the present time. However, the men do greatly outnumber the women as elders. The Presbyterian Church of England has granted women the right to hold office of elder for the past 30 years. In May of 1956 the first woman was admitted to the ministry by the General Assembly.

The Presbyterian Church in Ireland recognizes the right of women to hold the office of elder as well as to be members of church committees. However, women are not eligible to the office of the ministry.

The Presbyterian Church of Korea ordains women to the office of deacon. This church makes excellent use of these women in its calling ministry.

The Church of Christ in China, with which our church has worked in the past years, has for years ordained women to the office of elder. Missionaries tell of the very excellent work these women have performed. The Church of Christ in Japan and the Church of Christ in the Philippines make little distinction between the sexes in the work of the church. It is interesting to note that we have been doing in conjunction with the younger churches that which we are now contemplating in our own church.

On our own continent, the Canadian Presbyterian Church recently voted on a plan to grant ordination to women for the office of elder and deacon. This plan was defeated.

In our own country the Presbyterian Church in the United States, at its last General Assembly, heard a report on the subject of the ordination of women. At present the church is in the process of voting whether or not to admit women to the office of elder. The General Assembly of the Presbyterian Church U.S.A., at its last meeting received a report on the ordination of women. The Assembly voted to grant women full right to all offices. Recently the first woman was ordained to the ministry. The Evangelical and Reformed Church has ordained women to office since 1949.

When we move outside the churches of Reformed background, we find that in England the Baptist Union of Great Britain and Ireland make sex no bar to any kind of Christian service. The position of the Church of England is that the only official status for women is that of deaconess. The Congregational Union of England and Wales has no separate legislation concerning women ministers.

In the United States the major denominations ordaining women are the American Baptist Convention, the Congregational-Christian Church, the Disciples of Christ and the

Methodists. Ordination in the Methodist Church is not complete as women are not admitted to full membership in the annual conference. Some of the younger churches, as for example the Church of God, make no distinction between men and women as qualifications for Christian service.

The list of churches and their stand on this question is not complete. It simply points out that we are not alone in facing this problem.

It might be interesting to note the number of women in the Christian ministry. In 1951 there were 2,896 women clergy in the United States, a tiny fraction of the total number of ordained clergy. A large number of these were members of the fringe sects. Out of a total of 45,701 Methodist ministers, no more than 60 were women. In the Congregational-Christian Church, less than one fourth of the 239 ordained women are active as ministers. In England the Congregational Union of England and Wales lists 43 women ministers, 29 of whom are in full pastoral charge. If our experience would follow that of the above churches, we could expect no more than ten or fifteen women ministers by 1971. Granting the right of ordination seems no guarantee that women will crowd the offices of the church.

This article was prepared by Elder Andrew W. Meyer and the Rev. Lambert Ponstein for the committee of General Synod to study the ordination of women. Mr. Meyer is an elder in the North Park Church, Kalamazoo, Michigan, and the Rev. Lambert J. Ponstein is a professor of Bible at Hope College, Holland, Michigan.

III.

Ordination of Women and the Old Testament

By VERNON H. KOOY

While the question of the ordination of women properly belongs in the New Testament sphere, the Church, in regarding the entire Bible as "the rule of faith and practice," commits herself to study all problems from the whole of Biblical revelation. Thus a Biblical approach to this subject must take into account the Old Testament. This literature presents the following pertinent data:

I. The apex of God's creative activity was the human race, male and female (Gen. 1:26ff.), with the sexes complementary (Gen. 2:20ff.) and forming a unity (Gen. 2:23f., cp. Mt. 19:4ff., Mk. 10:6ff., I Cor. 6:16), each having its distinct place and function without priority and without independence. To the race as a whole God gave the command, "Be fruitful and multiply, and fill the earth and subdue it; and have dominion . . ." (Gen. 1:28, cp. Ps. 8:4ff.). The subjugation of women is viewed as the result of sin (Gen. 3:16). Nowhere in the Old Testament does it appear as part of the created order. One would expect this curse to be removed by redemption.

II. God's revelation came in a historical and cultural milieu in which male dominance was a part of the social structure. One cannot insist upon the absoluteness of any Biblical social norm. When cultural and social patterns change the Biblical forms must be reinterpreted.

III. God speaks and acts through special individuals upon whom He places His Spirit. In the Old Testament there were:

   A. Revealers of the divine will—through divination, sacrifice, ecstasy, spoken word, etc. (cp. Jer. 18:18, Ezek. 7:26). In this class we find:

      1. The priest, whose function was to divine by sacred lot to determine God's will and give instruction (torah). He was the holy person through whom the Israelite approached God in worship. He thus performed a dual function.

      2. The prophet, whose concern was the "word of the Lord." He was the divine spokesman, revealer of the divine counsel and activity (Amos 3:7). He also served as intercessor for the people before God (cp. Gen. 20:7, Jer. 7:16, 51:1).

3. The sage (and elder), endued with wisdom and able to counsel in accordance with the divine will and plan (cp. Jer. 18:18, Ezek. 7:26).

B. Those acting for God in a special capacity as: leaders of the people (e.g. Moses and Joshua), judges (judicators of lesser disputes), charismatics (as Ehud, Deborah, Gideon, Samson, Saul, etc.), and the king (as divine regent).

In both areas we find women serving. In the prophetic office we note such illustrious women as Miriam (Ex. 15:20f.), Deborah (Judges 4:4f.) and Huldah, consulted by king Josiah (II Kings 22:12ff., II Chron. 34:20ff.). Deborah held a three-fold office—prophetess, judge (dispensing justice in the hill country of Ephraim, Judges 4:4f.), and charismatic (inciting Barak to battle the Canaanites, she herself directing the battle, Judge 4:6ff.). Moreover, mediums (as the woman of Endor, I Sam. 28:7ff.) and false prophetesses (as Noadiah, Neh. 6:14) were consulted by the people and believed capable of disclosing the divine will. In one instance a woman sat on the throne of Israel and ruled for six years (II Kings 11:3).

While the occasions were few, God did not disdain to speak and act through women, and the people apparently recognized them as divine servants. It is not surprising that the numbers were few. It is rather remarkable, and therefore more significant, that there should have been any.

IV. The sacred offices of prophet, priest and king (those usually identified with the ministry) were neither indispensable nor permanent. When the prophetic office was degraded by those speaking "pleasing words" the true spokesman for God disclaimed any relationship to it (Amos 7:14, cp. Zech. 13:3ff.). The prophets described the sacrificial system as foreign to true worship (Jer. 7:22f., Amos 5:21ff., Mic. 6:6ff.), predicting the destruction of the temple (Jer. 7:1-15) that a proper worship might be established. With temple and sacrifice go the priesthood. Again, the royal office, promised as everlasting by covenant (Ps. 89:3f., I Chron. 17:12ff., II Chron. 6:16) is denied by some of the prophets as in keeping with the divine plan (I Sam. 8, 10:18f., Hos. 8-4, 12:9, 13, 13:9ff.). Moreover, these offices were not envisioned as directly passing over into the New Order. They were to be consummated in the coming of the ideal (cp. Deut. 18:15ff., Hos. 12:10ff., Zech. 6:12ff., I Sam. 2:35, Ps. 110:4, Isa. 9:1ff., 11:1ff., Mic. 5:2ff., Ezek. 34:23f. cp. also Isa. 42:6, 52:13ff.), which the New Testament rightly interprets as fulfilled in Jesus Christ. Whatever continuity these offices may have in the New Testament, their nature and qualifications would seem to be dictated by their fulfillment in Christ and not by the offices as constituted in the Old Testament.

V. While in the Old Testament specially called persons were endowed with the divine Spirit to act on behalf of the deity, there was envisioned a time when such would no longer be the case, but the divine Spirit would be poured out on all flesh, sons and daughters, manservants and maidservants alike, and all would prophesy (Joel 2:28f., cp. Jer. 31:31-34). This time the New Testament sees fulfilled at Pentecost (Acts 2:17ff.). One notes the absence of any distinction in the sexes.

VI. Whereas under the Old Covenant the male was the dominant figure and alone received the mark of membership (circumcision) in the covenant community, in the New Covenant the mark of membership (baptism) is enjoyed by both male and female, both equally a part of the community, there being no longer any distinction but "all are one in Christ" (Gal. 3:28).

VII. The ordained offices of prophet, priest and king (usually associated with the ministry) had a dual function—to act on behalf of both God and people. If there is any symbolism to be found in that a man can best represent the deity (masculine in Israel without any female counterpart) before the people, by a similar argument the representation of the people before God would seem most appropriately symbolized by a woman. One notes that Israel is known as the wife of God (e.g. Hos. 2:16, Jer. 3:8,

20, Ezek. 16:8), as a mother (e.g. Hos. 2:2, 5, Ezek. 16), and as a daughter (e.g. Isa. 1:8, Jer. 4:31, Ezek. 16:44, Mic. 4:8). Moreover this is fully in harmony with the symbolism of the Church as the "Bride of Christ."

Thus it appears to the committee that from the standpoint of the Old Testament there is nothing against the ordination of women. Although the occasions are not numerous, God did at times reveal His will through their ministry. Moreover, from the standpoint of symbolism there would seem to be a certain appropriateness in having women minister in a special office. This does not imply that the ministry of women would be identical with that of men. But, inasmuch as man and woman make a unit and God and people a unit, there would seem to be some point in having both the male and female elements represented in the ministry. It may be somewhat appropriate, thus, to permit the ordination of women, for "by nature the priestess is fitted to express the motherhood of the Church, to interpret the feminine aspect of the Word, the sacraments and pastoral care. As a priest is a father to the faithful, the priestess should be a mother to them." (C.C. Richardson, "Women in the Ministry," Christianity and Crisis, Dec. 10, 1951, p. 167).

The Rev. Vernon H. Kooy, Th.D., is a professor in the Department of New Testament at New Brunswick Seminary, New Brunswick, New Jersey. He has written the article for the Committee on the Ordination of Women.

IV.

The Ordination of Women and the Teaching of the New Testament

By RICHARD C. OUDERSLUYS

The question of ordaining women in the Reformed Church requires that due consideration be given the place which the New Testament assigns them in the church of Christ. And what is that place? Apparently it is one marked both by equality and inequality, by high honor and subordination. The puzzling fact is that whereas some Scripture passages declare that women took generous part in worship meetings, praying and prophesying, other passages command them to be silent.

Perhaps this should warn in advance the unwary that the question before us will not be solved by quoting a few texts, but rather by carefully examining and summarizing the total teaching of the New Testament. Now nothing approaching such an exhaustive study can be submitted in the columns of our church paper, but a few expository insights and results of such a study being made by Synod's committee can be presented. An attempt will be made in this first article to present briefly some comments on passages usually quoted as unfavorable to ordaining women. In a subsequent article, passages on the other side of the question will be dealt with.

The subordination of women. Our attention is rightly called to several passages of Scripture which make it clear that the wife is to be subject, subordinate to her husband (I Cor. 11:3; 14:34; Eph. 5:22, 24; Col. 3:18; I Tim. 2:11, 12; Titus 2:5; I Peter 3; 1, 5). The apostle Paul finds the basis of this subordination in the ordinance of creation (I Cor. 11:7-9; I Tim 2:13f), an order established for the duration of this age. In addition to this language about subjection, submission, subordination, Paul also speaks of the headship of man over woman (I Cor. 11:2-16). He declares "the head of every man is Christ, the head of a woman is her husband, and the head of Christ is God" (v.3). Now since this subordinate status of woman in the order of creation is relevant to the place of women in the church, let us examine the conception more closely. What is involved in this subordination? Does it connote ideas of restriction, suppression, in public meetings, in church worship? If so, why?

Paul presented his doctrine of "headship" (I Cor. 11:2-16) as part of his corrective counsel for certain worship disorders in the Corinthian church. Women were praying and prophesying in church meetings (vv. 5, 13) without their headcloth (veil). From the repeated references to "her head" and "her husband" (vv. 3, 5), it is apparent that married women are in view here. The only limiting and restrictive deduction which Paul makes from the "headship" doctrine is that women should wear their hair long and cover their heads with a headcloth when praying and prophesying. By doing this, in accordance with good social and church custom, they would show subordination to their husbands (heads). Paul even warns against drawing wrong conclusions from this headship doctrine, lest male pride try to enforce upon women some status of inferiority (vv. 11, 12). The entire passage, then, has to do with proper decorum for wives in church meetings and its impact upon the structure of marriage. Using their new freedom in Christ (Gal. 3:28) Christian wives were laying aside the headcloth in their praying and prophesying, and this might be understood directly or indirectly as a weakening of the structure of Christian marriage, and this Paul combats.

Now let us turn again to Paul's language about woman's subjection, submission, subordination. These terms in their original sense mean "to be placed in an order, to be under a definite (Greek word: tagmata) arrangement of things in order." Paul teaches that not women only, but all persons and things, the whole created order, stand under this divine subordination. All things have been put into subjection unto Christ (I Cor. 15:27, 28; Phil. 3:21), angels and authorities (I Peter 3:22), the church (Eph. 5:24). Children should be subject to parents (Eph. 6:1), slaves to masters (Titus 2:9; I Peter 2:13); believers to one another (Eph. 5:21), and the younger to the older (I Peter 5:5). In all of these relationships the principal requirement is a freely rendered subordination of one to the other in the spirit of Christian love and for Christ's sake. In some instances, the master-slave relationship, the state-citizen relationship, the New Testament also mentions the possession of power (*exousia*: authority) by the head over the subordinate. But significantly enough, nowhere does Scripture declare that husbands and fathers have power-authority over their children and wives. Nowhere does our Scripture declare that it is a woman's duty to obey her husband, unless one is ready to cite the indirect reference in I Peter 3:6 (Incidentally, this has bearing on the use of the word obey in the marriage form.) Nowhere does the New Testament tell man to subject woman to himself. In these matters, women are always exhorted to voluntarily acknowledge their husbands as their heads, to be subordinate to them, in order that "marriage might become something more than a battle between the sexes for power" (Zerbst-Merkens, *The Office of Woman in the Church*). Concern for the marriage relationship, then, is Paul's chief aim in stressing woman's subordination.

The silence of women. The demand for woman's subordination is also related to the command to keep silence in the church in I Cor. 14:34, 35 and I Tim. 2:11, 12, and this produces an expository problem that has exercised the commentators and scholars through the years. If taken literally, absolutely, this prohibition of speaking and teaching in church is the solitary exception to the rest of Paul's teaching with respect to the subordination of women. While various attempts have been made to reconcile Paul's teaching at these points, no single solution has gained general approval.

Paul's commands read as follows: "the women should keep silence in the churches. For they are not permitted to speak, but should be subordinate as even the law says" (I Cor. 14:34); "Let a woman learn in silence with all submissiveness. I permit no woman to teach or to have authority over men; she is to keep silent" (I Tim. 2:12). Concerning these commands, the following points deserve notice. For one thing, both passages refer to silence in church assemblies; clearly so in I Cor. 14 and probably so in I Tim. 2. For another thing, both passages refer to married women, and objection is raised against their decorum in church on the ground of its disturbing effect on the husband-wife relationship. This latter consideration again seems to be the prompting concern in Paul's demand for silence. Such a view gains support from Paul's statement that he does not permit women "to have authority over men." The verb "to have authority" means to act independently, to act on one's own authority. Now how did women's activity in church meetings by speaking ever give the impression of teaching and of lording it over their husbands? To understand this, we must keep in mind the informal nature of early church worship. What the New Testament terms "preaching" and "teaching" was largely argumentation and discussion, more dialogue than monologue. It was not like the formal, uninterrupted sermonizing and lecturing of our day. It has been convincingly shown (N. J. Hommes, *De Vrouw in de Kerk*) that the Greek words used to describe early preaching and teaching mean "to converse, argue, discuss." Paul's work in the synagogues was that of conducting discussions with question and answer periods (Acts 17:2, 17; 18:4, 19), and the same method was followed in his churches. This may explain the tragic episode at Troas where the young man Eutychus fell asleep at a third story window and tumbled to the ground (Acts 20:7, 8, 11). In this instance Paul should not be credited with an unforgiveably long sermon, but the Christian meeting with a discussion hour so interesting and provocative that it became unduly protracted in length. If the married women became over eager in asking questions and participating in the public discussions, this enables us to see why such activity would embarrass their husbands and even give the impression of lording it over their husbands. It explains Paul's command "to keep silent," and at the same time his command that married women reserve their questions and "ask their husbands at home" (I Cor. 14:34), and that they be content "to learn in silence" (I Tim. 2:11). Following his advice, Christian wives could still increase their knowledge, and yet avoid publicly embarrassing their husbands and prejudicing Christian marriage in the eyes of a public unsympathetic with these new expressions of Christian freedom.

It appears then, that the above passages ought not to be cited carelessly as though they settled this whole matter of admitting women to church offices. When the historical situation is rightly understood, these passages have nothing to do with church offices or women in general. Paul is concerned about the Christian decorum of married women in the public meetings of the church, in a time when social conditions were adverse to such startling expressions of freedom. A pair of texts, however, cannot settle a problem as fundamental as this one. What is needed is to set the problem in the total vision of the New Testament. The texts, then, of Corinthians and Timothy do not deal with women in general or with church offices. "Een veto voor de vrouw ten aanzien van het ambt is hier niet" (N. J. Hommes, *De Vrouw in de Kerk*).

The Rev. Richard C. Oudersluys, Ph.D., is professor of New Testament Language and Literature at Western Theological Seminary, Holland, Michigan.

IV.

The Ordination of Women on the Teaching of the New Testament

By RICHARD C. OUDERSLUYS

A new era for women dawned with the advent of Jesus Christ. The Gospel of Christ is also a gospel, news, good tidings for women. Their new status of dignity and importance is one of the conspicuous features of the early Christian movement.

Their inclusion in the early Christian movement. When Jesus Christ came into the world "born of the Virgin Mary" a new sanctity was at once imparted to motherhood, and with it came a new and higher conception of women's character and person (Luke 1:48). From the first, women were numbered among the followers of Jesus (Matt. 9:22; 15:28; 15:38; 26:7f). Those who accompanied Him on His mission tours are occasionally mentioned by name (Luke 8:2, 3), and still others unnamed are praised for their ministry to Him (Luke 8:3). Women figure in the scenes of the crucifixion of Jesus (Matt. 27:55, 56; Luke 23:49), and His resurrection (Matt. 27:61; 28:1; Luke 23:55, 56; 24:1, 9, 10, 22).

The Book of Acts makes mention of Sapphira, the wife of Ananias; Priscilla, the wife of Aquila; Tabitha; Mary, the mother of John Mark; the maid Rhoda; Lydia of Thyatira; the slave girl whom Paul freed from a spirit of devination; Damaris of Athens, and the four daughters of the evangelist Philip. In Romans 16 Paul mentions in rapid succession the following as prominent Christian workers: Phoebe, Prisca, Mary, Tryphena, Tryphosa, Persis, Julia, and the sister of Nereus. This Christian prominence of women stood in strong contrast to the depreciatory attitude of the Jewish and Gentile cultures and religions.

Their prominence in Christian activity. Not only were women recognized members of the Christian community, but active workers in it. This is the special point of Acts 21-8, 9 where it is said that Philip "had four unmarried daughters, who prophesied." This is the point of Paul's reference to Priscilla and Aquila as "my fellow-workers in Christ Jesus, who risked their necks for my life" (Rom, 16:3, 4). Other descriptions are noteworthy:

> "Mary, who worked hard among you" (Rom. 16:6); "those workers in the Lord, Tryphena and Tryphosa" (v. 12); "the beloved Persis, who has worked hard in the Lord" (v. 12); "Euodia and Syntyche . . . who have labored side by side with me in the gospel" (Phil. 4:2).

What work they did, we cannot determine precisely, to be sure, but it does scant justice to Paul's language to assume that they busied themselves chiefly in washing and ironing his shirts and preparing his tea.

It is a matter of record that in Corinth women were praying and prophesying (I Cor. 11:5, 13), and their eager participation in the discussion meetings was probably the prompting reason for Paul's command to "be silent" (I Cor. 14; I Tim. 2). The term Paul uses to describe Phoebe in Rom. 16:1 is not too clear. The Greek word *diakonon* may mean "deaconess" or "servant, helper." In his commentary on Romans, Origen said that the passage showed "that women also were set in the ministry of the church." Some early church fathers also understood I Tim. 3:11 to be a reference to women deacons, although the reference again is not indisputably clear. The "widows" mentioned in I Tim. 5:3-10 appear to be an official class. The term "enrolling" gives a strong impression of church office or order. That women did some teaching in the Christian groups seems fairly evident from Acts 18:26 and Titus 2:3.

Their equal status in the church. Woman's equal status with man in the kingdom of Christ is stated forthrightly by Paul in Gal. 3:28, "there is neither Jew nor Greek, there is neither slave nor free, there is neither male nor female, for you are all one in Christ Jesus." Wives are described as being joint heirs with their husbands of the covenant of grace and all its benefits (I Peter 3:7). Men and women alike are said to share in the service of praise and worship (Eph. 5:19; Col. 3:16), all are expected to teach and admonish one another (Col. 3:16), and all are said to share in the gifts of the Holy Spirit (Acts 1:14; 2:17).

But does this equal spiritual status cancel out the difference established between the sexes in creation? An answer to this question was attempted in our previous article. According to Paul's doctrine of subordination, creational differences continue valid, but they are set in the framework of Christian freedom, and woman's subordination is one of voluntary acknowledgment and practice out of Christian love and in the spirit of Christ. Moreover, as was noted before, Paul never adduces this doctrine of subordination except to conserve the institution of Christian marriage and to keep it from degenerating into a battle between the sexes for power. The New Testament does not adduce these creational differences as evidence or reason for denying women admission to church offices. The I Cor. 14 and I Tim. 2 passages are concerned with the proper decorum of married women in the public meetings of the church, and the creational differences between the sexes come into the discussion only because Paul does not want married women taking part in public discussions and thus jeopardizing Christian marriage.

But finally, does this equal status of women extend to office-bearing? Previously it has been pointed out that women did prophesy (I Cor. 11:5, 13; Acts 28:8, 9). But was the prophet a regular minister of the church? Some would deny it, reminding us that God called and inspired the prophets, and that the church did not elect them. Others affirm it, reminding us that many of the ministries of the early church were the result of grace-gifts of the Holy Spirit (I Cor. 12:8-11; 14:5. 29:33; Eph. 4:11). It seems quite clear from the texts just cited that prophets along with apostles and teachers held a spiritual office in the early church. What about teaching? Is there any evidence for women-teachers? Reference has been made before to Priscilla's instruction of Apollos (Acts 18:26) and to the teaching of older women

(Titus 2:3). The precise nature of their teaching cannot be determined. The speaking and teaching in church assemblies (I Cor. 14, and I Tim. 2) have previously been explained as asking questions and taking part in the informal church discussions.

All of this data is most startling, especially when we recall that the apostolic age was one in which male dominance was general in political, religious and social life. The gospel came into the world as good news, not as a new movement in sociology, and so we do not expect to read in the New Testament about a revolutionary attack on the existing social structure. A woman's emancipation movement in that time was not only impossible, but, if attempted, would have encountered disaster and would have been contrary to inherent character of the gospel. And so it is natural to find in the New Testament a situation of male dominance. Jesus called to discipleship and apostleship, twelve men. The church nominated two men to succeed Judas (Acts 1:23), appointed as deacons seven men (Acts 6:5). The sex of "bishops" and elders, as far as we can determine was male. This data, however, proves nothing concerning the divine will on the matter of admitting women to church offices, unless one is ready to recognize the social situation of the New Testament as binding in all particulars and for all time. The Scripture nowhere expressly forbids a woman to be an office-bearer, but on the contrary, actually emphasizes her inclusion, prominence and equal status with man in the church of Christ. Since the New Testament neither expressly commands nor forbids their admission to church offices, it would seem that this question before our church is largely one of practical theology, psychology and sociology.

The Rev. Richard C. Oudersluys is the professor of New Testament at Western Theological Seminary, Holland, Michigan. . . .

V.

The Offices and the Ordination of Women

By G. T. VANDER LUGT

Introduction

The objections raised against the admission of women to the offices in the Church are: (1) Citation of texts from Scripture, especially in Paul's letters, (2) the nature and function of women as unsuitable to the offices, (3) the nature and function of the offices themselves. The first has been studied in separate essays. The second can hardly be conclusive evidence against admission and is at best of secondary value. The third, however, is of primary importance. It is possible that the nature of the office is such that it implies conclusively that it can be held only by men. Hence, an exposition of its nature is given in this essay.

It does not lie in the scope of this essay to give a comprehensive analysis and exposition of its nature and function. Its scope is circumscribed by the question of women's eligibility. The question here discussed is whether the nature and function of the office as discerned in Scripture is such that by the nature of the case women should be excluded from serving in it, as our Constitution now excludes them.

Furthermore, the relative merits and demerits of the Presbyterial-Synodical as over against the Episcopal and Congregational systems will not be discussed, as lying beyond the purview of this study. Nor are we raising the question of the Scriptural correctness and inclusiveness of the four offices now recognized in our Constitution. (1).

1. The Constitution says: "The Offices in the Church are four: 1. The Office of Ministers of the Word. 2. The Office of Professors of Theology. 3. The Office of Elders. 4. The Office of Deacons." Article 1, Sec. 5.

It is the considered judgment of your committee, however, that while there are definite distinctions of function, the offices have essentially an identity of nature which makes it impossible to draw a line that is clear and decisive in determining the question of eligibility. In other words, if any office should be opened to women, all of them should be.

Accordingly, we sometimes speak of the office and at other times of offices. In the one case we think more of their oneness, in the other of their pluriformity.

I. The Context of the Office

The nature of the office must be seen in the context of the Church and the kingdom of God. The office is not something foisted upon the Church from the outside but something that stems out of the essential nature of the Church.

A. Jesus Christ and the Office

The essential nature of the Church is Jesus Christ, who is the unique office bearer. He is the servant of God, the mediator, sent into the world for its reconciliation (John 6:44, I John 4:14). Through His work and person He gathers into Himself a people and creates a fellowship of those who share in His mission through the Holy Spirit (I John 1:3). He is *the* ''minister'' of the New Covenant (Heb. 8:6) from whom every office in the Church is derived. ''It is not possible to speak of the office (Ambt) in the Christian Church without proceeding from Jesus Christ as the perfect office bearer. From Him alone is every office derived and to Him alone is clear what the character and significance of the office is. The office is the task God assigns to a person.''[1]

What needs emphasis here, first of all, is that Jesus Christ as God's servant by His person and mission creates the Church *as His servant*. She is the organ or means He uses to continue and complete His own service, ''the fulfillment of Him who fills all things with Himself'' (Eph. 1:23). Every office in and out of the Church is essentially a service of God and of His reconciling work in the world through Jesus Christ.

The service of Jesus Christ is primarily not a service for man (although that is included) but for God and for His kingdom; and every office derived from Him should be essentially a serving of God and of His concern with the world. Jesus Christ, His Church, the offices therein must be seen as means to God's end, the establishing of His Kingdom where He is recognized as king. A too soteriological emphasis does not do full justice to the Biblical meaning of the significance of Christ, His Church, and the offices. The full context is always eschatological—God's kingdom already present and coming. Only in this context will the significance and nature of the offices become clear.[2]

B. The Apostolic Office

As part of His work on earth Jesus Christ appointed Apostles, who represented Him. He chose them, delegated them, empowered them (Acts 10:41, John 6:70, 17:6). They stand between Christ and His Church in a unique way. They are the foundation upon which the Church is built, Jesus Christ being the chief cornerstone (Eph. 2:20). They are the witnesses to God's gracious act in Jesus Christ (I John 1:1-4). As such they occupy a singular, unique and unrepeatable place in the history of God's work of redemption. From Christ they receive a direct assignment, a specific authority to be His representatives, and a unique share in the once-for-all character of God's revelation (Acts 1:8, Matt. 28:18-20).

As we study the nature of the Apostolic office, we discern something of its structure. An Apostle is a person delegated to represent his sender (Jesus Christ) in the doing of a specific task to which he is called, to which he is bound (woe is me if I preach not the Gospel), from which he may not detract and to which he may not add, which he may not transfer to another but must carry out in person, and which he discharges in the name of, i.e., with the power of, his sender, to whom he is responsible and to whom he must give an account. The One sent is *as if* he were the sender. There is in the Apostolic office a functional identity with the office of Christ as if the Lord were doing the work Himself. ''He that receiveth whomsoever I send receiveth me; and he that receiveth me, receiveth Him that sent me,'' (Matt. 10:40, see also 16:19, and John 20:21).

The fact that all the Apostles were men does not, in our judgment, constitute a valid argument against women's eligibility to an office in the Church. In the first place, there is a once-for-allness, an unrepeatableness in the Apostolic office. There simply are no successors of the Apostles. They occupy a unique place in the history of God's redeeming purpose (See following Section C). Secondly, in the Apostolic Church, after the outpouring of the Holy Spirit, women as well as men take an active part in the various services, formal as well as informal, in the Church. They act as prophetesses, lead in congregational prayers, do works of charity, teach, do missionary work, and even later, may have administered sacraments (Acts 21:9, 18:26, Rom. 16:1-3, I Cor. 9:5, 16:19, Phil. 4:2f).

Moreover, to hold that the Apostles were appointed to their office because they were men and on that basis exclude women from office is to assume what needs to be proved. The sex of the Apostles is incidental, at least subordinate, (i.e., historically conditioned), to their election to their office. If the fact that they were men determines the nature of the office, then why not the fact that they were Jews or born in Palestine? What is essential is that Jesus Christ appointed them to be His representatives in laying the foundation of the Church.

C. Continuation of the Office in the Church

The Apostolic office lives on (1) in the Apostolic Word canonized as Scripture, and (2) in the Church, as a whole, where the work and mission of the Apostles spread out, diffused like light through a prism, in the services and ministries of the members and in the work of the office bearers. The Apostolic office was transferred to the Church in its total, corporate, institutional character as members and offices, and to the Canon as the authoritative Word.

It must, therefore, be maintained that the offices spring forth out of the midst of the fellowship of believers and functions in it, but it is not identical with it. The notion of an office has in it always the character of the specific, as something not shared by all. Out of the many, some are chosen or elected as representatives of Christ and His Word "over against" the others in the fellowship. A representative shares in the fellowship of believers in Christ but has in addition an election to a special task not identical with but for the sake of the ministries performed by the members of Christ's body.

There are those in the Church of Christ who maintain that the office has no status in Scripture over and above, (beyond, in addition to) the several ministries or services (diakoniai) of the members of Christ's Church. At best, they maintain, the office is but a specialization of services rendered by believers in the body of Christ. For them there is no office over and above the services of the members of Christ's Church. There is only this priesthood of believers.

Our Constitution, however, recognizes the office as legitimate and valid, as something other than and different from the various ministries which the Holy Spirit freely gives and inspires in members of Christ's Church. We believe that the offices were instituted by Jesus Christ for the ordering and direction of the ministries, for the upbuilding of His body. He is not only the head of His Church; He is also the subject of every office in His Church. The offices are the organs or means by which He is still active in His Church, in addition to His activity by the Spirit in the members of His Body (Eph. 4). The offices represent Christ in His threefold ministry, which He continues also now in His exalted state.

It is necessary to emphasize this twofold relation of Christ to His Church, (1) in the several ministries, and (2) in the formal offices. In the offices Christ is not so much in and with His people, as over against them.

Your committee maintains, therefore, that the question of women's eligibility can not be settled by virtually abolishing the *offices* in the Church of Christ, as some now do, and then hold that women are eligible because they already have ministries within the scope of the priesthood of all believers. Not only is the tradition of two millennia as also our Constitution against it, but especially, in our judgment, the weight of Biblical evidence. The Church has, through the years on the basis of Scripture, set aside some people of its membership to perform special functions to which they are called, for which they are ordained and legitimatized by the laying on of hands, and in which they are installed—and all this not simply as a concession to an outmoded and invalid tradition but as an acknowledgment by the Church that in its calling, ordaining, and installing it recognizes that God calls some of His people to a very special task for accomplishing His purpose in and through them. No one can take "this honor unto himself, but that he is called of God" (Heb. 5:4).

Your committee, therefore, has proceeded upon the premise that there is Scriptural evidence for the source and legitimacy of the four-fold office as distinct from and other than the ministries within the body of Christ performed by believers. The offices arise out of and within the scope of the various ministries but are not identical with nor a specialization of them. The question of women's eligibility is, therefore, here considered with reference to the formal offices specified and ordered in our Constitution.

II. The Nature of the Office

A. The Office as Instituted by God

When we consider the nature of the office in the New Testament, we must first of all emphasize that it is divinely instituted. The offices are not, ultimately, a creation of the Church. It is God who in Christ creates or institutes the offices and sovereignly chooses those whom He calls to serve in them as His representative. The offices are not of man's but God's making. See, for instance, what is said of Jeremiah's call (1:5) or of Paul's (first verse of all his Epistles). The calling is based upon the institution of the office, upon special grace for the person called, and upon a divine "setting apart" for an assigned task by the Lord of the Church. From Him also the one called receives authority and power, (and not from the Church) for and even over and over against the Church.

The words used in Scripture clearly indicate this character of the office. God—

gives—*didomi*—(I Cor. 3:5, 12:7, Rom. 12:6, Eph. 4:7, 8, 11)
appoints and places—*tithémi* (I Cor. 12:18, 28, Acts 20:28)
grants grace—*meridzo*—(Rom. 12:3, Eph. 4:7)
distributes—*diaireo*—(I Cor. 12:4, Heb. 2:4)
entrusts—*pisteuomai*—(Gal. 2:7)

All of these point in the direction of divine appointment and institution with the purpose of keeping the Church within the dimension of her divine calling and her Apostolic character. And the offices so instituted are for the equipping (katartismos) of the saints to the end that they may minister to the upbuilding of the Church and to the extension of the kingdom (Eph. 4:12). The saints, in turn, are admonished to receive the offices and officers gratefully, to recognize and respect those placed over them, and to submit themselves voluntarily to their rule or government (I Thes. 5:12-13, I Cor. 14:33, 15:23, and 16:15-16, Heb. 3:13, 10:25, 13:17, Col. 2:5, Rom. 13:1-7).

This divine institution does not mean that officers are to "lord" it over the Church (I Peter 5:3). The New Testament divests the offices of all earthly associations. Jesus Christ said clearly how those who represent Him to and before His Church are to conduct themselves (Luke 22:26, John 13:1-13). Even as He came not to be ministered unto but to minister, so they must serve. They are to be servants in behalf of the Church, always looking to "the pioneer and perfecter of their faith" (Heb. 12:2), humbly conscious of their divine calling. God is to remain sovereign and is to be glorified through them and their office.

If now the offices are instituted of God, can it be maintained that for this reason women can not serve? Does the fact that God instituted the offices for His own sovereign purpose, *ipso facto* mean that God does not equip and call women to the offices He instituted? It would seem that here, too, the Church of Jesus Christ must always remain humbly receptive to the leading of the Holy Spirit, who gives to every one (women as well as men) "grace according to the measure of the gift of Christ" (Eph. 4:7). The conclusion, therefore, seems warranted that the institutional aspect of the offices is not such as to exclude women from eligibility.

B. The Office as Representation

In the second place, Scripture clearly indicates that the offices as instituted have the character of representation and delegation. In the Old Testament prophet, priest, and king represented God to His people. They spoke and acted for Him and in His name, or better, He spoke and acted through them in their official capacity to which He called them.

Likewise, in the New Testament, an office means representation. This is supremely and uniquely true of Jesus Christ. He is God's new and unique instance of representation, the office bearer par excellence, who has a ministry "as far superior as the Covenant He mediates is better" (Heb. 8:6). He appointed and delegated the Apostles to represent Him as His special, unrepeatable servants in the ministry of reconciliation. Growing out of and continuous with their ministry there develops not only the ministry of believers in the body of Christ but also the ministry of the offices, both having the character of representation. Both are to reflect, mirror, illustrate, express Christ in His ministry but in different ways. The first represents Christ in the Church, the second Christ in, to, and for the Church.

All through Scripture there is in the idea of representation a strong emphasis upon the quality of subordination. We find it in the relationship of Christ to the purpose of God, of the Church to Christ, and of the official ministry to the Holy Spirit. This stress upon subordination is always set in the context of love and trust and mutual fellowship, wherein it exists and functions. The quality of subordination keeps representation within its proper limits. The members of Christ's Church and the office bearers must so live and conduct themselves that Christ may truly be the Head of His body, the All in All, even as God was in Him All in All. Every member and officer is to represent His Lord humbly in glad recognition of subordination.

An Analogy

Furthermore, the Bible uses an analogy to make clear the idea of representation. God's relationship to His people is symbolized by the relationship of a man to his wife. There is in Scripture a clear analogy between the relationship of God-humanity, Christ-Church on the one hand, and the relationship of husband-wife on the other. God has willed that His Covenant with man should be reflected and mirrored in the Covenant between husband and wife. See, e.g., Paul's discussion in Eph. 5:22-28.

The question, however, must be raised, what does this analogy signify? How must it be interpreted and what implications does it have relative to the question of women's eligibility to the formal offices?

1. The Divine Side of the Relation

The analogy expresses vividly, concretely, understandably that the relationship of God to His people, including officers in His Church, is not a symmetrical relationship, but an unsymmetrical one, involving a definite aspect of subordination. The one term in the relationship, God, is the originating personal ground of the relation as well as of the other term, man, who receives and can only return what he receives in humble service.

The word used in Scripture for subordination (hypotasso) is one open to a variety of interpretations ranging all the way from slavish, abject subjection that leaves no room for personal choice, to voluntary service of neighbor. And in between all sorts of nuances of meaning can be discovered.

To give some content to its meaning, we quote several passages where the word *hypotasso* is used in several forms. The Son "subjects Himself" to God (I Cor. 15:28). All things are "subjected" to the "One who does the subjecting," (verse 27). "Angels and authorities and powers are 'made subject' to Him," (I Peter 3:22). The Church is "subjected" to Christ (Eph. 5:24). Every person is to be "subject" to the governing authorities (Rom. 13:1, Tit. 3:1, I Peter 2:13). Children are to be "subject" to their parents (Luke 2:51, I Tim. 3:4, Eph. 6:1). The younger are to "subordinate themselves" to the elder (I Peter 5:5).

In regard to its use to express the relationship of man and wife, the Bible employs the word *hypotasso* six times, in I Cor. 14:34, Eph. 5:22, 24, Col. 3:18, I Tim. 2:11, Tit. 2:5, and I Peter 3:1, 5. In each instance it has the meaning of the wife's acknowledging and respecting her husband in his place, which she is not to usurp. She is to live in it, answering love with love. She can not usurp her husband's place without doing violence to the order of creation and of salvation.

In this specific relationship of husband to wife, the aspect of voluntary subordination is clearly a relationship between sexes. But the idea of sex is not a necessary aspect of the Scriptural teaching regarding subordination. Certainly in the relationship of Christ to God, of all things to God, of angels and powers to Christ, no biological structure and function is involved. And in the other instances mentioned above, the idea of biological differences is incidental, as males or females or both may be at either end of the relationship.

The symbolism of the husband-wife relationship as applied to the relationship of God in Christ to His Church must not be interpreted to mean that biological differences are of its essence. What is essential is the aspect of subordination that is to be evidenced in the relationship. God remains sovereign even though He enters graciously, of His own free will, into a covenant with man, elects him to a cooperating service in His Church and kingdom, and uses him in the fulfillment of His purpose. A person, even when elected, called, ordained, and installed in an office wherein he is to represent God, must not presume that he is God. He must never proudly usurp the place of the One who chooses him to be a representative. He may, because elected and chosen, speak in the name of his Sender, by His authority and power, act for Him and with Him and be His co-laborer, but he must always do so, knowing his place, which is one of subordination.

It would, therefore, seem that the symbolism used can not be employed as an argument for excluding women from office. Its use in Scripture is not in that direction. All it means to say is that whoever holds office (be he man or woman) must discharge his function in voluntary, glad, joyful subordination to His calling Lord.

2. The Human Side of the Relation

What has been said so far does not, however, exhaust the meaning of the analogy. The symbolism used in Scripture is applied to the Church, too. The Church, as well as the office in representing God, is to be subordinate to Christ. In it there are men and women. Men as well as women and women as well as men are to be subordinate to Christ, and as subordinate may represent Him. Hence, in the relationship of subordination, members of Christ's Church, both male and female, represent their Lord. If, then, the argument from the symbolism of subordination is to be used to exclude women from office, why not from membership in the Church? That conclusion, however, no one would draw from the given premises. It might even be argued that women would exemplify the relationship more acceptably than men, having learned something of its nature in the marriage relationship.

The office, it must be remembered, represents not only Christ in relation to His Church but also the Church in relation to Christ and God. This is also an aspect of representation, an aspect that needs emphasis when we use the symbolism of husband-wife as an analogy of the relation of Christ to His Church. There is not only the service of the Word in the broadest sense as representing God's ministry to His people but also man's needs, his prayers, his praise, his intercessions, his distress of body and mind. Christ, whom the office represents, is both God and man. And the offices in the Church must represent him in both of His natures, otherwise there is a kind of docetism in Church order.

This side of representation is a symbol of Christ's subordination to God. Here is an aspect of representation that is easily overlooked. There is a dissymmetry in the relationship. St. Paul in Eph. 5 in the same context in which he writes of a wife's voluntary subordination to her husband also writes of Christ's subordination to God, in representing His people. Even now He remains the Intercessor before God (Heb. 7:25, 9:24, Rom. 8:34, I Tim. 2:5, I John 2:1).

The offices in the Church, therefore, must also be a representation of this side of the relationship. God speaks to man and man must listen but man may also speak to God. The relationship, while unsymmetrical, has a polarity, a two-sidedness that we do not recognize sufficiently when we insist that Biblical symbolism always represents God as masculine. The Bible speaks of the Church as the Bride of Christ.

Again, it seems to your committee that seen from this side of the relationship the analogy used in Scripture to symbolize the relation between God and His people which the offices represent can not be used to exclude women from eligibility. We must always remind ourselves that in the order of salvation, i.e., in Christ, there is no male or female (Gal. 3:28) because both are there, both are baptized, both are members of His body, both serve their Lord. The old order is passed away, all things are become new in Jesus Christ, also man's approach to God. The order of creation is supervened by the order of recreation. The second is not a copy of the first but something new and should be represented by the offices.

In this representation the offices should manifest the quality of openness, receptivity, the freedom of the Spirit, who gives gifts (Charismata) to whom He will, and that may mean both men and women. Women have more regard for and sympathy with the personal, whereas man represents the more official, which may easily become, without the counterbalance of the personal, officiousness. The personal and the official are both aspects of representation. In fact, it may be argued that women, by their very nature and endowment, would express the personal side of the relationship more easily and adequately than men.

III. The Function of the Offices

The offices are clearly, all through Scripture, functional in nature. Their purpose lies not within themselves but beyond in the Will of God for His Church and kingdom. Christ chose to establish in His Church a special ministry to represent Him in the ordering, guidance, and direction of His body, of which He remains the head. This special ministry is clearly functional in character, for the order and government of the Church, its growth and edification. As Calvin says, Christ employs the office "just as an artificer makes use of an instrument in the performance of his work" (Institutes IV, III, I).

The form or structure this office developed in the course of history is not germane to this study. Scripture does not give us a fully developed Church-order. The Bible remains the good news of God in Christ. In it we find only seed thoughts regarding the office, which may be studied and systematized but always with care and tentatively. The form of the office is not biblically or theologically fixed, and determined.[1] The emphasis falls upon its representational and institutional nature, not upon its structure. Always there is an emphasis upon the continuous influence and action of the Triune God. God did not establish the Church and then let it develop or unfold from within. He is still active in it, directing and ruling, a blessed truth the fourfold office symbolizes.

This means that as the Holy Spirit leads the Church into the fullness of the salvation that is in Jesus Christ, the Church must ever remain amenable to the necessity of changing and developing its customs, ceremonies, and the structures of its life, under the guidance of the Holy Spirit. In this respect the Christian faith has been dynamic and must remain so. Calvin says in his commentary on First Corinthians that "a necessity may occur of such a nature as to require that women should speak in public."

The thrust of Reformation theology is in the same direction. It insisted as over against Rome that the office (as e.g., in the administration of the sacraments) is effective not because of the character of the office holder but because of the Holy Spirit who is operative in it. Here, too, the validity and efficacy of the office does not depend upon the person or the sex of the person. These remain incidental, part of its changing and developing form.

What, finally, is the content of this functional office? What does it involve, what duties and responsibilities are specified in our Constitution for and exercised in practice by those who are members of consistory and of the higher judicatories? Is there anything in what the offices cover that would exclude women from serving as office bearers? The question here raised is not whether the offices as described in our Constitution include what they should include, nor whether there should be four or more or fewer offices. Rather, the question is whether, accepting the status quo of the offices as now ordered and practiced, there is in them anything that would make it impossible or inadvisable to open the offices to women if qualified by the Holy Spirit.

At the outset, it should be emphasized that the fourfold office is a "service of the Word." The office of a minister is that but also that of an elder or of a deacon. Scripture is the source and norm of all knowledge of and communion in the new life in Christ. Inspired by the Holy Spirit, Scripture alone is authoritative for faith and life. The Church must live by the Word and, let us not forget, be judged by it. This living and being judged by the Word becomes visible and acquires form in the offices in the Church.

The content of these offices may be enumerated as follows:

1. The proclamation of the Gospel, the Word.
2. The Administration of the Sacraments.
3. Teaching—instruction in the Word.
4. Care of the sick, shut-ins, the sorrowing—"Pastoral" care.
5. Confirmation of marriage.
6. Conducting of funeral services.
7. The exercise of discipline—"Ruling."
8. Work with young people.
9. Care of the material and financial side of congregational life.
10. The organization and administration of the services to and of the congregation.
11. Choosing and appointing those who serve in various capacities in the Church.
12. Participation in the higher judicatories.
13. Representing the congregation in its relation to the government.

This enumeration lays no claim to exhaustiveness nor to a binding of the freedom of the Holy Spirit in the Church. These thirteen, or whatever the number, are not all equally primary. Some are clearly aspects of others. We believe the many responsibilities of the offices can be understood as essentially three main aspects of the service of the Word, comparable to Christ's threefold office of prophet, priest, and king.

The Word has a threefold mission to perform in the life of humanity and the world. (1) The Word must be spoken, interpreted, and sent forth as the Word of God that shall not return void (Is. 55). (2) Through the mission of the Word, creation and creatures must become recreated, to bear the image and stamp of the Holy, to become an offering unto God, and to manifest a fuller coming of His kingdom. (3) That Word proclaimed and exemplified must become authoritative and rule in the lives of men and in the world.

If this is the threefold ministry of the Word, is there anything in its function that would by the nature of the case exclude women from serving as "ministers" of the Word? Assuming, of course, the presence of the gifts of the Spirit, the necessary growth and maturity in the new life in Christ, and the required formal and informal training in certain women, can the Reformed Church in America maintain in the light of Scripture that God never calls upon them to serve Him in the offices? Does the function of the offices as described preclude the eligibility of women? This would be difficult to maintain in face of the fact that in the New Testament the Holy Spirit did qualify and use women in various formal capacities in the life of the Church.

Conclusion

Your committee is convinced that there is no sufficient Scriptural reason for insisting that the nature and function of the office is such that women should be excluded from eligibility. The fact that the Church may have been slow to recognize that the Holy Spirit does give women as well as men the necessary gifts for eligibility to office is no doubt historically and sociologically conditioned. Tradition, however, which is important in the life of the Church, must not be the determining factor in deciding the issue. The question really is, what does the Holy Spirit say now regarding this question to the Reformed Church in America?

VI.

The Ordination of Women

Practices in the Early and Post-Apostolic Church

By VERNON H. KOOY

Any discussion of the polity of the Apostolic Church must keep in mind that polity is, in a measure, conditioned by contemporary conditions and consequently the practice of the First Century A.D. is not, in itself, to be considered normative for the Church for all time.

With respect to the administrative and ministerial offices in the Apostolic Church one finds no uniform polity. The Church was early divided into two sections—Hebraist and Greek (often termed Pauline). Even as the requirements for membership, the ordering of worship and the conduct of life were somewhat different for each section so also quite possibly the polity of the Church. While the Twelve Apostles, along with James the Brother of the Lord, seemingly exercised a supervisory authority over the Church at its inception it is difficult to know how long such supervision pertained. Quite early they shared some of their authority with the Seven who, although appointed to "wait on tables," also exercised the functions of evangelists (Acts 6-8). Moreover, their specific task of overseeing the daily ministration appears to have been a local arrangement and did not establish an order of deacons for the whole Church (Cp. Acts 14:23 where elders alone are appointed in the Pauline Churches). Again the Twelve seem to have shared some of their supervisory authority with the elders (Cp. Acts 15:2, 6).

The lists of church officers in I Cor. (apostles, prophets, teachers, workers of miracles, healers, helpers, administrators, speakers in tongues; 12:27) and Eph. (apostles, prophets, evangelists, pastors and teachers; 4:11) reveal both variety and lack of uniformity. There does not appear to have been any common practice with respect to these positions. Nor do we find anywhere in the New Testament a provision to perpetuate these specific offices.

The offices in the Early Church can be divided somewhat into administrative and ministerial offices. In the Administrative Offices we find the apostles who ruled with the elders (Acts 15:2, 6). The apostles no doubt played a dual role. One notes a certain ambiguity in the word 'apostle' as it refers to a traveling evangelist (e.g. Acts 14:14, Eph. 4:11, Did. xi) and a witness to the resurrection (e.g., the Twelve together with James the brother of the Lord and Paul). Later the administrative offices seem to have been summed up in that of bishop, elder and deacon (cp. I Tim. 3, 5, Titus 1). The existence of a special order of Minister of the Word and Administrator of the Sacraments (as defined in our Constitution) does not seem to have been known. Quite possibly the administration of the sacraments was in the hands of many individuals. One is hard pressed to find an official "priesthood" in the Apostolic Church.

Ministerial offices, as determined by the varieties of spiritual gifts, did not seem to divide the people into clergy and laity, or men and women. Varieties of gifts tended to emphasize that all were essential to the Church and by their distribution God provided for the spiritual nurture of all the members. Paul, in persecuting the Church, was concerned to bring both men and women bound to Jerusalem (Acts 9:2). This implies women were as active as men in propagating the new faith, else why the concern. The charismatic gift of prophecy was likewise exercised by women (cp. I Cor. 14:4, 11:5, Acts 21:9). We have mention of Phoebe the Deaconess (Rom. 16:1) and a number of women co-laborers with Paul, who "worked hard for the Lord," as Priscilla who may have been a teacher (Acts 18:26, Rom 16:3), Mary (Rom. 16:6) and Tryphaena and Tryphosa (Rom. 16-12). Again there appears to have been an order of widows (I Tim. 5:3ff. cp. Acts 6:1, 9:39) which was no doubt set apart as an object of the Church's beneficence and to perform certain acts of service to the Church in return.

Nowhere do we find any attempt in the New Testament to sum up all these offices under one head. The offices of bishop and deacon existed alongside of the charismatic offices and may have been held in lesser honor. We note the exhortation in the Didache 'not to despise the bishops and deacons for they also render you the service of prophets and teachers' (Did. xv.), and in I Tim. ("If anyone aspires to the office of bishop he desires a noble task" 3:1). These offices may not have been as highly esteemed as those of apostle, prophet, teacher, worker of miracle, and healer and consequently often neglected.

As far as ordination by the "laying on of hands" and prayer is concerned one can make little case for this rite being reserved for special offices. Some Christians received the gift of the Spirit by this rite and thus full membership in the church with equipment for charismatic service (cp. Acts 8:17, 9:17, 19:6). Others were set apart for a special task by this ceremony (as deacons Acts 6:6, missionaries Acts 13:26). In the first instance women as well as men received this rite.

While nowhere does one find a woman appointed to the office of bishop, elder or deacon in the early Church (as would be expected) and consequently her sex played no prominent role in the leadership and government of the Church, women did possess and exercise spiritual gifts in common with the other members of the Christian community and were instrumental in propagating the faith, including preaching the word.

The transition from the variety of offices in the Apostolic Church to the three chief clerical offices in the Post-Apostolic Church—bishop, elder and deacon—is lost in obscurity. Whereas the regulations for bishop and deacon are marked in I Tim. (3) and there is a note that "the elders who rule will be considered worthy of double honor, especially those who labor in preaching and teaching" (5:17) the distinction between these administrative offices and the charismatic is not clear. By what process these were elevated to the chief offices of the Church is not mentioned. It is quite probable that it was a part of the movement toward catholicity in the Second Century.

One notes in the Post-Apostolic Church a movement toward hierarchy among the clergy with three chief offices: the bishop who presides in the place of God; the presbyters who preside in the place of the assembly of apostles; and the deacons who are entrusted with the ministry of Jesus Christ (Ign. to Magn. vi). In the Epistle of Clement to James (@ 300 A.D.) we have their separate functions listed as: the bishop is to preside over the people; the presbyters are to perform marriages, provide for widows and orphans, remove doubts and love all the brethren; the deacons are to be the eyes of the bishop inquiring into the conduct of members and checking the disorderly. A separate order of Catechists are to teach the word.

Besides these leading offices there appears to have been lesser orders of the clergy. The ordained orders are Deaconess (?), sub-deacon (in charge of the sacred vessels), reader (who read from the Holy Scriptures), and Singer (?). The unordained orders of church servants are: confessors, virgins, widows and exorcists (who possessed the gift of healing). (Cp. Apost. Const. VIII. sec. iii).

Among these offices we find three orders of women—deaconesses who were ordained, and virgins and widows who were unordained. The specific task of the deaconess seems to have been to keep the doors (possibly disciplinary guardian for women at services), to assist in the baptizing of women to maintain decency and propriety, to provide access for the women of the congregation to the deacons and bishop, and to administer charity to the women. They are not to do anything, however, which pertains to the offices of presbyter and deacon. (Cp. Apost. Const. II, xv. xvi. III xxviii).

The Virgins are called "the flower of the ecclesiastical order, the more illustrious portion of Christ's flock" (Cyprian Tr. II. 3). They are to be honored as the priestesses of Christ (Ign. to Tars. ix), being betrothed to Christ and are to take the vow to provide leisure for piety (Apost. Const. IV. xiv).

The order of Widows seems to have been established only as a group for church beneficence (even as the orphans). These are asked to give themselves to prayer on behalf of those who give alms and for the whole church (Apost. Const. III. v). They are to be honored as the altar of God (Ign. Tars. ix) and quite possibly had some service, on occasion, to render to the Church. Both widows and virgins are given a position ahead of other women at church worship and are under the supervision of the deaconesses. They are not to answer questions of faith except for the subversion of polytheism, not to teach or baptize or perform any of the functions of a priest. The ordaining of women priests was looked on as "one of the ignorant practices of Gentile atheism" (Apost. Const. III. viii).

In all this we note that none of the higher ecclesiastical or priestly offices were open to women. Orders for charity and piety were maintained but for the rest only one ordained functional office was open to women to maintain decency and propriety within the Church. Whether they were, in view of their ordination, considered an order of the clergy cannot be verified. It is possible ordination was to enable them to assist at baptism, in the distribution of alms, and in the exercise of discipline.

While one cannot on the basis of the practice of the Apostolic and Post-Apostolic Church make a strong case for the ordination of women, one does note that the social structure of Apostolic days required one ordained order of women for the well-being of the Church. This might seem to indicate that ordination was somewhat determined by social conditions, and while, for the most part, the ministry of the Church was in the hands of men there was a place for women to serve in an official capacity. This would seem to suggest that there is a place for the ministry of women in the Church of Christ.

Moreover, if the Proclamation of the Word, the Administration of the Sacraments and the Exercise of Discipline is a mark of the Church and the function of the clergy, then one notes from Apostolic and Post-Apostolic practice that women, in an ordained and unordained status performed these functions. In this regard they have unofficially been a part of the clergy.

Endnotes

Chapter V, Section I

1. J. L. Koole, *Liturgie en Ambt*, p. 72 Committee's translation.
2. Cf. Dr. A. A. Van Ruler's *Byzonder en Algemeen Ambt*.

Chapter 5, Section III

1. See the study "Practices in the Early and Post-Apostolic Church."

Notes: *The 1955 General Synod of the Reformed Church in America (approximately 350,000 members) authorized its president to establish the Committee on the Ordination of Women. This 1957 report from the committee includes a progress report issued in 1956 but mainly comprises six major papers on various aspects of the women's ordination questions. The report was adopted by the General Synod, and copies were sent to all the consistories of the church for study. The papers within the report recognize that a number of churches have granted ordination privileges to women, and asserts there are no great obstacles to women's ordination in the Bible. Of particular interest is the first paper, which briefly* *traces the history of the issue within the Reformed Church in America. The first overtures in support of women as deacons and elders were received in 1918, and further overtures came in 1921, 1922, 1932, 1936, 1941, 1942, 1945, 1951, and 1952 (at which time there were 13 different overtures on the topic). The paper also summarizes the various statements given during those years both supporting and opposing ordination.*

REFORMED CHURCH IN AMERICA

REPORT OF COMMITTEE ON ORDAINING OF WOMEN (1958)

Fathers and Brethren:

The Committee on the Ordination of Women has the privilege of submitting to you the following report. We are making hereby our third and last report, including one more study, which could not be included last year but which we believe should receive careful consideration and be given full weight in arriving at a decision regarding the question of the ordination of women in the Reformed Church in America. In addition to this report, your committee presents certain recommendations for action. First of all we present the report.

I

The Sociological Aspect of Ordaining Women

One may be convinced that there is no theological argument against the ordination of women, and that the offices should be opened to all who are called, both male and female. Yet the entire program might be defeated by the cultural pattern under which we live.

Women have had to struggle to gain recognition in all fields. One need simply to note the few women in the various professions. The same arguments were used against women entering medicine, law, or government service as are used today against women entering the service of the church. "These," says the International Federation of University Women News Letter are, "that women can not think logically, can not be objective, and seem ineradicable." However, these barriers are being broken. It is rather interesting that in communist countries this program is moving much faster than in our own country. Women doctors are as common as men in Russia. This can be explained by the necessity of using women to bring about a mechanized society. In our own country, World War II brought women into the factories in great numbers. The result has been that we now tolerate them in positions that once were reserved for men only. This same pattern seems to be followed in the church. We will accept women into the offices of the church when the cultural pattern of the day has removed the bias which is present. I think this is quite well understood by women. The Anglican Group for the Ordination of Women declared: "In our view the strength of the opposition to women lies less in theology than in psychological prejudice inherited from primitive times." In this paper I will approach the problem from this point of view.

First I would like to point out that this psychological prejudice does exist, and that it has been a stumbling block to full use of women in the church.

"Time" for October 21, 1957 reported some of the arguments used against women ministers at the meeting of the State Lutheran Church of Sweden. "A pregnant woman minister would not bring a proper austere authority to the pulpit." "The woman replied that fat male ministers are hardly more inspiring." One diehard stormed that he would never confess to a female because women were notoriously unable to hold their tongues. Dr. Maude Royden of London, in a letter to Christianity and Crisis (December 10, 1951) wrote: "It seems almost comic that the 'orthodox' should pour scorn on the erotic attraction that a handsome parson has for women, and at the same time speak of the sex atmosphere 'radiated' by women 'in a way which men do not,' and dilate upon the sexless impartial character which at present marks public worship.'' She continues. ''An Anglican Bishop married and with children, argued that it would be intolerable to have a woman standing at the altar 'where all the congregation could see her ankles'! And another Bishop pitied the priest who might have to walk into church behind 'a pretty red-haired girl acolyte.' A Congregational lady minister told me her marriage caused some concern among her congregation, but it was negligible compared with the outburst of filth which came when it was known that she was going to have a child. Oddly enough, these people did not realize that the experience of motherhood must enrich a woman's spiritual life.''

I bring these statements to your attention because they are so typical of the type of argument used against women in the offices of the church. We have no statistics with which to make a comparison between male and female ministers relative to dismissal because of moral causes. However, I am quite sure that the percentage figure in the Protestant Church would be such that women would not easily overtake their male co-workers.

''The equality of the sexes is still to a great extent a mere legal formality. The deeper significance of the term is still not known in the church. We may speak of being one in Christ, and that in Christ there is neither male nor female, but the actual practice of this is not yet a part of our Christian life. We do not yet 'in lowliness of mind let each esteem the other better than themselves.' The single, independent, working woman is not given the opportunity to do what she could do in the Christian Church. We still see her as a person of another sex, whose gifts may be great, but she must not reach a full status.'' (From ''Partnership Between Men & Women''—W.C.C.)

Since this is the cultural situation in which we find ourselves, what may we expect in the way of making a greater use of women in the church. I want to give you the experiences of a number of churches. The experiences will show you two things. One is that the cultural lag relating to women is still present in other churches, and the second is what we may expect in our own church.

A member of the General Council of the Congregational Christian Churches writes: ''In our own Congregational Christian Churches, I think that our experience with ordained women could be summarized not too unfairly as follows: Not more than one-third of the women ordained in our churches serve as the regular pastors of churches. Most of these pastorates are in relatively rural areas. The rest of our ordained women serve either as directors of Christian education, or as assistant pastors, or as the secretaries of various educational or women's boards in the denomination. It would seem to me that these figures indicate something of the reluctance of many churches to accept the ecclesiastical leadership of an ordained woman. At the same time, my own observation would compel me to note that many of the women who do serve as the regular pastors of churches perform their ministry with at least as high and perhaps a higher degree of effectiveness than would be achieved by many men in those specific circumstances.''

A correspondent from the United Christian Missionary Society writes: ''The Disciples of Christ have generally allowed their theology to follow in the wake of their sociological development. We have never had more than a handful of women ministers although we have long had many ordained women. Again, sociological reasons have been foremost. At present, we have approximately a dozen women as full practicing ministers. They are competent but have had a very difficult time, being limited to small rural congregations and with little possibility of improving their financial lot. We have noted much more resistance to women ministers among the women of the congregations than among the men. Traditionally we have recruited more girls for church vocations than boys. However, the fall-out has been tremendous for reasons of marriage, changing to teaching careers, etc. We are not now placing any great emphasis on the recruitment of girls to other than the ministry of Christian Education. These will be ordained if they complete their seminary education. As a matter of strategy we are moving our emphasis heavily to the men. Obviously, we are not making much noise about this because of very vocal opposition among the women's groups of our Communion. However, we feel that in the face of the sociological situation we can be responsible stewards in no other way. In sharing the experience of a group who has had long experience with the ordination of both sexes, I would say that we strongly believe in the right for women to be ordained, but feel it irresponsible to recruit girls to a profession that offers them only a second-rate opportunity."

The following is from the Congregational Board of Pastoral Supply: "The churches usually do not desire the services of a woman minister. The chances are that 95% of the churches would prefer, offhand, that their minister be a man. This offers an initial handicap to any woman in the ministry. Some of our women ministers are married and some are single. They work out this problem with the particular church and with their husbands, in terms of the total family situation. I have observed a good many such situations and feel that it has been very harmoniously dealt with. Concerning the problems growing out of confinements due to pregnancy, children and the adverse attitude of a certain segment of the community, we discover that these problems, in certain instances, have resulted in marked changes of plans for the person involved. There are problems involved, but comparable problems due to temporary illness of a male minister also occurs, and the disruption is, perhaps, no greater in one case than in another. There have been quite a number of women ministers seeking ordination and receiving it, who have later ceased to serve as parish ministers; due to the special problems involved. The percentage has perhaps been a bit higher than in the case of men, but there is no small percentage of men who also go into business and other phases of activity in connection with our Christian work and institutions. This office, and I believe our denominational leadership as a whole, would not keep any young woman in the dark regarding the difficulties and problems, provided she should seek counsel before entering upon this work. At the same time, we feel the door should be kept wide open lest we interfere with the operation of the Holy Spirit and the work of the Church. But I would repeat that we never paint a rosy picture to a young woman who contemplates entering the Christian ministry as a profession."

Mr. Riley B. Montgomery of the Disciples of Christ writes: "In our churches most of the ordained women are doing general or specialized types of work rather than the pastoral ministry."

The Salvation Army has perhaps answered the problem in the best way. Both the husband and wife must be officers in the Army. If the man marries a wife who is not an officer, his status goes to that of a layman. The same, of course, is true of women who are officers. Though this rule may seem to be very stringent, it has been the experience of the Army that they have lost very few men by this rule. In the corps itself, the woman is held to be subordinate to the husband, though both have had the same training. It has been the experience of the Army that the presence of a wife with equal training has been most helpful, especially in the field of counseling. The Army feels that there are many situations in which the wife could be far more valuable than the husband.

I think all this information, coming from churches which have had long experience with the ordination of women, seems to indicate that our problem is not with the ability of women to carry on the work, but rather with a culture which is not ready to receive women on an equal basis. Even in the cases of the churches—small rural—who have called women, we might well ask whether they would have done so, if they could have secured the services of a man. Their situation forced them to accept a woman as minister. This situation may also have forced a change of viewpoint relative to the woman as a minister, just as the situation in World War II rapidly changed our attitude toward women doing certain jobs, heretofore carried on by men only. Judging from the experiences of other churches, we can be quite sure that our own communion would have real difficulty in accepting women in the Christian ministry. I would judge that in our case the cultural lag—toward women in the ministry—would be greater.

It has been very difficult to find published material on the experiences of women who have been in the ministry. I received, however, a very interesting letter from a woman, who was ordained by the United Church of Canada. She will be working with her husband, who is a missionary in India. I must say that there was some real opposition to her ordination since the United Church requires that the ordinant shall give herself wholly to the work of the church. She is the mother of three children.

She writes that in her case there would be a real advantage in sending a married woman to work among the women and children in India, particularly because Indian culture suspects the single woman. Incidentally this matter of foreign culture also makes it necessary in some cases that members of the consistory shall be women. All cultures do not allow males to make pastoral calls on the female members of the congregation.

She writes further that there is a feeling in the United Church of Canada that some women have been ineffective, and that perhaps women should have only a limited sphere in the ministry. There is also the feeling that there have been a few notably successful women ministers. I quote the following sentence: "I think the general feeling among women is that it is too early to judge the effectiveness of women ministers on the small sample we have had, if we are comparing them with the best of men ministers, which seems to be the normal tendency." On this last statement I would quite agree with her. We always compare women with the successful minister, or elder, or deacon. We fail to take into account the number of men who are also mediocre.

She has the following to say about her own experience: "I myself have only experience as an unordained supply, and that before my training was complete. I was assigned to an Extension Council to help start two churches, one in a veterans' settlement and one in a city extension area. I received the fullest cooperation of the people and we did open a church in 1946 which is still functioning. My only other pastoral experience was a five months' mission field in 1941 from which families still keep in touch with me. I would say then, that a woman minister can come very close to her people and be of real help, but I think she must recognize that men still like to be led by men—and lots of women too!—and so plan to increase the lay leadership in her church as to provide for that. Of course, my husband and I feel that the ideal is a situation where a man-woman team works closely together, whether they be man and wife or whether they be in the same congregation with different functions, or whether they be neighboring pastors who organize their work so as to utilize the special gifts of each." I think a woman minister has to recognize certain limitations in breadth of service, which she may well make up to the church in depth, in special gifts, and in tackling social problems among women. It is still evidence of our male-dominated thinking that we consider some of the masculine gifts and abilities more desirable than the feminine ones in the ministry. I wonder when the final score is added up, if God will think so.

"Probably the greatest problems of a woman entering the ministry are with herself. Can she emotionally accept the prior call of her work, even above that of her children on occasion? For instance, my duties in India on one occasion required me to leave my 1 1/2 year-old with bronchial pneumonia in charge of a servant during the day, and on another occasion both of my young children with whooping cough, for a period of three weeks, during the day, with servants. Secondly, can she accomplish her work and still provide proper care for her children and sufficient time with them to give them a secure and happy childhood? Here the type of work to which she is assigned is of great importance, as is her husband's readiness to assume home responsibilities. I think the normal American pastorate could be managed with adequate household help, for the woman minister must realize she cannot run her home as well as care for a pastorate. That brings up the third major personal decision to be faced. Is she willing to work without financial gain? If she receives a salary, it will normally be spent in replacing her labors in the home. We simply must recognize that a woman minister is still a social pioneer, but that the need of the countless women who are seeking guidance from psychiatrists, from newspaper or magazine columnists and such like, instead of their pastors, makes the pioneering worthwhile. Before my marriage, I felt that when my training was complete, I would be able to handle a pastorate as effectively, and in the same way as a man. I now know that a woman has limitations—first, inexperience if she is single, and loneliness if she lives alone, which can make her lose objectivity, and secondly, energy and sometimes gifts of administration, and thirdly, the set 'tags' or mores which society places upon her, making it more difficult for her to be the impersonal counsellor men and women need. Yet I also know now that a man has limitations—a lesser degree of sensitivity, oftentimes a lesser interest in the nurture of the young of the church, and practically no entree into the deepest problems of women in his congregation. He also is handicapped by his sex. I have come to the conclusion that a full partnership of men and women in the ministry is a constructive thing, and even an urgent need in modern society."

From what I have been able to gain through reading, and there is very little from the practical side, I believe my correspondent has the best grasp of the problems involved. I would like to put down some statements:

1. A woman of equal ability will do as good a work as her male counterpart.
2. In some areas of work she will excel her opposite, in others he will excel her.
3. Problems raised by the presence of children will be greater for the woman minister than for the man.
4. The present attitude toward women in the ministry is of such a nature that it may well be said that it is the strongest deterrent toward her doing an effective job.

So far we have discussed only the ordination of women to the office of minister. However, the arguments against women in the other offices are substantially the same. The sociological barrier is the one that must be moved. If we could remove this barrier, the church could begin to make use of gifts which are unique with the women of the church. Many a minister has asked his wife for advice on specific problems. The Salvation Army has recognized the value of women officers to deal specifically with the problems of women. The male pastor simply is not taken into confidence by the women of his congregation. If we had women in the office of the elder we could make use of her special gifts. Much of the work of the deacons is of such a nature that women would far excel them in the execution of the office. I am thinking of the needs in the home in case of sickness or need.

In 1950, Canon Raven speaking at a Cambridge University Convocation made the statement that the church was fifty years behind the times in the relationship of men and women. When I think of the numerous times the New Testament refers to women in the church and their work, I am inclined to think that we are far behind the church of the first century.

I suppose we ought to ask ourselves a few questions. Ought we to wait until the social lag catches up to us before we ordain women to the offices? Or ought we to be in the forefront seeking to overcome this social lag? If the Church is convinced that women of equal ability can do equal work in the Church, and in some instances, work that a man can not do, we ought to make use of these women. A cultural lag ought not to stand in the way of allowing spiritual gifts to remain dormant.

II

Your committee was heartened by the serious consideration that was given in many parts of the Reformed Church in America to the studies submitted to the General Synod last year and distributed to the several consistories. Many of the responses received by the committee emphasized that while there might be serious practical blocks to the ordination of women, there was no Scriptural basis for excluding them from office. We believe that a forthright declarative statement to that effect by General Synod would indicate the real nature of the question that faces us in the ordination of women. The question is not theological but sociological and practical.

Accordingly, we *recommend* that General Synod make the following declarative

> statement: ''Scripture nowhere excludes women from eligibility to the offices but always emphasizes their inclusion, prominence, and equal status with men in the Church of Jesus Christ.''

Scripture everywhere emphasizes the oneness of man and wife. The two are one flesh. God made man male and female. These are two forms of being human. Each is specifically endowed by the Creator for the other's enrichment and well-being. They truly complement one another. The created differences mutually fulfill and enrich human life. God created man in His image, in the duality of male and female as the one human being, a partnership for the well-being of man's life. Man and woman need one another for their own fulfillment.

This oneness in duality or polarity of the created human world is not set aside in God's plan of redemption. Here, too, there is no evidence in Scripture that woman occupies an inferior position.

Your committee recognizes and acknowledges that even in the Church of Jesus Christ, sociological and practical difficulties make themselves felt and may for a time restrain Christians from translating what is considered right on the basis of Scripture into new forms of communal action, fearful of accepting the clearly-indicated responsibility of moving forward in response to the Spirit's leading.

Making women eligible to all the offices, even though scripturally sound, may arouse fears that the Church is not equal to her responsibility. We would not minimize the fears nor the practical difficulties and tensions the Reformed Church in America would face. We would like to point out, however, that in case the offices are opened to women as a policy of the Reformed Church in America, each congregation and each consistory retains the responsibility of deciding whether the Spirit of God is calling any woman to an office. The ultimate authority for calling, ordaining, and installing is on the local level. No deliverance of General Synod on the question of woman's eligibility to office will change the Reformed principle of church polity that the power of ordaining and installing rests in consistory and classis. This power and authority is in no way bound or restricted by the General Synod declaring that on the basis of its interpretation of Scripture, the offices in the church ought to be open to women as well as to men. Each consistory and each classis has the solemn responsibility of deciding whether practical difficulties and possible resulting tensions would restrain them from opening an office to a woman.

Moreover, your committee is convinced that the office in the Church of Jesus Christ is indivisible. The several offices are not independent of one another. While there are differences of accent, there is not a difference of essential nature. The three offices together represent the one office of Jesus Christ, the head of His Church, as Prophet, Priest, and King. Accordingly, to open, say, only one office, the office of deacon, to women would do violence to the essential oneness of the office in Christ's Church. The question basically is whether a woman in the Church can be ordained to represent Christ to His Church.

> Accordingly, your committee *recommends* that General Synod send down an overture to the classes, asking that they vote on the following proposal: The offices in the Reformed Church in America shall be open to women and men alike beginning with the year 1962.
>
> Your committee further *recommends* that should this proposal receive the necessary two-thirds vote of all classes and General Synod by declarative statement make it a policy of the Reformed Church in America, the necessary changes in the constitution and the liturgy be referred to the respective committees on constitution and liturgy for proper phrasing prior to their submission to the classes, which then, of course, will have to be voted on independently by the several judicatories

In its study of the question of the ordination of women, your committee has discovered that from time to time various irregular situations have arisen resulting possibly from an inadequate understanding of the nature of the office and the several ministries in the Church of Jesus Christ. There is lacking, we believe, in the Reformed Church in America, a clear grasp of the Biblical meaning of the office and of the ministries, which lack seems to indicate a need for further study to lead our denomination in thinking through once more, as was done in the time of the Reformation, the nature of the Church of Jesus Christ, the nature and function of the ministries, and the nature and function of the offices in the church.

> Accordingly, your committee *recommends* that a committee be appointed to make a fresh and Biblical study of the nature of the office and the ministries and their respective functions, and bring back a report to the General Synod.

Finally, since your committee has now finished the task assigned to it by the Synod of 1954, we recommend that the committee be discharged.

This report is respectfully submitted by the Committee on the Ordination of Women.

G. T. VANDER LUGT, Chairman
LAMBERT PONSTEIN
ANDREW W. MEYER
RICHARD C. OUDERSLUYS
VERNON H. KOOY

The Report of the Committee on the Ordination of Women was presented by its Chairman, Rev. Gerrit Vander Lugt. The report was received and considered seriatim. Recommendations #1 through #4 were adopted. A new recommendation was made requesting an appropriation in the amount of $600.00 for Committee Expenses. This was referred to the Committee on the Board of Direction. Recommendation #5 was adopted with the addition that the Committee be highly commended for their work. The report was adopted as a whole.

Notes: *This is the final report of the Committee on the Ordination of Women, including a paper on "The Sociological Aspect of Ordaining Women," which focuses on negative cultural attitudes as the main factor working against women in ministry. The General Synod adopted the proposed statement that Scripture does not exclude women from the ordained offices, and agreed to put to a church-wide vote whether to open those offices to women in 1962. That proposal was defeated.*

REFORMED CHURCH IN AMERICA

OVERTURE ON THE ORDINATION OF WOMEN (1970)

35. CLASSIS OF RARITAN, Show Biblical Cause re Women on Consistory

At the regular meeting of Classis Raritan, held on January 27, 1970 at 7:30 PM. in the High Bridge Reformed Church in High Bridge, New Jersey, the Rockaway Reformed Church of Whitehouse Station reported that its congregation had elected female elders and deacons to the consistory. The Middlebush Reformed Church reported they had done the same and had in fact ordained female elders and deacons to their respective offices.

At the same January 27 meeting the following motion was moved, supported, discussed and voted upon:

that the Classis of Raritan sustains the actions of the Rockaway Reformed Church and the Middlebush Reformed Church in electing and ordaining women to the office of Elder and the office of Deacon; and the Classis of Raritan OVERTURES GENERAL SYNOD TO SHOW CAUSE FROM BIBLICAL AUTHORITY WHY THESE CONGREGATIONS SHOULD NOT HAVE TAKEN THESE ACTIONS.

Two study papers were presented in support of this overture. These papers, too lengthy to publish, are in the hands of the Review Committee on Overtures.

35. CLASSIS OF RARITAN, Show Biblical Cause re Women on Consistory

By way of background, it should be reported that the Particular Synod of New Jersey took the following action on May 5, 1970:

> Whereas the Reformed Church in America has again voted down the ordination of women by having a majority of 29 classes vote for it and only 16 against it; and
>
> Whereas a classis under the jurisdiction of PSNJ, namely the Classis of Raritan, has sustained the action of two churches under its jurisdiction, the action being the election and ordination of women to the office of elder and deacon; and
>
> Whereas the Classis of Raritan has overtured the General Synod of the RCA to show cause from Biblical authority why these churches should not have elected and ordained women to the office of elder and deacon;
>
> I therefore move that PSNJ take action to keep this issue before the RCA by sustaining the action of Classis Raritan and by informing the General Synod of the RCA, before or on the day of its next meeting, that PSNJ supports the overture of Classis Raritan which deals with the Ordination of women.

While the "reasons" given for this overture plainly state that the Rockaway Reformed Church of Whitehouse Station and the Middlebush Reformed Church have ordained female elders and deacons, and while this is admittedly in violation of the *Book of Church Order, this is not the question before the committee or the Synod at this time. The question before us is whether or not the General Synod can show cause from Biblical Authority why these congregations should not have taken these actions.*

The Committee appointed a sub-committee to review the actions of General Synod which would relate to this matter. The most definitive statement is found in the Minutes of General Synod 1958, p. 328ff., which is a report of a Committee on the Ordaining of Women. This report was adopted by Synod. It plainly states that there is no Biblical cause for withholding ordination from women. To the best knowledge of the Committee, there is no other action of Synod at any time that would deny the offices to women on Biblical grounds. The essential contention of the Classis of Raritan is that the *Book of Church Order* is inconsistent with itself in restricting ordination as ministers, elders and deacons to men. The Preamble to the Book of Church Order states that, "The Holy Scriptures are the only rule of faith and practice in the Reformed Church in America." The Classis of Raritan would contend that the prohibition of women from the ordained offices of the church is not Biblical.

The contention might be made that since the *Book of Church Order* was written limiting the ordained offices to men, that therefore this constituted an interpretation of Scripture. This argument is weakened by the fact that Synod, in 1958, agreed that there was no Biblical cause for denying these offices to women. Therefore, we must agree that, according to the official actions of Synod to this date, there is no cause from Biblical authority why these congregations should not have taken these actions.

It is beyond the scope of the committee to suggest judgmental action concerning this matter, even though it is apparent that the Rockaway Reformed Church and the Middlebush Reformed Church are in admitted violations of the *Book of Church Order*. This violation is a disruption of the orderly process within the church and contributes to consternation in the church. It is the opinion of the committee that this violation should not serve as precedent in future procedures by the Classis of Raritan in this matter.

WE RECOMMEND no action. (ADOPTED).

Notes: *Included here are both the overture from the Classis of Raritan and the response of the Committee on Overtures. In 1970, tensions over the ordination issue were heightened when two different congregations elected female deacons and elders. The Committee on Overtures was pressed to provide biblical authority for the rule against female deacons and elders, but was unable to do so. It did restate that the ordination that had already taken place were against church order and should not be taken as precedents.*

Also in 1970, the Christian Action Commission issued a statement supporting the equality of women and their participation in ordained offices. These 1970 actions continued the now almost yearly stream of overtures in support of women's ordination. That stream included a 1964 overture that failed at the Synod meeting, a 1967 overture supported by the Theological Commission that failed in a church-wide vote, and another in 1968 that failed at the synod meeting. There were a number of overtures in 1969 that resulted in two church-wide votes; one to ordain women as ministers of the Word failed by four votes, and one to ordain women as deacons and elders failed by two votes.

REFORMED CHURCH IN AMERICA

RESOLUTION ON THE ORDINATION OF WOMEN (1971)

It was noted that 28 out of 44 classes had voted in favor of an amendment (Part II, Article 2, Section 8) to permit churches to ordain and install men *and women* as elders and deacons. Inasmuch as this was so close to expressing the needed two-thirds majority (30) and since this General Synod again confirmed with enthusiasm and joy the valuable contributions the women make to the work of the church, a motion was made from the floor that the General Synod of 1971 adopt the following as an amendment of the Government of the Reformed Church in America, as a rewording of Part I, Article 2, Section 9a and recommend it to the classes for their approval:

> "Elders and deacons shall be chosen from the members of the church in full communion who are at least twenty-one years of age." (ADOPTED)

Notes: *The 1970 proposal to permit women to be ordained as deacons and elders failed to capture the 30 votes necessary to meet the required 2/3 majority, but since the vote was close, it was once again adopted for a church-wide vote. This time the historic moment was realized, and in 1972 the amendment received exactly the 30 votes necessary for passage. Although this was a watershed in the Reformed Church's long struggle with the issue, the story was not yet complete. The Reformed Church has three types of ordination, and new debate focused on ordination as "minister of the Word."*

REFORMED CHURCH IN AMERICA

OVERTURE ON NON-PARTICIPATION IN THE ORDINATION OF WOMEN (1973)

37. Non-participation in Election/Ordination/Installation of Women to Office Particular Synod of Michigan.

    Whereas, the General Synod of 1972 has adopted a declaratory act in order to give final approval to an amendment to the Book of Church Order which will permit the election of women as elders and deacons;

    Therefore, the Particular Synod of Michigan overtures the General Synod, asking that, since the declaratory act is approved, the General Synod also approve a further amendment to the Book of Church Order, sending it to the classes for their concurrence, to amend Part I, Article II, Section 11, of the Book of Church Order, to add the following:

"No one who, by reason of conscience, cannot participate in the election, ordination, or installation of women to church offices, shall be expected to do so."

Reasons:

1. We recognize that many sincere Christians have been convinced over the centuries, and continue to be convinced today, that the Scriptures require that those who hold office in the church shall be men. And we do not sense that the process by which the RCA has altered its commitment to this historic position has been one of extensive theological study and developing consensus:
   a. The General Synod has had no theological study of the question laid before it since the publication in 1958 of a booklet of short articles, written by members of a special committee.
   b. At successive General Synods, there has been a variety of approaches to this question. The 1967 Synod sent to the Classes an amendment admitting women to all three offices of the church: minister of the Word, elder, and deacon. The Synod of 1969 sent a proposal approving the ordination of women only to the offices of elder and deacon. The Synod of 1970 sent an amendment empowering each Classis to decide whether women should be admitted to the three offices. And the Synod of 1971 has sent a proposal allowing women to be ordained as elders and deacons.
   c. Over the past few years, the approach used by advocates of women's ordination has often been to urge Classis members, in spite of their personal convictions, to relent and vote for a change which will let others have the right to elect women to the offices. This argument has been advanced by the President of General Synod, by various women's organizations, and by writers in the Church Herald, and we believe it has had some effect on the eventual outcome.
2. The drive for "equality" for women in the church could be carried to the place where a certain number of positions must be held by women. In the United Presbyterian Church, the Presbyteries have approved a constitutional amendment which, in effect, requires that half the elders and deacons in a congregation shall be women.
3. We are aware that the great majority of our sister denominations, Protestant, Roman Catholic, and Eastern Orthodox, not only in the United States but around the world, do not presently accept the ordination of women in church offices. Therefore, we believe it is reasonable for those who continue to share that conviction to have assurance that the Reformed Church will not allow situations to develop where anyone is expected to do that which is contrary to Scripture as he understands it. Rather, provision should be made so that anyone may legally decline to assist in the election, ordination, or installation of women to offices of government in the church, on the grounds of conscience.
4. In Christian charity, we must assume that the objection to the ordination of women is not on the basis of "male chauvinism" but on an understanding of Scriptural principles. Therefore, we feel the Reformed Church should accept in love and with respect those who continue to maintain such a view.

We recommend no action. (ADOPTED)

Non-participation by reason of conscience could be referred to many situations in life; one is always free to take such a course and to accept the consequences. Therefore, we do not believe that this one situation should be singled out to be provided with an amendment to the *Book of Church Order*.

Notes: *This 1973 overture asks for the provision of a conscientious objection clause for those who do not wish to participate in the ordination of women. This was denied. The irony of this overture is that similar wording would reappear in the 1980 "Proposal to Maintain Peace in Diversity in the RCA Concerning Women as Church Officers," as a key strategy in getting final legislation passed.*

REFORMED CHURCH IN AMERICA

DISPENSATION FOR JOYCE STEDGE (1973)

The following requests for Dispensations were reviewed by the Board of Theological Education. Except in those instances specifically indicated, the recommendation of the Review Committee is identical with the recommendation of the Board.

R-6 *We RECOMMEND that a dispensation not be granted to Elder Jacob Vander Meer.* (ADOPTED)

R-7 *We RECOMMEND that a dispensation from the academic requirement be granted to Elder Gilbert Van Beek and Elder Henry Vander Bilt.* (ADOPTED)(The Board of Theological Education recommended that a dispensation *not* be granted in these two instances.)

R-8 *We RECOMMEND that a dispensation from the professorial certificate not be granted to Martin Batts, Guy Safford and Norman J. Mol.* (ADOPTED)

R-9 *We RECOMMEND that dispensations from the professorial certificate be granted to Fred Herwaldt, Roy Ackermann, Frank Boerema, Donald De Kok, Donald Ringnalda, Jack D. Ritsema, Charles Van Engen, James Beukelman and Joyce Stedge.*

The consideration and actions on Recommendations R-9 were as follows:

A motion was made and seconded to adopt Recommendation R-9. An amendment was made and seconded to consider the granting of a dispensation from the professorial certificate to Mrs. Joyce Stedge separately.

A question was raised as to the constitutionality of the application of the Rockland-Westchester Classis and the recommendation of the Board of Theological Education relating to granting a dispensation from the professorial certificate to Mrs. Joyce Stedge. A ruling by the President was requested.

President Harry De Bruyn, after presenting reasons based on his interpretation of the BOOK OF CHURCH ORDER, ruled that the application and the recommendation were within the provisions of the constitution. (BOOK OF CHURCH ORDER, Part II, The Classis, Article 8, Section 8, p. 21, 22)

An appeal to the decision of the chair was made and seconded. Division of the house was requested. The vote was Yes - 152; No - 83) to sustain the ruling of the chair. The amendment to consider the granting of a dispensation from the professorial certificate to Mrs. Joyce Stedge separately was LOST.

Recommendation R-9 was ADOPTED.

*The following delegates, upon permission of the Chairman, recorded their votes as being against the granting of a dispensation from the professorial certificate for Mrs. Joyce Stedge:

John H. Alberts (Zeeland)
Cornelius Alkema, Jr. (South Grand Rapids)
John Lucasse (North Grand Rapids)
John Luinstra (California)
Sylvester Moths (West Sioux)

Frank J. Bahr (Raritan)
William Boersma (Holland)
James S. Boogerd (California)
Richard Brower (Zeeland)
Theodore Chandler (Bergen)
Sam Cnossen (California)
Jerome De Jong (Illiana)
Dennis De Korver (Muskegon)
Robert Gowens (Illiana)
B. Daniel Hakken (South Grand Rapids)
Louis Halbersma (Wisconsin)
David Hanson (Wisconsin)
Hans Harder (Passaic)
Martin Hoekman (North Grand Rapids)
John Hoekstra (Wisconsin)
Clarence Hoven (Pella)
Ralph Houston (Illinois)
Lambert Idema (South Grand Rapids)
Maurice Koets (South Grand Rapids)
Dirk J. Kolenbrander (Pella)
Mino Kooi (Illinois)
Paul Lanninga (Chicago)
B. Howard Legters (Rochester)
Clarence Norman (Illiana)
Eugene Osterhaven (Western Seminary)
Maurice Paterik (Chicago)
Herman Rosenberg (North Grand Rapids)
William Rosenberg (Pleasant Prairie)
James Sieperda (California)
David Smits (Zeeland)
Harold E. Snyder, Sr. (Raritan)
Richard Stadt (Illiana)
Tom Stark (South Grand Rapids)
Lester Ter Louw (Chicago)
Henry Teune (Ontario)
Raymond J. Teusink (Cascades)
John Tiggelaar (Zeeland)
Arnold Van Beek (Zeeland)
Everett Vander Weerd (California)
Alfred Van Dyke (Illiana)
John Van Harn (Holland)
Donald Veenendaal (Wisconsin)
John Verhoog (Zeeland)
William Wagenaar (North Grand Rapids)

Notes: *This decision to grant dispensation from the professorial certificate to a woman, Joyce Stedge, was the cause of considerable unrest throughout the following year. According to the Book of Church Order, a professorial certificate (or dispensation from one) "entitles" one to an examination for licensure and ordination. The professorial certificate, now usually called Certificate of Fitness for Ministry, is the last step prior to ordination, and signifies completion of academic and other requirements for ministry. As in this example, dispensations are typically given to a number of persons every year for reasons ranging from lack of sufficient number of units in Hebrew or Greek to completion of less than the required 24 months supervision of a senior pastor. In any case, the dispensation means that the technical requirements were not met for ordination, but that the rules have been waived in this instance. There were a number of interpretations of what it meant in the case of a woman. Some believed it to mean that Stedge could be ordained, and in fact she was ordained four months later, in October.*

REFORMED CHURCH IN AMERICA

REPORT AND RECOMMENDATION OF THE PRESIDENT'S CONSULTATION (1974)

At the 1973 General Synod a dispensation from the professorial certificate was granted to Mrs. Joyce Stedge. (MGS, 1973, p. 36, 37, R-9). Clarification was requested at that General Synod relating to the ordination of women as ministers of the Word in light of the action which had been taken. A response was made by Harry De Bruyn, President of General Synod, and by Marion de Velder, General Secretary, giving their opinion that the action of the 1973 General Synod, interpreting the word 'persons' in the Book of Church Order as meaning both men and women, gave permission to Mrs. Joyce Stedge to preach before Reformed Church congregations (as a licensed candidate), but that this does not necessarily mean that the door has been opened for women to become ministers of the Word within the Reformed Church. This was reported in the July 13, 1973, issue of the Church Herald.

A proposed amendment to Part I, Article 1, Section 3 to the *Book of Church Order* was adopted by the General Synod and was sent down to the classes for their approval. The Synod, when it adopted this amendment, requested that a cover letter be included with the amendments "informing the classes of the interpretation taken by the 1973 General Synod."

In October, 1973, Joyce Stedge was licensed and ordained as a Minister of the Word by the Classis of Rockland-Westchester and installed as Minister of the Word and pastor of the Rochester Reformed Church, Accord, New York by the Mid-Hudson Classis. A number of overtures and complaints were subsequently received relating to the ordination and installation. In order to clarify the situation, a meeting with the Executive Committees of the Rockland-Westchester and Mid-Hudson Classes was held on January 23, with Donald De Young, President of General Synod, and Marion de Velder, General Secretary.

At its February meeting, the GSEC authorized the President to call a consultation of representatives from the whole denomination, including chairmen or representatives from the Christian Action Commission, the Theological Commission, Church Government Committee, and Judicial Business Committee, GSEC representatives, 1974 General Synod delegates, and Particular Synod representatives.

The Consultation was held on April 16-17, 1974 with 49 representatives participating. The General Synod Executive Committee at its April 17 and 18 meeting adopted the following advisory statement which had been adopted by members of the Consultation:

> ***Advisory Statement to the General Synod Executive Committee***
>
> *The questions relating to the ordination of women to the office of the minister of the Word arising out of the 1973 General Synod have been under a continuing review by the General Synod Executive Committee, which has been deeply involved in the effort to clarify the situation and to maintain peace, unity and good order within the church.*
>
> *The General Synod Executive Committee authorized a President's Consultation, representing a broad spectrum of the church. It became clear to the Consultation that the decisions of the General Synod of 1973 relative to the questions of women and the office of the minister of the Word were understood in a variety of ways by the delegates to the General Synod and by the church, among which were the following:*
>
>> *Some members of the church believe that the actions of General Synod in granting a dispensation from the professorial certificate to a woman opened the office of the minister of the Word to women.*
>>
>> *Others believe that this action of General Synod opened the office of the minister of the Word only to that one woman.*
>>
>> *Others believe that all offices of the ministry were opened to men and women by the deletion of the word "male" from the BOOK OF CHURCH ORDER in 1972 (Part 1, Article 2, Section 9a).*
>>
>> *Other believe that the amendment to substitute "members" for "persons" was evidence that classes must vote a change in the BOOK OF CHURCH ORDER before women may be ordained to the office of the minister of the Word.*
>
> *We regret the pain and confusion which have resulted from these differences of interpretation. Because of these honest differences and the attendant confusion and*

lack of resolution concerning this issue in the mind of the church, the President's Consultation advises the General Synod Executive Committee to recommend that:

> *THE GENERAL SYNOD OF 1974 ADOPT AND REFER TO THE CLASSES FOR THEIR APPROVAL AN AMENDMENT TO THE BOOK OF CHURCH ORDER, PART 1, ARTICLE 1, SECTION 3, CHANGING "PERSONS" (which prior to 1973 in practice encompassed only men) TO "MEN AND WOMEN," AND THAT THE REST OF THE BOOK OF CHURCH ORDER AND THE LITURGY BE BROUGHT INTO CONFORMITY THEREWITH.*

R-10 *WE RECOMMEND that the General Synod adopt and refer to the classes for their approval an amendment to the Book of Church Order, Part I, Article 1, Section 3, changing "persons" (which prior to 1973 in practice encompassed only men) to "men and women," and that the rest of the Book of Church Order and the Liturgy be brought into conformity therewith.* (ADOPTED) (See Overtures Report, Pg. 93 and Editorial Committee Report. pg. 200).

The Executive Committee also adopted the following action for the implementation of the advisory statement presented by the President's Consultation:

"In regard to the process of involving the President's Consultation members in informing the classes on the significance and necessity for voting on the issue of ordaining women to the office of the minister of the Word:

1. That Dr. Louis Benes, Editor of the *Church Herald*, be asked to write a news report on the President's Consultation in concurrence with both Donald De Young, President, and Harry De Bruyn, Chairman of the GSEC.
2. That we encourage the President to include in his report to General Synod, a pastoral interpretation of the need for a change in the *Book of Church Order* in regard to the ordination of women to the office of the minister of the Word.
3. That a planning session of GSEC members be held at General Synod to determine how to involve members of the President's Consultation at classes sessions where the amendment is to be discussed.
4. That financing be made available for Consultation members who will visit classes in the fall.

Notes: *This is the report of the President's Consultation to the 1974 General Synod regarding various interpretations of the actions of the 1973 General Synod and the resulting ordination of Joyce Stedge in October, 1973. The 1974 General Synod received seven different overtures to rescind her ordination actions. These were tabled in favor of a church-wide vote on an amendment which would clarify the inclusion of women in ordination. The amendment fell two votes short of the 2/3 majority required for approval. A similar vote in 1975, on the recommendation of the Board of Theological Education, also failed, and two other votes in 1976 and 1977 failed as well.*

REFORMED CHURCH IN AMERICA

RULINGS ON ORDINATION OF WOMEN (1979)

The president called on the general secretary to clarify the nature of the matter before the Synod and to outline the options open to the Synod for dealing with the report of the Judicial Business Committee.

The general secretary stated that according to the *Book of Church Order*, the matters before the Synod were complaints, not appeals, and that the Synod would deal with the complaints as an assembly, not a judicatory. He then called attention to the possible options for the disposition of the report of the Judicial Business Committee as found in the *Book of Church Order* (p. 61, Item No. 7).

The general secretary's interpretation of the *Book of Church Order* was challenged. The president reled that the issues before the Synod were complaints.

> *VOTED: To sustain the ruling of the president.*
>
> (Cornelius Dunning requested that the record show that he is not in agreement with the decision that the matters be handled as complaints.). . .

In recapitulation, the matters properly before the Judicial Business Committee were as follows:

1. Should the complaint of the Rev. Martin L. Weitz against the action of the Particular Synod of New York upholding the action of the Classis of Brooklyn in ordaining Valerie DeMarinus Miller to the office of the minister of the Word be upheld or dismissed and the action of the Particular Synod of New York be confirmed or reversed?
2. Should the complaint of the Classis of Albany against the action of the Particular Synod of Albany reversing the action of the Classis of Albany in voting to ordain Joyce Borgman deVelder to the office of minister of the Word be upheld or dismissed and the action of the Particular Synod of Albany be confirmed or reversed?
3. Should the complaint of the Classis of Albany against the action of the Particular Synod of Albany directing the Classis of Albany not to ordain Joyce Borgman deVelder to the office of minister of the Word be upheld or dismissed, and the action of the Particular Synod of Albany be confirmed or reversed?
4. Should the complaint of Elder Henry L. Griswold against the action of the Particular Synod of New Jersey upholding the action of the Classis of Bergen in ordaining Louise Ann Hill-Alto to the office of minister of the Word be upheld or dismissed and the action of the Particular Synod of New Jersey be confirmed or reversed?

In what manner does a committee charged with the responsibility of earnestly and prayerfully pursuing these complaints seek to arrive at its final conclusion and recommendations? In the course of its long and deliberative examination of the substantive aspects of the complaints, it became increasingly clear that all recommendations of the Judicial Business Committee, and ultimately the final action of the General Synod, should properly and solely be based upon a consideration of the question of whether or not the *Book of Church Order* of the Reformed Church in America permits or does not permit the ordination of women to the office of minister of the Word.

The committee noted that the central point of the complaints is the definition and interpretation of the word "persons" as it is used in the *Book of Church Order* to define ministers of the Word. ("The ministers of the Word are those persons who have been inducted into that office by ordination in accordance with the Word of God and the order established by the church." *BCO*, Chapter I, Part 1, Article 1, Sec. 3.) The arguments of the complaints appears to be that the word "person" has some meaning other than that which it is given in contemporary usage. Since the committee could find no grammatical grounds offered for this interpretation, it addressed itself to the scriptural/theological and historical grounds presented in the complaints.

The committee first determined that the action of the General Synod in 1958 (*MGS*, p. 328) adopting a report of its Theological Commission, which unequivocally stated that it found no scriptural impediment to the ordination of women to any office in the church, established a position and precedent which still stands. It noted that within our good form of government, the General Synod is a permanent and continuing body whose decisions remain binding until and unless they are rescinded or modified at a subsequent session. The committee therefore considered the scriptural/theological question closed and not subject to debate unless action is taken to rescind the 1958 action of the General Synod.

The committee then addressed itself to the historical question. It found that it could not determine unequivocally what our forefathers meant when they used the word "person." One may infer certain meanings, but all that can actually be determined is that custom and practice saw no woman ordained for a specific period of time.

The committee then addressed the question whether this custom and practice is binding upon us today. The committee is of the opinion that this custom and practice is not binding on the church today. We have already noted that the theological question concerning the ordination of women was settled in the affirmative by the Synod of 1958. In a church such as ours, reformed and reforming according to the Word of God, custom and practice cannot take precedence over the declaration of the General Synod regarding the meaning of the Scripture.

The General Synod itself has not been bound by custom and practice, but has been guided by its understanding of the meaning of Scripture.

> First, it has repeatedly voted for amendments to the Constitution which would clearly and unequivocally declare all the offices of the church open to women.
>
> Further, on each occasion when such action was requested by the classes, the General Synod has in 1973 (*MGS*, p. 37) and again in 1977 (*MGS*, p. 168) granted dispensations from the professorial certificate to women; thus, opening the way to examination for licensure and ordination.
>
> And, it has in 1974 (*MGS*, p. 97) and in 1976 (*MGS*, p. 115f) taken no action on overtures which would have amended the *Book of Church Order*, Chapter 1, Part I, Article 1, Sec. 3, in such a way as to limit the office of minister of the Word to men only.

The committee discussed at length whether the amendments to the *Book of Church Order* proposed by the General Synod throughout the last decade themselves constitute a tacit acknowledgment by the General Synod that the *Book of Church Order* does in fact require amendment in order to permit the ordination of women to the office of minister of the Word. The committee noted that in 1974 the Classis of Brooklyn abstained from voting and recorded with the General Secretary its position that an amendment was not necessary. When a similar amendment was submitted to the classes by the following Synod, the Classis of Brooklyn agreed to participate in the amending process since the larger church deemed it wise and good but again recorded its opinion that an amendment was not necessary. It followed this same course for report to the Synods of 1976, 1977 and 1978. The committee concurs with the Classis of Brooklyn in its opinion that these recommended amendments were clarifying in nature rather than substantitive.

It should be noted further that in each instance of complaint the respective classes have followed due process leading to ordination. The *Book of Church Order* gives authority to the classis to examine and ordain a person to the office of minister of the Word providing the candidate has met all the requirements outlined in the *Book of Church Order* according to the judgment of the classis. It is our finding that in each instance the classes interpreted the *Book of Church Order* regarding the ordination of persons in good faith and without defiance; they exercised the prerogatives of the classis in the Reformed Church in following the procedure for car, examination, licensure and ordination of a candidate who has met all the requirements of the *Book of Church Order*. In each instance, all the carefully spelled-out steps of the *Book of Church Order* and all the requirements of prudent practice have been observed including certification of eligibility for examination by the agent or the General Synod itself.

Therefore, it is the finding of the Judicial Business Committee of this General Synod, that no deliberate, intentional or actual violation of the *Book of Church Order* took place on the part of the classes complained against. Moreover, we find that in each instance they acted in good faith and in accordance with the requirements of the *Book of Church Order*.

R-1.

To dismiss the complaint of the Rev. Martin L. Weitz against the Particular Synod of New York and to confirm the action of the Particular Synod of New York upholding the action of the Classis of Brooklyn in ordaining Valerie DeMarinus Miller to the office of minister of the Word. (ADOPTED)

R-2.

To sustain the complaint of the Classis of Albany against the Particular Synod of Albany and to reverse the action of the Particular Synod of Albany directing the Classis of Albany not to ordain Joyce Borgman deVelder to the office of minister of the Word. (ADOPTED)

R-3.

To dismiss the complaint of Elder Henry L. Griswold against the Particular Synod of New Jersey and to confirm the action of the Particular Synod of New Jersey upholding the action of the Classis of Bergen in ordaining Louise Ann Hill-Alto to the office of minister of the Word. (ADOPTED)

NOTE: Upon proper motion and adoption by the Committee, permission was granted for a minority report by Arthur L. Bridgeman to be appended to this report.

On a motion from the floor Synod:

VOTED: *To request the General Synod Executive Committee to present the decision relative to the ordination procedures of the several women to the whole denomination as soon as possible in the pages of the Church Herald; their statement to be set in a context that emphasizes our unity as Christ's church and our continuing need to seek to understand one another better, and that calls upon our people to pray that God's spirit will ever lead us as a church to a continuing larger service together.*

Minority Report Submitted by Arthur Bridgeman

The significant question to be decided by the Committee on Judicial Business in the matter of all complaints before the committee involving the ordination of women as ministers of the Word appears to be: "Does the *Book of Church Order* permit the ordination of women as ministers of the Word?" Since the Committee has decided this question in the affirmative, Arthur Bridgman requested that the record reflect his voting in the negative for the following reasons:

1. In the President's Report to the General Synod of 1977 President Louis Benes stated as follows (*MGS*, p. 29):

   The overture before us calls for resubmitting this proposed change to the classes again this year. The overtures committee will wrestle with this proposal, and come with a recommendation. My hope would be that we could wait a year before resubmission. I want, just now, to quote from a letter from the officers of this year's General Synod, of which I happened to be the author, and a co-signer. I believe that it still speaks to our present situation. "Some people will say that it (this proposed change) is unnecessary, because the present wording of 'persons' (in the *Book of Church Order*) clearly included women. The General Synod has, however, by its repeated recommendation of this proposed change in wording to the classes for their adoption indicated that it recognized that the traditional interpretation of this wording included men only, and that, for the sake of clarity and good order, the orderly process of amendment to the *Book of Church Order* should be followed in this matter."

2. Clear logic dictates that the meaning of the word 'persons' in referring to ministers of the Word could only mean male persons.

Up until 1972 the *Book of Church Order* referring to ministers of the Word used the word "persons" and as to elders and deacons provided that they "shall be chosen from the male members of the church in full communion."

The obvious question arises as to why it was necessary to restrict elders and deacons to male members of the church and not the ministers of the Word. The minister of the Word has generally been held to hold a higher office in the church than the elders and deacons. For instance, the installed pastor automatically becomes the president of the consistory.

It is the contention of those who have engaged in the ordination of women as ministers of the Word that the *Book of Church Order* in using the word "persons" never had prohibited it. However, this does not really face the question as to why ministers of the Word were referred to as "persons" whereas it was felt necessary to clearly restrict elders and deacons to male members of the church. To follow the reasoning of those who are ordaining women as ministers of the Word you would have to believe that in the long history of the Reformed Church in America it has always been allowable to ordain women as ministers of the Word, but not as elders or deacons. This is totally inconceivable and illogical. The only logical explanation is that it has been so generally accepted that ministers of the Word have been limited to male members of the church that it was never considered necessary to set it forth so clearly as with elders and deacons.

Notes: *The Committee on Judicial Business was presented with the ordination of several women to the office of Minister of the Word. By dealing with these as complaints and not appeals, the committee was able to make a ruling without submitting the issue of women's ordination to another church-wide vote. The committee interpreted the Book of Church Order as allowing the ordination of women, and thus sustained the ordinations already performed. This action was viewed by many opponents of women's ordination as constitutionally questionable.*

REFORMED CHURCH IN AMERICA

RESOLUTION ON WOMEN'S ORDINATION (1980)

Ordination of Women

From June, 1979, to April, 1980, the General Synod Executive Committee received communications from 14 individuals, 11 churches and 11 classes expressing concern about the action of the 1979 General Synod on the ordination of women to the office of minister of the Word.

Six of these communications were presented as overtures but were not accepted for the agenda by the GSEC since they alleged administrative error by the General Synod of 1979 and were thus judged to be complaints which are prohibited by the *BCO* (Chapter 11, Part III, Article V, Section 1). An additional reason for not accepting five of the overtures was that they asked the Synod either directly, or in effect, to rescind the judgment of the 1979 Synod on complaints submitted to it. Although the General Synod can, in most cases, rescind its legislative actions, it is not at liberty through legislative actions to rescind its judgments on complaints.

Nevertheless, through these letters and other means, the GSEC has recognized that many RCA members are dismayed because of General Synod's action concerning the ordination of women, even as others are encouraged. The GSEC also noted that the General Synod of 1979 addressed only the question of "whether or not the *Book of Church Order* of the Reformed Church in America permits or does not permit the ordination of women to the office of minister of the Word" (*MGS*, p. 67). The question of whether or not the *BCO* requires the ordination of women to the office of minister of the Word was not before the Synod.

Because the members of the Reformed Church are not of one mind on this question and because our differing opinions are rooted in strong convictions and are accompanied by deep feelings, the following recommendation is presented to the General Synod.

R-4.

(To call for careful avoidance of pressure which might lead either one who supports or one who opposes the action permitting the ordination of women to the office of minister of the Word to offend against his or her conscience, and to urge that no member of the church be penalized for conscientious objection to, or support of, the ordination of women.)

The advisory committee presented the following "Proposal to Maintain Peace in Diversity in the RCA Concerning Women as Church Officers" as a substitute for R-13:

To approve the following amendment to the *Book of Church Order* and refer it to the Editorial Committee:

a. Amend Part I, Article 1, Section 3 (*BCO*, p. 12) by substituting "men and women" for "persons."

b. Amend Part II, Article 2, Section 7 (*BCO*, p. 24) by adding the following:

If individual members of the classis find that their consciences, as illuminated by Scripture, would not permit them to participate in the licensure, ordination or installation of women as ministers of the Word, they shall not be required to participate in decisions or actions contrary to their consciences, but may not obstruct the classis in fulfilling its responsibility to arrange for the care, ordination, and installation of women candidates and ministers by means mutually agreed on by such women and the classis.

c. Amend Part II, Article 10 (*BCO*, p. 40) by adding a new section:

Section 15. Ministers of the Word shall not be pressured in such a way as to lead either one who supports or one who opposes, on scriptural grounds, the ordination of women to church offices to offend against his or her conscience. Nor shall any church member be penalized for conscientious objection to, or support of, the ordination of women to church offices. *Nor shall any minister of the Word or church member obstruct by unconstitutional means the election, ordination, or installation of a woman to church offices.* (ADOPTED AS AMENDED)*

Reasons:

1. To clarify and confirm through constitutional amendments the legality of the ordination of women as ministers of the Word.
2. To protect the rights of conscience of church members and officers and protect the rights of women candidates to ordination.
3. To bring peace in diversity in the RCA over the issue of women in church offices.

On a motion from the floor Synod:

VOTED: To instruct the Advisory Committee on Church Order to send a cover letter along with this recommendation to include:

*Substitution in light face type.

1. **background information which resulted in reaching this decision;**
2. **a statement to the effect that a vote by the classis in favor of this amendment is a vote recognizing who we are as a Reformed Church family—a people diverse yet united in Christ.**

3. **a statement to the effect that while certain RCA members may not be in favor of women's ordination personally, they are—by passing this amendment—saying they are in favor of being a member of a denomination that allows (ordination of women)** unity in diversity.*

VOTED: That the advisory committee instruct its subcommittee that drafted the substitute recommendation for R-13 to prepare the letter to be sent; that the letter be submitted to the advisory committee for approval; that the approved letter be reported to the General Synod; and that the approved letter be forwarded to the General Secretary's office for distribution.

The advisory committee presented for approval the following cover letter to be sent with the "Proposal to Maintain Peace in Diversity in the RCA Concerning Women as Church Officers" to all ministers and congregations.

To the Reformed Church Family:

A Proposal to Maintain Peace in Diversity in the RCA Concerning Women as Church Officers

After much deliberation as a committee, we adopted without dissent the enclosed proposal which was presented to the General Synod. After thorough discussion, the Synod adopted it with scarcely any dissent, followed by applause.

We believe that our committee and the Synod, representing varied views of the ordination of women, were satisfied that this represents a workable means of achieving peace with diversity in the Reformed Church in America. Because of our feeling of the tremendous importance of this action, we have asked the Synod for permission to share this information with you.

Sincerely in Christ,

THE ADVISORY COMMITTEE ON CHURCH ORDER

VOTED: To authorize the sending of the cover letter with the "Proposal to Maintain Peace in Diversity in the RCA Concerning Women as Church Officers" to all ministers and congregations.

*Addition in light face type.

Deletion in parentheses.

Notes: *This is a report by the Executive Committee recognizing that the previous year's actions did not resolve the issue of women's ordination, and that not everyone was satisfied with the means by which those actions took place. In an attempt to ease tensions and to satisfy both sides of the debate, an advisory committee presented a "Proposal to Maintain Peace in Diversity in the RCA Concerning Women As Church Officers." This proposal sought to amend this Book of Church Order by officially approving women's ordination (an attempt that had failed many times previously), but it also included a compromise statement for those who objected to the practice. This statement would allow conscientious objectors to women's ordination to not participate in ordination ceremonies as long as they agreed that they belonged to a church that permitted it. This is the same kind of statement that was denied by the Committee on Overtures in 1973. At the 1981 General Synod, it was reported that this resolution passed with the 30 votes required for a 2/3 majority. The long struggle which began in 1918 was, officially at least, over.*

SOUTHERN BAPTIST CONVENTION

RESOLUTION ON THE PLACE OF WOMEN IN CHRISTIAN SERVICE (1973)

Resolution No. 12—On the Place of Women in Christian Service

WHEREAS, The Scriptures bear record to the distinctive roles of men and women in the church and in the home, and

WHEREAS, Christian women have made and are making a significant contribution to the cause of Christ, and

WHEREAS, Christian women have been exhorted to redig the old wells of mission promotion and education in our churches by Kenneth Chafin, and

WHEREAS, There is a great attack by the members of most women's liberation movements upon scriptural precepts of woman's place in society, and

WHEREAS, The theme of the Convention is "Share the Word Now" and this Word we share is explicitly clear on this subject.

Therefore, be it *Resolved,* that we "redig" or reaffirm God's order of authority for his church and the Christian home: (1) Christ the head of every man; (2) man the head of the woman; (3) children in subjection to their parents—in the Lord.

Therefore, be it further *Resolved*, that we "redig" or reaffirm God's explicit Word that (1) man was not made for the woman, but the woman for the man; (2) that the woman is the glory of man; (3) that as woman would not have existed without man, henceforth, neither would man have existed without the woman, they are dependent one upon the other—to the glory of God.

Notes: *This 1973 resolution of the Southern Baptist Convention (approximately 14,000,000 members) came nine years after Addie Davis became the Convention's first ordained woman and one year after Druecillar Fordham became the Convention's first ordained black woman pastor. The resolution was brought by Mrs. Jesse Sappington, the wife of a Houston pastor. Passage of this statement, which reaffirms the woman's subjection to the man, unleashed considerable emotions on both sides of the issue.*

SOUTHERN BAPTIST CONVENTION

CONCERNING FREEDOM FOR WOMEN (1974)

Christian morality is at the heart of the faith we embrace, the gospel we preach, and the churches we serve. Particularly important to Christian morality development at this time are a careful consideration of freedom for women, race relations, integrity in government, and economic life.

I. *Freedom for Women.*—The good news proclaimed by the New Testament is that God has entered history through his son, Jesus, freeing human beings to reach their highest potential. At the beginning of his ministry, Jesus made the cause of human liberation his own, committing himself "to set at liberty those who are oppressed" (Luke 4:19).

The Bible champions human liberation. Paul, in reflecting upon the new life in Christ, wrote to the Galatians, "There is neither Jew nor Greek, there is neither slave nor free, there is neither male nor female; for you are all one in Christ Jesus" (Gal. 3:28).

Both men and women share the freedom which Christ gives. Historically, men have enjoyed far more freedom than women. Yet, men are not as free as God means for them to be, for when men keep women from being free, then both remain enslaved; and the work of Jesus Christ at this important point is made of no effect.

Injustice toward women persists to some degree in every institution in society: government, business, education, and the church. So imbedded is discrimination against women that it affects not only the hearts and minds of people in society but also the institutions and structures of society itself. Unequal pay for the same kind of work is an example of the injustices against women which ought to be intolerable to Christians. Even in our churches, women often have been kept from assuming places of leadership for which their abilities and their Christian commitment qualify them.

Just as it is sinful for men to discriminate against women, so it is sinful for women to refuse to accept the dignity God has bestowed on them.

To endorse the great concept of the human liberation of women in Jesus Christ is not to endorse the ideas or actions of every person who unfurls the women's liberation banner. Irresponsibility is no respecter of the sexes, and Christians must resist it no matter where it is found.

Encouraging women to achieve their God-intended potential need not be detrimental to the stability of the family and the spiritual health of the church. The home and the church have crucial responsibilities for teaching the equal worth as well as the distinctive roles of males and females.

Recommendation No. 1 Concerning Freedom for Women

In response to Christ's great call to freedom, we recommend:

1. That we reaffirm our commitment to the Bible's teaching that every individual has infinite worth and that, in Christ, there is neither male nor female, and that we endeavor to communicate these basic truths through Christian education, by precept and example, in church and at home;

2. That we work to develop greater sensitivity to both overt and covert discrimination against women and that we endeavor through religious, political, social, business, and educational structures to eliminate such discrimination; and

3. That our churches and our denominational agencies bear witness to the rest of society by rejecting discrimination against women in job placement, by providing equal pay for equal work, and by electing women to positions of leadership for which God's gifts and the Holy Spirit's calling equip them.

4. We recommend that the Southern Baptist Convention's Constitution and Bylaws, paragraph 5 [which is printed on pages 33-34 of the 1973 *Annual* of the Southern Baptist Convention as follows: "All Convention committees, boards and commissions shall include both ordained and lay persons as members. Not more than two-thirds of the members of any group should be drawn from either category."] of Bylaw 7 entitled "How Board Members, Trustees, Commissioners, or Members of Standing Committees Are Elected," be amended by adding as a move toward more equitable representation the following concluding sentence: *At least one-fifth of the total members shall be women.* [Since this recommendation involves a Bylaw change, it is understood that it requires a two-thirds vote of the Convention.]

5. We further recommend that this change be begun in 1975 and fully implemented no later than 1980.

Notes: *This resolution by the Christian Life Commission was challenged by Mrs. Jesse Sappington, who gained prominence in the previous year by her support of a statement in favor of the subordination of women. The Convention voted on the first three points separately from the fourth point. In both cases the resolution failed. The phrase "electing* *women to positions of leadership for which God's gifts and the Holy Spirit's calling equip them'' seemed to many to be a veiled affirmation of the ordination of women.*

SOUTHERN BAPTIST CONVENTION

RESOLUTION ON MISSIONARY QUALIFICATIONS (1974)

33. Tom Reynolds (Tex.) moved that the following be added to Article IX of the Constitution under the ''Missionary Qualifications'': ''All appointments, endorsements, etc., (including the military and industrial chaplaincy) whose function will be that of a pastor, which is restricted to males by Scripture, must meet those requirements as outlined in the New Testament.'' The motion was referred for later consideration, which was set at 11:40 A.M. the following day. (See Item 138). . . .

138. Tom Reynolds (Tex.) spoke in support of the motion he had offered (see Item 33). Discussion followed by Suzanne Coyle (Ky.) and Richard Jackson (Ariz.). A point of order was raised again from the floor about consideration of the motion to table still pending from the Tuesday evening session. The Chair declared that the messengers had sustained his ruling and that the consideration of the Reynolds motion would continue. James W. Kelly (Ga.) spoke to the motion. Howard Aultman (Miss.) moved the previous question. The motion passed. Since the result of a standing vote was in doubt, the vote was taken by ballot.

Notes: *This resolution would require that all positions beyond the local church that involve pastoring, such as chaplaincy, be limited to men. The Convention was evenly divided on this issue, as a standing vote did not result in a decision. The resolution eventually failed, but this did not mean the voters were in favor of women chaplains. Given the tenor of votes on similar issues, it more likely meant that they were not willing to infringe so strongly on local church prerogatives in ordination.*

SOUTHERN BAPTIST CONVENTION

STATEMENT ON WOMEN'S ORDINATION (1980)

Resolution No. 21—On Women

WHEREAS, Through responsibilities in the family and in multiplied avenues of service, women have made immeasurable contributions to the home, society, and the Kingdom of God, and

WHEREAS, Many women today are answering God's call for service within the home, in the church, and in the work-a-day world, and

WHEREAS, Contemporary pressures are forcing men and women to make difficult decisions regarding priorities and responsibilities,

Therefore be it *Resolved*, That we express gratitude to God for the contribution made by women in all avenues of service, and we call on Christian women to follow the pattern of Jesus and the teaching of the Scripture in determining priorities and responsibilities, and

Be it further *Resolved*, That we encourage all persons to be sensitive to the contemporary pressures facing women, and

Be it further *Resolved*, That for women who need or want to work outside the home we urge employers to seek fairness for women in compensation, advancement, and opportunities for improvement.

Be it finally *Resolved*, That this Convention, reaffirming the biblical role which stresses the equal worth but not always the sameness of function of women, does not endorse the Equal Rights Amendment.

Notes: *This resolution encourages unbiased treatment of women in the work world while at the same time refusing to open certain arenas to women. The same resolution was again passed in 1981.*

SOUTHERN BAPTIST CONVENTION

STATEMENT ON WOMEN'S ORDINATION (1983)

Resolution No.8—On Women

WHEREAS, The Bible teaches that men and women share in the dignity of creation, both being made "in the image of God" (Genesis 1:27); and

WHEREAS, Our Lord Jesus Christ by his attitude and actions affirmed the worth and dignity of women; and

WHEREAS, The Apostle Paul set forth in Galations 3:28 the principle of spiritual equality before God, declaring that in the grace of God "there is neither male nor female; for you are all one in Christ Jesus"; and

WHEREAS, Southern Baptist women have been and continue to be active, vitally involved, contributing members of the churches and of this Convention.

Therefore, be it *Resolved*, That we, the messengers to the Southern Baptist Convention assembled in Pittsburgh, Pennsylvania, June 14-16, 1983, express gratitude to God for the contributions made by Southern Baptist women in service to home, society, the missions enterprise, and the cause of Christ in general; and that we affirm those women who labor for the Lord and the churches in places of special service to which God has called them; and

Be it further *Resolved*, That for women who serve the Lord as homemakers, we affirm their special calling, honor them for their unique contributions to church and society, and support their right to financial security; and

Be it further *Resolved*, That for women who work outside the home, we urge all employers, including those Southern Baptist churches, institutions, and agencies which employ women, to seek fairness for women in compensation, benefits, and opportunities for advancement; and

Be it finally *Resolved*, That we encourage all Southern Baptists to continue to explore further opportunities of service for Baptist women, to ensure maximum utilization of all God-called servants of our Lord Jesus Christ.

Notes: *This resolution repeats a number of the ideas found in the 1980 and 1981 resolutions, but adds several new items that differ from those earlier documents. It emphasizes that both men and women share the image of God, and quotes the Galatians passage that is a favorite of those supporting women's ordination. The final section implies a willingness to discuss the ordination of women. The implications of this resolution apparently prompted the 1984 resolution as a clarification measure.*

SOUTHERN BAPTIST CONVENTION

STATEMENT ON WOMEN'S ORDINATION (1984)

Resolution No. 3—On Ordination and the Role of Women in Ministry

WHEREAS, We, the messengers to the Southern Baptist Convention meeting in Kansas City, June 12-14, 1984, recognize the authority of Scripture in all matters of faith and practice including the autonomy of the local church; and

WHEREAS, The New Testament enjoins all Christians to proclaim the gospel; and

WHEREAS, The New Testament churches as a community of faith recognized God's ordination and anointing of some believers for special ministries (e.g., I Timothy 2:7; Titus 1:15) and in consequence of their demonstrated loyalty to the gospel, conferred public blessing and engaged in public dedicatory prayer setting them apart for service; and

WHEREAS, The New Testament does not mandate that all who are divinely called to ministry be ordained; and

WHEREAS, In the New Testament, ordination symbolizes spiritual succession to the world task of proclaiming and extending the gospel of Christ, and not a sacramental transfer of unique divine grace that perpetuates apostolic authority; and

WHEREAS, The New Testament emphasizes the equal dignity of men and women (Gal. 3:28) and that the Holy Spirit was at Pentecost divinely outpoured on men and women alike (Acts 2:17); and

WHEREAS, Women as well as men prayed and prophesied in public worship services (I Cor. 11:2-16), and Priscilla joined her husband in teaching Apollos (Acts 18:26), and women fulfilled special church service-ministries as exemplified by Phoebe whose work Paul tributes as that of a servant of the church (Rom. 16:1); and

WHEREAS, The Scriptures attest to God's delegated order of authority (God the head of Christ, Christ the head of man, man the head of woman, man and woman dependent one upon the other to the glory of God) distinguishing the roles of men and women in public prayer and prophecy (I Cor. 11:2-5); and

WHEREAS, The Scriptures teach that women are not in public worship to assume a role of authority over men lest confusion reign in the local church (I Cor. 14:33-36); and

WHEREAS, While Paul commends women and men alike in other roles of ministry and service (Titus 2:1-10), he excludes women from pastoral leadership (I Tim. 2:12) to preserve a submission God requires because the man was first in creation and the woman was first in the Edenic fall (I Tim. 2:13ff); and

WHEREAS, These Scriptures are not intended to stifle the creative contribution of men and women as co-workers in many roles of church service, both on distant mission fields and in domestic ministries, but imply that women and men are nonetheless divinely gifted for distinctive areas of evangelical engagement; and

WHEREAS, Women are held in high honor for their unique and significant contribution to the advancement of Christ's kingdom, and the building of godly homes should be esteemed for its vital contribution to developing personal Christian character and Christlike concern for others.

Therefore, be it *Resolved*, That we not decide concerns of Christian doctrine and practice by modern cultural, sociological, and ecclesiastical trends or by emotional factors; that we remind ourselves of the dearly bought Baptist principle of the final authority of Scripture in matters of faith and conduct; and that we encourage the service of women in all aspects of church life and work other than pastoral functions and leadership roles entailing ordination.

Notes: *This resolution alters the apparent implications of the 1983 resolution by explicitly*

stating that, based on various Bible passages, women are not to be permitted to serve in ordained capacities. Because of the very loose authority the Convention wields over individual congregations, this resolution cannot force congregations to expel women pastors already in place, nor can it prevent congregations from ordaining others.

UNITED CHURCH OF CANADA

REPORT AND RECOMMENDATIONS OF THE COMMITTEE ON THE ORDINATION OF WOMEN (1928)

The Ordination of Women

Introduction

The Committee on the Ordination of Women was appointed by the Second General Council of The United Church of Canada (1926). This action was taken pursuant to the discussion in the Council of the following Memorial from the Conference of Saskatchewan:

> That the Saskatchewan Conference request the General Council to grant authority to this Conference to ordain Miss Lydia E. Gruchy to the Ministry of The United Church of Canada.

The question of the authority of the Council to take the action sought in the Memorial was laid before the Committee on Law and Legislation which reported as follows:

> Your Committee, having carefully considered the legal aspects of the motion with reference to the ordination of Miss L. E. Gruchy for the Ministry is of opinion that serious legal doubts exist regarding the right of The United Church of Canada, either by the General Council, or any Conference, to ordain women for the Ministry without complying with the provisions of the Basis of Union, Sec. 24, sub-Sec. 2 (a), Polity.

A Committee of the Council considered the Memorial and recommended as follows:

1. That the whole question of Ordination of Women to the Ministry be referred to the Presbyteries for their consideration and judgment, and for report to the next General Council.
2. That a Committee consisting of the Moderator, Revs. Geo. C. Pidgeon; Principal E.H. Oliver, C.W. Bishop, Prof. H.A. Kent, T. Albert Moore, W.T. Gunn, Hugh Matheson, E. Thomas and Prof. J.T. McNeill as Chairman, be appointed to prepare a statement for the information and guidance of the Presbyteries, which shall be submitted to the Executive Committee to be sent down to Presbyteries with the remit on Ordination of Women.

These recommendations were adopted. (See United Church of Canada Year Book, 1926, pp. 60, 80, 108, 114.)

After the Committee had begun its work it was charged by the Executive with the additional task of considering and reporting on the question of the membership of Women in Sessions, Presbyteries and Conferences, as indicated in the following extracts from Minutes:

Extract from Record of Proceedings, Year Book, Page 87.

Toronto West Presbytery, *re*election of women as members of session. (Basis, Polity, Par. B. 9 (a)). We recommend that this item be referred to the Executive Committee with instructions to investigate the legal aspects of this question, and to send down the information to Presbyteries.

Election of Women as Members of Session
Minutes of Executive Committee

A memorial to the General Council from Toronto West Presbytery, requesting that it declare whether women might be elected as members of Sessions, was referred to the Executive Committee with instructions to investigate the legal aspects of this question, and to send down the information to Presbyteries.

Resolved that the Remit concerning the legality of electing Women as Members of Session be sent to the Presbyteries after the Report of the Committee on Law and Legislation has been received by the Executive.

Ruling of Committee on Law and Legislation
May Women be Elected as Members of Session?

Under the Polity Division of the Basis of Union, part II-B, section 9, it is contemplated that the persons, who, with the minister or ministers, constitute the session shall be men, because sub-section (a) of section 9 is as follows:

> "The oversight of the spiritual interests of the charge by the minister (or ministers) and a body of men specially chosen and set apart or ordained for that work, who shall jointly constitute the session."

The above reference applies to charges formed subsequent to the union and to charges existing previous to the union which have adopted the plan of organization prescribed for pastoral charges formed subsequent to the union.

Extract from Minutes of Sub-Executive

On motion the Secretary was directed to forward this opinion to the Committee which is preparing a statement concerning the Ordination of Women for the information and guidance of Presbyteries, with the request that this Committee include in their report information on this subject for the consideration of the Presbyteries.

Official Position of Women

The request received from the Presbytery of Honan, asking that the ecclesiastical status of women in the Conferences and Presbyteries of The United Church be determined, which was before the Executive Committee last year, when much information was assembled concerning the status of women in each of the uniting Churches, and the whole question with this information referred to the General Council, with the suggestion that the question and information be remitted to Presbyteries. No action was taken by the General Council. On motion the question and information were referred to the Committee appointed to prepare a statement concerning the ordination of women, to report to the Executive Committee.

Section A

Women and the Ordained Ministry

I. Women's Work in the Church

In approaching the question of the ordination of women, it will be helpful to consider first the position of women in the Church during its formative stage. It is clear from the whole record of the gospels that in the mind, teaching and creative work of Jesus, men and women were spiritually equal. Women later received in common with men the gifts of the Spirit and were prominent in the activities of the Church. Their spiritual equality with men is indicated by St. Paul's words in Galatians 3: 26-28, which show that this equality is not restricted by race, social rank or sex;

> "For ye are all children of God by faith in Christ Jesus. For as many of you as have

> been baptized into Christ have put on Christ. There is neither Jew nor Greek, there is neither bond nor free, there is neither male nor female; for ye are all one in Christ Jesus.''

Equality of status, however, admits of diversity of function and this is seen in the recognition of various ministries, both of men and of women. Diversity of function, on the other hand, does not imply superiority or inferiority of status. It is evident from 1 Corinthians 2: 5, that praying and ''prophesying,'' or exhorting, were recognized activities of women in the Church. The restrictions elsewhere laid down by St. Paul upon certain ministries of women (1 Cor. 2: 3-16, 14: 34-36, 1 Tim. 2: 12) were designed to secure discipline, order and peace in the Church as it developed under the social conditions then obtaining. While these precepts embody an enduring principle for the conserving of order and discipline, they express that principle in terms relative to transient conditions, and ought not to be held as binding in detail under the vastly altered conditions of modern society, in which women may enjoy a larger sphere of social activity without going beyond what is seemly, modest and of good report.

In the early centuries of the Church the principal ministry of women was that of the diaconate. Originally the function of the deacons was the administration of alms, but in time they were also charged with preaching, teaching and the administration of baptism, and were ordained to their office as a part of the Universal Ministry. From Apostolic days women were admitted to the diaconate, their ministry being largely confined, in Hellenistic society, to work among women and children. In the Middle Ages the diaconate of women largely passed out of sight in the monastic sisterhoods, although it can be traced through monastic history by certain survivals. At the Reformation a diaconate of women was advocated, but was not established as a part of the Ministry. During the nineteenth and twentieth centuries women in various communions have rendered an increasing volume of service by public speech and organization, as well as by private ministrations. The Church has called to special office many of these workers, who devote their lives to the care of the poor and sick, and of neglected children, to various kinds of work in congregations and in home and foreign missions, and to other evangelical labors. Many of these women have served as deaconesses without ordination. But in certain communions movements have arisen for the ecclesiastical ordination to the diaconate of women as a part of the Ministry. The Lambeth Conference of Bishops of the Anglican Communion has resolved ''that the Diaconate of Women should be restored formally and canonically,'' and the Upper Houses of the Convocations of Canterbury and York have adopted a form for the Ordination of Deaconesses.

II. Doctrine of the Ministry

It is important at this point to consider the nature of the Christian Ministry. The office of the Ministry is a perpetual ordinance in the Church. By ordination the candidate is set apart to a Ministry of the Word and Sacraments; this being a Ministry of the whole Church and not merely of a part thereof. Concerning this Ministry of the Word and Sacraments, the position of the Church Universal, and of this Church has been, and is, that by ordination to the office, the functions and duties of the Ministry become the primary and life-long vocation of the ordained. He is to give himself wholly to this one thing. The calling is of such a nature that no other vocation of life can be primary. The Church and the young men who are ordained equally understand that their ordination is to a life-long service.

In the Primitive Church, as we have seen, the diaconate came to be regarded as a second order of the Ministry. At the Reformation the diaconate was retained in the Anglican Church as a part of the Universal Ministry, and it was continued in the Methodist Church at its formation on this Continent in 1784. The office is still retained in the Methodist Episcopal Church of The United States, and was continued in the main body of Canadian Methodism until 1833 and in one division of the Church until 1884. It appertains to this office to preach, teach, baptize and to perform such pastoral duties as may be required, by authority of the

Church. The office of the diaconate is life-long, but the Church has not held that its duties should always constitute the only life vocation of the ordained; a member of the diaconate may serve partly in the office, and partly in some other life calling. In fact the duties of the office may at times be such that a deacon who engages in another calling will thereby possess peculiar qualifications for the exercise of his ministry. A woman set apart to the diaconate would to the same degree dedicate herself to a life-long office; but in certain circumstances, such as marriage, she might without violation of obligations be by authority released, in whole or in part, from the duties of the office. In such case she would retain her status and could, if circumstances admitted, resume her active ministry.

III. Recommendations

Your Committee, having considered the proposals that have been presented for the admission of women to the Ministry, and the present situation of women's work in the Church as a whole, and especially in The United Church of Canada, is impressed with the desirability of giving fuller ecclesiastical recognition to certain ministries that are already exercised by women, and of calling forth the fullest service of women for the benefit of the Church.

It is the judgment of the Committee that in view of (a) the character of the Ministry as now constituted, (b) the possibility of controversy within the Church, and (c) the present state of the question in other Churches, no action should be taken at the present time on the proposal to ordain women to the Ministry of the Word and Sacraments. Their admission to the ordained diaconate would, we believe, satisfy the need that has inspired the memorial of the Conference of Saskatchewan.

It should be clearly understood that women qualified for and ordained to the diaconate would differ from the unordained deaconesses at present so usefully serving the Church, in these respects;

1. They would hold a regularly authorized position in the Ministry of the Church.
2. They would have relations to the Church Courts subject to such regulations as might be adopted.
3. They would have a higher academic standing than that now required for unordained deaconesses.

We therefore recommend as follows:

1. That the diaconate of women be recognized by The United Church of Canada as an order of the Ministry,* with authority to perform such pastoral duties as may be required, and in particular, to teach, to preach and where necessary to baptize.
2. That women manifestly called of God and adequately trained be ordained to this office.
3. That a Committee or Committees be appointed by the General Council to determine the conditions of admission to the ordained diaconate, and the relation of its members to the Church Courts, and to provide a course of training appropriate for candidates; which course should be comparable to that now prescribed for the Ministry while including training for special tasks.
4. That the members of the Deaconess Order as now existing be continued in their present work and retain their present status, and that subject to the regulations which may be adopted they may be admitted to the diaconate, but that the name of "deaconess" be conferred in future only upon women ordained to the diaconate.
5. That the fullest possible study of the subject of women's relations to the Church should be encouraged, and that all ministers should inform themselves and instruct their people concerning the history and present aspects of the subject, and the nature and implications of the above recommendations. The matter is one of such grave importance that no step

should be taken without the support of public opinion formed after due consideration in an uncontentious, truth-seeking and prayerful spirit.

N.B. These recommendations are submitted after full conference with the Committee responsible for the supervision of the Deaconess Order and with their general concurrence in so far as they relate to the future of the Deaconess Order.

We invite careful attention to the appendices accompanying this report.

For fuller study the following books are recommended:

Adeney, W.F., *Women in the New Testament*, London, 1906.

Bancroft, Jane, *Deaconesses in Europe*, New York, 1889.

Bardsley, C.C.B., *Women and Church Work*, London and New York, 1917.

Bingham, Joseph, *Antiquities of the Christian Church*, Vol. I, Oxford, 1855.

Charteris, A.H., *Women's Work in the Church*, Article in *Presbyterian Review*, Vol. IX (1888), p. 283 f.

Conference of Bishops of the Anglican Communion Holden at Lambeth Palace, July 5th to August 7th, 1920, p. 95 f, London, 1920.

Eckenstein, Lina, *Women under Monasticism*, Cambridge, 1896.

Golder, C., *History of the Deaconess Movement in the Christian Church*, New York, 1903.

Howson, J.S., *The Diaconate of Women in the Anglican Church*, London, 1886.

Kidd, Benjamin, *The Science of Power*, New York and London, 1918.

Lindsay, Thomas M., *The Church and the Ministry in the Early Christian Centuries*, New York and London, 1902.

Lodge, Oliver, et al., *The Position of Women Actual and Ideal*, London, 1911.

Ludlow, J.M., *Women's Work in the Church*, London, 1865.

The Ministry of Women, A report by a Committee appointed by His Grace the Archbishop of Canterbury, London, 1919.

On the Early History and Modern Revival of Deaconesses, in *Church Quarterly Review*, Vol. 47, p. 322 f. (Jan. 1899).

Picton-Turbervill, Edith, *Christ and Woman's Power*, London, 1920.

Robinson, Cecilia. *The Ministry of Deaconesses*, 2nd edition, London, 1914.

Royden, Maude, *The Church and Women*, containing chapter on *Women in Free Churches*, by Constance M. Coltman, London (undated).

Royden, Maude, *Women at the World's Cross-Roads*, New York, 1923.

Shäffer, Theodor, *Die Weibliche Diakonie*, 3rd edition, 3 vols. Potsdam, 1911.

Simpson, W.G. Sparrow, (Ed.) *The Place of Women in the Church*, London and Milwaukee, 1917.

Streeter, B.H. and Picton-Turbervill. *Women and the Church*, London, 1917.

Wheeler, Henry, *Deaconesses, Ancient and Modern*, New York, 1889.

Wordsworth, John, *The Ministry of Grace*, London and New York, 1901.

Section B

The Membership of Women in Sessions, Presbyteries and Conferences

The Committee has carefully considered this matter from the standpoint of the usage of the past, the terms of the Basis of Union, and the requirements of the work of the Church.

The present day tendency to admit women to all the rights of laymen in the Church Courts is exemplified in the Presbyterian Church of England and in the Church of England. In the Presbyterian Church of England women are eligible to the Eldership. "The Assembly also declares the office of the Eldership to be open to women on the same terms as to men, and authorizes their ordination as Elders in the same manner, and subject to the acceptance of the same formula as in the case of men, of women who are duly elected to that office." (Book of Order of the Presbyterian Church of England, 1922, p. 185).

The Conference of Bishops of the Anglican Communion, held at Lambeth (the Lambeth Conference), 1920, adopted the following resolution on the position of women in the Courts of the Church; "Women should be admitted to those Councils of the Church to which laymen are admitted, and on equal terms. Diocesan, Provincial, or National Synods may decide when and how this principle is to be brought into effect" (Lambeth Conference Report, 1920. p. 39).

In the Church of England by the "Church of England Assembly (Powers) Act, 1919," and under the "Rules for the Representation of the Laity" in Parochial, Ruri-decanal, Diocesan councils, and in the House of Laity women are eligible. It is enacted that "All members may be of either sex." (See Schedule to the Act, section II). In the Church of England women are eligible for the office of Churchwarden. (See Phillimore, Ecclesiastical Law, p. 1467; Blunt; The Book of Church Law, p. 256.)

The degree in which women have participated in bodies having ecclesiastical jurisdiction in the three uniting Churches is briefly indicated in the Appendices. The Basis of Union contains the following provisions which will be found relative to the matter:

Polity II. A.

4. In the management of their local affairs the various churches, charges, circuits or congregations of the negotiating Churches shall be entitled to continue the organization and practices . . . enjoyed by them at the time of the union, subject in general affairs to the legislation, principles and discipline of the United Church. Their representatives in the next higher governing body or court shall be chosen as at present.

8. Churches, charges, circuits, or congregations, received subsequent to the union, into the United Church, with the approval of Presbyteries, shall be entitled, if they so desire, to the privileges of sections 4, 5 and 7.

Polity II. B.9 (a).

The oversight of the spiritual interests of the charge by the minister (or ministers) and a body of men specially chosen and set apart or ordained for that work, who shall jointly constitute the session.

Polity II. B.14.

The members of the session, other than the minister, shall be chosen by those in full church membership, and shall hold office under regulations to be passed by the General Council.

Polity II. B.17 (2).

(It shall be the duty of the Official Board) to select representatives, in full church membership, of the pastoral charge to the Presbytery.

Polity III. 19 (2).

(The Presbytery shall consist of . . . .) the elders, deacons, leaders or other non-ministerial representatives of pastoral charges, within the bounds, equal in number to the number of ministers, etc.

Polity III. 20 (1).

It shall be the duty of the Presbytery: 1. To have the oversight of the pastoral charges within its bounds, review their records, and form new pastoral charges, or local churches.

2. To receive and dispose of petitions and appeals from the lower governing bodies or courts.

10. To select non-ministerial representatives to the Conference, etc.

Polity IV. 21.

The Conference shall consist of the ministers on the rolls of the Presbyteries within its bounds, and an equal number of non-ministerial representatives of pastoral charges chosen as provided for in sub-section 20 (par. 10.)

22. It shall be the duty of the Conference:

   2. To determine the number and boundaries of the Presbyteries within its bounds, have oversight of them, and review their records.

   3. To receive and dispose of appeals and petitions, subject to the usual right of appeal.

   8. To select an equal number of ministerial and non-ministerial representatives to the General Council.

I. Status of Women in Presbyteries and Conferences

a. Membership in Presbyteries.

Basis of Union, Polity II. A. 4, provides that in charges existing previous to the Union, "representatives in the next higher governing body or court shall be chosen as at present."

The bearing of this provision upon charges formerly of the Methodist Church, is indicated by the following enactment of the General Conference of 1922, (Discipline, Paragraph 91):

> The General Conference shall extend to women equal rights and privileges with men as lay members of the church.

In accordance with this provision women became members of District Meetings, Annual Conferences and General Conference.

In the Congregational Churches the situation is explained by the following paragraph in Appendix II. of this report:

> In the organization of the Congregational Union of Canada and of the Churches belonging to it, there is no difference made between men and women in the membership of the local church, the membership of the District Association, or the membership or office of the Congregational Union of Canada. Women have been delegates to the Associations and to the Union, freely appointed for many years. Women have been members of the Executive and Directors of the Foreign Missionary Society and of the Executive and General Committee of the Home Missionary Society.

Thus, in charges formerly of the Methodist Church and of the Congregational Churches of Canada, women are eligible for election to the higher governing bodies or courts.

In charges formerly of the Presbyterian Church in Canada, in which, (as stated in App.

II.) women "were not regarded as eligible, and as a matter of fact did not have a place on the Session," and which have not changed their plan of organization, the Basis does not provide for the election of women as representatives to Presbyteries.

In Polity II. B, with respect to charges formed subsequent to the Union, the Basis provides that "It shall be the duty of the Official Board, to select representatives, in full church membership, of the pastoral charge, to the Presbytery." (17) The words "in full church membership," obviously include women, and there is nothing in the Basis restrictive of this interpretation.

The eligibility of women for membership in presbyteries is further evident from Polity III. 19 (2), a provision applying to all charges in the Church, which describes the members of Presbyteries other than ministers as: "elders, deacons, leaders and other non-ministerial representatives of pastoral charges."

b. Membership in Conferences and in the General Council.

The provisions for representation in Conferences and in the General Council have general application. In Polity III, 20 (10), and IV, 21, the words "non-ministerial representatives" are used with respect to representatives in Conferences. In Polity IV, 22 (8), and V, 23, these words are used in respect to representation in the General Council. These words can only be interpreted as providing for the eligibility of all persons in full membership whether men or women, to become members of Conferences and of the General Council.

II. Election of Women as Members of Sessions

The opinion of the Committee on Law and Legislation on the provision of Polity II B, 9 (a), is: "It is contemplated that the persons, who with the minister or ministers constitute the session, shall be men." According to this interpretation, women are excluded from membership in the sessions of charges formed subsequent to the union.

In charges formerly of the Presbyterian Church in Canada there was, and while they maintain their former plan of organization under Polity II, A, 4, there remains, no provision for the election of women to sessions.

Thus, so far as both these classes of charges are concerned, the membership of women in sessions can be authorized only under new legislation, amending or declaratory.

Action of Presbyteries has revealed the need of explicit direction in this matter. It is to be noted that: (1) In a large proportion of the charges of the Church, women are eligible for membership in the local courts and as representatives to Presbyteries. In other charges they are excluded from both. In others they may be elected as representatives but may not be members of session. (2) Presbyteries, in which women are members, have the oversight of the pastoral charges, review the records of, and receive and dispose of petitions and appeals from, the sessions from which women are excluded. (3) Women who are members of pastoral charges in which they are ineligible for membership in sessions may be members of Conferences which receive and dispose of appeals and petitions from Presbyteries, and of the General Council, which receives and disposes of petitions, memorials and appeals from the lower courts.

Your committee would point out that these anomalies are mainly due to the necessities of a transitional period and it may be that this period is not yet completed. It is possible, however, that the United Church has already reached a stage at which it may wisely adopt a definite policy in the matter. The policy of admitting women to membership in all courts could be conveniently adopted by means of legislation amending or interpreting Polity II. A, 4, to make women eligible in charges where before the union they were not eligible, for membership in sessions and for representation in Presbyteries; and amending or interpreting II. B, 9, to make women eligible for membership in the sessions of charges formed after the union.

Minority Report

By Principal H. A. KENT

Ordination of Women to the Ministry

Reasons Against

1. It is at least doubtful whether more than a very few women in the Church are in favour of such a step.
2. The sphere of a woman in the ministry must in the nature of the case be limited. Nature being what it is there are things which a woman may not do and places where she may not go without loss of that womanliness which is her greatest possession.
3. Such a ministry would need to be confined to unmarried women. If not we should see a minister's home without family life and probably without children, or witness the not very edifying spectacle of the husband keeping house while the wife is engaged in public duties. Are we prepared to demand celibacy of the women ordained to the ministry, or to deprive them of their standing as ministers when they marry?
4. What the Church needs at the present time is not more femininity but more masculinity. Women's work in the Church is carried on with admirable zeal and faithfulness. What are the men doing? Will the work of the Church be made more attractive to strong virile manhood by the proposed ordination of women to the ministry?
5. If the United Church adopted such a proposal she would cut herself off from the great Churches of the Reformation, as well as from the practice of the ancient Church. Neither Rome, nor Canterbury, nor Geneva recognizes such a ministry. The adoption of the proposal to ordain women to the ministry would put the United Church of Canada out of touch with the Churches with whom she wishes to cultivate closer relations and might also produce a great deal of trouble and confusion within her own borders.
6. There is practically no demand in Canada to-day for the ordination of women to the ministry. A single case here and there is not sufficient to warrant the Church adopting such a proposal.
7. The Committee proposes that women be ordained to the Diaconate but not to the Presbyterate. As neither the United Church of Canada nor any one of the Churches which united to form it, has recognized a secondary order of the Ministry, this proposal practically means the ordination of women to the Ministry, but with the proviso that they are not permitted to administer the Sacrament of the Lord's Supper. Upon this I would offer the following observations:
   a. In the Roman and Anglican Churches, the diaconate is not perpetual. The deacon is a lower order of minister but it is clearly understood that his inferiority is temporary. He is on the way to being a Presbyter. The Committee's proposal means the perpetual inferiority of the ministry of women in the United Church of Canada.
   b. It is reasonable to maintain that the work of the ministry is such that women cannot give themselves to it as a primary vocation.
   c. It is unreasonable to say to the women of the Church "We will give you the same training as the men and will permit you to do the work of the ministry, only we will not allow you to dispense the Communion and to receive standing as Presbyters." Our Church has not a sacerdotal conception of ministry and sacraments and it would be unjust to the women of the Church to say to them, "We will admit you to the ministry, but in it you must always remain in a secondary position."

Concerning the Admission of Women as Members of Session

The Presbyterian section of the United Church of Canada has recently come through a storm of controversy. Much of this gathered around the eldership and its place in the United Church. My judgment is that it would not be in the interest of the peace and harmony of our Church at the present time to propose a revision of the Basis of Union in order to admit women to the eldership. Such a proposal would bring down "I told you so" from many quarters and might result in new losses in congregations which have already suffered heavily. It is true that the Basis of Union makes it possible for women to be members of the higher courts but not of Sessions. This is an anomaly. But it would be wiser to endure for a time an anomalous situation than to precipitate new difficulties.

(Signed) H. A. KENT.

Appendix I

The Ministry of Women—An Historical Sketch

Indicating to what ministries women have been set apart in the Christian Church, and what functions have been associated with these ministries.

I. In the Apostolic Age

In observing the position and tasks of women in the early Church it is important at all points to bear in mind the social environment in which the Church developed, and the presuppositions and established customs of Jewish and pagan society. In Judaism women were permitted to exercise prophetic functions, but were not admitted to the priesthood. With the rarest exceptions, they held no public office. Wives and mothers were respected for their service in the home, and this was regarded as the sole calling of women. They were related to society chiefly through their husbands and fathers whose chattels they were, in some degree, according to the Law. The extent of the rights and duties of a wife was determined largely by the amount of her marriage dowry. They were, however, accorded by custom a good deal of freedom of action, and unmarried women were not, as in the Greek world, necessarily regarded as immoral.

In Hellenistic society women held a place inferior to that accorded them in Judaism. Wives and daughters were secluded and kept in subjection to their husbands and fathers. In public places they appeared only with veiled faces. Violation of the code of female seclusion was a serious social offense. Unveiled women in public were recognized as prostitutes. Certain of the new cults had their priestesses, who were in general religious prostitutes. There was, of course, in the prosperous classes, and especially in a rapidly growing city of miscellaneous population like Corinth, a tendency to infringe the standards of social conduct; and under the emotional experiences of early Christianity, when enthusiasm ran high, the conduct of some of the Christian women was such as to cause anxiety to one who dreaded to see the Church misrepresented and misjudged.

The followers of Jesus included a number of women. The throngs which in certain instances attended Him were composed of both sexes. Some women believers were connected by ties of relationship with Jesus or the Apostles. Many were attracted by His healing and teaching ministry. Women converts in certain instances contributed by their means (Luke 8:3). While neither the Twelve nor apparently the Seventy included women, some women were distinguished among His believing followers for their personal devotion.

Throughout the history of the Church much of women's Christian service has been rendered within the sphere of private and home life. The Church has prospered through Christian motherhood. With this immeasurably important aspect of women's contribution to the Church, this study has nothing directly to do.

The Church as mother of her children and nurse of sick souls, with her compassion and humane enterprise, has always availed herself of the varied services of women. The functions of women in their public service to the Church, were, in the Apostolic Age, with some degree of clearness differentiated into the offices of *Deaconess, Widow and Prophetess.*[1]

Deaconesses

The diaconate of men and women in the Apostolic Church partook of a common character and may be rightly regarded as one office. It arose (as is generally agreed) as a result of the need of officers to administer alms (Acts 6: 2-4), and was characteristically a ministry of relief and consolation to the sick and dependent. Stephen is represented as preaching; and though this may not have been a necessary function of the diaconate, it was not excluded. Spiritual qualifications are indicated in Acts 6: 3; 1 Timothy 3: 8. As the orders of the ministry were more clearly defined, the deacon was recognized as being in holy orders, though subordinate to the presbyter, with whom he was often directly associated in his labors. Still later the (male) diaconate was recognized as an order of the hierarchy, and became in most instances a stage in the ministry antecedent to admission to the presbyterate. It then largely lost its special character as a ministry to the sick and poor.

Phoebe is described in Romans 16:1 as a *diakonos* of the Church which is at Cenchrea. The usual significance of this word when applied to a man is "deacon," and the description of Phoebe's services in the context here strongly points to the rendering "deaconess" rather than "servant" as in A. V. Origen in his commentary on Romans says: "this passage shows that women also were set in the ministry (or diaconate, *diakonia*) of the Church.[2]

In 1 Timothy 3:8-11 the qualifications for deacons are given, and these are immediately followed by: "Even so must women (not as in A. V. *their wives*) be grave," etc. The natural interpretation of this passage is that it sets forth some of the requirements for women in the diaconate.

Most scholars are in agreement with Lightfoot in the opinion that in the New Testament "the female diaconate is as definite an institution as the male diaconate."

It is impossible to describe in detail the functions of the deaconess in the Apostolic Church. Phoebe is described by Paul as "a succourer (or patroness) of many and of mine own self." The qualifications for the office given in 1 Timothy 3 ("grave, not slanderers, temperate, faithful in all things") resemble those of the male diaconate rather than of the episcopate or presbyterate. As Miss Robinson says:

> "The qualifications required of both the men and women Deacons refer to character, rather than to fitness for special duties. Their lives must be simple and well-disciplined, commending the faith which they profess. But it is not required of them as of the Bishop, that they should be 'apt to teach' or able to rule. Their mission is to serve. Seriousness, sincerity, self-denial, trustworthiness, these are what the Church requires of her servants. 'Faithful in all things' is the motto of the diaconate."

Widows

The place of the widows as a special group is exhibited in Acts 6:1 and 1 Timothy 5:3-16. From v.9 of the latter passage it is evident that at Ephesus an official roll of their names was kept. The age of admission to the ranks of the church widows is here set at sixty years. They were not an order, as were the deaconesses. The reason of their enrolment was that they received aid from the church. C. H. Turner observes "The widows correspond not to sisters of charity but to inmates of our almshouses." Their service consisted of prayer and devotion and exemplary behavior. Their function was "not that of Martha, but that of Mary."

Prophetesses

The "four daughters of Philip that did prophesy," Acts 21:9, were representative of a class of women who edified the Church by their utterances. St. Paul endeavored to place prophecy, especially that of women, under sober restrictions, and in some passages seems to exclude the function of the prophetess altogether. Women are prohibited from teaching in 1 Timothy 2: 12. The passage in 1 Cor. 14: 34 has been held to refer to the interruption of the worship by the conversation of women,[3] but the passage as a whole seems to require the interpretation of the opening words, "Let the women keep silence in the churches," in the sense of a prohibition of public speech in congregations assembled for worship. On the other hand 1 Corinthians 11:5 implies permission of women to prophesy if their heads are covered according to the custom. There is nothing to indicate whether in this passage the Apostle is thinking of prophecy in the general meetings of Christians, to which pagans were admitted, or not.

The Apostle apparently does not attempt to frame a uniform and consistent rule, but strongly inclines to repress what appears to him as a dangerous freedom.

It is evident from all the passages in which St. Paul lays down restrictions and prohibitions respecting the public ministry of women, that he had in mind the customs of Hellenistic society in which the Christians were constantly subjected both to temptation and to criticism, and that he feared the danger of immodesty and scandal. In the conditions of modern society no comparable danger attends the public ministry of women.

The ministry of the prophetess like that of the prophet was charismatic. It was perpetuated as distinct for a considerable period beyond the Apostolic Age.

II. From the Apostolic Age to the Fifth Century

The ministry of women was affected by the process by which in course of time the Ministry of the Word and Sacraments took on the character which has become traditional. The duties of women in the ministry came to be more clearly defined; explicit regulations were made regarding their qualifications and the conduct of their work, and forms for their admission were provided.

Deaconesses

Pliny's expression in a letter to Trajan from Bithynia c. 112, *ancilla quae ministrae dicebantur*, may not improbably refer to regular deaconesses, who in this case happened to have been drawn from the slave class. The Ignatian Epistles, in a non-genuine section, refer to "the guardianesses of the holy gates, the deaconesses in Christ." The reference is to their duties in welcoming and conducting to their seats the women worshippers as they entered the churches. The *Apostolic Constitutions*, which gather up traditions of the second, third and early fourth centuries, ascribe to ministering women a considerable range of duties.

Information regarding the deaconess is found in the following passages from Book III of this collection:

> "Wherefore, O Bishop, appoint thy fellow-labourers and workers of life and righteousness, Deacons well-pleasing to God, those whom out of all the people thou dost approve as being worthy and full of activity for the needs of the ministration (*diakonia.*) And appoint also a Deaconess (*diakonissan*) faithful and holy, for the services (*hypēresias*) of the women. For there are times when to certain houses thou canst not send a man (that is a) Deacon (*andra diakonon*) because, of the unbelievers: thou shalt send therefore a woman (that is a) Deaconess (*gynaikos diakonon*) because of the imaginings of the wicked. For indeed for many needs do we need a woman (that is a) Deaconess (*gynaikos diakonon.*) And first, when women are baptized (lit. enlightened) the Deacon shall anoint only their forehead with the holy oil; after him the Deaconess (*hē diakonos*) shall fully anoint them: for it is not necessary that women should be seen by men. But only in the laying on of hands the Bishop shall anoint her head, even as priests and kings of old were anointed: not that those who are now baptised are ordained (*Cheirotonountai*) priests, but as Christians (so called) from Christ (i.e. the Anointed One), a royal priesthood and a holy nation, God's

> Church, the pillar and support of the bridechamber, who once were not a people, but now (are a people) beloved and elect."

After a description of the deacon's duties we read:

> "And let the deaconess be diligent in taking care of the women; but both of them ready to carry messages, to travel about, to minister and to serve. . . . Let them not be ashamed to minister to those that are in want."

Again, of troublesome widows it is said:

> "But those widows which will not live according to the command of God, are solicitous and inquisitive what deaconess it is that gives the charity and what widows receive it. And when she has learned these things she murmurs at the deaconess who distributed the charity. . . ."

In Book II, XXVI we read:

> Let your Bishop preside (lit. sit first) over you, being honoured as with the honour of God, wherewith he governeth the Clergy (*kiēros*) and ruleth the People. And let the Deacon stand by him, as the Powers do by God; and let him minister to him in all things blamelessly; even as Christ doing nothing of Himself doth always the things that are pleasing to the Father. And let the Deaconess (*hē diakonē*) be honoured by you as a type of the Holy Spirit, doing and uttering nothing without the Deacon; as neither doth the Paraclete do or speak ought of Himself, but glorfying Christ waiteth upon His will. And as it is not possible to believe on Christ without the teaching of the Spirit, so without the Deaconess let no woman approach the Deacon or the Bishop. And let the Presbyters be reckoned by you as a type of us, the Apostles: let them be teachers of Divine Knowledge. . . . And let your Widows and Orphans be counted by you as a type of the Altar: and let the Virgins be honoured as a type of the Altar-of-Incense.

The reference to the Holy Spirit is a modification of the teaching of the earlier Syriac Didascalia, which simply says "and the deaconess shall be honored by you in the place of the Holy Spirit." A subordination of the deaconess to the deacon is explicitly asserted in the Apostolic Constitution; it is probably implied in the earlier work by the argument regarding the Trinity.

The earliest form for the ordination of deaconesses is also contained in this work, and is as follows:

> I, Bartholomew, enjoin: Oh, Bishop, thou shalt lay thy hands upon her, with the Presbytery and the deacons and the deaconesses standing by; and thou shalt say: Oh God, the Eternal, the Father of our Lord Jesus Christ, the Maker of man and woman, who didst fill with the Spirit Miriam and Deborah, and Hannah and Huldah, who didst not disdain that Thine Only-begotten Son should be born of a woman; Thou that in the tabernacle of witness and in the temple didst appoint the women-guardians of Thy Holy gates: Do Thou now also look on this Thy handmaid, who is appointed unto ministry (or, "unto the office of a deaconess": *eis diakonian* and give to her (the) Holy Spirit and cleanse her from all defilement of flesh and spirit, that she may worthily accomplish the work committed unto her, to Thy glory and the praise of Thy Christ, with whom to Thee and the Holy Spirit be glory and worship, world without end. Amen."

In regard to the qualifications for office the *Apostolic Constitutions* provide that "the deaconess be a pure virgin; but if not then a widow once married, faithful and honorable." Epiphanius adds a class of "women once married living in continence." It is evident that the deaconesses were mainly recruited from the young unmarried women and from widows.

Fourth and fifth century information on the female diaconate is abundant for the Eastern Church. The laws of Justinian indicate that there were at this period forty deaconesses in the service of the Great Church at Constantinople alone. From the correspondence of Chrysostom we learn many facts about individual deaconesses. Most of those whose names are known to us (e.g. Pentadia, Silvina, Sabiniana, Olympias) were widows who devoted their talents, and in some instances their wealth, to the Church. Outstanding among these is Olympias, to whom as "the most reverend and religious deaconess," Chrysostom addressed a large number of his letters. She was distinguished for her lavish almsgiving, hospitality, and devout and ascetic manner of life.

Elsewhere in the East deaconesses were widely employed. In certain instances they engaged in teaching. In the beginnings of monasticism deaconesses often held a place of honor and authority in the ascetic sisterhoods. Gregory of Nyssa tells of one Lampadia "placed over the choir of the virgins in the standing of the diaconate."

In regard to the age of admission of deaconesses we may quote from Miss Robinson's statement (*Ministry of Deaconesses* p. 74 f.):

> "As a safeguard against a want of steadfastness on the part of those holding this office, the age fixed for admission was much more advanced than that required for the rest of the clergy. The Emperor Theodosius (A.D. 390) enacted that none should be accepted save such as were sixty years of age, and had borne children. This seems to remind us of the Western confusion between the Deaconesses and the Widow; for it is said to be 'according to the precepts of the Apostle.' The Council of Chalcedon (A.D. 451) fixed the age at forty, after 'careful testing,' and this decision is repeated by the Council in Trullo, at the close of the seventh century. Justinian, in his earlier laws, named fifty as the lowest age, but afterwards fixed it at forty. No doubt the Bishops varied it at their discretion. Olympias is described as a young widow at the time of her ordination."

From the extracts above cited it appears that in the period before Constantine deaconesses held a recognized position in the East. They exercised a ministry to women especially in connection with the anointing in the rite of Baptism. In Oriental society, as in some mission fields to-day, the seclusion of women limited the pastoral service of the male ministry, and required that certain duties of visitation and pastoral care should be undertaken by deaconesses. They were responsible, jointly with the deacons, (to whom they are sometimes regarded as subordinate in authority) for the distribution of alms.

Sometimes confusion of deaconesses with virgins and widows—the classes from which they were recruited—occurred; but ordinarily the deaconess was distinct, and she alone of ministering women was ordained.

In the West, however, the diaconate of women was apparently unknown in this period. Jerome illustrates the passages Romans 16: 1, 1 Timothy 3: 9 by reference to contemporary deaconesses "in Eastern parts." The functions of the deaconess were in the West performed by (unordained) members of the order of widows and of that of the professed virgins. In North Africa women "however learned or holy" were strictly forbidden "to teach in an assembly of men." (A. D. 398).

Widows

The *Apostolic Constitutions* and other documents of the period abundantly show the continuity in the Church of the "order of widows." They are repeatedly referred to as an order, though it is explicitly stated that they are not to be ordained with the laying on of hands. Apart from the emphasis on the duty of widows to pray for those who have given alms in her support, and for the whole Church, "the widow's place is that of a recipient of alms,"—"not an order of ministry but the objects of ministry." (C. H. Turner) The widows were a numerous class in both East and West, and often grave problems arose in the administration of the alms. It is a notable feature of the history of the Church that this faithful but economically unproductive class was held in respect, given the dignity of ecclesiastical recognition, and supplied with the means of a decent livelihood. Some ministerial functions are given to Widows in the "Apostolic Church Order" and the "Testimony of Our Lord," documents which show a Montanist trend. (See Wordsworth, *Ministry of Grace*, p. 271f.)

Virgins

The increasing asceticism of the age gave additional importance to the class of virgins. Communities of virgins and ascetic widows began to be formed, and these came to be regulated by strict rules which gave them a permanent character. Bingham (*Antiquities*, Vol II, p. 397) notes:

> "The ecclesiastical virgins were commonly enrolled in the canon or matricula of the Church—that is, in the catalogue of ecclesiastics—as we learn from Socrates, who speaks of them under that title. And hence they were sometimes called *canonica, canonical virgins*, from their being registered in the *canon* or books of the Church. They differed from the monastic virgins chiefly in this, that they lived privately in their father's houses, and had their maintenance from their fathers, or in cases of necessity from the Church; but the others lived in communities, and upon their own labour, as we learn from the third Council of Carthage and the writings of St. Austin."

The virgins were consecrated even when they remained residents of their own homes, in some instances at an early age—sixteen or seventeen—(Bingham, p. 401, cites canons: See Wordsworth *Ministry of Grace*, p. 293); but the imperial laws gave liberty to marry to those who had taken the obligations of virginity before the age of forty. Marriages of vowed virgins were visited with ecclesiastical penalties, but were not annulled. The *Pseudo-Clementine Epistles* indicate that virgins were engaged in works of mercy, but the evidence for this elsewhere is slight. Their course of life is highly praised by the church fathers and they were given a place above the widows by some writers.

Prophetesses and Teaching Women

The prophetic office was maintained with diminishing importance through most of this period, and was frequently exercised by women. The Montanist movement was largely promoted by women prophets. This movement tended to discredit prophecy in general, and particularly prophecy by women. Says Harnack (*Mission and Expansion of Christianity*, Vol II, p. 230):

> "It was by its very opposition offered to Gnosticism and Montanism that the Church was led to interdict women from any activity within the Church, apart, of course, from such services as those rendered to those of their own sex."

Tertullian expressly taught that women were forbidden to speak or to teach. The Carthaginian synod of 398, as already noted, forbade them to teach in assemblies of men. The so-called Gallican Statutes, c.500, repeat this prohibition. Private teaching by gifted women still frequently occurred, and there are evidences that instructresses of the celibate women were not always deaconesses. Among the educated Roman women whom Jerome guided in asceticism, was Blaesilla, whose intellectual powers made her in his opinion "a rival of Origen." Blaesilla's mother and sister, Paula and Eustochium, assisted Jerome in his biblical studies. Marcella, who headed a community of ascetic women in her own home at Rome, was consulted by priests on points of theology. Macrina, the sister of St. Basil and Gregory of Nyssa, was highly esteemed for her "philosophy" or knowledge of Christianity. She instructed Basil in the Gospel when on returning from his studies he was "puffed up beyond measure with the pride of oratory."

We may conclude that while, especially in the West, ecclesiastical recognition of the teaching office of women was withdrawn, exceptionally gifted women still found a teaching function, either in their private circle of acquaintance, or in the rising monastic institutions for women.

III. In the Middle Ages

The outstanding fact of the ministry of women in the Middle Ages is the place of women in monasticism. The ascetic orders absorbed all the official ministries of women which the early Church possessed. There is evidence that attempts were made from the fifth century onward to obtain the recognition of deaconesses in the West, chiefly in Southern Gaul, which was peculiarly under Eastern influence. The Council on Nimes, 394, violently condemned the ministrations of women which had been introduced, apparently by Manichaeans recently come from Eastern parts. The Council of Orange, 441, enacted that "women are on no account to be ordained"; and this was repeated in another Gallican Council (Epaône) in 517. Again the Council of Orleans; 533, determined that: "To no woman hereafter shall the diaconal benediction be entrusted, by reason of the frailty of their sex." By 567 the title *diaconissa* is applied by a Council of Tours, to the wives of the deacons, "which seems to show," says Miss Robinson, "that the true deaconess has disappeared." Later, however, the order obtained recognition at Rome. The earliest mention of Roman deaconesses is in a notice of the year 799. A Roman form "for the making of a deaconess" of this period has been preserved, as also English liturgical fragments of the sort, coming from the eighth and the eleventh century. Near the end of the tenth century we find reference to a deaconess who is at the head of a convent in Capua. "Probably by this time the Western deaconess was entirely monastic, and hardly distinguishable from the nuns among whom she lived," (*Ministry of Deaconesses*, p. 90). The order also lapsed in the East, and the last medieval deaconess known by name is one Aeria, of Hellenopontus Amisus, who died in 1086. Locally in both East and West, vestiges, and in some instances the name, of the office, survived. The abbesses of Benedictine nunneries were sometimes called deaconesses, e.g., by Abelard. Some scholars hold that the abbess is the deaconess with changed functions. The relation of the deaconess to the consecrated nuns, particularly of the Cistercian order, is more clearly indicated, both by liturgical forms and by vestments (*Ministry of Women*, p. 168 and p. 305f.) Yet it cannot be said that the female diaconate was maintained in any monastic office.

The sisterhoods which arose, chiefly in the Netherlands, in the late Middle Ages, especially the Beguines (twelth century) and the Sisters of the Common Life (fourteenth Century), offered to women a lay ministry. They were composed of unmarried women and widows, and engaged in educational and relief work, and nursing. In the former individuals were sometimes paid for their services; no permanent vows were imposed. In the latter the community was more closely knit. The daughters of burghers were sent to their houses to be instructed in household arts and in the care of the sick. Such sisterhoods, rather than the monastic houses, correspond to the ministering women of the early Church; but they received no ordination.

In some heretical and sectarian groups, notably the Cathari, deaconesses were retained. They appear also in the *Unitas Fratrum*, and in its outgrowth, the Moravian Church, in which they were restored in 1745.

IV. In the Reformation and Puritan Period

The Reformation was accompanied by a fresh interest in the institutions of the early church, and some attention was given by the Reformers to the ministry of women. Their interest in the subject was partly aroused by conditions following the dissolution of many nunneries, and partly followed from their fresh studies of the New Testament. The Vulgate rendering of *gunaixas* in 1 Timothy 3: 11 by *uxores* still determined Reformation commentaries on that passage, and so prevented a sound exposition of the place of deaconesses in the Apostolic Church. They were generally confused with widows.

Protestant sisterhoods resembling the Sisters of the Common Life appear in the sixteenth century at Keppel and Walsdorf and in therefugee Reformed Church at Wesel. Among nine departments of service enumerated in connection with the Walsdorf institution, the word "deaconesses" is used of those who took care of the poor and sick of the neighborhood. At

Wesel too, deaconesses engaged in caring for the sick. It does not appear that these so-called deaconesses were differentiated except in function from the other sisters, or that they were ecclesiastically set apart to their office. Indeed at Wesel they might be married women, serving with the consent of their husbands.

Calvin in his Commentary on Romans, in explanation of Phoebe's ministry, at once jumps to the passage in 1 Timothy 5, and regards the office of Pheobe as that of the class of widows. He speaks of her, however, as "bearing some public office in the Church." The following passage from the Institutes (IV., III.9), throws additional light on Calvin's view:

> The care of the poor was committed to deacons, of whom two classes are mentioned by Paul in the Epistle to the Romans, "He that giveth, let him do it with simplicity"; "he that showeth mercy, with cheerfulness," (Rom. 12: 8.) As it is certain that he is here speaking of public offices of the Church, there must have been two distinct classes. If I mistake not, he in the former clause designates deacons, who administered alms; in the latter, those who had devoted themselves to the care of the poor and the sick. Such were the widows of whom he makes mention in the Epistle to Timothy, (1 Tim. v.10). For there was no public office which women could discharge save that of devoting themselves to the service of the poor. If we admit this, (and it certainly ought to be admitted,) there will be two classes of deacons, the one serving the Church by administering the affairs of the poor; the other, by taking care of the poor themselves. For although the term *diakonia* has a more extensive meaning, Scripture specially gives the name of deacons to those whom the Church appoints to dispense alms, and take care of the poor, constituting them as it were stewards of the public treasury of the poor. Their origin, institution and office, is described by Luke (Acts 6. 3.) When a murmuring arose among the Greeks, because in the administration of the poor their widows were neglected, the apostles, excusing themselves that they were unable to discharge both offices, to preach the word and serve tables, requested the multitude to elect seven men of good report, to whom the office might be committed. Such deacons as the Apostolic Church had, it becomes us to have after her example."

He evidently regards the office of the diaconate male and female as one, and approves the diaconate of women, as being scriptural; although the functions of the women deacons are to be limited to the "care of the poor and sick" as distinct from the "administration of alms," or the control and management of church funds. In point of fact, however, the diaconate of women was not revived in Geneva, or in the Reformed churches generally.

An attempt was made to restore the order of deaconesses, at an early stage of the Reformed Church of the Netherlands. The matter came up from the congregation of Wesel, which as we have seen had appointed deaconesses, to the classis of Wesel, and was under discussion for some time. The classis in 1580 favored the restoration of the office, making it open to widows only, as being the scriptural rule. The General Synod of Middleburg, to which it was then referred, decided against the reform, "on account of various inconveniences," but urged the wives of the deacons and other good women to perform such services as were to be assigned to deaconesses. Thus the movement remained entirely local.

Women obtained no official position in the Reformed Churches of England or of Scotland. In the English Presbyterian movement led by Thomas Cartwright, we see the intention to revive the female diaconate. After the conference attended by sixty Puritan ministers at Cockfield, resumed at Cambridge and again at London, Cartwright and Travers published a statement of the conclusions reached (1586). These include:

> *Of Collectors for the Poor, or Deacons:*
>
> "Touching deacons of both sorts, viz. men and women, the church shall be admonished what is required by the apostle; and they are not to choose men of custom or course, or for their riches, but for their faith, zeal, and integrity; and that the

> church is to pray in the meantime, to be so directed, that they may choose them that are meet.
>
> "Let the names of those that are thus chosen be published by the next Lord's day, and after that their duties to the Church, and the Church's duty toward them; then let them be received into their office with the general prayers of the whole Church."

There is, however, no indication of the actual revival of the deaconess order in Cartwright's circle.

Discussing the ministry, in controversy with Whitgift, Cartwright moderately advocates the office of widow, which he identifies with the female diaconate. A. F. Scott Pearson thus sets forth his argument (Thomas Cartwright and Elizabethan Puritanism, p. 98):

> The deacon, according to Cartwright, is not a minister, but an office-bearer, who has charge over the poor. Cartwright suggests that the existing collectors should become deacons. Of deaconesses or widows he does not speak with his usual dogmatic confidence. He observes that there was greater need of them in the early Church because of the "multitude of strangers through the persecution, and by the great heat of those east countries, whereupon the washing and suppling of their feet was required; yet forsomuch as there are poor which are sick in every church, I do not see how a better and more convenient order can be devised. . . . If such may be gotten, we ought also to keep that order of widows in the church still. I know that there be learned men which think otherwise, but I stand upon the authority of God's word." He further says, "The perpetuity of that commandment touching widows remaineth in that sort it was given, that is, upon condition."

Deaconesses appear in Puritan congregations in the Netherlands. A document of the Amsterdam refugee congregation of the year 1589 proposes "Relievers or Widows" to minister to "the sick, lame, wearie, and diseased such helpful comforts as they need, by watching, tending and helping them." In Governor William Bradford's "Dialogue between some Young Men born in New England and sundry Ancient men that Came out of Holland and of Old England," 1648, as quoted in A. Young, *Chronicles of the Pilgrim Fathers*, 1841, we find the following:

> "They had for their pastor and teacher those two eminent men before named, and in our time four grave men for ruling elders, and three able and godly men for deacons, one ancient widow for a deaconess, who did them service many years, though she was sixty years of age when she was chosen. She honored her place and was an ornament to the congregation. She usually sat in a convenient place in the congregation, with a little birchen rod in her hand, and kept little children in great awe from disturbing the congregation. She did frequently visit the sick and weak, especially women, and, as there was need, called out maids and young women to watch and do them other helps as their necessity did require; and if they were poor, she would gather relief for them of those that were able, or acquaint the deacons; and she was obeyed as a mother in Israel and an officer in Christ."

Nothing is said here of the ordination of deaconesses, though something may be implied in the words "an officer in Christ."

It has sometimes been held that the introduction of deaconesses in the Amsterdam congregation was due to Mennonite influence, since that body had restored the office. It seems at least as probable that it was due to the teaching of Cartwright and his sixty associates of 1575-76, or to a fresh study of Scripture.

In 1642 John Robinson published in England "A Brief Catechism concerning Church Government," which advocates "deaconesses or widows" who are "to tend to the sick and impotent with compassion and cheerfulness."

Deaconesses of the kind contemplated by Cartwright and Robinson were to hold an ecclesiastical office. This office was clearly distinguished from the Ministry of the Word and Sacraments. Yet they would have a recognized place in the Church and were to be "received into their office with the prayers of the whole church."

The deaconess movement originated by Pastor Fliedner, of Kaiserswerth, in 1836, was of a different type, and took the form of a sisterhood whose members stood ready to aid the Church, but were not ecclesiastically controlled or locally attached to it.

It may be added that the Non-jurors approved of the deaconess order and the "Compleat Collection of Devotions" published in 1734 and reprinted in P. Hall; *Fragmenta Liturgica*, Vol. VI., contains (p. 293) "the Form and Manner of Ordaining Deaconesses." The Collect contains the words: "didst admit thy servant Phoebe and others into the order of deaconesses." The candidate, who must ordinarily be not less than forty years of age, is presented to the bishop by the deacons, and questioned by the bishop and ordained with the imposition of his hands. The following question contains a description of the office resembling that in the Apostolic Constitutions:

> Bishop. It appertaineth to the office of a Deaconess, to assist at the baptism of women; to instruct (in private) children and women who are preparing for baptism; to visit and attend women that are sick and in distress; to overlook the women in the Church, and to correct and rebuke those who behave themselves irregular there and to introduce any woman who wanteth to make application to a Deacon, Presbyter, or Bishop. Wilt thou do all this faithfully, diligently, and willingly?

The whole office follows the same model as that for the ordaining of deacons which precedes it in the collection. There is no evidence that deaconesses were ever actually set apart among the Non-jurors.

V. The Modern Revival of Women's Work

Deaconesses

The Reformed churches failed to institute the deaconess order, and the local employment of deaconesses at Wesel ceased in 1610. The institutions at Walsdorf and Keppel, on Lutheran ground, were discontinued a short time afterwards.

It does not appear that any effort was made to restore the order prior to the nineteenth century. There is evidence that for some time before Fliedner's enterprise began, proposals of the kind had been made by individuals, and that the labors of the Roman Catholic Sisters of Charity during the Napoleonic Wars directed the attention of Protestants to the subject. Pastor Friedrich Klönne of Bislich published a pamphlet advocating the institution of deaconesses in 1820, and the proposal was favored by the statesman, Baron von Stein. In 1835 a periodical devoted to the advocacy of the revival of the order of deaconesses appeared, only to cease publication immediately. Its sponsor, Count Adalbert von der Recke-Vollmerstein, aimed at the restoration of the order with all its original ecclesiastical recognition and functions.

Meanwhile, Theodor Fliedner had begun his remarkable pastorate at Kaiserswerth. While travelling to collect money for his impoverished charge Fliedner saw relief institutions at work in Holland and England. The work of Elizabeth Fry in particular impressed him with the value and possibilities of women's service. He also witnessed with great admiration the work of deaconesses among the Mennonites.

The beginnings of deaconess work under Fliedner were in connection with service to female convicts. It was soon enlarged to include nursing of the sick among the poor. In 1836 a Deaconess Society was formed with a constitution, and Gertrude Reichard, the daughter of a physician, took the obligations of the order. Despite the opposition of those who accused him of Romanizing, Fliedner's work grew with great rapidity, and daughter institutions began to be formed. At his death in 1864 there were thirty "mother-houses," or centres of deaconess work, directly connected with Kaiserswerth.

The modern deaconess movement in all lands is principally due to the direct influence of Fliedner or to the imitation of his work. In respect to organization the Kaiserswerth deaconesses constituted a sisterhood, governed by a board of directors. Only Protestant unmarried women or childless widows were eligible for admission. They passed through a period of probation and training, and were admitted to the order only after a vote of the members already in the mother-house. They retained their property, and the right to retire from their calling. They were ordained with the imposition of hands, in which two sisters participated with the pastors. The vows involved "childlike obedience" to "the authority of the superiors of the deaconess institution," but made no mention of Church authority. The work of the deaconesses was chiefly nursing and the relief of the poor and unfortunate. Those qualified might also engage in teaching. Piety was cultivated, and the "quiet half-hour" for common but silent devotion in the chapel was observed. Deaconesses were taught to pray with their patients and to read and apply the Scriptures in their ministry. They were expected to give at least five years of service, but they were at liberty, in exceptional circumstances, to retire even before the expiration of that time. "I will have no vows," said Pastor Fliedner. As a bond of union they had their common use of a Bible Manual and of a specially prepared book of sacred song.

It is clear that the Kaiserswerth deaconesses constituted a voluntary sisterhood, largely self-governing and not ecclesiastically controlled in any way. They cannot be regarded as a part of the Ministry of the Church as were the deaconesses of the early Church. Pastor Fliedner's claim to have them regarded as a revival of the deaconess order rests only on their similarity to the early deaconesses in the kinds of service undertaken. The further step of attaching them to the ranks of the official Ministry, as women deacons, was not taken.

The Kaiserswerth sisterhood has been reproduced in the deaconess institutions that have arisen in the various evangelical Churches of Britain and America, though with considerable modification. There has been much variety in the degree in which community life was practised; and in many cases the deaconess has found her closest bond not with the sisterhood, but with the local congregation by which she was employed. But in general the deaconess has not been admitted to the diaconate as an order of ministry.

The associations of women devoted to charity formed by Elizabeth Fry and Florence Nightingale owed something to Fliedner's work. Dr. Pusey was among the first of Church of England leaders to take steps for the organization of sisterhoods, and he formed a group of religious women in 1847 at Regent's Park. A number of similar institutions arose. Their aim was rather mutual edification than ministry to others. The desire to revive the deaconess order was expressed in the setting apart by Bishop Tait, of London, of Catherine Elizabeth Ferard in 1861. Miss Ferard became the head of a diocesan deaconess training institution, and this was the model of many in other dioceses. In 1871 a body of "Principles and Rules," signed by the two archbishops and eighteen of the bishops, was issued, in which a deaconess is defined as "a woman set apart by a Bishop, under that title, for service in the church."

This rule restricted the use of the word "deaconess" to ordained women. But the deaconesses were not yet ordained to an office which can be fully identified with the early diaconate of women. In certain instances the obligation was taken to serve only "for the space of three years at least." The Convocation of Caterbury in 1891 resolved to encourage the formation of deaconess institutions and the work of deaconesses, in view of the fact that they had "proved their efficiency in the Anglican Church, wherever the order had been revived." The language here quoted assumes that the order had been revived; and this is again assumed in an utterance of 1897. But the point is challenged in a scholarly article in the *Church Quarterly Review* for January, 1899.

In the Churches of the Anglican communion the form for the ordination of deaconesses in no case contains a vow of celibacy, and a degree of impermanency is in some instances recognized.[4] Yet the office is generally looked upon as a life vocation which excludes the idea of marriage. The head deaconesses, Siddall and Barker, write:

> "For the Deaconess believes that she is pledged to a lifelong ministry, and that she is, therefore, not free to enter into relationships or undertake duties which would permanently interfere with her special ministry in the Church. Though, for example, it might be right for her, with the bishop's consent, to give up her work temporarily, in order to minister to one to whom she owed a special duty, such as an aged or invalid parent, it would not be consistent with her vocation to lay aside her ministerial office and return to private life. This precludes her from marriage: not because she considers the marriage state in any sense inferior, but because it would make demands upon her which would prevent her from exercising her ministry as a deaconess. Marriage is a life vocation, by which a woman is set apart for the sacred duties of motherhood, which must always have the first claim on her life. The two vocations of the deaconess and the wife are therefore mutually exclusive.
>
> The deaconess does not take the negative vow of celibacy, but her ordination implies to her the positive vow of lifelong service for the Church, as has been the rule from the first days. It follows from this that a woman should not be ordained until she has fully tested her vocation. As a general rule a deaconess is not ordained under thirty, and in some dioceses the age-limit is higher. As a further testing a woman is often required to serve as a lay-worker before being presented for ordination."

A Committee of the Lambeth Conference of Bishops of the Anglican Communion appointed to consider the ministry of women, in 1920 interpreted the ordination of deaconesses in that communion as "conferring Holy Orders." The Conference resolved: "That the time has come when in the interest of the Church at large, and in particular of the development of the Ministry of Women, the Diaconate of Women should be restored formally and canonically, and should be recognized throughout the Anglican Communion." It favored including in the duties of a deaconess: "to read Morning and Evening Prayer and the Litany, except such portions as are assigned to the priest only, in Church; and in Church also to lead in prayer, and under license of the Bishop to instruct and exhort the congregation." (Conference Bishops of the Anglican Communion, 1920, pp. 39-41.)

In "the form and manner of making of Deaconesses" adopted by the Upper Houses of Convocations of Canterbury and York and contained in the proposed revision of the Anglican Prayer Book issued February 7, 1927, the description of the office of a deaconess is as follows:

> "It appertaineth to the Office of a Deaconess, in the place where she shall be appointed to serve in things both temporal and spiritual, to minister to the welfare and happiness of those to whom she is sent; to give instruction in the Holy Scriptures and in the Christian Faith, and to help the Minister of the Parish in his work of preparing candidates for Baptism and Confirmation; to assist at the administration of Holy Baptism; to advise and pray with such women as desire help in difficulties and perplexities; to intimate the names of those who are in need, sickness, or other distress unto the Minister of the Parish, and to be at his disposition in the work of relief and succour to the parishioners."

The candidate is authorized "to execute the Office of a Deaconess in the Church of God." Similar forms of ordination have been widely used in dioceses of the Church of England and of the Protestant Episcopal Church.

In a recent letter to the *Church Times* a Bishop of the Anglican Church says: "It is not generally known, I think, that the preparation of candidates for the Order (of Deaconesses) has been undergoing drastic revision during the last few years, and that now there are coming into the ministry of the Church (though, alas, in too few numbers!) women of knowledge and capacity, highly trained and entirely suited for responsible tasks, both at home and abroad."

In the Methodist Episcopal Church deaconesses are consecrated with the use of the words: "I admit thee to the office of a deaconess in the Church of God." Provision is made in the

Discipline for leave of absence, and for honorable discharge, and also for Associate Deaconesses who receive appointments for a limited period of time. (Discipline 1924, pp. 199, 191.)

Women as Teachers and Preachers

The varied and valuable work of women in many departments of modern church organization is too well known to require extended notice here. Women have succeeded not only in the detailed tasks which they have undertaken, but also in the administration of missionary, relief and educational work. They have come to hold a place in the councils of many Churches, including our own.

While the higher ranks of the teaching profession have not been open to women on equal terms with men they have done a great deal of work of elementary teaching, and in some instances have given notable service in the universities. In religion and theology they have rarely found a teaching opportunity, but they have taken increased advantage of the opportunity of publication, and through books and articles a few women have accredited themselves in the company of authoritative theological writers.

The prophetic ministry has also been resumed by a few women in the Churches of the Reformation. Quakers and Independents in England recognized the office of the woman preacher, and despite much obloquy and legal hardship a number of courageous women served the cause of religion by public preaching. Methodism utilized the preaching as well as the teaching talents of women. "God owns women in the conversion of sinners," said Wesley, "and who am I that I should withstand God?" Women served among Wesleyan Methodists as class leaders, local preachers, and itinerants.

The Wesleyan Methodist Church is governed by the following resolution:

> "The Conference is of opinion that the cases in which it is desirable that women should preach among us are exceptional. Where, however, a woman possesses special gifts, and gives evidence of having received a Divine Call to the work of preaching, liberty should be given her for the exercise of other gifts. But in all such cases the preaching of women shall be subject to the following conditions:
>
> 1. They shall not preach in the circuit where they reside until they have received the approbation of the Superintendent and Quarterly Meeting. In the case of Wesley Deaconesses the permission of the Warden and the Committee of the Wesley Deaconesses Institute is equivalent to and shall take the place of that of the Superintendent and Quarterly Meeting.
>
> "2. Before they go into any other circuit they shall have a written invitation from the superintendent of that circuit, and a recommendatory note from the superintendent of their own circuit.
>
> "N.B. So far as possible the preaching of women shall be restricted to neighbourhoods in which there is no special opposition to such preaching. (Minutes of Conference, 1901, pp. 365, 366.)"

In 1922 a committee of the Wesleyan Methodist Church, on "Women and the Ministry" reported that in principle "The Committee is not aware of any function of the ordained ministry for which a woman is disqualified on the ground of her sex, but it is felt that in practice the system of the itinerant ministry, peculiar to Methodism, raises special difficulties, and the Committee is seeking to explore other avenues for the service of women to the Church." Women are eligible to become fully accredited Local (or Lay) Preachers on the same conditions as men. Wesley Deaconesses play an important part in the life of the Wesleyan Church. (Constance M. Coltman, in A. Maude Royden's The Church and Women, p. 119f.)[5]

The Presbyterian Church of England in its Assembly of 1921 declared by a majority that "there is no barrier in principle to the admission of women to the ministry;" and received in 1922 the report of a Committee of which a majority were of the opinion:

> That the Church would be following not only the trend of our time but the direction of the liberating spirit of God if we opened our ministry to women (ibid., p. 118).

Presbyteries, however, proved unfavorable to the step, and the Assembly of 1923 declined to give the question further consideration "at the present time."

In the Congregational Churches of England and Wales there is no bar to the admission of women to the Ministry. A few women have been ordained to the full Ministry, and some are at present serving in the pastorate.

Women took part in the National Mission conducted by the Anglican Church in 1916; though not without opposition to their being permitted to speak in consecrated buildings. One of the Lambeth resolutions of 1920 permits unordained women, "duly qualified and approved by the Bishop, to speak in consecrated or unconsecrated buildings," though not in the "regular and appointed services" of the Church. No official regularizing of the preaching of women has taken place, however.

The General Conference of the Methodist Episcopal Church in 1924 received the report of a Commission appointed in 1920 to consider the expediency of granting to women ordination and admission to the General Conference. The Commission declined to approve of these measures on the grounds of the connexional polity which "guarantees to every effective minister a church and to every self-supporting church a minister," and of the "indifference of the Church at large to the matter." The Commission, however, recommended "that the General Conference enact such measures as shall provide for the ordination of women as local preachers." The Conference resolved: "that all disciplinary provisions relating to Local Preachers and to their ordination as Deacons and Elders shall be so construed as to include women, and that any verbal alterations in the Discipline thereby made necessary, be effected." In a footnote on p. 183 it is stated that the provisions in the sections on Local Preachers "include women, except in so far as they apply to candidates for the travelling ministry."

Appendix II

Status of Women in the Three Churches Previous to Union and in their Foreign Fields

The following report was compiled by Dr. W. T. Gunn, Dr. James Endicott and Principal Alfred Gandier, at the request of the Executive of the General Council for information only, and was presented to the Executive at its meeting on March 18, 1926.

I. Status of Women in the Congregational Union of Canada

In the organization of the Congregational Union of Canada and of the Churches belonging to it, there is no difference made between men and women in the membership of the local church, the membership of the District Association, or the membership or office of the Congregational Union of Canada. Women have been delegates to the Associations and to the Union, freely appointed for many years. Women have been members of the Executive and Directors of the Foreign Missionary Society and of the Executive and General Committee of the Home Missionary Society.

Deaconess Order

No such order, as far as my memory goes, has ever been officially approved by the Union, but local churches, in a number of cases, have employed women workers, who were given the title of Deaconess, and in several churches there were Boards of Deaconesses, as well as Deacons, the duties being somewhat similar to those of the Boards of Deacons, but dealing more especially with the care of the women and children and relief work of the church.

Ordination

While there is no record of the ordination of women to the ministry in any of the records of the Congregational Union of Canada, yet women have been ordained by the Congregational Churches of the United States. In the regulations of the Congregational College of Canada there is nothing which would prevent women from taking the College Course or from sitting as a member on the Board of Governors or taking part as a representative in the annual meeting. As a matter of fact, there is no record of any such appointment, although there is a Ladies' Auxiliary Committee in connection with the Board of Governors. The Congregational College of Canada, in connection with the Co-operating Colleges, in Montreal, has prepared possible courses for training women for the work of deaconesses and foreign missionary work.

In the Congregational Union of England and Wales, there have been several cases in which women have been ordained to the ministry. In one case a husband and wife were both ordained and recognized as joint pastors of a church.

Report Concerning Church Organization in the United Church Mission Field, Angola, West Africa

The work in this field has been carried on in co-operation between the American Board of Commissioners for Foreign Missions and the Canada Congregational Foreign Missionary Society and Woman's Board. All missionaries going out from Canada were commissioned as members of the American Board. The work on the field was divided according to agreement, though the organization, while separate as to each station, is united as one Mission.

The organization on the field consisted of a Missionary Council. This met annually, electing its own officers, including the Treasurer of the whole field, who acted as banker for all the work and the missionaries' personal accounts. This Conference met annually and had an Executive which met when needed.

Every missionary who had passed his or her first year examination in the native language was called a "voting missionary," but not all missionaries attended the Annual Council. One delegate was sent for each two missionaries on each station, and an additional missionary if there were three or any odd number of missionaries on the station. The missionary, the missionary's wife, the doctor, the doctor's wife, and the regularly commissioned industrial or agricultural missionaries, with their wives, had each a vote and held the same rank in the Mission Council. At the Annual Meeting of the Conference, all missionaries who attended were usually allowed the "voting" privilege.

The Canada Congregational Women's Board, in 1925, changed from its previous relation to the Woman's Board of Missions of the Congregational Churches of the United States to being an auxiliary to the Canada Congregational Foreign Missionary Society, and it is now merged in the Woman's Missionary Society of The United Church of Canada.

Organization of the Native Church

Separate and independent churches have been organized in all the Mission Stations and at some of the out-stations, while the Church of Chiyuka, ordinarily worshipping separately, is organically part of the church at Chisamba, and meets there once a month for Communion.

The local church is organized with native pastor and elders. No native pastors have as yet been ordained. The Communion Service is always conducted by one of the missionaries. Once a year there is held a conference of native Christians. This includes also representatives from the Brethren Mission to the north and north-east of our group of stations. It has no authority over the local church, but is composed of duly appointed representatives from each church, together with such visitors as may desire to come. As a matter of fact, the attendance runs well up over a thousand. Each local church appoints, in proportion to its membership, a certain number of delegates, both men and women. At the meeting of the Conference there are sessions of the women delegates by themselves and sessions of the men by themselves, with joint sessions as a whole for subjects of common interest. At both these separate sessions and the united session, while all can be present and take part, any matter requiring a vote can only be voted upon by the regularly appointed delegates. While the missionaries are at these conferences and take part for help and guidance, it does not seem that they have any formal ecclesiastical connection.

The matter of ordination of native pastors has been agitated for some years past, and it would seem that the time was close at hand for this.

Mission Stations are built upon concessions given to the Mission on homesteading terms by the Portuguese Government. The Government of the concession is practically in the hands of the missionaries and the elders of the native church.

Under the care also of the missionary and the elders of the church are the elders in charge of out-stations and their people, who usually arrange with their people to come to the central mission church for Communion once a month.

II. Status of Women in the Methodist Church

Equal Status

According to the latest Discipline, namely that of 1922, the status of women in the Church was stated as follows (Par. 91):

> "The General Conference shall extend to women equal rights and privileges with men as lay members of the Church."

This enactment makes it clear that women have all the rights and privileges that other lay members of the Church possess in all the courts of the Church.

Women and the Ministry

At the same General Conference a lengthy discussion arose on the report of the referendum—"Women and the Ministry." That is to say, the question had been opened for consideration, by the special action of the previous General Conference, in all the Quarterly Official Boards of the Church during the quadrennium, and votes were taken of official members as to the advisability of the General Conference taking action making it possible for women to be ordained into the Christian ministry. An amendment, and an amendment to the amendment, were offered but finally the original recommendation of the Committee on Memorials was adopted, which reads as follows (Page 378):

> "That in regard to the results of the referendum on the admission of women to the ministry, the judgment of the Committee is that the General Conference, whatever its convictions might be, would not be warranted in officially declaring the door open, and making any disciplinary changes that might be involved. In view, however, of the facts that nearly half of the official boards refrained from voting, that the majority was small, and that any proposal to enter untrodden paths naturally arouses hesitation and uncertainty, it is our judgment that the door should not be declared to be closed finally, but that the Church should wait for clearer indications of the Will of the Great Head of the Church in this matter."

Deaconess Order

For many years there has been an organization in the Church known as the Deaconess Society of the Methodist Church, and the object is stated in Paragraph 312 of the Discipline, which reads as follows:

> "The object of this society shall be to foster the interests of the Deaconess order; to

conduct a training school; to promote the establishment of Deaconess Institutions; to secure adequate maintenance for deaconesses and Deaconess Institutions.''

Women in the Foreign Mission Fields:

a. *Under the Woman's Missionary Society*—Great liberty has been enjoyed by the women of the Methodist Church in the development and carrying out of the work of the Woman's Missionary Society. In the collection and expenditure of funds and in the selection of missionary candidates and in many other respects in practice there has been almost complete independence of action. It is true that according to the letter of the Discipline the powers of the Woman's Missionary Society are actually more restricted than they have generally been in actual practice. All the women working under the Woman's Missionary Society in any given Mission Field are members of their own Women's Council and in this Council all members enjoy equal status. All the work carried on by the Woman's Missionary Society in any foreign field comes under the review of their own Council, and recommendations, policies and estimates for work, and such like, are referred directly from the Council to the Home Board of the same Society. There is special provision of the Discipline (Par. 412) which states:

> ''The Mission Council of the Woman's Missionary Society shall meet in joint session with the Council of the General Missionary Society at least once in the year, for consultation in regard to matters of common interest, with the view of promoting harmony and co-operation between the agents of both societies.''

b. *Under the General Board of Missions*—All single women at work in the Foreign Mission fields under the General Board, enjoy equal status on their respective Mission Councils and the various Committees of the Mission, with the men missionaries. It has not been the practice of the Methodist Board to give the wives of missionaries voting powers on the Council or on its Committees, but they are generally accorded the privilege of Corresponding Membership in the Council. In the matter of the Central Stations in China, however, all the workers, wives included, constitute the Local Committees and on these Committees the women have equal status with the men.

The West China Mission Council at its meeting in 1925 forwarded the following memorial to the General Board with respect to the standing of wives of missionaries:

> ''Whereas the wives of our missionaries are, while discharging their household duties, also actively engaged in various forms of missionary work, and
>
> Whereas we as a Council are doubtless losing a great deal in effectiveness because they are debarred from participation in the deliberation of Council, and
>
> Whereas the wives of missionaries in other societies are recognized as members of the Mission, and
>
> Whereas wives of missionaries are already eligible for membership in the General Council of our church.
>
> Resolved, that this Council recommend to the Home Board and to the General Council of the United Church of Canada, that the wives of our missionaries be given the status of missionaries but without salary; it being understood that this implies:
>
> 1. That their names be included in the list of members of Council.
> 2. That they be entitled to the privilege of debate and the right to vote in all meetings of our Mission.''

After some consideration the following resolution was adopted by the General Board:

> ''That this matter be referred to the Japan Mission Council and to the General Council of the United Church.''

The following paragraph affecting the status of wives of missionaries in the matter of electing delegates to the General Conferences from the foreign fields was adopted (Discipline 125):

> "For the purpose of electing delegates to the General Conference from the Missions in Japan and China, special meetings composed of the missionaries of the General Board and their wives, and the missionaries of the Woman's Missionary Society, shall be convened in Japan and China, respectively, during the year in which the General Conference is held. These meetings shall be deemed in each case to be an Annual Conference for the purpose of electing delegates to the General Conference, and shall proceed with these elections in the same way as an Annual Conference. Delegates to the General Conference from the foreign mission fields shall be chosen from among those who shall be on furlough when the General Conference to which they are elected delegates, shall meet."

III. Status of Women in the Presbyterian Church in Canada

Women who were members in full communion of the Presbyterian Church in Canada always had equal rights and votes with men in all congregational meetings, but they were not regarded as eligible for the eldership, and as a matter of fact did not have a place on the Session. Not being members of the Session, they were never elected as representatives of the congregation to Presbytery, and therefore had no place in the membership of Synod or Assembly.

In 1908, the General Assembly instituted an order of deaconesses by adopting the report of a special committee in the following terms:

1. That the Assembly sanction the institution of an Order of Deaconesses for the Presbyterian Church in Canada, the Order to consist of women trained for the service and devoting their whole time thereto, and of godly women of mature years, sober-minded, thoroughly tested in the school of experience, and devoting themselves to the work as the faithful elder does to his. But inasmuch as there is already a recognized title by which women workers in the foreign field are known, it is not advisable that the term "Deaconess" be applied to these.

2. That the Assembly direct that the Ewart Training Home in Toronto be an institution for the training of women for the missionary and deaconess work of our Church, and for affording them a Home under helpful Christian influences during the period of their training, also for providing a temporary home for women missionaries and deaconesses on furlough and for deaconesses engaged in work in its vicinity, as far as this does not interfere with its primary object as a training home.

3. That the Assembly direct that on the completion of the course of training, a diploma be granted to the graduates of the Home, and on the appointment of such graduates to work under the Foreign Mission Committee or the Home Mission Committee or to Parochial work, they shall be designated to their work as Missionaries, or Deaconesses, as the case may be, by a Presbytery. Such designation is not, however, to be regarded as an ordination, nor shall any pledge of perpetual service be exacted, but each worker shall be free to retire from her work upon notice duly given to the Committee under whose direction she is laboring.

4. Instead of Deaconesses receiving, as in the case of some Churches and organizations, a guaranteed home and support for life with simply a spending allowance while in the work, she shall receive from the Committee or Church Court employing her, a remuneration based, as in the case of foreign missionaries, upon what is necessary for comfort and health, and for making some provision for age. This amount will vary with the cost of living in different localities, and with the nature of the services in which she is engaged, but in no case should it be less than a minimum to be fixed by future legislation.

5. Provision for aged and infirm deaconesses shall be made by the Church under the same general rules as those now in effect regarding women missionaries in the foreign fields, namely, when a deaconess, through infirmity or age, retires from service with the sanction of the Committee in charge of Deaconesses' Work, she shall receive from the funds provided by the Church for deaconesses' work, after ten years' service, an annuity of fifty dollars, and five dollars for each additional year of service up to forty, but no annuity shall exceed $200.00 per annum. In event of her marriage the annuity ceases.

Note—The designation of a deaconess was expressly declared by the Assembly of 1908, not to be ordination.

To the General Assembly of June, 1921, there came a reference regarding the "admission of women to Theological Colleges as regular students with a view to ordination." This reference was referred to a committee to report to next Assembly. The report of the Committee was adopted by the Assembly of 1922 and ended with the words, "the Assembly is not prepared to direct that women be ordained to the office of the ministry." Since that time no action has been taken by the Presbyterian Church in Canada. The whole finding is as follows:

> "Reference from the Assembly of June, 1921, regarding 'Admission of Women to Theological Colleges, as regular students, with a view to ordination.'"
>
> This raises the question of the ordination of women to the holy ministry. The Assembly is not prepared to foreclose this question either positively or negatively. It desires, however, to direct attention to the following considerations.
>
> 1. It is a matter of history that a ministry of women existed both within the Apostolic Church and in the Church of the immediately succeeding centuries; but there is no evidence that ordination in the full sense of the term was bestowed upon women. It is true, that the laying on of hands was practised with respect to deaconesses, but it was distinctly understood that this did not carry with it full ministerial function. No precedent therefore can be quoted for the ordination of women, while at the same time the authority of primitive practice cannot be regarded as absolutely binding upon the modern Church.
> 2. Present-day instances of the ordination of women can be quoted; yet they are not so numerous that an argument for the introduction of the practice in our own communion should be based upon them, and there is no evidence of a wide-spread demand for the ordination of women throughout the membership of our Church.
> 3. The Assembly recognizes gladly and thankfully the ministry of women whether in an official or non-official capacity, in very many departments of the Church's work. Congregational activities depend very largely on the devotion and sacrifice of multitudes of women, both younger and older. The Church at large owes to such servants of Christ an overwhelming debt of gratitude. In more specialized directions women have proved their gifts for organization and administration, for evangelism and missionary enterprise, for social service and for teaching and preaching. The Assembly would mention with high acknowledgment, the excellent work accomplished through the Church's order of deaconesses. In parochial service our deaconesses have acquitted themselves with highest efficiency; some of them have taken charge of Mission fields in the West, with the warmest approbation, both of the people and of the Missionary Conveners and superintendents.
>
> The inference from these facts, however, that the whole work of the pastorate can be fully performed by a woman does not indubitably follow. There is no question here of withholding from women rank or privilege which men jealously confine to themselves. Nor is the question to be settled by an *a priori* view of the nature of

> ordination or the validity of sacraments. The question is really two fold and concerns the nature of the task on the one side, and the possibility of effective service on the other. In view of the variety, the intimacy, the gravity and the burdensome nature of the work of the Ministry on the one side and in view of the limitations, necessarily involved in the fact of sex on the other, the Assembly is not prepared to direct that women be ordained to the office of the Ministry.

The status of women in the Foreign Mission Fields of the Church is set forth in the following statement:

Honan

The Presbytery of Honan directs the work of the Mission.

At each meeting of Presbytery, it resolves into a Committee of the Whole, giving all the ladies—W.M.S. and wives of Missionaries—the right to take part in the discussions and vote on all Mission matters. The Committee of the Whole rises, reports progress and its resolutions almost without exception are confirmed by the Presbytery.

From the beginning of the Mission, Presbytery has dealt with all matters usually dealt with by Mission Councils in the other fields. There never has been a Mission Council for either men or women in the Honan Mission. One anomaly is the continued existence of two Presbyteries—one exclusively foreign and the other largely Chinese (certain missionaries are recognized members of the Chinese court, i.e., any Evangelistic missionary who has at least one elder in his district.) Some of the best men for executive work who are engaged in institutional work are therefore excluded.

South China

A Council governs the Mission. This Council is composed of the male missionaries and W.M.S. missionaries.

Matters relating to women's work are dealt with by a women's sub-committee and the recommendations sent on to the Council for final action. The wives of missionaries are given full voting power in the sub-committee, but have no vote in the Council. The W.M.S. ladies, of course, have full membership in the Council.

Formosa

A Mission Council governs the work.

In the past there were three Councils—Men's, Women's, and a Union Council. Early in 1925 one Mission Council was formed. The Council resolves into a Committee of the Whole, thus giving the wives of missionaries an opportunity of taking part in the discussions. The actions taken are ratified by the Mission Council. Single ladies are full members; wives of missionaries have no vote in Council.

Korea

A Mission Council governs the work.

Male missionaries and W.M.S. ladies who have passed their first year's language examination have full voting powers. At the meeting of Council in July, 1925, wives of missionaries were given a vote.

Central India

A Mission Council governs the work in India.

Action taken July 8, 1924, *re* formation of "The Mission Council"—

"The Mission Council agrees to dissolve and herewith does dissolve the Council as at present constituted, to meet with the members of the Women's Council on Friday, July

18th, 1924, at 12 o'clock noon, to form the new Mission Council on the basis already determined, and sanctioned by the Foreign Mission Board and the Women's Missionary Society of the Presbyterian Church in Canada.''

A motion similar to the above was passed by the Women's Council.

Membership

All the present members of both Councils shall be members of the United Council. For the future those missionaries, men and women (including wives) appointed by the Home Board, who pass their First Language Examination, shall become members of Council. Council may, in special circumstances, receive as full members missionaries who have not passed the qualifying test.

British Guiana

The Mission Council is the governing body. Men, and Single Women have full membership. The married ladies have no vote in Council, but attend in an advisory capacity.

Trinidad

The Mission Council directs the work, and is composed of the male missionaries and single women missionaries.

Ordination of Women

While your Committee feels that owing to certain misunderstanding on the part of some Presbyteries concerning the question submitted and the indifference toward the matter displayed by others—the mind of the Church about the ordination of women has not been fully disclosed,—nevertheless on the basis of the returns received from Presbyteries your Committee submits, that while a large section of the Church, probably indeed a majority, regards the ordination of women to the full ministry of word and sacraments as an ideal towards which the Church should move, an unmistakeable majority, in the existing circumstances of The United Church, is opposed to any such step being taken at the present time.

Your Committee also find that there is no such demand for the creation of a diaconate, ordained to the Word and one Sacrament, either for women alone, or for both men and women, as would justify the creation of that order of the ministry within The United Church of Canada.

On the other hand, your Committee feel that there are anomalies in the relation of women to Church Courts, in especial, to Sessions, which ought, if possible, to be removed. They find that the ordination of women to the eldership is already the practice in other Churches to which we are affiliated, and that the sole bar to their ordination in our Church is the legal interpretation of the relevant section in the Basis of Union, and that, if that were removed, no obstacle would remain which would prevent constitutionally elected women from serving in all courts of the Church, and they are of opinion that the General Council should devise means whereby that obstacle should be removed.

Your Committee therefore recommend:

1. That the General Council take no action in the matter of the ordination of women to the ministry; but puts itself on record as holding that there is no bar in religion or reason to such ordination.
2. That the General Council do not create a diaconate ordained to the Word and one Sacrament.
3. That the General Council remit to the Committee on Law the question of the ordination of women to the eldership.

a. To determine whether by a declaration of Council the word "men" in 2B, 9A of the Basis of Union may not legally be held to include women or,

b. To devise a means whereby, under the Barrier Act, the necessary change may be secured.

Your Committee cannot conclude without expressing the hope that every encouragement will be given to the existing order of Deaconesses to develop their educational training, and their special aptitudes for the wonderfully valuable work which they do. They hope that Deaconesses employed by congregations will be members of Official Boards and of Sessions, when that is legally possible, in order that they may be eligible for the higher courts of the Church, and that thus wisely and with regard to the harmony and well being of the whole Church, they may enter into that larger sphere to which their gifts of insight and service entitle them.

C. T. Scott, *Chairman* Nellie L. McClung, *Secretary*.

Remit, Ordination of Women

The Secretary presented the report of the action of the Presbyteries on the remit regarding the Ordination of Women:

CONFERENCE	Favorable	Opposed	Approve Principle But Advise Defer Action	Favorable Diaconate	Opposed Diaconate	No Report
Newfoundland	. .	. .	4	. .	. .	. .
Maritime	5	4	4	2	2	5
Montreal and Ottawa	2	. .	. .	. .	. .	3
Bay of Quinte	1	2	4	3	. .	. .
Toronto	2	5	4	1	. .	1
Hamilton	. .	4	. .	. .	. .	5
London	1	3	2	. .	. .	1
Manitoba	6	1	1	1	. .	2
Saskatchewan	8	7	2	4	1	. .
Alberta	6	5	. .	1	1	5
British Columbia	1	3	2	1	1	1
	32	34	23	13	5	23

Moved by Rev. G. W. Kerby, seconded by Rev. W. L. Armstrong: That the report be referred to the Sessional Committee on Ordination of Women. Carried.

Women and Sessions

The Secretary presented the report of the action of Presbyteries on the remit regarding the eligibility of women for election as members of sessions, as follows:

CONFERENCE	Favorable	Opposed	Approve Principle But Advise Defer Action	No Report
Newfoundland	. .	. .	. .	4
Maritime	6	4	. .	8
Montreal and Ottawa	1	. .	. .	4
Bay of Quinte	2	. .	. .	7
Toronto	3	4	2	3
Hamilton	5	1	. .	4
London	1	1	. .	3
Manitoba	5	. .	. .	5
Saskatchewan	10	. .	. .	7
Alberta	8	1	. .	6
British Columbia	1	2	. .	4
	42	13	2	55

Moved by Rev. J. E. Peters, seconded by Rev. Charles Hackett: That this report be referred to Committee dealing with Ordination of Women. Carried.

Report, Committee on Ordination of Women

The Committee preparing the statement concerning the Ordination of Women was instructed to complete its report, and given authority to print sufficient quantities to send to Presbyteries with the remit of the General Council concerning this question, and also a copy to each minister throughout the Church.

James Endicott, *Moderator.*
T. Albert Moore, *Secretary.*

Endnotes

Section A

*It is beyond the province of the Committee to recommend the similar recognition of the diaconate of men as part of the Ministry. We recognize that such a step might be regarded as logically consequent upon the adoption of the Committee's recommendations: and that for certain reasons, some of which have come to the notice of the Committee, the diaconate of men might be found advantageous to the work of the Church. It would for example afford a means of regularly authorizing the employment of men, not qualified for the full Ministry, whose special gifts might be thus made available to the Church.

Appendix I

[1] *Virgins* were in the Church of the first century a social class, but apparently not an organized and specially consecrated sisterhood with definite tasks. Cf. 1 Corinthians 7: 25-28. The *Presbytis* (*presbutis*) in Titus 2: 3 seems to mean not a presbyteress in any ecclesiastical sense, but simply a woman of advanced years. Apparently the same meaning attaches to *presbutera* in 1 Timothy 5: 2.

[2] In later usage, as in the Apostolic constitutions, the forms *hē diakonos, hē diakonissa* are interchangeable.

[3] This interpretation offers a parallel to the following passage in the Canons of Hippolytus: "an inspectress is to be appointed over the women, that they be not unchaste nor lovers of

pleasure nor prone to laughter, not talk at all in church, because it is the house of God. It is not a place of conversation, but a place of prayer with reverence.''

[4] e.g., in the phrase ''as long as you shall hold this office,'' in the form in use in the dioceses of Pennsylvania and New York.

[5] After this report was in print the action taken by the Conference of the Wesleyan Methodist Church, 1927, has come to our knowledge. The Conference resolved as follows:—

> In view of the difference of judgment between the two sessions of the Conference, in regard to the proposal for the admission of women to the ministry, and of the wide divergence of opinion in the Representative Session, and having regard to the declaration of the Pastoral Session that the serious practical obstacles to the admission of women to our itinerant ministry, interposed both by our organization and traditions, do not admit immediately of any complete solution, this Representative Session of the Conference, realizing that the importance and difficulties of the subject demand for it further consideration, remits the whole question to a Committee, directing it to explore the possibility of suggesting such arrangements as shall secure larger opportunities for the exercise of the gifts of consecrated women in the service of Christ, and the further development of the diaconate of women in the ministry of the Church. Such a Committee shall confer, if desired, with any corresponding Committee appointed by the Pastoral Session.

(Editor's note: Portions of the preceding statement originally appeared in Greek; these phrases were transliterated to English to aid the reader.)

Notes: *Printed here is the 1928 report of the Committee on the Ordination of Women of the United Church of Canada (approximately 2,186,000 members), followed by the committee's summation and recommendations to the General Council and a survey of the Presbyteries on the issue, which was ordered to accompany the committee's report. The report begins by noting that the topic of women's ordination arose in 1926 when Lydia E. Gruchy sought ordination in the Saskatchewan Conference. In its main study, the committee followed the lead of the 1920 Lambeth Conference of bishops of the Anglican Communion by recommending that female deacons be ordained. In its final summary and recommendations, however, the committee noted that a majority of the church's members was opposed to any ordination of women, a fact which caused the committee to reverse itself and instead bolster the existing order of deaconess (in which women were not ordained). The committee did believe there was sufficient sentiment towards the eventual ordination of women and that ''there [was] no bar in religion or reason to such ordination.'' The possibility of using legal means to open the door for female applicants in the future was also mentioned.*

UNITED CHURCH OF CANADA

VOTE RESULTS ON THE ORDINATION OF WOMEN (1935)

Remit, Ordination of Women.

A report was presented in regard to the Remit on the Ordination of Women; seventy-five Presbyteries have sent in their reports; of which sixty-one have voted in favor, and fifteen have voted against the proposed amendment to the Basis of Union. The final date to receive reports is June 1st, 1935.*

Endnote

*The vote on the Remit, ''The Ordination of Women'' (Proceedings, General Council, 1934, page 26) on June 1st, 1935, was as follows:

Conference	No. of Presbyteries	For	Against
Newfoundland	6	1	1
Maritime	18	7	8
Montreal and Ottawa	5	4	1
Bay of Quinte	7	3	4
Toronto	12	8	4
Hamilton	7	5	1
London	8	5	2
Manitoba	10	10	—
Saskatchewan	18	16	2
Alberta	16	14	2
British Columbia	7	6	1
Total	114	79	26

Notes: *In the seven years following the report of the Committee on the Ordination of Women, attitudes changed considerably within the United Church of Canada. Instead of opposing ordination, church members now approved the practice by a three to one majority. As a result of this vote, Lydia Gruchy was ordained in St. Andrew's United Church, Moose Jaw Presbytery, in 1936, 10 years after her original petition for ordination.*

WORLD COUNCIL OF CHURCHES

CONCERNING THE ORDINATION OF WOMEN (1964)

Foreword

At the third Assembly of the World Council of Churches in New Delhi, 1961, the Department on Faith and Order was requested to establish a study in conjunction with the Department on Cooperation of Men and Women in Church, Family and Society, on the theological, biblical and ecclesiological issues involved in the ordination of women. The Department on Cooperation, which from its beginning has been keenly interested in the question, warmly welcomed this request.

Consequently, in preparation for the Fourth World Conference on Faith and Order in Montreal, 1963, the two Departments jointly gathered the material which makes up the contents of this booklet, including: an introduction summing up the issues involved, a statement drawn up by a small consultation, two papers on the scriptural evidence, and three personal comments from representatives of various traditions.

At Montreal, these papers were presented as study material for the Section on "The Redemptive Work of Christ and the Ministry of His Church." The Section recommended that the study of this question be continued under the title "Women in the ministry and the ministries". The two Departments are aware of the fact that the material herein submitted represents only an initial stage of the full study to be undertaken. But it is for this very reason that they have decided to publish and present it now to the Churches for wider reflection.

Geneva, February 1964.

The Ordination of Women

Initial Statement by Dr. Lukas Vischer
(Research Secretary, Department on Faith and Order,
World Council of Churches)

The question whether women can undertake the responsibilities of a pastor in the Church is not a new one. It came up from time to time in earlier centuries. A careful enquiry into the history of the office of deaconess, and the importance of widows in the Christian Church, would bring to light some interesting facts in this connection. But during the last few decades it has cropped up in an entirely new way. In earlier centuries the question was more peripheral and could be dismissed fairly easily. But more recently a much more fundamental question has been raised: does the life of the Church adequately reflect the great truth that *in Christ there is neither male nor female*? Does the Order of the Church adequately express this truth? There is growing insistence that women should assume more responsible functions in the life of the Church; this demand has grown particularly strong within the ecumenical movement, in which so many women have played a leading role. It is typical, for instance, that women spoke at the very first World Conference on Faith and Order (1927). Six women issued a statement, which was recorded in the Minutes: "that the right place of women in the Church is one of grave moment and should be in the hearts and minds of all". They pointed out that if the Church seeks deeper unity it must re-examine the question of the relationship between men and women, and that the mission task makes it imperative to put to better use *all* the gifts available in the Church. They deliberately refrained from raising the problem of church order in this connection. But already at that time it was clear that it would be impossible to avoid facing the question later.

The churches are therefore confronted by a new question, which they must answer in the light of their understanding of the Gospel. It is clear, they are bound to come to different conclusions. For since the churches are divided on questions of Faith and Order, they approach a new question like this from different assumptions. The assumptions of some churches are such that they hesitate even to examine the question at all. They do indeed see the need for examining the relationship between men and women, and giving women the position in the Church which God intended. But in the light of the truth they think it is clear that the ministries of the Church should be restricted to men. They are therefore inclined to say that the problem of ordination cannot be raised at all. If the relationship between men and women requires a fresh expression in the Church (they say), at any rate a solution should not be sought at this point. On the other hand, other churches see no fundamental obstacle to examining the question. In the light of their ecclesiology and of their understanding of Scripture they are convinced that the form of church order can never claim to be final: it must be modified in obedience to Christ in a new age where the situation is changed. They are therefore prepared to consider changes which involve a great change from the traditional forms. It must, however, be added that even in cases where this readiness exists, no agreement has yet been reached. The solutions proposed by the different churches differ widely in many respects, and again one realises how different are the assumptions from which the churches approach the question. Some churches draw a careful distinction between different forms and grades of religious office, allowing women a certain restricted place, with careful reservations. Other churches place men and women on an equal footing, in every respect. In some churches great difficulties are involved in overcoming the obstacles; in others the ordination of women for all the functions of the ministry is taken for granted.

We are confronted by a great variety of answers, some in direct opposition to others, and it is clear that this question has brought out a difference between the churches which did not exist centuries ago, at any rate not in this way. But should not precisely a question of this kind show that the churches form a fellowship? Can the churches allow their divisions to continue, because they arrive at different decisions? Must they not explore every possible avenue, in order to arrive at a common answer?

Or at the very least, must they not take their decisions in living fellowship with other churches, so that the particular course taken by one church is comprehensible to the other churches? The churches which refuse to admit the question of the ordination of women at all will at first be tempted to say that the churches which do so are deepening the divisions within Christendom, owing to their arbitrary decisions. But is it permissible for them to pass judgement in this way? They recognise that the Holy Spirit is also at work in other churches. Must they not therefore consider the possibility that the course taken by another church may be important for them also? Should they not re-examine their own teaching and approach, in view of the attitude of that other church? And are they not obliged to express more clearly in what way they are safeguarding the cooperation of women in the Church? The churches which are prepared to consider the ordination of women will at first be tempted to regard the other churches as conservative and traditionalistic. They will tend to think that the refusal to consider ordination of women is due to lack of respect for women. But is such a view admissible? If these churches take the ecumenical fellowship seriously, must they not see the importance of continuity in the life of the Church, and what a responsibility it is to introduce a new element at any point? Must they not take serious account of the testimony of the churches which want to preserve that continuity? And are they not forced by their testimony to express more clearly how they think of preserving it? At any rate it is of great importance that the churches should not isolate themselves from one another in their attitudes.

It is essential to say this, as becomes still clearer if we take a few examples showing how the question of the ordination of women affects the unity of the Church. We select three examples:

a. In the Lutheran Church of Sweden, the introduction of the ordination of women led to serious upheavals, and these differences have given rise to a deep cleavage which has still not been overcome. There were long struggles before the decision was taken (in 1958), and although public discussion ended when the first three women were ordained (in 1960), the tension still continues. It is significant that the request to study the question at the ecumenical level came from Sweden.

b. Not only did the discussion about the ordination of women endanger the unity of the Church of Sweden. It also had certain repercussions upon the relations to other churches, especially the Church of England. The Church of England has intercommunion with the Church of Sweden. The fact that the Church of Sweden has retained the Apostolic Succession made this intercommunion possible. When the ordination of women was considered in Sweden, the Church of England asked itself whether the same close relations could be maintained in the future, and many Anglican theologians expressed their misgivings. Actually, however, the relations between the two Churches do not seem to have deteriorated.

c. Differences about the question of the ordination of women naturally constitute a considerable difficulty in some negotiations for union. One example of this is the negotiations between the Congregational Union of Scotland and the Church of Scotland. In one report published by the Congregational Union the question of the ordination of women is mentioned as one of the main obstacles to the union of the two churches. "If the Congregational Union were to stand fast on the principle of Women in the Ministry, then there could be no question of organic union of the two denominations in the immediate future". (Congregational Union of Scotland, Annual Assembly, 7th-11th May 1962, p. 35.) Mention is indeed made of the fact that the question is being discussed in the Church of Scotland, and that it may possibly be taken up again later on. At the same time, however, it is explained that the Congregational Union must try to find a realistic solution in the existing situation.

Another example is the plan for union in North India and Pakistan (1957). It does not actually propose the ordination of women, but a comment reads as follows: "The question of the admission of women to the ordained ministry is left for the consideration of the Synod of the Church" (p. 17). This remark drew the following comment from the Lambeth Conference (1958): "Clearly, any autonomous Church can if it so desires consider this question, and therefore the proposed Churches of North India and of Pakistan would inevitably have freedom to raise the matter in their own Synods if they so desired. The admission of women to an Order of Deaconesses would raise no difficulty. If, however, the Churches of North India and Pakistan were to decide to ordain women to the presbyterate this would raise a grave problem for the Anglican Communion, the constituent Churches of which might well find themselves unable to recognize the ministry of a woman so ordained''. (Stephen F. Bayne, *Ceylon, North India and Pakistan*, 1960, p. 193.)

Many more examples could easily be given. But the few given above suffice to show how important the question is for the unity of the Church.

As we have already seen, the problem of ordination arises in different forms in the different churches. We must revert to this point, in conclusion. We are not dealing with a question to which some churches say ''No'', and others say ''Yes''. The basic attitude is much more complicated, and many different points of view have to be considered, if one is to understand and appreciate the attitude of the different churches. How do the churches understand the nature of the Church? What form does the ministry take? Is it divided into different grades, or is there only one form of ministry? And how is the theological significance of the ministry defined? What is the teaching about ordination? What functions are attached to the different ministries, and what functions are transmitted by ordination? What is the predominant view of the Bible? How are the biblical passages concerning the position of women in the Early Church interpreted? And lastly, what is the prevailing view of the relationship between men and women in the Church, and how is this view expressed in practice? All these factors have a definite influence on the answer which a church arrives at, and one immediately realises that every church is likely to consider the question in a different way, according to its own Christian convictions.

It is therefore extremely important that in an ecumenical discussion the question should be couched in sufficiently wide terms from the very outset. We shall achieve no result if we simply ask ourselves whether or not the office of priest or pastor can be assumed by a woman. We must regard the question in its whole setting, and the conversation must provide occasion for a basic consideration of important ecclesiological, hermeneutic and anthropological questions. If the question is phrased too narrowly, it will be answered by an irreconcilable ''Yes'' or ''No'' and the arguments for and against the ordination of women will serve as heavy artillery in the fray. But if we consider the problem in its broad context, and the factors in every separate church, a solution may appear in unexpected places. Many churches which are inclined to reject the idea can be led to a modified attitude by consideration of the anthropological basis. And many churches which seem to see no difficulties at all about the ordination of women may find themselves obliged to re-examine the whole question of ecclesiology and of the ministry. When it comes to an exchange of views of this kind, the question of the ordination of women must not be regarded as ''a fresh difficulty'', to be tackled against one's will. It may rather prove to be a blessing for the ecumenical fellowship of the churches.

The Ordination of Women: An Ecumenical Problem

(Report of a consultation organised by the Department on Cooperation of Men and Women in Church, Family and Society and the Department on Faith and Order, in Geneva, 10th-12th May 1963).

Introduction

At the Assembly of the World Council of Churches, in New Delhi, 1961, the Committee dealing with the questions of the Department on Faith and Order expressed an urgent request to the Working Committee on Faith and Order ''to establish a study of the theological, biblical and ecclesiological issues involved in the ordination of women''. The initial request was made with the situation in the European churches in mind. But in the general discussion it was emphasised that this study must not be restricted to Europe. At the same time the hope was expressed that it would be undertaken "in close conjunction with the Department on Cooperation of Men and Women in Church, Family and Society". The proposal was accepted by the Working Committee of Faith and Order at its meeting in Paris, which decided to place the question of the ordination of women on the agenda of the Fourth World Conference of Faith and Order, to be held at Montreal, Canada, from the 12th to 26th July, 1963.

This decision was felt to be necessary because the problem is of practical concern to an increasing number of churches. Many churches welcome women to the ordained ministry and have found the policy advantageous. Others, having adopted this policy, face serious internal tensions. In others, the policy is under discussion and provokes heated debate. The matter frequently becomes acute in negotiations for church unity. And even apart from formal negotiations, it affects the mutual relations of churches which ordain women to those which do not. It would be wrong, therefore, to view this issue as a result of feminist demands or agitation by a few enthusiasts. It concerns the total understanding of the ministry of the church and therefore has deep theological significance.

The range of the discussion and the urgency of the problem is something new in Christian history; it has been occasioned by social and cultural movements, although the solution of the problem requires theological decision. Social and cultural movements have their proper place as a challenge to translate Christian doctrine into possible new forms of church life and church order. It is true that the danger must be avoided of accommodating Christian truth to the current ideology, but we must also say that God may use secular movements for showing his will to us.

In our day there has been a rediscovery of two theological factors particularly relevant to our present study: a new insight into the nature of the wholeness of the body of Christ and a better understanding of the meaning of the partnership of men and women in God's design.

a. It is a basic tenet of the New Testament that the whole body is called to witness to the name of Christ; all members—men and women—have therefore their appropriate ministry to which they are called by him. This basic Christian truth was for many centuries overlaid. It has been rediscovered in our own day by all parts of Christendom.

b. It is an essential element of the Christian message that man and woman are created in the image of God and are therefore of equal dignity and worth before him. The developments in our time have shown us that this truth has not always been sufficiently understood and emphasized. All the churches are confronted with the necessity of finding a new expression for this basic truth.

It is in this context that the question of the ordination of women is raised. Even the churches which oppose such ordination will realize that these new theological emphases have a relevance for them. The question involves many controversial points of exegesis, of dogmatic formulation and of ecclesiastical life. We have concentrated upon some of these.

Exegetical considerations

Many are of the opinion that the evidence of the New Testament speaks clearly against admitting women to the ministry. However, it should be seen that the New Testament is not always used in the appropriate way in the discussion of this issue.

Modern historical research on the Bible has given us a new awareness of the extent to which the biblical witness is conditioned by and oriented to historical situations. Therefore biblical teaching cannot be abstracted from the historical context in which the books have been written. The Bible is not a collection of proof texts, and questions cannot be answered by quoting single passages. Therefore if we are confronted with problems of today's world we cannot find the answer by quoting single passages. Every question must be understood and answered in the light of God's revelation in Christ which is the centre of Scripture. This methodological principle is very important for the discussion of ordination of women. Both supporters and opponents tend to quote single passages for or against such ordination. However, it should be clear that no answer is given by a single reference, e.g. to Gal. 3 or I Tim. 2. An answer can be given only by taking into consideration the whole of the Bible and the historical situation to which each single passage refers.

Sometimes it is said that the ''biblical doctrine on men and women'' does exclude any consideration of admitting women to the full ministry. But the New Testament does not contain a developed doctrine on this relationship. As the New Testament in all its parts witnesses to Christ, it is not concerned to establish a system of doctrine. Every question with which the Church is confronted is answered by referring to the central reality of Christ. The centrality of Christ even makes possible the use of different anthropological statements in the Bible. Therefore one cannot speak of New Testament doctrine on men and women and draw conclusions from such a doctrine we think is established. We have to examine the new situation in which we live in the light of Christ's Lordship.

If the passages in the New Testament dealing with the position of women in the Church are seen in their historical contexts, it becomes clear that they are written with a particular intention and in view of a particular danger for the Church. For example, it is important to see that the passages of the Pastoral Letters have in view the danger that by the public activity of women marriage could be dishonoured. It is the intention of the New Testament which we have to seek in examining its literal content. Right exegesis does not consist of imposing biblical formularies on a given situation but of interpreting it in harmony with that intention. And though we have to avoid carefully any arbitrary freedom, this principle is of great importance.

Modern research has led also to a new understanding of the relation between the Old and the New Testaments. The results of historical research do not allow us to interpret Old Testament passages according to the methods sometimes used in the New Testament period. For example, we are no longer able to use the method of interpretation we find in I Cor. 11 and I Tim. 2. This does not mean that these passages are for us empty of meaning. They are still significant. But we discover their meaning for today only by distinguishing between the intention of the Apostle's arguments and his patterns of presenting them.

Modern exegetical research has led to a deeper understanding of the eschatological character of the Christian message. The statements on the relationship of men and women are to be understood in this perspective. If it is stated that men and women are equal, it is said in view of the Eschaton. This does not mean that the differentiation of the sexes ceases to exist. We live in and are faithful to the order of creation, but at the same time the order of nature has been overcome by this new dimension. Men and women are not living any more either in isolation or in a restricted togetherness. They have received a new freedom also from the domination by their sexual nature. It is in this freedom that in the New Testament new forms of ministry are possible for men as well as women. It is in the same freedom that celibacy is offered as a way of life to men and women. It is important to take into serious consideration this eschatological dimension of the Church's life. Though the Church lives in historical continuity with its origins, it is always called to open itself anew to the future and to give a fresh expression to its eschatological message.

These exegetical considerations apply equally to two larger but related questions: the message of the Bible regarding the Christian ministry and the meaning of ordination. These two questions are answered in various ways by our churches. They must now subject these answers afresh to critical examination in the light of recent research on the Bible and on the early centuries of Christian history. Unable to venture into this vast field, this committee expresses its hope that discussions of the ordination of women will be carried on in close connection with discussions of the ministry and of ordination, and that concern for the former will strengthen concern for the latter.

Dogmatic considerations

The Bible views the persons of the Trinity as beyond the sphere of sex, which is fundamental only to human kind. This affirmation is specially clear for the person of Yahweh in the Old Testament who was carefully distinguished from the pagan background of gods and goddesses. But it is also true for the person of Jesus Christ, who is image of the new man (including men and women), and for the person of the Holy Ghost. Therefore, as the ministry is the announcement to the world of the trinitarian reality and work, we must renounce the argument in favour of the masculinity of ecclesiastical ministry on the basis of the fact that God is called Father or that Jesus Christ is incarnated as male. This argument was used neither in the biblical sources (e.g. by St. Paul or St. Peter) nor in the early tradition. It distorts the parabolic and symbolic language in which trinitarian formulas describe the divine mystery and identifies language with reality and thereby literalizes the action of the tri-une God; thus it obscures the soteriological purpose of the ministry as a function of the body of Christ by overstressing the significance of the sex of the minister as a person in the created order.

Sometimes it is said that the subordination of the woman to the man is inherent in the order of creation and that therefore it would be a violation of God's order of creation for a woman to take a public responsibility. Some biblical passages seem to indicate such an understanding of subordination, and it is rooted in Christian tradition. But it is doubtful that it can be maintained. The image of God is presented in the Bible as the coexistence of man and woman. They are called together to dominate the world of creation (Genesis 1, 2). Their relationship is to be understood as complementarity rather than as subordination. The more we are aware that the meaning of creation is disclosed by God's redemptive work in Christ, the more we realize that God created man and woman in partnership. It is true that Paul refers to Genesis 2 when he reminds the woman to be subordinated. But reading the New Testament as a whole it becomes clear that the first emphasis is laid on complementarity. It seems therefore evident that subordination does not belong to God's order of creation but is part of the good order in society commonly accepted in Paul's time.

In recent times there is in many churches a new emphasis laid on baptism as the consecration to a new life of witness and service to the world. This emphasis is to be seen in close connection with the calling of the whole people of God. It inevitably raises anew the question of the relation between baptism and the consecration to the special ministries in the Church. Many churches teach that ordination is a sacrament clearly to be distinguished from baptism; other churches consider ordination as a setting apart within the baptismal grace. However, all churches see a close relation between baptism and the ministry, and if it is true that baptism leads to participation in the ministry of the whole Church, explanation must be given on what grounds a baptized woman, who shares all the privileges given through baptism, can be excluded from the ordained ministry.

Many churches argue that the original apostolate was composed solely of men, that the ordained ministry of the Church is derived from and dependent upon the apostles, and that therefore the ordination of women would compromise the apostolic heritage of the Church. It is true that Jesus appointed twelve men as his apostles, and that the earliest Church did not nominate a woman to replace Judas, even though women had been eye-witnesses of the Lord's work and the first bearers of resurrection tidings. But the masculinity of the apostolate may be understood theologically more as a fulfillment of God's promise to Israel than as a divine law governing the future of the Church. In the twelve the structure of the old Israel, with its patriarchs and tribes, was represented and fulfilled. The apostolate brought the Old Covenant to its authentic consummation, so that Gentiles might share in the glory promised to Israel. (It may be noted that no Gentile was included among the apostles, although this fact has not excluded them from the Church's apostolicity.) At any rate, it is by no means clear that the preservation of an apostolic ministry should forever exclude women (or Gentiles) if there are cogent theological reasons for including them.

The ministry of the Church consists in the edification of the body of Christ in order to witness to the world through administering the sacraments and preaching God's word. It is to be doubted whether the New Testament offers sufficient theological support for drawing a sharp distinction between these two ministries and, e.g., allowing a woman to participate in all the church ministries with the exception of presiding over the Eucharist. Does it show any interest in the qualification of those who should administer the sacraments? It seems clear at least that St. Paul did not separate the sacramental from the non-sacramental ministry. He was far more concerned with the effectiveness of all the gifts of the Spirit in edifying the Church and in the reconciliation of the world.

Ecclesiastical life

Since it is impossible in the New Testament to obtain any concrete direction concerning the ordination of women other than the fact that they were not of the apostolic band, the question must be faced in view of a radically changed situation whether their exclusion from the ordained ministry rests upon divine law or upon human tradition. Some churches see divine law being promulgated through the tradition which has come down to them in the body of Christ. Others would question whether forms of ministry rightly belong to the tradition. There is therefore a call for a re-examination at this point of the value and content of ecclesiastical tradition. In this re-examination of their traditions and canon law, the churches should be aware both of the valid historical reasons for the shape of their old tradition and of the non-theological influences (such as out-dated patterns of sexual prejudice) which have entered all traditions.

The churches are faced today with the need to discover new forms of ministry to meet situations which did not confront them in the past. It is clear that women as well as men are called to take their place in these new forms of ministry which may differ considerably in form and function from any ministry the Church has yet known. It is the duty of the churches to seek such forms. In doing so, they may find that the ordination of women is the right response to new opportunities. This problem poses itself in most concrete terms in some of the younger churches.

The problems raised by the ordination of women are too new for the churches to have reached a common mind on this matter. This means that they will be acutely felt in the field of inter-church relations, especially where churches which take a more traditional view are contemplating union with churches which believe that in ordaining women they have been led by the Spirit. When the churches seriously face the theological issues involved, it is much to be hoped that whatever decision an individual church reaches there will be no accusation of heresy but that its decision will be accepted by others as a genuine effort to follow the guidance of the Holy Spirit.

Moreover, in reaching its own decision, each church should consider not only its obligation to its own members and its responsibility for avoiding internal schism but also its loyalty to all churches in all countries. All policies regarding the various ministries are ultimately subject to the authority of Him from whom the one Church has received its ministry as a gift. Each church accordingly must decide not only its own way of obedience, but must also determine its attitude towards the status of ministers in churches whose obedience has taken a different path. Each must make its decision in the freedom which Christ has given from the Law, in the love which will not cause others to stumble, and in hope for the consummation of God's kingdom on earth.

Possible points for discussion

Can it be said that

—churches face today a new situation with regard to the relationship of man and woman?

—all churches have insufficiently expressed the calling of the whole Church, and need to find new ways of expressing the sending of all church members, both men and women?

—the issue of the ordination of women concerns all the churches, those opposing change as well as those considering new steps?

—the biblical evidence does not speak either clearly in favour of, or against, admitting women to the full ministry?

—that biblical passages are always to be seen in their historical context and should be understood rather in their intention than in their literal content?

Can we agree that some arguments against admitting women to the ministry are invalid, e.g.:

—because God is father, only man can be ordained?

—because Christ chose only men as apostles, it would be against his will to include women in the apostolic ministry?

—the subordination of woman to man belongs to the order of creation?

Can we agree that the following points need to be re-examined by the churches:

—the relationship between baptism and ordination?

—the evidence of the New Testament, and especially of the Early Church, on the position of women in the Church?

Can we say that

—the churches recognize in charity the decisions taken in this matter by other churches?

—the churches opposing the ordination of women are obliged to rethink the position of women in general?

—the churches accepting such ordination without difficulties have to re-examine their understanding of the ministry in the Church?

Names of the participants at the Consultation

The Rev. Dr. Hans Thimme, Chairman;
Dr. Marga Bührig;
The Rev. H.R.T. Brandreth;
The Rev. Dr. André Dumas;

WCC Staff

Dr. Madeleine Barot;
The Rev. William H. Clark;
The Rev. Dr. Paul Minear;
The Rev. Father Paul Verghese;
The Rev. Dr. Lukas Vischer.

Notes: *Printed here is the foreword and first two chapters of the World Council of Churches' 1964 study, "Concerning the Ordination of Women." These sections highlight the particular role the World Council has played in the discussion of this issue, acting as a forum where global trends have been surveyed and different church polities have met. The World Council was created to facilitate ecumenical activities, and by the 1960s the fact that women were ordained in some churches and not in others began to block dialogue and strain relations. The council is not in a position to dictate a preferred stance, but helps churches consider issues in a world context.*

WORLD COUNCIL OF CHURCHES

EXCERPTS FROM "WHAT IS ORDINATION COMING TO?" (1970)

Introduction

The Consultation on the Ordination of Women, held in Cartigny near Geneva from September 21-26, 1970 under the auspices of the World Council of Churches was unique in the history of ecumenical encounters. The meeting brought together 25 participants from 6 continents representing 8 different traditions. They included Roman Catholics and one Orthodox Bishop. This conference was given its mandate in 1968 by the Uppsala Assembly, which stated:

> "(We) realise that the question of the admission of women to holy orders has been the subject of several studies. We urge that these be continued, especially taking into account the experience of the increasing number of churches which now ordain women, so that in the light of this experience there may be further theological reflection on the ecumenical implications of this development."

This volume contains the three reports from working groups. The Consultation voted to adopt the conclusions and recommendations, to be transmitted to the WCC member churches and to the WCC itself for action. Some papers that were presented to the Consultation have been included too.

Preparation and Planning

During the preparation for this Consultation a survey was sent to ordained women in order that we could obtain some of their experiences. The report of this survey is also included in the volume.

Several people from different cultural and denominational backgrounds were requested to prepare background material for this Consultation. A resumé of these papers has been made.

Fresh Perspective in the Churches

In the churches there is a discernible movement to take the ministries of women with greater seriousness. Now about 72 of the constituent churches of the WCC ordain women. Women who were pioneers in this field have fought through difficulties and won battles which have now made life easier for the next generation of ordained women. The eighteen women, seven of them ordained in their churches, confirmed this statement.

No church which has proceeded to the ordination of women has ever had cause to reconsider its decision. Rather the experience has been one of enrichment and greater adequacy in developing flexible forms of ministry. The actual experiences of such churches is of great importance, since so many forbodings are grounded merely in theoretical possibilities, untested by actual experience of the work of ordained women. It is important to note that there were still psychological and sociological problems affecting women differently in their cultures. Some of the American participants were affected by the climate and the strong impact of the women's liberation movement.

It became evident in our discussions that in all the churches the old barriers remain untouched because even after ordination women still had no opportunities for leadership and very few were involved in decision-making.

There was an agreement that theological arguments from scripture and tradition which were previously thought to be decisive are no longer able to sustain their traditional interpretations, which projected a subsidiary role for women in the scheme of creation and redemption. Instead, attention is given to mankind's basic oneness. It is male and female together who are made in the image of God.

The highlight of the Consultation was the closing High Mass according to the Liturgy of the Church of Sweden. All the members of the Consultation felt they could participate. The Orthodox Bishop, who did not receive the elements, pronounced the blessing at the close of the service. This was a moving experience to many of the consultants, especially those who had never received communion from a woman pastor.

Women's Rights and Roles in Different Cultures

To ask whether women should be ordained is not simply to ask whether there should be an *extension* of existing forms of ordination. It is to raise the whole question of the value of ministry and ordination as these have been known down the centuries. Preparatory papers . . . though not as representative of all backgrounds as we would have wished, indicate some of the questions being raised against different cultural backcloths.

Continuity: An Alternative Angle

A Canadian contribution looking to the same source, focused on the continuity of the *dynamic* of the Church itself, rather than on the continuity of a particular shape of authority:

> "On Easter Morn there were eleven men "set apart" (but surely not formally ordained to a Ministry of Word and Sacraments in the congregation), but there were no three-level ministries, no congregations, no "church" as we know it, no scriptures, no rituals, ecclesiastical structures, canons, or forms of any kind. All we have was one day proposed by or grew out of the needs of a particular situation in a particular age as something "new"—was examined prayerfully, tested theologically, and, under God, judged to be "good" for its time; thus did tradition grow and continuity become established. In every age God is in His Church to reform it—reformation is an on-going process. Under that process the Church has discarded surely as much as it has kept."

Public Attitudes

In Finland, a swing in social and in church congregational attitudes pressured the Church into re-examining the conception of ministry as a whole and, in particular, the ministry of women theologians:

> "According to a Gallup-inquiry in the beginning of 1970, public opinion has clearly changed and is taking a more positive swing towards the ordination of women. In 1958 the supporters of the ordination of women numbered 44% and the opponents 34%. Now, the corresponding figures are 66% and 12%."

An African contribution points out that it is not African traditions but Western traditions which offer a stumbling-block:

> "In view of the place that African traditional life gives to women especially in religion, one often wonders if the apathy in some of the 'prophet' movements towards the priesthood of women is not more an influence from their mother churches than from African religion and African way of life. If this is true, then as soon as the Mission Churches which are the parent bodies of the 'prophet' movements adopt a more concrete and concerted attitude towards the ordination of women, many of their seceded groups constituting the 'prophet' movements may also rethink their stand on the question of the ordination of women." Further contributions also ascribe the low rating of women in the Historic Churches in Africa to *imported* Western assumptions about women's place.

Images and Stereotypes

Part of the difficulty which people in many cultures have to contend with, to get the ordination of women even considered seriously, is the image people already have firmly fixed in their minds. A contribution from Korea makes it clear that there exist not only stereotypes of the "good religious man", but of the "good religious woman". The legend of the "Bible Women" illustrates this:

> "Bible Women" was a name given to a group of ladies who played important roles, especially in the field of evangelical ministry, in the early days of Christianity in Korea. These ladies worked devoutly for the Church; their sole concern was concentrated on serving God and spreading the Gospel. Personal security or personal welfare was of no concern for them. They lived poorly and walked around in old-style dresses and shoes. Eventually, the devout attitude and the old-style appearance became the historical symbol of women church workers. However, young girls of today can no longer accept the ideal of the "pious looking" Bible Women.
>
> On the other hand, aged people who occupy the majority of the church pews still cherish the image of the "Bible Women" in the old days; and they are not sure whether they can give due respect to young girls fresh from the Seminaries. Therefore, churches are often hesitant to appoint young seminary graduates to the important positions in the Church. This situation diminishes job opportunities."

Over against this, a Swiss contribution suggests that there is something behind traditional stereotypes; but that it does not imply the superiority-inferiority interpretation so often instinctively given:

> "If the Christian Church regards man's activity and intelligence as the only elements needed for building up society, it will fail to avail itself of the great contribution which women have been quietly making to the Church for many centuries. It is the element of *community* which women have always created in the family and in the home. If more attention were paid to this gift, many situations would become more humanized. The gift which women possess of creating contacts must be recognized as an essential element in the building up of society. Women must be regarded essentially as building stones for creating community in the Church."

From Finland it is observed that changes in the social image of different types of work produce change in their instinctive classification as male or female:

> "The image of a profession, and not its tasks, determines if it is regarded as a male or female profession. Many religious groups have already long ago accepted women as preachers, but not as leaders of worship. . . .
>
> In the background there may be an identification phenomenon. To many persons a clergyman represents the authority of father and mother in a family. A pastor's role may be based especially on the father-identification.
>
> However, society has already been secularized to the extent that the pastor hardly any more represents an object of identification. Also the mixing of roles in the modern family has influenced the matter. It is no longer clear that father and mother images in the family can be distinguished, at least not according to the sex.

The Canadian paper, noting the dramatic change in the position of women in society and in the home, suggests that the Church is allowing itself to be landed with an image of mere obsolescence:

> "This has led and lends increasingly to the demand in society for equal rights in employment and complete acceptance for the woman "worker" in Western society, which, left unheeded by the Church, gives it the appearance of holding on to the status quo of an era now past - an image it does not need. This should then lead to a more open approach on the part of all denominations to the question of opening the ordained (or unordained as it may be) ministry of the Church to both men and women."

Influences of Culture and Tradition

In African culture the 'prophet' movements have provided elements of spontaneity which have given room for movement in traditions which might otherwise be too inflexible:

> Mbiti remarks (*African Religions and Philosophy*) "There are in their own ways attempts by African people to 'indigenize' Christianity and apply it in ways that perhaps spontaneously render Christianity both practical and meaningful to them." If, therefore, the 'prophet' movements in black Africa are a deliberate attempt by traditional Africans themselves to make an impinging culture (i.e. Christianity, a rather happy coincidence for our purpose) meaningful and relevant to them, then the Christian Church in thinking out the question of the ordination of women, cannot make light of the view of these movements on this vital issue as a whole, more particularly in the African context."

Several contributions on African society speak both of the status that women have had; and of the barrier of "uncleanness" considered to exist as long as menstruation takes place:

> "In certain African tribes women have always had great influence. Among the Lovedu of the Transvaal the Rain Queen ruled. The Ashanti and the Swazi are amongst those tribes where women were traditionally dominant. Many societies were matrilineal or matriarchal. In West Africa women who trade successfully in the market often become richer than their husbands, and have considerable influence. The majority of tribes, it is true, were patriarchal and polygamy was practised. A woman could not inherit property. Men, not women, made up the Elders' Council, and led the religious ceremonies. Yet in a polygamous society women were held in respect; their status was assured. In some societies they were consulted, as diviners or prophetesses, not unlike the O.T. prophetess Deborah, and others."

Whereas, among the Kikuyu

> "If women were permitted to participate in the offering of the sacrifice, which was a lamb of a certain colour, they were only women beyond childbearing age, and so considered to be immune from worldly mischief, and regarded as mothers not of individuals, but of the community."

This new potential status of women produced by the menopause is mentioned several times. In fact, they even dress like men, said one report.

Non-Theological Factors

Sometimes an anticipation of practical difficulties rules out of court a serious consideration of the possibility of ordaining women in some parts of Latin America.

> "The Methodist Church of Brazil does not have women pastors. . . . Evidently the Church has not yet had the opportunity of gaining experience in this matter, and its objections therefore concern the problem of residence, the problem of the femininity of women, which renders them incapable of facing certain situations peculiar to the pastoral ministry, and other problems of a practical nature.
>
> Peru has had two women deaconesses (parish assistants) who had carried out a full pastoral ministry, but in spite of this experience, there are no ordained women pastoral ministers in Peru. The attitude of the Church is nonetheless favourable, particularly as a result of the good work done by the women just mentioned. There has been no discussion in this country as to the theological arguments for or against the pastoral ministry of women, and there exist only practical considerations which in some circumstances might create difficulties, such as maternity, attitude or occupation of the husband, care of the household, transfers, etc."

In other parts of that continent there seems to be promise of progress but the speed of change is a snail's pace:

> "In Argentina there is one woman pastor, but the attitude of the congregations and of the Church itself is still somewhat reserved. It is felt there that this ministry is still rather new and that conditions are therefore not yet ripe for passing judgment on such a service. There are no discussions in Argentina on this account, nor are there objections on theological grounds, and those of a practical nature come from persons who have not yet freed themselves from certain social prejudices of another epoch.
>
> In Uruguay there is one woman pastor. The attitude toward this ministry in the interior of the country has not given rise to any difficulty. In Hontevideo, on the other hand, there has been an atmosphere of waiting, I would even go so far as to say surprise, but certainly no resistance. The Church authorities have always given stimulus to this ministry."

In some cases the road is cleared for the ordination of women in principle, but suspected practical difficulties have blocked the way to implementation:

> "The Valdensian Church of Rio de la Plata, following a year of postponement, during the course of which the problem was studied, gave its approval to women ministers, in close liaison with the Valdensian Church of Italy, at the District Conference held in Argentina in March 1963. . . . Yet women who are in this situation (i.e. equipped) right now in Uruguay have still not been ordained. . . . The strongest arguments have referred to family difficulties, to the problem of movement, that is to say, nocturnal visits, worship and meetings. . . ."

The fear of a feminized church was seen to be at the root of some male attitudes. A paper from Switzerland probes behind such reactions:

> "It is certainly a fact that men (both simple and educated men) often manifest such reactions, when they think they see any threat to their own unquestioned superiority. But this aggressive attitude must be understood as such. Men of the younger generation have already learnt how to cooperate with women much better, in many ways. But women also have difficulty in accepting such cooperation based on equal status. For centuries they have been man's "helpmates", who adapted themselves to him. They have learnt to be man's "*anima*" figure (as C.G. Jung calls it). A long process of maturity is required in order to grow out of this role and to become a conscious, independent personality. . .. For this reason women are needed as pastors who have achieved this inward maturity, and who can help other women to develop into complete personalities."

The lowly social position of women in some societies is simply reproduced in church order.

> "There are no women pastors in Bolivia. . . . The Church in general does not look upon this ministry with much favour. But this attitude, once again, is not due to certain theological or practical considerations but rather to social ones, as women in this country occupy a position far inferior to men."

In other societies where this has once been true, a change has been taking place. By virtue of educational opportunity previously denied them, women are assuming quite new responsibilities and assuming positions of leadership:

> "Today African society is in an in-between stage. One of the most fascinating aspects of modern East Africa is the emergence of a highly educated female elite. Their number is small but their achievements in daily life, as well as on the national level, deserve great esteem. Most of them have been born into a traditional rural family, have overcome the severe obstacle of their environment, reached a high educational level, (often an academic degree at an East African or overseas university) and stand out in professional life, being by no means inferior to men in energy, intelligence, efficiency and idealism. Their lives are characterized by a multiplicity of roles and tasks; they manage demanding urban households, including the care and education of the children, they have responsible, mostly full-time jobs,

social obligations deriving from their husbands' and their own professional positions, and, additionally, most of them are engaged in some voluntary activities in the service of 'nation building'.

Because there are relatively few educated women, all those who are educated and well-trained become involved in a multiplicity of activities wherever their participation is required."

Leadership Roles

Where, in parts of Africa, women assume positions of leadership in religious movements, this is often the reassertion of a prophetic role which once characterized their tribal tradition. It is in conflict with, rather than an interpretation of, forms of Christianity imported from the West. Thus it is said:

> "First we note that a considerable number of the Independent Churches in Africa have been started by women, Legio Maria in Kenya, Mai Chaza in Umtali, and the Lumpa Church in Zambia, have each been started by women. For others which have been founded by women see D. Barrett "Schism & Renewal in Africa", p. 148.
>
> Both Marie-Louise Martin and Dorothy Lehman make the point that if the 'Historic' Churches had adopted a more liberal attitude towards women like Mai Chaza and Alice Lenshina, the churches might have gained much, and the wrong teaching that followed in the churches they established might have been prevented.
>
> D. Barrett notes an interesting point in regard to separatist movements, "From the Montanist movement onwards, the history of enthusiasm is largely a history of female emancipation." He remarks also "Women in independent churches have come into a prestige and authority that they never knew in their parent bodies." D. Lehman refers to women in Independent Churches of the Zionist type who are ordained and who administer the sacraments."

Within the historic churches themselves in Africa, where they cannot be effectively run by men, women step forward and do the needful:

> "Churches in rural areas are often made up three-quarters of women. In some rural areas 'Historic' Churches are 'run' by women. True, a man lay-reader or elder preaches and leads the service, but the women 'run' the Church. "We do the work the men do not like. We raise the money, we visit the sick, we cater for special functions, providing the tea, the food. We do not shout; we just keep quiet. Men like to feel superior; we let them feel so". So a great deal turns on the women. In this way women have a very great influence; when women challenge or rival the men in positions of leadership it can lead to conflict."

These remarks were made by leading women, members of their churches, each one active in society in Nairobi today. It is clear they recognize they have power now, although they let the men feel superior and important. This same group feels that women should be 'more to the fore' in the 'Historic' Churches. They should be ordained, having had an appropriate training, and they should preach and lead services. Each knew of women who preach now and are said to be well accepted. (It was interesting to learn that two African Roman Catholic Sisters preach regularly). More women should be on Church Committees from Parish level up to highest Synod or equivalent Councils.

This point is expanded and developed in another contribution from Africa:

> "In the religious sphere both men and women are ritual specialists. Parrinder observes in his *African Traditional Religion* that women may be "mediums or devotees who are 'possessed' with the spirit of a god or ancestor" and that the "majority are women". . . . Above all, African women are priestesses. For instance among the Dogon of the Sudan and the Ewe of West Africa priestesses are as prominent as priests in performing religious ceremonies. As a result Parrinder in his

> work already cited, categorically states "The Psychic abilities of women have received recognition and scope to a much greater degree in African religion than they have in Islam and Christianity where they are still barred from the priesthood. African priestesses may work in conjunction with men like the Hebrew prophetesses Hulda and Anna and they may have complete charge of a sanctuary like Deborah to which men as well as women may come."

> "Harold Turner makes a reference in his work on the Church of the Lord (Aladura) to the ministry of women in that group. He says that a woman can supercede a man in the ministerial hierarchy because "If both husband and wife are trained ministers the senior of the two in the ministry says benediction in worship even if she should be the wife." Some other of the movements which have no ministry of women, give great prominence to women in the running of their groups: for instance The Eden Revival Church and The Faith Praying Brotherhood Circle in Ghana."

In my view the instances cited above from both African traditional life and the 'prophet' movements suggest that the question of the inferiority of women in African thought and life is much exaggerated. For instance, we have discovered that in practically all African societies women can be religious leaders discharging the duties of ritual or sacred specialists. They may even rank higher in importance than their male counterparts. At an important point in the cult of the ancestors among the Ashanti of Ghana the chief, as the officiating ritual specialist, cannot proceed with the rites if the Queen Mother is not present. Among the Southern Ewe people of West Africa, it is the prerogative of female ritual specialists only to particularize a reincarnated ancestor and perform the principal reincarnation rite.

Because of the place of religion in African societies, an accepted leadership must be religiously founded. In other words, the voice of God automatically becomes the voice of the people. The leader must have a charisma in Max Weber's sense, for instance. The leader in African concept is voluntarily respected, accepted and followed because of the source of that element in the authority - the SACRED - which he now wields. Once this happens, leadership in Africa is accepted without question, be the leader a man or a woman. Without this African concept of leadership, women like Alice Lenshina cannot have such large support at least from men.

The ordained are set apart because of the relation that their contact with the super-natural now confers on them. But this does not put them in a class that makes them feel unnecessarily superior to others. It is only when the priests and priestesses are discharging their sacral duties that they are 'other' because essentially they are not regarded as themselves in that state but the super-natural himself so to speak. However, usually it is hard to tell ritual specialists and other members of society apart when they are engaged in activities other than religious.

Disabilities Suffered

The Pressure to Remain Single

The pressures on ordained women to remain unmarried amounts to a severe handicap. In Korea:

> "Generally, each year, seven to eight women receive their B.Th. degree from the Methodist Seminary after completing four years' theological studies and training in practical fields of ministry. However, most of these seminary graduates are quite hesitant to proceed with the programme for ordination. Some seminary graduates choose to become ministers' wives rather than to become ministers themselves. This actually seems to provide opportunities for those who want to marry and also use their education and training. Some other graduates get jobs in schools and offices of Christian institutions. Only one or two graduates are admitted to positions assisting in local churches."

In Latin America, restrictions are implicitly imposed in some instances, and thoughtful arrangements made in others:

> "Although it is true that in none of these countries must women take vows of celibacy in order to be ordained in the pastoral ministry, in Chile they are not allowed to pursue their ministry following marriage, whereas in Uruguay marriage does not put an end to the eclesiastical ministry. The Methodist Church of Uruguay always favours a desire on the part of women pastors to become 'localized' following marriage, that is, to give up the itinerant ministry practised in the Methodist Church but to retain the possibility of remaining in a given city in which to carry out their ministry."

The Finnish report says:

> "In the Church you can perceive . . . a latent demand for celibacy. It concerns all workers of the Church, but it is most clearly felt in regard to women. The image of an ideal servant of the Church is that of a person having no private life."

Inequality in Finance and Decision-Making Opportunities

Expectation of the celibacy of ordained women is related to finance in many parts of the world. The Finnish report states:

> "The latent expectation of celibacy is also to be observed in the stipulations where the privileges of the office of lectors differ from those of the ministry of men. Both have the same salary, but the housing provision of a lector is smaller than that of a pastor. Lectors are expected to live within the territory of the congregation, but sometimes they are provided with a residence which is too small for a family.
>
> Furthermore, "equal pay" is not reached, because lectors' positions are not placed in the same category as the highest paid pastors' vacancies, e.g. those of the pastors in charge of vicars in congregations."

From Korea it is reported:

> "Another serious problem that discourages women participants in the church ministry is the economic treatment, which is quite unfair. Women ministers are paid about one half of the salary that men minister get, even when the women have equal education and experience doing the same kind of work. The usual excuse for the lower pay is that women ministers are single and can live with less money. But actually the pay they get is insufficient even to provide for sufficient life necessities and tools for their vocation, such as books and periodicals, etc.

From Latin America comes the following:

> "In the three South American countries where there are women pastors, that is, Chile, Argentina and Uruguay, they receive the same salary as men, but according to a report received from Chile, there is a marked difference between the situation in that country and in Uruguay. It is interesting to note that, although the Valdensian Church has accepted the pastoral ministry of women and has given women the same opportunity as men to answer the call of God to perform a similar service, there is a decided difference in the salaries received by men and women. Although equality exists as regards rights, opportunities and responsibilities, men are paid higher salaries for the exercise of similar functions."

The point is frequently made that women are kept out of representative positions and positions of responsibility in the structures of the churches, even when the status for some individual women is advanced. Thus the Korean paper says:

> "It is recognized that women members are a great working force sustaining the Church. . .. However, there is little representation by women at conferences or

> national assemblies, although churches have a higher membership of women than men."

After an examination of the position of women in the historic churches in Africa, one background paper goes on to say:

> "The writer has no figures, but knows that only one or two women are members of Synod/'top' committees. But six years ago there was not one woman preaching or leading worship, and it is only in the last 3-4 years that African women have taken on from missionaries in 'woman's work'.
>
> We see then that women are *beginning* to take a part in leading services, in preaching, assisting at Holy Communion, and also in 'top' committees."

Latin America offers one clear instance of where practice caught up with theory:

> "Since 1920, the Methodist Church has had women who have exercised a full pastoral ministry. Yet they did not become members of the Annual Conference, like their masculine colleagues. However, since the Conference of May 1956, this distinction based on sex has been completely eliminated, and women now enjoy an equal status with men in the ministry of this Church."

On the same continent, an instance of complete equality, and a matching of status in society with status in the Church is noted:

> "In Chile at present there are women pastors each of whom is in charge of a parish, their pastoral duties being carried out in the cities. In this country we find that the social, political and legal status of women, as well as their position in the Church is identical to those of men. Women have access to the pastoral ministry, with all the responsibilities, opportunities, and privileges of man. The attitude of the congregation toward such a ministry is really favourable, owing in particular to the excellent work which has been accomplished there."

New Forms of Ministry

The paper from Switzerland points to new expressions of the life of the Church not only in traditional ways but in "new service-groups" and in "mission-cells" and notes that:

> "Special posts are being created side by side with that of the pastor, and all these people are cooperating in building up parish life."

It would appear that there is more hope for a full use of the gifts of women through the growth of a variety of forms of ministry than through the creation of special posts such as "lector".

A new form of ministry which was described in some detail was that of Lector in the Evangelical Lutheran Church of Finland. The following paragraphs describe some of the main features of this special form of ministry brought into being to accommodate women:

> "The lectors are mainly responsible for the work among women and youths and also for instruction at confirmation schools. In addition to these tasks the lectors are active in many sectors of parish work. . . .
>
> When estimating their own work the women theologians seem to be very unsatisfied. 60% of them are of the opinion that they spend too much time on the inner groups of the parishes. They want to search for new possibilities for meeting and serving people outside the traditional forms of parish activity. Especially they want more possibilities for pastoral care, for group and case work, for activities in the form of discussions and lectures on contemporary themes, building contacts with groups outside the congregations, e.g. with secular women's organizations. They also want to plan a training project for the congregation in order that a great part of the work may be led by laymen.

Ordination is not considered to be a cure-all or even an advantage:

> Many theologians are afraid of ordination, as it would mean undertaking all traditional pastors' duties. The image of the clergyman making continually speeches has no attraction. After ordination the women theologians would not have the same freedom as they have now for developing their own work and for specializing in the obligations that they feel to be important. Also the image of ordination as giving some special characteristics to the ordained person can unconsciously cause hesitation. It would perhaps mean losing one's own personality and freedom, and isolation from other people. Very often the lectors say that they don't like to have any ordination because they want to remain ''ordinary people''. . . .

Group Reports

Report of Group 1

1. *The discussion on the ordination of women to the ministry has changed.*

   The approach to the problem is now very different. In the last few years the atmosphere has changed. A number of new elements have entered the picture. The most important are the following:

   a. The number of churches which ordain women to the ministry has considerably increased. While in 1960 a few member churches of the World Council of Churches were ready to ordain women to any of their ministries the figure has reached in 1970 ca. 70. Some churches have opened new areas of ministry to women.

   b. The question has become an issue of serious discussion in a larger number of traditions, while in 1960 in some traditions the question had not even been considered. In theological discussion this is particularly true for the Roman Catholic church (cf. resolution 12 of the Congress of Theologians at Brussels). The Lambeth Conference in 1968 asked for consultations with other churches.

   c. In view of the tradition of the church, previously theological arguments from scripture and tradition have been used negatively but now the weight of the theological arguments in favour of the ordination of women is strongly felt. In an increasing number of churches the burden of proof is with those who are opposed to the ordination rather than with those who affirm its appropriateness and necessity.

   d. The argument has often been used that a change of practice with regard to the ordination of women would threaten the growing unity among the churches. Churches wanting to introduce the ordination of women were advised not to create a new reason of division. This argument has lost much of its significance. Though it is still felt to be relevant (e.g. R.C. Church and Orthodox) it is more and more recognised that the ordination does not necessarily threaten the cohesion of the ecumenical fellowship. As the ecumenical movement claims to be a movement of renewal the churches engaged in it must be prepared to face change and to respect the decisions of other churches.

2. *Why has the nature of the discussion changed?*

   It is not sufficient to note these changes. The question must be asked: why have they occurred in this relatively short time? It is impossible to give an exhaustive picture. The following aspects may be underlined:

   a. There has been in recent years a more radical emphasis on renewal and the necessity of change in the church. Only a few years ago the reference to the need of unbroken continuity with the past carried more weight than today.

   b. All patterns of ministry are being challenged by the development of the contemporary society. Ministers are fulfilling more and more functions they were not originally ordained for. They are fulfilling tasks which are also fulfilled by women though the women have not been ordained. The distinction between ordained and unordained becomes unclear.

c. The experience of churches in which women are ordained is generally positive. None of these churches has found any reason to reconsider its decision.

d. Probably even more important than all these reasons is the fact that the understanding and the experience of the relationship of men and women has further changed in many societies. There is less importance attached to preconceived images of the role to be fulfilled by either men or women. It has become more and more a matter of course that women may fulfill the role of leadership.

3. *Weight of argument in favour of ordination increasingly felt.*

Obviously, the different confessional backgrounds play a significant role in determining the approach to the question of ordination of women. There is growing consensus that many of the theological arguments which have been used in the past do not carry real weight. Where the churches differ on the question it is mainly because of their different theological attitude to the Tradition. Churches which hesitate ask: Is it not necessary to maintain in this respect the unbroken continuity with the apostolic times? Does the pattern of the ministry constitute part of the Tradition which must be kept unchanged or can change be introduced? We notice three attitudes:-

a. The attitude represented by the Orthodox Church: Owing to the normative character of tradition, the Orthodox Church does not raise the problem of a reconsideration of the accession of women to the priesthood. But this does not imply, as historical evidence suggests, that women must necessarily be excluded from all kinds of ministry in the church.

b. According to the attitude represented by the Roman Catholic Church the question is being reopened. Up till the 20th Century the Roman Catholic Church expressed her position on the place of women in the church in Canon Law, ''*Solum mas est subjectum ordinationis*''. Theologians gave the following arguments:-

In the New Testament the ministry of *episcopoi* and *presbuteroi* is given only to men and never to women;

Tradition is against the ordination of women to the episcopate and presbyterate;

Ratio Theologica: Bishops and priests are called to represent Christ—the bridegroom—towards the community His bride.

In the last few decades among a number of Catholic thinkers (especially but not only women) there has been growing criticism of the traditional view. They refer to Paul's doctrine that in Christ ''there is no male and female, but you are all one person in Christ Jesus'' (Gal. 3:28). Several theologians have re-examined the traditional doctrine, not least in the light of experience and developments in other churches. The background of this re-examination is the fresh approach in Roman Catholic theology to the question of the relation of scripture and tradition, and a more dynamic ecclesiology.

c. According to a third attitude represented by the Reformed Churches the change came about both by a fresh understanding of the biblical revelation as well as a new appreciation of the way in which the Holy Spirit guides the Church today. There is a growing difficulty in refusing ordination to women simply on biblical and theological grounds.

Among Anglican and other Christian Churches a variety of attitudes can be found but everywhere there is the same tension between the tradition against the ordination of women and a new questioning of the validity of this attitude.

4. *Positive Considerations for the Ordination of Women.*

a. *The basic oneness of man and woman in creation and redemption*—According to the doctrine of creation, man, homo, in the duality of male and female, is made in the image of God, i.e. neither man alone nor woman alone.

   In the order of redemption, this relationship is re-affirmed in the dealings of Jesus with men and women alike giving them new personal identity and dignity.

b. *The significance of Baptism*—Both men and women, by virtue of their baptism, are engrafted into Christ and called to be members of His body. This means that all baptised persons share in the royal priesthood of the Church. When considering the pluriform and differentiated ministries based on the total priesthood of the body there is no theological reason for introducing barriers at this point on grounds of sex.

c. *The Calling of women to the historic ordained ministry*—The fact is that in an increasing number of churches some women believe themselves to have been called and this call has been ratified by the Church and sealed in ordination. In other churches women believe themselves to have been so called and are asking to have this call tested. This is a new factor which does not question the past working of the Holy Spirit, but requires a new obedience from the churches.

d. *The Wholeness of the Church*—The health and effective functioning of the body require the full and free participation of all the members. This is also true within the ministry which is maimed without the participation of women.

e. *Sociological factors*—In view of sociological developments which have in many cases outpaced the Church, the Church may be in danger of bearing witness to, or even perpetuating, a past concept of freedom now overtaken by events. Rather, the Church may discern in sociological movement the working of the Holy Spirit.

5. *Partial Solutions*—The question would be clouded by discussing only that part of the ministry thought to be suitable for women, e.g. the diaconate, orders of women, lectors. Rather, the question must be posed whether there is *any* function in the Church which cannot be fulfilled as well by men as by women.

   To allow unordained women to exercise functions normally fulfilled by ordained men is questionable.

   On the other hand, it may be that in the providence of God a forward movement may come through such anomalous situations, or *experiments*, if the Church is willing to face the realities of the situation and change her law *ex post facto*.

6. *The discussion of the ordination of women occurs when ordination itself is being questioned in many churches.*

   Creative thinking about ordination has been encouraged by what has been called by some, the eschatological aspect of the church and by others the need to think with the future always in mind, with the mark of hope always predominant. Our conviction is that the church of our grand-children is as important as the church of our grand-fathers. The church is something given once and for all and it is also moving towards fullness, a realisation of itself as one and holy and apostolic. This is a dynamic view in contrast to a static view; it has enabled the thinkers of the Vatican II Council to be loyal to the tradition of their Church and at the same time to give a positive value to other Christian churches.

   This fresh approach has consequences for the doctrine of the ministry. The major changes in thinking about ordination in the last 10 years have been seen in the emphasis on the Church as People of God, the ministry of all Christian people, called by some 'the priesthood of all believers', stress on the ministry of the laity as well as the clergy, and great concern for a variety of ministries, in which the ministry of the full-time parish priest is seen as one among many, not as normative for all. Radical changes in society have led to radical changes in the practice of ministry, such as group ministries and specialist ministries.

The ordination of women, if accepted today, would be within a church whose understanding and practice of its ministry is developing. The ordination of women would further this development. The comment of the Lambeth Conference in this context is apt, "The New Testament does not encourage Christians to think that nothing should be done for the first time." (Lambeth Conference Report, 1968, p. 106). The Ministry of the whole people of God could be immensely strengthened if women were enabled to share the task, equally with men. It is our experience that when churches, even at cost to established customs, make one change in what they believe to be obedience to the will of God, renewal of life by the Spirit may follow in other areas as well.

The present crisis in the failure of men to offer for ordination in many though not in all countries has been suggested as a reason against ordaining women at the present moment. Is the question of the ordination of women yesterday's question? We do not think so for the reasons set out elsewhere in this report and also because we believe that in the development of the practice and understanding of ministry, women will have an essential role. The Church which seeks to be the people of God, a sacrament or sign of His work in the world must be a body where there is full cooperation between men and women. Today this is only possible if the ordination of women is permitted.

Taking into account these arguments and in the context of developing thought about the Church and its ministry, the ordination of women should be seen as one mark of dynamic renewal. Education of all members of the church is necessary if divisive controversies are to be avoided and changes accepted with goodwill. We believe that the ordination of women may be a part of the joyful renewal to which we are called.

Report of Group II.

Psychological and Sociological Factors in the Ordination of Women

Introduction

The task of our section was to articulate the experiences, joys and difficulties of women who are ordained, in a world and a church where vigorous processes of renewal and change are offering new opportunities of service to both men and women. To this end we have received through written case-histories and personal sharing of experience much factual material, and have considered elements which appear to be common in various parts of the church and the world.

It is a source of joy that all the women serving in ordained ministries have spoken of the deep satisfaction they have found in their work. We have heard evidence from Sweden, France, Africa, Scotland, Germany, the United States of America, Switzerland, New Zealand and South America, among other countries, that women are exercising adventurous and creative ministries in many fields. They serve as parish pastors, chaplains in prisons, hospitals, industrial missions and universities, in youth leadership, in missionary enterprise to affluent city suburbs and African communities. They hold responsible posts in education and administration, and have clearly demonstrated their competence in these and other areas.

Nevertheless, it is also clear that very often they have had a long struggle for the right to serve, and that particularly the first generation of women ordained to the ministry in every church has had serious difficulties to overcome.

One important fact not always recognised is that many of the problems thought to be attached to the ordination of women, are in reality common to all women living in a rapidly changing world, especially to those in professions; and many are common to the ministry in general, male and female. The intimate relation that exists between the church and society is seen in the reflections of social change in the churches. There are changes in the Church that affect the nature of the ministry in general as well as the ministry of women. In addition there are experiences common to all members of the community, or to all professions, or to any particular category of persons, such as pioneers and innovators.

Changes in Society

One of the chief marks of the age in which we live is the pervasiveness of change in almost every part of the world society and every sector of most societies. Many of these changes are very important for the human condition, but have less significance for the ordination of women. We identify those which have particular relevance to the topic.

The tide of rising expectations for life is clearly moving in all races, among the poor in many societies, and is being evidenced among women. No racial group seems content with second-class citizenship even when their position is better than that of a sector elsewhere. Not content with visions, the depressed and oppressed are beginning to see that they can force change.

The women of the churches have also experienced these rising expectations and increased their demands. At the same time other social and technical developments are combining to bring about a radical alteration in views of human sexuality. Analyses of this sexual revolution are abundant. The implications for the ordination of women are a part of the social scene and are important factors bringing the issue to the fore in a fresh way.

The challenges to nearly every form and locus of established authority are another significant societal development. The churches have not escaped the demands for participation in governance by the repressed segments of the community. The challenge to established authority by the request of women for the rite of ordination is at the heart of the problems which are the concern of this consultation. The powers that have repressed women in general are particularly challenged by the ordination of women, even where ordination is requested in order that women may serve where their vocation calls them to serve.

Finally, major upheavals in many social structures are of immediate relevance for the ordination of women. For example, structural changes in families due to changes in life style, family size and life expectancy, free many women from family duties during the years of their greatest vigour and competence. Work place, reward, and duration immediately affect economic structures and the work of men and women. Some of the factors that appear to be associated with the ordination of women are actually the impact of these and other social changes. It is inevitable that these changes will also be involved with pressures for and of the ordination of women. But even where women are not ordained and continue to be more or less repressed, the resisting social group will have to cope with such change. Further, we feel that the Church and the churches are impoverished and handicapped in becoming fully Christ's Church as long as half (and more!) of its constituency is treated as less than full members and citizens.

Church - Pressure or Reflection?

In society, as we have noted, change is occurring all the time. In the Church we too often find change occurs only as a result of pressure from outside. Too often, the Church, having resisted change, is regarded as irrelevant to the needs of the people. Those members of the Church who are engaged in the life and witness of their church are keenly aware of tension here.

People involved in the pressures of business, labour processes and material aspects of life are feeling increasingly aware of need for a spiritual dimension which may lead to clarification of the meaning of life. This groping is sometimes revealed in small groups and cells seeking to find new ways of radical obedience to the gospel. If the Church is to respond to and be enriched by such groups, its rigid structures of the past must be opened up, and movements towards unity welcomed.

The last decade or two have seen an exciting rediscovery of the theological concept of the Church as the whole people of God, and influences commonly thought of as democratic are seen at work here. Within the existing church leadership, the people of God or 'laos' experience increasing frustration. It is felt by the 'laos' as a whole, but in particular by women who frequently find a great discrepancy between the attitudes of the secular world and of the Church. In an increasing number of areas of secular society they may enter positions of full responsibility, whereas in the structures of the church they still experience male domination almost everywhere. In many branches of the church the chairmanship and membership of committees are mainly male. Churches need to show a greater readiness to enable and encourage women to take their full share of responsibility in all areas of church and community life.

Ministry

As has been said above, many of the difficulties of a woman minister are not peculiar to her, but are common to the ministry in general. As a consequence of the changing task of the Church today, the task of the minister becomes more complicated. Both ministers and congregations need to help each other to perceive the new demands being made on them, and what the role of the minister should be.

Increased opportunities of specialisation and team ministry offer new and fascinating challenges to ministers who do not find themselves suited to parish work. The traditional expectations of a congregation have often forced the minister into a role he did not wish to fill. Here a woman pastor may be at an advantage, because often the congregation does not have such clear ideas of what her role may be. It is to be hoped that in the future both men and women will be more able to work according to their own talents and interests, and to develop a ministry of service which extends their personal capacities.

All ministers face crises of identity both in the beginning of their work and during the whole period of their ministry. It is recognised that some people may have entered the ministry for wrong reasons - men and women alike. Motives could include unworthy ideals of priesthood, power seeking, and the contest of the sexes: women wanting to reach a position they do not have, and men to hold privileges they have because of their sex. We believe it is important for all ministers to have the opportunity of working through their questions and difficulties with professional assistance, to enable them to see their own particular gifts and weaknesses.

A woman minister may encounter curiosity, uncertainty and even suspicion to a greater degree than a man both from parishioners and male colleagues. Much depends on her own personality and ability to cope with these stresses, particularly in the early stages of her ministry.

Some of the stress arises from the fact that questions of marriage and celibacy may be even more acute for her in many societies than for her male colleagues. Few churches, it seems, legally require their ordained women to remain single, and in some marriage and leave over the child-bearing period are straightforward. Others in fact make it very difficult for a woman to marry and exercise her ministry. It is recognised that it is not a simple question of whether celibacy is mandatory or not, but we believe hidden pressures should not be exerted on women as such. Both men and women may consider themselves to have a vocation to celibacy, but we do not believe it should be compulsory for either. While marriage presents certain practical difficulties for a woman in some positions in the church, particularly perhaps in a parish rather than in specialist fields, the single person has other problems to resolve in order to become a mature personality.

Why ordination?

We have observed that the societies we live in are still organised by the ideas and principles of men. But it is being realised in a growing way that women are people (human beings) as well as men!

It is essential for the Church to demonstrate to the world the oneness of the Body of Christ by including women equally in the ordained ministry. Therefore the churches have to take seriously the fact that women as well as men believe themselves to be called by God to the ministry. We may even see the work of the Holy Spirit in the pressures of various kinds, inside and outside the churches, offering plenty of opportunity for all kinds of ministries of ordained women.

We are well aware of the splendid service given in the past by women in various orders and ministries. But these ministries have also been the source of much frustration both to the women themselves personally and in pastoral relationships, because they were always subordinate and secondary.

If we believe both men and women are called in their baptism to be full members of the people of God, then the ordination of women to the full ministry is essential as a sign and a consequence of this wholeness.

Specific factors.

Women who are ordained suffer from the fact that they live in a church and society which for hundreds of years has been patriarchal. In that pattern they feel they have only a limited place and fixed role, and to find a new identity they must push against high walls. Very often they sense attitudes of unconscious superiority among men, especially when, as by ordination, they have entered fields traditionally thought of as male. They are confronted with conservative ideas of women and family, both in male colleagues and in parishioners male and female, and with old stereotypes such as physical and mental feebleness, unpredictability, lack of nervous stamina and the like.

They also have to face in church and tradition the myth of the unholiness or uncleaness of the female. Such myths have no place in the modern world. In the nature and biology of women there are factors where flexibility in planning of work is helpful, but this is a minor problem. In the secular professions it is dealt with quite satisfactorily.

Also, it has sometimes appeared that women had to be more competent and work twice as hard to be thought half as good as those who had the advantage of being male. In almost every case those women who feel called by God to serve in the ordained ministry have to prove their capacity time and again, to win acceptance for their cause and their right to serve in this field. They have frequently accepted denial of the possibility of marriage, suspicion of their motives and their womanhood, the hostility offered to those who serve outside of an accepted role, and some loneliness - not to mention lower salaries. But they have done so because they believed themselves called and equipped to share in this ministry. It is notable that the second generation of ordained women do not appear to feel they have had to go through such experiences.

Where the ordained ministry is open only to men, we consider a whole dimension of human experience and life to be missing. The Church and society are both composed of men and women, and it is likely that a ministry including men and women will best serve them. Team and specialist ministries are certain to develop much more effectively in the future, and women bring different and valuable attitudes, insight and experience to a team based on the responsible partnership of men and women. We would not wish to suggest that qualities of warmth, sensitiveness in personal relationships, skill in healing and reconciling, are at all the monopoly of women, but there is some evidence that these qualities are expressed in different ways by men and women.

It has also been suggested that the more mechanised cultures, particularly those of the west, have lost something of the primitive sense of the wholeness of life. So they reveal a dichotomy between the sacred and the secular, the world of the intellect and the world of the emotions and senses, which is not characteristic, say, of African communities. It may be that women because of their different education and experience over the centuries can bring a contribution towards a restoration of the sense of community and the wholeness of personality in the life of the Church and of theology.

It is a source of real joy to us that where women have been permitted to serve in the ordained ministry they have frequently found warm acceptance by congregations. Our case histories have shown that many of the fears entertained in prospect have proved to be ungrounded; and also that the practical problems foreseen and cited in opposition were quite capable of being worked through satisfactorily.

In sum, we believe that women, both lay and ordained, are sharing in the exhilarating experience of renewal which is growing in the churches. We believe that the Church must surely be aware of the need to use for mission all the gifts at her disposal, for the building up of the people of God and the service of the world. Women may have been given different gifts, a distinct understanding of the mind of Christ, but they are doubtless equal in love for him and devotion to his Church and people. We believe that ultimately one's acceptance as a person determines one's acceptance as a minister. If the call, gifts and graces of God reveal themselves in his servants, male and female, God's people will be served and he will achieve his purposes in and through them.

Report of Group III - Initiatives for Change

It is an irony that the Christian church which has been at the forefront of the liberation of the human spirit, bringing a new freedom and dignity to men and women in many societies is now the very institution which, by holding women back from participation in the ministry, appears to sanction a view of women as subordinate. We believe that discrimination against women in Church and society is a form of dehumanisation. Thought patterns, institutional structures or practices which dehumanise persons (whether women, youth, blacks, etc.) is contrary to God's will, an affront to the Almighty, and blasphemy in the eyes of many in society, secreting a venom which can poison and paralyse the Church. Understandably, some traditions find great difficulty in looking afresh at this question; however, the right ecumenical attitude is surely *not* for one church to refrain from change because another church has not moved, but to declare that discrimination cannot be permitted in any part, and attempt to persuade towards the truth those parts which still practise and indeed institutionalise discrimination. Within confessions, a Church may be called to lead her sister Churches into a fuller understanding of women's ministry and a greater readiness to explore and manifest this ministry.

The reasons behind dehumanization are complex. Age-old superstitions about women persist in the Church in spite of the witness and model of Jesus Christ in his earthly ministry. Ignorance, fear of and resistance to change and the unknown have been decisive factors. Men have been architects of a Church structure that has rigidly segregated Christians by sex. Many want to keep it that way, men, because they command power; women, because they have been habituated to submission.

Religious orders and creative forms of service specially designed for women have given, and will continue to give valuable avenues of service. But whatever benefit derived from these ministries, the Church must not evade the central issue, which is to remove *all* barriers and to set women free to seek fresh forms of service, responsibility and authority in the Church.

Many churches ordain women who claim and give evidence of a call of the Holy Spirit. The ministry of these women is bearing fruit in the Church. Such full appropriation of the gifts of women is also visible in human society, where they are gradually being freed to find and express their complete identities in positions of authority and service, not in opposition to, but in full creative relationship with men. We rejoice that this activity of the Holy Spirit, in both Church and world, is thus continuing the evolution of Christian tradition in the direction of a fuller humanity for *all*.

Recommendations

We ask the World Council of Churches to bring to the attention of the appropriate authorities the following recommendations:-

1. That current data be assembled immediately, accurately reflecting the involvement of women in the ministries of member churches and other denominational groups, by a research project, and staff to be appointed within the structure of the W.C.C., and that such data, with its evaluation, be communicated to the member churches through appropriate councils and committees and to interested groups and individuals.

   That this be regarded as a short-term project, to be funded by special appropriations or gifts.

2. That the W.C.C. recruit and appoint women in increasing numbers to all committees, commissions and executive staff positions.

3. That the Faith and Order Commission consider the report of this Consultation as a prime order of business and remind the Churches that the composition of the Commission itself is evidence of discrimination.

4. That, in order to educate opinion within the churches, the Education Renewal Fund Committee be requested to consider the production of a film documenting and interpreting the current work of women in the ministries of the world-wide church.

We recommend that institutions and faculties of theological education should:

1. Recruit and appoint women to teaching positions in the full range of theological disciplines.

2. Design courses of study to create serious encounter with sociological and theological factors present in current trends toward freedom and a new society, based on a right understanding of the doctrines of creation and redemption.

3. Review their programmes of scholarship aid and recruitment practices, so as to encourage women to pursue advanced theological studies.

   We further recommend that the Theological Education Fund Committee seriously consider these recommendations.

We urge the member churches to:

1. Make more fruitful use of the abilities and gifts of trained women in all forms of ministry.

2. Experiment boldly beyond the ecclesiastical and sociological limits normally present, in order that the contribution of women may have maximum effect.

3. Maintain a climate of education and discussion on the contribution of women to the ministry of the church, and more specifically on the ordination of women, through educational curricula and church publications.

   And further, we urge member churches which already ordain women, to examine their ecclesiastical procedures for systemic discrimination, to ensure that ordained women are indeed placed in positions of responsibility and decision-making.

Summary Report on Survey on Ordination of Women

The Department on Cooperation of Men and Women in Church, Family and Society conducted a survey in order to gather data for the Consultation on the Ordination of Women. The survey was based on findings from questionnaries sent to 100 women, fifty-six of whom responded.

Protestant and Eastern Orthodox Churches

Source of Information

The replies came from three African, two Asian, and eight European countries as well as from North America, namely:

Canada
France
Germany
Kenya
England
Wales
Sweden
Holland
Scotland
New Zealand
Switzerland
South India
Zambia
South Africa
U.S.A.

Nine of the replies were joint responses. Our of the total of fifty-six responses, forty-three of the women were fully ordained and thirteen were not ordained but were in full-time employment by the church.

A number of specific questions were raised to which the answers could be relevant to the evaluation of the current policies and practices of the member churches of the World Council of Churches. This report addresses itself to these general and specific issues, related to our present needs.

Questions had to do with:

a. Special problems women had experienced with respect to ordination;

b. The interviewees' perception of the existence or non-existence of discrimination with respect to women in a number of areas of women pastors' lives, e.g. special dress required, salary, allowances, types of work, provisions for part-time jobs for *married* women, roles in decision-making bodies of the churches;

c. Relationships with parishioners and male colleagues;

d. Further questions related to theological, psychological and sociological problems.

It is important to mention that the survey was not intended to reflect the world situation but was only a 'spot-check' based on the personal contacts that have been made by the Department.

We have no comparative regional figures concerning the numerical strength of ordained women as such figures did not seem necessary for the purpose of this survey. In the regions included in the survey, ordination seems to be affected more by men-women relationships as they persist in the traditionally patriarchal societies than by church traditions exclusively. Economic and educational patterns of the churches, each in its place, seem to reflect those of the prevailing society.

Developments

There has been a marked increase of ordained women since the Second World War. Out of the 239 member churches of the WCC, 68 churches now ordain women. It should be noted though that the bulk of our member churches (Anglican and Orthodox Churches) have not changed their views on ordination.

The survey showed that in terms of numbers of ordained women, 39% of those who answered the questionnaire were ordained in the last decade while only 7% were ordained between 1940-1950.

***Tables of our Survey Showed the following*:**

A. Year of Ordination

Pre 1940 4
1940-1950 3
1950-1960 9
1960-1970 21

B. Churches which ordain women

United Church of Zambia
Church of Scotland
United Church of Canada
Church of Sweden
Canadian Baptist Church*
Gereformeerde Kerken in Nederlands*
Church of the Brethren
Tsonga Presbyterian Church (Swiss Mission in South Africa)*
Remonstrant Brotherhood
Evangelisch-reformierte Landoskirche von Appenzell ARH
Eglise réformée du Canton de Berne
Nederlandse Hervormde Kerk
Congregational Church in England & Wales
Eglise Nationale Protestante de Genève
Evangelisch-reformierte Kirche, Baselstadt
Eglise Réformée de France
Evangelisch-reformierte Landeskirche des Kantons Zürich
Baptist Union of Great Britain and Ireland
United Presbyterian Church, U.S.A.
Kirche von Berlin-Brandenburg
Methodist Church of New Zealand
Evangelisch-reformierte Landeskirche des Kantons Aargau
Eglise Libre du Canton de Vaud

*Not a member church of the WCC

C. Churches which do *not* ordain women

Anglican Church of Canada
Church of the Province of East Africa (Anglican)
Eglise Réformée Evangélique du Canton de Vaud
Church of South India
Eglise Réformée Evangélique du Canton de Neuchâtel

Functions

Special attention was directed to the kind of work that ordained women do. The figures below indicate the related priorities according to the actual time spent:

Preaching	70%
Pastoral Visiting	55%
Administration	55%
Teaching	61%
Counselling	44%
Administering the Sacraments	53%

Women's Work	44%
Youth Work	43%
Chaplain to Institution	22%
Urban Industrial Work	4%
Social Work	20%

Between 3-9% of their time was spent in other forms of ministry.

The idea of special ministries which are more suitable for a woman, the belief that one's sex would be a greater advantage at times, was completely rejected by 90% of the interviewees.

One question that was raised in the replies was whether some of these functions should actually be carried out by ordained persons. The comments made indicate that there is a challenge of adaptation to the changing circumstances of our work and life.

It is encouraging to note that 82% of the churches do employ *married* women for full-time professional work and only 16% actually refuse to employ married women. Another new factor is that 47% of the churches now have *part-time* jobs for married women pastors. Twenty-five of the fifty-six women replied to say that the policies in their churches are being changed so that married women pastors can be employed.

Discriminatory Practices

Having been given the chance to be ordained and granted that the status and opportunities were the same as those of men in the church, the percentage of women in positions of leadership is low. The analysis showed that only 28% of the women have any possibilities of being in charge of their ministry or team where they work.

Two replies indicated that although the person was able to be a member of the local or parish council she was not entitled to be a member of the policy decision-making body at the higher or national level.

There are practically no discriminatory practices on the basis of sex in basic salary and security, but there are a few discrepancies in allowances. The overall ''quantitative'' equality of the treatment of men and women who are in ordained ministry is generally the same in most churches.

Ecumenical Problems

The ordination of women has been mentioned as one of the obstacles to negotiations for church union. 55% of the women who replied agreed that this was true in their situations, but still it was not considered to be the major issue. When the Lutherans in Sweden decided to permit the ordination of women, they were afraid that their relationships with the Church of England would be strained, but there has been no significant crisis in nine years.

Psychological and Sociological Problems

The statements of a large majority of those interviewed related essentially to psychological and sociological problems, and 60% of the replies indicated that, of the two, psychological problems were predominant. These lay deeper and were less easily defined than the sociological problems. A descriptive analysis of evidence of such problems has been given in the case-studies and comments from these ordained women: they varied from relationships with male colleagues, relationships with colleagues' wives, 'father-and-mother figure' complexes, to 'sex identity'.

It would be a mistake to associate these psychological and sociological problems with the church only. Many of them stem out of the society's traditions and education. Comments from replies indicated that some of the psychological problems can be changed. Many attitudes people have about women pastors can be changed by experience.

Conclusion

This report does not, nor could provide exact statistics on this issue, because it was not intended to be a scientific survey.

Special thanks must be given to those people who answered the questionnaires, although the terminology and the phrasing used was not always understood.

Ordination of Women — Member Churches of W.C.C. — Aug.'70

	Africa		Asia		Australasia		West Europe		East Europe		North America		Latin America		TOTALS	
	Do	Do Not	Do	Do Not	Do	Do Not	Do	Do Not	Do	Do Not	Do	Do Not	Do	Do Not	Do	Do Not
Anglicans		5		3		2		4			2	2		2		18
Baptist		1		3	1*		1	1	1	1		2			4+1*	8
Congregational	1	2		1u	3*		4	1u			2				5+3*	2
Disciples	1			1	2		1								6	1
Independent		1		1							1					2
Lutheran		4		2			6	4	3	6	3	2		2	10	20
Methodist	1	3 1p	1	1	2		1*	2				1		3	7+1*	10
Pentocostal														2		2
Old Catholic								4		2		1				7
Eastern Orthodox		1		2				3		7		3				16
Orient Orthodox		2		4						1	2	1				8
Reformed	1	10	5	11 3u	1	4	11	3	2	2 1p	2	3	1		23	33
United	2	2	2	5			1	2		1	1+2			2	7	12
Others		2					2	2	1p					1u	3+2*	4
TOTALS	6	33	8	33	9	6	27	25	6	20	15	15	1	11	72	143

* In principle but not yet in practice   u Unknown at time of completion   p Probable

Protestant and Eastern Orthodox Churches

Notes: *Printed here are the introduction, first chapter, and reports and summaries from the 1970 World Council of Churches publication, "What is Ordination Coming To?" Whereas the 1964 World Council paper was part of a preliminary exploration of the subject, this paper is based on the fact that the number of member churches ordaining women increased from a few to approximately 70. The report, then, is less theoretical and serves more as a survey of the impact and results of women's ordination. It notes that "no church which has proceeded to the ordination of women has ever had cause to reconsider its decision." The survey in the last report of member churches around the world is valuable in showing the spread of ordained women beyond North America and western Europe.*

Jewish Groups

Organized Jewish religious communities in the United States involve approximately half of the nation's six million Jewish citizens. The communities are generally divided into three main branches—Orthodox, Conservative, and Reform. Each branch has approximately one million adherents. Additionally, the Reconstructionist Movement claims about 40,000 members. Of these groups, only Orthodox Judaism does not ordain women as rabbis. The changes, however, have not come easily. Reform Judaism, the most liberal of the groups, expressed its approval of women as rabbis as early as 1922, and yet did not ordain its first women rabbi until 1972. Conservative Judaism ordained its first woman rabbi in 1985. For Judaism, a large concern has been how much change the tradition can handle without jeopardizing its religio-cultural distinctiveness.

CENTRAL CONFERENCE OF AMERICAN RABBIS

STATEMENT ON WOMEN'S ORDINATION (1922)

Responsum on Question, "Shall Women be Ordained Rabbis?"

JACOB Z. LAUTERBACH.

The very raising of this question is due, no doubt, to the great changes in the general position of women, brought about during the last half century or so. Women have been admitted to other professions, formerly practiced by men only, and have proven themselves successful both as regards personal achievement as well as in raising the standards or furthering the interests of the professions. Hence the question suggested itself why not admit women also to the rabbinical profession?

The question resolves itself into the following two parts: first what is the attitude of traditional Judaism on this point, and second, whether Reform Judaism should follow tradition in this regard. At the outset it should be stated that from the point of view of traditional Judaism there is the following important distinction to be made between the rabbinate and the other professions in regard to the admission of women. In the case of the other professions there is nothing inherent in their teachings or principles which might limit their practice to men exclusively. In the case of the rabbinate on the other hand, there are, as will soon be shown, definite teachings and principles in traditional Judaism, of which the rabbinate is the exponent, which demand that its official representatives and functionaries be men only. To admit women to the rabbinate is, therefore, not merely a question of liberalism, it would be acting contrary to the very spirit of traditional Judaism which the rabbinate seeks to uphold and preserve.

It should be stated further, that these traditional principles debarring women from the rabbinate were not formulated in an illiberal spirit by the rabbis of old out of a lack of appreciation of women's talents and endowments. Indeed the rabbis of old entertained a high opinion of womanhood and frequently expressed their admiration for woman's ability and appreciated her great usefulness in religious work. Thus, e. g. they say: "God has endowed woman with a finer appreciation and a better understanding than man." (Niddah 45b). "Sarah was superior to Abraham in prophecy" (Tanhuma Exodus beginning) "It was due to the pious women of that generation that the Israelites were redeemed from Egypt" (Sotah 11b) and "The women were the first ones to receive and accept the Torah" (Tanhuma Buber, Mezora 18, p. 27a); and "They refused to participate in the making of the golden calf." These and many other sayings could be cited from rabbinic literature in praise of women, her equality to man and in some respects, superiority to him. So that we may safely conclude that their excluding of women from the rabbinate does not at all imply deprecation on their part of woman's worth.

But with all their appreciation of woman's fine talents and noble qualities, the rabbis of old have also recognized that man and woman have each been assigned by the Torah certain spheres of activity, involving special duties. The main sphere of woman's activity and her duties centered in the home. Since she has her own duties to perform and since especially in her position as wife and mother she would often be prevented from carrying on many of the regular activities imposed upon man, the Law frees her from many religious obligations incumbent upon man, and especially exempts her from such positive duties the performance of which must take place at certain fixed times, like reciting the Shma, or at prescribed seasons, like Succah.

(M. Kiddushin I, 7).

wkl mswt 'šh šhzmn grmh 'nšym hyybyn wnšym ptwrst

This fact, that she was exempt from certain obligations and religious duties, necessarily excluded her from the privilege of acting as the religious leader or representative of the congregation, *šlyh sbwr* She could not represent the congregation in the performing of certain religious functions, since, according to the rabbinic principle, one who is not personally obliged to perform a certain duty, cannot perform that duty on behalf of others and certainly cannot represent the congregation in the performance of such duties. *kl š'ynw mhwyb bdbr 'ynw mwsy' 't hrbym ydy hwbtn* (R.H. III, 8, Berokot 20b).

On the same principle she was expressly disqualified from writing Torah scrolls. Since she could not perform for the congregation the duty of reading from the Torah, the text prepared by her was also not qualified for use in connection with the performance of that duty (Gittin 45b Mas. Soferim I, 14). Women were also considered exempt from the obligation to study the Torah (Erubin 27a; Kiddushin 29b-30a). Some rabbis even went so far as to object to women studying the Torah (M. Sotah III, 4). This opinion, of course, did not prevail. Women were taught the Bible and given a religious education and there were some women learned in the law even in talmudic times. But to use the phrase of the Talmud (M. K. 18a) *'šh by mdrš' l' šqyh'* women were not to be found in the *byt hmdrš* in the academies and colleges where the rabbis assembled and where the students prepared themselves to be rabbis. Evidently, for the reason that they could not aspire to be rabbis, the law excluding them from this religious office.

This law that women cannot be rabbis was always taken for granted in the Talmud. It was considered to be so generally known and unanimously agreed upon that it was not even deemed necessary to make it a special subject of discussion. The very idea of a woman becoming a rabbi never even entered the mind of the rabbis of old. It is for this reason that we find only few direct and definite statements to the effect that women cannot be rabbis. Only occasionally when the discussion of other questions involved the mentioning of it, reference, direct or indirect, is made to the established law that women cannot act as judges or be rabbis. Thus in a Baraita (pal. Talm. Shebuot. IV, i 35b and Sanhedrin IV, 10, 21c) it is stated: *hry lmdnw šh'šh 'ynh dnh* "We have learned that a woman cannot act as judge, i.e., cannot render decisions of law." The same principle is also indirectly expressed in the Mishnah (comp. Niddah VI, 4 and Shebuot IV, i). In the Talmud (Gittin 5b) it is also indirectly stated that a woman cannot be a member of a Beth Din, i. e., a rabbi, or judge. For there it is taken for granted that she could not be one of three who form a tribunal or *byt dyn* to pass upon the correctness of a bill of divorce or of any other document. (See Rashi ad. loc.)

In the Midrash Num. R. X, 5, it is also quoted as a well known and established principle that women may not have the authority to render decisions in religious or ritual matters, *šhnš'm 'ynm bnwt hwr'h.*

These talmudic principles have been accepted by all medieval Jewish authorities. Maimonides, Yad, Sanhedrin II, 7, declares that the members of every tribunal or *byt dyn* in Israel, which means every rabbi, *Dayyan* or *More Horaah* in Israel, must possess the same qualities which characterized the men whom Moses selected to be his associates, and whom he appointed judges and leaders in Israel. These qualities, Maimonides continues, are expressly stated in the Torah, as it is said: "Get you from each one of your tribes *men*, wise and understanding and full of knowledge, and I will make them heads over you." (Deut. I, 13). Maimonides here has in mind the idea, entertained by the rabbis of all generations, that the rabbis of each generation continue the activity and are the recipients of the spirit of those first religious leaders of the Jewish people. For, as is well known, *Moshe Rabenu* and the seventy elders who formed his council were considered the prototypes and the models of the rabbis of all subsequent generations (comp. Mishnah R. H. II, 9). Likewise, R. Aaron Halevi of Barzelona (about 1300 C.E.) in his Sefer Ha Hinuk (Nos. 74,75,77,79,81,83) as well as Jacob Asheri in Tur Hoshen Mishpat VII and Joseph Karo in Shulhan Aruk, Hoshen Mishpat VII, 3, all expressly state the principle that a woman cannot officiate as judge or rabbi. It hardly need be stated that when some of the sources use in this connection the term judge *dyyn* they, of course, mean rabbi for which Dayyan is but another name. In rabbinic terminology the functions of a rabbi are spoken of as being *ldyn wlhwrwt* to judge and decide religious and ritual questions. And even in our modern rabbinical diploma we use the formula *ywrh ywrh ydyn ydyn* giving the candidate whom we ordain the authority to judge and decide religious questions and to give authoritative rulings in all religious matters.

To be sure, the rabbis do permit the women to be religious teachers, like Miriam, who according to the rabbis, taught the women while Moses and Aaron taught the men (Sifre Zutta quoted in Yalkut, Shimeoni Behaaloteka 74i end) and Deborah whom the rabbis believed to have been merely teaching the law (Seder Elijahu R. IX-X Friedmann, p. 50, compare also Tossafot B. K. 15a s. v. *'šr tśym* and parallels). Some authorities would put certain restrictions upon women even in regard to her position as teacher (see Kiddushin 82a and Maimonides, Jad. Talmud Torah II, 4) but in general the opinion of the rabbis was that women may be teachers of religion (see Hinuk 152 and comp. Azulai in Birke Joseph to Hoshen Mishpat VII, 12); and as a matter of fact, there have always been learned women in Israel. These women-scholars were respected for their learning in the same manner as learned men were respected. (See Sefer Hasidim, 978 and comp. also Sde Hemed I, letter Kaf No. 99) and some of these women scholars would occasionally even give lectures in rabbinics, but they have never been admitted to the rabbinate since all the rabbinic authorities agree, at least implicitly, that women cannot hold the office of a rabbi or of a *šlyh sbwr* and cannot perform any of the official functions requiring the authority of a rabbi.

This is the attitude of traditional Judaism towards the question of women rabbis, a view strictly adhered to by all Jewry all over the world throughout all generations even unto this day.

Now we come to the second part of our question, that is, shall we adhere to this tradition or shall we separate ourselves from Catholic Israel and introduce a radical innovation which would necessarily create a distinction between the title rabbi, as held by a reform-rabbi and the title rabbi in general. I believe that hitherto no distinction could rightly be drawn between the ordination of our modern rabbis and the ordination of all the rabbis of preceding generations. We are still carrying on the activity of the rabbis of old who traced their authority through a chain of tradition to Moses and the elders associated with him, even though in many points we interpret our Judaism in a manner quite different from theirs. We are justified in considering ourselves the latest link in that long chain of authoritative teachers who carried on their activity of teaching, preserving and developing Judaism, and for our time we have the same standing as they had (Comp. R. H. 25a). The ordination which we give to our disciples carries with it, for our time and generation, the same authority which marked the ordination given by Judah Hannasi to Abba Areka or the ordination given by any teacher in Israel to his disciples throughout all the history of Judaism.

We should, therefore, not jeopardize the hitherto indisputable authoritative character of our ordination. We should not make our ordination entirely different in character from the traditional ordination, and thereby give the larger group of Jewry, following traditional Judaism, good reason to question our authority and to doubt whether we are rabbis in the sense in which this honored title was always understood.

Nor is there, to my mind, any actual need for making such a radical departure from this established Jewish law and time honored practice. The supposed lack of a sufficient number of rabbis will not be made up by this radical innovation. There are other and better means of meeting this emergency and that is, by the rabbis following the advice of the Men of the Great Synagog, to raise many disciples and thus encourage more men to enter the ministry. And the standard of the rabbinate in America, while no doubt it could be improved in many directions, is certainly not so low as to need a new and refining influence such as women presumably would bring to any profession they enter. Neither could women, with all due respect to their talents and abilities, raise the standard of the rabbinate. Nay, all things being equal, women could not even rise to the high standard reached by men in this particular calling. If there is any calling which requires a whole-hearted devotion to the exclusion of all other things and the determination to make it one's whole life work, it is the rabbinate. It is not to be considered merely as a profession by which one earns a livelihood. Nor is it to be entered upon as a temporary occupation. One must choose it for his lifework and be prepared to give to it all his energies and to devote to it all the years of his life, constantly learning and improving and thus growing in it. It has been rightly said that the woman who enters a profession, must make her choice between following her chosen profession or the calling of mother and homemaker. She cannot do both well at the same time. This certainly would hold true in the case of the rabbinical profession. The woman who naturally and rightly looks forward to the opportunity of meeting the right kind of man, of marrying him and of having children and a home of her own, cannot give to the rabbinate that whole-hearted devotion which comes from the determination to make it one's lifework. For in all likelihood she could not continue it as a married woman. For, one holding the rabbinical office must teach by precept and example, and must give an example of Jewish family and home life where all the traditional Jewish virtues are cultivated. The rabbi can do so all the better when he is married and has a home and a family of his own. The wife whom God has made as a helpmate to him can be, and in most cases is, of great assistance to him in making his home a Jewish home, a model for the congregation to follow.

In this important activity of the rabbi, exercising a wholesome influence upon the congregation, the woman rabbi would be deficient. The woman in the rabbinical office could not expect the man to whom she be married to be merely a helpmate to her, assisting her in her rabbinical activities. And even if she could find such a man, willing to take a subordinate position in the family, the influence upon the families in the congregation of such an arrangement in the home and in the family life of the rabbi would not be very wholesome. Not to mention the fact that if she is to be a mother she could not go on with her regular activities in the congregation.

And there is, to my mind, no injustice done to woman by excluding her from this office.

There are many avenues open to her if she choose to do religious or educational work. I can see no reason why we should make this radical departure from traditional practice except the specious argument that we are modern men and, as such, we recognize the full equality of women to men, hence we should be thoroughly consistent. But I would not class the rabbis with those people whose main characteristic is consistency.

Discussion

Rabbi Levinger: I feel very strongly on this question. When we look at the various denominations in this country who are opposed to ordaining women as ministers we find that they are those who like the Episcopalians and Catholics look upon their ministers as priests. To us the Rabbi is merely a teacher and preacher. The question is not whether there are a great many women who want to become rabbis. Perhaps there are none at all. But we are called upon to act on a matter of principle and if in the next thirty or forty years we produce but one Anna Howard Shaw, we want her in the rabbinate.

Rabbi Witt: I was present at the meeting of the Board of Governors when the matter came up, and it was decided to refer it to the Conference. After reading the response that was prepared by Rabbi Lauterbach I feared that there would be much opposition. I trust that our action in this matter will be unanimous. It is not a matter of tradition at all. I must confess I was not in the least interested in Rabbi Lauterbach's presentation. It seemed reactionary to me. I did not feel that it was the proper presentation of the subject.

I need not say that I honor Dr. Lauterbach for the learning contained therein but the point he presents is not the point at issue. We have witnessed the revolution in the status of woman. Five years ago I had to argue in favor of women's rights when that question came up in the Arkansas legislature, but I did not feel that there would be need to argue that way in a liberal body of men like this.

There is a principle involved, and I hope that the stand we take will be one in line with all the progressive tendencies of our day: That we will have the vision to see what is before us and from the standpoint of to-day shall we say to women that they shall not have the right to function as we are functioning?

The question is, Have they the qualifications to function as spiritual leaders? What does it require to be a spiritual guide? It requires a great spirit and the quality of leadership. Some women have it and some women have not. Some men have it and some men have not. If we had a great leadership we would not have the questions which were so ably presented yesterday among the practical questions of the ministry. The one thing that was stressed was that if we had devoted leaders who could inspire following all the problems would vanish.

I believe that this body of men should do nothing that would stand in the way of any forward movement in behalf of the womanhood of America. I cannot believe that a religion that is so splendidly spiritual and forward-looking as our religion will stand in the way of such a movement. I feel that this Conference can only act in one way, and that is to fall in line with what is the destiny of the women of the future.

Rabbi Weiss: In a large measure I agree with the previous speakers. I agree with all that has been said in favor of ordaining women as rabbis. I believe I am second to none in the rabbinate in the matter of idealism. But a vast measure of compromise must enter into all situations of life. I do not believe that we can have life exactly as we would like to have it. There is a vast debt due to cold, austere justice, but there are fourteen million Jews in the world and they must be considered. In the City of New York alone there are a million and a half who look upon you with a degree of respect but who have their own mode of procedure and who would look upon any radical action on your part as a line of cleavage in the House of Israel. I merely mean that we should proceed slowly. I believe that some compromise can be effected such as allowing women to be teachers or superintendents, but I believe that it were unwise at the present time to have them ordained as rabbis. Let me give one concrete illustration. Suppose one were to sign a marriage document. To many in New York today such a ceremony would hardly be recognized as binding.

Rabbi Brickner: There is much merit in what Dr. Lauterbach has said. He has not stressed the question of opinion, but the question of practicability. Modern psychologists agree that women do not differ from men so much in intellect. In fact experiments prove that women are the peers of most men. There are women occupying positions in modern industry in which she could not be equaled by many men. It is not a question of equality. All that Dr. Lauterbach has said, has already been said against women entering other professions. The question with us is one of practicability. The tendency in modern Judaism is to conserve Jewish values. We wish to be in touch with the masses of Jewish people. When I came away from Toronto the other day I clipped from the newspaper the vote of the Methodist Church in Canada. It represents the liberal traditions in Canada. And yet it voted by a small majority against permitting women into the ministry. It is not a question of principle or equality—on that we are all agreed. It is purely a question of practicability.

Rabbi Charles S. Levi: The matter before you is not a matter of the hour, but a matter of all times. It is a matter that touches upon the acknowledged leadership of our people, and reaches the lives of uncounted thousands of our American co-religionists. We are the links in the chain of time. We are the spokesmen who give expression to the great truths which bind the past to the future, and it is for us to keep alive the chain of tradition.

Rabbi Rauch: I listened with great interest to Dr. Lauterbach's presentation and was at first inclined to agree with him but as he proceeded it struck me that there was a great omission. He gave a fine presentation of the traditional point of view and even hinted at certain modern needs, but I regret to say that he failed to touch on what reform Judaism has to say on the subject. And yet our whole interpretation of religious life is supposedly based on the principles of reform Judaism. Now what has the philosophy of reform Judaism to say in regard to woman? I know from experience because I was born in an orthodox environment. There was a very clear line of distinction between the boy and girl, and the education given to the boy and girl. The boy had to learn Scriptures while the girl was not expected to learn them. Many duties were imposed upon the boy, few upon the girl. This went on for centuries. What happened when reform came in? One by one the barriers separating the boy from the girl educationally began to be broken down. We admitted the girls into the same schools, and we tried to teach them the same things. Even in the important ceremony of barmitzva we brushed aside the traditional point of view and we said that the girl should be educated and confirmed the same as the boy. And in our congregations, which is the practical side of our religious life, we have given to women exactly the same status as the men. In my own congregation women conduct the summer services and they conduct them just as well if not better than they used to be when we got some one temporarily for the summer. In every line of endeavor in our temples we have proceeded on the theory that woman is the equal of man. What do they ask us to do? They want us to make it possible for women to work along the same lines as we men are working. We do not ask privileges for them. Let there be the same demands, the same rigorous training and let the congregation decide whether the woman is doing the work well or not. I do not think that our cause will be hurt by a liberal attitude.

Rabbi Englander: Personally I was surprised to learn that the Board of Governors submitted this question to the Conference. I thought that after the faculty, a body composed of the teachers, had taken action that would be sufficient guidance for action on the part of the Board of Governors. However, I wish to touch on one argument which has been raised to the effect that if we admit women as rabbis we would tend to create a schism in Israel. During all the conferences in recent years there are many actions that we would not have taken had we feared this. We would not have set ourselves on record against Zionism. Had fear been taken into consideration we would not have taken a stand on many subjects. Twenty years ago this Conference put itself on record favoring absolute religious equality of women with men. Are we going back on our own action? In spite of all the arguments advanced by Dr.

Lauterbach, the faculty set itself on record as favoring the ordination of women although it stated that at the present time it believed it was impractical for women to enter the rabbinate. But I do not believe that the question of practicability is for us to decide. The only question before us is, shall we in the light of reform Judaism put ourselves on record in favor of admitting women to the rabbinate.

A motion is made that further discussion be discontinued.

Rabbi Morgenstern: I do not care to express any opinion upon this subject, because you can readily understand, inasmuch as this question has been submitted by the college authorities to the Conference to get an expression of opinion, I am here rather to listen than to offer any opinion I myself may have. I realize that the time of the Conference is very precious and that you cannot afford to give more time than is necessary to the discussion of this question, but I believe that the question is of such importance that it ought to justify the expenditure of as much time as may be necessary for a thorough discussion of the question. Several of the men lay emphasis upon the significance of the principle of not breaking with Catholic Israel. We have heard the arguments but there are several valuable thoughts which have not yet been presented. And there is one phase of the question which has not been adequately discussed. We can all accept the opinion of Dr. Lauterbach as authoritative, namely, from the point of view of traditional Judaism the ordination of women would not be permitted. We need not discuss that. But the practical aspect of the question has not been discussed. Namely, is it expedient, and is it worth while?

Rabbi Abrams: I cannot feel but in thorough sympathy and agreement with Rabbi Lauterbach. We are paying too much attention to what is being done by other denominations. It is the spirit and practice of Israel that should guide us. It would be a mistake to break with the traditions of the past.

Rabbi Raisin: It seems to me that the question resolves itself into three parts. First, what is the principle? Second, is it consistent? Third, is it practical?

As a matter of principle women ought to be ordained as we now recognize that they are entitled to the same privileges and rights as men. Our ancestors never asked, is it practical? They asked, is it the will of God? And thus they settled the question for themselves. But we must ask the question, is it in keeping with the tradition of the past? In the whole paper of Rabbi Lauterbach we do not find the statement that women could not be ordained as rabbis. Indirectly we inferred that she may not be ordained because we do not find any women who were ordained. At the most sentiment was against it, but sentiment was against women going into many of the professions even to-day. But that does not mean that they should not be ordained or could not be according to traditional laws.

What is our ordination to-day? In spite of our claim that we are the descendants of the ancient rabbis, we must admit that the function of the modern rabbi is entirely different from the function of the rabbi of old. In olden times, he was the judge. That was his chief function. Preaching and teaching were secondary. If we were to lay claim to be lineal descendants of the ancient teachers we must go to the prophets of the Bible. We are the followers of the prophets more than of the rabbis. And if we would follow the example of the women of the Bible, we would find that many women served as prophets and that during Talmudic times many of them taught. So we are not inconsistent with the past, if we put ourselves on record as favoring the ordination of women.

Rabbi Joseph L. Baron: I enjoyed thoroughly the scholarly paper of my teacher on the negative view of the question, and I shall not deny that the admission of women into the rabbinate will, like any innovation, shock some people and call forth opposition and ridicule. But I wish to point out several flaws in the negative argument. Professor Lauterbach intimates that the matter has hitherto never arisen as a practical issue because it has been taken for granted that a woman cannot, in the capacity of rabbi, carry out, or represent the people in, a function in which she is not personally obliged to participate. How, then, can we infer from this that with the full entry of woman in all the religious functions of home and synagog, she must still be denied the privilege of ordination? We broke with tradition long ago when we granted women an equal standing with men in all our religious functions.

I disagree entirely with the remark that by taking the proposed step, we shall create a schism. The Russian Jews, to whom reference has been made, do recognize and follow women leaders, as in the radical factions. And if women are not recognized as leaders in the orthodox synagog, let us not forget that neither are we recognized as such. There is a distinct difference made, even in the Yiddish terminology between a *Rav* and a *Rabbi*. Again, we broke with tradition long ago when we declared that a rabbi need not be an authority on questions of *Kashruth*; and I need not mention which, from the point of view of orthodoxy, is the greater offense.

When I received the responsum of Dr. Lauterbach a week or two ago, I inquired as to the attitude of the members of a Unitarian Church in Moline, where a woman has been officiating for about half a year, and the reply was very favorable. That minister is not falling behind her male predecessors in her zeal and ability in handling all the problems of the church. So, as to the practicality of the matter, I believe that should be left entirely with the individual congregation.

Rabbi James G. Heller: I do not believe that the Conference has the right to appeal to its duty to "Catholic Israel" in order to settle this question. In the past many decisions have been taken which evidenced no regard for mere keeping of the peace. The one question at issue, the one question that should be discussed by this Conference, is whether in principle the admission of women into the rabbinate is desirable, and whether it is in accordance with the historic teachings of reform Judaism. The entire content of Dr. Lauterbach's responsum can, to my mind, be summed up in that very logical inconsistency to which he refers toward the end of his paper in so laudatory a manner. He must complete the syllogism contained in his remarks. Since traditional Judaism, Orthodoxy, did not require women to perform certain duties or functions, did not permit them to share in certain duties or functions, did not permit them to share in certain religious acts, it could not allow them to become teachers of these same duties. And, per contra, since reform Judaism requires and asks of women the performance of every religious duty in the catalog, it cannot deny them the right to become teachers and preachers.

Rabbi Samuel S. Cohon: I wish to call your attention to the fact that in other professions there is a great deal of prejudice against women even where they administer with considerable success. You would imagine that women would welcome the services of women physicians. But in actual practice it is stated that women are more bitterly opposed to female practitioners than are men.

In the legal profession we also know that in many instances women are debarred from practice. But I believe that many of us who realize how much our wives have helped us, how they have co-operated with us, how they have borne many of the responsibilities also realize that they should be given the opportunity to assume this work on their own accord if they so desire. Of course there will be prejudice against women in the rabbinate but if one congregation is found that will welcome a woman the opportunity should be granted.

Rabbi Frisch: We have made greater departures from tradition in reform Judaism than the one which is before us so we can afford to dismiss this question without further discussion. But I regard the ordination of women as the last step in the removal of restrictions in the Jewish faith. She is fitted by temperament and by all of her qualifications to the position of teacher and she has been granted the right to participate in all our congregational activities as the equal of man. Civilization has had cause to regret every restriction which it has placed in the way of those who wanted to be free.

I have been wondering whether we are not denying ourselves a new source of strength, a new source of inspiration by our reluctance in admitting women to the rabbinate. I recognize the handicaps, but I believe that the women who surmount the obstacles will be greater spirits than the men who are in the rabbinate to-day. Will it be any greater reproach for a woman to give up the ministry for the sake of maternity than it is for a man to give it up to seek a livelihood in other work? I think it will be for a nobler reason. If we get women into our midst as rabbis I believe that we will be enjoying some of the inspiration and strength which we feel we need. So I plead that we place ourselves on record as in full sympathy with a further emancipation of women by their ordination as rabbis in Israel.

Rabbi Stern: Emotionally I am conservative and I do not like to break with the past, but I cannot agree with Rabbi Lauterbach in this instance. Is it not essential for us first to decide what is the principle? I believe the practical will take care of itself. It is very interesting to note that in the city of New York a professor in the Seminary, the rabbi of an orthodox congregation had a Bar Mitzva of girls. This is very interesting and shows that the other wing of Judaism is also making progress.

A motion that the opinions of members which have been sent in should be read was introduced. The motion was lost.

Rabbi Morgenstern: I think there is one possible source of information that we have not heard from and whose opinion would be very helpful to us. I mean the wives of the rabbis present. It would help us to get an expression of opinion from the women, if some of the wives would be willing to give us their ideas based on many years experience in this work. I would ask that opportunity be given to the ladies to express their opinion.

It was moved that the courtesy of the floor be extended to any of the ladies present who cared to take part in the discussion.

Mrs. Frisch: When I entered the hall this morning, I was opposed to the ordination of women as rabbis. I am now in favor of it. I have been much impressed with what I have heard.

The reason I was opposed to the ordination of women was what you would call the practical reason. I now feel that whatever practical reasons I may have had cannot be compared in value with the matter of principle which has been mentioned here this morning.

The practical reason that I had in mind was that I as a wife and mother did not understand how a woman could attend to the duties which devolve upon a rabbi and at the same time be a true home-maker. Candidly, I do not see at this moment how it can be accomplished. I cannot solve this question, but there may be some women who would prefer a life of celibacy in order to minister to a congregation.

Personally I am selfish enough not to be willing to give up the happiness of wifehood and motherhood for this privilege, great though it be. But I love the work of the rabbinate so much that could I have prevailed upon myself to forget the joys that come with wife-making I should have become a rabbi. And I do not believe that privilege should be denied women and it behooves us to go on record as being in favor of this movement.

Miss Baron: I am connected with Jewish work in New York City and I know that since the Jewish woman has entered the work it has intensified the value of Jewish education; and I believe that should the Jewish woman enter the rabbinate she will be able to intensify the religious feeling of our people.

Mrs. Berkowitz: I am more than satisfied to be the silent member of our partnership, but I believe it is the function of women to give spiritual value to the world and especially the Jewish woman imbued with the Jewish spirit will naturally bring a certain quality to the ministry which some of our men lack. I think that might be enlarged and strengthened and therefore I should like to see our women become rabbis if they wish to do so.

A motion that action on this resolution be postponed until next year was lost.

A motion that a referendum vote of the members of the Conference be taken was lost.

A motion that this resolution be referred to the Committee on Resolutions was lost.

Rabbi Joseph Leiser: The objections of Professor Lauterbach concerning the admission of Jewish women to the rabbinate are inadequate. His thesis, that the rabbinical profession is a career and involves the totality of life to the preclusion of even the function and offices of motherhood, is not valid and is no more applicable to the Jewish woman as rabbi than it is to the Jewish woman as lawyer, doctor, dentist, newspaper writer, musician, business woman or teacher. In all these trades and professions, Jewish women are actively engaged beyond the consideration or limitations of sex, and independent of previous sex-taboos. As a profession, the rabbinate ought to be open to women on a parity with that of man, providing women receive a degree for academic training carried on according to approved standards.

But my objection to the position maintained by Prof. Lauterbach rests on more fundamental contentions than of sex discrimination in the rabbinate. The Professor fails to analyze the rabbinate in the light of its function and activity in the world to-day. He carries over into America, a modern America, the methodology and outlook of an orthodox rabbi whose function is that of a lawyer, one who renders decisions in an ecclesiastical court from codes drawn up by established standards of behavior. Orthodox Judaism rests upon laws of conformity. One discharges his duties. One learns them and fulfills them, whereas reform Judaism releases the individual to enable him to realize his own nature and therefore allows him to contribute whatever there is implanted within his soul and mind to humanity.

This difference in motivation is translated to the profession of the rabbi, as it is interpreted in reform Judaism.

The mere repudiation of the authority of the Talmud and Schulhan Aruk is not sufficient to constitute one a reform rabbi nor does the accepting of it make one an orthodox rabbi. To be sure, the orthodox rabbi is learned in the law, since the very nature and constitution of his profession require it. But the reform rabbi is not primarily a legal expert. The modern rabbinate has become an institution, just as the synagog has developed other functions than those pertaining to worship and the discharging of ceremonial observances. In these days it serves more than one purpose and therefore requires more than one type of professional labor.

The variety of activities that are now released in the ordinary synagog calls for a number of workers all of whom must be filled with the knowledge of God. The new work recently developed in the synagog appeals particularly to the woman who by nature and training is singularly fitted to undertake it.

It will be said in rebuttal that, while the need and utility of these modern activities within the synagog may require the professional assistance of woman these functions do not require the training and professional equipment of a rabbi.

This is a mistake. Mere inclination provides access to those qualities of emotionalism and undisciplined enthusiasm which endanger the assistance of a woman. Professional training is required for the expert in the religious institution of the synagog. In the department of education as our synagogs are elaborating them a Jewish woman is particularly well qualified, providing her training in rabbinics is grounded in a thorough knowledge of the literature.

A Jewish woman is the logical adjunct to young people's societies and organizations, and no synagog is complete without these new features.

The social activities of a congregation are dependent on the social instincts of a woman. Her rabbinical training enables her to link up these activities with tradition and provides the background of Jewish consciousness to this work.

The pulpit and whatever pertains to it is, and remains, a plane wherein man is by nature and temperament best qualified, although not exclusively so. Nor is woman by reason of self limitations, disqualified. Viewing the rabbi in the light of a prophet and the man of vision, he more than woman responds to this unusual endowment. Men are prone to be idealists. They are quick to see visions. They are the dreamers. To men is given the gift of prophecy but not exclusively, as the careers of Hulda and Deborah testify. Men are called upon by God to be pathfinders, liberators, protagonists of right, brandishing the shining sword of justice before the hosts of evil-doers. In the defense of right, men will face the outrages of the world alone.

On the other hand, women are conservative, and seldom are impelled to stand forth and proclaim these eternal convictions. They are pacifists, importunists, moderators, trimming their sails to whatever winds blow on the seven seas of thought. Remember, that while it was due to the merit of women that the children of Israel were redeemed from Egypt, it was only merit not the fierce rebellion of a Moses, saying, ''Let my people go free!'' that wrought the miracle.

Were the woman as rabbi merely confined to pulpit discourses and the formal aspects of ceremonials, her admission to the profession would be inept and otiose. The synagog, however, has enlarged its tent cords ofservice. It is an institution of which the pulpit is part, not the totality. Being only a feature of the institutional labor, there are spheres of activity in the synagog that can not only be filled by woman, but are primarily her province.

Rabbi Neumark: I. ''This fact that she was exempt form certain obligations . . . she could not . . . represent the congregation in the performance of such duties. (R. H. III, 8; Berakot 20b)''. Against this argument is to be said:

First: The traditional functions of the rabbi have nothing to do with representation of the congregation in the performance of certain religious duties from which women are freed. There are certain categories of men, such as are deformed and afflicted with certain bodily defects, who could not act as reader, but could be rabbis for decisions in ritual matters and questions of law. The same holds true of people with a ''foreign accent'' in Hebrew.

Second: Women are not free from the duties of *Prayer, Grace after meal*, and *Kiddush*, and they can read for others,—cf. Mishnah and Bab. Gemara Berakoth 20a, b. Thus even in our modern conception of the function of the rabbi which includes reading, woman can act as representative according to traditional law. (Of course, ''Tephillah'' here is used in its technical meaning—''Eighteen-Prayers''—, while the Prayer in its general meaning of Divine Service had the Sh'ma in its center from the obligatory reading of which woman was free. But no orthodox Jew ever waited with the obligatory reading of the Sh'ma for the public service; it has, at least in post-talmudic times, always been done right in the morning privately.

Third: The practice within reform Judaism has decided in favor of admitting women as readers of the Divine Service. And since we are interested in the traditional law on the subject only in order to take from it a clue for reform practice, this argument would be of no consequence even if it were valid as it is not: If woman is to be debarred from the rabbinate in orthodox Judaism because she cannot serve as a reader, then the only logical consequence would be that reform Judaism which has decided in favor of the woman reader, should disregard the orthodox attitude, and admit woman to the rabbinate.

II. The reason why a Torah Scroll written by a woman was considered unfit, is not, as Dr. Lauterbach claims, because she could not be reader of the Torah, but quite a formal one: Whosoever has not the obligation of binding (T'phillim), has not the fitness of writing (a Torah-Scroll—Gittin 45b; Men. 42b). The above reason is given in Sopherim I, 13, but there, woman is not debarred from writing a Torah-Scroll (I have before me ed. Berdyshew 5657—one-volume Talmud and 12 vol. Talm. ed. Wien, Anton Schmidt, 1832).

III. In Babli Moed Katan, 18a, it is not said that ''women were not to be found in the academies and colleges where the rabbis assembled and where the students prepared themselves to be rabbis.'' It is only said: *'šh by mdrš' l' škyh'* ''a woman is not *often* to be found in the Beth-ha-Midrash.'' The academies and colleges of those days were not institutions for training of rabbis, but institutions of learning, most of whose students were pursuing other vocations. A woman in those days was supposed to keep away from all public places, such as courts, and the like, and even, as much as possible, from the streets:

kl kbwdh bt mlk pnymh

IV. As to the direct question of the legal situation, I have discussed that matter in the opinion which I have submitted to the faculty of the Hebrew Union College. I want to add the following remarks: I. The statement of Jerush. Synh. 21c and Sheb. 35b, that woman cannot serve (occasionally) as judge, is not from a Baraitha, as Dr. Lauterbach claims; but occurs in a discussion between two Amoraim. 2. *lmdnw* does not mean ''we have learned'', but is a technical term for an inference on the virtue of an hermeneutical rule; in this case a *gzrh šwh*. 3. Nowhere in talmudic but always by *tny'* literature is a Baraitha introduced by *tny lmdnw* and the like. 4. The emphasis on ''men'' in the quotation from Maimuni is *not* justified.

V. As to the practical question of the advisability to ordain women at the Hebrew Union College, I do not believe that the orthodox will have any additional reason to object. They themselves employ women in their schools as teachers and readers, and more than this our woman rabbi will not do. In fact the entire question reduces itself to this: Women are already doing most of the work that the ordained woman rabbi is expected to do. But they do it without preparation and without authority. I consider it rather a duty of the authorities to put an end to the prevailing anarchy by giving women a chance to acquire adequate education and an authoritative standing in all branches of religious work. The practical difficulties cannot be denied. But they will work out the same way as in other professions, especially in the teaching profession, from the kindergarten to post-graduate schools. Lydia Rabbinowitz raised a family of three children and kept up a full measure of family life while being a professor of bacteriology. The woman rabbi who will remain single will not be more, in fact less, of a problem than the bachelor rabbi. If she marries and chooses to remain a rabbi, and God blesses her, she will retire for a few months and provide a substitute, as rabbis generally do when they are sick or meet with an automobile accident. When she comes back, she will be a better rabbi for the experience. The rabbinate may help the women, and the woman rabbi may help the rabbinate. You cannot treat the reform rabbinate from the orthodox point of view. Orthodoxy is orthodoxy, and reform is reform. Our good relations with our orthodox brethren may still be improved upon by a clear and decided stand on this question. They want us either to be reform or to return to the fold of real genuine orthodox Judaism whence we came.

It was moved and adopted that the President appoint a committee to formulate a statement which shall express the sentiment of the Conference on the subject of the ordination of women as rabbis.

The following statement was submitted, and was adopted by a vote of 56 to 11:

> The ordination of woman as rabbi is a modern issue; due to the evolution of her status in our day. The Central Conference of American Rabbis has repeatedly made pronouncement urging the fullest measure of self expression for woman as well as the fullest utilization of her gifts in the service of the Most High and gratefully acknowledges the enrichment and enlargement of congregational life which has resulted therefrom.
>
> Whatever may have been the specific legal status of the Jewish woman regarding certain religious functions, her general position in Jewish religious life has ever been an exalted one. She has been the priestess in the home, and our sages have always recognized her as the preserver of Israel. In view of these Jewish teachings and in keeping with the spirit of our age, and the traditions of our Conference, we declare that woman cannot justly be denied the privilege of ordination.

HENRY COHEN, *Chairman*,
HENRY BERKOWITZ,
BARNETT R. BRICKNER,
MAX HELLER,
JACOB LAUTERBACH,
MORRIS NEWFIELD,
LOUIS WITT.

(Editor's note: Portions of the preceding statement originally appeared in Hebrew; these phrases were transliterated to English to aid the reader.)

Notes: *The Central Conference of American Rabbis is the representative rabbinical group of Reform Judaism (approximately 1,200,000 members). This 1922 discussion on the ordination of women as rabbis indicates that a large majority (56 to 11) of conference members were in favor of it. Despite this, however, women were not immediately ordained to the rabbinate. In fact, the central conference was still discussing the issue in the 1950s, and it was not until 1972 that a woman was actually ordained.*

CENTRAL CONFERENCE OF AMERICAN RABBIS

STATEMENT ON WOMEN'S ORDINATION (1955)

The Ordination of Women

Colleagues, I am taking the liberty of bringing back for your consideration a question we answered in the negative long ago, before many of the younger members of this Conference were rabbis; namely, the ordination of women.

In the discussion that took place in 1922 I expressed my opposition to such a proposal. But since then our needs have changed, and I have changed my mind. Many Christian Protestant denominations have also changed their minds and now ordain women.

The Harvard Divinity School will now admit women as regular students beginning next fall. They will be permitted to take the course leading to the degree of Bachelor of Theology as well as advanced study for the degrees of Master of Theology and Doctor of Theology, which will qualify them for ordination by their respective denominations. The General Assembly of the Presbyterian Church just recently broke a 167-year old tradition by voting four to one recommending the ordination of women as ministers. The Presbyterians said they found that the Bible does not contain any prohibition against ordaining women.

I know that Reform is more than Biblio-centered, but is there anything in our missing Reform *Shulhan Aruch* that prohibits us from ordaining women? Does it not accord with our liberalism? The Reform Movement pioneered in granting equality to women. Women not only sit on our Boards, but soon one of the oldest Reform congregations will elect a woman as its president. Why should we grant women degrees only in Religious Education, qualifying them to be educational directors yet denying them the prerogative to be preachers as well as teachers? They have a special spiritual and emotional fitness to be rabbis, and I believe that many women would be attracted to this calling.

Furthermore, there is a shortage of rabbis. New congregations are increasing; and many a small town languishes for want of a spiritual leader. I do not intend that this proposal should lead to immediate discussion, but I do recommend that a committee be appointed to re-evaluate this subject and bring in a report at the next Conference.

With reference to recommendation 10, we recommend that in the spirit of the statement adopted at the Cape May Conference of 1922 and the recommendation of the President a committee be appointed, as proposed by the President, to restudy the question of the ordination of women and report at a forthcoming Conference.

Notes: *This section of the Message of the President of the Central Conference of American*

Rabbis notes that whereas other major groups were ordaining women and the 1922 Central Conference itself went on record in favor of it, a committee should be formed to restudy the matter. That recommendation was approved.

CENTRAL CONFERENCE OF AMERICAN RABBIS

REPORT ON THE ORDINATION OF WOMEN (1956)

To the Central Conference of American Rabbis,

COLLEAGUES:

This report for which you asked covers an issue which was long ago explored and resolved by this Conference. All we bring is reinforcement of the same arguments which convinced this body in 1922, or contemporary enlightenment regarding them.

The CCAR was brought into being by Isaac M. Wise in 1889. At one of the early meetings of this Conference, just three years after its creation, on July 10, 1892, the following resolution was adopted: "Whereas we have progressed beyond the idea of a secondary position of women in Jewish congregations, we recognize the importance of their hearty cooperation and active participation in congregational affairs; therefore be it resolved that women be eligible to full membership with all the privileges of voting and holding office in our congregations." This early resolution demonstrates that the CCAR began its history with the determination that men and women shall have equal status in Reform Jewish affairs.

In submitting this report on the ordination of women on an equal basis with men, sixty-four years after the aforementioned resolution was approved, this Committee is simply meeting its assignment from the 1955 Conference to reexamine the already settled subject of the religious equality of the sexes in Reform Judaism, with special reference to the unqualified acceptance of women as our colleagues in the rabbinate.

Since that 1892 resolution was passed, this question was subjected to another critical review by the Conference, a review that preceded what we present today by thirty-four years. The issue arose in the 1922 meeting of the Conference when Dr. Jacob Z. Lauterbach wrote a responsum on the question, "Shall Women be Ordained Rabbis?" Dr. Lauterbach argued the traditional orthodox position against their ordination. Among other arguments, his opinion that ordination of women might jeopardize the authoritative character of our traditional ordination ranked highly. Dr. David Neumark, rejecting Dr. Lauterbach's position, argued at this same Conference, "You cannot treat the Reform rabbinate from the Orthodox point of view. Orthodoxy is Orthodoxy and Reform is Reform. Our good relations with our Orthodox brethren may still be improved upon by a clear and decided stand on this question. They want us either to be Reform or to return to the fold of real genuine Orthodox Judaism whence we came."

After lengthy debate, the following statement was submitted and was overwhelmingly adopted by the convention: "The ordination of woman as rabbi is a modern issue; due to the evolution in her status in our day. The Central Conference of American Rabbis has repeatedly made pronouncement urging the fullest measure of self-expression for woman, as well as the fullest utilization of her gifts in the service of the Most High and gratefully acknowledges the enrichment and enlargement of congregational life which has resulted therefrom.

"Whatever may have been the specific legal status of Jewish woman regarding certain religious functions, her general position in Jewish religious life has ever been an exalted one. She has been the priestess in the home, and our sages have always recognized her as the preserver of Israel. In view of these Jewish teachings and in keeping with the spirit of our age and the traditions of our Conference, we declare that woman cannot justly be denied the privilege of ordination.'' Dr. Lauterbach, flexible and pliant in his thinking, along with young Rabbi Brickner, now President of our Conference, were among the seven men who officially signed this document as it was submitted to the 1922 convention.

In his presidential message in June, 1955, Dr. Brickner wrote, ''I am taking the liberty of bringing back for your consideration a question we answered long ago. The Reform movement pioneered in granting equality to women. Why should we grant women degrees only in religious education, qualifying them to be educational directors, yet denying them the prerogative to be preachers as well as teachers? They have a special spiritual and emotional fitness to be rabbis, and I believe that many women would be attracted to this calling.''

Our President continued with the recommendation, subsequently accepted by last year's Conference, that a Committee be appointed to reevaluate this subject, and to present a report to this 1956 Convention. The Committee, consisting of the rabbis whose names are signed below, did indeed give this subject resolute scrutiny and study. We examined the issue in the light of the age-old traditions of our faith and in the light of the sixty-four year old traditions of this Conference. These are the facts we reviewed.

The recognition of women as of equal status with men goes back to the very beginning of the liberal movement in Judaism in Germany long before it spread to America. At the ''Conference of the Rabbis of Germany'' which took place in Frankfort on the Main in July, 1845, it was stated that, ''One of the marked achievements of the Reform movement has been the change in the status of women. According to the Talmud and the Rabbinic Code, woman can take no part in public religious functions but,'' the rabbis of this convention added, ''this Conference declares that woman has the same obligation as man to participate from youth up in the instruction in Judaism and in the public services, and that the custom not to include women in the number of individuals necessary for the conducting of a public service (a *minyan*) is only a custom and has no religious basis.'' This opinion was expressed to the Frankfort Conference by Rabbi Samuel Adler.

At the Breslau Rabbinical Conference held in July, 1846, the Conference agreed, ''that woman be entitled to the same religious rights and subject to the same religious duties as man.'' In accordance with this principle, the rabbinic body made the following pronouncements: ''That women are obliged to perform religious acts as depend upon a fixed time *mswh šhzmn grmh bh*, in so far as such acts have significance for our religious consciousness. That the benediction *šl' 'śny 'šh* which owed its origin to the belief in the religious inferiority of woman be abolished. That the female sex is obligated from youth up to participate in religious services and be counted for *minyan*.''

It was at this Breslau Conference that Einhorn said, ''It is our sacred duty to declare with all emphasis the complete religious equality of woman with man in view of the religious standpoint that we represent, according to which an equal degree of natural holiness inheres in all people the distinctions in sacred writ having therefore only relative and momentary significance. Life, which is stronger than all theory, has already accomplished something in this respect, but much is still wanting for complete equality, and even the little that has been achieved lacks still legal sanction. It is therefore our mission to make legal declaration of the equal religious obligation and justification of woman in as far as this is possible. We have the same right to do this as had the synod under Rabbenu Gershom eight hundred years ago, which passed new religious decrees in favor of the female sex.

The denial to women of equal status with man in the performance of all religious duties, obligations, and functions is clearly a survival of the oriental conception of woman's inferiority. To condemn woman to the role of a silent spectator, an auditor, in the synagogue while granting her an important voice in the home is illogical and unnatural in an occidental society; it is incongruous with the customs, standards and ideals of our age. It is true that in Orthodox Judaism the oriental conception of woman's inferiority is codified in the *Shulhan*

Aruch, but Reform Judaism has long maintained that these paragraphs do not express its liberal view. The emancipation of woman applies to life within the synagogue as well as to life outside the synagogue.

In view of woman's parity with man, we believe that the unwarranted and outmoded tradition of reducing woman to an inferior status with regard to ordination for the rabbinate be abandoned. Specifically, we believe that she should be given the right to study for the rabbinate, that she should be ordained if and when she has properly completed the course of study, and that she should then be admitted into the CCAR upon application for membership.

The question before us is purely academic at this time. We have no particular case in point. We are drawing a general pattern, not a specific tracing. We are establishing a principle which may be applied as the need arises in the future. We believe that the time has long since passed when a person's sex should constitute a bar to self-expression in any area of human endeavor. The only proper passport to participation in any profession is adequate training and proven capability, regardless of sex. During the last few centuries, the position of women has undergone an enormous revolution. At long last, we must remove the final barrier in her way to becoming a teacher in Israel, a rabbi, of an equal status with men.

This attitude reflects the unaltered conviction of this Conference. It has been the consistent judgment of this body, with each reopening of the subject, for it is in harmony with the high esteem and respect in which women of virtue and valor have always been held in Israel. The opposing viewpoint that would limit woman's activity to a separate and segregated area of expression was refuted and rejected by rabbis generations ago. Furthermore, the religious equality of women with men can be assumed as universally confessed in all liberal denominations. A number of Protestant Christian denominations such as the Unitarians, the Universalists, the Presbyterians and others have already taken the step to ordain qualified women as ministers. We are not among the first liberal religionists to take this step.

As members of the CCAR, we are in two areas, that of traditional attachment and that of liberal influence. We hear the hour strike on both clocks. We know both arguments. But assuming that we wish to extend the horizons of our faith, we should proceed to remove from woman the degradation of segregation. As liberal rabbis who are concerned with the refinement of Jewish practices, and who are sensitive to the currents of today's thinking, we can reach no other decision about the ordination of women. A modern rabbi with discerning eyes and sensitive conscience must, we believe, support those contentions.

Therefore, this Committee recommends to this Conference that it endorse the admission into the HUC-JIR of educationally and spiritually qualified female rabbinical students. We further recommend that, when a woman shall have satisfactorily completed the course of study leading to ordination as rabbi, as prescribed by the faculty, the CCAR shall endorse her ordination as a rabbi in Israel. Lastly, we recommend that the CCAR welcome into its ranks any woman who has been ordained as a rabbi, who may apply for membership in this professional association.

Respectfully submitted,

JOSEPH L. FINK, *Chairman*
LOUIS BINSTOCK
BERYL D. COHON
MAURICE N. EISENDRATH
ALFRED L. FRIEDMAN
NELSON GLUECK
JAMES G. HELLER
FERDINAND M. ISSERMAN

(Editor's note: Portions of the preceding statement originally appeared in Hebrew; these phrases were transliterated to English to aid the reader.)

The report was discussed and a motion was passed to table action so that those who have an opposite point of view may have an opportunity to present a report.

Notes: *The committee formed in 1955 to study the ordination of women made this report to the Central Conference of American Rabbis. As in 1922, the recommendation was to allow women rabbis based on applicable Reform precedents from as far back as 1846. While the recommendation was tabled to allow opposing viewpoints to be heard, little formal discussion of the issue ever occurred. Instead, the decision was simply made to ordain women, and on June 3, 1972, Sally Priesand became the first woman rabbi.*

CENTRAL CONFERENCE OF AMERICAN RABBIS

STATEMENT ON WOMEN'S ORDINATION (1973)

8. Equality of Women in Reform Judaism And The Equal Rights Amendment

Historically, the Reform Movement was the first in Judaism to assert the religious equality of women. We are proud, too, that there are no logical impediments barring women from any post or office in Reform Judaism, and that women have made effective contributions in various offices, including the office of president of some congregations and the Rabbinate itself. Despite this, inequities persist. Very small numbers of women are elected to our governing bodies. Very few are enabled to contribute in full measure their skills, energies, and creativity to a movement in which, by rights, they should be full partners.

We therefore call upon all members of the CCAR and all our congregations to implement without delay the following program:

1. Initiate measures assuring wider participation of women as officers, members of Boards of Trustees, nomination committees, and participants in every area of synagogue life.

2. Review all religious school programs, practices, and textbooks, both in our schools and in the synagogue at large, to assure that the teaching received by our children will firmly establish that in Reform Judaism both sexes share equally in responsibilities and opportunities, unhampered by the prejudices of earlier times. If necessary, the congregation should bring inequities to the attention of the National Commission on Jewish Education.

3. Support the proposed Twenty-seventh Amendment—the Equal Rights Amendment—to the Constitution of the United States, which would render unconstitutional discrimination on the basis of sex, and we urge our congregations and affiliates to press for adoption of the Amendment. This Amendment states that equality of rights under the law shall not be denied or abridged by the United States or by any state on account of sex, and gives Congress the power of enforcement.

The Equal Rights Amendment recognizes the inherent rights and concomitant responsibilities of women as co-equal with men. If adopted, it would rectify long-standing injustices which have deprived women of education, employment, and financial opportunities equal to those of men, as well as end discriminatory public laws which have contributed to a second-class status for women in American society.

The resolution was adopted.

Notes: *This 1973 resolution in support of the Equal Rights Amendment mentions the presence of women rabbis to illustrate Reform Judaism's position in favor of the religious and civic equality of women.*

CENTRAL CONFERENCE OF AMERICAN RABBIS

WOMEN IN REFORM JUDAISM (1975)

WHEREAS the Central Conference of American Rabbis is a professional organization we address ourselves to special concerns of the rabbinate as a profession, and

WHEREAS the Reform movement has ever affirmed the religious equality of women, and

WHEREAS the Central Conference of American Rabbis has expressed its support of the Equal Rights Amendment, and

WHEREAS we firmly believe that women should be full and equal partners in all areas of synagogue and community life,

BE IT THEREFORE RESOLVED that we express our concern that, despite the basic principles of our Movement, there are still Reform congregations in which family memberships are listed by the man's name only. We call upon all members of the CCAR to review all policies and programs of our synagogues and communal institutions to insure that men and women share equally in responsibilities and opportunities.

BE IT FURTHER RESOLVED that we urge all our members and congregations to nominate, elect and appoint qualified women to positions of leadership within the synagogue and community, to invite women to participate in every aspect of synagogue ritual including *Aliyot* and the privilege of carrying the Torah during the *Hakafot*. We call for greater sensitivity to the feelings and needs of women in liturgical language and practice. We stress the need to provide customs and ceremonies which are meaningful to both men and women. We urge our congregations to institute a *Bat Mitzvah* ceremony which is comparable in every way to the existing *Bar Mitzvah* ceremony and to introduce other life-cycle ceremonies for females equivalent to those now conducted for males. We emphasize the importance of encouraging young girls to participate in the life of the synagogue.

BE IT FURTHER RESOLVED that we call upon all members and congregations to review their religious school curricula and textbooks to be certain that traditional stereotypes are not being reinforced without presentation of new role models and that young girls are not being made to feel that their place is solely in the home. We direct the Commission on Jewish Education to develop new materials which stress the numerous contributions women have made to Judaism and humanity and which emphasize the possibilities that exist for female participation within the Jewish community.

BE IT FURTHER RESOLVED that we express once again our total support of the ordination of women. We call upon the Hebrew Union College-Jewish Institute of Religion to continue to seek qualified female candidates for the rabbinate and cantorate, and we urge our congregations and all others who employ Rabbis and cantors to choose their spiritual leadership not on the basis of sex but in terms of individual ability and competence.

BE IT FURTHER RESOLVED that we call upon the HUC-JIR, the UAHC, the WUPJ and the CCAR to nominate, elect and appoint more women to their governing bodies in keeping with the historic commitment of our Movement to the religious equality of women.

Notes: *This 1975 resolution, three years after the first woman rabbi was ordained, reaffirms support not only for the ordination of women, but also for the restructuring of rituals, practices, and hiring trends to be more sensitive to the participation of women.*

RABBINICAL ASSEMBLY

RESOLUTION REGARDING WOMEN AS RABBIS (1975)

XIV. Resolution Regarding Women as Rabbis

The Rabbinical Assembly, in Convention assembled, hereby declares its desire to admit to membership in the Rabbinical Assembly, qualified applicants regardless of sex.

It further calls upon its members to work toward an end to discriminatory treatment in their individual synagogues.

It was duly moved and seconded that this proposal be adopted as a Convention resolution. During the discussion of this proposal, Rabbi Yaakov Rosenberg made the following amendment: "The Rabbinical Assembly, in Convention assembled, instructs its administration to do everything in its power to bring our influence to bear upon our alma mater, to make sure that the Jewish Theological Seminary of America admit qualified applicants to the Rabbinical School." Rabbi Rosenberg's amendment was duly seconded. After further discussion, during which opinions were expressed both in favor of and in opposition to the proposal and the amendment, Rabbi Herschel Portnoy moved that the discussion of the proposal concerning the acceptance into membership of women rabbis be tabled until a time when the entire membership of The Rabbinical Assembly will first have been notified that the discussion will take place, and that a vote will be taken, so that all of our colleagues may carefully consider the matter and exercise their vote. This motion to table was duly seconded, and passed.

Notes: *The Rabbinical Assembly is the representative rabbinic group of Conservative Judaism (approximately 1,000,000 members). 1975 witnessed this first proposal within the assembly for the admittance of women rabbis, but the issue was tabled for further discussion.*

RABBINICAL ASSEMBLY

RESOLUTION ON RABBINICAL MEMBERSHIP (1976)

BE IT RESOLVED that the Rabbinical Assembly direct its Committee on Membership to consider applications for membership in the Rabbinical Assembly of otherwise qualified candidates regardless of their sex.

BE IT RESOLVED that the Rabbinical Assembly call upon the Jewish Theological Seminary of America to admit otherwise qualified candidates to the Rabbinical School regardless of sex.

The Rabbinical Assembly calls upon the United Synagogue of America and its affiliated congregations to move with expedition to bring about full equality, regardless of sex, within the Synagogue.

This resolution was tabled.

Notes: *This resolution to admit rabbis regardless of sex was tabled, as was the previous year's resolution.*

RABBINICAL ASSEMBLY

STATEMENT ON WOMEN'S ORDINATION (1977)

I. The Role of Women

The Resolutions Committee has revised its resolution as follows:

WHEREAS the Conservative movement initiated educational policies of equal intensive Jewish education for our daughters and our sons, and

WHEREAS the Conservative movement pioneered the ceremony of Bat Mitzvah to accord ritual expression to women, and

WHEREAS The Rabbinical Assembly has supported equal status of women within the synagogue, and

WHEREAS two major rabbinic seminaries now ordain women, and

WHEREAS we recognize the enormous potential for enhancing our people by utilizing the wisdom and commitment of our people, regardless of sex, and

WHEREAS Article III of the Constitution of The Rabbinical Assembly provides that all "upon whom the title of Rabbi has been duly and properly conferred by a recognized rabbinical seminary or by Semikha; provided, however, that they have the secular training equivalent to the requirement for a college degree" shall be eligible for membership.

BE IT RESOLVED that The Rabbinical Assembly encourages the Jewish Theological Seminary of America to consider and to admit to the Rabbinical School all qualified candidates regardless of their sex.

After discussion, the following substitute resolution was presented from the floor, was duly seconded and adopted.

BE IT RESOLVED that The Rabbinical Assembly respectfully petitions the Chancellor of The Jewish Theological Seminary of America to establish an interdisciplinary commission to study all aspects of the role of women as spiritual leaders in the Conservative movement.

BE IT FURTHER RESOLVED that this study commission, whose membership shall reflect the pluralism and diversity of the Conservative movement, shall be responsible for a progress report on its findings to be presented to the Executive Council of The Rabbinical Assembly in the spring of 1978 and for a final report and recommendation at the 1979 convention of The Rabbinical Assembly.

Notes: *This proposal to admit women rabbis was still unsuccessful, and a substitute motion was adopted to ask the Jewish Theological Seminary of America to have a commission study the matter.*

RABBINICAL ASSEMBLY

FINAL REPORT OF THE COMMISSION FOR THE STUDY OF THE ORDINATION OF WOMEN AS RABBIS (1979)

I. Preamble

The deliberative body issuing this report was formed at the behest of the Rabbinical Assembly, which, at its annual convention held in May 1977 in Liberty, New York, passed the following resolution:

> Be it resolved that the Rabbinical Assembly respectfully petitions the Chancellor of The Jewish Theological Seminary of America to establish an interdisciplinary

> commission to study all aspects of the role of women as spiritual leaders in the Conservative Movement.
>
> Be it further resolved that this study commission, whose membership shall reflect the pluralism and diversity of the Conservative Movement, shall be responsible for a progress report on its findings to be presented to the Executive Council of the Rabbinical Assembly in the spring of 1978, and for a final report and recommendation at the 1979 Convention of the Rabbinical Assembly.

The formation of the Commission was announced in October 1977 by Gerson D. Cohen, Chancellor of the Jewish Theological Seminary of America, and Chairman of the Commission. Shortly thereafter, the Commission convened a series of meetings which continued throughout 1978, and which will be described below. With the submission of this final report to the 1979 Convention of the Rabbinical Assembly, the Commission terminates its career.

The fourteen men and women who accepted invitations to serve on the Commission represented a wide array of disciplines, backgrounds, and geographical regions. Their names follow:

1. Gerson D. Cohen (Chairman), Chancellor, The Jewish Theological Seminary of America.
2. Haim Z. Dimitrovsky, Professor of Talmudic Exegesis, The Jewish Theological Seminary of America.
3. Victor Goodhill, Professor of Otologic Research, University of California at Los Angeles.
4. Marion Siner Gordon, Attorney, Royal Palm Beach, Florida, and Lenox, Massachusetts.
5. Rivkah Harris, Assyriologist, Chicago, Illinois.
6. Milton Himmelfarb, Editor, *American Jewish Year Book*, and Director of Information, American Jewish Committee, New York, New York.
7. Francine Klagsbrun, Author, New York, New York.
8. Fishel A. Pearlmutter, Rabbi, Congregation B'nai Israel, Toledo, Ohio.
9. Harry M. Plotkin, Attorney, Washington, D.C.
10. Norman Redlich, Dean, New York University School of Law.
11. Elijah J. Schochet, Rabbi, Congregation Beth Kodesh, Canoga Park, California.
12. Wilfred Shuchat, Rabbi, Congregation Shaar Hashomayim, Westmount, Quebec.
13. Seymour Siegel, Professor of Theology, The Jewish Theological Seminary of America.
14. Gordon Tucker (Executive Director), Assistant to the Chancellor, The Jewish Theological Seminary of America.[1]

The first task which the Commission faced was the definition of the problem it was to consider, and an interpretation of its mandate. Although the resolution of the Rabbinical Assembly was intentionally broad, referring as it did to "all aspects of the role of women as spiritual leaders in the Conservative Movement," it was decided at the outset that this Commission would deal specifically with the question of whether qualified women may and should be ordained as rabbis by the Rabbinical School of The Jewish Theological Seminary of America. Ruled outside of the scope of the Commission's deliberations were such issues as the investiture of women as cantors, and more general forms of ritual participation and leadership. The question of whether women already ordained by a recognized rabbinical seminary ought to be considered for membership in the Rabbinical Assembly, although related to the main question, was considered by the Commission to be subordinate to it. In any event, it was the Commission's understanding that the sense of the 1977 Rabbinical Assembly Convention was that any action by the Rabbinical Assembly on membership procedures for women should and would be deferred until the Commission reported its findings on the question of ordination at the Seminary, and until the Seminary's faculty took action on the basis of the report. Thus, the Commission's inquiry focused on the posture it would recommend to the Seminary with respect to female applicants to its Rabbinical School.

This final report on the Commission's activities will have the following form: first, the procedures which were followed will be described. Then, the specific areas of inquiry will be treated, and a summary of the evidence gathered and the subsequent discussion will be provided. Following that, the recommendation of the majority of the Commission on the main question will be presented and elaborated, along with some additional recommendations which the Commission felt a responsibility to offer at this time. Finally, a separate section will contain those opinions and recommendations of members of the Commission which diverged from the majority view.

II. Procedures

Several operating principles were established at once at the Commission's initial meeting on December 12, 1977.

1. Each member of the Commission had been invited to serve by dint of personal experience and expertise, and not as a representative of any organization or institution to which he or she belonged.
2. The Commission would actively consult as wide a sampling of the constituency of the Conservative Movement as possible: rabbis, organizational leadership, synagogue leadership, and to the extent that it was possible, individuals as well.
3. The Commission would approach the main question from the perspectives of the many disciplines which impinged upon it. Those included *halakhah*, ethics, economics, sociology, psychology, and education. Pragmatic and symbolic considerations were also deemed to be important objects of deliberation.
4. Most important, despite the acknowledgment of the many facets considered relevant to the inquiry, the Commission was unanimous in its commitment to the following guideline: *no recommendation would be made which, in the opinion of members of the Commission, after having heard the testimony of experts, would contravene or be incompatible with the requirements of halakhah as the latter had been theretofore observed and developed by the Conservative Movement.* Thus, the Commission not only committed itself to recognizing the primacy of the role played by the *halakhah* in Conservative Judaism but in effect decided that in matters which profoundly affect the future course of the Movement, *halakhic* considerations and constraints must be of primary significance.

The specifics of procedure for the life of the Commission were as follows:

a. The meeting of December 12, 1977, in New York determined operating guidelines and was otherwise devoted to a general discussion of the issues to be considered.

b. A second meeting took place over a three-day period in New York, from March 12 to March 14, 1978. During that time, invited testimony was heard from the leadership of the Rabbinical Assembly, the United Synagogue of America, and the Women's League for Conservative Judaism. Those who presented testimony were thoroughly questioned by Commission members. The first extensive discussion of the *halakhic* dimensions of the issue took place at this meeting, and several members undertook to research that particular aspect thoroughly in the ensuing months, in keeping with the Commission's insistence on conformity with Jewish legal norms. Plans were made for establishing lines of communication with the general constituency of the Movement, the implementation of which will be described in the paragraphs immediately following.

c. Public meetings were arranged for various locales in North America, at which all persons affiliated with the Conservative Movement were invited to present testimony before several members of the Commission. These meetings were not for the purpose of counting "votes" pro or con, but rather for the purpose of gathering information on the problems which concerned the rank and file of the Movement, and the arguments which were being formulated by the laity. It was felt to be a fundamental principle of Jewish practice that any decision concerning Jewish usage, even an *halakhically* based decision, must take account of what will be reasonably acceptable to the community. Accordingly, meetings were set up as follows:

   a. Vancouver, British Columbia, on July 20, 1978.

   b. Los Angeles, California, on September 5-6, 1978.

   c. Minneapolis, Minnesota, on September 13, 1978.

   d. Chicago, Illinois, on September 14, 1978.

   e. Washington, D.C., on September 17, 1978.

   f. New York, New York, on November 1-2, 1978.

   g. Toronto, Ontario, on November 22, 1978.

   h. New York, New York (for members of the faculty and student body of The Jewish Theological Seminary of America) on December 3, 1978.

All of the above-mentioned public meetings were taped, and the transcripts have been made available to the public upon request. Arguments which were heard in the course of these meetings will be incorporated in the discussion of the substantive issues below: Nevertheless, some general, qualitative observations on these meetings should be made at this point:

i. Although no tally was made, or indeed ever contemplated, it was manifest that the overwhelming majority of those who chose to testify at these meetings strongly favored the ordination of women.

ii. It became equally clear that women are very much interested in continuing their drive toward full religious equalization with men; moreover, many young women are seriously interested in the rabbinate as a career.

iii. By and large, those women who aspire to become Conservative rabbis have a strong commitment to traditional values and law. In fact, many of those women could probably be characterized as having a pattern of religious observance lying near the more traditional end of the spectrum of Conservative Jewish practice.

iv. The Conservative communities, as they were represented at these public meetings, seem to be prepared to accept, even if gradually, rabbinic leadership by women.

Needless to say, these observations must be considered in the light of the uncertainty concerning just how representative a sampling of the community were those who took the trouble to testify at the hearings. In spite of the fact that there was fairly wide and general publicity in advance of each meeting, there was evidence that, for whatever reason, some persons who would oppose the ordination of women did not take the trouble to attend the hearings. On the other hand, those who did make the effort to testify probably constituted a better sampling of those Conservative Jews who have strong feelings on the subject, and that in itself is significant. In that connection, the following should be noted: the Commission took great satisfaction and pride in the fact that in community after community across North America, Conservative Jews were motivated by this issue to seriously contemplate their own personal stances not only with respect to the issue at hand, but also with respect to Jewish commitment generally. In many cases, people took the initiative in reading and studying about the issue, and in that sense, the Commission's enterprise was an educative force in the community.[2]

The Commission met again in New York on December 6-7, 1978. During those two days members shared and discussed the results of their own researchers and investigations, considered new evidence from various sources (e.g., the regional hearings, and the unsolicited communications which were addressed to the Commission fairly steadily throughout its lifetime), and eventually arrived at tentative conclusions. Subsequently, Commission members communicated via the mails and the telephone in order to arrive at the final version of this report.

Thus, the Commission was active for slightly less than fourteen months, during which time it met as a complete body for six full days, convened six public hearings plus one hearing for the Seminary community, received considerable testimony, both solicited and unsolicited, and itself commissioned a scientific survey of the Conservative laity on the issue being confronted.

III. The Issue

There are certain aspects to the question at hand regarding which it was at once established that there was unanimity among members of the Commission. These are some of the more obvious considerations which come to mind: the ability and willingness of women to perform rabbinic duties as well as men, the right to equal job opportunities, the right to pursue a career of one's choice. Indeed, it could be said that with respect to the context in which general feminist issues are discussed, there was never any serious dispute among Commission members, nor apparently within the community either. There were and are, for example, many men who fully accept the fact that their wives are pursuing careers, as well as women actually pursuing careers, who nevertheless oppose the ordination of women.

It was therefore determined at the outset that this could not be treated solely as a feminist issue. From that point of view, there was plainly very little to discuss. The complexity of the issue at hand stemmed from the fact that, although there is general agreement concerning the questions which characterize general feminist debates, there is still a wide range of other considerations of which account must be taken. Those considerations include some peculiar to the rabbinate, to Jewish practice in general, and to Conservative Judaism in particular. It was about these special considerations that discussion and debate revolved.

A. Halakhic Considerations

As indicated above, the demands of *halakhah* led the list of matters to be resolved. Even though the Commission was not charged with developing an *halakhic* stance or approach for the Conservative Movement, its commitment to the notion that legitimacy within Conservative Judaism must be measured first and foremost by an *halakhic* standard made theoretical discussions concerning the processes of *halakhah* indispensable.

The Commission eventually adopted the classical position which had been embraced by the religious leadership of the Conservative Movement since its founding. That stance maintains that the body of Jewish law is not uniform in texture, but is rather composed of materials which fall into two main categories, usually referred to as *de-oraita* (biblically ordained) and *de-rabbanan* (rabbinically developed). That which is *de-oraita* can be considered to be the very core of the system, which holds it in place and provides a frame of reference. It therefore must be treated as inviolable. Tampering with what is *de-oraita* is tantamount to destroying the core of the Jewish pattern of life as it has existed for millennia. There is positive precedent for doing so only in the most dire of circumstances, and even then with extreme caution and conservatism.

The much greater (that is, in terms of volume) overlay which is *de-rabbanan*, on the other hand, comes with procedures for change and development. What is *de-rabbanan* can develop, is in fact meant to develop, as the conditions of the Jewish community change.

That is what ensures the vibrancy and the continuity of the *halakhah* as the coordinate system which roots all Jewish communities.

It is a commonplace among Conservative Jews that the recognition of the flexibility and fluidity of the *halakhah* is one of the hallmarks of Conservative Judaism, and this is certainly true. It is equally the case that this recognition constitutes in many ways a major distinction between Conservatism and Orthodoxy. Yet it ought not to be forgotten that there are important similarities between Conservatism and Orthodoxy which need reemphasis. In particular, it cannot be stressed too strongly that the strength of Conservative Judaism depends as much on its continuation as a movement devoted to tradition as it does on its continued devotion to *halakhic* development. The two are inseparable in classical terms, and the centrality of tradition expresses itself in the conditions under which development becomes acceptable. Those conditions include:

1. The core which is *de-oraita* may not be altered or displaced. The general principles of, for example, *kashrut* or *Shabbat* could never be displaced as central pillars of Conservative Judaism.
2. Development in the domain of *de-rabbanan* must not be abrupt or discontinuous, must be rooted in traditional exegetical methodologies, and above all, must be ratified by the community of the committed and the informed.
3. The impetus for development in what is *de-rabbanan* must come from *within* the community of the committed and the informed, and not be an external influence originating outside the concerned Jewish community.

When the Commission determined that it would not recommend anything which would contravene the *halakhah*, it was to this view of the *halakhic* process that it was appealing. Faithfulness to this process constitutes, in the opinion of the Commission, a *sine qua non* for legitimacy within the Conservative Movement. Of course, the view outlined above is not univocal or free of ambiguities. Indeed, there is a certain amount of inherent ambiguity attending all three of the conditions lately listed. There is, in fact, no clear-cut demarcation line between *de-oraita* and *de-rabbanan*. Nevertheless, the existence of gray areas does not negate the fact that the areas which are clearly black or white are well distinguished, and it certainly does not preclude the use of criteria which give rise to those gray areas. Given the obvious fact that some ambiguities will be unavoidable, the alternative would be paralysis, which could not possibly serve the cause of *halakhah*.

Once agreement was reached on the philosophical and theoretical level, the specific *halakhic* problems which arise were addressed. As is well known from the recent literature on this issue, there are a variety of *halakhic* criteria which have traditionally distinguished between men and women. Primary among these are the following:

1. According to some sources, women may be ineligible to be appointed to any office of communal responsibility in the Jewish community.
2. Women are exempted from the obligation to study Torah (except for the acquisition of knowledge concerning obligations they do have), although there is no problem presented by their voluntarily assuming that obligation.
3. Women are exempted from positive time-dependent commandments, with a few notable exceptions. The most relevant commandments under this category for purposes of this Commission are those relating to public worship, for exemption from performance raises problems concerning eligibility to discharge the obligation of another person who cannot claim exemption.
4. Women are traditionally ineligible to serve as witnesses in judicial proceedings, including the execution of documents determining personal and familial status.
5. Women are, by virtue of (4) above, considered by most traditional authorities to be ineligible to serve as judges.

All of these sex-role distinctions of the *halakhah* were discussed and researched by members of the Commission. The results of those deliberations will now be summarized:

The role of the rabbi as we know it today is not one which is established in classical Jewish texts, but rather is one which has evolved through social need and custom. Consequently, there is no specifiable *halakhic* category which can be identified with the modern rabbinate, nor with the currently accepted mode of ordination. Ordination at the Jewish Theological Seminary of America is done in a way which is nearly indistinguishable from the granting of an academic degree at the successful completion of a course of study. Of course, it still has a profound religious and symbolic significance not shared by any academic degree. In other words, issues relating to ordination are not *halakhic* issues per se, though it is certainly true that there may be serious ramifications of decisions concerning ordination which can lead to a confrontation with certain *halakhic* principles. Strictly speaking, point (1) above is general enough to present an *halakhic* problem concerning ordination. That point has its origin in a passage in the *halakhic* midrash on the Book of Deuteronomy, the *Sifre*. On the verse in Deuteronomy 17:15, "You shall be free to set a king over yourself," the *Sifre* comments, "A king and not a queen." Extrapolating from this comment, Maimonides in *Laws Relating to Kings* 1:5 says, "Only men may be appointed [to positions of authority] in Israel."

Insufficient as Halakhic Barrier.

After considering the opinion of Maimonides on this matter, the Commission decided that it was beset by numerous ambiguities and uncertainties and should not be accounted as an immutable provision of the *halakhah*.

The modern rabbinate cannot be analogized to an appointment on the order of magnitude of the ancient monarchy. The many obvious high-level appointments of women in modern Jewish life indicate the passing of this principle from general Jewish usage. The Commission therefore determined that this *halakhah* as formulated by Maimonides was insufficient to pose an *halakhic* barrier to the ordination of women.

With respect to point (2) above, the Conservative Movement has already taken the strongest possible stand in favor of obligating women to study Torah on a basis equal to that of men. The Movement's introduction of *Bat Mitzvah* half a century ago, its educational programs in Camp Ramah, United Synagogue Youth, Leaders Training Fellowship, and last but not least, the schools of the Jewish Theological Seminary of America, all bear witness to that stand. Indeed, the history of the Conservative Movement on the issue of the religious education of women not only vitiates the force of point (2), but actually constitutes a consideration in favor of ordaining women, as will be noted below.

Points (3), (4), and (5) are a group in several respects. First, they have all been dealt with to some extent by a constituent arm of the Conservative Movement. Second, they are all *halakhic* sex-role distinctions which are secondary to the issue of ordination, as will be explained. Third, although they are secondary to the ordination issue *logically*, they are closely connected to the rabbinic role *practically*. These points accounted for most of the *halakhically* based discussions during the Commission's proceedings.

Matters of *halakhic* import in the Conservative Movement have always been channeled through the Rabbinical Assembly Committee on Jewish Law and Standards (henceforth: the Law Committee). That Committee's composition and rules of procedure have varied considerably over the years, but it has consistently defined itself as a panel which primarily makes recommendations on the basis of legal scholarship; its decisions have binding power on Movement leaders only when a very strong consensus condition is met. For the past several years, the operating rule has been that only a position held by all but two or fewer members of the Committee is binding; a minority position with three adherents on the Committee becomes a legitimate option for Conservative congregations and rabbis. Despite inevitable disagreements concerning one or another of the Law Committee's decisions, nearly universal respect has been accorded to the principle of legitimate option. Accordingly, in considering the proper course for the entire Conservative Movement on a matter such as the one under scrutiny, the history of the Law Committee's treatment of some of the related questions must be looked into.

The Law Committee published a majority decision in 1955 which allowed women the privilege of an *aliyah* at Torah-reading services. Although this practice is far from universal in Conservative congregations, it is a practice which is growing and which was legitimated by the 1955 decision. In 1973, the same committee issued a majority responsum which permitted congregations to count women as part of the *minyan* for public worship. This practice has likewise not nearly become universal, but the number of congregations which have been accepting it is steadily growing. Finally, a *minority* report in 1974 declared that women should be permitted to serve as witnesses in legal proceedings, including the signing of *ketubot* and *gittin*. Since that minority report was issued by six committee members, the rules of the Law Committee imply that it is a legitimate option for rabbis and congregations in the Conservative Movement. Thus, the Commission established that the practices referred to in points (3), (4), and (5) had already been declared by the Committee on Jewish Law and Standards of the Rabbinical Assembly to be *halakhically* acceptable options within the Conservative Movement. Hence the Commission determined that its resolution of the ordination issue could not lead to a possible contravention of a binding standard for the conservative Movement.

More important than the foregoing observations was the fact that irrespective of what one's *halakhic* view is on the matter of a woman performing these practices, they are strictly secondary to the issue of ordination. A wide variety of functions are viewed as part of the role of the rabbi today. Among these are teaching, preaching, counselling, officiating at religious ceremonies, representing the Jewish community, etc. Leading a prayer service as the *shaliah tzibur*, receiving an *aliyah*, or even signing a *ketubah* or *get* as a witness are not among these essential functions. A rabbi supervising divorce proceedings might be entitled to sign the *get* as a witness, and may on occasion do so as a matter of convenience, but surely it is not the rabbi's role qua rabbi to do so. Similar observations would apply to other forms of testimony and to the various roles associated with public worship which have been mentioned. The simple fact is that the rabbinate, as noted above, is not defined or circumscribed by *halakhic* strictures. Hence there can be no direct *halakhic* objection to the conferral of the title "rabbi" upon a woman, together with all the rights and responsibilities to perform the functions essentially connected to the office. In connection with this, the Commission noted that it is a commonplace to ordain *Kohanim*, even though officiating at a funeral, which can pose *halakhic* problems for a *Kohen*, is popularly viewed as a rabbinic function.

One objection raised against this analysis was given very serious consideration by the Commission. It was as follows: granted that the religious functions in question are logically distinct from the role of the rabbi, they are certainly connected closely enough in practice to be a serious cause for concern. Specifically, it is unreasonable, according to this objection, to ordain a woman, place her in a pulpit in a small community, and expect that she will not lead prayer services, sign legal documents affecting personal status, etc. The very inevitability of one event following on the heels of the other might make the two inseparable for the purposes of this discussion.

In the course of lengthy consideration of this objection, the Commission noted several things: (a) As indicated above, previous Law Committee decisions have resolved the problems concerning the practices in question for many members of the Conservative Movement. Indeed, there are already many congregations giving *aliyot* to women and counting them in a *minyan*, and there are Conservative rabbis who, in accordance with the minority responsum of the Law Committee, allow knowledgeable women to sign *ketubot* and *gittin*. (b) Even for those who do not accept the lenient positions on these issues (and this group is largest on the question of testimony, where a good number believe that a female serving as a witness is contrary to biblical law), the objection is still not connected to ordination itself, but rather to an assessment of what is quite likely to happen given a certain job situation in a certain place. The Commission decided that there was little point in speculating on such matters, particularly given the fact that with the increased education and activism of women in the Conservative Movement, the act of ordination itself would not be likely to significantly affect the prevalence of practices which are not universally accepted. Excessive concern over possible objectionable effects of an unobjectionable action (i.e., ordination), where those effects are objectionable to only part of the community, and are not caused solely by that action, can easily degenerate into an *ad infinitum* list of potential objections. (c) Observations (a) and (b) taken together make it clear that there is no cogent argument on *halakhic* grounds for denying a sincere, committed woman the opportunity to study for and achieve the office of rabbi.

In closing this section on *halakhah*, the Commission notes that in the medieval period, the spiritual leadership of women was not unknown. One bit of evidence for this is to be found in the fourteenth-century work of a Spanish rabbi, known as *Sefer Hahinukh*, which assumes that a woman is eligible to perform the most basic of the classical rabbinic functions, viz., deciding specific matters of law. Section 152 of that treatise, which deals with the prohibition of deciding matters of ritual law while intoxicated, notes that the prohibition "applies to males, as well as to a knowledgeable woman who is eligible to give such instruction."

To summarize, then: The *halakhic* objections to the ordination of women center around disapproval of the performance by a woman of certain functions. Those functions, however, are not essentially rabbinic, nor are they universally disapproved, by the accepted rules governing the discussion of *halakhah* in the Conservative Movement. *There is no direct halakhic objection to the acts of training and ordaining a woman to be a rabbi, preacher, and teacher in Israel.*

The problems associated with ancillary functions were deemed by the Commission to be insufficient grounds for denying a considerable and growing group of highly talented and committed Jewish women the access they desire to the roles of spiritual and community leaders.

B. Ethical Considerations

Although there was some discussion on the subject, there was no agreement among Commission members concerning precisely what the relationship is or ought to be between *halakhah* and ethics. One general observation was, however, agreed upon. In many areas of Jewish law, the developmental history of the *halakhah* exhibits a strong tendency to approach ever more closely an ideal ethical state within the parameters and constraints of the *halakhah*. Indeed, echoing the opinion of Rav that the *mitzvot* were given us in order to "refine us," the Commission accepted the view that the commandments have among their chief purposes the ethical perfection of the individual and of society. The basic ethical principle underlying the democratic society in which we live—a principle that has deep roots in our biblical-rabbinic tradition—is that each person should have at least a legally equal opportunity to pursue a chosen career. This principle should be followed within the Jewish community more especially where no specific *halakhic* violation is involved. Since there is no specific *halakhic* argument against ordaining women, denying a Jewish woman the opportunity to serve the Jewish community and the cause of Torah as a rabbi merely because she is a woman would be ethically indefensible.

One ethical objection considered by the Commission was actually rooted in sociology and economics. That objection invoked the possibility, or even the likelihood, considering the initial experiences of other movements which have ordained women, that female Conservative rabbis might at first face great difficulty in finding congregational positions. This argument then maintained that it is unethical to train people for a profession with the knowledge that they will find it extremely difficult to practice that profession and thereby fulfill their aspirations and earn a livelihood. The Commission dealt with this objection in several ways. First, it was noted that the results of the public hearings which were held in the fall of 1978 did not indicate that most congregations would be unreasonably reluctant to hire a female rabbi. On the contrary, there was growing evidence, gathered at the Commission's hearings and through the United Synagogue of America, that the receptivity to female rabbis in the communities was much higher now than it had been several years ago. Apparently, familiarity with the issues, as well as the presence and visibility of some ordained women over the last six years had taken effect. At any rate, the assumption of a bleak future in the job market seemed quite unjustified, particularly given the fact that the Conservative Movement is experiencing a shortage of rabbis to serve its congregations.

In addition, the Commission questioned whether job placement was a legitimate ethical issue. Many graduate and professional schools in all fields train students year after year despite wide fluctuations in the job market. While the size of an entering class should certainly not be excessively out of line with what the market can absorb, there is nothing unethical about providing an opportunity for a person to train for his or her chosen profession despite possible difficulties in locating a suitable job situation. What could be improper is withholding information about the realities of the job market, but that is certainly not a serious possibility.

A more serious ethical concern was voiced many times by many interested parties. This objection concerned the right of a minority to have its commitment to conscience respected. Specifically, it was argued as follows: when the Law Committee decided certain *halakhic* issues by means of majority and minority reports, those whose consciences directed them to the more traditional position could still feel comfortable and legitimate, while respecting their colleagues' right to choose the position which they felt was mandated by the relevant factors. Were the Seminary to begin ordaining women, however, it would be the first time that the central academic institution of the Movement would have entered the arena to take a public stance on an issue of *halakhah*, a stance which could *ipso facto* become the standard for the Movement. Those who opposed the ordination of women on religious grounds would then have no legitimate option but to silently acquiesce in the decision, or to leave the Movement.

The sincerity and the frequency with which this argument was raised led the Commission to consider it very carefully. Having done so, the Commission recognized that there would indeed be some unavoidable uneasiness whatever its recommendation would be. Nevertheless, there were three points which were found to mitigate some of the strength of this objection:

1. This objection partially hinges on the assumption that there are serious matters of *halakhic* import connected with a decision by the Seminary to ordain women, and that these are serious enough to create difficult crises of conscience. Because of the analysis given in the previous section of this report, it was felt that this objection was overstated.

2. The objection apparently is intended to argue that the Seminary faculty should not be taking a stance, so as to avoid foreclosing the legitimacy of the opposing view. It fails to take into account the fact that at this point, for the Seminary faculty not to vote to change the status quo would *in itself* be a stance on the issue. Moreover, it has been the observation of the Commission that there are commitments to conscience among those who favor the ordination of women which are as strong as those among opponents of that decision. The reality is that the Seminary faculty, irrespective of what it does, is going to give rise to some uneasiness in some quarters. This is not to say that one position is obviously better than another, but it does obviate the force of this objection to action on the part of the Seminary faculty. The important issue which does arise out of this is the need to assuage the uneasiness and ensure that it is only a temporary reaction to a decision of great import.

3. Finally, this objection reveals a bias, which has often been expressed to the Commission, against the Seminary faculty taking a stand on *any halakhic* matters affecting the Conservative Movement. This bias was of particular concern to the Commission, and was discussed on several occasions. It was ultimately the consensus of the Commission that on an issue such as the present one, one which will affect the very nature of the American rabbinate, and which manifestly will not go away if ignored, it is rather the unavoidable responsibility of the Seminary faculty to get involved and take a stand. The Commission assumes that the stand which the faculty will find it necessary to take on any *halakhic* issue will be a thoroughly informed stand, and that the decision which it now must of necessity make on the issue of ordaining women will be based not only on the careful study of this report, but on the examination of all other data available to it which relate to this issue.

The most compelling ethical argument heard by the Commission was one in favor of ordaining women, and it was heard from members of the Conservative laity in many different parts of North America. As noted in the previous section, the Conservative Movement has a proud history of educating females in Jewish Studies from the earliest ages on a perfect par with males. In fact, it is worth considering for a moment what it is like today for boys and girls to grow up in a committed Jewish home identified and affiliated with the Conservative Movement. Such a boy and girl would both be given the very same Hebrew or Day School education from the outset. Both would prepare for *Bar* or *Bat Mitzvah* ceremonies and in most cases perform the same functions in the service. Both would likely receive intense Judaic training at Camp Ramah. They would proceed to Hebrew High School, join LTF and/or United Synagogue Youth. In many congregations, they would participate in public worship equally through adolescence, building on their acquired Jewish skills. They would seek out the same reinforcement of their Jewish values while away at college, and form a more sophisticated intellectual commitment to Judaism. That commitment would in some cases be strong enough to generate a desire to study for the rabbinate at the Seminary of the Conservative Movement. Suddenly, discontinuously, at this point, the female is differentiated from the male in being unable to fulfill the education she was given and encouraged to pursue in the way she chose to fulfill it.

This scenario was not an abstract creation, but rather was the actual testimony of many parents who, confronted by the problem, were unable to explain the sudden differentiation to their daughters. In considering this increasingly common phenomenon, the Commission felt that it was morally wrong to maintain an educational structure that treats males and females equally up to the final stage, but distinguishes between them at that stage, *without a firm and clearly identifiable halakhic reason for doing so*. In such a case, the Commission felt that the secondary *halakhically* related issues dealt with in the previous section paled even further in significance. On balance, the ethical arguments *coupled with the absence of halakhic counter-argument* were considered by the Commission to constitute a strong case for the training and ordination of women as rabbis at the Jewish Theological Seminary of America.

C. Other Considerations

A good deal of other evidence came to the attention of the Commission and was discussed by it. Most of it tended to support a decision to recommend the training and ordination of women as Conservative rabbis. These blocks of evidence fall under a variety of rubrics and will be summarized in this section.

1. Preliminary data from the survey commissioned by this body indicated that, in absolute numbers, a majority of the laity of the Conservative Movement was ready to accept women in the role of congregational spiritual leader.
2. Those persons who testified at the regional hearings convened by the Commission represented an extraordinary range of backgrounds, talents, professions, and ages. In all, a considerable majority of these strongly favored the ordination of women in the

Conservative Movement. Another fact which came to light as a result of the hearings was that there are more women interested in pursuing this career out of genuine commitment to the traditional Jewish community than had been assumed.

3. Although the opinions of members of the psychological profession previously reported in the literature were mixed, those professionals in the field who made contact voluntarily with the Commission were overwhelmingly positive and encouraging on the issue of ordination.

4. Two United Synagogue congregations are currently being served in some rabbinic or quasi-rabbinic role by a woman, and both communicated, through official leadership as well as through individual congregants, their satisfaction with that situation.

5. The student body of the Seminary's Rabbinical School, when surveyed by the Student Government, expressed support for the admission of women to the Rabbinical School by an affirmative vote of 74 percent.

6. It became clear as well that a decision not to ordain women would mean the neglect if not the rejection of a pool of talented, committed, and energetic women who could eventually represent 50 percent of the potential spiritual leaders, and who could play a major role in revitalizing Jewish tradition and values in the Conservative Movement. Indications are that the Movement cannot afford the cost of refusing to take advantage of that leadership talent at the present time.

There was one other major consideration which was voiced many times, and could best be classified under the category of "symbolism." This point was raised by many persons who believed on substantive grounds that the ordination of women was both correct and defensible, but who feared what they termed the symbolic break with tradition that such a move would represent. For exponents of this argument, the symbolic result of admitting women to the rabbinate would be a blurring of the ideological lines which have divided Conservatism from more liberal Jewish movements. That, it is claimed, would destroy the main attraction of the Conservative Movement, to wit, the coexistence of authenticity of tradition with a critical view aimed at developing that tradition within the framework of *halakhic* norms.

The Commission took this argument most seriously, but concluded that it was insufficient to militate against ordaining women. The reason for this conclusion was that, by the Commission's own commitments and chosen procedures, a recommendation in favor of ordination would be based on a thorough and predominant commitment to *halakhah*. In a case such as this, where a recommended development is consistent with *halakhah*, and manifestly to the advantage of the community, symbolic considerations must not be allowed to block that development. To be sure, the symbolic considerations must be taken very seriously, but rather as a challenge to educate the community to the extent that it is evident to all that the development is in consonance with the historical ideological commitments of Conservative Judaism, and does not represent an ideological shift. It is hoped that this report will constitute a first step in that process of education.

IV. Recommendations

Based on its overall commitment to *halakhic* authenticity, and all of the evidence and reasoning which have been summarized or alluded to in this report, the signatories to this majority opinion recommend that qualified women be ordained as rabbis in the Conservative Movement. Specifically, the recommendations are:

A. That the Rabbinical School of the Jewish Theological Seminary of America revise its admission procedures to allow for applications from female candidates and the processing thereof for the purpose of admission to the ordination program on a basis equal to that maintained heretofore for males.

B. That this revision of policy be accomplished as quickly as possible, preferably so as to allow applications from women for the academic year beginning in September 1979.

C. That the Jewish Theological Seminary of America take steps to set up appropriate apparatuses for the recruitment, orientation, and eventually, career placement of female rabbinical students.

D. That the major arms of the Conservative Movement immediately begin discussion of procedures to be followed to educate the community concerning issues raised in this report so as to ensure as smooth and as harmonious an adjustment to the new policy as possible.

In making these recommendations, the Commission is making no recommendation in regard to traditional practices relating to testimony, and no implications concerning such practices should be drawn on the basis of this report.

The following members of the Commission join in supporting the above majority report:

Gerson D. Cohen
Victor Goodhill
Marion Siner Gordon
Rivkah Harris
Milton Himmelfarb
Francine Klagsbrun
Fishel A. Pearlmutter
Harry M. Plotkin
Norman Redlich
Seymour Siegel
Gordon Tucker

Minority Opinion

Although the signatories to this section are in sympathy with many of the arguments and sentiments expressed by our colleagues on the Commission, and embodied in the majority opinion given above, we remain opposed to the ordination of women as rabbis in the Conservative Movement. Since many of the reasons for this conclusion have already been discussed or at least mentioned earlier in this report, we shall simply list briefly our motivations for arriving at this recommendation.

A. Our main thrust has to do with certain *halakhic* problems which cannot in our opinion be separated from the question of ordination but flow from it almost inexorably. Not all congregations accept the view that women may be counted in a *minyan*, receive *aliyot*, or lead the service in liturgical prayer as a surrogate for others. Many more congregations and many Jews outside our Movement may be affected by practices in connection with testimony relating to marriage and divorce, where the laws are restrictive in the case of women. You cannot, within the present climate of the Conservative Movement, ordain women and expect that they will not at some point infringe on these *halakhic* restrictions in the performance of their rabbinical duties.

B. We fear the possible disruption of the unity of the Movement. One of the consequences of a decision to ordain women might very well be the violations of *halakhic* principles adhered to by others in the Movement, which in turn would result in the untenable position of individual rabbis being unable in good conscience to recognize the validity of marriages, divorces, and conversions supervised by one of their colleagues.

C. A decision to ordain women would mark the first time in recent history that the Seminary had entered the arena of *halakhic* decision-making. The centrality and authority of the Seminary would perforce be a uniformizing influence which could have the unfortunate effect of foreclosing the options of minorities wishing to remain within the Movement.

D. Finally, we are concerned that at a time when American Jewish youth seem to be turning more toward traditional values, and to an authentic *halakhic* life-style, this would seriously compromise the traditional image of the Conservative Movement, and the Jewish Theological Seminary of America as an authentic *halakhic* institution. We feel strongly that such matters of symbolism must be taken as seriously as possible, for a wrong decision on an issue of this magnitude will, in our opinion, alienate many more *halakhically* committed people than it will attract.

For these reasons, we recommend to the leaders of the Conservative Movement that appropriate roles be created for Jewish women short of ordination so that their commitment and talents may be a source of blessing and not of unnecessary controversy.

The following members of the Commission join in supporting the above minority opinion:

Haim Z. Dimitrovsky
Elijah J. Schochet
Wilfred Shuchat

Endnotes

[1] As executive director, Rabbi Tucker was also responsible for the writing of this report, which was carefully reviewed and approved by the signatories to both the majority and minority opinions.

[2] A survey of the Conservative Jewish community of a more scientific nature was considered to be desirable as well. As a result, very generous professional assistance was secured from two quarters. The first was the market research firm of Yankelovich, Skelly, and White, which designed a questionnaire and a tabulation plan, and provided advice on methods of choosing a sample and distributing the questionnaires. Special thanks are due to Ms. Florence Skelly and Mr. Arthur White, as well as to their associates, Mr. Sanford Deutsch and Ms. Ann D. Clurman. Second, Dr. Saul Shapiro lent his assistance in programming and running the tabulation of the completed questionnaires. In all, fourteen Conservative congegations were sent some 300 questionnaires each. The Commission only had the benefit of some preliminary results, due to some unavoidable delays in the processing of the data. However, fully tabulated and cross-correlated results have now been obtained, and the Commission hopes that the bodies which will bear the responsibility for considering, debating, and perhaps implementing the recommendations made herein will consult those results in the process.

Notes: *This report by a group of faculty members of the Jewish Theological Seminary of America to the Rabbinical Assembly takes a clear stand in support of the ordination of women. The commission determined that there were no overwhelming obstacles to the ordination of women within the* halakhah, *the Jewish heritage of oral and written law, adherence to which, as a strong but flexible system, is the hallmark of Conservative Judaism. Three of the fourteen commission members disagreed and signed a Minority Report. Their objections centered upon the* halakhic *principles of some which might be infringed upon by the activities of women rabbis, and by the various disruptions which might occur in the Conservative Movement.*

RABBINICAL ASSEMBLY

RESOLUTION ON THE DECISION TO ORDAIN WOMEN (1979)

WHEREAS The Rabbinical Assembly, in Convention assembled, commends Dr. Gerson Cohen, the Chancellor of the Jewish Theological Seminary and the members of the Commission for the report on Ordination of Women as Conservative Rabbis, and

WHEREAS this recommendation will be advocated to the Seminary faculty, and

WHEREAS the Seminary faculty will make its decision on this matter within one year, and

WHEREAS many members of The Rabbinical Assembly will not have had the opportunity to hear or read the report of Chancellor Cohen prior to the end of this convention, and

WHEREAS it has been the tradition of the Conservative movement that no one institution attempt to unduly influence the modus operandi of another, therefore

BE IT HEREBY RESOLVED that The Rabbinical Assembly will take no action on the question of the ordination of women or on the Commission recommendation prior to the study of the report by the full membership and the study, analysis and decision of the Seminary faculty on the recommendation.

This recommendation was duly seconded and adopted.

Notes: *Having received the commissioned report on the ordination of women as rabbis, the Rabbinical Assembly decided to withhold comment until the whole seminary faculty had a chance to vote on the report.*

RABBINICAL ASSEMBLY

STATEMENT ON WOMEN'S ORDINATION (1980)

II. The Ordination of Women

WHEREAS the Jewish Theological Seminary of America's Faculty Senate has tabled the motion for admission of qualified women into its Rabbinic ordination program;

THE RABBINICAL ASSEMBLY URGENTLY PETITIONS the Seminary and its authoritative bodies to discuss and vote on the motion tabled with all deliberate speed.

Without wishing to dictate to the Seminary Faculty its position in any way, THE RABBINICAL ASSEMBLY GOES ON RECORD as favoring the ordination of women.

Notes: *Despite an original position of hesitation in 1975, the Rabbinical Assembly eventually offered clear support for the ordination of women and urged the faculty of the Jewish Theological Seminary of America to vote on the issue. That vote was finally taken on October 24, 1983, and was 34 to 8 (with one abstention) in favor of admitting women to the rabbinical program. The first Conservative woman rabbi was ordained in 1985.*

Other Religious Bodies

North America is now home to many groups which are neither Christian in the traditional sense (i.e. Catholic, Protestant, or Eastern Orthodox) nor Jewish. Other practices include Hinduism and Buddhism from Asia, Islam from the Middle East and elsewhere, the Latter-Day Saint tradition native to the United States, and those that follow other traditions, both ancient and modern. Some of these groups, like Islam, do not allow women to serve as religious leaders, and there has been little significant dialogue within Islam on that topic. For other groups, the lack of a formal ordination process eliminates much of the controversy. A good representation of a nontraditional group is provided by the Reorganized Church of Jesus Christ of Latter Day Saints. Its office of priesthood differs, for example, from the mainstream Christian tradition because it is open in one way or another to much of the membership, including women. When controversies do arise in these groups, however, arguments for and against women's ordination are similar to those presented in Christian, Protestant, or Jewish communities.

REORGANIZED CHURCH OF JESUS CHRIST OF LATTER DAY SAINTS

REPORT OF THE COMMITTEE ON THE ROLE OF WOMEN IN THE CHURCH: MINISTRY AND OFFICE (1973)

Ministry and Office

It would be hardly responsible to attempt any appraisal of the role of women in the Church without considering the matter of ordination. It is not too difficult to affirm that all members of the Church, male and female, share a common *calling* (connecting the source of their sense of vocation), a common *ministry* (indicating the character of the activity), and possibly even a common *priesthood* (indicating the orientation of the activity: on behalf of others). However, the matter of *office*, which has to do with differentiated role is a matter at issue.

This committee believes that there is considerable difficulty in holding to a view of the exclusion of women from the differentiated roles of *office* on any theological grounds. While it may be possible to affirm that "all are called" in terms of the Doctrine and Covenants statement, it is hard to escape the conclusion that, in practice, some are called more than others, and some are excluded from some callings, upon grounds that bear investigation.

Two possible difficulties may be foreshadowed at this point. In the first place, the argument from *precedent* or *silence* may be invoked. That is, the contemporary scriptures are silent upon the matter, except for the customary use of the generic *men*, and no precedent can be called upon citing an instance of ordination, unless the terminology employed with respect to Emma Smith is strained. In response to this we must consider the strong, and probably determinative influence of traditional expectations as a factor dictating against the possibility in the past. It is submitted that this is by no means of itself a persuasive argument: the inferential response to revelatory experience on the part of presiding officers is very much influenced by precedent and expectation.

In the second place, it may be suggested that any consideration to extend the right of office to women would raise substantial practical problems. In light of the fact that the ordination of women would signify a departure from long-established patterns and mental-set, it is only to be expected that problems would arise. It is certain that the breaking out of its Jewish mold of the early Christian church did not proceed without much anguish and readjustment. The operative question was not, and should not now be, "what is easy?" but "what is faithful?"

The Committee wishes to emphasize that no study of the question should be started from the question, "should we ordain women?" Rather the starting point should be a doctrine of creation and an understanding of personhood, set alongside and seen in terms of the calling of God to all persons to be the church, fully and equally.

However, it is at this point that the Committee feels it reaches the limits of its commission. Any specific recommendations would need to be established on the basis of a carefully articulated and comprehensive theological understanding of ministry. They would require perspectives upon such questions as:

a. What are the parameters of the meaning of such concepts as *ordain, priesthood, calling, set apart*?

b. How does *office* relate to the foregoing?

c. How is *authority* to be understood?

c. How do theological, historical, sociological and ecclesiastical considerations relate to these concepts?

It would appear that up to the present time our understandings and practices have been grounded in implicit and largely unexamined presuppositions rather than upon carefully and coherently stated positions. For this reason the Committee is of the opinion that a careful study, preferably in the form of a *World Church Seminar*, should form a necessary correlate to the study of the role of women, since the two concerns are essentially related.

We acknowledge the brevity of this report. A number of questions and concerns have been explored at greater depth than this paper reflects. The Committee would be pleased to be available for personal conversations with respect to any of the considerations or proposals included.

By way of conclusion, the Committee would like to express the feeling that the matters under consideration have taken on the character of urgency in view of the weight of concern which can no longer (if it ever could have been) be dismissed as fadism or extremism. Either to delay or to make premature foreclosures upon the future would appear to diminish the impact of a prophetic church.

Notes: *This is an excerpt from the 1973 "Report of the Committee on the Role of Women in the Church," of the Reorganized Church of Jesus Christ of Latter-Day Saints (approximately 200,000 members). In this brief look at the issue, the committee notes that the question cannot be dismissed as "fadism or extremism," and supports further careful study.*

REORGANIZED CHURCH OF JESUS CHRIST OF LATTER DAY SAINTS

RESOLUTION AND LETTER ON THE ORDINATION OF WOMEN (1976)

1141. Whereas, Resolution 564, adopted April 18, 1905, is no longer responsive to the needs of the church; and

Whereas, A limited number of recommendations for women to be ordained to the priesthood have been submitted through adminstrative channels; and

Whereas, We are restricted from processing these under the provisions of Resolution 564 arrived at by common consent; and

Whereas, After research, consultation, and prayerful consideration of many factors, we find no ultimate theological reason why women, if it were thought wise to do so, could not hold priesthood; and

Whereas, Acceptability by those to whom ministry is offered is a significant factor and to some extent would be determined by existing cultural and sociological conditions; therefore be it

Resolved, That Resolution 564 be rescinded; and be it further

Resolved, That consideration of the ordination of women be deferred until it appears in the judgment of the First Presidency that the church, by common consent, is ready to accept such ministry.

(The Conference ordered an explanatory letter of the First Presidency to be published, and this was printed on pages 265-266 of the 1976 *Conference Bulletin.*)

Letter from the President to Headquarters and Field Administrators

Dear Co-workers:

Since the distribution of the proposed resolution entitled "Ordination of Women" we have received some inquiries the nature of which lead us to believe that some additional information may be helpful.

We are appreciative of the fact that this is a fairly complex issue, and it is our desire to avoid misunderstandings of our intent. In this spirit we are offering some additional comments to aid administrative officers and others in interpreting the meaning of the resolution.

At the World Conference in 1970 a resolution was presented which ended with the following paragraph:

> "Resolved, That the World Conference of 1970 ask the First Presidency to provide a clarifying statement on the ordination of women to priesthood which can serve as a guideline to the church in this matter."

The resolution was laid on the table.

Since that time, however, the question of the ordination of women has increasingly been raised in the church, and during the last inter-Conference period two formal recommendations for the ordination of women to priesthood offices have been referred by administrative officers to the First Presidency. As a result it is the belief of the First Presidency that we do need to give some direction and leadership to the church in this matter.

It is our conviction that the question of the ordination of women to priesthood is not addressed in the Scriptures, and our basic theology does not give us a firm basis for resolving this matter. Section 24 of the Doctrine and Covenants was addressed to Emma Smith and does indicate that she be ordained to "expound Scriptures, and to exhort the church, according as it shall be given thee by my Spirit,'' but it does not indicate an ordination to priesthood.

It is the belief of the First Presidency that the role of women relative to priesthood has been largely determined by historical, psychological, and sociological factors of society. The roles of men and women are not less significant because they have been culturally determined, and certainly these are important in the church as well as to other aspects of society. It does mean, however, that the society itself is free to make decisions about cultural changes.

It is, therefore, our belief that the church is free to discuss and determine in a responsible way questions relative to the ordination of women.

The First Presidency do have deep concerns about this matter, however. Firstly, we are greatly concerned about the divisive effects of this consideration in the church. It is our belief that the ordination of women is not a crucial factor in the development of the church now. Whatever values there might be in determining the question either for or against the ordination of women are small as compared to the harm that would be done by polarizing the church and causing estrangement over this issue. Time and thoughtful consideration in the spirit of mutual concern and love will help us resolve the matter without conflict.

Secondly, a decision on this matter based upon ''rights'' and imposed by a small legislative majority upon the remainder of the church violates the spirit of priesthood. Priesthood is a burden to be accepted for the blessing of the people and for achieving God's purposes. It is not a right to be claimed and demanded. Therefore, no matter what the proper resolution to this problem may be, a bitter controversy over the matter would do violence to the concept of priesthood.

For the reasons mentioned above we have proposed a resolution on the ordination of women to the coming World Conference which we feel would be in the best interests of the church. Firstly, this resolution would rescind G.C.R. 564, thus taking from our legislative actions a resolution which we believe is offensive to many people.

Secondly, the resolution recommends that further Conference consideration of the question of the ordination of women be deferred, thus giving time for thoughtful discussion of the issue to take place hopefully leading in time to a greater spirit of unity among the church membership on the matter. Although the consideration of this question can be initiated by the appropriate jurisdictions, quorums, or delegate bodies of any succeeding World Conference, it would be our hope that the matter will not be pressed prematurely. If at some later period we feel it wise to introduce the matter to the World Conference we will do so. In any event the church should be reassured that the First Presidency have no intention to approve the ordination of women until the World Conference takes some action to provide for it.

The First Presidency

Notes: *Printed here is the approved 1976 General Conference resolution and the explanatory* letter *which was ordered to accompany it. The resolution opened administrative channels for the future consideration of ordained women, but postponed such consideration until the First Presidency and the church judge the timing to be appropriate. The letter from the First Presidency implies that there may be some future affirmative action, but not until it is clear such action will not have a harmful divisive effect upon the church.*

REORGANIZED CHURCH OF JESUS CHRIST OF LATTER DAY SAINTS

REPORT OF THE STUDY ON THE ORDINATION OF WOMEN (1984)

H-1

Report of the Study on the Ordination of Women

This report contains the following elements:

Part I—The Task Force's analysis of the findings of a survey of church members and leaders throughout the world

Part II—The Task Force's study of the perspectives of various national, cultural, and ethnic groups where the church is established. . . .

We respectfully submit this report to the 1984 World Conference. The data and information contained in it indicate that considerable diversity of opinion exists within the World Church on this issue. This is reflected not only in results of our own internal survey but also in the studies of other persons and groups which have focused on the larger populations in which Saints constitute a relatively small minority. Such diversity represents both polarized segments of populations and other persons who are seeking honestly to receive further light on the subject.

We trust that our efforts are in keeping with the intention of the Conference, and we stand ready to respond to additional inquiries. A complete copy of the data gleaned from the use of the survey instrument is on file in the World Church Library, along with a more complete analysis of our findings. These will be available for perusal by serious students.

THE TASK FORCE

Carol Anway
Tom Edmunds
Ardis Everett
Duane G. Graham
Irene Jones
John P. Kirkpatrick
Jeri L. Shumate
Alan D. Tyree

Part I

Introduction. This paper (Part I) reports results of a survey which was conducted in response to the directive of the 1982 World Conference to ". . . assess the opinions of leaders and members throughout the church on the issue of the ordination of women." The survey included a representative sample of church leaders and members throughout the church in more than twenty nations.

Procedures. A task force appointed by the First Presidency planned and conducted the study. A questionnaire was written with the intention of examining attitudes toward ordination of women. This was written, field-tested in a local congregation, revised, and used in the survey. . . .

The sampling of subjects for this study was a complex procedure. The ideal would have been to draw a random sample of adequate size from each nation in which the church is established. Seldom in survey research can the ideal be realized, however, and in this instance some modifications were necessary. The technique used and the resulting sample are described in this section.

Because of demands relating to distance, illiteracy, and variations of language and culture, sampling techniques varied slightly from nation to nation. Survey materials were sent directly to a random sample of 1,076 persons in Canada and the United States. Of those persons, 430 (40 percent) were identified as "leaders." The distinction between leaders and nonleaders was given by the following operational definition: a "leader" is a person who holds a position in the pastoral unit, stake, district, or national church as a presiding officer or assistant, as leader of a major program area, or in some other leadership position. The sample of 430 was drawn at random from the population of such leaders as listed in the computerized records of the World Church. The remaining 646 persons were drawn at random from the computer file listing of church members in the United States and Canada over the age of fifteen years.

Direct mailing from headquarters to persons in jurisdictions outside Canada and the United States was not possible. In general the following procedure was used, with slight variations in some nations. Jurisdictional administrators (region administrators, national church presidents) were provided the necessary printed materials and were asked to administer the survey in their jurisdictions. Specific directions were given for subject sampling and for handling data in order to provide as much consistency as possible. Samples were to be drawn randomly if possible, and if random selection was not possible the samples were to include the desired variety of sex, age, and leadership. Both leaders and nonleaders were to be included. Jurisdictional leaders were to provide translation of materials if needed. Selection of these subjects thus was not in strict accordance with a random design, but the sample was adequately representative to support the conclusions stated subsequently in this report.

The following table shows numbers of subjects selected, grouped by nation or geographic area. Response totals and rates are also shown.

	No. Sent/ Requested	**No. Returned**	**Response Rate**
United States, Canada	1,076	496	46.1%
Australia, New Zealand	150	42	28.0%
French Polynesia, Fiji	56	47	83.9%
Asia	34	26	76.5%
Europe	54	29	53.7%
Africa	30	17	56.7%
Latin America/Caribbean	60	45	75.0%
Totals	1,460	702	48.1%

Because the legislation called for a study of opinions of both leaders and members, two separate subject subsamples were drawn. The first was a sample of designated leaders. The second was a sample of members which included both leaders and others not designated as leaders. The numbers of leaders and nonleaders are shown in the following table. Note that while 39 percent of the total sample drawn were leaders, about 73 percent of the responses were from leaders. This is the result of the response rate from leaders being much higher than the response from nonleaders. This results in a weighing of responses toward the leadership perspective. The overall response rate was 48.1 percent.

	No. Sent/ Requested	No. Returned	Response Rate
Leaders	570	510	89.5%
Nonleaders	890	192	21.6%
Totals	1,460	702	48.1%

Several demographic variables other than leadership were also examined in this study. Numbers of responding subjects associated with each of these variables are shown in the following tables.

Number of years the respondent has been a member of the church:		
Fewer than 15 years	135	(19.2%)
15-29 years	201	(28.6%)
30-44 years	208	(29.6%)
45-59	86	(12.3%)
60 or more years	25	(3.6%)
Information not available	47	(6.7%)

Whether respondent is a member of the priesthood		
Not Ordained	172	(24.5%)
Ordained, Aaronic	84	(12.0%)
Ordained, Melchisedec	399	(56.8%)
Information not available	47	(6.7%)

How frequently the respondent ordinarily attends church activities:		
Seldom or never	22	(3.1%)
1-4 times monthly	89	(12.7%)
5-10 times monthly	309	(44.0%)
More than 10 times monthly	235	(33.5%)
Information not available	47	(6.7%)

Whether respondent holds a leadership role in the jurisdiction:		
No leadership position	179	(25.5%)
Presiding officer/assistant	331	(47.2%)
Leader of major program	77	(11.0%)
Other leadership position	115	(16.4%)
Total in leadership position	523	(74.5%)

Sex of the respondent:		
Male	495	(70.5%)
Female	160	(22.8%)
Information not available	47	(6.7%)

Age of the respondent:

Fewer than 30 years	96	(13.7%)
30-44 years	201	(28.6%)
45-59 years	238	(33.9%)
60-74 years	99	(14.1%)
75 years or more	21	(3.0%)
Information not available	47	(6.7%)

Number of years of formal schooling completed by the respondent:

8 or fewer years	41	(5.8%)
9-12 years	179	(25.5%)
13-16 years	223	(31.8%)
More than 16 years	212	(30.2%)
Information not available	47	(6.7%)

Nation of respondent's residence:

Canada	33	(4.7%)	United States	463	(65.9%)
Haiti	21	(3.0%)	Dominican Rep.	7	(1.0%)
Honduras	4	(0.6%)	Fr. Polynesia	47	(6.7%)
Mexico	3	(0.4%)	Austr./N. Zealand	42	(6.0%)
Brazil	4	(0.6%)	Philippines	9	(1.3%)
Argentina	2	(0.3%)	British Isles	20	(2.8%)
Peru	4	(0.6%)	Fed. Rep. Germany	6	(0.9%)
India	8	(1.1%)	The Netherlands	2	(0.3%)
Taiwan	4	(0.6%)	France	1	(0.1%)
Japan	5	(0.7%)	Nigeria	14	(2.0%)
Zaire	3	(0.4%)			

A substantial difference exists between the number of male and the number of female respondents to this survey. There are two reasons for this. One is that the total sample consisted of two subsamples; one of leaders and the other of general membership. The leaders were mostly men and the general membership sample was almost equally divided between men and women. The merger of the two groups created a sample somewhat heavily weighted with males. In addition, the leaders responded to the survey at a somewhat higher rate than did the nonleaders, thus weighting the total even more heavily with males.

Analysis of the data consisted of these steps:

- Responses were totaled for each item and each demographic variable.
- Those totals were converted into percentage equivalents.
- Response patterns and differences related to demographic variables were identified.

Results. The results reported here are limited to those which relate directly to the issue of ordination of women, as directed by the Conference action. The survey also included items related to participation of women in occupational and church-related roles. The full report of the research project includes this additional information.

Items 45 to 50 of the questionnaire relate to attitudes toward six different hypothetical approaches to ordination of women. Respondents were asked to mark an option on a five-level scale. The scale was a continuum representing a range of attitudes, as follow:

- Strong opposition to the suggestion was indicated by marking A.
- Moderate opposition was indicated by marking B.
- A position of neutrality, or no opinion, was indicated by marking C.

- Moderate approval of the suggestion was indicated by marking D.
- Strong approval was indicated by marking E.

For analysis the two levels of opposition were merged into one ''oppose'' response category, and the two levels of approval were merged into one ''approve'' category. The following comments, therefore, refer to those three alternatives.

Of the six stated approaches to the ordination of women, the highest approval rate (55 percent) was given to the suggestion that women not be ordained, but that their contributions be utilized more widely in all functions except those which explicitly require priesthood ordination. The second highest approval rate (45 percent) was given to the suggestion that the current predominant practice relative to ordination be maintained. It should be noted that the percent who expressed opposition to maintaining the current predominant practice (39 percent) was nearly as high as the percent who expressed approval. Approximately one-third (32 percent) of the respondents expressed approval of providing for ordination of both men and women. The suggestion to set apart women to specific functions through the laying on of hands, but without ordination, was approved by 26 percent of the respondents. The remaining two suggested alternatives received less support. The number of neutral responses ranged from 9 percent to 19 percent on these items. A neutral response may be interpreted as indecision—perhaps as an openness to await direction from leadership before taking a position.

Conclusions. The following are major conclusions drawn from this research:

1. Approximately one-third of the respondents to the survey indicated their approval of the suggestion that both men and women should be eligible candidates for divine call to the priesthood. The probability of a person's holding this view is related somewhat to his/her position relative to various demographic variables. Those subgroups who are more likely to approve ordination of women are persons who are younger and persons who have completed more years of schooling. A slightly higher percentage of leaders than of nonleaders expressed approval of ordination of women (leaders—33 percent; nonleaders—30 percent).

2. Approximately one-half of the respondents (49 percent) indicated their opposition to the suggestion that both men and women should be eligible for priesthood call. Persons who have had fewer years of schooling are markedly more opposed than persons having more schooling. A somewhat lower percentage of leaders than of nonleaders expressed opposition (leaders—48 percent; nonleaders—59 percent).

3. Approximately 13 percent of the respondents expressed a neutral position on the issue of ordination of women. This may be interpreted as a willingness to await leadership or direction through the prophet before taking a position on this issue. Some respondents so indicated in their responses to the questionnaire. There may also be other reasons for their neutral stand.

4. The number of respondents who wish to see the contributions of women utilized more widely in many roles in the life of the church is substantially greater than the number who have experienced women serving in those roles. This survey provides evidence of widespread support for the contributions of women being utilized more widely in the life of the church.

5. The suggestions that ordination of women should be authorized for some priesthood offices only, and that priesthood offices should be created which are open to women only, received approval of only 12 percent and 10 percent, respectively of the respondents.

Part II

A second task of the committee was to ''examine the perspectives of different national, cultural, and ethnic groups throughout the church on the issue of the ordination of women.''

To accomplish this task thoroughly would require a large budget with the employment of several persons skilled in gathering and interpreting public and private opinion in many different cultures. These resources were not available to the committee. Neither has this specific task been undertaken by any other agency of which we are aware.[1]

The issue of ordination is closely related to other social and economic issues affecting women, so attitudes and opinions about women in the society and the marketplace are reflected in the ecclesiastical systems as well. In all areas of the world, attitudes and practices toward women have been changing. Alvin Toffler, a leading futurist, includes the changing sex roles as one of the important factors in the transformation of society. He says, "The world-wide movement for a change in sex roles and for the recognition of women's rights is a part of this historic transformation that will touch every conceivable aspect of our lives over the next twenty-five or thirty years" (United Nations, p. 8). Nevertheless, societal attitudes still vary between cultures in which the RLDS church is located, and a closer look at those variances will provide increased understanding of the distinctions found in the task force study.

Western Nations

The Western nations in which our church is established (Europe, Australia, Canada, United States) have experienced patterns of change in the roles and status of women in society during the last three decades that are quite similar to each other. Women have gone into professions and jobs that at one time were occupied almost exclusively by men. As greater numbers of women have moved into full-time professions, the number of women clergy has increased except where churches have legal or traditional barriers to full participation by women.

A comprehensive study by Carroll, Hargrove, and Lummis (1983) indicates that in recent years there has been a large influx of women into the ranks of the ordained clergy in American Protestant churches. By the end of the 1970s about half of the seminarians in the master of divinity programs at most mainline Protestant seminaries were women (Carroll, p. 107). More women than men seminarians experienced difficulty in becoming ordained. Also there were inequities in the job market both in positions and salaries (Carroll, p. 138). The study pointed out that although women clergy are generally paid less and have greater difficulty in obtaining sole or senior pastor positions than do men in the same denominations, there is comparatively little difference between the two groups in terms of feeling accepted by the laity and the people's confidence in their ability.

In the United Kingdom, studies have been made of the opinions of representative groups of the Church of England regarding the ordination of women. One survey[2] indicated a wide range of opinion but no changes were made in church policy.

Women are not ordained in the Church of England. The archbishop has said he sees no theological objection to ordination of women, but feels it would jeopardize his church's relationships with Rome and Constantinople. The Roman Catholic and Orthodox churches are resolutely against the ordination of women to the priesthood. This view would be predominant in any country where these churches constitute the majority of Christianity in that country.

Betty Thompson made this statement in the book *A Chance to Change*:

> In both Eastern and Western Europe and in North America the concerns about women and work and new roles for both women and men predominated. The concern for ordination (which is more prevalent in North America and Europe) and the deeply felt discrimination in theology and church structures against women raised a question there about whether women could remain in strong patriarchal churches.

The feelings indicated above are reflected in this study. In Canada, 30 percent supported maintaining the predominant current practice, while 52 percent agreed with providing for ordination of both men and women. Also 39 percent agreed with setting women apart to specific roles or functions, but not to ordain them.

European respondents strongly agreed (72 percent) with utilizing women more widely without ordination. Thirty-four percent agreed with providing ordination for both men and women, and 30 percent agreed with maintaining the predominant current practice. Of all groups surveyed, European respondents agreed most strongly (52 percent) with setting women apart to specific roles or functions.

Forty-eight percent of respondents from Australia-New Zealand strongly agreed with providing for ordination of both men and women, and utilizing women more widely (45 percent). Of all groups surveyed they were the least supportive of maintaining the predominant current practice (17 percent). Thirty-three percent agreed with setting women apart to specific roles or functions.

In the United States 48 percent of the respondents agreed with maintaining the predominant current practice, and 57 percent agreed with utilizing women more widely. Thirty-one percent supported the idea of providing ordination for both men and women, while 21 percent agreed with setting women apart to specific roles or functions.

Developing areas of the world show some similarities in their attitudes toward the roles of women, but some very distinct differences also appear. The remainder of this report will therefore deal individually with Asia, Africa, and Latin America.

Asia

In Asia, women have traditionally held certain positions associated with power within the religious structures. These are often in roles of mediums or spiritual diviners through whom a person might offer prayers, contact the spirits of the dead, make vows, or purify a home. These roles are found particularly in India and Japan, and except for these highly specific functions women do not enjoy the same degree of power as do the men in the same faiths.

Since World War II specifically, but beginning in the nineteenth century, many new religions have emerged in Japan. Women have founded a large number of these new religions, but "the pattern of strong female leadership does not continue once the movements have been established. Nor do the new religions advocate dramatic changes in sex roles or power relationships between women and men" (Falk, p. 175). Overall, Asian women have been expected not to upset male dominance.

These attitudes would seem to correlate well with the findings of this study. Though a fairly high percentage of the respondents from Asia would like to see the current practice maintained or see women utilized more widely without ordination (38 percent each), a larger number agree with providing for ordination of both men and women (54 percent), recognizing some priesthood offices as open to women (54 percent), or setting women apart to specific roles or functions (46 percent). While in society as a whole Asian women have maintained traditionally a high level of subservience, within the religious settings there continues to be a high degree of interest in participation by women.

Africa

The Third World nations often find themselves caught up in political and social upheaval to the extent that matters of survival and basic existence take precedence over issues of religion and theology. More precisely, some peoples in Africa and Latin America live in an atmosphere of turmoil, confusion, and sometimes terror, their individual governments changing hands in a constant succession of military despotisms. It is not surprising that the question of ordination of women is not a burning issue for them. Nevertheless, some familiarity with general religious attitudes in these areas will help us understand how the concept might be viewed by these populations.

Women have traditionally held considerable power in some tribal religions of Africa. These roles have been symbolic and ritualistic ones not unlike those found in Asia. This appears to be true for the entire African continent, even though there is a wide variance of forms of religion. Women hold high positions in the spiritual communities as healers, diviners, and ceremonial leaders. Even in the new religions which have sprung up, women have retained their positions as mediums and their symbolic power, allowing for a parallel and complementary development of male and female ritual leaders. In some countries women do not, however, hold other official positions in the society.

Even the positions of leadership women currently hold in the various religious structures seem at present to be threatened. "The complexities of the contemporary situations [in Africa] often lead to traditionalistic and revivalistic responses in which women reassume the trappings of conventional roles with more force than before in a symbolic effort to reconstitute a lost sense of community" (Hock-Smith, p. 4). Though in some individual nations women are advancing in their involvement in society, in many others the progress continues to be slow. In Sierra Leone women have served as cabinet ministers and as U.N. delegates, while Nigerian women achieved the right to vote only as recently as 1979.

Again, these observations correlate well with the findings of the task force. Though a high number of the Africa respondents agreed with maintaining the predominant current practice (71 percent) but utilizing women more widely (65 percent), a relatively high number (47 percent) also agreed with setting women apart to specific roles or functions. A significantly smaller number (6 percent) agreed with providing ordination for both men and women. It should be emphasized again that with the high level of national strife and poverty which most of these nations face, maintaining livelihood and a sense of community become more important than the development of individual status.

Latin America

Several factors affect Latin American attitudes. One is the concept of male *machismo*, defined by Mexican psychiatrist Dr. Jorge Segura Millan as an "attitude . . . based on the inferiority complex manifested extrovertly as superiority" (Liebman, p. 49). It is perhaps the most extreme example of male dominance/female subservience in existence today. Partly because of this attitude, the Christian church in general, in spite of its great numbers and apparent political force, has in the past failed to be a potent force for social justice.

Latin America is one of the strongest bastions of the Roman Catholic faith in the world today. In many countries it is the one faith accepted and adopted by the government which is often structured around the church as the core. Yet in many of the Latin American countries a state of military rule has existed for some time. With that military rule has come a tendency toward oppression and harassment of the people. In this setting the Roman Catholic Church has sought new meaning and purpose as it attempts to reconcile its political ties with its call to minister to those in need.

With these two thoughts in mind, it is easier to understand why the issue of women's roles is not a crucial one in Latin America. In recent years in some places, the Roman Catholic Church has chosen to align itself with the poor and oppressed, taking a definitive stand against the military states. This has meant direct harassment leveled at the church itself, including kidnapping, torture, and murder of its clergy and lay personnel. There has, in addition, been a trend of gradually diminishing numbers of clergy in Latin America. A unique development has been the attempt of religious women (sisters) to fill this void in working directly with the rural communities. These women carry, particularly in Latin American countries, "immense responsibilities in pastoral work without enjoying even the most minimal participation in the ecclesiastical power structure" (Levine, p. 202).

Again we see this information correlating well with the responses found in the task force study. Sixty percent of the Latin American respondents agreed with maintaining the predominant current practice, while only 7 percent agreed with providing ordination for both men and women. There was a fairly high level of agreement (36 percent) with the idea of utilizing women more widely.

Summary

A variety of feelings exist even within the countries that show certain trends. In the midst of that variety, however, there remains an undercurrent of unity in thought regarding the roles of women within their churches. The following quote from the book, *A Chance to Change: Women and Men in the Church*, summarizes those feelings:

> In reading the thirty-year-old study on *The Service and Status of Women in the Churches* by Kathleen Bliss, it is evident that while the same theological arguments are still used against the participation of women in the leadership of the churches and that some churches have not changed at all, the world picture is quite different. Because of . . . the insistence by tens of thousands of women that they share in all the responsibilities of church and society, there is a new attitude both among women themselves and toward their participation by men. The single most important change is simply that many, mostly anonymous, women have come to believe "I am because I participate" and they are no longer content to be the silent majority.

Further in-depth research is needed that reports specifically on the status of women in regard to different national, cultural, and ethnic groups throughout the countries where the church is organized. Only then can there be adequate reporting as to the feelings of acceptance of ordination of women in various areas of the world. Because of the push of the women's movement in the more developed countries, it is likely that the acceptance and desire for this kind of participation in the church is higher there than in the developing nations where tradition is more rooted, and where the struggle for existence is of primary concern.

Endnotes

[1] Sources contacted included the League of Women Voters, the United Nations, the National Organization for Women, and standard library references.

[2] In June 1971 the Standing Committee of the General Synod of the Church of England invited Miss Christian Howard to produce a survey of the present state of opinion about the ordination of women to provide background information for the Anglican Consultative Council meeting in 1975.

Notes: *The 1982 World Conference meeting called for a study to determine the feeling within the church on the issue of women's ordination, which resulted in this report. The survey found the membership fairly divided, with about 30 percent in favor, 55 percent against, and 13 percent neutral. The study also noted a tremendous amount of change worldwide in the understanding of women's roles, and urged further study.*

REORGANIZED CHURCH OF JESUS CHRIST OF LATTER DAY SAINTS

"INSPIRED DOCUMENT" BY PRESIDENT WALLACE B. SMITH (1984)

Section 156

President Wallace B. Smith submitted the following document to the quorums, councils, and orders of the church, and to the World Conference, convened at Independence, Missouri, on April 3, 1984. Major aspects of the document centered in (1) the release of Apostle Charles D. Neff and the call of Geoffrey F. Spencer to the Council of Twelve, (2) the purposes of the temple in the Center Place, (3) analysis and fuller comprehension of priesthood calling and commitment to servant ministries, (4) opening the way for the full participation of the church's women in relation to those ministries, including priesthood, and (5) a reemphasis of the vital role of every member in bringing to pass the cause of Zion. The World Conference on April 5, 1984, voted acceptance of the document as God's will for the church, and provided for its inclusion in the Doctrine and Covenants.

President Smith included the following statement as an introduction to the document:

> *"As I have continued to seek for greater understanding of the divine will in my role as prophet of the church, the burdens of that office have not become easier. In seeking to address some of the difficult and potentially divisive issues facing the church today, I have found myself spending much time in prayer and fasting, importuning the Spirit on behalf of the church.*
>
> *"Because of the nature of that which I am now presenting, I have sought over and over for confirmation. Each time the message has been impressed upon me again, consistently and steadily. Therefore, I can do no other than to bring what I have received, in all humility, and leave it in your hands, believing with full assurance that it does truly represent the mind and will of God."*

To the Councils, Quorums, and Orders of the Church, to the World Conference, and to the Church:

1. It is my will that Charles D. Neff be released from the Council of Twelve Apostles. His long association with the developing national churches, beginning with the Orient field in 1960, has been a great blessing to the church. Likewise, his leadership in the council, especially in regard to field organization and structure, has been of particular value in a time of expanding witness of my gospel. Now, in order to pursue his continuing interest in human and community development in emerging countries, he should be allowed to retire and be afforded the honor of superannuation.

2. To fill the vacancy in the Quorum of Twelve, Geoffrey F. Spencer is called to be an apostle in my church. In this office and calling his strong pastoral sense and unique ministerial gifts will enrich the church, and he should be ordained without delay.

   The Spirit prompts me to say further by way of guidance to the church:

3. My servants have been diligent in the work of planning for the building of my temple in the Center Place. Let this work continue at an accelerated rate, according to the instructions already given, for there is great need of the spiritual awakening that will be engendered by the ministries experienced within its walls.

4. a. Indeed, these ministries shall be the means of great blessing for you, my people, if you will heed the counsel of my servants of the First Presidency who are rightly charged with the responsibility of developing the specific details of these ministries.

   b. The priesthood offices already provided for in my church have always had the potential of supplying these blessings. Some of their functions, however, will be expanded and given additional meaning as the purposes of temple ministries are revealed more fully.

5. a. The temple shall be dedicated to the pursuit of peace. It shall be for reconciliation and for healing of the spirit.

   b. It shall also be for a strengthening of faith and preparation for witness.

   c. By its ministries an attitude of wholeness of body, mind, and spirit as a desirable end toward which to strive will be fostered.

   d. It shall be the means for providing leadership education for priesthood and member.

   e. And it shall be a place in which the essential meaning of the Restoration as healing and redeeming agent is given new life and understanding, inspired by the life and witness of the Redeemer of the world.

6. Therefore, let the work of planning go forward, and let the resources be gathered in, that the building of my temple may be an ensign to the world of the breadth and depth of the devotion of the Saints.

The following is also presented as the voice of the Spirit:

7. a. Hear, O my people, regarding my holy priesthood. The power of this priesthood was placed in your midst from the earliest days of the rise of this work for the blessing and salvation of humanity.

b. There have been priesthood members over the years, however, who have misunderstood the purpose of their calling. Succumbing to pride, some have used it for personal aggrandizement.

c. Others, through disinterest or lack of diligence, have failed to magnify their calling or have become inactive.

d. When this has happened, the church has experienced a loss of spiritual power, and the entire priesthood structure has been diminished.

8. a. It is my will that my priesthood be made up of those who have an abiding faith and desire to serve me with all their hearts, in humility and with great devotion.

b. Therefore, where there are those who are not now functioning in their priesthood, let inquiry be made by the proper administrative officers, according to the provisions of the law, to determine the continuing nature of their commitment.

9. a. I have heard the prayers of many, including my servant the prophet, as they have sought to know my will in regard to the question of who shall be called to share the burdens and responsibilities of priesthood in my church.

b. I say to you now, as I have said in the past, that all are called according to the gifts which have been given them. This applies to priesthood as well as to any other aspects of the work.

c. Therefore, do not wonder that some women of the church are being called to priesthood responsibilities. This is in harmony with my will and where these calls are made known to my servants, they may be processed according to administrative procedures and provisions of the law.

d. Nevertheless, in the ordaining of women to priesthood, let this be done with all deliberateness. Before the actual laying on of hands takes place, let specific guidelines and instructions be provided by the spiritual authorities, that all may be done in order.

10. Remember, in many places there is still much uncertainty and misunderstanding regarding the principles of calling and giftedness. There are persons whose burden in this regard will require that considerable labor and ministerial support be provided. This should be extended with prayer and tenderness of feeling, that all may be blessed with the full power of my reconciling Spirit.

11. a. Dear Saints, have courage for the task which is yours in bringing to pass the cause of Zion. Prepare yourselves through much study and earnest prayer.

b. Then, as you go forth to witness of my love and my concern for all persons, you will know the joy which comes from devoting yourselves completely to the work of the kingdom. To this end will my Spirit be with you. Amen.

WALLACE B. SMITH
President of the Church

INDEPENDENCE, MISSOURI. April 3, 1984

Notes: *The Reorganized Church has a hereditary prophetic office occupied by the descendants of Joseph Smith, Jr., and since 1958, Wallace B. Smith has filled that office.*

These president/prophets occasionally receive revelations which may then be added to the Book of Doctrine and Covenants. *President Smith received this revelation in 1984 and presented it to the 1984 World Conference. The document, which authorizes women in the priesthood, was voted upon and overwhelmingly accepted, and now is in Section 156 of the* Book of Doctrine and Covenants.

Acknowledgments

"Can Women Serve in the Ordained Ministry?" Reprinted with permission of the Evangelical Lutheran Church in America, from *Can Women Serve in the Ordained Ministry?*

"Concerning the Ordination of Women." Reprinted with permission of the World Council of Churches, from *Concerning the Ordination of Women.*

"Excerpts from 'What is Ordination Coming To?" Reprinted with permission of the World Council of Churches, from What is Ordination Coming To?

"Final Report of the Commission for the Study of the Ordination of Women as Rabbis." Reprinted with permission of the Rabbinical Assembly, from *The Ordination of Women as Rabbis: Studies and Responsa.*

"Report of the Commission on the Comprehensive Study of the Doctrine of the Ministry." Reprinted with permission of the Evangelical Lutheran Church in America, from *Report of the Commission on the Comprehensive Study of the Doctrine of the Ministry.*

"Report on Ordination of Women." Reprinted with permission of the Evangelical Lutheran Church in America, from *Report on Ordination of Women.*

"Report on the Ordination of Women." Reprinted with permission of the Central Conference of American Rabbis, from *Yearbook of the Central Conference of American Rabbis.*

"Reports from the Committee on Inter-Church Relations." Reprinted with permission of the Evangelical Lutheran Church in America, from the *1972 Convention Report of the Committee on Inter-Church Relations.*

"Resolution on Rabbinical Membership." Reprinted with permission of the Rabbinical Assembly, from *Proceedings of the Rabbinical Assembly.*

"Resolution Regarding Women as Rabbis." Reprinted with permission of the Rabbinical Assembly, from *Proceedings of the Rabbinical Assembly.*

"Statement on Women's Ordination." Reprinted with permission of the Rabbinical Assembly, from *Proceedings of the Rabbinical Assembly.*

"Statement on Women's Ordination (1922)." Reprinted with permission of the Central Conference of American Rabbis, from *Yearbook of the Central Conference of American Rabbis.*

"Statement on Women's Ordination (1955)." Reprinted with permission of the Central Conference of American Rabbis, from *Yearbook of the Central Conference of American Rabbis.*

"Statement on Women's Ordination (1973)." Reprinted with permission of the Central Conference of American Rabbis, from *Yearbook of the Central Conference of American Rabbis.*

Index to Organizations, Statements, and Subjects

Citations in this index refer to page numbers; page numbers rendered in boldface after an organization name indicate the location of that organization's statement(s) within the main text.